TRIESTE, 1941–1954

TRIESTE, 1941–1954

The Ethnic, Political, and Ideological Struggle

BOGDAN C. NOVAK

THE UNIVERSITY OF CHICAGO PRESS
Chicago and London

Standard Book Number: 226-59621-4
Library of Congress Catalog Card Number: 73-96068
The University of Chicago Press, Chicago 60637
The University of Chicago Press, Ltd., London
© 1970 by The University of Chicago
All rights reserved. Published 1970
Printed in the United States of America

TO MY WIFE, MARIA

CONTENTS

MAPS	ix
TABLES	xi
FOREWORD	xiii
PREFACE	xv
GUIDE TO PRONUNCIATION OF SLAVIC TERMS	2
1. Italian Versus Slav: A Setting for Conflict	3
2. A Quarter-Century of Ferment (1914–1941)	23
3. Fascist Victory and Yugoslav Resistance (1941–1943)	46
4. The Adriatic Littoral: German Occupation and the Collaborationists (1943–1945)	70
5. Resistance to German Occupation (1943–1945)	89
6. The Julian Region on the Diplomatic Front (1943–1945)	120
7. The Liberation of Trieste	133
8. The Forty Days (May 1–June 12, 1945)	161
9. The Two Worlds of Allied and Yugoslav Military Occupation	202
10. The Peace Treaty and the Free Territory of Trieste	240
11. The Ascendancy of Italy in Zone A	268
12. Consequences of the Cominform Resolution	314
13. Italo-Yugoslav Negotiations: A Solution Frustrated (March 1951–March 1952)	353
14. Steps toward a Final Solution (March 1952–June 1953)	381
15. From Violence to Compromise (June 1953–October 1954)	418
BIBLIOGRAPHY	473
INDEX	495

MAPS

1. Julian Region: Ethnic Map — 5
2. Julian Region: Boundary Proposals, 1946 — 243
3. Julian Region: 1945–1947 — 261
4. Free Territory of Trieste: Zones A and B — 269

TABLES

1. AMG Schools in the Julian Region (December 1945) — 217
2. Organization of the AMG — 295
3. Electorate and Votes in Zone A, FTT (1949) — 306
4. First Administrative Elections in Zone A (June 1949) — 306
5. Percentage of Votes for or against Italy (1949) — 310
6. Places of Birth of Voters Registered in Trieste (1949) — 311
7. Administrative Elections in Trieste (May 25, 1952) — 395
8. Administrative Elections in Muggia (May 25, 1952) — 396
9. Administrative Elections in Rural Communes (May 25, 1952) — 397
10. Pupils in Slovenian and Italian Zone A Schools (1945–1955) — 411

FOREWORD

As Professor Novak reminds his readers in chapter 1, the region at the head of the Adriatic Sea, where Slav, Italian, and German speaking peoples abut upon one another and where easy passes over the Alpine mountain barrier connect Europe's southern coastlines with the Danube and central Europe, is a strategically sensitive area that has been fought and quarreled over for centuries.

Between 1941 and 1954 the struggle took the form of an angry confrontation between a revolutionary Yugoslav regime and first the Axis, then the Western powers. On several occasions, threatening military moves seemed about to precipitate violence between Tito's Partisans and the Anglo-American troops that had occupied part of the region in the spring of 1945. The situation was further complicated by domestic political and ideological factors. Italian nationalism confronted international revolutionary communism, inside Italy as well as abroad. Croat and Slovenian nationalisms collided with Italian nationalism, and at the same time chafed against the Yugoslav harness which the Partisan movement had resurrected from the ruins of the interwar Yugoslav state. Finally, the Great Powers loomed over the entire scene, fencing for position in Italy, in Yugoslavia, and in Europe as a whole.

Professor Novak brings special qualities and years of preparation to the task of analyzing and recording these complexities. He was born and educated in the area and lived in Trieste during most of the period with which he deals in this book. He was thus a first-hand witness of events and took some pains to collect fugitive materials—handbills, proclamations, newspapers and the like—that helped in the preparation of this work. Having witnessed and experienced the struggle, he is able to understand and recall the fierce passions that were spent so freely on both sides and can follow the ebb and flow of events with an easy mastery of detail that historians who depend entirely on records can scarcely hope to equal.

But there is an even rarer and more important quality to Pro-

FOREWORD

fessor Novak's performance. He maintains an admirable detachment from the partiality of the protagonists, yet does so without sacrificing a lively human sympathy for all who found themselves caught up in the turbulence of the time. The whole pattern of his life contributed to this capacity for irenic detachment. Born a Slovene, he was no Titoist; educated in Slovenian, Italian, and American universities, he was no Italian nationalist. Yet he could not fail to take a lively interest in the fate of his native land, and he had the intellectual energy and vision needed to distill what he knew and could discover into the pages of this book.

The result is an admirable historical study: richly detailed, breathing the stuff of human reality, yet set in the broadest context of international as well as local political movements. An earlier form of the work was accepted as a Ph.D. dissertation at the University of Chicago. In its revised and perfected form, the work retains the best qualities of a monograph, but combines them with the wider sweep and scope of vision that young thesis-writers usually lack. It is a pleasure and an honor to introduce such a work to the public.

WILLIAM H. MCNEILL

PREFACE

Trieste stands as a symbol of the Italian-Yugoslav border dispute of 1941-54. The struggle of course embraced a much larger zone than this north Adriatic city, namely the Julian Region. The present work deals with the Julian Region only to September 1947; after that date it limits itself to the Free Territory of Trieste (FTT). Moreover, the narrative focuses on internal affairs in the Julian Region and the FTT, especially as they flared into ethnic conflict accentuated by national feeling, and into a clash of Western and Eastern ideologies. Events of wider international scope enter the account only when they made a signal impact on the local population.

For the reader's benefit, some terms need clarification. In particular, one must distinguish between an ethnic group (or people) and a nation, between the latter and a state, and consequently between a national and a citizen.

Various ethnic groups or peoples occupying their own delimited areas on the continent of Europe developed through the centuries their own language, and material and spiritual traditions which found expression in their own particular culture. The nineteenth century added national consciousness. An ethnic group became aware of the qualities that had made it unique, and this historical process transformed the group into a nation. A politically divided nation might then aspire to unify and form its own national state. Such was the case with Italy. Slovenes and Croats of the Habsburg empire, on the other hand, sought cultural and political identity by demanding that Austria-Hungary transform itself into a federal state with self-government for them. Failing to achieve their aim, the Slovenes and Croats united with Serbia to establish a new state, Yugoslavia. Thus, while Italy exemplifies the national state, Yugoslavia is a multinational state made up of four nations—Slovenes, Croats, Serbs, and Macedonians. There is no single Yugoslav nationality.

Nationalism and the democratization of European society have profoundly affected frontier-making in our time. Newly awakened nations cannot willingly accept a state boundary that

PREFACE

severs one part of the nation from the whole. Ideally the border must correspond to the ethnic line separating two nations. But border between the states had somehow to leave the smallest hard to draw. The Julian Region was just such a zone. The new border between the states had somehow to leave the smallest possible number of Italians outside the Italian state, and at the same time the smallest number of Slovenes and Croats outside Yugoslavia.

Ideology, in the form of competition between the beliefs of communism and Western democracy, added further complexity to the border solution. The Communists during World War II organized and usurped all power in the Yugoslav National Liberation Movement and later established their own communist regime in Yugoslavia, and the Italians overthrew their fascist dictatorship and formed a pro-Western democracy.

The four major powers—France, Great Britain, the Soviet Union, and the United States—having decided to draw the new border themselves, realized that the Italian-Yugoslav frontier would also mark the line separating the Eastern communist bloc from Western pro-democratic nations. In supporting Yugoslav claims the Soviet Union saw a chance to extend the communist system further toward the west. But the Western powers were equally determined to prevent such communist expansion. Hence ideology and the ensuing East-West rivalry among the Great Powers had a profound impact on the solution of the Trieste problem.

Yugoslavia effectively used both nationalism and ideology when entreating the support of the people of the Julian Region. She appealed to the national consciousness of Slovenes and Croats and expected them to demand unification with the majority of their nation in Yugoslavia. But she also beseeched the Italian workers of the region to prefer a socialist Yugoslavia to bourgeois capitalist Italy. Italy rightly anticipated that a substantial part of the Italians of the region would desire to remain united with her. It was also expedient for Italy to point out that she had a democratic government prepared to give broad minority rights to non-Italian ethnic groups, while depicting Yugoslavia as a communist dictatorship.

International events, nationalism, and ideology, together

PREFACE

with Yugoslav and Italian propaganda, profoundly affected the people in the Julian Region. The majority of Slovenes and Croats, mainly but not exclusively for nationalistic reasons, preferred Yugoslavia. They formed a strong political group which supported Yugoslav territorial claims. A minority among them, however, felt quite uneasy because of the communist regime in Yugoslavia. Many Italian workers living in the industrial centers of the region preferred Yugoslavia too, for ideological reasons, as long as Yugoslavia remained a member of the Soviet bloc. Other Italians of the Julian Region formed their own political groups and supported Italian territorial demands. Yet some Italians and Slovenes living mostly in the city of Trieste favored neither Italy nor Yugoslavia. They advocated establishment of a free Trieste state. In their view an independent Trieste would best preserve the city's historic role as the chief import-export harbor for central European lands. At the same time a free Trieste would function as a friendly link between Italy and Yugoslavia. The independentists, as this third group was called, considered economic well-being more important than nationalism and ideology. They never became a decisive political force because in the Trieste dispute nationalism played a much greater part than economic considerations.

All of these problems are incorporated into the chronological account. Chapters 1 and 2 acquaint the reader with the historical background. The subsequent chapters can be grouped into the following broader units: chapters 3-6 describe the war period (1941-45), chapters 7-10 deal with the postwar era up to establishment of the Free Territory of Trieste in 1947, and chapters 11-15 trace the story of the Free Territory until its dissolution in 1954.

My research concentrated primarily on events in the life of the Italians, Slovenes, and Croats of the Julian Region and the Free Territory of Trieste. Inasmuch as international affairs were to be viewed merely as a framework for better understanding the internal situation, I refrained from original research in this field. Instead I consulted Italian, Yugoslav, British, American, French, and German secondary works. In preparation for writing the last chapters describing the struggle for dismemberment of the FTT, I added to this literature newspaper articles and printed documents. I obtained the excellent work of the Sorbonne professor Jean-Baptiste Duroselle after most of the present book had already been written.[1] I consulted Duroselle's work, however, in preparing the last chapter of the present book, as is evident in the footnotes.

In reconstructing the events that took place in the Julian Region and the Free Territory of Trieste, I not only examined printed source material, newspapers, pamphlets, and books, but could draw upon personal experience, having lived in the area from December 1946 until the summer of 1951. In addition, I interviewed many inhabitants of the region. I did not, however, have the opportunity to examine the rich Italian, Slovenian, and Croat unprinted source collections in the archives of Trieste or those of Yugoslavia, though I of course checked almost all of the printed and some unprinted source material available in the United States. It was also impossible for me to obtain the local Trieste, Italian, or Yugoslav newspapers. Instead I depended largely on paper clippings, which I began to collect when living in Trieste. I was fortunate to have access to two additional private collections of paper clippings, pamphlets, and books, one of Professor Joseph Velikonja and the other of Professor Vlado Rus. In addition I acquired the works published in Europe, the United States, Canada, and Argentina by Slovenian, Croat, and Serbian émigrés so that I could present their viewpoints, especially for the war period. The reader will thus become acquainted with both communist and anti-communist interpretations.

I must express my gratitude to all who so generously helped me in one way or another during the research and writing. With their financial assistance my brother Slavko Lou Novak and Dr. Victor Cercek enabled me to pursue my doctoral studies at the University of Chicago, where I conducted my research on the Trieste problem resulting in my Ph.D. dissertation. Under the able guidance of Professor William H. McNeill and the challenging environment of the University of Chicago, my views shifted from the polemical to a level in which objectivity and historical

1. *Le Conflit de Trieste: 1943–1954*, vol. 3 of *Etudes de cas de conflits internationaux* of the Centre européen de la dotation Carnegie pour la paix internationale (Brussels, 1966).

PREFACE

truth were the goals. I am also indebted to Professor Joseph Velikonja, with whom I consulted many times and who prepared the maps for the book.

At the University of Toledo I am grateful to President William S. Carlson and Vice-President Archie N. Solberg for the financial help and summer research fellowship which enabled additional research. Furthermore I thank for help and encouragement the late Dr. Duane D. Smith, Dean Jerome W. Kloucek, Dean Noel L. Leathers, Professor Randolph C. Downes, Chairman Melvin C. Wren, Mr. Victor Ullman, Mr. Jerry L. Morrow, and many others. I am especially in debt to Professor Arthur R. Steele for his time and encouragement. Professor Steele spent uncounted hours in editing the manuscript, trying to transform it into smoothly flowing English in such a manner that the original style and meaning would not be lost. This task required many discussions with me but Professor Steele never lost heart and continued until the work was accomplished. Indeed, I am very fortunate to have such a good friend.

During my research I profited from the beneficial help and advice of the staffs of many libraries. I extend my thanks to the University of Chicago Library; the Library of International Relations, Chicago; the Chicago Public Library; the Newberry Library, Chicago; the Midwest Inter-Library Center, Chicago; the Cleveland Public Library, Cleveland, Ohio; the Library of Congress; and the University of Michigan Library, Ann Arbor. At the University of Toledo Library I express my gratitude to the former library director, Mrs. Mary M. Gillham, and to the director, Mr. Patrick T. Barkey. I especially want to thank Mr. John M. Morgan for his much appreciated cooperation and efficient administration of the Interlibrary Loan Section.

I also wish to acknowledge Mrs. Marjorie Managhan and Mrs. Alice Mills for their clerical help and Mrs. Elaine Knutson for the final typing of the manuscript.

Clarification of two more problems of a technical nature may be helpful. The Julian Region, as every ethnically mixed territory, has more than one geographical name for each locality. In the north, for example, is the Slovenian-Italian Trst-Trieste, and Gorica-Gorizia, and in the south the Croat-Italian Rijeka-Fiume and Pula-Pola. Many places have in addition a third,

PREFACE

German name, such as Triest for Trst-Trieste and Görz for Gorica-Gorizia. To avoid confusion only one name is usually used in the present work, based upon the political allegiance of the locality since 1954. For places in Italy the Italian name is given and for those in Yugoslavia the Slovenian or Croat version. Consequently the Italian name is used for Trieste and Gorizia and the Croat form for Rijeka and Pula.

TRIESTE, 1941–1954

GUIDE TO PRONUNCIATION OF SLAVIC NAMES

č — is pronounced as ch in church
ć — is a softly pronounced č
dj — is a softly pronounced dž
dž — is pronounced like a hard j in John
j — is pronounced as y in yes
š — is pronounced as sh in she
ž — is pronounced as zh in azure or measure

1
ITALIAN VERSUS SLAV: A SETTING FOR CONFLICT

THE LAND

The heat of national feeling and the intrigues of ideological strife helped ensnare Trieste after World War II in a maze of the greatest complexity. The maze had not been built in a day and the way out was long. If one is to comprehend the difficulties faced by the Triestines, he must begin at the beginning—with a study of the people involved and the nature of the land they lived in.

Though our attention will eventually turn to the Free Territory of Trieste—the municipality and its immediate environs—it is necessary to consider first the problems of a larger zone we shall call the Julian Region. This area embraces, in general, the land between the Italo-Austrian border of 1866–1918 and the Italo-Yugoslav frontier established in 1920, known as the Rapallo line. Italians call the region Venezia Giulia; to Slavs the proper term for a nearly equivalent zone is Julijska Krajina, or the Julian March. Both expressions are heavy with emotional, nationalistic connotations.

The term Venezia Giulia was coined in 1863 by the Italian linguist Graziadio Ascoli, who proposed that Austrian land then being sought by Italian patriots be called Tre Venezie, or Three Venices. One of the three would be Venezia Giulia, named after the Julian Alps, to remind the Italian people of the glorious role played by the Romans (Julius Caesar) as well as by Venice in the Adriatic.[1] In practice, the name was not much used until near the end of the nineteenth century, but became widely known during peace negotiations after the First World War. At this same time Croat and Slovenian writers adopted the term Julian March.

Both terms, Venezia Giulia and the Julian March, exclude the Dalmatian city of Zadar (Zara) and the Dalmatian islands which

1. "Venezie, Tre," *Enciclopedia italiana*, 35 (1937): 78, 90; Viktor Novak et al., *Oko Trsta* (Around Trieste) (Belgrade, 1945), pp. 374–75.

ITALIAN VERSUS SLAV

went to Italy in 1920 by the Rapallo Treaty. Venezia Giulia does, however, include the city of Rijeka (Fiume), which went to Italy in 1924, while the Julian March includes Venetian Slovenia, which became a part of Italy in 1866. The principal difference between the two terms is that Venezia Giulia includes Rijeka but excludes Venetian Slovenia, and, vice versa, the Julian March excludes Rijeka and includes Venetian Slovenia.

In Austria before World War I there was no administrative unit corresponding to Venezia Giulia or the Julian March. During this time three entire Austrian provinces and parts of three others formed the geographical unit later known as Venezia Giulia. From north to south they were the following: the Kanal Valley (part of Carinthia), the County of Gorizia-Gradisca, the Idrija and Postojna districts (parts of Carniola), the Free City of Trieste, Istria, and Rijeka (part of Hungary). Nor under Italy, after World War I, did Venezia Giulia form an administrative entity. The Kanal Valley in the north and a few border villages in the west went to Udine Province situated west of Venezia Giulia. The rest of Venezia Giulia was divided into four Italian provinces, namely, Gorizia, Trieste, Pola, and Fiume.

Slovenian and Croat works have used still another geographical division based partly on the old Austrian administrative provinces and partly on an ethnic division between Slovenes, Croats, Italians, and Germans. According to their reasoning, the Kanal Valley is part of Slovenian Carinthia which formed the southern part of the old Austrian Carinthia. The Slovenian part of the Austrian county of Gorizia-Gradisca, the Free City of Trieste, and the Slovenian part of Istria came to be called *Slovenska Primorska, Slovensko Primorje,* or briefly *Primorska,* meaning Slovenian Coastland or Slovenian Littoral. The term Slovenian Littoral does not include a small territory of the southwestern part of the Austrian province of Gorizia-Gradisca which has an Italian ethnic majority. The Idrija and Postojna districts are part of Carniola, the central Slovenian province. The Croat part of Istria (the greater part of Austrian Istria) is usually referred to as Istria or Croat Istria. The city of Rijeka is part of the Croat Littoral and not of Istria. The term Venetian Slovenia is applied to Slovenian land west of the Italo-Austrian border of 1866–1918, which from

This map is based on the results of the 1910 and 1921 censuses. Communes that had a Slavic majority in both censuses are marked Slavic (Slovenian or Croatian) territory; those that had an Italian majority are included in ethnically Italian territory. In western Istria, communes with a Slavic majority in 1910 and an Italian majority in 1921 are included here in Italian territory. Professor A. E. Moodie drew a similar line on an ethnic map of the Julian Region in his work, *Italo-Yugoslav Boundary*, p. 85. (Joseph Velikonja, professor of geography at the University of Washington, helped me prepare this map.)

1866 on became part of the Italian province of Udine, and is claimed by Slovenes as their land.

The Julian Region links the Italian plain of the Po Valley with the Danubian basin. Several low passes between the lofty Alpine crests in the north and the start of the Dinaric range along the Adriatic in Yugoslavia constitute a natural gateway of great strategic value; whoever controls these passes dominates the entrance into both the Po and Danubian basins. The Celtic Illyrians, for instance, fought with all their might, but without success, to keep the Romans out of the passes and hence out of the Danubian region. The Romans in turn built a defense along the passes to halt barbaric invasions, and only after destroying these bulwarks could the barbarians pour into Italy. The lessons of ancient times were not lost on later foes. This explains why both Italy and Austria fought for the Julian Region in the latter part of the nineteenth century, and, after dismemberment of the Austrian empire, why the new neighbors, Italy and Yugoslavia, took up the struggle.[2]

Censuses of 1910 and 1921 showed that the Julian Region had close to a million inhabitants in an area of a little over 900,000 hectares (about 3,500 square miles).[3] The region is mostly mountainous and poor, and dotted with many small valleys. A natural limestone formation known as the Karst keeps the mountains and hills devoid of soil, and only the valleys have land reasonably good for crops. There the rural inhabitants—one-half of the population —make their homes. The cities and towns housing the other half are led by Trieste, which between the two world wars had about a quarter million people. Of the other principal cities, Rijeka had over 50,000 inhabitants, Gorizia close to 40,000, and Pula over

2. For a more detailed geographical-strategic study of this region see A. E. Moodie, *The Italo-Yugoslav Boundary: A Study in Political Geography* (London, 1945).

3. Austria, Statistische Zentralkommission, *Österreichische Statistik*, n.s., vol. 1, no. 2: *Die Ergebnisse der Volkszählung vom 31. Dezember 1910* . . . (Vienna, 1914), p. 43, cited hereafter as *Census 1910;* Italy, Ministero dell'economia nazionale, Direzione generale della statistica, Ufficio del censimento, *Censimento della popolazione del regno d'Italia al 1° dicembre 1921,* vol. 3: *Venezia Giulia* (Rome, 1926), p. 208, cited hereafter as *Census 1921;* V. Novak et al., pp. 142–52.

30,000. Most of the remaining towns along the Istrian coast ranged in size between 5,000 and 15,000 inhabitants.[4]

THE PEOPLES

Geographic-strategic importance gives but one clue to explain why Germans, Italians, and Slavs have struggled for the Julian Region. From the era of the migration of nations the land has been ethnically mixed. The Slovenes and Croats settled down in the rural districts, while Italians clustered in the cities and Istrian coastal towns, cultivating only the immediate vicinity. German administrators and, later, German commercial classes also settled in the cities, and during the latter part of the nineteenth century Germans of the Austrian empire sought to build a land bridge from Carinthia to Trieste. But after dismemberment of the Austrian empire the final contest for the Julian Region was confined to Italians and Slavs. In this latter clash the ethnic factor played an important role.

Generally speaking, the region's population is about half Slavic and half Italian, and nationalist writers on either side have had to use countless devices to make their folk a majority. Austria took censuses every decade from 1880 through 1910; Italy conducted several beginning in 1921, but only its first one gave an ethnic breakdown. Yugoslavia took a census of Istria in 1945.[5] Usually only the Austrian statistics of 1910, showing a Slavic majority, and the Italian census of 1921, which confirmed Italian hopes of preponderance, enter into the argument as, for example, at the peace conference after World War II.

A practical difficulty stems from the fact that the Julian Region had administrative units under Austrian rule different from those imposed by Italy. By including some of the border dis-

4. *Enciclopedia italiana,* Appendix 1 (1938), p. 1069, Appendix 2 (1949), pp. 566, 953, 1072; Bogdan C. Novak, "The Ethnic and Political Struggle in Trieste, 1943-1954" (Unpublished Ph.D. dissertation, University of Chicago, 1961), p. 452.

5. For the Austrian census of 1910 listing different ethnic groups see *Census 1910,* p. 43; for the Italian census of 1921 see *Census 1921,* p. 208; and for the Yugoslav census of 1945 see L'Institut Adriatique, *Cadastre national de l'Istrie d'après le recensement du 1er octobre 1945* (Zagreb, 1946), pp. 586, 588–89, cited hereafter as *Census 1945.*

7

tricts, or by leaving them out, one could vary the ratio of Italians and Slavs. To complicate the issue, the ethnic tables of the Austrian census of 1910 listed different ethnic groups only for Austrian subjects. Thus, many citizens of Italy living in the Julian Region were tabulated simply as "foreigners" without further identification. In the Italian census of 1921, where only the ethnic origin of Italian subjects was shown, many citizens of Yugoslavia were thrust into the same anonymity. Obviously, the ethnic tables of the census of 1910 failed to record the true number of Italians, just as the Italian census of 1921 incorrectly portrayed the size of the Slavic population.[6]

Subjective, emotional factors make the picture still more confusing. Differing concepts of nationality, peculiar to the area, will illustrate the point. Numerous Slovenes and Croats, migrating to the Italian-dominated cities, rejected their mother tongue as a language of peasants, and began to speak Italian. To be an Italian —a city-dweller—brought prestige. And, even if the urban Slav continued to speak Slovenian or Croat in his home, he had to learn Italian for use during working hours. Employment in an Italian business or household and dealings with Italianate local officials wrought an obvious influence. Italian authors thus contended that anyone proclaiming himself Italian, though of Slavic origin, belonged to the Italian ethnic group. Slavic writers naturally criticized reliance in the various censuses on the speech used in everyday life (*Umgangssprache—lingua d'uso*), rather than on the mother tongue (*Muttersprache*), as the means of determining nationality.

6. The Austrian census of 1910 gives one statistical table for the ethnic groups and another for the foreigners. Austrian subjects were listed according to their ethnic origin (*Umgangssprache*) in *Census 1910*, p. 43. Foreigners living in Austria were broken down according to their citizenship: in Austria, Statistische Zentralkommission, *Österreichische Statistik*, n.s., vol. 2, no. 2: *Die Ergebnisse der Volkszählung vom 31. Dezember 1910* ... : *Die Ausländer* ... (Vienna, 1913), p. 7. The same method is used in the Italian census of 1921. One statistical table listing ethnic groups is published on p. 208, and another listing foreigners according to their citizenship is printed on p. 191 of *Census 1921*. Thus by consulting both statistical tables (for ethnic groups and foreigners) it is possible to establish the number of Italians living in Austria in 1910 and the number of Slovenes and Croats living in Italy in 1921.

THE PEOPLES

The Austrian census of 1910 reflected a growing national consciousness among Croats and Slovenes in the Julian Region, and thus, to Slavic writers, was the best one to use. But even here they had many reservations.[7] They pointed out that an initial count taken in Trieste in 1910 (largely by Italian employees of the local administration), showed only 36,208 Slovenes. After Slovenian protests, a second tally in the same year raised the total to 56,910.[8] The Slavs, however, stressed that even this figure was incomplete, for the second census was never finished because of Italian objections—Austria, fearing to irritate its fellow member of the Triple Alliance, had succumbed to Italian protests.[9]

Italian writers in later years charged, on the other hand, that Austrian authorities had favored the Slavs in the population count of 1910 by using Slavic employees to collect data in the rural districts. These persons, especially in Istria, registered as Croats many Italians who possessed Slavic names. Furthermore, as we know, many Italians—subjects of Italy, that is—were agglomerated into the count with the indistinct status of foreigners. Italian writers therefore held that previous Austrian censuses, which had shown a larger proportion of Italians, were closer to the truth.[10]

7. For the Yugoslav viewpoint see: L'Institut Adriatique, *La Marche Julienne* (Sušak, 1945); V. Novak et al.; Pero Digović and Frano Goranić, *La Haute Adriatique et les problèmes politiques actuels: Fiume, Istrie, Goritie, Trieste* (Lausanne, 1944); Lojze Berce, *Budućnost Trsta u svetlu njegove prošlosti: Tragedija jedne luke i jednog naroda pod Italijom* (The Future of Trieste in the Light of Its Past: The Tragedy of a Port and of a Nation under Italy) (Belgrade, 1948). These are only some of the more important works. Many others exist and the pamphlet literature is especially abundant.

8. V. Novak et al., p. 118. The number of both Slovenes and Croats was 59,319 according to this correction (ibid., p. 125).

9. The Slavic writers, moreover, claimed that according to parish books registering births, marriages, and deaths, as well as parliamentary election results, the number of Slovenes in Trieste could be established at about 80,000. For this see: *Marche Julienne*, pp. 61–71; Francis Gabrovšek, *Jugoslavia's Frontiers with Italy* (New York, n.d. [during World War II]), pp. 27–34.

10. For the Italian viewpoint see: *La Frontière Italo-Yugoslav* (Rome, 1946); Ferdinando Milone, *Il confine orientale* (Naples, 1945); Sator, *La popolazione della Venezia Giulia* (Rome, 1945); Carlo Schiff-

9

They found support in the Italian census of 1921, which returned the proportion of Italians to Slavs to the general pattern of older Austrian statistics. The census of 1921 was conducted by the Italian government after the Julian Region had become part of the Italian kingdom by the Treaty of Rapallo of 1920. It was the only Italian census to list the population by ethnic groups, and it showed an Italian majority.

Yugoslav supporters raised many old and new objections to the 1921 census. Ethnic groupings had again been counted according to the language of everyday life—a familiar Slavic accusation. Italian annexation of the Julian Region psychologically hindered the growth of a national consciousness among the Slovenes and Croats in the cities—an ethnic awareness that had been slight to begin with. Those who had married Italians, or who wished to advance on the social scale, and many others subject to Italian economic or cultural influence, found an advantage in proclaiming themselves Italians. At the same time, many Slovenes and Croats migrated to Yugoslavia for economic or national reasons, or because they feared Italian persecution which began to erupt in 1919. Simultaneously, many Italians entered the Julian Region for the first time as civil servants, replacing German and Slavic employees, or as workers seeking positions in the newly acquired territory. Italy was always overpopulated and the new lands offered a chance for work, especially to many Italians of the southern part of the kingdom, where it was hardest to find a job.

Slavs after World War II found a true picture of the ethnic condition only in the Yugoslav Istrian census of 1945, which rested on the proclaimed nationality of every individual.[11] Italians opposed this census because it was taken during a time of tension, when both countries were seeking to claim the Istrian Peninsula. Moreover, Yugoslav authorities had administered the census while the Yugoslav army occupied Istria. Many Italians had migrated from Istria to Italy, or to Zone A of the Julian Region which was

---

rer, *Sguardo storico sui rapporti fra Italiani e Slavi nella Venezia Giulia*, 2d rev. ed. (Trieste, 1946); and by the same author, *La Venezia Giulia* (Rome, 1946). Besides this there exist an abundant number of books and pamphlets from the times of the peace conferences after the first and second world wars.

11. See the introduction in *Census 1945*.

THE PEOPLES

under Allied administration, in order to escape Yugoslav Partisan persecutions. At the same time, many Croats and Slovenes, who were not natives of this region, came to Istria as members of the Yugoslav army. The Italian writers further pointed out that many inhabitants of Istria were arbitrarily classified without their consent as Slovenes or Croats because they had Slavic last names, though they thought of themselves as Italians. The Italians had their claims reinforced when experts of the four Great Powers, visiting the Julian Region in 1946, did not recognize the validity of the Yugoslav Istrian census either.

In spite of all the confusion, one can obtain a reasonably clear focus by looking at the matter geographically. Italians are mostly limited to the cities, Istrian coastal towns, and to the rural districts of the western Istrian coast. The Slavs inhabit the greater portion of the rural territory, the Slovenes in the north, including a tiny section of Istria, and the Croats in the south. There is little problem in drawing an ethnic line, running north to south, from the Austrian border to the Adriatic Sea. Except for the Kanal Valley and the Tarvisio district, where a German minority exists, the land east of the ethnic line is an almost compact Slovenian settlement. West of the line is Italian in complexion.[12]

It is harder to plot an ethnic line from Trieste toward the south of the Istrian Peninsula. Here, Trieste and the small coastal towns have an Italian majority. The same is actually true for the rural area, for Italians are in the majority in many communes and districts, but this is often because the number of Italians in towns exceeds the entire Slavic rural population of the same commune or district.[13]

12. Note that the western neighbors of the Slovenes are not the Italians, but the Friulians, speaking their Rhaeto-Romanic (Ladin) language. There were never great disputes between the Slovenes and the Friulians; on the contrary, they lived in a friendly relationship. Note also that the Italo-Slovenian ethnic line does not coincide with the old Italo-Austrian border of 1866–1918. Venetian Slovenia lies west of that border, while the ethnically mixed land of the Kanal Valley lies east of the old border. Moreover, the Italian territory southwest of Gorizia also lies to the east of the old border. Though this latter area has always had an Italian majority, some Slovenian villages were also located there.

13. Another neo-Latin people, besides the Italians, is also present in Istria. This group settled down in Istria during the fifteenth and

ITALIAN VERSUS SLAV

In Italian municipal tradition the rural district belongs to the city. The city is the center of a geographic unit, the seat of administration and of the economy; by comparison, the rural hinterland counts for little. Because the major cities of the Julian Region had an Italian majority, according to this interpretation the entire region was Italian, and should be part of Italy. The Slavs always stress instead the importance of land, a concept derived from their history. The Slovenes and Croats in Istria were peasant peoples without political leaders of their own. They were ruled by foreigners, German or Italian, but the peasants' land was Slavic. The city was merely the seat of the foreign ruling class and belonged to the land that engulfed it. This concept, applied to the Julian Region, meant that all the land compactly settled by Slavs was theirs, including the cities, despite the Italian majority in them. Hence, the Julian Region was Slavic and must be united with Yugoslavia.

THE ECONOMY

Another factor—the economic—directs our attention especially to Trieste. Prior to the nineteenth century it had been only a small port trading with other Adriatic cities. In the fourteenth century the municipal council had asked for Habsburg protection, to avoid Venetian control, and the city remained until 1918

---

sixteenth centuries, together with Slavic, Albanian, and Greek refugees, after the extension of Ottoman power over the Balkan peninsula. Schiffrer calls this neo-Latin group Istrorumeni (Istro-Rumanians), and gives their number as 8,501 *(Venezia Giulia,* pp. 57–59, 122). According to Schiffrer they are living in a few villages of the Pazin (Pisino) and Rijeka districts. Their villages are islands in Croatian land and they all therefore speak Croatian besides their neo-Latin language. The Italian census of 1921 listed only 1,644 people speaking this language (Rumanian) *(Census 1921,* p. 208). Because of the above reasons this neo-Latin group has been included in Croatian territory on our ethnic map.

In addition to the neo-Latin group there are the so-called hybrids in western Istria. Schiffrer gives the number 28,370 for them *(Venezia Giulia,* p. 122). Moodie (p. 85) marked them as Italianized Slavs on his ethnic map. On our ethnic map this group is included in Italian ethnic territory.

THE ECONOMY

beneath the wing of the Habsburg eagle, except for a time under Napoleon's rule (1809-13).

The city's rapid expansion began in the nineteenth century. By 1857 a railroad had linked the city to its hinterland and, after Austria's loss of Venice in 1866, Trieste became the single significant port in the Habsburg empire. The opening of the Suez Canal (1869) and the development of Austrian industry further boosted the traffic of Trieste. Influence of the port spread not only throughout the empire but to Bavaria and Switzerland as well.[14]

Trieste came under Italian rule for the first time after World War I, a point from which Yugoslavs traced the decline of the city's exports and imports. Not only had Trieste never been part of the Italian economic community, they said, but now trade was declining because the natural link between port and hinterland was broken. The obvious answer was to join Trieste to its immediate hinterland—that is, to Yugoslavia.

Italians denied the validity of this view. They pointed out that dissection of the Austrian empire had brought an end to the economic unity of Trieste's hinterland. The newly created national states in central Europe were devising economic policies to fit their own national interests. New political borders brought new customs barriers, and the former economic unity of central Europe was destroyed. Moreover, some new states had established import and export connections with north European ports, using the cheaper river routes. Thus, the decline of Trieste's trade after World War I could be laid to the changed political and economic situation in central Europe, and not to Italian rule over the city.

Italy, in fact, as its supporters maintained, spent large sums between the wars to overcome the crisis caused by decomposition of the economic unity of central Europe. The government transformed Trieste into an industrial city and absorbed the unemploy-

14. The Yugoslav and Italian works listed above in nn. 7 and 10 have chapters on the economic significance of Trieste. For a more detailed economic study see the Italian works: Pierpaolo Luzzatto-Fegiz et al., *L'economia della Venezia Giulia* (Trieste, 1946); Giorgio Roletto, *Il porto di Trieste* (Bologna, 1941); and by the same author, *Trieste ed i suoi problemi* (Trieste, 1952). The Yugoslav Vladimir V. Pertot published on the same topics *Trst, medjunarodni privredni problem* (Trieste: An International Economic Problem) (Belgrade, 1954).

ment of the port. Thus, in the eyes of Italians, they had a just title to Trieste on economic grounds. But this claim was supported, of course, by an even stronger argument—the undoubted Italian ethnic majority in the city.

THE RISE OF NATIONALISM

The era of nationalism, in the second half of the nineteenth century, injected a new emotional factor into the Trieste milieu. Leaders of the Italian Risorgimento, in their drive for a unified national state, were first to assert their claims to the Julian Region. As early as 1845, the Piedmontese military headquarters proposed an Italian frontier with Austria to run along the Alps and the eastern shore of the Adriatic Sea, incorporating the Julian Region and part of the Croatian Littoral.[15] This represented a geographic-strategic border. But the planners also knew that such a frontier would include other persons than Italians living in the hinterland of the Julian Region. At that time these people had not yet developed a national consciousness, and the Piedmontese drafters felt sure they could easily be absorbed into an Italian community. The above formulation of the eastern Italian national border is significant, for the Italian government demanded almost the identical line from the Entente powers in 1915 for strategic and ethnic reasons.[16]

15. Angelo Vivante, *Irredentismo adriatico* (Florence, 1912), p. 59.
16. Not all Risorgimento leaders supported this line, which represented maximal Italian demands. Whether for political or ideological reasons, Giuseppe Mazzini indicated, at different times, different lines for the Italian eastern border. In 1857, he insisted on a line along the Alpine peaks to Trieste; in 1860, he was for an ethnic line along the Isonzo River, and in 1871 he included also the Istrian Peninsula as far as the city of Rijeka. (Giuseppe Mazzini, *Scritti editi e inediti* [Imola, 1931–41], 59:35; 69:61; 92:159.) Cavour also expressed different opinions at different times. In 1860 he stated that only the province of Venezia should be demanded from Austria. But on his deathbed he changed his mind and declared that the duty of his generation had been to reunite Rome and the Austrian province of Venice with the Italian kingdom, while the future of Istria and the Tyrol was a task belonging to the next generation. (Vivante, pp. 60–64; Aurelio Ciacchi, "Cavour e la Venezia Giulia," *Trieste,* no. 13 [May–June 1956], p. 49.)

RISE OF NATIONALISM

The Italian Risorgimento achieved its first great triumph in 1861 when the Kingdom of Italy was proclaimed. In the ensuing period, until 1866, Risorgimento leaders concentrated on annexing the Austrian province of Venice, though during this time the first pamphlets were also published claiming the Julian Region and Dalmatia for Italy. After the war of 1866, Italy acquired Venice, and a new border now divided Austria from Italy until the end of World War I.[17]

Three regions still remained in Austria for Italian patriots to covet: Trentino, Venezia Giulia, and Dalmatia. To the Irredentists, the Risorgimento was unfulfilled until these regions could be joined to Italy.[18] This radical nationalism and imperialism, though characteristic of Europe in the late nineteenth century, went far beyond the basic ideas of the Risorgimento as expressed by Giuseppe Mazzini, who had envisaged a united Europe based on a brotherhood of equal nations, whether large or small.

Irredentists spread their views by means of special literature, and formed cultural organizations on both sides of the border. They also carried out terroristic attacks on Austrian political figures, most notably an attempt on the life of the Austrian emperor Francis Joseph by Trieste-born Guglielmo Oberdan in 1882. Oberdan was executed by Austrian authorities, and the Irredentists and Italians of Trieste got their first martyr.[19]

17. In 1866 Italy gained Venetian Slovenia. The Venetian Slovenes were separated from Slovenes living in Austria and came under Italian rule before the Slovenian rebirth movement took place. Hence, they did not take part in the Slovenian national movement.

18. This land was called "unredeemed Italy" or Italia Irredenta. The movement working for the unification of Italia Irredenta with the Italian kingdom was hence called Irredentism. For a more detailed analysis of the Irredentist movement see: Mario Alberti, *L'irredentismo senza romanticismi* (Como, 1936); Ruggero Fauro, *Trieste: Italiani e Slavi; il governo austriaco; l'irredentismo* (Rome, 1914); Attilio Tamaro, *Trieste: Storia di una città e di una fede,* 2d ed. (Milan, 1946). All these works are written in a pro-Irredentist vein, while the previously mentioned work of Angelo Vivante, who was a socialist, condemned the Irredentist movement.

19. Vivante, pp. 93–94. In older Italian books and in German literature his name is spelled Oberdank. Contemporary Italian literature uses only Oberdan.

The principal aim of Oberdan and his Irredentist friends was to prevent an Italo-Austrian alliance, but his sacrifice was in vain. Italian prime minister Agostino Depretis was unwilling to let the Irredentists spoil improved Italo-Austrian relations, just established by the Triple Alliance. He disbanded all Irredentist organizations in Italy, but could not destroy the movement. Around 1890 new Irredentist groups arose, the most significant being the Lega Nazionale.

The Lega Nazionale played an important role in the Julian Region where the Irredentist movement was both underground and legal. Its main aim was to aid Italian private schools in ethnically mixed territories. Especially by its cultural work, the Lega strengthened the Italian national consciousness, and Slovenes and Croats came to regard it as the main factor in Italianization of the Slavic population in this region.

Toward the end of the century the Irredentists joined hands with the new wave of Italian nationalism inspired by Gabriele d'Annunzio. They could thus reach a broader stratum of the Italian people and increase their importance as a pressure group on the Italian government.

Principal support in the Julian Region for the Irredentists came from Italian intellectuals in Trieste and Italian inhabitants of Istrian coastal towns. The commercial population of Trieste, on the other hand, did not give the movement strong endorsement.[20] The Irredentists accused the bourgeoisie of being too cosmopolitan, interested only in economic advancement, and lacking in national consciousness. History helps to explain the difference. Trieste had been a part of Austrian lands from the fourteenth century, whereas the Istrian coastal towns were for centuries attached to the Venetian Republic and came under Austrian domination only after Napolean's defeat in 1814–15. Intellectual and economic ties with Venice and Italy were much stronger in Istria than in Trieste.

Whatever the wishes of bourgeois Triestines, the Irredentists and other Italian nationalists demanded that Trieste and Gorizia be added to the kingdom of Italy and helped create a myth that all of the Julian Region was Italian because of the Italian majority in these cities. By the time of World War I, this propaganda had

20. See, for example, Alberti, p. 32.

RISE OF NATIONALISM

helped persuade the government to accept Irredentist claims as goals of Italian foreign policy.

As for the Slovenes, at the beginning of the nineteenth century they were an almost unknown agricultural people. Only after 1848 did they assert themselves as a separate national group of the Austrian empire with their own cultural, political, and economic bodies. Several factors account for this development.[21]

One was the ideological influence of nationalism, common to Europe. Early in the nineteenth century a small but devoted nucleus of educated Slovenians accepted the new idea of the brotherhood of nations. The realization that they were Slovenes, different from Germans, tied them together in a common desire to awaken the Slovenian national consciousness. Before 1848, this movement was limited to the Slovenian intelligentsia, students, and a small circle of the bourgeoisie.

Liberation of the peasants in 1848 from the remnants of feudalism further helped to promote the Slovenian national movement, as a more numerous group of intelligentsia and bourgeoisie came into being. Only after 1860, however, did the national movement actually begin to spread among the Slovenian peasant masses. In the next twenty years, cultural, political, and economic organizations were founded which embraced the entire nation.

The movement centered in Ljubljana, capital of the Austrian crownland of Carniola, which became the political and cultural seat of Slovenia. The Slovenian Littoral in some respects also played a leading role, for it was here that the peasants first absorbed the national idea. At great meetings, known as *tabori*, organized out-of-doors, speakers appealed to the peasants to join in a common struggle to gather all Slovenian lands into one ad-

21. The rise of Slovenian and Croat nationalism is described in the following works, among others: Berce, *Budućnost Trsta;* Digović and Goranić, *La Haute Adriatique;* V. Novak et al., *Oko Trsta; Marche Julienne;* and Vivante, *Irredentismo adriatico.* For a more detailed study on the rise of Slovenian nationalism see: Fran Zwitter, "Narodnost in politika pri Slovencih" (The Nationality [Problem] and the Politics of the Slovenes), *Zgodovinski časopis* (Historical Review), 1 (1947): 31–69; Ferdo Gestrin and Vasilij Melik, *Slovenska zgodovina, 1813–1914* (Slovenian History, 1813–1914) (Ljubljana, 1950); Josip Mal, *Zgodovina slovenskega naroda* (The History of the Slovenian Nation) (Celje, 1928).

ministrative unit. In such a "United Slovenia," still a part of the Habsburg empire, cultural, economic, and political direction would be in Slovenian hands.

The Slovenian political fight against German and Italian domination could be successful only if supported by self-conscious and economically independent Slovenian small farmers and bourgeoisie. The need for aid to accomplish this end was especially clear in the Slovenian Littoral. Self-help cooperatives emerged, to prevent the selling of land at auction because of delinquent taxes. Cooperative savings and loan associations lent money to Slovenian peasants with minimal interest rates. The small farmer became more nationally conscious, and began a systematic attempt to keep land from passing into Italian or German hands. The same cooperative banks also supported Slovenian commercial houses and small shops in Gorizia and Trieste. Hence, the cooperative system linked the small farmers and bourgeoisie and became the backbone of the Slovenian national movement. By the end of the century the Slovenian Littoral could claim a sizable number of nationally conscious farmers and a small but relatively strong Slovenian bourgeoisie.

For various reasons, the Croat national rebirth movement in Istria did not have the same success. In 1867, when the Austrian empire broke into two political units, Croat lands were divided between Vienna and Budapest; Croatia proper came under Hungary, while Dalmatia and Istria formed a part of Austria. Thereafter, Croat nationalism became involved in a struggle for "historical rights" against Magyar nationalists and paid little attention to Istria. Rather, it was the Slovenian national movement which at this time influenced the Istrian Croats. With the help of Slovenian national leaders from Trieste and northern Istria, the Istrian Croats established their own cultural, economic, and political organizations on the Slovenian model.

The Italian and Slavic national movements were bound to collide, for both claimed the entire Julian Region. Clashes occurred especially in education and politics. Slovenian and Croat nationalists regarded the private schools of the Lega Nazionale as the most dangerous means employed to Italianize the Slav population. To counterbalance the evil effects of Italian private schools, the Slovenes and Croats each formed their own Association of St.

RISE OF NATIONALISM

Cyril and Methodius, which organized private schools in the Slovenian Littoral and Istria—Slavic counterparts of the Lega Nazionale.[22] Politically, Italian and Slavic nationalists competed in local administrative elections and in balloting for representatives to the parliament at Vienna. The Austrian electoral system, which divided the residents into different classes (*curiae*) based on the amount of property owned, favored the Italian city population. Though the Slovenes and Croats did well in the rural districts, they could never elect a number of councilors in the cities proportional to their national strength. In 1907, however, the Austrian government introduced universal manhood suffrage for parliamentary elections and put all votes on an equal basis, whether cast by wealthy city dwellers or by poor peasants. In parliamentary elections the Slavic rural majority could now fully counterbalance the Italian predominance in the cities, and from that time on, Slovenian and Croat parties successfully challenged the Italians in the Julian Region.

The old curiae system, however, continued in use for local administrative elections. This system enabled the Italians to retain control over city administrations, especially in Trieste.[23] Consequently, Italian bourgeois parties, though professing a liberal ideology, defended the old nonliberal electoral system, while the Slavic and socialistic parties stood for introduction of general manhood suffrage for local administrative elections. While the Slavs and socialists were not successful in bringing about a change on the local level, the new electoral law used in parliamentary elections had politico-social consequences, and ethnic ones as well.

The Slavs also gained from empire policy in another sense. Though Austria had no desire to promote Slavic nationalism, she welcomed for obvious reasons every attack by the Slavs on Italian claims to the Julian Region.

22. The Association of St. Cyril and Methodius was organized not only for the Slovenian Littoral but also for Southern Carinthia and Southern Styria, where it tried to counterbalance similar German scholastic associations, whose aim was to Germanize the Slovenian territory in an effort to establish a German land bridge to the Adriatic.
23. For an analysis of the election procedures in Trieste see: Vasilij Melik, "Volitve v Trstu, 1907–1913" (Elections in Trieste, 1907–1913), *Zgodovinski časopis*, 1 (1947): 70–122.

INDUSTRIALIZATION AND THE SPREAD OF SOCIALISM

Tensions inherent in the rise of Italian and Slavic nationalism were offset by new socialist movements that were gaining significance in the 1890s. The beginning of industrialization and the extension of port facilities in Trieste in the second half of the nineteenth century had created a new and numerous working class of varied ethnic origins, mostly Italian and Slovene. Socialist leaders, in a fight for better economic and social conditions, sought to unite the workers of whatever nationality in a common socialist struggle against the bourgeois capitalist enemy.

The socialist movement in Trieste patterned its organization and ideology after that of the Austrian Social Democratic party. This party was a federation of six virtually independent social democratic parties—German, Czech, Polish, Ukrainian, Yugoslav, and Italian—representing the different national or ethnic groups in those parts of the empire ruled from Vienna.[24] Two of these parties centered in Trieste, the Yugoslav and Italian, the former having been founded in 1896 and the Italian a year later.[25] Up to 1909 each party participated separately in elections, under an agreement in which the Italian party was to present candidates in the city and the Yugoslavs enter elections in villages outside the city. Members of both parties were urged to support the other's candidates. From 1909 on, Italian and Slavic socialists presented a single slate in which two Slovenian candidates had been placed on the common list for city offices, and one Italian on the common list for the surrounding area.[26] Each party formed its own professional bodies, cooperatives, and cultural organizations.

Ideologically, both parties followed the revisionist trend, supporting the concept that socialism should be achieved by peaceful means through parliamentary procedure and the introduction of democracy. To attain these goals, the socialists would participate

24. The Hungarian part of the empire was not included.
25. Ivan Regent, *Poglavja iz boja za socializem* (Chapters from the Struggle for Socialism), 3 vols. (Ljubljana, 1958–61), 3:21; Ennio Maserati, "Il socialismo triestino durante la grande guerra," *Trieste,* no. 64 (Nov.–Dec. 1964), p. 8.
26. Regent, 3:24–28.

in elections, fight for the introduction of universal suffrage for both sexes, and demand that the government be responsible to parliament.

The Austrian socialists sought to preserve the Austrian empire, whose economic unity they held to be of more importance than any aspirations for independent national states. They did, however, propose to reorganize the empire into a federation of autonomous administrative units corresponding to the ethnic boundaries—in other words according to the example of the Austrian Social Democratic party. While supporting the ethnic groups for this limited purpose, the socialists condemned nationalism both inside and outside the autonomous socialist parties. Perhaps in an effort to overcome these nationalistic tendencies, the Austrian socialists strongly asserted that the primary goal of socialism was international unity of the proletariat in a common struggle against their capitalist enemy.[27] Nationalism, in fact, was pictured as an offshoot of bourgeois capitalism.

In the Julian Region the socialist movement was confined principally to Trieste. By condemning nationalistic extremism, whether Italian or Slavic, it laid the foundation for closer Italo-Slavic cooperation between the workers, which would in time play a vital role in this region. But the presentation of common election lists by Italian and Slavic socialists provoked violent attacks from both Italian and Slovenian nationalists. The Italian socialists were accused of pro-Slavic sentiments, and the Slavic socialists of betraying Slovenian interests.[28] These attacks had some influence on the socialists. Although stressing internationalism, some socialist leaders on both sides became infected by nationalism. World War I and the postwar period aggravated the situation. Nationalism and new radical internationalism would one day split the socialist ranks of both parties.

27. Ibid., pp. 7–30; Maserati, *Trieste,* no. 64, pp. 8–10. See also Regent, 1:9–122, which is a selected collection of his articles published during 1906–14. Regent was one of the leaders of the Slovenian socialists in Trieste. Cf. Giuseppe Piemontese, *Il movimento operaio a Trieste dalla fondazione alla fine della prima guerra mondiale* (Udine, 1961), written by an Italian Communist.

28. See, for example, Fauro, pp. 212–38; Regent, 1:113–19.

ITALIAN VERSUS SLAV

Aside from those following the socialist path, many Slavic and Italian people were captivated by one of a series of myths: the myth of an Italian Venezia Giulia, the myth of a Slovenian Littoral, and the myth of a Croatian Istria. These fantasies all obscured the real situation. But Italians, Slovenes, and Croats who had never visited the Julian Region believed the myths to be true and were prepared to fight to conquer or defend these lands. World War I would give them the opportunity.

2
A QUARTER-CENTURY OF FERMENT
(1914-1941)

THE PACTS OF LONDON AND ROME

When World War I began, Italy, though a member of the Triple Alliance, remained neutral. Wooed by both Entente and Central powers, she was in a position to bargain. Moreover, as time went by and neither side could win a decisive battle, the Italian advantage tended to grow.

On April 8, 1915, after long negotiations between the ambassadors of Italy and the Central Powers, the Italian foreign minister Sidney Sonnino outlined his final demands. Italy would remain neutral if given the Trentino region of the Austrian South Tyrol, the western section of the Kanal Valley, and a portion of the county of Gorizia-Gradisca including the city of Gorizia. At the same time, the city of Trieste and environs would become a neutral independent state.[1] But Austria was resigned to only minor border changes, as the Italian ambassador in Vienna, Giuseppe Avarna, reported to Sonnino on April 16. She would cede to Italy, after the war, only the Italian-speaking part of the South Tyrol and a small southwestern corner of the county of Gorizia-Gradisca.[2] On May 19, Karl Macchio, the Austrian ambassador in Rome, made a stronger effort to keep Italy neutral. In a letter to the Italian prime minister Antonio Salandra he offered no new territories, but agreed to immediate Italian annexation of the lands

1. Sonnino to Avarna, April 8, 1915, in Italy, Camera dei deputati, Atti parlamentari, Legislatura XXIV, Sessione 1913-1915, *Documenti diplomatici presentati al parlamento italiano dal ministro degli affari esteri (Sonnino): Seduta dal 20 maggio 1915: Austria-Ungheria* (Il libro verde) (Rome, 1915), doc. 64, pp. 55-56. (English edition [London n.d.], pp. 82-84.)

2. Ibid., doc. 71, pp. 58-59 (English ed., pp. 86-89); René Albrecht-Carrié, *Italy and the Paris Peace Conference* (New York, 1938), pp. 23-24.

promised in the report of April 16.[3] Austria, however, was too late, for Italy had meanwhile received a better offer from the Entente.

From March 1915 on, Italy had been dealing with the Entente powers—Great Britain, France, and Russia.[4] The outcome was an agreement signed in London on April 26, 1915, the London Pact, promising Italy almost all the Austrian territory claimed by the Irredentists except the city of Rijeka and parts of Dalmatia.[5] Besides the South Tyrol and the county of Gorizia-Gradisca, Italy would receive Trieste, Istria, and parts of Carinthia, Carniola, and Dalmatia.[6] In return, Italy assured the Entente that she would enter the war on their side in a month, which she did on May 23, 1915.[7]

The London Pact was secret. But after Italy came into the war on the Entente side, the Slovenes and Croats began to suspect that the Entente powers had promised Italy more Austrian land than Italy had originally claimed. Knowing Irredentist demands, they feared the worst. Austria was quick to benefit from this anxiety. She lined up principally Slovenian, Croat, and Bosnian troops for defense of the Italo-Austrian border, pointing out that the Slavs were really fighting for their own land. This appeal to Slavic nationalism was indeed effective. Even though Austria had sent only a small force into the area, the Italian army could advance but ten miles in the first two years, which brought them only halfway to their goal, the occupation of Trieste. Then, after

3. For the text of Macchio's offer see Albrecht-Carrié, pp. 342–44.
4. Ibid., pp. 25–29.
5. For the text of the London Pact see: "Agreement between France, Russia, Great Britain and Italy, Signed at London, April 26, 1915" in Great Britain, *Parliamentary Papers*, vol. 51 (*Accounts and Papers*, vol. 25: State Papers), Cmd. 671, Miscellaneous, no. 7 (1920) (London, 1920). The treaty was signed by Sir Edward Grey, Britain's principal secretary of state for foreign affairs, by Marquis Guglielmo Imperiali, Italian ambassador in London, by Count Alexander de Benckendorff, Russian ambassador in London, and by Paul Cambon, French ambassador in London. Cf. H. W. V. Temperley, ed., *A History of the Peace Conference of Paris*, 6 vols. (London, 1920–24), 4:287–96.
6. A free hand was also granted to Italy in Albania as well as an equal participation in the division of Turkish possessions and German colonies, should such a division take place.
7. Albrecht-Carrié, p. 34.

PACTS OF LONDON AND ROME

her armies were relieved of Russian pressure, Austria started, with the help of German troops, a great offensive in the fall of 1917, and the Italian army had to retreat far into old Italian soil, back to the Piave River.[8]

Many leaders in Slovenian, Croat, and Serbian political and cultural life escaped from Austria when World War I began. In exile they formed the Jugoslovanski odbor (the Yugoslav Committee) which advocated a new Yugoslav state to unite all Slovenes, Croats, and Serbs living in Austria with the Serbs of Serbia and Montenegro.[9] Likewise, representatives of other nationalities from the Austro-Hungarian empire formed their own national committees and demanded creation of their own independent states. They found favor in influential circles among the Entente powers, though no official policy was ready to recommend independence. In any case, a great movement began. The common goal of all the national committees was dismemberment of the Austro-Hungarian empire. Italy, especially after her retreat to the Piave River, was ready to support the movement as long as it did not conflict with her own territorial aims. Thus she now favored the work of all these bodies except the Yugoslav Committee. Nonetheless, the need for agreement on future frontiers between Italy and a possible new Yugoslav state became urgent as a feeling developed during the winter of 1917-18 that Austria might ask for a separate peace.[10]

8. Temperley, 4:184; Berce, pp. 175-77.

9. Two Croat political leaders, Frano Supilo and Ante Trumbić, organized these émigrés into the Yugoslav Committee in London in 1915. In the same year the committee published its program for a united Yugoslavia (see Jugoslav Committee in London, *The Southern Slav Programme* [London, 1915]). For more information on the work of the Yugoslav Committee see Milada Paulova, *Jugoslavenski odbor: Povijest jugoslavenske emigracije za svjetskog rata od 1914-1918* (Yugoslav Committee: History of Yugoslav Emigration during the World War, 1914-1918 (Zagreb, 1925); Dragovan Šepić, *Supilo diplomat: Rad Frana Supila u emigraciji, 1914-1917 godina* (Supilo the Diplomat: The Work of Frano Supilo in Exile during the Years 1914-1917) (Zagreb, 1961). Cf. Temperley, 4:175; Albrecht-Carrié, pp. 43-44; and Ivo J. Lederer, *Yugoslavia at the Paris Peace Conference: A Study in Frontiermaking* (New Haven, 1963), p. 5.

10. Lederer, pp. 27-28.

There thus arose in the Italian parliament a group supporting an understanding with the Yugoslav Committee. In December 1917 Andrea Torre, the leader of this group, established the first contact with the Yugoslav Committee in London. Then, during a visit to London in January 1918, the new Italian prime minister Vittorio Orlando met with the president of the Yugoslav Committee, Ante Trumbić, and invited him to Rome. In February Orlando appointed Torre as chairman of a parliamentary committee for cooperation with the subject peoples of the Habsburg empire and, as a result, Torre met Trumbić in London on March 7 and concluded an agreement on future Yugoslav-Italian relations. They then arranged for a congress of oppressed nationalities of Austria to meet and further define this accord.[11]

The Congress of Oppressed Nationalities convened in Rome on April 8–10, with the Italian prime minister Orlando officially greeting the Italian, Yugoslav, Czechoslovak, Polish, and Rumanian representatives in an opening speech. On April 10, 1918, the Torre-Trumbić agreement was enlarged to become the Pact of Rome.[12] The first three provisions applied to all nationalities subjected to the Austrian empire, while the last four dealt in particular with Italo-Yugoslav relations. These last articles explicitly stressed that the unity and independence of the Serbs, Croats, and Slovenes was of vital interest to Italy, just as Italian national unity was of prime importance to the Yugoslavs. The future boundaries should be settled amicably "on the basis of the principle of nationality and of the right of peoples to determine their own fate." Ethnic minorities remaining in either of the two states were to be "recognized and guaranteed the right to have their language respected, as well as their culture and their moral and economic interests." It should be noted that the Pact of Rome was not signed officially by the Italian government, though Prime Minister Orlando had welcomed the delegates. Moreover, nothing was said about the London Pact.

The news spread quickly. The Slavs greeted the new pact

11. Temperley, 4:293–95; Albrecht-Carrié, pp. 44–47; Lederer, pp. 29–31.

12. For the Italian text of the Pact of Rome see Giovanni Amendola et al., *Il patto di Roma* (Rome, n.d. [ca. 1919]). An English translation is to be found in Albrecht-Carrié, pp. 347–48.

with thanksgiving, for they were convinced it meant the end of the secret London Pact. On May 16 a great demonstration took place in Prague, and, in August, another in Ljubljana (Slovenia) in favor of the Pact of Rome, signaling the start of Austrian internal disintegration. In Italy, however, the Pact of Rome met with divided sentiment. Socialists and some progressive liberals favored it and sought friendly relations with the neighboring Slavs. Prime Minister Orlando was also sympathetic, at least for the nonce. But nationalist and Irredentist groups were greatly disturbed, as was foreign minister Sidney Sonnino. They felt that territorial promises given in the Pact of London to Italy were endangered, if not lost altogether. In general, the lower classes in Italy supported the Pact of Rome, while the bourgeoisie defended the London Pact.

After World War I, with the Austro-Hungarian empire actually dismembered, the problem was no longer theoretical. Italy had a new neighbor on her eastern border, the Kingdom of Serbs, Croats, and Slovenes, later called Yugoslavia. The time had come for hard bargaining to begin.

A BORDER DECIDED, A PROBLEM UNSOLVED

At the end of the war, Italy, one of the victorious powers, occupied former Austrian lands roughly up to the line promised her in the London Pact of 1915. However, Italian troops also penetrated east of this London line—as in the Tarvisio district of Carinthia, the Postojna and Cerknica districts of Carniola, and the city of Rijeka (Fiume).[13] At the Paris peace conference in 1919, Italy demanded all the lands occupied by her forces: more territory than promised in the London Pact. She claimed the entire Julian Region because it would give her "natural boundaries," and because of the definite Italian preponderance in the urban centers of Trieste, Gorizia, Pula, and Rijeka. Here was a clear statement, except for Rijeka, of the Italian concept that the land belongs to the city. Italy claimed Rijeka on the ground that

13. For a more detailed account of how Italian troops tried to occupy as much territory as possible east of the London line, including the Slovenian capital of Ljubljana, and how much money the Italian army was prepared to spend with the approval of the Italian government to break up the Yugoslav unification, see Lederer, pp. 54–78.

the city had an Italian majority which at the end of the war had voiced its wish to be joined to Italy.[14]

The additional demands, especially for Rijeka, weakened Italy's position in the eyes of France and Great Britain. President Woodrow Wilson, who objected to all secret treaties, added a further complication. If Italy did not adhere to the London Pact, the other Great Powers were free to discuss the claims of both Italy and Yugoslavia to the Julian Region. The Yugoslavs, in support of an ethnic line as the future Italo-Yugoslav border, pointed out that Italy had agreed to the ethnic principle in the Pact of Rome of April 1918. Italians at the peace conference, however, stressed that the Pact of Rome had been signed by individual Italian political and cultural figures, not the Italian government.

The new border claimed by Yugoslavia would run along the old Italo-Austrian frontier with a small modification in the south. The western part of the Friulian flatland, that is, west of the line from Cormons to Monfalcone, including both of these cities, would go to Italy. All territory east of that line would become part of Yugoslavia. This would give Yugoslavia the Tarvisio district (the eastern part of the Kanal Valley), the entire county of Gorizia, and Istria, Rijeka, and Dalmatia. It would include such cities as Gorizia, Trieste, Pula, and Rijeka as well as the coastal towns in western Istria where Italians were in the majority. In claiming the Italian cities and towns, the Yugoslavs stressed their familiar view that these represented mere Italian islands in ethnically Slovenian or Croatian lands. The Yugoslavs also claimed Trieste and Rijeka for economic reasons. The port should belong to its hinterland, by whose resources it had been built and for which it performed its functions. Rijeka, they also noted, had been assigned to Croatia in the London Pact. The Yugoslav memorandum pointed out that President Wilson's "right of self-determination" applied to entire nations, not individual territorial units, thus counteracting the petition signed by the Italians of Rijeka demanding to be joined to Italy.[15] The Yugoslavs did not

14. Italian demands were stated in "The Italian Memorandum of Claims," dated February 7, 1919, reprinted in Albrecht-Carrié, pp. 370–87. For analysis of this memorandum see ibid., pp. 96–103.
15. *Memorandum Presented to the Peace Conference, in Paris, Concerning the Claims of the Kingdom of the Serbians, Croatians and*

A BORDER DECIDED

seek Venetian Slovenia, for it had been part of Italy before World War I, and they knew that Italy as a victorious power would not cede any of her own soil.

Yugoslavia occupied a difficult position at the peace conference. On December 1, 1918, the unification of the Serbs, Croats, and Slovenes was proclaimed. The new state had still to work out the proper relationships among these three ethnic components and to organize a constitutional form of government. When the peace conference started, the new state was not yet recognized by the Great Powers, largely due to Italian resistance. Italy also refused to recognize the Yugoslav representatives at the peace conference, so they were seated as the Serbian delegation. Italy argued that only Serbs could be classified as an Allied force, for the Slovenes and Croats had been her enemies and therefore a defeated nation, and should be treated as such. Moreover, Italy refused the Slovenes and Croats the right to present their border proposals to the Council of Ten, or later to the Council of Four (Great Britain, France, Italy, and the United States), which would make the final decisions. Italy also insisted that the Italo-Yugoslav border could be discussed and established only by the four Great Powers.[16] Later, however, the Great Powers recognized the new state and the Yugoslav delegates defended their demands before the Council of Four.[17]

Italy's position was also precarious. By demanding territory beyond that promised in the London Pact, she faced loss of the support of Great Britain and France. But if, for example, the Italian government should abandon its claim to Rijeka, this would endanger its position at home. While Italy had entered the war under the slogan "Trentino [South Tyrol] and Trieste," by 1919 Italian nationalists had added Fiume (Rijeka) to their de-

Slovenes (Paris, 1919); *Frontiers between the Kingdom of the Serbians, Croatians and Slovenes, and the Kingdom of Italy* (Paris, 1919); cf. Temperley, 4:207–10; and Lederer, pp. 94–96, 103–7.

16. See, for example, Temperley, 4:296–98; Albrecht-Carrié, pp. 106, 116–17, 122–23.

17. The United States was the first (February 5, 1919) officially to recognize Yugoslavia, followed by Great Britain and France on June 1 and June 5, respectively. Italy recognized Yugoslavia on June 28, 1919, when signing the Versailles Treaty. (See Lederer, p. 205.)

29

mands. Fiume became a symbol. Any Italian government not acknowledging this new emotional factor would face a vote of no confidence on the part of the Italian parliament.[18] Trieste would play a similar role after World War II.

The only man who could start proceedings for a compromise line was President Wilson. As the United States was not a partner to the London Pact, the president could deal freely with Italy for concessions. The solution of the American delegation, the Wilson line, ran in a north-south direction similar to the old London line, but somewhat to the west. Beginning in the north, the two lines ran along together up to the Idrija district, but here the Wilson line turned west of the London line so as to leave the Idrija and Postojna districts and the eastern shore of Istria to Yugoslavia. This solution would secure the railway connections of Rijeka–Št. Peter–Postojna–Ljubljana to Yugoslavia while the county of Gorizia, Trieste, and most of the Istrian Peninsula would go to Italy. All the rest of the territory, including Dalmatia and the city of Rijeka, would become part of Yugoslavia.[19]

It should be stressed that the Wilson line represented a compromise, not an ethnic division. It would have left to Italy 370,000 Slovenes and Croats, while only 75,000 Italians would remain in Yugoslavia.[20] In this instance, President Wilson did not apply his ethnic principle and the right of self-determination. By the ethnic principle Italy would get only the amount of territory she could have received from Austria-Hungary for her neutrality. Although the line proposed by Wilson meant a loss of ethnic territory for Slovenes and Croats, it was better for them than the London line.

To the Yugoslavs the Wilson line represented the absolute minimum. The Italians were not prepared to leave Rijeka to Yugoslavia and wanted at least part of Dalmatia, which had been promised in the London Pact. From April 1919 to January 1920 the Great Powers offered various compromise solutions by which

18. Albrecht-Carrié, pp. 102–3.
19. "Wilson's Memorandum to Orlando, April 14, 1919" in Albrecht-Carrié, pp. 445–47; cf. Temperley, 4:289–300.
20. "American Territorial Report, January 21, 1919," in Albrecht-Carrié, p. 365. Instead, according to the London line, over 750,000 Slovenes and Croats would go to Italy, and only about 4,000 Italians to Yugoslavia (cf. Temperley, 4:302, 304).

A BORDER DECIDED

Dalmatia would go to Yugoslavia except for one or two Italian cities, while Rijeka would become an international city under protection of the League of Nations. President Wilson countered these plans with an answer of his own. He accepted the idea of an international Rijeka but demanded that instead of the city alone a larger territory should be internationalized to be known as the Free State of Rijeka. This new state would include, besides Rijeka, all the disputed territory between his Wilson line and the line claimed by the Italians. Though Wilson agreed to some minor corrections in favor of Italy in southern Istria, he otherwise remained firm. Neither of the two succeeding Italian governments —those of Vittorio Orlando and Francesco Nitti—accepted these proposals, and the Paris peace conference ended leaving the Italo-Yugoslav border to a future solution.[21]

After January 1920 the Italian position constantly improved. Great Britain and France, who by now had tired of the affair, left Italy to settle the question by direct dealings with Yugoslavia. Italy reinforced her position by continuing to occupy even more territory than she claimed. The new Italian government of Giovanni Giolitti made it clear that if the Yugoslavs would not accept Italian demands, Italy would retain all territory in which her troops were stationed. Most important, Woodrow Wilson, the only hope for the Yugoslavs, who was ill and nearing the end of his second term of office, would not be a presidential candidate again. The new Democratic candidate, James Cox, supported Wilson's foreign policy, but his Republican rival, Warren G. Harding, was opposed. The Italians wisely waited for the election returns before opening final negotiations with Yugoslavia. With a victory on November 2, 1920, for the Republican party, Italy could act without fear of President Wilson's veto.[22] In the face of these conditions the Yugoslavs negotiated the Treaty of Rapallo from November 8 to 12. The treaty was signed November 12, 1920, ten days after the

21. For a short summary of these negotiations see Temperley, 4:300–327; and Berce, pp. 181–93. The works by Albrecht-Carrié and Lederer, cited above, deal in detail with the role of Italy and Yugoslavia respectively at the Paris peace conference.
22. See Albrecht-Carrié, pp. 298–304; Berce, pp. 193–98; Lederer, pp. 301–6.

Republican victory in America.[23] Under this treaty Italy received the Kanal Valley (including the Tarvisio district) in the north. The border then ran between the London line and the line of Italian occupation, leaving the entire Julian Region to Italy, while Dalmatia went to Yugoslavia, except for the city of Zadar and a few islands. Two of the three main islands in the bay of Rijeka went to Italy. The city of Rijeka with a small surrounding territory (20 square kilometers) was made into the state of Rijeka, whose independence was guaranteed by both Italy and Yugoslavia.

The Treaty of Rapallo failed to satisfy either Italian nationalists or Slovenes and Croats. The Italian foreign minister, Count Carlo Sforza, who signed the treaty for Italy, was attacked by Italian nationalists, who said he had sold out Dalmatia to Yugoslavia.[24] Slovenes mourned the Rapallo Treaty because one-third of Slovenian land and people came under Italian rule, a great loss for such a small nation. The Croats were also distressed that they had lost Istria, some Adriatic islands, and Rijeka. Yugoslav writers particularly stressed that by the Treaty of Rapallo over a half-million Slovenes and Croats came under Italian rule, without guarantee of any minority rights, while the rights of the Italian minority in Dalmatia were set forth in detail.

The Treaty of Rapallo did not actually solve the Rijeka question, for the territory was in the hands of the poet and ardent Italian nationalist Gabriele d'Annunzio, who refused an order of the Italian government to evacuate. His rule had begun in September 1919. After the fall of Orlando's cabinet in June of that

23. For the English text of the Treaty of Rapallo see "Recognition by His Britannic Majesty's Government of the Treaty of Rapallo of November 12, 1920, between the Kingdom of Italy and the Kingdom of the Serbs, Croats and Slovenes" in Great Britain, *Parliamentary Papers*, vol. 43 (*Accounts and Papers*, vol. 25: State Papers), Cmd. 1239, Miscellaneous, no. 12 (1921) (London, 1921). The above treaty was signed by Giovanni Giolitti, C. Sforza, and Ivanoe Bonomi for Italy, and by Mil. R. Vesnitch [Vesnić], Dr. Ante Trumbić, and Costa Stoianovitch [Kosta Stojanović] for Yugoslavia.

24. See, for example, Giulio Benedetti's attack on Sforza in his work *La pace di Fiume: Dalla conferenza di Parigi al trattato di Roma* (Bologna, 1924), pp. 103-4; for greater detail see Carlo Sforza's two works: *Pensiero e azione di una politica estera* (Bari, 1924), and *Jugoslavia: Storia e ricordi* (Milan, 1948).

year, Italian nationalists had become alarmed over the future of their demands and over Rijeka in particular. An incident broke out in Rijeka, started by young fanatics who attacked French occupation soldiers. The peace conference sent a special commission to investigate. Meanwhile, D'Annunzio, a veteran of World War I, began to gather volunteers in the Julian Region, organized from young Irredentists, nationalistic army veterans with the tacit support of some members of high Italian military circles, and with financial help from the bourgeoisie of Trieste.[25] To the last named, previously known for their cosmopolitan character under Austrian rule, it had now become evident that Trieste would go to Italy. Hence, they felt that the second largest port of the eastern upper Adriatic—Rijeka—should belong to Italy too. Otherwise, all middle European trade might be directed to a Yugoslav or independent Rijeka, which would greatly diminish the import and export trade of Trieste and be detrimental to the well-being of Trieste's bourgeoisie.[26] In September 1919, while peace negotiations still continued in Paris, D'Annunzio entered Rijeka with his volunteers and took over the government. A year later, in September 1920, he occupied the nearby islands and proclaimed the Italian Regency of Quarnero (Reggenzia Italiana del Carnaro).

When D'Annunzio defied Premier Giolitti and refused to evacuate Rijeka after the Treaty of Rapallo was signed, the Italian government established a blockade. On Christmas Day of 1920 Italian troops and D'Annunzio's volunteers clashed, and D'Annunzio was forced to leave Rijeka. Italian soldiers entered the city on January 18, 1921, and in April the Italian administration held

25. Temperley, 4:307–9, 334–35; V. Novak et al., pp. 368–73. For more detail see Benedetti, *La pace di Fiume,* a contemporary pro-Fascist work, and two more recent works: Paolo Alatri, *Nitti, d'Annunzio e la questione adriatica, 1919–1920* (Milan, 1959); and Ferdo Čulinović, *Riječka država: Od londonskog pakta i danuncijade do Rapalla i aneksije Italiji* (The State of Rijeka from the London Pact and [the Period of] D'Annunzio to Rapallo and the Annexation to Italy) (Zagreb, 1953). Of the last two the first is an Italian work covering in detail the period from 1919 to 1920, the second a Yugoslav work covering the period from 1915 to 1925.

26. Claudio Silvestri, "Una repubblica delle Tre Venezie con presidente il Duca d'Aosta," *Trieste,* no. 35 (Jan.–Feb. 1960), pp. 25–27.

a free election. The independentist party won, but nationalist fanatics burned the election results. The Italian government finally established order by October, when Riccardo Zanella, the leader of the independentists, took over the local government. His administration lasted only five months, for on March 3, 1922, the nationalists and Fascists organized armed resistance and Zanella and members of his government had to flee. On March 21, 1922, nationalists under Attilio Depolli formed a provisional government. Meanwhile, Benito Mussolini had come to power in Italy. In September 1923 he sent his emissary to Rijeka to accept the government of that city from Depolli.

By 1923 it was evident that Rijeka would not become an independent state, and Mussolini, in order to legalize its position, began negotiations with Yugoslavia for a partition. On January 27, 1924, the Treaty of Rome was signed, ending the state's existence. Italy took under her sovereignty almost all of the city itself, plus a narrow strip connecting it to Italian territory. The northern portion of the state of Rijeka and the eastern part of the city, called the Delta, situated between the Eneo (Rečina) River and a canal, as well as Baroš pier went to Yugoslavia.[27]

The Rijeka events in 1919 were an object lesson for Trieste after World War II. To both Italians and Yugoslavs the affair was proof that to gain a territory one must occupy it by force. A de facto occupation is better security than awaiting settlement at a peace conference.

PERSECUTION OF SLAVS AND SOCIALISTS

Extreme Italian nationalists began to persecute Slovenes and Croats in the Julian Region as soon as the Italian army occupied it in 1918.[28] It is understandable that they would fear all forces

27. For the text of the Treaty of Rome and its attachments see Benedetti, pp. 283–306.
28. As soon as Italy occupied the Julian Region, during the latter part of November 1918, General Pietro Badoglio, deputy to General Armando Diaz, the commander-in-chief of the Italian army, prepared a program on how to break Slavic resistance to an Italian annexation of the occupied territories. This program was approved by Prime Minister Orlando, Minister for Foreign Affairs Sonnino, and Commander-

opposed to a union of the Julian Region with Italy. A large Slavic population in this section spelled danger to Italian claims—a danger enhanced by Slovenian and Croat demands for a plebiscite to decide the future of the territory.[29]

The unsettled border situation, together with divergent economic and nationalistic interests in the Julian Region, provided a fertile ground for creation of the first Fascist units, at a time when Fascism in Italy had yet to become an important political force. These units, called shock troops (*squadre d'azione*), comprised the most ardent supporters of Italian Irredentism. They came from

---

in-Chief Diaz on December 9, 1918, and communicated to Badoglio. (See Lederer, pp. 71, 73, 75.)

29. A detailed description of these persecutions is to be found in the following Yugoslav works: Lavo Čermelj, *Life-and-Death Struggle of a National Minority: The Yugoslavs in Italy*, trans. F. C. Copeland, 2d ed. (Ljubljana, 1945); Institute for International Politics and Economics, *Italian Genocide Policy against the Slovenes and Croats: A Selection of Documents* (Belgrade, 1954), hereafter cited as *Italian Genocide Policy*; Ive Mihovilović, "Talijanska kolonizacija Julijske Krajine: Dokumenti" (Italian Colonization of the Julian March: Documents), *Anali jadranskog instituta* (Annals of the Adriatic Institute), 1 (1956): 117–56. Dr. Lavo Čermelj is a well-known Slovenian expert on the persecutions of the Yugoslav minority in Italy. The second work is a collection of documents related to the persecutions. The article of Mihovilović deals with the economic side of the persecutions, based on new documents obtained by the Yugoslavs after World War II.

These persecutions are confirmed also by Italian works. See, for example: Gaetano Salvemini, *Racial Minorities under Fascism in Italy* (Chicago, 1934); and articles dealing with specific topics published in the review *Trieste* after World War II, by Elio Apih, "Il fascismo a Trieste," *Trieste*, no. 7 (May–June 1955), pp. 38–43; Carlo Schiffrer, "Fascisti e militari nel incendio del Balkan," no. 55 (May–June 1963), pp. 15–18; by the same author, "Chiesa e stato a Trieste durante il periodo fascista," no. 58 (Nov.–Dec. 1963), pp. 4–8; and by Claudio Silvestri, "Mons. Bartolomasi e il problema slavo," no. 57 (Sept.–Oct. 1963), pp. 14–15.

The persecutions were acknowledged by Fascist writers themselves, who glorified the local Fascist leaders for transforming the Julian Region into an Italian zone. See Michele Risolo, *Il fascismo nella Venezia Giulia: Dalle origini alla marcia su Roma* (Trieste, 1932).

the lower middle classes who, for a long period, had been fighting off Slavic nationalism and the internationalism of the workers. The Irredentists, demanding as their supreme goal unification of the Julian Region with Italy, had volunteered to fight in the Italian army during World War I. After the war, many regarded the fruits of their victory as being in danger and became Fascist propagandists and organizers under the leadership of Francesco Giunta. They were joined in terrorist activities by their younger brothers, high school students, who had been too young to participate in the war and regarded themselves as otherwise deprived of a chance at the heroism and glory ascribed to their older brothers. Indeed, these squadre d'azione were destined to become the elite of the Fascist movement. Monetary aid supplied by the upper bourgeoisie and tacit support of local authorities encouraged the formation and activities of these Fascist groups.[30]

Giunta and his Fascists used an incident occurring in the Dalmatian city of Split to incense public opinion against the Slav nationalists. On July 12, 1920, Croat nationalists clashed with Italian sailors in Split, resulting in the death of an Italian officer and a sailor. Giunta called a meeting for six o'clock the following evening in the Piazza Unità, the main square in Trieste. During the gathering, in which he described the Slavic danger with emotion, the Fascists mortally wounded a youth called Nino with a knife. Giunta immediately claimed that Slav nationalists had killed Nino and appealed to the audience to revenge the Split incident and now the death of this boy. He started to march with his Fascists toward the Hotel Balkan, headquarters of the Slovenian cultural, political, and economic organizations in Trieste, also known as the Slovenian National Home (Slovenski narodni dom). That evening Giunta and his squadrists burned down the home with the support of Italian nationalists. Italian occupation troops stationed in nearby barracks to prevent disorder joined the Fascists in assaulting the Slovenian building.[31]

The signing of the Treaty of Rapallo in November 1920 did not stop persecution of Slovenian and Croat minorities. Rather, as

30. Carlo Schiffrer, "Il fascismo al termine della parabola," *Trieste,* no. 56 (July–Aug. 1963), p. 15; Risolo, pp. 31–33.
31. Schiffrer, *Trieste,* no. 55, pp. 15–18; cf. Čermelj, pp. 147–52; Risolo, pp. 56–62.

PERSECUTION OF SLAVS AND SOCIALISTS

Fascism came into power, the mistreatment grew more intense and systematic. Slavic sources describe many incidents occurring between the two world wars. For example, the Slovenian political leaders and many outstanding intellectuals were sent to the Lipari Islands, where they remained interned until freed by Allied forces during World War II. The same treatment befell Slovenian and Croat priests, who were the cultural and political leaders of the Slavic peasants in their rural parishes. To avoid such a fate, many Slovenian political figures and intellectuals escaped from Italy to Yugoslavia.

Slovenian and Croat public and private schools became Italian state schools with Italian as the only language of instruction. The Slovenian and Croat press and publishing houses were suppressed and their political parties abolished. The old geographical names, in completely Slovenian or Croat regions, were either translated from Slavic into Italian or replaced with new Italian designations. Likewise, personal names were changed from Slavic to Italian. The introduction of Fascist syndicalism served to destroy Slovenian and Croat economic establishments. The once flourishing Slavic cooperative system collapsed. Without their own financial institutions, many Slovenian and Croat peasants became indebted to Italian banks, from which they borrowed to pay taxes or to repair their buildings damaged during World War I. When the peasants were unable to repay these loans, Slovenian and Croat farms became the property of Italian banks, which in many cases sold them at public auction. Later the Fascist government organized special agricultural institutions solely to assure that such farms would come into Italian hands. Thereafter a systematic colonization of Slovenian and Croatian land began.

Furthermore, many former Austrian civil servants of Slavic origin migrated after World War I to Yugoslavia in fear of Italian terrorists. Others who remained were transferred by the Italian civil service from the Julian Region to central or southern Italy, and their places filled by Italian civil servants coming from Italy. This fact helped to change the ethnic composition of the Julian Region in favor of the Italians. The aim of all these measures was to make the region completely Italian and, in line with this plan, use of the Slovenian and Croat tongues was forbidden in all state institutions and public places, including churches.

The persecutions and Italianization policy dealt a blow to Slovenian and Croat ethnic groups; but, on the other hand, the oppression also united all political factions and strengthened Slovenian and Croat national consciousness. Hence, the first Slavic resistance groups emerged—various terroristic organizations, seeking unsuccessfully to assassinate Mussolini and other Fascist leaders. Many were captured by the Italian police or escaped to Yugoslavia. The Extraordinary Military Tribunal handled the cases of those who fell into the hands of the Italian police, and in 1929 these Fascist authorities executed a young Croat from Istria, Vladimir Gortan.[32] He became a hero and a symbol of Croat resistance in Istria. A year later four Slovenian youths were condemned by the Extraordinary Military Tribunal and shot in Basovizza, a Slovenian village belonging to the Trieste commune.[33] These "Basovizza victims" became a further symbol.

Slavic nationalists were not alone in facing persecution by Italian nationalists and Fascists after the First World War; socialists met the same fate. For one reason, it was felt the socialists could change the political balance by allying with one or the other of the two nationalistic parties. There were three major political groups in Trieste. The Italian nationalists represented a little less than half the population, the Slovenian nationalists slightly less than a quarter, and the socialists a little more than a quarter. An alliance of socialists and Slovenian nationalists could undermine the plurality of the Italian nationalists. The latter understandably watched with suspicion any move of the socialists, and grew more insecure and fanatical.

32. Čermelj, pp. 193–95. Four associates of Gortan were sentenced to thirty years' incarceration.

33. Čermelj, pp. 195–99. The four executed were: Ferdinand Bidovec, Fran Marušič, Zvonimir Miloš, and Alojz Valenčič. There were other trials, but the two mentioned in the text are the best known ones. For other trials see ibid., pp. 199–209. The last of the trials took place in 1941 after Italy had occupied Yugoslavia. Čermelj was among the accused, one of the reasons being publication of the above-named book. This last trial he described in *Ob tržaškem procesu 1941: Spomini in beležke* (About the Trieste Trial in 1941: Recollections and Notes) (Ljubljana, 1962). He was condemned to death but the sentence was commuted to life imprisonment. See chapter 3, under "Resistance in the Julian Region."

PERSECUTION OF SLAVS AND SOCIALISTS

A second reason for Italian nationalist hostility was the socialists' support of an independent Trieste—even though they later reversed their stand. From the spring of 1918 on, as the Austrian empire faced an internal crisis that was a sign of impending dissolution, the Austrian socialists called for reorganization of the empire into a federation of national states. But by the fall of the same year, when the Austrian nationalities began to demand independent national states, the majority of Triestine socialists proclaimed themselves in favor of an independent Trieste. In line with their Austrian tradition, the Trieste socialists regarded the port as economically linked to its hinterland. To perform its economic function Trieste should be independent. In this way it would serve all of the new states formed out of the Austrian empire.[34] But after the Italian occupation of Trieste early in November 1918, the former Austrian-Italian Social Democratic party decided to join the Socialist party of the kingdom of Italy. This decision signaled their agreement that Trieste should belong to Italy.[35]

In contrast, the majority of the Austrian-Yugoslav Social Democratic party continued to support an independent Trieste. Consequently, in April 1919 they assumed the new name of Independent Slovenian-Croat Socialist party of the Julian March. But when it became apparent that the Great Powers would assign Trieste to Italy, the Slovenian socialists in Trieste also reversed their position. Thus, in September 1919 the Slovenian-Croat Socialist party joined the Italian Socialist party.[36] By this move the Slovenian socialists in Trieste accepted the inevitable fact that Trieste would go to Italy. Up to that time each of the two Triestine socialist groups, Italian and Slav, had had their own socialist organization. Now they merged, and from that time on there was

34. Maserati, *Trieste,* no. 64, pp. 8–10; Regent, 1:129–31, 146; 2:11–26; 3:54–56. Valentino Pittoni, representing the majority of the Italian Social Democratic party, made his declaration favoring an independent Trieste in Vienna on October 17, 1918 (Maserati, *Trieste,* no. 64, p. 10). Edmondo Puecher, representing a small minority, was of the opinion that Trieste should go to Italy (ibid., p. 9). Dr. Henrik Tuma and Ivan Regent, representing the majority of Yugoslav Social Democrats, favored an independent Trieste, while Dr. Josip Ferfolja and Rudolf Golouh urged that Trieste should go to Yugoslavia (Regent, 3:54).
35. Maserati, *Trieste,* no. 64, p. 10; Regent, 1:143.
36. Regent, 3:57.

only one socialist party in Trieste. The Slovenian nationalists attacked the Slovenian socialists, accusing them of betraying the Slovenian national interest at a time when peace negotiations were still going on. The Italian nationalists on their part were not convinced of the socialists' sincerity, mistrusting them for their longtime stand on behalf of an independent Trieste.

But the Italian nationalists had a further ground for their fears—a suspicion that the Slovenian socialists would inject a more pronounced left-wing radicalism into the unified socialist party. In truth, it was this radicalism which had made the Italian nationalists afraid of the socialists in the first place. The origin of socialistic radicalism could be traced to the victory of the Bolshevik revolution in Russia, which confirmed the majority of the socialists in their belief that a world revolution would soon introduce a new socialistic order. Democracy and parliamentarianism belonged to the past. These new socialistic tenets naturally frightened the bourgeoisie, who formed the backbone of the Italian nationalists in Trieste.

The Fascists ably exploited this bourgeois fear to their own advantage in Italy and especially in Trieste. Terrorizing the Slavic population in the Julian Region with their armed bands, they appeared as the true defenders of Italian national interests. Moreover, the same Fascist armed bands fought against the general strikes, which were fomented by socialists seeking to crush the old socio-political order. The Fascists forced the workers to stay at their jobs or ran the trains and factories themselves. The bourgeoisie supported such actions, either tacitly or in the open, convinced the Fascists were the only possible force to prevent a socialist takeover. Two well-known episodes will illustrate the scope of Fascist attacks against the socialists.

In the first days of September 1920 the socialists in Trieste proclaimed a general strike to coincide with a similar movement in Italy. One of the workers was killed in a clash between the strikers and Fascists. Socialists then organized a great funeral procession which was again attacked by the Fascists. In the melee the Fascists overthrew the hearse and wounded a few workers. Public opinion was indignant. An attack on a funeral procession was unheard of. Utilizing this public reaction against their opponents, the socialists decided to annihilate the Fascists. They raised barricades in San Giacomo, a living quarter of Trieste's working class. The Fascists assaulted the barricades, but were too weak to take them. The Italian occupation army then came to the support of the Fascists and flattened the barricades with a few artillery shots.[37]

A second and greater clash occurred in October of the same year. Toward the middle of the month the socialists proclaimed another general strike in Trieste, seeking to honor Soviet Russia and her October revolution. But the move united in opposition all Italian groups defending the established order. Using the moment when Italian opinion had thus turned against the socialists, the Fascist armed bands demolished the socialist headquarters in Trieste and the printing offices of their newspaper, *Il Lavoratore*.[38]

The clash between socialists and Fascists caused an open split in the Socialist party itself. A moderate section condemned the revolutionary tactics of the left wing as dangerous to the socialist movement. The radical left, on the other hand, was convinced that the time was ripe for a revolution and that socialism in Italy would before long be victorious. Hence, it supported a radical policy to undermine the unstable bourgeois society. The final outcome among the socialists in Trieste and the entire Julian Region was a victory for the radical wing.[39] The Slovenian socialists, except for a few intellectuals, joined the radical left, convinced that a socialist victory was near. Such a victory would bring all of Europe into a confederation of free socialistic republics, and result

37. Claudio Silvestri, "Il socialismo a Trieste dopo la prima guerra mondiale," *Trieste*, no. 21 (Sept.–Oct. 1957), pp. 30, 32; Risolo, pp. 78–85; Regent, 1:375–76. According to Silvestri it was a minor clash. Risolo, a Fascist author, glorified the clash as a decisive battle for the Fascists with twelve dead and over two hundred wounded. Regent merely registered the event as one among the Fascist attacks on the socialists and Slavs.

38. Silvestri, *Trieste*, no. 21, p. 31; Risolo, pp. 123–29; Regent, 1:376.

39. The split into two major groups, the moderate socialists (revisionists) and radical left (maximalists) went back prior to World War I. In Trieste the leaders of the Italian moderate socialists were Valentino Pittoni, Edmondo Puecher and others. Giuseppe Tuntar was the leader of the Italian radicals. Ivan Regent and Dr. Henrik Tuma were the leaders of the Slovenian radicals. See Maserati, *Trieste*, no. 64, pp. 8–10; Silvestri, *Trieste*, no. 21, pp. 29–32; and Regent, 2:23–24; 3:58.

in true freedom for all oppressed nationalities, including the Slovenes. Moreover, in such a new socialist Europe, Trieste would be a free state serving its natural hinterland.[40] Without doubt the Slovenian and Croat socialists contributed to the victory of the radical wing of the party in the Julian Region. As a result, during the Livorno congress of the Socialist party in January 1921, this radical majority of socialists from the Julian Region joined with the dissenting socialists from other parts of Italy to form the Italian Communist party. From this time on there were two parties, Socialist and Communist, in the Julian Region, the latter being the stronger.[41] This split affected the Italian socialists, while the Slovenian and Croat socialists entered en bloc into the new Communist party.[42] Italo-Slavic cooperation in the Socialist and later in the Communist party had important consequences during and after World War II.

Instead of bringing forth the socialist revolution, the split of socialist forces contributed to the Fascist victory in 1922. This development put an end to the legal existence not only of the Communists and Socialists but other Italian and Slovenian parties as well.

ITALO-YUGOSLAV RELATIONS

Though Mussolini spoke in favor of good Yugoslav-Italian relations at the time the Treaty of Rome was signed in 1924, the persecution and denationalization of the Slovenian and Croat minority in the Julian Region embittered relations between the two neighboring states. Numerous migrations of Slovenes and Croats from the Julian Region to Yugoslavia created a strongly organized Slovenian and Croat irredentism which took care that the Italian persecutions became known to as many people as pos-

40. These ideas typical of leftist radicalism were expressed, for example, by Regent in his articles published during August 1918 and November 1920 and reprinted in his *Poglavja iz boja za socializem,* 1:123–233.

41. Ibid., 1:234–45, 250–64; 2:53–61, 65–68; Silvestri, *Trieste,* no. 21, p. 31.

42. Only a few intellectuals did not join the Communist party, among them Dr. Tuma.

ITALO-YUGOSLAV RELATIONS

sible.[43] Slovenes and Croats grew bitterly disposed toward Italy and Italians. Fascist support of the Croat pro-Fascists led by Ante Pavelić was regarded as an indication that the Fascist government wanted only an opportune moment to intervene in Yugoslavia's internal affairs. Strong suspicion existed that Italy would support the creation of an independent Croatian state with Pavelić as head of the government. An alliance of Macedonian and Croat terrorists killed King Alexander of Yugoslavia in 1934, while he was visiting France. Though the terrorists were trained in Hungary, the protection given by Italy to their leaders and especially to Pavelić further strengthened the belief of Yugoslavs that the Fascist government was the sinister power behind the assassination. It is not suprising that Yugoslav writers described the Julian Region as a bridgehead for Italian Fascist expansion over the Balkans.[44]

The Italian Fascist government watched with equal apprehension the development of organized irredentism in Yugoslavia. The Italians were shocked by the violent Yugoslav reaction against the condemnation of Slovenian nationalists in Trieste by the Extraordinary Military Tribunal in 1930. To show their resentment some Croat nationalists demolished the heads of the lions on monuments built by the Venetians when they had controlled Dalmatian cities.[45]

43. The organization and the work of Slovenian and Croat émigrés from the Julian Region are described in Ivan Regent et al., eds., *Slovensko Primorje in Istra: Boj za svobodo skozi stoletja* (Slovenian Littoral and Istria: The Struggle for Liberty through the Centuries), prepared under the direction of Juraj Hrženjak (Belgrade, 1953), pp. 158-67, hereafter cited as *Slovensko Primorje in Istra*.

44. Italo-Yugoslav relations are well described in Milan Marjanović, *Borba za Jadran 1914-1946: Iredenta i imperijalizam* (The Struggle for the Adriatic, 1914-1946: Irredentism and Imperialism) (Split, 1953). Cf. the German work, Joseph März, *Die Adriafrage* (Berlin, 1933), pp. 5-19, 297-317, 327-43.

45. A typical Fascist work, blaming Yugoslavia for bad Italo-Yugoslav relations and glorifying the good will of the Fascist government to establish friendly relations between the two countries is Gabriele Paresce, *Italia e Jugoslavia dal 1915 al 1929* (Florence, 1935), especially pp. 269-320. The work of Virginio Gayda, *La Jugoslavia contro l'Italia: Documenti e rivelazioni*, 2d ed. (Rome, 1941) describes the Yugoslav irredentist groups, accusing them of anti-Italian propa-

43

The Mussolini government also viewed nervously the extension of French political and economic interests into the Balkans. The pacts of friendship between the Little Entente (Yugoslavia, Rumania, Czechoslovakia) and France, as well as the signing of the Balkan military alliance (Greece, Turkey, Bulgaria, and Yugoslavia), greatly increased French influence. These factors, together with a Yugoslav economic blockade against Italy during the Ethiopian war, prevented a friendly relationship between Italy and Yugoslavia.

However, the changed international situation, the rise of Nazi Germany and her claims to Austria, combined with economic stress caused by the war in Ethiopia, in time brought a partial improvement of Italo-Yugoslav relations. In 1937 a five-year nonaggression pact was signed, in which Italy was to allow the Slovenian and Croat minority to use their language in the Julian Region. Though the agreement remained a dead letter, the treaty did introduce economic cooperation and exchange between the two states. Yugoslav irredentists bitterly attacked the treaty and, as a result, the Yugoslav government introduced harsh controls over the irredentist organizations. Their activities were strictly supervised, some of the groups were disbanded, and some of their leaders confined. By these acts the irredentist publications and meetings directed against Italy had been curbed, but the hostile sentiment against her nurtured by Slovenes and Croats remained unchanged.

Shortly after the Italo-Yugoslav treaty was signed, Italy consented to German annexation of Austria. Consequently Nazi Germany became a neighbor of Yugoslavia. Moreover, the Italo-Yugoslav nonaggression treaty did not prevent Italy from attacking Yugoslavia in 1941 as an ally of Germany. Rapid victory, at this stage of World War II, secured more by German than Italian arms, opened to Italian occupation a broad band of Slovenian and Croat as well as Montenegrin territory along the shores of the eastern Adriatic. Italy thus acquired not only all the lands once demanded by Italian Irredentists, but extended her territory and influence beyond any frontiers dreamed of in the nineteenth cen-

---

ganda, terrorism, and training for war against Italy. This is another characteristically Fascist book.

tury. The Adriatic Sea could now properly be called mare nostrum. But success was only temporary, bringing new disillusionments, hardships, and finally defeat to Italy. At the same time, Fascist imperialism provoked a strong Slavic underground to fight against Italian occupation armies and administration, both in the new territories and in the Julian Region.

3
FASCIST VICTORY AND YUGOSLAV RESISTANCE (1941-1943)

YUGOSLAVIA, 1941: DISSECTION AND COUNTERACTION

Once Hitler had trampled on Austria and Czechoslovakia, Italy seized the chance to do likewise in lands east of the Adriatic. She occupied Albania in April 1939. Then, having entered World War II as a German ally in June 1940, she launched an assault against Greece in the following October. On April 6, 1941, Italy and Germany attacked Yugoslavia, and by the end of that month, both Yugoslavia and Greece had fallen. Italy now ruled the entire Adriatic coast.

Yugoslavia disappeared from the map of Europe. The German and Italian foreign ministers, at a meeting in Vienna, April 20 to 22, 1941, carved up the country between them, and dealt out pieces to Hungary, Bulgaria, and Albania. They allowed the Croats to form an independent state, including Bosnia and Herzegovina, though ruled by the rightist followers of Ante Pavelić. In July 1941, Montenegro proclaimed its independence, but under Italian occupation, and in August the government of a diminished Serbia came into being under German control with General Milan Nedić as prime minister. In reality, Italian and German spheres of interest encompassed the entire region. The Italian included the whole Adriatic hinterland, namely Southern Slovenia, Southern Croatia, Dalmatia, Bosnia-Herzegovina, Montenegro, and Albania. All territory to the north, northeast, and east came under German influence.[1]

The Vienna agreement marked the greatest extension of Italian power and influence over the Adriatic hinterland. Fascist

---
1. Werner Markert, ed., *Jugoslawien* (Cologne, 1954), pp. 102-5, 109.

Italy proudly asserted that she was following in the footsteps of her Roman ancestors in building an empire.

The concentrated attack of Italy and Germany, beginning April 6, 1941, had stirred up great confusion in Yugoslavia. The king and government left for Greece after authorizing General Danilo Kalafatović to sign an armistice. He did so on April 17. Two days later the Yugoslav government stated in Athens that it would battle the Axis on the side of Great Britain until final victory. After the Greek defeat, the Yugoslav government-in-exile went to Jerusalem, from whence it was transported to London.[2]

However unimportant the Yugoslav statement may have seemed to the conquerors, it offered a warning that the administration of Yugoslav territory would not be a peaceful one. Shortly, in fact, two important resistance movements were formed: the Chetniks and the Partisans.

The Chetnik movement began with Yugoslavia's defeat in April. Many officers of the Yugoslav army retreated into the mountains with chosen volunteers to continue the war against the new occupants. After contacts had been established among the first isolated groups, all recognized former Colonel Draža Mihajlović as their leader, and in May he set up his headquarters in Ravna gora, Serbia.[3]

The Chetniks stood for restoration of the prewar political

2. Ibid., pp. 101-2; Constantine Fotitch [Fotić], *The War We Lost: Yugoslavia's Tragedy and the Failure of the West* (New York, 1948), pp. 97, 106. The government was known as the royal government, London government, or the government-in-exile. The author of the book, Fotić, was Yugoslav ambassador to the United States before and during the war.

3. Branko Lazić, *Titov pokret i režim u Jugoslaviji: 1941–1946* (Tito's Movement and Government in Yugoslavia: 1941–1946) (Munich, 1946), pp. 17–20. Lazić's work is a pro-Chetnik analysis of the Partisan movement. Another pro-Chetnik work is Radoje L. Knežević, ed., *Knjiga o Draži* (A Book about Draža), 2 vols. (Windsor, Ont., 1956). This is a collection of essays written by former members of the Chetnik movement about Draža Mihajlović. For a critical analysis in English of the civil war in Yugoslavia, see Charles Zalar, *Yugoslav Communism: A Critical Study*, prepared for U.S., Senate, Subcommittee of the Committee on the Judiciary, 87th Cong., 1st sess. (Washington, D.C., 1961), pp. 55–116.

and social order. In January 1942, Mihajlović became war minister in the Yugoslav government-in-exile, though staying in Yugoslavia to keep up his struggle against the intruders and also against the Partisans.[4] Serbia remained the stronghold of Chetnik forces, though they also formed armed bands in other parts of Yugoslavia.

The second resistance movement, called Partisans for short, entered the fray after June 22, 1941, the day Germany attacked the Soviet Union.[5] The official name of this communist-sponsored underground was the National Liberation Movement; the Partisans, as its armed units, derived their name from the word *party* (i.e., Communist party).

The Partisans fought for a new communist order in a federative Yugoslav republic. Their leader was Josip Broz, alias Tito, the secretary general of the Yugoslav Communist party. The Partisans organized autonomous provincial National Liberation committees for Slovenia (September 1941), Serbia (November 1941), Montenegro (February 1942), Croatia (March–June 1943), Bosnia-Herzegovina (November 1943), and Macedonia (August 1944). These were the embryonic revolutionary governments of the future six federated republics of Yugoslavia.

In November 1942, the first assembly of Partisan delegates meeting in Bihać appointed an Antifašističko veće narodnog oslobodjenja Jugoslavije (Anti-Fascist Council for the National Liberation of Yugoslavia) or AVNOJ. The council became the supreme

4. Fotitch, p. 156; Zalar, pp. 80–84.
5. Partisan literature instead stressed that the resistance had actually begun with Yugoslavia's defeat in April. From April to June 22 was the period of preparation for armed resistance, but the actual armed resistance began after Germany's attack on the Soviet Union. For this see, for example, Metod Mikuž, *Pregled zgodovine narodnoosvobodilne borbe v Sloveniji* (Survey of the History of the National Liberation Struggle in Slovenia), 2 vols. (Ljubljana, 1960–61), 1:95–170. On the other hand, the anti-Partisan writers underline the fact that the Partisans would never have fought against German military forces if Germany had not attacked the Soviet Union. The same writers point out that Partisan resistance began only after June 22, while the first clashes between Chetniks and Germans occurred in May 1941. See Lazić, pp. 19–27; Zalar, p. 80.

RESISTANCE AND REACTION IN SLOVENIA

authority for all of Yugoslavia and elected from its members an executive committee. A year later AVNOJ met at Jajce where it elected a Presidium, a new name for the Executive Committee, to act when AVNOJ was not in session. The Presidium in turn elected the Yugoslav National Liberation Committee which was a de facto federal government for the Partisan movement with Josip Broz-Tito as chairman and commissar of war.[6]

Two underground movements pursuing such different aims could not avoid a mutual clash, and the conflict in turn unleashed civil war in Yugoslavia. In this fight the Partisans were attacked not only by Chetniks but by other armed groups that came into existence with support of the occupation forces.

RESISTANCE AND REACTION IN SLOVENIA

The same day that Germany and Italy attacked Yugoslavia, April 6, 1941, representatives of Slovenian "organized and recognized political parties" formed a National Council as the supreme authority for Slovenia during the war and foreign occupation. The following parties participated: Slovenian People's party (Catholic), Yugoslav National party (liberal), National Radical party, Independent Democratic party, and Yugoslav Socialist party.[7] The first two had been the leading Slovenian parties. The

6. Zalar, pp. 96–100; William Jones, *Twelve Months with Tito's Partisans* (Bedford, Eng., 1946), pp. 123–25. Besides Tito there were sixteen other commissars or ministers in the Yugoslav National Liberation Committee.

7. France Škerl, "Politični tokovi v osvobodilni fronti v prvem letu njenega razvoja" (Political Trends inside the Liberation Front during the First Year of Its Development), *Zgodovinski časopis*, 5 (1951): 17. For some other pro-Partisan works see: Franta Komel, *Narodno-osvobodilna borba v Sloveniji* (The National Liberation Struggle in Slovenia) (Maribor, 1960); and Franček Saje, *Belogardizem* (White Guardism) (Ljubljana, 1951). The following are anti-Communist works: Matija Škerbec, *Krivda rdeče fronte* (The Guild of the Red Front) (Cleveland, 1961); *Vetrinjska tragedija* (The Tragedy of Vetrinje) (Cleveland, 1960), published by Zveza Slovenskih protikomunističnih borcev (The Union of Slovenian Anti-Communist Combatants), cited hereafter as *Vetrinjska tragedija*; France Grum and Stane Pleško, eds., *Svoboda v razvalinah: Grčarice, Turjak, Kočevje* (The Wreck of Liberty: Grčarice, Turjak, Kočevje) (Cleveland, 1961); Bor. M. Karapandžić,

49

former governor *(ban)* of Slovenia, Marko Natlačen, was elected president of the council.

Anti-Communist sources state that the Communist party refused to join the National Council.[8] Partisan writers, on the other hand, claim that the party was not invited. When, they say, the Central Committee of the Slovenian Communists demanded representation, the other parties declined on the ground that the Communist party had been illegal in Yugoslavia and that only recognized parties should share in making decisions.[9]

On April 10, independent Croatia was proclaimed, thus isolating Slovenia from the rest of Yugoslavia. Marko Natlačen, president of the National Council, met two days later in Celje with the German general Lantz, who occupied northern Slovenia, to ask that German troops take over all of Slovenia and prevent its being partitioned. General Lantz disavowed his authority to make such a decision, though he promised to notify the German government of these Slovenian wishes. But Natlačen's mission failed. The same day Fieldmarshal Wilhelm Keitel ordered the temporary partition of all of Yugoslavia.[10]

Keitel's directive, confirmed by the German and Italian foreign ministers at the Vienna meeting from April 20 to 22, allocated a small part of northeastern Slovenia—Prekmurje—to Hungary. The Germans occupied the rest of the north, and Italians all of the south. Later the Germans annexed their part of Slovenia to the Third Reich, eliminating all Slovenian political and cultural

---

Kočevje Titov najkrvaviji zločin (Kočevje, the Bloodiest Crime of Tito) (Cleveland, 1959); Lado Bevc, *Na braniku za sokolske ideale* (In Defense of Sokol [Falcon] Ideals) (London, 1965); Vladimir Kozina, *Communism as I Know It* (Piedmont, Calif., 1966).

8. Cf. *Vetrinjska tragedija*, p. 9.
9. Cf. Škerl, *Zgodovinski časopis*, 5:17.
10. Ibid., pp. 21–22; Mikuž, *Pregled zgodovine*, 1:48–52. Keitel acted according to directions issued by Hitler, April 12, 1941, about the partition of Yugoslavia. For this see ibid., p. 52; Yugoslavia, Beograd, Vojno-istoriski institut (War-Historical Institute), *Zbornik dokumenata i podataka o narodno-oslobodilačkom ratu jugoslovenskih naroda* (Collection of Documents and Data of the National Liberation War of Yugoslav Nations), 7 pts. (Belgrade, 1949–57), pt. 2, 2:543–47. This edition of official documents in the Serbo-Croat language will be cited as *Zbornik* (Belgrade).

institutions and prohibiting use of the Slovenian tongue. During the summer of 1941, the Slovenian intelligentsia and clergy were expatriated to Serbia and about twenty to thirty thousand peasants transported to Silesia. The land was given to German peasants who had been a minority group in Kočevje in the Italian-occupied zone of Slovenia.[11]

After the unsuccessful meeting with General Lantz, the National Council accepted an Italian proposal to establish the Provincia di Lubiana (Province of Ljubljana), in the southern, or Italian, part of Slovenia. The province was formally created on May 3, 1941, and the Italian government nominated Emilio Grazioli, a Fascist officer in the Trieste region, as high commissioner. Italians filled the top administrative jobs, though the lower places remained in Slovenian hands.[12]

The Province of Ljubljana became a part of Italy, although the inhabitants were not made Italian citizens and could not be conscripted to fight for Italy. The old Italo-Yugoslav border remained, and to cross it required a special permit. The Italian government assured the Slovenian people of the new province that it would respect the Slovenian language, as well as cultural and political institutions. This concession did not, of course, apply to Slovenes in the Julian Region, for they had been under Italian dominion for years.

Slovenian political leaders saw in the new province an asylum from German persecution, and a place to escape the turmoil of war. This proved to be an illusion. Ljubljana Province became, instead, the center of civil conflict.

11. For a contemporary account of German atrocities in Slovenia see Kazimir Zakrajšek, *Ko smo šli v morje bridkosti* (When We Entered the Ocean of Sorrows) (Washington, D.C., 1942). The author had been a missionary worker among Slovenian immigrants in the United States. He left Slovenia as an American citizen after the Italian occupation, entering the United States in the fall of 1941. At that time he was asked by the State Department to prepare a report on conditions in Slovenia and Yugoslavia. The above work is a more detailed elaboration of his report about the situation in Slovenia.

12. Mikuž, *Pregled zgodovine*, 1:60–62; John A. Arnež, *Slovenia in European Affairs: Reflections on Slovenian Political History* (New York, 1958), p. 83.

The disruption of the idyll of peace came from the Communist party, which condemned the work of the National Council as opportunistic and against the welfare of the Slovenian people. The National Council, according to Communist sources, satisfied only the desires of the bourgeoisie. With no one else to defend the "people," the Communist party had to assume the role. Thus, on April 27, 1941, they gave the impetus to organization of the Anti-Imperialist Front, directed against any kind of imperialism, including the English. The Front comprised representatives from the following parties and groups: the Communist party, the left wings of the Yugoslav National party (liberals) and the Christian Socialist party, and a group of progressive intelligentsia. The Communists had fashioned a close tie with these groups before the German attack on Yugoslavia, through the Organization of Friends of the Soviet Union, founded after Yugoslavia had established diplomatic relations with Russia in May 1940.[13]

After Germany attacked the Soviet Union on June 22, 1941, the Anti-Imperialist Front took the new name Osvobodilna fronta, or OF (Liberation Front).[14] It confined itself at first to propaganda to gain support of the people for a fight against the German and Italian intruders. For that purpose, local Narodno-osvobodilni odbori (National Liberation committees) were organized in the city of Ljubljana and in the villages. Except for the Communist party, the political groups that joined the Liberation Front very soon lost their identity. The Communist party became director of the Liberation Front and vanguard of the fight against occupation. Thus, as in Russia, where the Communist party represented the leadership and the soviets the mass organization, so in Slovenia the Liberation Front was the mass movement and the Communist party the leadership circle.

How could the Communist party, representing a tiny minority, assume control of Slovenian resistance? Many factors are involved, but one above all deserves note. The Communists were the only ones with a strong underground apparatus, for their party had been illegal and persecuted by the Yugoslav government. All other political and cultural bodies had been easily disbanded by occupation forces. The Communists thus used their experience in

13. Škerl, *Zgodovinski časopis*, 5:29–30.
14. Ibid., pp. 33–34; Mikuž, *Pregled zgodovine*, 1:95–155.

underground work to take quick advantage of the other parties. After a few months of propaganda, the Liberation Front had enough members to assemble its first small armed bands. They took the name of Partisans, a term later applied to the entire Communist-led underground. Throughout 1942 the Partisans attacked enemy garrisons in small villages and then quickly disappeared into the forests. Not until 1943 did they begin to control larger rural sections. These areas had no strategic significance for the occupying forces, who thus did not seriously try to expel the Partisans. It is further significant that lands held by the Partisans were mostly in Italian-occupied sectors.

In such liberated territories the Partisans established their new administration. The local village liberation committees, by replacing the old municipal (communal) councils, transformed themselves from propagandist into administrative agencies. An increase of "liberated" territory brought into existence higher authorities, namely district and regional liberation committees. Slovenski narodno-osvobodilni odbor (the Slovenian National Liberation Committee) represented the highest Partisan authority for Slovenia.[15] This committee recognized the federal Executive Committee of AVNOJ as its superior, and the highest Partisan authority for Yugoslavia.[16]

At first the leaders of the traditional Slovenian political parties did not take Partisan propaganda seriously—until Italian soldiers began to burn villages after Partisan attacks on their garrisons. The clerical and liberal leaders then pointed out to the people that Partisan appeals to fight for liberation were not aimed at the Axis intruders, but designed to win popular support for the

15. To be exact, the name of the highest Slovenian Partisan authority was Slovenski narodno-osvobodilni odbor or, in short SNOO, from September 16, 1941, until February 19, 1944, when it was renamed the Slovenski narodno-osvobodilni svet (Slovenian National Liberation Council) or SNOS. For this see: Zalar, p. 98; Inštitut za zgodcvino delavskega gibanja v Ljubljani (Institute for the History of the Labor Movement in Ljubljana), *Dokumenti ljudske revolucije v Sloveniji* (Documents of the People's Revolution in Slovenia), 2 vols. (Ljubljana, 1962–64), 1:116, hereafter cited as *Dokumenti*.

16. See above, this chapter, end of section "Yugoslavia, 1941."

FASCIST VICTORY AND YUGOSLAV RESISTANCE

Liberation Front which would then be used to insure a Communist victory after the war.

Although the traditional leaders lacked a formal party structure, their condemnation of Partisan movements spelled danger to the Communists.[17] The Partisans answered with a series of terroristic attacks against well-known figures of the parties with which they disagreed. Partisan propaganda tried to justify the violence by accusing the former leaders of opportunism or of direct collaboration with the occupying forces.[18] The list of assassination victims included persons from the local village level up to the former governor Marko Natlačen. These acts, occurring from the fall of 1941 until the fall of 1942, mostly in Italian-controlled Ljubljana Province, greatly demoralized the conservative population. In the long run, however, they caused a violent reaction against the Partisans, and drove the conservative forces into open collaboration with the Italians, through Vaške straže (the Village Guards) and Legija smrti (the Legion of Death). Communists and their opponents have each tried to explain how and why these collaborationist units came into being.

According to anti-Communist sources, the Partisans at first had little success among the peasants. The majority belonged to the Catholic party and did not trust the Communists. Moreover, by tradition they opposed war or guerrilla fighting. But when the Partisans began to attack Italian garrisons, and the Italians in reprisal burned down villages, shot hostages, or transported the people to concentration camps, the peasants became involved. To avoid Italian persecution, many peasants left for the mountains where they were persuaded peacefully, or by force, to join the Partisans. The peasants thus were beset by two dangers: if they

17. Partisan documents (nos. 24, 71, 74, 80, 88, 98, 126, 127, 137) issued from the end of August 1941 to the end of February 1942 (reprinted in *Dokumenti,* vol. 1) amply illustrate this fear of the "criminal atrocities of the Slovenian reaction."

18. The anti-Communist sympathizers were convinced that the terrorist acts were possible only with Italian support. They stressed that the Italians never captured a single Partisan terrorist though the province was filled with Italian garrisons. Moreover, the Partisans were on good terms with Italian soldiers and police forces. (Cf. Grum and Pleško, pp. 13–20.)

remained in their villages they were exposed to Italian retribution; if they left the villages and sought refuge in the mountains, they were forced against their will to join and fight for the Partisans.[19] To overcome this precarious position and still stay on their land, the peasants spontaneously organized defenses. Equipping themselves with weapons they had hidden after the collapse of the Yugoslav army, they guarded their villages during the night to prevent Partisan attacks and avoid Italian countermeasures. In the beginning the Italians were unaware of these tactics, but when they found out they did not oppose them. The first Village Guards were recognized in the early summer of 1942, and from that time on Italian troops supported them with food and ammunition.[20]

The Legion of Death was formed at about the same time as the Village Guards, by anti-Communist youth, onetime members of Catholic or Liberal parties, in order to protect the lives of their leaders and to fight against the Partisans. For the first purpose the members organized a police force in the city of Ljubljana. But the name Legion of Death was later generally given to the mobile detachments that pursued the Partisans in the forests.

The Partisans explained the formation of both the Village Guards and the Legion of Death from a Marxian perspective.[21] The Catholic and Liberal parties had played a miserable, opportunistic role during the first days of war and foreign occupation. Both parties had helped to create Ljubljana Province in order to

19. The anti-Communists stressed that Partisans attacked villages to get new fighters for their Partisan units and not to fight against Italian garrisons. Moreover, the Partisans were on good terms with local Italian commanders and often drank with them in village inns. (Škerbec, pp. 12–13.)

20. Cf. Grum and Pleško, pp. 23–26.

21. The official Italian name for both the Village Guards and the Legion of Death was Milizia Volontaria Anti-Comunista (MVAC). For a detailed Partisan description of the Village Guards and the Legion of Death see Saje, pp. 273–310, 417–81, 517–641. To a large degree, Saje's information is based on confessions extracted from the imprisoned anti-Communists and on testimony given before the Communist people's courts. Because of this fact, anti-Communist writers have questioned the reliability of his information.

continue the bourgeois social order. By this means, they offended national pride and caused a moral depression among the people, who remained without political leadership to give them faith in the future. Creation of the Liberation Front by the Communist party removed this feeling of resignation. With new hope the people looked toward the Liberation Front and its leader, the Communist party, which became not only the vanguard of the working class but also a guide to the entire nation. Neither major bourgeois party was pleased by this development. The Catholic and Liberal parties, bitter enemies before the war, united against the Liberation Front and the Communists, and in so doing collaborated with the Italian occupying forces.[22] After the first successes of the Partisans, the leadership of the Catholic and Liberal parties decided to create bands to fight against them with Italian approval and support. The Village Guards and the Legion of Death had thus been organized by the party leaders and did not reflect spontaneous opposition by the peasants. The Partisans called both formations Bela garda (White Guard), a name used by the Bolsheviks for the forces that fought against them in the Russian civil war.

Besides the Partisans, the Village Guards, and the Legion of Death, the last two being formally recognized by Italian authorities, there existed also the above mentioned Slovenian Chetniks. The first Chetnik guerrilla units were organized in April 1942. At that time the representatives of the prewar political parties united into the Slovenska zaveza (Slovenian Alliance) which was an underground continuation of the National Council created a year before. The Slovenian Alliance was to be the supreme political authority for Slovenia, and recognized the Yugoslav government in London as its legal representative.[23]

To protect the anti-Communists from Partisan massacres and to fight against Italian troops the Slovenian Alliance organized illegal military formations, set up along party lines. These were Slovenska legija (the Slovenian Legion), Sokolska legija (the

22. Škerl, *Zgodovinski časopis,* 5:13–51.
23. *Svobodna Slovenija-Eslovenia libre,* August 31, 1967; Mikuž, *Pregled zgodovine,* 1:303–15. The first work is a weekly newspaper published in Buenos Aires, Argentina, by Slovenian émigrés, hereafter cited as *Svobodna Slovenija.*

Falcon Legion), and Narodna legija (the National Legion). The first comprised members of the Slovenian People's party (Catholics), the second, the Liberals and Socialists, and the third, members of smaller parties and people without party affiliation. Every legion had its own command. All three recognized Draža Mihajlović as supreme commander and formed the Slovenian Chetnik movement. The Partisans called them Plava garda (the Blue Guard) to distinguish them from the White Guard which was directly supported by Italian officials. This movement never developed much military strength. No legion had more than a handful of men in the mountains. The rest of their forces were organized to prevent a Communist seizure of power after the war, and Chetnik activity was limited to underground organization and propaganda. The legions on many occasions received their military supplies from the Village Guards and the Legion of Death. The Chetnik legions did not attack the Italians and the Italian forces did not pursue them.[24] This mutual neutrality and the fact that the Chetniks were supplied at least from time to time by the White Guard, proved to the Partisans that the Chetnik legions were collaborating with the Italians.

RESISTANCE IN THE JULIAN REGION

Partisans and Chetniks also competed in the Slovenian Littoral, where the situation favored the development of illegal organizations. The Italian entry into World War II in 1940 had aroused new hopes for unification with Yugoslavia among the Slovenian minority. Slovenian nationalists organized small terrorist groups that attacked Italian ammunition depots. Italian authorities brought sixty intellectuals, terrorists, and Communists to trial in Trieste in December 1941, before the Extraordinary Tribunal. The group was accused of plotting the assassination of Benito Mussolini as well as committing acts of military sabotage. Nine defendants were condemned to death and five actually executed.[25]

24. Grum and Pleško, pp. 12–13, 19–23, 28–33; Mikuž, *Pregled zgodovine*, 2:338–47, 353–55.
25. See above, n. 33, chapter 2.

In the meantime the first Slovenian Communist propagandists had entered the Slovenian Littoral. Many had been born in, or were onetime residents of, the region. In the summer of 1941 they illegally returned to stimulate active mass resistance against Fascism under the banner of the newly formed Liberation Front of Slovenia. How could the Slovenian party enter and organize itself and the Liberation Front in the Slovenian Littoral, when formal jurisdiction over Communist activity in the area was the prerogative of the Italian Communist party? And how did the Soviet Communist party and the Comintern regard the situation? During this period no Communist party had taken so important a step without Stalin's consent. The answers to these questions are yet incomplete. Tentatively, however, some assumptions can be made from material published by Metod Mikuž, the Slovenian expert on the history of the National Liberation Movement, based on selected Partisan documents.[26]

The Slovenian Communist party justified its action by quoting the April 1934 agreement of the Austrian, Italian, and Yugoslav Communist parties in Moscow under the presidency of George Dimitrov, secretary of the Comintern. According to this agreement all three parties recognized the right of self-determination of the Slovenian people and pledged to support their struggle for unification of Slovenian territory, which had been divided among Austria, Italy, and Yugoslavia.[27] The original aim of the accord

26. Metod Mikuž, "Boji Komunistične partije Jugoslavije za zahodne meje od 1941 do 1945" (The Struggles of the Communist Party of Yugoslavia for the Western Boundaries from 1941 to 1945), *Zgodovinski časopis*, 12–13 (1958–59): 7–24; Mikuž, *Pregled zgodovine*, 1:291–98, 385–90, and 2:216–26, 316–22, 329–30. For an Italian account see Luigi Longo, *I comunisti italiani e il problema triestino* (Rome, 1954), pp. 5–10. This is a reprint of Longo's article published in the review *Rinascita* in December 1953. See also Mario Pacor, *Confine orientale: Questione nazionale e resistenza nel Friuli-Venezia Giulia* (Milan, 1964), pp. 173–84.

27. The agreement was published in the underground organ of the Italian Communist party, *Stato Operaio*, no. 4 (1934), pp. 349–51. It was reprinted in *Delo* (Work), organ of the Central Committee of the Slovenian Communist party, no. 1 (1948), pp. 66–68. (Cf. Mikuž, *Pregled zgodovine*, 1:293.)

was to create an independent Slovenian workers' and peasants' republic, which could join any of the neighboring states (Yugoslavia, Austria, or Italy) in which a Communist regime might be victorious.[28]

Important also was the fact that Umberto Massola, alias Quinto, a member of the Central Committee of the Italian Communist party, had lived in Ljubljana as a guest of the Slovenian party from 1940 on. After Germany attacked the Soviet Union in June 1941, Massola-Quinto left for Italy and became temporary secretary of the Italian Communist party. A portion of the first monetary support for his activities in Italy came from the Slovenian party. Moreover, the Slovenian and Yugoslav Communist parties were Massola-Quinto's communication links with the Comintern and the Soviet Union, at least until the Italian armistice in September 1943.

Before Massola-Quinto left for Italy, he agreed that Slovenian Communists could organize their party and the Liberation Front in the Slovenian Littoral and advised that they cooperate closely with the local Slovenian and Italian Communists in a common struggle against the Fascists. However, Massola-Quinto insisted that the local Italian Communists remain independent and under the direction of the Central Committee of the Italian Communist party.

There were thus two Communist parties—Slovenian and Italian—in the Slovenian Littoral. Though they seem to have reached no general agreement, piecemeal accords for the period ending in September 1943 provided that only the Slovenian party, the Liberation Front, and their Partisan units would be organized in the territory in which Slovenes lived. In the coastal towns of Trieste, Muggia, Koper, Izola, and Monfalcone, both Slovenian and Italian parties would be in existence. Both groups would support a common underground against the Fascists, but each would preserve its independent local party organization, subordinated to the national Central Committees. It was also agreed that the Italians should form their own Partisan regiments, but remain temporarily under Slovenian command until there were

28. *Svobodna Slovenija*, August 31, 1967; Pacor, p. 275. This original aim was denied by the Slovenian Communists in 1942. See *Dokumenti*, 1:295–96.

FASCIST VICTORY AND YUGOSLAV RESISTANCE

enough Italian Partisans for independent action. As events developed, the Slovenian Partisans controlled most of the territory, the Italians being limited to the coastal urban centers. In the long run, this favored the Slovenian Partisans. The Comintern confirmed these accords, which meant that Stalin had agreed to organization of the Slovenian party in the Slovenian Littoral.

More difficult was a question regarding the political future of the Slovenian Littoral. The Italian Communist party recognized in its declaration of January 1942 the right of self-determination and the unification of Slovenian territory—but only in principle. Trouble arose over concrete delimitation of the former Italian territory which would go to Slovenia. In general, the Italian party consented to unification of the compactly settled Slovenian sector of the Slovenian Littoral with a future Yugoslavia. It disagreed, however, that Trieste, Monfalcone, and the Istrian coastal towns necessarily formed a part of Slovenian territory. The people here should have the right to determine which state they preferred to join. The Slovenian Communist party, on the other hand, demanded that the entire Slovenian Littoral, including Trieste and the coastal towns, should go to Slovenia and Yugoslavia, and that Venetian Slovenia and other parts of Udine Province, at one time settled by Slovenes but later Italianized, should also go to Slovenia.[29] By September 1943, at the time of the Italian armistice, the leaders of the two parties had not yet agreed on the future frontier, and negotiations continued.

From the summer of 1941 to the end of July 1942, the Communists organized their party in the Slovenian Littoral, and also the first committees of the Liberation Front. To gain support of the Slovenes, the Communists sent into the Littoral members of other political groups participating in the Liberation Front. These agitators appealed to Slovenian nationalism, stressing this

29. Pacor, pp. 173–84; Yugoslavia, Vojnozgodovinski inštitut jugoslovanske ljudske armade (War-Historical Institute of the Yugoslav Peoples Army), *Zbornik dokumentov in podatkov o narodno-osvobodilni vojni jugoslovanskih narodov* (Collection of Documents and Data of the National Liberation War of the Yugoslav Nations), pt. 6, *Borbe v Sloveniji* (The Struggles in Slovenia), 12 vols. (Ljubljana, 1953–65), pt. 6, 5:86–87. This is the Slovenian edition of *Zbornik* (Belgrade) and will be cited as *Zbornik*.

moment as the most opportune in which to fight for unification of all Slovenian land by joining the Liberation Front and the Partisans. Some Slovenes did join, while others were sympathetic to both Partisans and Chetniks. To many Slovenes the Liberation Front marked only a continuation of the old national resistance to Fascism and foreign rule. In rural districts, unlike Ljubljana Province, the Liberation Front did not encounter great opposition, as non-Communist Slovenes for a long time had been without political or cultural organizations to lead a struggle against communism.

Significantly, at this time the Communists did not propagate ideas for a new social order and did not come into the open as Communists. Their party organization was to be unknown to the non-Communist Partisans and followers of the Liberation Front, a fact clearly underlined in a letter sent by the Central Committee of the Slovenian Communist party on November 16, 1942, to its Provincial Committee for the Slovenian Littoral.[30]

By the summer of 1942 about one hundred Partisans were actually participating in sabotage and approximately one hundred local committees of the Liberation Front existed to spread propaganda and collect food, clothing, medicine, and arms for the Partisan units. Fascist authorities knew of this favorable disposition toward the Liberation Front and Partisans. In his speech in Gorizia on July 31, 1942, Mussolini warned the Slovenes that the strong hand of Roman justice would destroy the Communist conspiracy in the Julian Region as well as in Slovenia and Yugoslavia.[31] Coincident with these warnings came the first actions in the Slovenian Littoral by the regular army and Fascist militia. Seven villages in the valley of Vipava (Vipacco) were burned.[32]

This military action did not, however, destroy the Partisan movement. On the contrary, new recruits poured in as the first period, that mainly of propaganda and small sabotage actions, ended and the second period, that of organized struggle, began. From the summer of 1942 on, the Partisans directed their attacks especially against the vital railroad connections on the Trieste-

30. *Zbornik*, pt. 6, 4:274.
31. Gabrovšek, p. 49. For directions given to the Italian army by Mussolini see *Zbornik*, pt. 6, 3:559–64.
32. V. Novak et al., p. 402.

Villach-Vienna and the Trieste-Ljubljana-Vienna lines. The Partisan units, still small, were constantly on the march in order to avoid enemy encirclement, and therefore as yet controlled no given territory. Nevertheless, because of the ever present Partisan menace, the Italians had to divert the Divisione Giulia, which had been ready to leave for the Russian front, into a fight against the Partisans in hopes of eliminating them once and for all.

This large-scale military action began in November 1942. It was preceded by mobilization of the entire male population, including boys thirteen to fifteen years old, into special Italian battalions which were sent to southern Italy, Sicily, and Sardinia, to get them out of the way, because the Slovenian and Croatian people could no longer be trusted by Italy after the attack on Yugoslavia of April 1941.[33]

The outcome was quite different from what the Italians had hoped. The Partisan detachments managed to escape destruction and, in fact, increased in size. Mobilization of the people for deportation, the burning of villages, and similar atrocities caused a flight into the forests where the refugees joined the Partisan units.

In the spring of 1943 the Partisan forces were for the first time able to cross the old Italo-Austrian frontier of 1866 and penetrate into Slovenska Benečija (Venetian Slovenia) and Friuli, where they distributed anti-Fascist propaganda.[34] The growth of the Partisan forces went hand in hand with the spread of local Liberation Front committees. In the fall of 1942, a small Provincial Liberation Front Committee was formed for the Slovenian Littoral, and by December it had increased in size. In the following February, the first conference of delegates of the Liberation Front was held, and during this time a new, enlarged Provincial Committee was elected, with one Italian representative.

Local members of the Italian party living mostly in Trieste and the coastal towns, however, were inactive up to the summer of 1943. They regarded any organized resistance as premature, and dangerous to the existence of the party itself because of Fascist vigilance. The Italian party in June 1943 organized its Littoral Committee for Trieste (Comitato Litorale di Trieste PCI). This was the local (provincial) committee of the Italian party with

33. Ibid., pp. 402–3; *Slovensko Primorje in Istra,* pp. 362–63.
34. Mikuž, *Pregled zgodovine,* 2:318–19.

activity limited to the city of Trieste and the surrounding coastal towns of Monfalcone, Muggia, Koper, and Izola. In the same fashion as the Slovenian Liberation Front, the Italian party created a mass organization for the same coastal territory, called the Action Committee of the National Front (Comitato Fronte Nazionale d'Azione).[35] This was undoubtedly the result of negotiations between the Slovenian and Italian Communist leadership and the Comintern, which urged the Italian party in the Slovenian Littoral to act. It must be noted also that this happened at a time when Great Britain had sent her first military observers to the Tito Partisans in Yugoslavia, in the spring of 1943. This recognition by the Western Allies increased the prestige of Yugoslav and Slovenian Partisans in the Slovenian Littoral and stirred the Italian Communists to action.

To summarize: Beginning in the summer of 1943, Communist activity in the Slovenian Littoral was divided into two parts. In the rural Slovenian section only Slovenian Partisans, the Liberation Front, and the Slovenian Communist party operated. In Trieste and the surrounding coastal towns both Communist parties, Slovenian and Italian, existed. Here both built up their own mass organization, the Liberation Front for the Slovenes, and the Action Committee of the National Front for the Italians.

Meanwhile, during 1942 and 1943 the Chetniks set up encampments in the mountains along the old Italo-Yugoslav border, from which they sent propaganda to the Slovenian Littoral. They appealed to national solidarity and promised to fight for unification of the Slovenian Littoral with Yugoslavia. At the same time, the Chetniks condemned the Partisan movement, which they saw as dividing the nation and fighting on behalf of Communist interests only.[36] The Chetniks had the disadvantage of being latecomers. In the eyes of the Partisans, the Chetniks were the ones creating disunity. Moreover, the Chetniks were accused of tacit collaboration with the Italians. After recognition of Tito's Partisans by the Western Allies, the Chetniks began to lose in popularity. From the summer of 1943 the majority of people probably

35. Ibid., 2:321–22.
36. Ibid., 1:386.

favored the Liberation Front, and the Partisans became the only important Slovenian underground.

To the city of Trieste itself, the Slovenian Communist party had sent delegates in July and August 1941 to organize the local Triestine Slovenian Communists into their own Slovenian party, but the task was difficult. As soon as the city organization began active work, Fascist authorities arrested the leaders. At least three times new men had to replace the old leadership and to begin again from scratch.[37] The great difficulties of the Slovenian Communist city organization could be at least partially ascribed to the ethnic character of Trieste, for here the Slovenian Communists worked in a predominantly Italian city.

After establishing the Slovenian party organization, the Communists tried to develop the city committees of the Liberation Front, and for that purpose got in touch with Slovenian intellectuals in Trieste. In 1941 the Slovenian intellectuals and bourgeoisie in Trieste formed an illegal National Council, later headed by Dr. Jože Ferfolja. However, an agreement was reached only after September 1943, for this group to participate in the Liberation Front.[38]

Because of the reluctance of the leaders of the Slovenian intellectuals and middle class to join the Partisan Liberation Front, the Slovenian Communists had to appeal directly to individual Slovenes. In 1942, they succeeded in organizing the first city committees of the Liberation Front, and in November of the same year the first district committee of the Liberation Front for Trieste.

From the beginning of 1941 the Slovenian Communist party had urged the leaders of the Italian party to begin action against Fascism. The Italian leaders, however, were convinced that the time was not yet ripe. Dissatisfied with this position, the Slovenian party began to invite individual Italian workers to join the Partisan units. How much success the Slovenian Communists had in this recruiting is still not clear. It seems, however, that not many Italian workers enrolled in the Slovenian Partisan units.

Toward the end of December 1942 at a joint meeting with the Slovenian Communists the Italian Communists agreed to

37. *Slovensko Primorje in Istra*, pp. 456–57.
38. Ibid., pp. 458–59.

participate in the common struggle against Fascism. A positive result was the formation of Delavska enotnost–Unità Operaia (Workers' Unity), a mixed Italo-Slovenian organization for workers employed in Trieste's big factories. It was designed to foster the struggle against Fascism and recruit soldiers for the Partisan units. With the reorganization of the local Italian Communist party in June 1943, Trieste became the seat of the Comitato Litorale di Trieste PCI and of its mass organization Comitato Fronte Nazionale d'Azione.[39] Fascist vigilance, however, kept the membership and activities of all these underground organizations in Trieste quite limited. Their important efforts began only after the Italian armistice in September 1943.

Up to the fall of Mussolini in July 1943, democratic forces in Trieste were inactive. Italian and Slovenian democratic leaders looked toward London rather than Moscow. The Slovenian National Council in Trieste favored the Yugoslav London government and could not be induced to join the Communist-sponsored Liberation Front. The same was true for Italian democratic leaders. They became more and more convinced that Italy would lose the war and Fascism would disappear. The same feeling spread among the Italian armed forces. But little more than occasional private discussions took place among the leaders of pre-Fascist Italian parties.

Before the summer of 1943 the Chetniks had many sympathizers in Trieste, especially among the middle class and intellectuals. They listened to the London radio, were in favor of the Yugoslav exiled government in London, and hoped that after the war the Slovenian Littoral together with Trieste would be united with the rest of the Slovenes in Yugoslavia. These sympathizers preferred the royal underground, the Chetniks, but probably, like the Italian democrats in Trieste and the coastal towns, did not participate in any active organization. However, pro-Chetnik sentiment must have been quite strong. Partisan documents show that the Slovenian Communists were aware of, and regarded as detrimental to their own movement, these pro-Western and pro-Chetnik feelings.

39. Comitato cittadino dell'U.A.I.S., *Trieste nella lotta per la democrazia* (Trieste, 1945), pp. 45–46, hereafter cited as *Trieste nella lotta*; *Slovensko Primorje in Istra*, pp. 457–58; Mikuž, *Pregled zgodovine*, 2:321–22.

If any organization of the pro-Chetnik movement existed among the Slovenes in Trieste it is hard to establish, as there are no published works about it. On the other hand, a large amount of literature exists glorifying Partisan activities. This factor could easily create an exaggerated picture of Partisan strength in comparison with the Chetnik forces.

The situation was different in the southern Julian Region, that is to say, in Istria, Rijeka, and the nearby islands. This land, which I shall refer to as Istria, was regarded by the Yugoslav Communists as Croatian. It was the task of the Croat Communist party to organize the underground. Their work was much more complicated than that of Slovenian Communists in the Slovenian Littoral, because of a different political situation.

After the collapse of Yugoslavia in April 1941, Slovenia had been divided among three occupation forces, but Croatia, though of limited size, became an independent state. Thus while Slovenian Communists were urging the Slovenes to support a national liberation struggle against foreign occupation forces, Croat Communists could hardly appeal to such sentiments. True, the Croats were dissatisfied with their pro-Fascist, so-called Ustashi government, headed by Ante Pavelić, and disliked Italian occupation of some parts of the Croatian coast, but they still regarded their independent state as the realization of an old national dream. Thus, at first the Communists had to rely on their own strength. The only support they received came from the Serbian minority, which had left for the mountains to avoid Ustashi persecutions. But many of these Serbs favored the royalist cause and refused at least in the first year or so to cooperate with the Communists.

The Croat Communists formed the first Partisan units out of their own membership in the last part of 1941 and the beginning of 1942. They were later joined by some Serbs and a very few democratic Croats. While the Slovenes had their own Liberation Front and Partisan units by the summer of 1941, the Croat Liberation Movement could be organized on a broader base only in June 1943, into the Provincial Anti-Fascist Council of National Liberation of Croatia (Zemaljsko antifašističko vijeće narodnog oslobodjenja Hrvatske), referred to as ZAVNOH in Yugoslav literature.[40]

40. Zalar, p. 98.

As to their position in Istria, the Croatian Communist party had no agreement similar to that of April 1934, which had been used by the Slovenian party in discussions with Massola-Quinto.[41] Furthermore, it is still doubtful that Massola-Quinto, in his talks with the Slovenian Communists, had agreed that the Croat party could be organized in Istria. Only in the summer of 1942 did the Comintern send two letters to the Yugoslav Communist party, urging the organization of Partisan units in Istria, which would be supported by both the Croatian and Italian parties. With these letters the Comintern confirmed, at least indirectly, the right of the Croat Communists to organize their own party in Istria.[42] Finally, it should be added that the western shore of Istria had an Italian population, which preferred an Italian government, even if Fascist, to a foreign Communist movement. To a lesser degree, this was also true for local Italian Communists, who were of course opposed to Fascism but did not like to come under a foreign state, even though it were Communist.

Taking all the above factors into consideration, it can be understood why in Istria the Croat Communists encountered greater difficulties than their Slovenian comrades, were slower to organize their party, and still slower to organize their National Liberation Movement.

For a year after the summer of 1941 the Croat party tried to create its own cells in Istria. The work was hard, as there were no Croatian Communists there, and the rural Croat population lacked educated leadership. Most of the towns were Italian, and there the workers belonged to the Italian Communist party. The Croat Communists had first to educate their own cadres in the towns and rural districts. They eventually succeeded in organizing some cells of their party and some small Partisan detachments out of recruited Communist members. From time to time the Slovenian Partisans gave a helping hand, and by the summer of 1942 the first large Partisan unit, named "Vladimir Gortan," was formed in Istria.[43]

41. For an account of events in Istria during 1941–43 see *Slovensko Primorje in Istra*, pp. 201–55; Pacor, pp. 173–84.
42. See *Zbornik* (Belgrade), pt. 2, 5:166; Mikuž, *Zgodovinski časopis*, 12–13:13–14.
43. *Slovensko Primorje in Istra*, pp. 229–30.

FASCIST VICTORY AND YUGOSLAV RESISTANCE

The Croat Communists were unsuccessful in winning over the Istrian Italian Communists to start armed resistance against Fascism or to support Croatian Partisan units. Italian Communists, as in Trieste, argued that it was too early to start an armed uprising. They pointed out that the struggle of the Croat Communists in Istria had a nationalistic rather than a proletarian character, because the Croat Communists accepted too many peasants into their Partisan units. Furthermore, there was no guarantee that these peasants would not turn their arms, at an opportune moment, against the Communists and ally with the bourgeoisie against the workers. The Istrian Italian leaders again and again stressed that they would cooperate with the Croatian Communists only after an agreement was reached at the top level between the Central Committees of the Yugoslav and Italian parties or when they received instructions from the Comintern to support the Croat party and to join Croat Partisan units.[44]

Until September 1943, there was no agreement between the Istrian Italian and Croat parties similar to the one in the Slovenian Littoral. Because of this the Croat Communists also appealed directly to Italian workers to join in their fight against Fascism. Through bypassing the leadership, the Croat party finally succeeded in gaining some followers among the Istrian Italian Communists and workers, who joined the Croat Partisans.

Only in March 1943 was the Croat party in Istria able to establish a provincial party leadership, and the provincial organization of the National Liberation Movement came into being in August, two months after its superior the National Liberation Council for Croatia (ZAVNOH) had been formed.[45] The Croat Communists thus organized the provincial leadership of their party and of their liberation movement in Istria about a year later than did their Slovenian comrades in the Slovenian Littoral. In the summer of 1943, the Croat National Liberation Movement began to publish a Croat underground journal in Istria. This was *Glas Istre* (the Voice of Istria). Previously journals and pamphlets had been sent to Istria from Croatia proper.[46]

Unlike the Slovenian Littoral, where both the Italian and

44. Ibid., pp. 231–33, 242, 248–49.
45. Ibid., pp. 241, 247.
46. Ibid., pp. 252–55.

Slovenian Communists and their liberation movements were operating, Istria had only one active underground by September 1943, led by the Croats. The Italian Communist leadership in Istria remained inactive.

Many Croats and some Italians in Istria, as was the case in the Slovenian Littoral, sympathized with the Western Allies. Some Croats in Istria, disillusioned by the Ustashi regime in Croatia, favored the Yugoslav London government. They hoped that it would come home as a victor after the war. The triumph of the Allied forces would return parts of the Croatian Littoral and Dalmatia, which at this time was under Italian occupation, and would unite Istria with Croatia and Yugoslavia. This sentiment was stronger in Istria and in parts of Dalmatia than in Pavelić-controlled Croatia. For Istria, as well as for the Slovenian Littoral, there is no documented evidence of an organized royal underground. The Croat Chetniks, however, were encamped along the old Yugoslav border of Istria. Their propaganda must have been effective enough to cause worry to Partisan sources.[47]

Little activity can be ascertained among Italian democratic forces in Istria up to September 1943. The Italian democrats hesitated to oppose Fascism which at that time seemed to most Italians the only guarantee that Istria would remain Italian, because they were aware of the Croat demand to unite Istria with Croatia. Nationalism, then, underlay the sentiments of the Italian Communists as well as democrats. The same was true, of course, for the Croats and Slovenes, whatever their political beliefs.

47. Ibid., p. 242.

4
THE ADRIATIC LITTORAL: GERMAN OCCUPATION AND THE COLLABORATIONISTS (1943–1945)

GERMAN ADMINISTRATION

In 1943, by a turn of the fortunes of war, the Julian Region got a new master. Mussolini fell on July 25, to be replaced by a military government under General Pietro Badoglio. A month and a half later, on September 8, Italy signed an armistice with the Allied powers and the Soviet Union.[1] As Italian troops in the Julian Region lay down their arms and hurried home, the Partisans acted quickly to occupy all of the area except the cities of Trieste, Pula, and Rijeka. For a short time they gloried in their dominion, until German troops in September and October forced a retreat deep into the mountains and forests. The Germans would rule the Julian Region from then until the end of the war.

The amazingly thorough and rapid dissolution of the Italian army and its failure to defend any part of this vital section of its eastern frontier, gained at such a cost in World War I, have aroused much argument among Italians. Fascists throw the blame entirely upon a Badoglio government intent only on seeking an armistice. Non-Fascists indict a Fascist regime that rewarded "party" generals who, confused by the downfall of Mussolini, sought salvation by collaborating with the Germans. Both sides miss a significant point.

1. Italy signed the armistice on September 3. The unconditional surrender was made public on September 8. Later, on September 29, more detailed terms of surrender were signed. On this see: Winston S. Churchill, *The Second World War*, 6 vols. (Boston: Houghton Mifflin Company, 1948–53), 5:110–13, 195; Diego de Castro, *Il problema di Trieste: Genesi e sviluppi della questione giuliana in relazione agli avvenimenti internazionali, 1943–1952*, 2d ed. (Bologna, 1953), pp. 90–91.

GERMAN ADMINISTRATION

The Italian army in the Julian Region was on ethnically non-Italian terrain, where a native Partisan guerrilla force was daily gaining in strength. Isolated in their cities, the Italians could not form guerrilla bands against either the Germans or the Slavs. Herein lay the principal reason for Italian soldiers to throw down their arms, abandon their places, and try to cross the Isonzo River, on the other side of which they could feel secure and at home.[2]

The Germans, having assured the conquest of most of the terrain, formed the Adriatisches Küstenland (Adriatic Littoral) out of the Julian Region, the provinces of Udine (Friuli) and Ljubljana, and the Dalmatian coast and Adriatic islands. All civil

2. For a description of events happening around September 8, see, for example, the following works of Italian pro-Fascist and democratic writers, and of Yugoslav anti-Communist and Partisan authors. Pro-Fascist: Giovanni Esposito, *Trieste e la sua odissea: Contributo alla storia di Trieste e del "Litorale Adriatico" dal 25 luglio 1943, al maggio 1945* (Rome, 1952), pp. 31–67; and Bruno Coceani, *Mussolini, Hitler, Tito alle porte orientali d'Italia* (Bologna, 1948), pp. 7–22. Italian democratic: Antonio Santin, *Trieste 1943–1945: Scritti, discorsi, appunti, lettere presentate, raccolte e commentate a cura di Guido Botteri* (Udine, 1963), pp. 16–27; Biagio Marin, "Coscienza nazionale," *Trieste*, no. 2 (July–Aug. 1954), pp. 14–15; Ercole Miani, "La resistenza nella Venezia Giulia," *Il Ponte*, 4, no. 4 (Apr. 1948): 339–45; G. F. [Galliano Fogar], "La politica tedesca nel Litorale Adriatico," *Trieste*, no. 3 (Sept.–Oct. 1954), pp. 19–21, and no. 4 (Nov.–Dec. 1954), pp. 23–26; Pacor, pp. 185–99. Yugoslav anti-Communist: Matija Tratnik (pseud.), "Temna zarja na Primorskem" (Gloomy Dawn over the Littoral), *Koledar Svobodne Slovenije, 1951* (Calendar of "Svobodna Slovenija," 1951), p. 114, calendars hereafter cited as *Koledar-Zbornik;* "Ob dvajsetletnici: Iz zapiskov zareškega župnika" (For the Twentieth Anniversary: From the Notes of the Parish Priest of Zarečje), serialized in *Vestnik-Noticiero*, 15, no. 8 (Aug. 1964) to 17, no. 6–7 (June–July 1966). The monthly journal is published by the Union of Slovenian Anti-Communist Combatants in Buenos Aires, Argentina. Hereafter cited as *Vestnik*. Partisan works: "Mobilizacija in oborožitev primorskega ljudstva ob kapitulaciji Italije" (The Mobilization and the Arming of the People of the Littoral at the Time of the Italian Capitulation), *Ljudska pravica*, Sept. 21, 1947; France Škerl, *La battaglia delle popolazioni del litorale per il potere popolare* (Ljubljana, 1945), pp. 6–19; Documents nos. 9 and 67 (*Zbornik*, pt. 6, 7:20, 112–16), are characteristic; *Slovensko Primorje in Istra*, pp. 256–70, 378–89.

authority came into the hands of the German Supreme Civil Commissariat for the Adriatic Littoral, with its seat in Trieste.[3]

During the month of October 1943 the Germans set up their administration. Dr. Friedrich Rainer, the Gauleiter (governor) of Carinthia, was named supreme commissary, and Dr. Wolsegger became Regierungspresident (president of the civil service) and vice-supreme commissary.[4] Lower-level posts remained in the hands of the native population, though subject to control by German overseers. The Italian Bruno Coceani was nominated as *prefetto* (prefect) of Trieste Province and supervisor of all other Italian prefects of the region, who would be appointed later. Cesare Pagnini, also an Italian, was designated mayor of Trieste, the largest city and center of the Adriatic Littoral.[5] Each of these functionaries had a counterpart in the Deutscher Berater (German adviser), who represented the supreme commissary. Thus in Trieste Dr. Rudolf Hinterregger became the agent of the supreme commissary on the provincial level functioning as an adviser to Coceani, and, on the municipal level, Herr Schranzhofer was made adviser to Pagnini.[6]

Though Ljubljana Province formally comprised a part of the Adriatic Littoral, the Germans granted it special status. Leon Rupnik, a former Yugoslav general, became president of the province, directly responsible to the supreme commissary. He was therefore not under supervision of Prefect Coceani, although Ljubljana Province continued to use Italian currency and received food supplies from Italy. And, despite the fact that Coceani maintained private connections with Mussolini's new Fascist

---

3. The decree concerning the formation of the Adriatic Littoral was signed on October 1, 1943, and published in the first number of the Official Gazette for the Adriatic Littoral on October 15, 1943. The decree was translated and printed in *Zbornik,* pt. 6, 7:557–58.

4. Rainer, as governor of Carinthia, remained in Klagenfurt, the capital of Carinthia, and seldom appeared in Trieste. Wolsegger, stationed in Trieste, was Rainer's right-hand man, executing his orders (cf. Esposito, p. 97).

5. Coceani, pp. 29–30. Note that Duroselle (p. 128) is spelling Wohlsegger instead of Wolsegger.

6. Fogar, *Trieste,* no. 3, p. 20; Esposito, p. 97. Santin (pp. 40 and 62) is spelling Hinteregger instead of Hinterregger.

Republic established in September 1943 in the north of Italy, the Adriatic Littoral remained under German civil and military control. This relationship signified de facto separation of the Adriatic Littoral from Italian administration. In the event of a German victory, the Nazis apparently intended that the Julian Region, at least up to the old Italo-Austrian border, would become a part of the German Reich.[7]

The German heads of government, such as Rainer, Wolsegger, and the S.S. commander, General Odilo Globocnik, were onetime officials of the Austrian empire. Their underlings had likewise been Austrian subjects, thus emphasizing the old ties between Trieste and Vienna. To accentuate these links, the Germans prepared a radio program in Trieste: "Trieste saluta Vienna" (Trieste Greets Vienna). Reopened, too, was the Heim der Deutschen (German Home), a cultural and political center for former Austrian Germans in Trieste. In the same vein, *Die Deutsche Adria Zeitung* (the German Adriatic Newspaper) was published in Trieste. Of course, this pro-Austrian policy was not one pursued merely by a few German officials, but a plan approved by the Nazi leaders to gain support for Hitler's Germany among pro-Austrian circles of the Triestine bourgeoisie.[8]

To enlist the aid of the local population, the Germans exploited Italo-Slavic animosities. They recognized the existence and language rights of all ethnic groups. Their official gazette was published not only in German but in the two principal languages spoken in each area—Italian and Slovenian in Gorizia and Trieste, and Italian and Croatian in Istria and Dalmatia.[9] The Germans nominated Slovenes and Croats to the local administration, and allowed Slovenian and Croat schools to be established, thus re-

7. F. W. Deakin, *The Brutal Friendship: Mussolini, Hitler, and the Fall of Italian Fascism* (New York, 1962), pp. 613–17.

8. Coceani, pp. 72, 229–31; Elio Apih, "La stampa nazista a Trieste," *Trieste*, no. 9 (Sept.–Oct. 1955), pp. 25–27; Carlo Ventura, "Goebbels e il Litorale Adriatico," *Trieste*, no. 27 (Sept.–Oct. 1958), pp. 26–30; and by the same author, *La stampa a Trieste, 1943–1945* (Udine, 1958), pp. 48–67.

9. At the same time the German government denied the national existence of the Slovenes in Southern Styria (Northern Slovenia), annexed to greater Germany in 1941.

versing the policy in force under Italian Fascist rule. In this way the Germans secured some Slovenian and Croat support. At the same time, of course, these concessions to the Slavs greatly alarmed Italian nationalists. To protect as far as possible Italian interests and the Italian character of the Julian Region, many Italians also collaborated with the Germans. Especially in Trieste, this response involved two groups: the one led by Coceani and the new Partito Fascista Republicano (the Fascist Republican party or PFR).

ITALIAN COLLABORATIONISTS

One would have expected the Germans to choose their prefects and other Italian administrators from the ranks of the newly organized Republican Fascist party, that is from those who remained faithful to Mussolini. But just the opposite was true. While the Germans reinstated Mussolini and his Republican Fascists in northern Italy, they refused to recognize the new prefects appointed by Mussolini in the Adriatic Littoral. Instead the Germans made their own choices, as with Coceani in Trieste, a fact which seemed further to emphasize their intent to separate the Adriatic Littoral from Mussolini's Republic.

The great Slavic uprising under the leadership of Tito's Partisans immediately after the armistice, and the German occupation which followed, convinced Coceani that Italy faced two great dangers: Slavic and German. He stated in his works published after the war that he had not believed an ultimate German victory possible. For him the German danger was transient; the Slovenes and Croats posed the long-term threat. Coceani had chosen the lesser evil and collaborated with the Germans. He thus kept local administration in the hands of Italians, thereby protecting Italian interests which might be used to organize Italian resistance against the Slavs after the war. Coceani further explained that had he refused to work with the Germans, the latter would have themselves taken over the administration or would have appointed some old pro-Austrian Triestine in his place.[10]

Coceani affirmed that in accepting the appointment of prefect he had been able to stem Germanization of Trieste by invoking

10. Coceani, p. 32.

the pre–World War I practice of legal resistance. Among other things, he had prevented the deportation to Italy of Italians who had not been born in the Adriatic Littoral, a policy the Germans canceled only after Coceani's intervention.[11] But as prefect he could also oppose the German policy of establishing Slovenian schools, cultural institutions, and administration in his province. While working with the Germans, Coceani tried to create a strong Italian bloc which, sheltered by the German army, would be able to prepare for defense of the Julian Region against a Yugoslav takeover at the end of the war.

In pursuit of his aims Coceani tried to revive the old Irredentist tradition. He supported or reestablished the cultural institutions, magazines, and newspapers that had been prominent in the fight of Italian Irredentists against Austria, some of which had been suspended during the Fascist regime. Like old Irredentists, Coceani urged the Italians to subordinate their political differences to the one historic necessity, namely, that the Julian Region remain united with the future Italian state. While recognizing the existence of different political groups, he urged them to form a single bloc, which could then defend the Julian Region primarily against annexationist designs of Yugoslavia. Toward the end of the war Coceani also convinced Mussolini that this was the only sensible course to follow in the Julian Region. Consequently, in March 1945 Mussolini himself urged all Italians to cooperate. As reported by Coceani:

> The order given by Il Duce was to establish contacts with the representatives of the Comitato di Liberazione [Italian

---

11. Ibid., pp. 73–74, 141, 210–11; Esposito, pp. 66–67. Among other anti-Italian plans the German authorities even discussed with General Rupnik the creation of a Slovenian state embracing the Slovenian Littoral (consisting of the provinces of Gorizia, Trieste, and the part of the Province of Udine claimed by the Slovenes) and the Province of Ljubljana. The offer was tempting, since the Slovenes would thus reach a boundary west of the Isonzo River, but General Rupnik declined the proposal because the German authorities would not permit Southern Styria and their part of Carniola inhabited by Slovenes to be united with the new Slovenian state. (This information was given to the author in 1945 by a person who had been closely connected with the Rupnik government.)

underground] and with all the Italian parties, including the Communists, to create a bloc of Italian forces against the annexationist designs of the Slavs.[12]

Constantly keeping in mind the end of the war, Coceani requested the Germans to permit his group to form its own police force in Trieste. Finally the Germans granted permission, and Mayor Pagnini organized the Guardia Civica, which, according to Coceani, could be used at the end of the war for the defense of Trieste against the advancing Yugoslavs. Suspecting that the Guardia Civica and Fascist military bodies in the Adriatic Littoral might be too weak for such a defense, Coceani urged the Germans to allow the Fascist military units from Mussolini's Republic to be transferred to the Adriatic Littoral.[13] But the Germans refused this request and held firm to de facto separation of the Adriatic Littoral from Italy.

Coceani's followers were old Fascists who for various reasons had refused to join the Republican Fascist party organized by Mussolini after the armistice. Obviously, there was bound to be constant tension between Coceani's group and the Republican Fascists. The Germans had entrusted the administration to Coceani's group, whereas the Republican Fascists had thought it should be in their hands. Moreover, the Republican Fascists stood for one-party rule, and had refused Coceani's plan for a national bloc composed of all Italian political groups. Finally, Coceani's followers were looked upon as traitors to Mussolini. Nonetheless, aside from these tensions, there were constant contacts between the two groups.

In the Adriatic Littoral the Germans permitted the Republican Fascists to organize their party and have their own military formations (of course under German supervision), which were used to fight the Partisans. In Trieste the Republican Fascists were allowed to have their own secret police, known for its persecution of the Italian and Slovenian underground.[14] While differences, or

12. Coceani, p. 222. Cf. Esposito, p. 138.
13. Coceani, p. 88.
14. For more information on the *Partito Fascista Republicano* in Trieste see Esposito, pp. 137–38; Teodoro Sala, *La crisi finale nel Litorale Adriatico, 1944–1945* (Udine, 1962), pp. 118–32.

rather jealousies, existed between Coceani's group and the Republican Fascists, they both had been nursed by Fascist ideas and both collaborated with the Germans because they thought it the best defense for Italian interests in the Adriatic Littoral. However, not all Italians agreed. There were those who opposed both groups, not for want of nationalistic sentiment, but because they opposed both the old and new Fascist ideologies and because they felt that collaboration with the Germans could bring only disaster to Italian interests. These Italians formed their own underground, the Comitato di Liberazione Nazionale (CLN), which will be discussed in the following chapter.

ANTI-COMMUNISTS IN LJUBLJANA PROVINCE

The fall of Fascism and the Italian armistice enabled the Slovenes of the Julian Region to express publicly their nationalistic feelings and their various political views. The result was a threefold split into Partisan, Catholic, and Liberal groups. Each could look for advice, guidance, or help to a similar parent organization or movement in the abutting Ljubljana Province. Hence the events taking place in Ljubljana Province exerted an even greater impact than before on political movements in the Slovenian Littoral.

By September 1943 in Ljubljana Province the struggle between Communists and anti-Communists had been going on for more than a year.[15] The Partisan forces, experienced in guerrilla fighting, had a united leadership in the National Liberation Front, with a clearly designed political goal—to obtain power and to introduce a Communist regime. Communist discipline prevented dissent in political organization and permeated the Partisan armed forces.

Although the anti-Communist forces were brought together by their fear and hatred of communism, their support of the royal Yugoslav government-in-exile, and their recognition of General

15. For more information about the events in Ljubljana Province see the following works: Saje, pp. 757–91, and Mikuž, *Pregled zgodovine*, 2:338–55. Both works are pro-Partisan. Major Karl Novak's article, "Pokret otpora u Slovenačkoj" (The Resistance Movement in Slovenia), in *Knjiga o Draži*, ed. Knežević, 1:317–32, defends the Chetnik point of view. Grum and Pleško's work gives a general anti-Communist account.

Mihajlović as supreme commander of all Yugoslav armed forces at home, there their unity ended. In contrast to the Partisans, they suffered from a severe diversity in political organization and goals. Their military strength lay in the Village Guards (numbering about 6,500 men), legally recognized by the Italians, and in the much smaller semi-illegal Chetnik force of about 350 men.[16] Political leadership of anti-Communist activity remained in the hands of the Slovenian Alliance, an underground committee composed of representatives of the prewar political parties.[17] The Catholic party, the strongest of the three principal political parties, played a predominant role, because, among other things, the great majority of the Village Guards were also members of this party. The other two main political parties combined (Liberal and Socialist) were much weaker than the Catholic party alone and thus had to make concessions to it. Each political party had its own underground organization—the Slovenian, Falcon, and National legions.[18] As before, the legions concentrated on political propaganda, and recruited and organized their followers into units which were to enter an armed struggle only at the end of the war,

16. The term Village Guards, as used herein, includes the Legion of Death, except when the latter is specifically mentioned. The official number of Village Guards was 6,500 (Grum and Pleško, p. 64); about the same number is given by pro-Partisan works (Saje, p. 708; and Komel, p. 92), while Major Novak estimated them as 10,000 strong. Novak's mistake occurred as the result of his enumeration of the entire Catholic force included in the Slovenian Legion, which would mean 6,500 Village Guards and about 3,500 organized reserve members of the Slovenian Legion. (Cf. K. Novak, *Knjiga o Draži,* 1:319, 322, 327.)

17. One must keep in mind that the leadership of these political parties had been greatly reduced in size and quality during the war, thus moving some lesser leaders to the top leadership. Some old leaders had been abroad in Great Britain, the United States, and Switzerland. Others, mostly from Northern Slovenia, had been in German prisons and camps, or had been expelled to Serbia and Croatia by the Germans from 1941 on. Still others had been killed by the Partisans, as mentioned above.

18. According to K. Novak (*Knjiga o Draži,* 1:319) the Slovenian Legion numbered 10,000 men and the Falcon Legion, 1,000. He gave no figures for the National Legion, mentioning only that it was a smaller group.

at which time each party hoped to achieve its political aims by means of its own armed units. The Catholic party stood for a democratic federal Yugoslavia with self-government (autonomy) for Slovenia while the majority of Liberals and Socialists favored a return of the prewar centralistic form of government. Hence the diverse anti-Communist forces of the Slovenian Alliance formed two larger groups—autonomists and centralists. The former included the legally recognized Village Guards and the underground Slovenian Legion, whereas the centralists controlled the Falcon and National legions and the small Chetnik guerrilla force.

These political differences became accentuated during 1943 because of the centralistic tendencies of Major Karl Novak whom General Mihajlović had appointed as his representative in Slovenia and commander of the Chetnik military units. The autonomist Catholic party was quite reluctant to recognize the unlimited military authority of a commander known for his centralistic sympathies or to recruit volunteers for him. Hence the Slovenian Alliance and the Catholic party recognized Major Novak as the commander of Chetnik guerrilla units but demanded that he submit to directives of the Slovenian Alliance. Major Novak instead insisted that he was subordinate only to General Mihajlović and supreme over all anti-Communist forces. This status would make him above and independent of political parties and the Slovenian Alliance. As this question was never properly settled, it hindered the recruitment of Chetnik guerrillas.

In the spring of 1943, General Mihajlović had urged Major Novak to enlarge his Chetnik force, whereupon the major asked the Catholic party to enroll half of the Village Guards in his Chetnik units. The Catholics refused. Major Novak thereafter tried to persuade individual commanders of the Village Guards to join. Again, he had no luck. In time the Falcon and National legions did recruit some of their members for his forces, thus increasing Chetnik strength from 50 to about 350 men, but though the Slovenian Legion also finally promised to help, no recruits appeared.[19] During these decisive days the anti-Communist movement clearly demonstrated the presence of two foci, one procen-

19. K. Novak, *Knjiga o Draži*, 1:329–30.

tralistic, commanded by Major Novak, the other autonomist, under the leadership of the Catholic party.

Both anti-Communist groups were aware that the fall of Fascism might well signal the final defeat of Italy. In this assumption they were correct. However, a naïve belief in a British landing in Istria, as a consequence of Italian surrender, cost them dearly. All the plans prepared by the anti-Communists for eventual capitulation took for granted such a British landing, which would also mean the final liberation of Slovenia. Even had their differences been resolved, this attitude would have prevented, very probably, the establishment of a united anti-Communist military command because each group was eager to present itself to the British as the representative of the majority of the people.

The Catholic party's plan called for the Village Guards and recruits from the Slovenian Legion, at the time of Italian surrender, to be proclaimed the Slovenian National Army, forming part of the Royal Yugoslav Army. The Catholic party chose Colonel Ernest Peterlin as commander of this new army. The entire force was to assemble at Turjak, an old medieval castle some fifteen miles southeast of Ljubljana. There the combatants would be reorganized into newly formed battalions. The old Village Guard commanders, mostly former Yugoslav reserve officers, would be replaced by onetime Yugoslav career officers who had not collaborated with the Italians. From Turjak the Slovenian National Army would march toward Istria to meet the British.

But when the Italian armistice came, on September 8, 1943, the anti-Communist factions, except for the Legion of Death, stood little chance in the face of swift action by the Communists—despite the initial anti-Communist edge of some 7,000 men against only 2,500 Communists.[20]

The Partisans had indeed acted quickly. They had immediately sent their representatives to individual Italian commanders demanding surrender to the Partisans of all heavy and light armament. Claiming to be the only underground legally recognized by the Allied forces, the Partisans convinced the Italian commanders to surrender to them. Moreover, the Partisans invited the confused Italians to join their units and fight on their side against the Germans, their common enemy. The British liaison

20. Grum and Pleško, pp. 36–37.

mission to the Partisans proved of great help in persuading reluctant Italian commanders.[21] Thus, in a few days the Partisans became the best equipped and best supplied force in Ljubljana Province. By getting new volunteers and through forced mobilization their armed units increased to some 6,000 men.

Within one day after the armistice, in fact, the Partisans had ended Chetnik hopes of obtaining the surrender of Italian units. Just before that time, the strongest Chetnik unit, numbering about 200 men, had begun to move eastward toward the Croatian border, where they planned to unite with a stronger Chetnik force advancing from western Croatia. Both groups were then to proceed toward Istria in hopes of meeting the British army. But before the forces could unite, on September 9 the Partisans encircled the Slovenian Chetniks at Grčarice, and after a short but ferocious fight the Chetniks surrendered.

Meanwhile, the Village Guards, who were to concentrate around Turjak, remained in theory the strongest military force. But they had been scattered all over Ljubljana Province, garrisoned in larger villages and towns. Accustomed to guard duty (except for the Legion of Death) they were not used to forced marches and had never before operated as a large group. What proved to be worse, very few commanders actually received the order to concentrate their forces at Turjak.

The result was great confusion, which left only half of the original members to engage in fights with the Partisans. Some of the Village Guards remained at their posts until subdued by the Partisans one by one. Other units simply dispersed. Only two concentrations occurred, one in the eastern part of the province, centering around the Legion of Death, and the other at Turjak. The first may have numbered some 1,500 men. Though left without direction and cut away from the force gathered at Turjak, the Legion of Death, the best of the Village Guard mobile detachments, repulsed all Partisan attacks and later became the nucleus of the newly created Domobranci force. The second group, gathered at Turjak, totaled about 1,600. These men had come because their commanders had received the order for concentration, or

21. Major William Jones, a British liaison officer with the Slovenian Partisans, describes in his book (pp. 101–4) one such negotiation in which he participated.

ADRIATIC LITTORAL

they had joined the rest to feel secure in a larger group. At Turjak also was the remnant Chetnik force of some 150 men.

The Turjak force, however, was immediately torn apart by a serious crisis over the future command. Colonel Peterlin had remained in Ljubljana and lost contact with Turjak. Hence, the senior officer, Colonel Josip Dežman, a Chetnik, called a meeting of all officers present to choose a new commander for the entire force at Turjak and to appoint commanders for the new battalions. But the officers could not agree. The old Village Guard commanders refused to recognize Colonel Dežman as supreme commander and were not prepared to relinquish their posts to the newly arrived professional officers. Moreover, the old commanders suspected a maneuver of the Chetniks to control the entire armed force. The result was another split. Meanwhile, news had arrived of the Partisan troops' approach. The Village Guard commanders decided to retreat into the castle and defend it against the Partisans. About half of the gathered force, some eight hundred men, followed. The other half went with professional officers to occupy nearby strategic positions with their center in Zapotok village. This was the ultimate mistake made by the anti-Communists. By dividing their forces, they became numerically weaker than the Partisan units which began to encircle them.

The Partisans attacked Turjak with the artillery and tanks the Italians had surrendered to them. Many of the tanks and cannon were operated by Italian soldiers who had joined the Partisans. The Turjak force resisted the Partisan siege for a week, but on September 19 had to surrender.

The Zapotok units also had to retreat before the greater Partisan forces. They finally broke through the Partisan encirclement and, with some losses, reached the city of Ljubljana, where they surrendered to the Germans.

When negotiating for the surrender of Chetniks at Grčarice and of Village Guards at Turjak, the Partisans had promised an amnesty for all, including the commanders. But they did not keep their word. The prisoners were brought to Kočevje, a city surrounded by forests in the southeastern part of Ljubljana Province. There, the officers were put before the Partisan people's court, condemned to death, and executed between October 10 and 15, 1943. Many other prisoners known for anti-communism were executed without a trial. The rest were put in so-called working battalions, or were enrolled in Partisan units. Many placed in the working battalions were also secretly executed.

Meanwhile, Ljubljana, less than a mile from the Italo-German border of 1941, was occupied by the Germans, who were rushing their troops from there to Trieste and further toward southern Italy. The mayor of Ljubljana happened to be a former Yugoslav army general, Leon Rupnik, who had been an officer of the Austrian army before World War I. He established the first contacts with the newly arrived Germans and, after negotiations, agreed to collaborate. In turn, they appointed him president of Ljubljana Province, as mentioned above. Both the Germans and General Rupnik were interested in the destruction of Partisan power. With the Germans' approval and under their supervision, General Rupnik built, out of the remaining forces of the Village Guards, Chetniks, and new volunteers, a new military force called the Domobranci (Home Guards). The Home Guards were much better equipped and organized than the former Village Guards. They had a unified headquarters, with Colonel Franc Krenner as their chief commander. They were divided into village and town garrisons, and mobile battalions which were in constant pursuit of the Partisans. By the end of the war, the entire force numbered about ten to fifteen thousand men, quite sizable for a province of three hundred thousand inhabitants. Besides a good military organization, the Home Guards had an efficient secret police to clear out Partisan underground organizations, and a strong propaganda apparatus to unmask Communist goals in legally published newspapers. General Rupnik was further able to free his force from meddling by political parties. The single goal of the Home Guards was to defeat the Partisans.

Ironically, while collaborating with the Germans, the Home Guard soldiers were pro-British and pro-American in their sentiments. In combating the Communists, they deeply believed the Home Guards were performing a valuable service for the Western allies. According to Home Guard thinking, the alliance between the Soviet Union and the Western Allies would break down after the defeat of their common enemy, the Germans, for it was an unnatural alliance of democratic forces and Communists, accidentally formed after the German attack on Soviet Russia, and not the result of voluntary action by either partner. The Home Guards continued to support the royal Yugoslav government-in-exile in

London and were convinced that both the royal Yugoslav and British governments tacitly approved the Home Guards' struggle against communism, the future enemy of all. Events in Greece further strengthened these beliefs.[22]

The blow the Partisans had delivered to the anti-Communist forces and the establishment of the Home Guards brought a new sobriety to the three political parties. The old quarrels ended. The Slovenian Alliance continued to exist, and the parties represented in it finally agreed on a common political program by accepting the federalistic views of the Catholic party. Slovenia would become an autonomous state and part of a federal Yugoslavia under the rule of King Peter II. While giving moral support to the Home Guards and their struggle against communism, the Slovenian Alliance avoided collaboration with the Germans, hence remaining underground. The Slovenian Alliance also adopted a plan of action similar to the one the Catholic party had prepared for September 1943. Toward the end of the war the Slovenian Alliance would call a Slovenian parliament composed of deputies who had been members of the last prewar Yugoslav legislature. Here a new provisional Slovenian government would be proclaimed. The Home Guards and new volunteers would form the Slovenian National Army, for which the provisional government would appoint a commander who would have to follow its directions.

After the September disaster Major Novak resigned, whereupon General Mihajlović appointed Colonel Ivan Prezelj, alias Andrej, as his representative in Slovenia. Colonel Prezelj displayed better diplomatic sense than Major Novak in dealing with the political parties. This change introduced a new period of more friendly cooperation between him and the Slovenian Alliance. He retained a small underground Chetnik organization.

COLLABORATION IN THE SLOVENIAN LITTORAL AND ISTRIA

Returning to the Slovenian Littoral, we should recall that no Slovenian anti-Communist movement existed there prior to Sep-

22. For the British relationship toward the Greek Communist and anti-Communist forces see Churchill, 5:532–52; 6:108–14, 283–325.

tember 1943. The Partisans were the sole organized group because, for more than twenty years, the Italians had denied to the Slovenes not only political rights but even their ethnic existence. The primary goal of Littoral Slovenes was therefore unification with the Slovenes living in Yugoslavia. Slovenes of the Littoral firmly believed that this would be achieved after the war. The Partisans, who had come first to the Slovenian Littoral, exploited this sentiment for their own purposes by stressing that a strong unified underground built around the Partisans would achieve this national goal. This development also explains why the Littoral Slovenes had supported the great Partisan uprising after the armistice and fought against the Germans in Partisan units without regard to political or ideological beliefs.

After the destruction of Italian administrative and military authority, the Partisans organized their own administration in the short interval before the Germans took over. During this period the Partisans unmasked themselves. While proclaiming the unification of the Littoral with Yugoslavia and fulfilling the old Slovenian national demands, the Partisan administration indicated that the true rulers of a future Yugoslavia would be the Communists and their fellow travelers, and that the other political groups might remain excluded from any position of power. The news of the Partisan massacre of Village Guards and Chetniks in Ljubljana Province further confirmed fears that the Partisans were fighting primarily for a Communist victory.[23]

Thus, when the new German masters showed a certain willingness to recognize some Slovenian rights, the anti-Communists decided to collaborate with them toward the end of 1943. In this policy, the Slovenian anti-Communists pursued two main objectives: first, to achieve as many political and cultural rights for the Slovenes as possible, and second, to prevent a Communist victory after the war by fighting against the Partisans.

As they had to face a well-established Partisan underground, which ably exploited Slovenian national sentiment, the anti-Communists who collaborated with the Germans in the Slovenian Littoral remained relatively small in number. Though they had the same political and ideological goals as the Home Guards in

23. "Ob dvajsetletnici," *Vestnik,* 15, no. 8 (Aug. 1964) to 17, no. 6–7 (June–July 1966).

Ljubljana Province, the Littoral anti-Communists, at the insistence of the Germans, had to form a different armed force called the Primorska narodna straža (Littoral National Guard). The Home Guards from Ljubljana Province did help them as much as the Germans permitted, and in December 1943 Colonel Tone Kokalj came from Ljubljana to take command of the National Guard. He established his headquarters in Trieste.[24] The fact that each of the two organizations was limited to its own province proved detrimental to the growth of anti-Communist strength and enabled a pursued Partisan unit to escape from one province to the other.

The National Guard did achieve some of its political and cultural goals, though its work was much easier in Gorizia than in Trieste Province. In the former, the newly appointed prefect, Count Marino Pace, was a tolerant man favoring cooperation between Italians and Slovenes. Much different was the situation in Trieste Province, where Coceani's extreme Italian nationalism prevented any cooperation with the Slovenes.

In the city of Gorizia, a Slovene was appointed vice-mayor; a Slovenian newspaper, *Goriški list* (Gorizia's Paper), started publication; and a Slovenian secondary school opened. In the Slovenian districts of the province, Slovenian elementary schools were organized and Slovenes took over the local administration. Slovenes became mayors presiding over the village and town councils formed by Slovenes.

In Trieste Province, Prefect Coceani pursued the opposite policy. According to Coceani's own report, Colonel Kokalj met with him on April 19, 1944. Kokalj wanted reinstatement of all institutions suppressed by the Fascists. Besides the reopening of Slovenian schools and participation in the administration, he asked for restoration of certain buildings destroyed or confiscated in Trieste: the National Home, the printing establishment "Edinost," school buildings once owned by the St. Cyril and Methodius Association, and Slovenian libraries and cultural centers. Giving various excuses, Coceani refused all Slovenian demands.

Because of his firm opposition, the Slovenes appealed to the Germans. The latter permitted Slovenes in rural parts of Trieste

24. Tratnik, *Koledar-Zbornik, 1951*, pp. 145–51; Coceani, pp. 133–37, 207–8, 215–18.

Province the same rights they enjoyed in Gorizia. But, with the exception of radio programs in the Slovenian language, the Slovenes still got no concessions in the city of Trieste. Even the small considerations greatly alarmed Coceani. In his talk with Mussolini, he lamented that the Slovenian tongue and Slovenian singing could be heard again in the streets and public places of Trieste.

Because of the struggle between the Partisans and anti-Communists, the Slovenian democrats had little opportunity to develop a noteworthy movement in the Julian Region. Prior to the Fascist period they were, in the main, adherents of the Liberal, Socialist, or Catholic parties. During the first years of the war they hoped that the royal Yugoslav government would satisfy their principal desire for unification of the Slovenian Littoral with Yugoslavia. In the summer of 1943 after the fall of Fascism, Liberals and Socialists, who had traditionally formed the two strongest parties in Trieste, organized the Slovenian National Council, with Dr. Jože Ferfolja agreed upon as the temporary chairman.[25] In Gorizia Province, which had been the stronghold of the Catholic party, no formal council was created though the Slovenian clergy held informal discussions about what should be done in the future.[26]

A strong democratic front was not realized in either Trieste or Gorizia, having been forestalled by the organization of the Littoral National Guard. Democrats who considered communism a greater danger than Nazism supported the National Guard. Others who condemned collaboration with the Germans joined the Partisans. In the fall of 1943 the majority of the National Council of Trieste entered the Partisan movement, whereas the democrats of Gorizia either joined the National Guard or remained inactive until the end of the war (though the feelings of the latter were more on the side of the Partisans). This polarization of the democratic movement likewise dispersed the forces from which the main support might have come for a Slovenian Chetnik movement. Hence the Chetniks were condemned to impotence in both Ljubljana Province and the Slovenian Littoral.

The Germans applied the same policy in Istria as in the

25. *Slovensko Primorje in Istra,* pp. 458–59.
26. "Ob dvajsetletnici," *Vestnik,* 17, no. 3-4-5 (Mar., Apr., May 1966): 97–107, and 17, no. 6–7 (June–July 1966): 147–55.

Slovenian Littoral, ruling it from Trieste as part of the Adriatic Littoral. In sections with an Italian majority, they left the Italian administration. Where Croats predominated, they were allowed to organize their administration from a district level downward. Following this pattern the Germans appointed an Italian prefect (Ludovico Artusi), and a Croat vice-prefect (Bogdan Mogorović) for Pula Province, which included most of Istria.[27] Both Italians and Croats also organized their own military forces, which fought together with the Germans against the Partisans.

At the same time the pro-Fascist Ustashi government of Croatia had been pressing the Germans to separate Istria from the Adriatic Littoral and to unite it with Pavelić's Croatian state, a design ardently opposed by both the Italians in Istria and Mussolini's Republican government. Faithful to their policy of gaining support from both ethnic groups, the Germans promised Istria at one time to the Croats and at another to the Italians. Although Istria remained part of the Adriatic Littoral, the Germans allowed the Ustashi to work among the Istrian Croats. Operating from a center at Pazin in Istria, the Ustashi organized the Croat Home Guards, opened and administered Croat schools, and began to spread pro-Croat propaganda over all of Istria.[28]

As 1944 drew to an end, two other groups came to Istria in retreat before the advance of the Russian army and Yugoslav Partisans. One was the Serbian armed force which, under command of General Milan Nedić and Dimitrije Ljotić, had collaborated with the Germans in Serbia. The other was the Serbian Chetniks. They had separated from General Mihajlović and, retreating through Croatia, had reached Istria. Both groups settled down in Istria and the Slovenian Littoral with German approval and fought against the Partisans.[29]

27. They were appointed Dec. 2, 1943 (Esposito, p. 67).
28. *Slovensko Primorje in Istra, pp.* 272–73; Pacor, pp. 208–10.
29. *Slovensko Primorje in Istra,* pp. 272, 318; Bor. M. Karapandžić, *Gradjanski rat u Srbiji, 1941–1945* (The Civil War in Serbia, 1941–1945) (Cleveland, 1958), pp. 396–401.

5
RESISTANCE TO GERMAN OCCUPATION (1943-1945)

YUGOSLAVIA: TITO TRIUMPHANT

The policy of the pro-Communist forces in the Julian Region from 1943 to 1945 depended upon the fortunes of war, the relationships among the Great Powers, and the agreements between the Italian and Yugoslav Communist parties.

The Italian surrender strengthened Tito's Partisans everywhere. What has been said about the Julian Region and Ljubljana Province was equally true for all of Yugoslavia. The Italian army in Yugoslavia surrendered relatively peacefully to the Partisans because most of the Italian commanders had received instructions from the Allied High Command in the Middle East to do so.[1] By this move, a great quantity of armaments fell into Partisan hands. Bosnia remained the stronghold of the Partisans, and they were relatively potent also in Slovenia (the Slovenian Littoral and Ljubljana Province) and in Montenegro. In Serbia, on the other hand, the Mihajlović Chetniks retained absolute control of the underground forces.

The Partisans' improved position at home was crowned with further success in the international field, achieved at the Teheran conference in late November and the early days of December 1943. It is true that very little is known about what was discussed and agreed upon at Teheran regarding Yugoslavia. Nonetheless, actions taken by Great Britain and Soviet Russia after the Teheran conference, together with explanations given by British Prime Minister Winston Churchill and by Milovan Djilas, at that time

1. Fotitch, p. 209; cf. also David Martin, *Ally Betrayed: The Uncensored Story of Tito and Mihailovich* (New York, 1946), pp. 219-20.

89

a leading Yugoslav Communist, warrant the following description.[2]

Before leaving for Teheran, Churchill had received false reports about Partisan strength—the first success of Tito's international propaganda, which deceived not only a few progressive intellectuals, but the British foreign office and Churchill himself.[3] These false reports convinced Churchill that the Partisans had been the only underground seriously fighting the Germans and that the Partisans enjoyed overwhelming support of the Yugoslav people. Based on this information, at the Teheran conference Churchill proposed an agreement on Yugoslav affairs. Here it was probably decided that all guerrilla forces should unite against the Germans. Tito's Partisans would become the only recognized underground force to receive British military support. The Chetniks should join Tito's Partisans, and in return Tito would assure the British that he would not use their arms to fight the Chetniks, except in self-defense. Tito would also make no attempt to introduce communism into Yugoslavia. Further, Tito's Liberation Movement and the Yugoslav royal government would form a coalition to act as the recognized provisional government of Yugoslavia.[4]

Churchill and Stalin easily agreed on the formation of only one Yugoslav underground. Their common goal was to defeat the Germans in the quickest way possible, and such a united underground would of course have an improved chance of success in fighting the Germans. Besides, Churchill felt, a united Yugoslav front would give the royal Yugoslav forces some say in a future Yugoslav state. Stalin had another goal. He was convinced that this agreement would in the long run benefit Tito and the Communist cause. Tito would be in control of all the armed forces during and after the war, and, according to Stalin, he who controls the armed forces also controls politics.

After the Teheran conference, Stalin urged the Yugoslav Communists to compromise with England and the royal Yugoslav government. A good illustration of Stalin's aims is contained in

2. Churchill, vols. 5, 6; Milovan Djilas, *Conversations with Stalin* (New York, 1962).
3. Martin, pp. 34–46; Zalar, p. 105.
4. Churchill, 5:467–68.

his statement of June 1944 to Djilas, then on an official visit in Moscow. "Do not refuse to hold conversations with Šubašić [prime minister of the royal Yugoslav government]—on no account must you do this. Do not attack him immediately. Let us see what he wants. Talk with him. You [Yugoslav Communists] cannot be recognized right away. A transition to this must be found. You ought to talk with Šubašić and see if you can't reach a compromise somehow."[5] On the same occasion Stalin urged Yugoslav Communists to avoid anything that might alarm the English into thinking that a revolution or an attempt at Communist control was going on in Yugoslavia.[6]

The Teheran agreement on Yugoslavia was a deal between Churchill and Stalin. President Roosevelt knew about it but was not a party to it.[7] Stalin had never trusted Churchill. He suspected that Churchill was trying to prevent a Communist victory in Yugoslavia. Later, after Teheran, Stalin constantly warned the Yugoslavs to be extremely cautious when dealing with the English, and to be aware of English duplicity. In a June 1944 conversation with Djilas, Stalin hinted at the possibility that the English might try to kill Tito, as they, according to Stalin, had killed a Polish general who had opposed British plans: "They [the British] were the ones who killed General Sikorski in a plane and neatly shot down the plane—no proof, no witnesses."[8]

Churchill, upon his return from Teheran, put heavy pressure on the Yugoslav king, Peter II, to dismiss his government and to recognize Tito as the sole leader of the Yugoslav underground. In line with this plan, Churchill ordered in the first days of December that all British aid to the Chetniks should end and be instead directed entirely to the Partisans. The Partisans thus became by the end of December 1943 the only recognized and supported Yugoslav underground. In the first months of 1944 Churchill notified Tito about these changes.[9]

Ironically, at exactly the same time that Churchill had put the heaviest pressure on the Yugoslav royal government and on King Peter to recognize Tito, the Partisans suffered great defeats at home. In the spring of 1944, the Germans decided to evacuate

5. Djilas, p. 74.
6. Ibid., p. 73.
7. Ibid., p. 63.
8. Ibid., p. 73.
9. Churchill, 5:467-76.

their troops from Greece. For this move they needed safe routes and hence decided to crush the Partisans. In the last days of May 1944, the Germans launched a parachute attack on Tito's headquarters in Drvar, Bosnia. Only by the heroic fight of Tito's personal guard, which was almost completely annihilated, did Tito and his staff manage to escape. Later a British plane flew Tito to Bari, Italy, from where he was taken by a British destroyer to the island of Vis in the Adriatic. On Vis, Tito established his new headquarters, protected by the British navy against enemy attack.[10] During the early summer of 1944 German troops, retreating by land, shattered the Partisan units in Bosnia. Meanwhile, German troops transported by sea disembarked in Rijeka and Pula, causing heavy losses to Partisan units in Istria and western Croatia.[11]

Nevertheless, the Partisans continued to be successful in the international field. On May 17, 1944, the Yugoslav King Peter gave in to the pressures of the British prime minister. The King dismissed the government of Dr. Božidar Purić and on June 1 appointed the former governor (*ban*) of Croatia, Dr. Ivan Šubašić, as prime minister with the task of forming a new government.[12] Before doing so, Šubašić visited Tito on the island of Vis and concluded an agreement on June 16, 1944. Tito demanded that his Partisan movement be recognized as the only legal resistance. All other forces should come under his command. Tito also opposed King Peter's return to liberated territory in Yugoslavia during the war. Tito however agreed that the Yugoslav people should decide the future form of government and the socio-economic order in a free election after the war. According to the agreement, Šubašić should form a new Yugoslav government-in-exile, composed of progressive democratic elements, which would accept this agreement. It was decided further that a joint government would be formed later out of members of Tito's National Liberation Council and members of the Yugoslav government-in-exile.[13] After his

10. Martin, pp. 238–41; Vladimir Dedijer, *Tito* (New York, 1953), pp. 217–21.
11. *Slovensko Primorje in Istra*, p. 318.
12. Churchill, 5:476–78; Zalar, p. 107; see also Knežević, 2:120–35.
13. U.S., Department of State, Foreign Relations of the United States, Diplomatic Papers, *The Conferences at Malta and Yalta, 1945*

return from Vis, Šubašić formed on July 12 his royal government of six members including two Serbs, two Croats, and two Slovenes.[14]

In the first days of August 1944 Tito and Šubašić met Prime Minister Churchill in Italy.[15] Churchill was interested in two questions: Would Tito meet King Peter, and what would be the postwar political system in Yugoslavia? On the first issue Tito answered that he had nothing against meeting King Peter, but preferred not to do so at present. On the second issue Churchill reported: "Tito assured me that, as he had stated publicly, he had no desire to introduce the Communist system into Yugoslavia. ... I asked Tito if he would reaffirm his statement about Communism in public, but he did not wish to do this as it might seem to have been forced upon him."[16] Here Tito acted as advised by Stalin. At this same meeting it was agreed that the Yugoslav royal navy and air force, up to then fighting with British units, should come under Tito's command.

After the Tito-Churchill meeting, King Peter, still under pressure, decreed on August 26 the abolition of the command of General Mihajlović and recognized Marshal Tito as the sole leader of the resistance in Yugoslavia.[17] Moreover, in a broadcast from London on September 12, 1944, Peter appealed to all Serbs, Croats, and Slovenes to support and join the National Liberation army under the command of Marshal Tito.[18]

By September 1944 Tito and his Partisans had won an important diplomatic and political victory. For his vague promises, Tito had been recognized as the sole commander of all military units, becoming the de facto ruler of Yugoslavia. He had achieved what he wanted. From then on, he showed no interest in forming a coalition government with Šubašić. This question was postponed until a later time.

(Washington, D.C., 1955), pp. 250–54, hereafter cited as *Conferences at Malta and Yalta*.

14. Zalar, p. 109.
15. Churchill, 7:88–93.
16. Ibid., pp. 89–90.
17. Zalar, p. 109.
18. For the full text of the broadcast see Knežević, 2:118–19.

After his victory in the international field Tito registered his first great success at home, owing to the advances of the Red army. By September 1944, Rumania and Bulgaria had accepted armistice terms and Russian troops approached the Yugoslav border. On September 21, Tito secretly, without British knowledge, left Vis on a Soviet plane. He stopped at Marshal Tolbukhin's headquarters in Rumania and then flew to Moscow. Here Tito and Stalin agreed that Soviet troops would help Tito to occupy Serbia and expel the Germans from Belgrade; thereafter Soviet troops would leave Yugoslavia.[19] According to this agreement Tito became the sole master over Serbia. After October 20, 1944, he established his headquarters in liberated Belgrade.[20] His Partisan units were transformed into the regular Yugoslav army. Though Tito's army still had to liberate the western parts, there was no doubt after October 1944 that Tito and his Communists would have the upper hand in Yugoslavia.

Churchill, who hoped to retain some influence over Yugoslavia, was alarmed when Tito disappeared from Vis.[21] On October 9, 1944, when Churchill went to Moscow, he again discussed the Balkan situation with Stalin. Stalin accepted Churchill's proposal that Yugoslavia should remain a sphere of interest for both Russia and Great Britain according to a fifty-fifty principle.[22] But this agreement did not diminish Tito's power at home. When under pressure to fulfill his promises to Šubašić and to form a coalition government, Tito always found new excuses for postponement. In March of 1945, when preparing for occupation of the Julian Region, Tito realized a coalition government might be to his advantage. Such a coalition might encounter less opposition from the Western Allies when the Yugoslav army occupied the Julian Region. Consequently on March 7, 1945, the new coalition government was formed, headed by Marshal Tito. It was composed of twenty-eight ministers, but of these, only five were royalists while twenty-three belonged to the Partisans. Though Yugo-

19. Dedijer, pp. 230–32.
20. Zalar, p. 110.
21. Churchill, 6:230; Fitzroy Maclean, *The Heretic: The Life and Times of Josip Broz-Tito* (New York, 1957), p. 241.
22. Churchill, 6:226–28.

ITALY: THE ALLIES AND THE UNDERGROUND

slavia had a coalition government, there was no doubt the Communist party and the Partisans remained in absolute control.[23]

Equally important were the events occurring in Italy. After the armistice, when the Germans took over almost all the Italian peninsula, the Allied forces launched a hard struggle to push them out. Progress was uneven and slow. By October 1943 the Allied forces were in possession of the peninsula south of Naples. From here they progressed during the fall half way to Rome. At this point the Allied offensive stopped at Cassino. Not before the spring of 1944 did the Allies break the German defenses and continue toward the north. Rome fell on June 4, just two days before the Allied invasion of Normandy. From Rome northward the front moved slowly and in the fall of 1944 stopped again on the hills overlooking the north Italian flatland. Here the Germans dug in, on what was known as the old Gothic line. Not before the spring of 1945 was this line broken and a new Allied offensive, the last one, finally able to liberate all of Italy—after the Allied landing in Normandy the Italian front had become of secondary importance.[24]

Italian politics and the Italian resistance movement in German-occupied territory were of course conditioned by the advance of the Allied forces in the Italian peninsula. Up to the time when the Allies entered Rome in the first days of June 1944, Italian political life had been in great confusion. In the liberated south the Allies recognized King Victor Emmanuel and his government headed by Marshal Pietro Badoglio who had signed the armistice. The leaders of the pre-Fascist political parties, on the other hand,

23. Zalar, p. 111.
24. For a more detailed account see: Roberto Battaglia, *The Story of the Italian Resistance*, trans. and ed. P. D. Cummins (London, 1957); Massimo Salvadori, *Storia della resistenza italiana* (Venice, 1955); Leo Valiani, *Tutte le strade conducono a Roma* (Florence, 1947), written by a leading member of the Action party; Luigi Longo, *Un popolo alla macchia*, 2d ed. (Verona, 1952), written by a leading member of the Italian Communist party; and Raffaele Cadorna, *La riscossa: Dal 25 luglio alla liberazione* (Milan, 1948), written by a professional soldier and the supreme commander of the joint guerrilla forces.

declined such recognition, on the ground that both the monarch and Badoglio had been closely connected with Fascism. Badoglio's government, however, survived these attacks because Prime Minister Churchill supported it. Not until President Roosevelt urged a new government for Italy did Churchill agree that the king should be replaced by the heir to the throne, Prince Umberto, and a new government formed—but this should take place only after the Allies captured Rome.[25]

The leaders of the pre-Fascist parties were strong in the north. Here they organized an Italian resistance movement against the Germans. By this act their importance increased. They were no longer regarded as heads of pre-Fascist parties, with doubtful popular support, but leaders of important underground forces, a fact which Churchill himself recognized.

The first meeting of leaders of the pre-Fascist parties had taken place in Rome in the first days after Italian surrender in September 1943. Here they constituted the Central Committee for National Liberation under the chairmanship of Ivanoe Bonomi.[26] The Central Committee was composed of representatives of six pre-Fascist parties: the Communist, Action (progressive republicans), Socialist, Christian Democratic, Republican, and Liberal. This committee acted as the supreme political body for Italian resistance in the part of Italy occupied by German forces. Soon in each of the northern provinces a similar provincial or city Committee of National Liberation (Comitato di Liberazione Nazionale, or CLN) was formed. Unlike the Yugoslav National Liberation Movement, where all individual parties ceased to exist except that of the Communists, the Italian CLN became only the supreme common political forum of all the parties, each of which retained its own political organization and guerrilla forces. The Communists were thus only one of the six parties, having but one vote against five in the CLN.

The guerrilla forces sprang into existence from two sources—scattered army bands that went into the hills, and units created by individual political parties represented in the CLN. The first,

25. Churchill, 6:496–99, 501–5; Salvadori, pp. 99–100.
26. For two different accounts of this see: Giulio Andreotti, *De Gasperi e il suo tempo: Trento, Vienna, Roma* (Milan, 1956), p. 138; and Longo, *Un popolo,* p. 56.

headed by staff officers, were conservative and royalist, and favored Badoglio's government. Among the second the most numerous were the Garibaldi units organized by the Communist party. Next came the Justice and Liberty (Giustizia e Libertà) units of the Action party. The socialists formed Matteotti units, named after the socialist martyr Giacomo Matteotti, murdered by the Fascists in 1924. Christian Democrats organized Il Popolo units, which were much weaker, as were those of the Liberals and Republicans.[27]

At first the Allies did not take the Italian guerrillas seriously, for various reasons. The first units were badly organized and sometimes more a hindrance than a help to the Allied forces. Many of the guerrilla units belonged to the Communist or other left-wing parties, which made them suspicious in the eyes of the Allies. The Allies did cooperate with the guerrilla bands up to the time their area was liberated and then disarmed them, disbanding their units or sending them to special camps.[28]

Though suspicion of the political views of the CLN and the guerrilla forces did not completely disappear until the spring of 1945, the Allied position toward the CLN improved after the capture of Rome.[29] As previously agreed, in the first days of June 1944 the old King Victor Emmanuel abdicated and his son Umberto became regent (*luogotenente*). The Badoglio government resigned and the chairman of the Central Committee of the CLN, Bonomi, became prime minister of a new coalition government.[30] To be sure, the powers of the Italian government were limited indeed. The highest authority remained in the hands of the Allied supreme commander, and the Allied Military Government (AMG) took over the civil administration.[31] With the approval of the

27. Salvadori, p. 96; Geoffrey Cox, *The Road to Trieste* (London: William Heinemann, 1947), p. 147; all quotations from this book are reprinted by permission.
28. Cox, pp. 146-49.
29. Ibid., p. 149; Cadorna, p. 175.
30. Salvadori, p. 101.
31. For more details see C. R. S. Harris, *Allied Military Administration of Italy, 1943-1945*, a vol. in *History of the Second World War*, ed. J. R. M. Butler. United Kingdom Military Series (London, 1757).

Allied supreme commander the Italian government could perform only such functions as were not reserved to the AMG.

After the liberation of Rome the CLN of Milan emerged as the factual leader of resistance in northern Italy. It became known as the Comitato di Liberazione Nazionale Alta Italia (the Committee of National Liberation for Upper Italy) or CLNAI. In this case only five political parties formed the committee, the Republican party having no representative. Alfredo Pizzoni, alias Longhi, a man without political affiliation, became its chairman, and Ferruccio Parri, alias Maurizio, its most dynamic personality. He was the commander of the Justice and Liberty units of the Action party. Luigi Longo, alias Italo or Gallo, represented the Communists in the CLNAI and was commander of the most numerous and best organized Garibaldi units.[32]

As the Communists and the Action party controlled about 70 percent of all guerrilla forces, the CLNAI had a left-wing preponderance. The military bands composed of royalist and conservative elements suspected that the leftist parties planned to introduce socialism after the war by using a common front (the CLNAI) to achieve their goal. In the eyes of the Western Allies this split was harmful to the common struggle against the Germans and Fascists, and they urged the groups to unite to achieve better military results.[33]

In the first part of June 1944 the CLNAI took action in this direction. It invited all the guerrilla bands to form a joint force, called the Corpo Volontari della Libertà (Corps of Volunteers of Liberty) or CVL.[34] Each guerrilla unit was to retain its individuality but had to recognize in military matters the authority of a joint command. The CLNAI invited a professional soldier, General Raffaelle Cadorna, to come from Rome and organize the command. This move provided an opportune moment for the Allies to gain some control over the guerrilla forces and over the left-oriented political parties in northern Italy. The Allies approved the project, gave General Cadorna instructions and mon-

32. Salvadori, pp. 101–3.
33. Cadorna, p. 116.
34. Longo, *Un popolo,* p. 226.

etary help, and parachuted him into northern Italy on August 12, 1944.[35]

After two months of hard negotiations General Cadorna got the leaders of the three most important guerrilla groups, the Communists, the Action party, and the military bands, to recognize a joint military command. A professional soldier was to be the supreme commander with two vice-commanders, one belonging to the Communists and one to the Action party. The arrangement proved to be a great success. Then, at the end of October, the representatives of the Communists, Action party, and military bands, together with the chairman of the CLNAI, went to southern Italy to conclude an agreement with the supreme Allied commander for Italy, General Henry Maitland Wilson.[36] By this accord of December 7, 1944, the CLNAI was recognized by the Allies as the supreme underground authority for northern Italy and the legitimate representative of the Italian government. The Allies also promised monetary help and military supplies. General Wilson approved the appointment of General Cadorna as the supreme commander of the CVL, and Longo, a Communist, and Parri of the Action party as vice-commanders. However, the agreement stressed that the CVL was to obey directives given by the CLNAI as well as those of the supreme Allied commander. Moreover, after the retreat of the Germans, the CLNAI would agree to transfer all of its authority to the Allies in the liberated areas and together with the CVL promised to obey all of the orders issued by the Allies, including those to disband and turn over weapons.

35. Cadorna, pp. 113–20; Salvadori, p. 101.
36. For the English text of the agreement see U.S., Department of the Army, Office of the Chief of Military History, *United States Army in World War II*, Special Studies, Harry L. Coles and Albert K. Weinberg, *Civil Affairs: Soldiers Become Governors* (Washington, D.C., 1964), pp. 541–42. Hereafter cited as Coles and Weinberg. The agreement with an accompanying letter from General Wilson to CLNAI is reprinted also in Cadorna, pp. 176–78. Note that Salvadori (p. 103) gives December 17, 1944, as the date the agreement was signed. This might be a printing mistake because on December 12, 1944, Marshal Alexander had already taken over the position of supreme Allied commander from General Wilson. (See Harold Alexander, *The Alexander Memoirs, 1940–1945*, ed. John North [New York, 1962], p. 141.)

RESISTANCE TO GERMAN OCCUPATION

Under such conditions there was little hope for the Communists to take over. The question remains as to why they signed such an agreement though they had the most numerous guerrilla force. The answer may well lie in a widespread rumor of August 1944 that the Western powers and Soviet Russia had agreed on dividing Europe into two spheres of influence.[37] Italy, according to this train of thought, belonged to the Western sphere, which would mean the Italian Communists must renounce their revolutionary goals at least for the time being.

THE JULIAN REGION: COMMUNIST COMPETITION AND COOPERATION

Yugoslav Partisan activity in the Julian Region from 1943 to 1945 continued to depend upon agreements between the Central Committees of the Italian, Slovenian, and Croat Communist parties. The last two negotiated in the name of the Yugoslav Communist party of which they were autonomous, constituent parts.

These agreements reflected Stalin's directives, the successes or failures of the Communist movement in Yugoslavia and Italy, and the different aims pursued by each participant. The Yugoslav (Slovenian-Croat) party sought exclusive control over the entire Julian Region, as well as Venetian Slovenia and, if possible, Friuli, which made up the Italian province of Udine. Its ultimate aim was to annex these territories to Yugoslavia after the war. The Italian party resisted these demands as long as possible, but the closer to the end of hostilities, the greater became the Italian concessions. One trend was easy to see: the more the Communists achieved power in Yugoslavia, the more the Italian Communists conceded.

A series of proclamations began to disturb the old relationship between the Italian and Yugoslav Communist parties in the Julian Region immediately following the Italian armistice of September 8, 1943. Three days later the Liberation Front for the Slovenian Littoral proclaimed annexation of this land to Slovenia, which would in turn become part of a free and democratic Yugo-

37. Allied (Control) Commission, Headquarters, Public Relations Branch, *A(C)C Weekly Bulletin*, 1, no. 19 (Aug. 13, 1944): 2, hereafter cited as *AC Weekly Bulletin*.

slavia; on September 16, the Slovenian National Liberation Committee confirmed this action of its provincial subsidiary.[38]

Meanwhile, Croat and Istrian Italian Communist party delegates agreed in Pazin on September 12–13 that Istria should be a part of Croatia in a free and democratic Yugoslavia. The Italian Communists would institute an autonomous section of the Croatian party, as well as autonomous Italian sections of the National Liberation Movement and other mass organizations. Thus the entire Partisan underground in Istria came under control of the Croat Communist party and the Croat National Liberation Movement though it is unlikely that all Istrian Italian Communists were pleased by this development. The Croat National Liberation Committee for Istria proclaimed the annexation of Istria to Croatia on September 13 and a week later the Liberation Council for all of Croatia (ZAVNOH) confirmed the decision. On November 29, 1943, the Yugoslav National Liberation Council (AVNOJ) ratified both the Slovenian and Croat proclamations, which would annex practically the entire Julian Region to Yugoslavia.[39]

Worth special notice is the fact that none of these proclamations had been published in the name of the Communist parties, but rather by the various mass organizations—the National Liberation committees and councils. In reality, of course, it was the Slovenian and Croat Communist parties who aspired to exclusive control over the Communist organizations, Partisan activities, and liberation movements of the entire Julian Region. Moreover, no specific boundaries were outlined to show what territory was meant by such a term as the Slovenian Littoral. Since the Slove-

38. The proclamation issued September 16, 1943, is reprinted in *Zbornik*, pt. 6, 7:101; see also the article "Že leta 1943 so naša narodna predstavništva pravno izvedla priključitev Slovenskega Primorja in Istre k Jugoslaviji" (Already in the Year 1943 our National Representatives Had Legally Accomplished the Annexation of the Slovenian Littoral and Istria to Yugoslavia), *Ljudska pravica*, Sept. 21, 1947.

39. The AVNOJ decree was published in *Ljudska pravica*, Sept. 21, 1947; for the proclamation of the National Liberation Committee for Istria and for the decree of ZAVNOH see *Slovensko Primorje in Istria*, pp. 263, 265. Cf. M. K. Bulajić, *Pitanje Trsta u svjetlosti novih dogadjaja* (The Question of Trieste in the Light of the New Happenings) (Belgrade, 1950), p. 12.

nian Littoral had never been a political-administrative unity, any interpretation was possible. It could or could not include Trieste and Venetian Slovenia.

Though broad autonomy was guaranteed to the Italian minority, including use of their language, schools, press, and a free cultural development, the Central Committee of the Italian Communist party criticized the Yugoslav proclamations in letters of October 6, 1943, and January 5, 1944. The Italian Communists objected first to not having been consulted before proclamation of the decrees annexing Istria and the Slovenian Littoral to Yugoslavia.[40] They then condemned the decrees as tactically wrong, as stimulating Slavic and Italian nationalism and thereby leading to Slavic-Italian clashes instead of a unified struggle against the common Nazi and Fascist enemies. The disputes would strengthen the Slavic and Italian reactionaries, who would try to exploit the friction. Finally, these decrees would damage the position of the Italian Communist party in Italy proper, where it would be accused by bourgeois parties, with whom it was allied in the Committee for National Liberation (CLN), of selling out Italian interests in the Julian Region.[41]

After the letter of January 5, 1944, lengthy negotiations began on local and national levels between the Yugoslav and Italian parties. Istria very soon dropped out of consideration. From available data it would seem that the Italian party gave up Istria, where before September 1943 only the Croat Partisan movement had existed, and accepted local agreements concluded between the Italian and Croat Communists. Thus the Croat party remained the leader of the Istrian pro-Communist forces, with autonomous sections provided for the Italian Communists, Partisans, and mass organizations.

The Slovenian Littoral was another matter. Here the Italian party demanded independence for its own party, Partisans, and

40. Which, according to Mikuž (*Zgodovinski časopis,* 12–13:15) was not true. On August 20, 1943, Edvard Kardelj, a leading Slovenian and Yugoslav Communist, notified Massola-Quinto that the Slovenian Liberation Front would demand unification of Trieste with Slovenia and asked for a discussion of the subject with the Italian party.

41. Mikuž, *Zgodovinski časopis,* 12–13:15–16, 17–18; Pacor, pp. 277–78; Bulajić, p. 12.

JULIAN REGION: COMMUNIST COMPETITION

mass organizations, especially in Trieste and the coastal towns where Italians were in the majority. The Slovenes might use the principle of self-determination in the Slovenian Littoral, but the Italians demanded the same rights in predominantly Italian sections. When the Slovenian party sought to claim that Trieste and Venetian Slovenia were an integral part of the Slovenian Littoral, the matter was carried to the head of the Comintern in Soviet Russia, George Dimitrov. On March 28, 1944, he answered, above his famous signature "Ded," that he regarded the territorial dispute as politically premature. It ought to be solved only after defeat of the common enemy.[42]

This rebuke from on high caused the Yugoslav party to retreat on April 4, 1944. Agreement on new borders was postponed until more could be known about the forms of the future Yugoslav and Italian governments. Meanwhile the Slovenian party, Partisan units, and mass organizations would have control in all areas of compact Slovene settlement, while the Italians could do the same in sections of high Italian concentration such as Friuli. In mixed regions, Trieste, and the coastal towns, each party would remain independent within its own ethnic group. A liaison committee (Comitato di Collegamento), composed of delegates from both parties, was to settle problems of common action against the enemy. Italian Partisan units in the Julian Region would be responsible to parent Partisan units in Italy, but when operating in territory of the Slovenian Partisan Corps they would obey its headquarters. Slovenian Partisans were to be permitted to function in Venetian Slovenia and Friuli under the same conditions.[43] The agreement within the Communist parties was paralleled by an accord between the Slovenian Liberation Front and the Italian National Liberation Committee for Upper Italy (CLNAI) in Milan.[44]

As has been mentioned, between spring and autumn 1944 the position of the Yugoslav Communists greatly improved. Tito's Partisan movement became the only recognized underground in Yugoslavia and Tito's meeting with Stalin in late September assured him of Russian help in liberating Serbia. The prospects

42. Mikuž, *Zgodovinski časopis,* 12–13:20.
43. Ibid.; Pacor, p. 278.
44. See below, this chapter, "The CLN and Democratic Resistance."

were good for a Communist victory in Yugoslavia. Just the opposite was true for the Italian Communists.[45]

These changing factors influenced the decisions reached by the new secretary of the Italian Communist party, Palmiro Togliatti, and the leading Slovenian and Yugoslav Communist, Edvard Kardelj, in mid-October 1944. Their agreement was transmitted to the local Italian party in Togliatti's letter of October 19. The outcome marked a great victory for the Slovenian Communists in the Slovenian Littoral. Togliatti pointed out that it would be good for communism to have Tito's Yugoslav army occupy the entire Julian Region. This move would keep out Anglo-American troops, and the Partisan units would not be disarmed by the Western Allies as had happened in Italy, for Yugoslav troops were recognized as Allied forces. Besides, a reactionary bourgeois regime would not be established. Togliatti further stressed the need for the local Italian party to cooperate with its Yugoslav comrades in setting up a people's government after the liberation. To achieve this goal the local Italian party should work with the Yugoslav Communists in all places where Italians lived, especially in Trieste. Here, in preparation for the day of victory, leadership of the people must fall into progressive Italian hands willing to cooperate with the Slovenian Liberation Front and the Yugoslav liberation army. A campaign must also begin for an Italian Partisan army, which would retain its autonomous national character, but become a part of the Yugoslav liberation army and Partisan units. The Yugoslav party agreed to an individual Italian mass organization in Trieste alongside a Slovenian one, each autonomous at all levels except at the top, where a joint Supreme City Liberation Committee would make needed decisions.[46] Istria was not mentioned in the agreement, but the Italian party there had already become an autonomous section of the Croat Communist party.

Although it was evident that the Yugoslav Communist party and liberation movement were supreme in the Julian Region, the Italian Communist party refused to acknowledge that Trieste or Venetian Slovenia should go to Yugoslavia after the war. The

45. See above, this chapter, "Italy: The Allies and the Underground."
46. Mikuž, Zgodovinski časopis, 12–13:23; cf. Pacor, pp. 295–96.

Yugoslavs could have their organizations in Venetian Slovenia, but the area's destiny must await the end of hostilities.

In withholding a final decision and seeking a compromise procedure, both parties were following the directive from Moscow. The concern of Soviet Russia at this time was primarily to fight the common enemies—Nazi Germany and Mussolini's Fascist Republic of Northern Italy. The Soviet Communist party had no interest in a dispute between the Yugoslav and Italian parties about Trieste and Venetian Slovenia, a quarrel which would only weaken its hand in the bigger struggle. Acting on their own the Slovenian and Croat parties, however, were not above pursuing the greatest possible gains laid open to them by the October agreement. They hoped to leave no doubt in the Julian Region and in the minds of the Great Powers that the entire territory, including Trieste and Venetian Slovenia, should go to Yugoslavia after the war.[47]

In the first days after the Italian armistice a mass uprising occurred in the Slovenian Littoral under Partisan leadership. For reasons discussed before, Slovenes of all political beliefs supported the Partisans and greeted the Partisan proclamation which had decreed the unification of the Slovenian Littoral with Yugoslavia. Upon the dissolution of the Italian military force Slovenes armed themselves with abandoned Italian weapons and joined the Partisans, for they knew that a hard campaign could be expected against them by the Germans. This proved to be true. The struggle was a bloody one. Many were killed and much property destroyed. The German offensive drove the hard core of the Partisans away from the populated centers and from railroad lines. The Partisans retreated deep into the forests, where they continued their struggle with arms and propaganda.[48]

In addition, the Partisan monopoly on Slovenian national sentiment began to be challenged by the anti-Communist National Guard. Hence, the Liberation Front forbade its followers to cooperate with the Guard in any way, such as sending their children to the new Slovenian schools or participating in the Slovenian administration, dominated by sympathizers of Kokalj's

47. Cf. *Slovensko Primorje in Istra,* pp. 462–63.
48. Ibid., pp. 378–81; Škerl, *La battaglia,* pp. 6–19.

National Guard. Moreover, the Liberation Front proclaimed Kokalj's forces to be collaborationists and traitors. And since, in the Slovenian Littoral, the Partisans had been the first to launch their propaganda, and had established their political movement, created their committees of the Liberation Front, and organized their fighting units against the Italians even before the Italian armistice, many Slovenians naturally continued to follow the Partisans.

During the years 1943 to 1945, German units, the Slovenian National Guard, Italian Republican Fascists, and, in 1945, Serbian troops, all launched attacks against the Partisans. The Partisans survived, however, by using all possible tricks. By the end of June 1944, for example, German troops surrounded a concentration of Partisans—four to five thousand men—in the Bača valley, from whence there was no escape because of high mountains. The few exits were strongly protected by the Germans. In this desperate situation, the Partisans concluded an agreement with the German command for the Adriatic Littoral. The Partisans promised not to attack railroad connections between Trieste and the hinterland, and the Germans in turn agreed to stay away from territory controlled by the Partisans. Thus, though the German forces had the Partisans surrounded in the Bača valley, the Germans retreated on July 5, 1944, and the Partisans saved the main body of their troops in the Slovenian Littoral. How long this agreement remained in effect is still not known, but its importance was demonstrated by promulgation in the German, Slovenian, and Italian languages and posting at all railroad stations between Trieste and Postojna.[49]

The surrender of Italy marked the third stage of Partisan organization, which previously had moved from propaganda to small Partisan units harassing the Italian army and now had reached the stage of an organized army and the formation of governmental authority over a definitely controlled territory. Now in

49. Tratnik, *Koledar-Zbornik, 1951,* pp. 147–48. However, this agreement did not last long. In the late summer and fall of 1944 new fighting broke out among Germans and Partisans, according to Partisan sources (*Slovensko Primorje in Istra,* pp. 408–14). Cf. also Franc Zorec-Kocelj, "Pogodba med Nemci in slovenskimi partizani" (Agreement between the Germans and the Slovenian Partisans), *Vestnik,* 16 (June 1965): 143–45.

JULIAN REGION: COMMUNIST COMPETITION

villages narodno-osvobodilni odbori (National Liberation committees) or NOO were elected by a mass assemblage of the people of the locality. The village committee was the lowest administrative unit. Up the hierarchical ladder came the district committees, and a provincial committee for the Slovenian Littoral.[50] This provincial committee was subordinated to the supreme Partisan authority in Slovenia which was called the Slovenian National Liberation Committee until February 19, 1944, when it was renamed Slovenski narodno-osvobodilni svet (Slovenian National Liberation Council) or SNOS.

Before the summer of 1944 the local, district, and provincial committees had been appointed from above, but after that time they were elected from below. This gave the entire Partisan movement a more democratic outlook. However, the elections in reality merely confirmed most of the committees which had been appointed before. The president of the provincial committee for the Slovenian Littoral was, for example, before September 15, 1944, the Slovenian writer France Bevk. Other important members were Dr. Jože Vilfan and Dr. Aleš Bebler. The same persons remained president and leading members respectively of the elected provincial committee after that date. It should be added that the election was not secret, the vote being taken by a show of hands. It was also a direct election only on the village level. District and provincial committees were elected indirectly by delegates chosen by the lower echelons.[51]

50. The name of the provincial committee was until January 13, 1944, Narodno-osvobodilni svet (NOS) (National Liberation Council). From that date to September 15, 1944, the name changed to Pokrajinski odbor osvobodilne fronte (POOF) (Provincial Committee of the Liberation Front). From September 15, 1944, on it was called Pokrajinski narodno-osvobodilni odbor (PNOO) (Provincial National Liberation Committee). These changes indicated that the provincial council was first an autonomous body, then became incorporated into the Slovenian Liberation Front, and finally emerged again as an autonomous body. These changes without doubt reflected different policies of the Slovenian Communists toward their Italian comrades. (For two different interpretations of these changes see: *Slovensko Primorje in Istra*, pp. 391, 394; Tratnik, *Koledar-Zbornik, 1951*, p. 145.)

51. *Slovensko Primorje in Istra*, pp. 392–94.

During the second half of September 1944 the provincial committee for the Slovenian Littoral established people's courts, its own finances, relief services, care for wounded Partisans, food supply, and education. In the fall, when the new school year 1944-45 began, the Council reopened 248 Slovenian elementary schools with 290 teachers.[52]

This new Communist-led regime was actively supported by the people. Previous administrations had been Italian or Austrian, in both cases foreign. The administration and schools established by the National Guard had been denounced as the work of collaborators. The Partisan administration, instead, was looked upon as entirely Slovenian, especially since the Communists did not stress their communist aims. It is true that some question was raised about the red star placed on the Slovenian tricolor (white-blue-red), but this was explained as a sign that the Communist party was fighting together with the entire Slovenian nation. Besides, did not the National Liberation committees take in all sorts of ideologies? Were not the well-known Slovenian writer France Bevk (a left-wing intellectual), the president of the provincial committee, and the Slovenian priest Anton Bajt a member of that committee?[53]

But this was only the visible side of the picture. Real power remained in the hands of the secretaries of the Liberation Committees on all levels, and these officials were all assisted by trained Communists in the posts of political commissars. A small but disciplined Communist party remained the real ruler behind the mass organization of the Liberation Front and National Liberation committees.[54]

Knowing well the value of propaganda, the Liberation Front issued many newspapers in the Slovenian Littoral in a village close to Gorizia. For over a year, beginning in 1944, the main underground newspapers for all of Slovenia were published there. This was true of *Ljudska pravica* (People's Right), the organ of the

52. Berce, p. 149.
53. Cf. Škerl, *La battaglia,* p. 11.
54. The same was true for the auxiliary organizations of the Liberation Front, the Slovenska protifašistična ženska zveza (SPŽZ) (Union of Slovenian Anti-Fascist Women) and Zveza slovenske mladine (ZSM) (Union of Slovenian Youth).

Slovenian Communist party, and of *Slovenski poročevalec* (Slovenian Reporter), the voice of the Slovenian Liberation Front. For the Slovenian Littoral other local newspapers appeared, such as *Partizanski dnevnik* (Partisan Daily), *Primorski poročevalec* (Littoral Reporter), *Delo* (Work), *Kmečki glas* (Peasant's Voice), and others.[55]

In their pamphlets and newspapers, the Partisans condemned the chauvinism of the Littoral National Guard and constantly proclaimed Italian-Slovenian brotherhood. Judging from the repeated stress placed upon this issue, it was probably the least convincing point of the entire Partisan program. Nonetheless, it bore fruit in that some Italians were induced to join the movement.

The Italians who joined the Partisan movement in the Slovenian Littoral came from two different geographical areas—from Italian industrial centers along the coast (Trieste, Monfalcone, Muggia), the so-called mixed territory around Trieste, and from Friuli, Venetian Slovenia, and Gorizia.[56] The Italian Communists, socialists, and progressive republicans organized their own Communist-led Garibaldi formations. The most known of these were Brigata d'Assalto Garibaldi-Trieste, Brigata Fontanot, and Brigata Garibaldi-Natisone. The history of the first, better known as Brigata Triestina, went back to the days immediately after the armistice: In September 1943 the workers from the Trieste area had formed their first Brigata Proletaria (Proletarian brigade). After the German offensive of September and October against the Partisans, the surviving members joined with other Italian Partisan groups, and in April 1944 formed the Triestina brigade. When the membership increased, a new brigade, Fontanot, was formed in December 1944.

The Triestina brigade continued to fight together with the Slovenian Partisans organized into the IX Korpus (Ninth Corps) operating in the Slovenian Littoral. The Fontanot brigade was

55. Berce, p. 146; see also *The Julian March, Iuliĭskaia Kraĭna, la Marche Julienne* (Ljubljana, n.d. [1946]), for photographic reproductions of title pages of different newspapers published in Julian Region.

56. See: Bruno Steffè, "Le formazioni partigiane a Trieste e nella Venezia Giulia," *Trieste*, no. 66 (Mar.–Apr. 1965), pp. 19–21; Pacor, pp. 190–92, 200–202; *Slovensko Primorje in Istra*, pp. 424–26.

made part of the Slovenian Seventh Corps fighting in Ljubljana Province.

Also in eastern Friuli the Italian anti-Fascists formed their first Garibaldi battalion in September 1943. By June 1944 the number of volunteers had greatly increased, and six Garibaldi battalions joined together into the Garibaldi-Natisone brigade. The brigade united in September 1944 with the Italian royal and Catholic Partisans of the Osoppo brigade, forming jointly the Garibaldi-Osoppo division. The Slovenian Partisan units fought together with the pro-Communist formations of Garibaldi-Natisone in eastern Friuli.

Following the October agreement of 1944 between the Slovenian and Italian Communists, Garibaldi-Natisone broke with the Osoppo Partisans and in December joined the Slovenian Ninth Corps as the Natisone-Garibaldi division. In March 1945, the Triestina brigade also united with the Garibaldi-Natisone division, which then had four Italian brigades.

This Slovenian-Italian brotherhood in arms against the Nazi and Fascist forces so ardently required by Soviet Russia brought closer political contacts among the Slovenes and Italians in the ethnically mixed coastal territory around Trieste. Over and above Unità Operaia (Workers' Unity), a mixed Italo-Slovenian labor organization, there came into being other Italian auxiliary organizations quite parallel to those created by the Slavs, such as Donne Antifasciste Italiane (Anti-Fascist Italian Women) and Gioventu Antifascista Italiana (Italian Anti-Fascist Youth). These various organizations published their own newspapers in Trieste, such as *Unità Operaia-Delavska enotnost* (Workers' Unity), the journal of the Partisan labor union of the same name; *Il Lavoratore* (The Worker), organ of the Italian Communist party; and *Bollettino* (Bulletin), of the Italian Friends of Yugoslavia.[57]

Through their organizations and propaganda, the Partisans collected from Trieste alone, up to the end of the war, over fifty million lire. They arranged for medical help and relief services and prepared a thorough net of Partisan supporters in Trieste, ready to come into the open as soon as the war ended.[58]

In Istria during the years 1943 and 1945 there existed only

57. Berce, pp. 143, 146. 58. Ibid., p. 141.

one Communist party, one National Liberation Movement, and one Partisan underground, as had been the case before the Italian armistice. The party, the Liberation Movement, and Partisans were Croat with autonomous sections for Italians as already indicated.

The Partisan units in Istria remained relatively weaker than in the Slovenian Littoral. The German forces, and the Italian and Croatian units fighting with them, controlled larger sections, especially along the western coast where the Italians formed the majority of the population. The growth of the Partisan units was slow, and only in April 1944 did the first one, Vladimir Gortan, increase to such a degree that it became a brigade. In June of the same year a second Istrian brigade was formed. In the late summer both brigades had to retreat from Istria to Slovenia and Croatia. In Croatia, a third Istrian brigade was formed. At the end of August 1944, all three brigades became organized into the Forty-third or Istrian division, the highest army unit in Istria. The Italian Partisans had their own battalion, Pino Budicin, formed in April 1944, named after a left-wing leader of the Italians in Istria who had been executed by the Germans. The Italian battalion was made a part of the first Partisan brigade, Vladimir Gortan, and later of the 43rd division.[59]

The Croat National Liberation Movement elected its local district and provincial committees for Istria. They became the administrative authority in the liberated territory. In July 1944 a liberation movement was organized for the Italians in western Istria and Rijeka—L'Unione degli Italiani dell' Istria e di Fiume (the Italian Union for Istria and Rijeka). This also was a partial retreat, according to the Cominform directive mentioned above. This Italian union was an autonomous organization forming part of the Croat National Liberation Movement. National Liberation committees in the western parts of Istria, where the Italians lived, were formed by both Italians and Croats.[60] The National Liberation committees organized Croat schools, their own people's courts,

---

59. *Slovensko Primorje in Istra*, pp. 293, 308, 318–20; Steffè, *Trieste*, no. 66, pp. 19–21.
60. *Slovensko Primorje in Istra*, p. 317; Pasquale de Simone, "I comunisti italiani a Pola di fronte al problema nazionale," *Trieste*, no. 57 (Sept.–Oct. 1963), pp. 16–18.

and a cooperative economy in territory controlled by the Partisans.⁶¹ These committees also published newspapers and propaganda material. The best-known weekly was the *Istarski vjesnik* (Istrian Herald) and the monthly *Glas Istre* (Voice of Istria), both issued in the Croatian language. For the Italians, *Il Nostro Giornale* (Our Newspaper) was published beginning in the month of December 1943, edited by an Italian Communist, Vicenzo Gigante, alias Ugo. Later in the summer of 1944 still other journals appeared for Croats and Italians.⁶²

THE JULIAN REGION: THE CLN AND DEMOCRATIC RESISTANCE

Sincere Italian democrats of the Julian Region who opposed Fascism and the German occupation formed in Trieste their own underground, known, just as in Italy, as the CLN—the Comitato di Liberazione Nazionale (Committee for National Liberation) and linked in a slight fashion with the Italian committee. Its position was difficult. Its members were of course directly exposed to persecution by the German authorities and by the Republican Fascist secret police. Should they try to escape into the hinterland, they would have to face up to Tito's Partisan forces, who controlled this part of the Slovenian Littoral and Istria.

An alliance with Tito's Partisans for a common fight against the Germans and Fascists would mean at least a tacit renunciation of the CLN's claim to the Julian Region. On the other hand, to assert this claim would bring the CLN closer to Coceani's collaborationist group, whose principal aim was defense of the Julian Region in the face of a Slavic conquest, and such an alliance would mean a betrayal of the CLN's democratic anti-Fascist beliefs. Hence, the CLN had to find a solution somewhere between its nationalistic and democratic anti-Fascist sentiments.

The first Committee for National Liberation had been formed in Trieste after the Italian armistice by leaders of five pre-Fascist parties (Action party, Christian Democrats, Liberals, Socialists, and Communists). Because its seat was in Trieste, it

61. *Slovensko Primorje in Istra*, pp. 264–67, 273, 276–78, 285–86, 297, 301–3, 312–17, 322–25.
62. Ibid., pp. 276, 321–22.

JULIAN REGION: CLN AND DEMOCRATIC RESISTANCE

came into contact mainly with representatives of the Slovenian National Liberation Movement rather than with the Croats. Its leadership was arrested three times (December 1943, September 1944, and February 1945) by the Germans and the Republican Fascist police, but each time a new committee was formed.[63]

Coceani states that the CLN at first endorsed his legal resistance to the German occupation, but refused his invitation to help organize a unified Italian bloc against a possible Slavic conquest.[64] The CLN did agree, on the other hand, to cooperate with the Slovenian Liberation Front. The proposal for this alliance had come from the latter body as a result of the urgent appeal of the Russian Communist party to form the broadest possible resistance movement by incorporating all anti-Fascist forces.

The Slovenian Liberation Front also desired the agreement as a precaution in case Anglo-American troops should land in Istria, in order to secure Slovenian claims at least over those parts of the Slovenian Littoral controlled by Slovenian Partisans. There were widespread rumors of such a landing, which would bring Trieste and its communication lines with Vienna and the rest of Austria under Anglo-American domination. Such control would secure to the Western Allies at least all territory west of the Vienna-Ljubljana-Trieste line, and prevent a Russian drive beyond this point. Slovenian Communists were afraid that Anglo-American occupation of the Slovenian Littoral, and possibly Slovenia, would greatly diminish their chances to win the struggle for political power in Yugoslavia. They suspected that these Anglo-American forces would favor the old parties and the old social order, which could mean a victory of the Chetniks over Tito's Partisans.[65]

63. Pacor, p. 217; Ennio Maserati, *L'occupazione jugoslava di Trieste, maggio-giugno 1945* (Udine, 1963), p. 30.

64. Coceani, pp. 271-72.

65. Vladimir Dedijer wrote, concerning this (*With Tito through the War: Partisan Diary, 1941-1944* [London, 1951], pp. 245-46): "As for our attitude towards such an invasion [of the Western Allies]—it is clear enough—if the landing is aimed at weakening the invader [the Germans], we shall assist it with all in our power. But if, on the other hand, the British land to crush our movement [Partisans], aiming at landing in force, after we have got the enemy out, and beaten those who helped the Germans, that will constitute intervention, trampling on the

Yet another reason is advanced, this time in Italian literature, for these negotiations.[66] Because of the setbacks the Partisans suffered in the spring and early summer of 1944 in Yugoslavia and Istria, they were looking for an alliance with the Italian underground.[67] There might be still a further reason for these dealings with the CLN, not mentioned in Yugoslav or Italian literature: the Slovenian Liberation Front was hoping to find out how much of the Julian Region a democratic Italian government would be prepared to cede to Yugoslavia in future peace conversations.

It is significant that the Slovenian Liberation Front at first had bypassed the CLN of Trieste and negotiated with the Committee for the National Liberation of Upper Italy, hoping probably for better results. The first meeting of representatives of the Slovenian Liberation Front and the CLNAI had taken place in Milan on June 8 and 9, 1944.[68] The CLN of Trieste had been invited but was not able to send its delegates in time. The three-man Slovenian delegation was composed of Dr. Anton Vratuša, alias Urban, for the Communist party, a Mr. Vran for the Liberation Front, and Franc Štoka for Workers' Unity. The Slovenian delegation made it clear that it regarded the Julian Region as Yugoslav territory, in accordance with the AVNOJ decree of November 1943. The CLNAI, however, would not accept the AVNOJ decree as applicable to the entire Julian Region though it did agree to accept annexation of the parts of the Julian Region compactly settled by Slovenes and Croats. A similar right was to be recognized for Italians by the Slovenian Partisan authorities. The problem of mixed territories would be resolved after the war according to the principles of self-determination and ethnic composition. Further, the CLNAI agreed that both sides should cooperate during the war, on a parity principle, in the common struggle against Fascism and Nazism.

The results of the meeting were published on June 10 in the *Manifesto alle popolazioni italiane della Venezia Giulia* (Mani-

---

basic principles of the Atlantic Charter, on our national rights, an attack on our independence, and we should resist."

66. See, for example, Carlo Schiffrer, "La resistenza a Trieste nel panorama europeo," *Trieste,* no. 66 (Mar.–Apr. 1965), p. 18.

67. See above, this chapter, first section.

68. For a description of this meeting see Pacor, pp. 284–86.

JULIAN REGION: CLN AND DEMOCRATIC RESISTANCE

festo to the Italian People of Venezia Giulia) issued by the CLNAI and sent to the local committees of the CLN in the Julian Region. The manifesto urged all the Italians of the Julian Region to join the CLN and fight together in a united front with the Slovenian Liberation Movement against the Nazi-Fascist forces.

The CLN in cities and towns of the Julian Region outside of Trieste accepted the manifesto as the basis for cooperation with the Slovenian Liberation Front. But the CLN of Trieste, except for the representative of the Communist party, protested loudly. The majority of Trieste's CLN objected to the ethnic principle and the principle of self-determination according to which the new border would be drawn after the war. It did not recognize the Slavs' right to annex to Yugoslavia all the territories compactly settled by Slavs. The CLN of Trieste made it clear that the entire Julian Region should remain united with Italy. If the CLNAI declined to accept the principle of an undivided Italian Julian Region, the CLN of Trieste would feel free to sever its connections with the CLNAI.[69]

To clarify the differences with the CLN of Trieste and to achieve cooperation between the Slovenes and Italians in Trieste, the CLNAI called a second meeting which took place in Milan from July 16 through 19, 1944.[70] Present were seven members of the CLNAI, three delegates from the CLN of Trieste, and two from the Slovenian Liberation Front, twelve men in all. No agreement was reached on the territorial question. The representatives of the Slovenian Liberation Front remained firm in demanding recognition that the entire Julian Region had been annexed to Yugoslavia by the AVNOJ decree. The majority of the CLN of Trieste, except the Communist delegate, refused to confirm the annexation to Yugoslavia of the territory compactly settled by Slovenes (in opposition to the manifesto of June 10) but accepted the ethnic and self-determination principles. Because of the deadlock it was agreed that the meeting had no authority to decide

69. Ibid., pp. 286–88.
70. The second meeting is described by Pacor, p. 288; by Giuliano Gaeta, a delegate of CLN of Trieste representing the Action party, "Chi a tradito la fratellanza," *La Voce Libera*, July 16, 1947; by the same author, "La posizione di Luigi Frausin," *Trieste*, no. 7 (May–June 1955), pp. 15–16; and by Mikuž, *Zgodovinski časopis*, 12–13:29–30.

about a future Yugoslav-Italian border. This question should be solved after the war at the peace conference according to ethnic and self-determination principles.

On Slovenian-Italian cooperation, it was agreed that the CLN and the Slovenian Liberation Front would support each other against Germans, Italian Fascists, and all collaborating forces. The struggle against the Nazi-Fascist enemy would be under the direction of the CLN in territory compactly settled by Italians (Friuli) and directed by the Slovenian Liberation Front in lands compactly settled by Slovenes. In mixed zones (Trieste and the coastal towns) coordinating committees would be created by the CLN and the Slovenian Liberation Front to direct the struggle against the common enemy. These committees would take over administration of the mixed zones after the war as provisional local governments. They were to be organized on the parity principle.

So far the talks concerned only the Slovenian Littoral. To the argument that the CLN represented the entire Julian Region, and that an agreement therefore should be concluded between the Italians, Slovenes, and also the Croats, the Slovenian representatives answered that they had no mandate to speak in the name of the Croats. This position confirmed the opinion that the Yugoslav Communists were not interested in any dealings over Istria, which was apparently already in their hands for sure. The Yugoslav Communists were primarily concerned about Trieste and the surrounding coastal towns—the territory which had not been recognized as Yugoslav in the April negotiations with the Italian Communist party.[71]

According to the Milan agreement a Comitato Antifascista di Coordinamento (Anti-Fascist Coordinating Committee) was established in Trieste, composed of six members. Two represented the CLN; two, the Slovenian Liberation Front; and two, the mixed Italo-Slovenian Workers' Unity.[72] The pro-Communists thus had a majority, as the Workers' Unity had been a creation of the Slovenian Liberation Front. The Coordinating Committee met only three times (August 6, 16, and 23). New quarrels broke out between the CLN and the Slovenian Liberation Front. One of them was over differing interpretations of the term "mixed terri-

71. Gaeta, *La Voce Libera,* July 16, 1947.
72. Mikuž, *Zgodovinski časopis,* 12–13:30.

tory." The Slovenian Liberation Front defined it as limited to coastal towns: Trieste, Monfalcone, Muggia, Piran, Izola, and Koper. The CLN insisted on a broader hinterland, where it could organize its own committees and Partisans. Also supporting these CLN demands now was Luigi Frausin, who represented Trieste's Italian Communists in the CLN.[73] Soon after the third meeting Frausin was arrested by the S.S. police. At the beginning of September 1944 other members of the CLN were also seized. Some Italian sources expressed the suspicion that Frausin and other members of the CLN had been betrayed to the Germans by Slovenian Communists because of their opposition to Yugoslav claims in the Julian Region.[74]

On September 4, 1944, came a third and last meeting in Milan between the Slovenian Liberation Front and the CLNAI. Formally a new agreement was signed, confirming the old points accepted previously.[75] Actually, this was the last time the Slovenes tried to get confirmation of their claims to the entire Julian Region from the CLNAI, and they failed again. As the CLNAI was acting as the underground authority for Bonomi's Italian government, the Slovenes concluded that the future Italian democratic government would equally oppose their claims to the entire Julian Region. Moreover, the Churchill-Tito meeting in August 1944 further confirmed the fears of the Slovenes that the Western Allies might also oppose Slovenian claims to the entire Julian Region.[76] Hence after September 4, 1944, the Yugoslav Communists realized that their future control over Trieste and the coastal towns was very much in doubt. In the eyes of the Yugoslavs a well-organized CLN claiming at least the Italian coastal parts of the Julian Region would be a danger to their pretensions. Therefore the CLN should be weakened.

In accord with this policy, the representative of the Slovenian Liberation Front in Milan cancelled on September 25 all agreements concluded between the Front and the CLNAI. Attacks on the Slovenian Liberation Front by individuals and groups form-

---

73. Pacor, p. 289; Schiffrer, *Trieste,* no. 66, p. 18; Giovanni Paladin, "L'inizio della 'Porzus' giuliana," *Trieste,* no. 7 (May–June 1955), pp. 21–22.

74. Cf. Paladin, *Trieste,* no. 7, p. 22.

75. Mikuž, *Zgodovinski časopis,* 12–13:30–31.

76. See chapter 6, first section.

ing part of the Italian resistance under control of the CLNAI were given as pretext. The representative of the Slovenian Liberation Front, however, said the Front would continue to support "true" Italian democratic forces fighting for liberty and democracy.[77] The same policy to weaken the CLN was pursued in Trieste.

After the arrest of Trieste's Italian Communist leader Frausin, the Slovenian Communists' greatest interest was to see that the next Trieste Italian Communist representative would cooperate more closely with them. The arrest of Frausin had occurred at the end of August—before the Kardelj-Togliatti agreement was concluded in the middle of October 1944.[78] In accordance with this agreement the new leader of the Italian Communist party was a pro-Yugoslav who supported the Yugoslav claim to the Slovenian Littoral. The Italian Communist representative to the CLN in October 1944 demanded recognition by the CLN of the fact that the majority of the people in the Slovenian Littoral, including the Italians, had requested unification with the new democratic Yugoslavia, and also demanded that a representative of the Slovenian Liberation Front be accepted into Trieste's CLN. The CLN rejected these two conditions, and, as a result, Trieste's Italian Communists abandoned the CLN.[79] This was an important event. From October 1944 on, the local Italian Communist party supported the formation of a pro-Yugoslav Coordinating Committee of all the anti-Fascist forces, but without the CLN.[80] This weakened the CLN greatly. But was not this the aim of the Yugoslav Communists? In a Coordinating Committee with a strong CLN the Yugoslav Communists would never prevail. Moreover a Coordinating Committee dominated by a strong CLN would be in favor of an Anglo-American, and not a Yugoslav occupation of the Julian Region—exactly what the Yugoslav Communists were trying to prevent.

With the resignation of the Italian Communists from the CLN, that body altered its policy. After the arrest of the leaders of the second CLN, the third CLN committee issued a proclamation on December 9, 1944, which was diffused through the press and

77. Mikuž, *Zgodovinski časopis,* 12–13:31–32.
78. See this chapter, "The Julian Region: Communist Competition."
79. Carlo Schiffrer, "La missione storica del C.L.N. giuliano," *Trieste,* no. 7 (May–June 1955), p. 15.
80. Cf. *Slovensko Primorje in Istra,* p. 462.

JULIAN REGION: CLN AND DEMOCRATIC RESISTANCE

radio by the Roman democratic government.[81] It stated that the Italian democratic parties represented in the CLN of Trieste would defend the old Italian frontier, which had been stained by the blood of the best sons of Italy fighting as allies of England, France, and the United States against the old enemies, Austria and Germany, in the First World War. They, however, promised cultural autonomy for the Slovenian and Croat minorities. Naturally, this declaration brought the CLN position very close to that of Prefect Coceani, and lent weight to the Partisan charge that Italian chauvinism was the main reason the local Italian Communist party had refused to work with the CLN.

The CLN, however, did not join Coceani's national bloc for defense of the Julian Region. The anti-Fascist and pro-Western democratic aims of the CLN could not be denied, but there are strong indications, blown out of proportion by Yugoslav literature, that connections existed among the members of the CLN and Coceani, as well as Mayor Pagnini. The Yugoslav Communists saw in this a confirmation of a bourgeois Italian conspiracy against the interests of Tito's Yugoslavia. What in reality happened was that the CLN hoped to take power peacefully from Coceani after the end of the war. The CLN looked backward, in this case, to the events of World War I, when such a peaceful transition from Austrian to Italian authority occurred in Trieste and in the entire Julian Region.[82]

Thus, nationalistic aspirations of both the CLN and the Slovenian Liberation Front in the Julian Region prevented an alliance between the two. Each tried to guarantee either a pro-Italian or pro-Yugoslav solution. Although nationalism played a large role on both sides, the ideological difference should not be minimized. One side stood for a Western democratic ideal, and the other for a Communist social order. These were, of course, not the last contacts of the CLN with the Slovenian Liberation Front in Trieste.

81. For the text see "Il patto del 9 dicembre 1944," *Trieste*, no. 7 (May–June 1955), pp. 11–12.

82. A pro-Western National Committee for all of Slovenia, formed on May 3, 1945, in Ljubljana, hoped to achieve a similar peaceful transition of political authority from General Rupnik at the end of the war.

6

THE JULIAN REGION ON THE DIPLOMATIC FRONT (1943–1945)

YUGOSLAVIA AND ITALY: CLAIMS AND COUNTERCLAIMS

All during the war, and especially after the Italian armistice, both Yugoslavs and Italians busily issued papers setting forth their respective claims to the Julian Region. No sooner had the royal Yugoslav government-in-exile been established in Jerusalem than its Slovenian and Croat experts began to prepare and publish pertinent data, first in Jerusalem and then in London, where the government eventually settled, and finally in the United States and elsewhere. Slovenian demands were, in general, the same as those aspired to at the end of World War I, namely the unification with Yugoslavia of the Slovenian Littoral, the Kanal Valley, and Venetian Slovenia.[1] Croatian ex-

---

1. The following is a list of the more important publications of the Yugoslav royal government or by individual Slovenian experts working for the government. The publications are listed in chronological order. (*a*) Royal Yugoslav Government-in-Exile, *Memorandum on the Slovene Territorial Claims at the Moment of the Establishment of the New Boundaries of the Yugo-Slav State* (At the Seat of the Royal Yugo-Slav Government, May 1, 1941). (*b*) *Ethnography of the North-West Frontier of Yugoslavia with Germany on the North and Italy on the West*, ed. G. M. S. Leader (London, 1942). This is a collection of ethnographical maps of American, British, Yugoslav, Swiss, Italian, and German origin. (*c*) Ivan M. Čok, *Memorandum of the Committee of the Yugo-Slavs from Italy: About the Yugoslavs, That Is Slovenes and Croats, under Italy, and Their Aspirations and Claims* (New York, 1942). Mr. Čok was president of the National Committee of Yugoslavs from Italy, and was born in the Julian Region; he served as an expert for the Slovenian minority in Italy with the royal Yugoslav government. (*d*) Ivan M. Tchok [Čok], *The Problem of Trieste*

CLAIMS AND COUNTERCLAIMS

perts pressed their claims to Zadar, all the islands along the eastern shore of the Adriatic, Rijeka, and Istria.[2] On their side Tito's Partisans through the National Liberation committees and councils proclaimed the annexation of the Slovenian Littoral and Istria to Yugoslavia.[3] The Yugoslav-Italian negotiations in the first half of 1944 and the subsequent agreements could be regarded as a Yugoslav Partisan trial to find out how much of the Julian Region the new Italian government was prepared to cede to Yugoslavia.[4]

To obtain recognition by the Great Powers of these unilat-

(Ridgefield, Conn., 1943). A pamphlet of 24 pp. (*e*) Francis Gabrovšek, *Jugoslavia's Frontiers with Italy*. Gabrovšek, a native of Trieste Province, was one of the Slovenian experts of the royal Yugoslav government. (*f*) Yugoslav Government-in-Exile, Information Department, *The Yugoslav-Italian Frontier: Trieste and Hinterland,* foreword by John Parker, M.P. (Yugoslav Document no. 3: London, n.d. [1943]). In addition, at least two works published by English writers sympathetic to the Yugoslav cause should be mentioned: Joseph Clissold, *The Slovenes Want to Live* (New York, n.d. [1943]). Joseph Clissold was a former attaché to the British consulate in Zagreb, Yugoslavia. A. E. Moodie, *Slovenia, An Area of Strain* (Yugoslav Document no. 4; London, n.d. [1943]). This is a reprint of a lecture delivered on June 1, 1943, to the members of Le Play Society.

2. From the Croatian side, two outstanding works, published by Pero Digović, a representative of the Croatian Peasants party sent to Switzerland during the war, should be mentioned. Pero Digović, *La Dalmatie et les problèmes de l'Adriatique,* intro. Ivan Meštrović (Lausanne, 1944); Pero Digović and Frano Goranić, *La Haute Adriatique et les problèmes politiques actuels,* a work already cited. This work was written by Digović while in exile during the war. He used material prepared by Josip Roglić, Matko Rojnić, Rudolf Maixner, Ive Mihovilović, Ante Iveša, and Lavo Čermelj, and, in order to protect them, adopted the pseudonym Frano Goranić. Later, in 1945, the above-mentioned authors published their material in *Marche Julienne*. (For this see Fran Zwitter, "Bibliografija o problemu Julijske krajine in Trsta: 1942–1947" [Bibliography on the Problem of the Julian March and Trieste: 1942–1947], *Zgodovinski časopis,* 2–3 [1948–49]: 269).

3. See chapter 5, "The Julian Region: Communist Competition."

4. See chapter 5, "The Julian Region: The CLN and Democratic Resistance."

eral acts was one of Tito's aims on his visit to Italy in 1944.[5] On August 10 he conferred with General Henry M. Wilson, the Allied commander of the Mediterranean theater. The next day he met with Marshal Harold Alexander, then commander of the Eighth Army, at Lake Bolsena, north of Rome.[6] At the Bolsena conference both parties agreed that Yugoslav troops would meet with Allied forces at a line passing generally north of Rijeka, leaving the port of Rijeka and territory east of this line under control of Marshal Tito, while the troops of Marshal Alexander would control the Julian Region.[7]

This agreement would seem to draw the line along the railway running north from Rijeka toward Yugoslav territory and would leave only the district of Postojna to Tito, with almost all of the Julian Region coming under Allied control.

The following day Tito met Winston Churchill for the first time, but the frontier problem was not discussed. On the morning of August 13, however, when Tito conferred with General James Gammell, chief of staff to General Wilson,[8] he received a memorandum on the Julian Region asserting the intention of the supreme Allied commander "to impose Allied military government in the area which was under Italian rule at the outbreak of war, which automatically suspends Italian sovereignty."[9]

On the afternoon of the same day Tito met with Churchill for the second time. Present also was Ivan Šubašić, the new prime minister of the royal Yugoslav government-in-exile. Both Tito and Šubašić protested against the memorandum and explained that the Yugoslavs regarded the Julian Region as their territory. Moreover, they pointed out that introduction of an Allied Military Government would also mean continuation of the Italian civil administration of the region, while in many sections the Partisans

   5. For other aims see chapter 5, first section.
   6. Dedijer, *Tito,* pp. 216–17.
   7. "Background Statement on Alexander-Tito Talks," released by Allied Military Headquarters, Rome, May 19, 1945, reprinted in *New York Times,* May 20, 1945. The date of the Bolsena meeting is given in the above communiqué as July 1944, although all other works give the date as being in early August 1944.
   8. Churchill, 6:88–90.
   9. Ibid., p. 90.

CLAIMS AND COUNTERCLAIMS

had already introduced their own rule. Tito therefore demanded that the Yugoslavs be at least permitted to participate in the Allied administration of the region.

Churchill replied that any territorial changes would have to be approved by the president of the United States, who was against such alterations in time of war. Further, said Churchill, the Allied powers ought not to discourage the Italians now making a useful contribution to the war. Thus the best solution was to have an Allied military government administer the territory until the question could be decided at the peace conference. In regard to Yugoslav participation in the Allied administration, Churchill urged Tito and Šubašić to prepare a joint proposal.[10]

Apparently the entire problem had been left in a state of confusion, a line of division having been decided at Lake Bolsena and then denied by General Wilson and Churchill two days later. It was not surprising that Tito returned to his headquarters on the island of Vis dissatisfied with his failure to get any promises concerning the Julian Region.

A month later, in a speech of September 12 at Vis, Tito repeated his claims to Istria and the Slovenian Littoral but did not outline a future border. The slogan first used here and so often repeated later by the Partisans was, "We don't want what is another's, but we won't give up what is ours."[11]

The events of autumn 1944 opened a new possibility that Tito would side with the Soviet Union and become a tool in her hands for the westward expansion of communism.[12] Recognizing these changes, the British foreign minister, Anthony Eden, proposed during the Crimean conference at the beginning of February 1945 that a clear line be drawn through the Julian Region, as failure to do so could result in confusion and tension should the Allied forces meet Tito's there. He proposed to leave Trieste and a line of communication to Austria, via Gorizia, in Allied hands, and allow the rest of the territory to go to Tito in accordance with the ethnic principle. The representatives of the United States, who wished all territorial questions to be left for the peace conference, and those of the Soviet Union, who probably hoped

10. Ibid., p. 91.
11. Mikuž, Zgodovinski časopis, 12–13:11.
12. Chapter 5, first section.

123

that Tito's forces would ultimately occupy the whole region, did not agree to Eden's idea, and no decision was made.[13]

During February 22–26, 1945, Field Marshal Alexander, who in the meantime had replaced General Wilson as the supreme commander of the Mediterranean theater, stopped at Belgrade to arrange for coordinated operations between his Allied force and Tito's troops in the Julian Region. According to the Allied communiqué issued in Rome almost three months later, the discussions between Tito and Alexander had the following tenor: Marshal Alexander stressed the need for the Allies to occupy Trieste and the railway connections with Austria, thus in turn necessitating an Allied military administration of the entire Julian Region west of the 1939 Italo-Yugoslav border. Although expressing accord with such control, Tito argued that the civil administration already established by the Partisans should be recognized by the Allied military authorities, with the understanding that local officials would be responsible to the latter.[14]

In contrast to this Allied communiqué, Yugoslav sources described the Tito-Alexander meeting only in general terms. *Borba,* the official organ of the Communist party of Yugoslavia, merely reported that the parties discussed the coordination of future military operations, the provision of supplies for the Yugoslav army, and the administrative arrangements to go into effect when the Allied and Yugoslav forces met.[15]

Apparently, Marshal Alexander was ready to propose a new line of demarcation, running from about fifteen miles south and east of Trieste toward the north and northeast, following east of Ajdovščina, Gorizia, Kobarid, and Tarvisio to the Austrian border. Doubt exists as to whether the plan was ever presented to the

13. *Conferences at Malta and Yalta,* pp. 888–89. Unfortunately the map on which the line was drawn was not attached to the published text. From the text, however, it would appear that the line proposed by Eden was close to the Morgan line adopted in May–June 1945. The Eden line may have run just a little east of the Morgan line.

14. "Background Statement," *New York Times,* May 20, 1945.

15. *Borba,* Feb. 27, 1945, cited in Janko Jeri, *Tržaško vprašanje po drugi svetovni vojni: Tri faze diplomatskega boja* (The Trieste Question after the Second World War: Three Phases of the Diplomatic Struggle) (Ljubljana, 1961), pp. 74, 98 n. 35.

Yugoslavs, because of objections by the United States, but in any case it was clear to Tito that the Western Allies were opposed to his occupation of the entire Julian Region, and especially of Trieste.[16]

After all these discussions, Tito apparently saw that he could gain possession of the entire Julian Region only by armed occupation. The leading figures of the new Tito Yugoslav government and the Yugoslav press lost few opportunities to pound home Yugoslav demands for all of the Julian Region. The urgent necessity to occupy the territory as soon as possible was confirmed by the crescendo of Italian propaganda then sounding forth, demanding the retention of all of the Julian Region by Italy. It seemed the turn of the Yugoslavs in April 1945 to follow the practice of D'Annunzio and his volunteers at Rijeka, namely, to pursue military conquest of disputed territory in order to put a fait accompli before the Allies.

After the 1943 armistice, succeeding Italian governments, thoroughly aroused by Yugoslav pretensions to the Julian Region, directed their efforts to defeat these claims. Their first line of argument was that according to the armistice, the Allied powers were bound to occupy all Italian territory within the frontiers of 1939.[17] Because both Yugoslavia and Italy were seeking the Julian Region, neither should participate in occupation of the disputed territory. The final settlement would be reached at the peace conference after the war, before which time neutrality of the disputed region ought to be guaranteed by Anglo-American military occupation without any promises to either party. Italy counted on having, by the time of the peace conference, a change in status from former enemy to ally, which would strengthen her cause.

Pursuing this strategy, Italy declared war on her former ally Germany, in hopes of gaining the status of an Allied power. Although the United States was quite prepared to grant her this position, Great Britain was firmly opposed and Italy remained

16. Harris, pp. 331-32; Jeri, pp. 74-75; Mikuž, *Zgodovinski časopis*, 12-13:36-37; *Archiv der Gegenwart* (1945), pp. 112, 235, cited in Mikuž, *Zgodovinski časopis*, 12-13:36. This new line of Alexander's seems to be very similar to that proposed by Eden, if not identical.
17. De Castro, pp. 90-92, 109.

only a co-belligerent.[18] Even so, it marked a partial success for Italian diplomacy.

With acknowledgment as a co-belligerent, Italy now tried to reestablish normal diplomatic relations with Great Britain, Russia, and the United States, but again only the United States responded in full. While Great Britain and Russia went only so far as to accept representatives of the Italian government, the Italians were able to reopen their embassy in Washington in February 1945.[19] This too marked an important forward step, for Italy now had agents in the capitals of the Allied powers able to observe all changes of sentiment, express Italian viewpoints, and place Italian propaganda about the Julian Region in foreign newspapers. This advantage was especially valuable in the United States, where large groups of Americans of both Italian and Yugoslav descent resided.

To prevent premature action by the Allies, Italy steadily insisted that the best way to handle Yugoslav-Italian disputes was by direct negotiation between the parties involved. To show its goodwill, in August 1944 the Italian government first sent its spokesmen to Dr. Miha Krek, representing the royal Yugoslav government in Rome. However, the Allies had just recognized Tito's government, and the Italians were forced to change their tactics quickly and seek contact with Tito in order to establish proper diplomatic relations.[20]

The Tito administration, however, still regarded Italy officially as a defeated nation, a stand which promised more success for Yugoslavia at the conference table than if Italy were recognized as an ally. Here, too, the Yugoslavs were only imitating the Italians who, at the Paris peace conference in 1919, insisted that the Slovenian and Croat delegates be treated as representatives of a

18. Ibid., pp. 91–92, 95; Winston S. Churchill, *The Second World War* (London: Cassell & Co., 1954), 5:168–76. Whenever the London edition is used the publishing company's name will follow the author's. When only the author's name is given, the reference is to the Houghton Mifflin edition.

19. Alberto Tarchiani, *Dieci anni tra Roma e Washington* (Verona, 1955), p. 23. The author was the first Italian ambassador in the United States after World War II.

20. De Castro, pp. 104, 514–15.

defeated power, and postponed official recognition of the new state.

Rebuffed by the Tito regime, Italy finally turned to Russia, asking her good offices to persuade Yugoslavia to establish friendly diplomatic relations. Here, too, Italy was without success, although the Russians did promise to help.[21]

News from the Yalta conference and the Tito-Alexander meeting in February 1945 thoroughly alarmed the Italian government. It suspected some agreement concerning the future partition of the Julian Region had been made in favor of the Yugoslavs. But toward the end of March and during April 1945 confirmation came from Washington and London, as well as from the Allied Military Commission in Italy, that the Allied forces would occupy the entire Julian Region.[22]

Certain well-known Italian figures, such as the historian Benedetto Croce and Gaetano Salvemini and the former minister Carlo Sforza, now began to agitate in favor of the Italian government. Press reports in Italian and foreign newspapers backed their statements, and comments favorable to Italian claims appeared. The chief agent demanding recognition of the old Italo-Yugoslav border was, however, the Comitato Giuliano (Julian Committee), formed by refugees from the Julian Region on July 25, 1944, a week after the second agreement between the CLNAI and the Slovenian Liberation Front had established cooperation in the war against Fascism.[23]

On September 22, 1944, in a now celebrated speech backing the aspirations of the Comitato Giuliano, Benedetto Croce, following the point of view expressed by Carlo Sforza at a conference held a month before in Rome, elaborated on the theme that the main cities of the Julian Region, namely Trieste, Gorizia, and Rijeka with their overwhelmingly Italian majority, represented the very centers of the economy and industry of that zone and could not possibly be separated from it. The Julian Region could not be taken away from Italy, continued the argument, because the Treaty of Rapallo, which recognized Italy's annexation of the Julian Region, had been entirely the result of a compromise in

21. Ibid., p. 515.   22. Ibid., pp. 108–9.
23. Ibid., pp. 106–7; see chapter 5, "The Julian Region: The CLN and Democratic Resistance."

which Italy gave up Dalmatia in consideration of Yugoslavia's renouncing the Julian Region.[24]

Salvemini was more willing to compromise, for in October 1944, he defended the Wilson line proposed by President Wilson at the Paris peace conference in 1919. This solution would be championed by the Italian government in 1945.[25]

To the leader of the Milan CLNAI, Ferruccio Parri, who visited Rome toward the end of 1944, these optimistic views were a surprise. Knowing the real situation in the Julian Region from his dealings with the Slovenian Partisans, he said that Italy would be lucky to retain her border even on the Isonzo River.[26] That division would leave the Friulian part of the Julian Region to Italy, while the rest of the territory, including all of the big cities, would go to Yugoslavia.

Despite all obstacles, the Comitato Giuliano worked in the Irredentist tradition and by January 1945 was able to arouse the Italian press to active support of its nationalistic claims. Thus began a sharp duel between Yugoslav and Italian newspapers, each defending its respective demands.[27] The struggle did not remain limited to the press. It aroused national sentiments, which burst out in public demonstrations in Rome during the last part of March and the first days of April. The demonstrators demanded that the entire Julian Region remain Italian. The culmination of this emotionalism came on April 8, 1945, when a bomb exploded in front of the headquarters of the Yugoslav Partisan representation in Rome.[28]

24. De Castro, p. 106. There were 20,414 Italians (17,989 with Austrian and 2,425 with Italian citizenship) in Dalmatia according to the Austrian census of 1910. Of this number, by the Rapallo Treaty, 12,283 Italians living in the city of Zadar and the Dalmatian Islands went to Italy, according to the Italian census of 1921. This left not more than 10,000 Italians in Yugoslavia at best. There remained 368,876 Slovenes and Croats (351,744 with Italian and 17,132 with Yugoslav citizenship) in Italy, according to the Italian census of 1921, which did not favor the Yugoslav minority. (See B. C. Novak, pp. 439-41, 455.) The Rapallo Treaty left, therefore, about 10,000 Italians in Yugoslavia and 369,000 Slovenes and Croats in Italy. If this was a compromise, it was certainly not favorable to Yugoslavia.

25. De Castro, pp. 107-8.
26. Tarchiani, p. 52.
27. De Castro, pp. 107-8.
28. Ibid., pp. 70, 516-17.

The Communist leader of Italy, Palmiro Togliatti, condemned these manifestations. He reminded his fellow citizens that it was Italy that had attacked Yugoslavia, and that it was up to democratic Italy to establish peaceful and friendly relations with the new democratic Yugoslavia. From Yugoslavia itself came scathing invective against the demonstrations as having been inspired by Fascist supporters, and sharp demands for a purge of all such elements endangering the continued war efforts of the Allied nations as well as the future peace.[29]

THE POLICY OF THE GREAT POWERS

Great Britain was the nation most directly interested in the coming balance of power in the Mediterranean and Balkans, and hence was concerned about the future of Trieste. The aim of the United States was first to win the war; territorial settlements must await a postwar conference. The Soviet Union at the beginning of the war was preoccupied in defense of her own soil, though Stalin was already devising ways to prevent a future invasion of the Soviet Union. Her frontier should therefore be extended toward the west, and friendly regimes established along her borders. But the Soviet Union did not urge such a solution until the last years of the war when her armies began to repulse the German invader. From the spring of 1944, and especially at the Yalta conference, Stalin pressed for agreement between the Big Three (Great Britain, the United States, and the Soviet Union) about a future division of the world into spheres of interest. Churchill was prepared for such negotiations, convinced that only in this way could a clear line between East and West be established. Franklin Roosevelt, on the other hand, opposed any agreement of this nature, but made concessions to Russian demands at Yalta with regard to the future Russian western border. Roosevelt, however, opposed confirmation of any territorial claims of other countries, including Yugoslavia.[30]

29. Ibid., pp. 572-73.
30. For a more detailed description see: William H. McNeill, *America, Britain and Russia: Their Cooperation and Conflict, 1941-1946*, a volume of the *Survey of International Affairs: 1939-1946*, edited for the Royal Institute of International Affairs by Arnold Toynbee (London, 1953), pp. 313-75, 402-33, and 454-566.

JULIAN REGION ON THE DIPLOMATIC FRONT

Declarations of the Great Powers to Yugoslav and Italian representatives concerning their claims to the Julian Region form a part of the same picture. There was some speculation among Italians that Great Britain had promised the Yugoslav government the Julian Region, or some parts of it, in 1941, to prevent a Yugoslav-German alliance.[31] To clarify this point I asked the Slovenian representative in the Yugoslav government, Miha Krek, whether the British government or Churchill had made a promise. In a letter of May 19, 1960, Dr. Krek made the following statement:

> Officially, neither the British Government nor Mr. Churchill ever promised that we would receive our Littoral from Italy after the war. Because of a *Putsch* we had entered the war without any international pre-arrangements. As early as our stay in Jerusalem our [Yugoslav] government, at our [Slovenian] instigation, had issued its declaration that the liberation of all Slovenes was a goal of its war policy. When we arrived in London the members of the British government told us privately that we could be hopeful that we probably would obtain from Italy after the war whatever Yugoslavia would justifiably demand.[32]

As early as December 1941, when Stalin had mentioned to Eden that Yugoslavia should be rewarded after the war with parts of Italian territory claimed by the Slovenes and Croats, the British answer was the same, that is, that Yugoslavia should get what she could rightfully claim.[33] Great Britain's position was therefore clear. Yugoslavia should lay claim to the Julian Region at the peace conference, which would decide on "just demands."

Promises made by the United States were in the same general vein. President Roosevelt assured the Yugoslav ambassador, Konstantin Fotić, on September 7, 1943, that injustice done in 1919 to

---

31. See for example Gaetano Salvemini, "Trieste and Trst," *Free Italy*, 1, no. 4 (Apr. 1945): 9; Amadeo Giannini and Gino Tomajuoli, eds., *Il trattato di pace con l'Italia* (Milan, 1948), p. 69; P. A. Quarantotti-Gambini, *Primavèra a Trieste: Ricordi del '45* (Milan, 1951), pp. 248, 276–77.

32. My translation. The Slovenian original is in my possession.

33. Churchill, 3:628, 630.

Yugoslavia would be corrected after the war.[34] The same result emerged from the Churchill-Tito-Šubašić conversation on August 13, 1944, when Churchill gave the Yugoslavs to understand that the question of the Julian Region was to be settled at a postwar peace conference.[35]

The Italian government meanwhile feared Churchill might have promised to the Yugoslavs at least some parts of the Julian Region. To find out if their fears were justified the Italian undersecretary for foreign affairs, Marchese Visconti Venosta, addressed a letter on August 15, 1944, to the acting chief commissioner of the Allied Control Commission, Captain Ellery Stone of the United States, asking for advance information on measures to be taken in the Julian Region at the moment of German collapse. A copy of the letter also went to the English ambassador, Sir Noel Charles. On September 11, Captain Stone answered that the supreme Allied commander intended to set up an Allied military government in the Italian provinces of Bolzano, Trento, Rijeka, Pula, Trieste, and Gorizia. But, the answer stressed, the final disposition of these territories would be a matter of postwar settlement.[36] This statement probably expressed both the American and British viewpoints, as it came from headquarters of the Allied Control Commission in which both parties were represented.

Until autumn 1944 the British and American policy was to occupy the entire Julian Region and to postpone the final solution until after the war. Both powers clearly stated this intention to Yugoslavia and Italy. However, the events of the fall of 1944 changed the attitudes of the two Western Allies. By then the danger of an extension of Communist power toward the West had become greater. The Western powers were cognizant of the relatively rapid advances of the Soviet army and of the liberation of eastern Yugoslavia, where Tito established his Communist government. Not so far back, Churchill had perceived this danger. Time and again he had urged a landing of the British and American forces in Istria from whence the Allied troops would push northward through the Ljubljana gap to Vienna. By October 15, 1944,

34. Fotitch, p. 212.
35. See this chapter, first section.
36. De Castro, p. 105; Harris, p. 329.

Churchill had to abandon this plan when President Roosevelt and the American chiefs of staff opposed it.[37]

Because of this changed situation Tito's chances to occupy the entire Julian Region looked good during the last months of 1944. More so when in October the Italian Communist party agreed to such an occupation. Churchill was aware of this development. Moreover, he suspected that the Soviet Union might support Tito in his desire to occupy the entire region. It was to save part of the Julian Region from Communist occupation and to avoid a future dispute that Anthony Eden, speaking for Great Britain, proposed at the Yalta conference his line of division. But, as we know, such a line was opposed by President Roosevelt and not acted upon by Stalin.

The Yalta conference did not remove the distrust and disagreements between the Great Powers. Instead, after the conference the first signs of future division of the world into two blocs became evident. Between the Yalta conference and mid-April, it was also clear that Tito's Yugoslavia had become a part of the Eastern bloc. The members of the royal government, which made the compromise with Tito, were losing importance in Yugoslavia. On the other hand, during his visit to Moscow from April 10 to 12, 1945, Tito concluded a treaty of friendship with Russia. At the same time, the Russian army newspaper, *Red Star,* published Yugoslav demands for the Julian Region, a further confirmation of Russian support.[38]

England was prepared to divide the Julian Region in the beginning of 1945—witness Eden's proposal at the Yalta conference and Marshal Alexander's talks with Tito. Subsequent events, however, convinced Churchill that the area should be occupied by Allied troops as soon as possible to check the advance of the Communist Eastern bloc. The United States this time agreed with Churchill.

The month of April therefore found the Western Allies under Alexander, supreme commander of the Mediterranean forces, and Tito's regular Yugoslav army in sharp competition to see who would first occupy the Julian Region.

37. Churchill, 6:159, 224–25.
38. Markert, p. 119; De Castro, pp. 111–12; Herbert Feis, *Churchill, Roosevelt, Stalin: The War They Waged, and the Peace They Sought* (Princeton, 1957), p. 627.

7

THE LIBERATION OF TRIESTE

THE END OF MUSSOLINI AND HITLER

As early as February 1945 General Karl Wolff, commander of the German S.S. forces in Italy, contacted the American Intelligence Service in Switzerland to find out the Allied terms for surrender of German troops in Italy. For that purpose General Wolff met on March 8 with Allen Dulles, head of the American Intelligence Service in Zürich. Here it was arranged for General Wolff to talk to the British and American generals. This encounter took place on March 19, and General T. S. Airey and General L. L. Lemnitzer, the British and American chiefs of staff for Italy, made clear to General Wolff that nothing but an unconditional surrender of all German forces would satisfy the Allies.[1]

Meanwhile, in early March 1945, General H. von Vietinghoff became commander-in-chief of all German forces in Italy, replacing Field Marshal A. Kesselring who had become commander-in-chief of German forces on the Western front. Moreover, on April 20, Hitler set up two general commands which were to take over the defense of Germany in case Berlin should fall. Admiral Doenitz would take charge of both military and civilian authority for northern Germany, and Field Marshal Kesselring would become military commander for the entire south. This was the omen of German collapse.[2]

On April 24 General Wolff returned to Switzerland with full powers from General von Vietinghoff to agree to an unconditional surrender of all German forces in Italy. He was instructed to send two plenipotentiaries to Allied headquarters in Italy. Here, on April 29, they signed the document of unconditional surrender in the presence of high American, British, and Russian officers. The surrender went into effect on May 2. It is noteworthy that Stalin

1. Churchill, 6:441.
2. Ibid., pp. 410, 522, 532.

opposed a separate German surrender on the Italian front up to the last moment.³

The CLNAI, the Italian underground for northern Italy, proclaimed a general insurrection to begin at 6 A.M. on April 25, 1945. The same day in Milan, Mussolini met with the leaders of the CLNAI, who asked for unconditional surrender. Later, but still on April 25, Mussolini left the city. The same day, around 7 P.M., leaders of the CLNAI met with the German representative Wolff, who asked for the terms of surrender in the name of General von Vietinghoff, supreme commander of German troops for Italy. No agreement was reached. However, the Fascist Republican units and Germans began to evacuate Milan. On April 26, fighting in Milan continued and on April 27 the Partisan troops entered Milan, liberating it. The first Allied troops entered the city only on April 30, 1945.⁴

Mussolini, who had left Milan for Switzerland on April 25, was captured near the Swiss border by Italian Partisans on April 27. The next day he was shot and his body sent to Milan where it was hung head down on meat-hooks in Loreto square.⁵

On April 30, Hitler received the news of Mussolini's death. At 3:30 P.M. of the same day he shot himself in order not to fall into the hands of Russian troops which were already fighting in the streets of Berlin. Before his death Hitler appointed Admiral Doenitz as his successor.⁶

THE CONTENDING FACTIONS

Near the end of April 1945, when the evidence began to mount that the war in Europe was almost over, five distinct groups in Trieste carefully watched events preparing for the day, and adopting positions they felt would best achieve their goals.

Excluding the German occupation forces, the contenders in

3. Ibid., pp. 526-27. For more detail see Allen Dulles's own account of these negotiations in his book *The Secret Surrender* (New York, 1965).

4. Valiani, pp. 337-53. From Valiani's description it is not clear if the German representative Wolff was identical to General Karl Wolff. This would be impossible according to Dulles (pp. 188-94).

5. Longo, *Un popolo,* p. 437; Churchill, 6:527-28.

6. Churchill, 6:533-34.

Trieste were: (1) the Republican Fascists; (2) Prefect Coceani's supporters; (3) the Comitato di Liberazione Nazionale (CLN); (4) Tito's Partisans and the Italian Communists; and (5) anti-Communist Slovenes organized into the Littoral National Guard, plus Serbian troops who had retreated in the face of the Russian advance.

Despite internal differences, all Italian groups but the Communists conceded their first duty to be a defense of Italy's eastern border against Slavic occupation. Coceani's followers called it the historical imperative. Against this bloc was arrayed the Slovenian Liberation Front, joined by Italian Communist forces, whose main objective was to annex Trieste and the whole of the Julian Region to the new Communist Yugoslavia. Nationalism thus impelled both factions, but the Slovenian Liberation Front and the Italian Communists sought a new communist social order as well. In a most difficult position between these two principal opponents lay the anti-Communist Slovenian nationalists and Serbian troops, who could join neither side.

During March 1945 the Republican Fascists (PFR) abandoned their policy of one-party rule. In the last days of April they agreed to join Coceani's group, the Comitato di Salute Pubblica (Committee for Public Welfare), so that all Italian forces would be defending Trieste against the approaching Yugoslavs.[7] This plan offered at least to the lower ranks of the PFR a unique chance to escape prosecution for a pro-Fascist and pro-German past and for crimes committed during the war.

As the end of German control drew near, the leader of the PFR, Bruno Sambo, on April 28, 1945 agreed to hand over to Mayor Pagnini all weapons in his armory.[8] It was further agreed that the Republican Fascists joining the Committee for Public Welfare would abandon their Fascist insignia (fasces, black shirt, and short two-edged sword) for the Italian tricolor armband and the customary Italian army uniform.[9]

Inasmuch as Coceani's plan for the defense of Trieste was never realized, as a result of the refusal of the CLN to participate, some of the Republican Fascist units disintegrated, while others

7. *Trieste nella lotta,* p. 76.
8. Coceani, p. 300.   9. Ibid., p. 303.

retreated together with the German S.S. and police forces beyond the Isonzo (Soča) River. When, on April 30, 1945, the CLN launched a major uprising against the Germans, some of the Republican Fascists may have joined the action, though it is not known what part, if any, they actually played. But in transferring their arms to the mayor they made it possible for these weapons to be used by the CLN.

The second group competing for power embraced all supporters of Prefect Coceani and Mayor Pagnini. The CLN, while anti-Fascist in principle, found it nonetheless expedient to keep in touch with the administration of these men, and relations between leaders of the two factions remained friendly until the end of World War II. Because of their extreme nationalism, Coceani's group refused an anti-Communist alliance with the Slovenian and Serbian troops, even though it would have hindered the advance of Tito's Partisans and consequently the spread of Communism. One may thus affirm that Coceani's followers were not primarily anti-Communist, but advocates of anti-Slavic nationalism.

As we know, in March 1945 Coceani induced even Mussolini to support a united Italian front, including Italian Communists, against the Slavic danger.[10] Beginning in March and during all of April 1945 Coceani and Pagnini prepared to put their plans into action. On April 4, they tried to get military commitments from Mussolini's Republican Italy to meet the concentration of Tito's Partisans intending to occupy Trieste.[11] It was at this time that Mussolini sent his personal messenger to Rome to ascertain whether any militia or Republican Fascist troops, sent to fight against Tito's forces in Venezia Giulia, would be treated as regular troops and protected by the Italian democratic government of Rome.[12] Upon being reached in that city, Raffaele de Courten, admiral and minister of the navy in Ivanoe Bonomi's government, gave a positive reply, but the answer came too late, arriving in the last days of April when Mussolini's government was already disintegrating.[13] This episode, reported by Coceani and by Attilio

---

10. See chapter 4, "Italian Collaborationists."
11. Coceani, p. 266.   12. Ibid., p. 267.
13. Ibid. Coceani based his account on the story of Attilio Tamaro, a Fascist historian of the Julian Region and Trieste.

Tamaro, if true, is significant because it shows that the democratic government in Italy was prepared—or at least its military circles were prepared—to use even Fascist troops to defend the Julian Region against the Yugoslavs.

More important than these overtures to Mussolini were Coceani's preparations to foster Italian unity in Trieste itself. He states that leaders of the CLN approved his plans for an all-Italian bloc headed by the Comitato di Salute Pubblica. Coceani thus remained in contact with the leaders of the CLN, Antonio Fonda-Savio ("Manfredi"), commander of the CLN volunteers, Biagio Marin, and Ercole Miani, while Mayor Pagnini did the same with his former schoolmate Carlo Schiffrer, representative of the Socialist party in the CLN and a liaison between the CLN and the resistance movement in northern Italy.[14]

At a meeting of over five hundred prominent members of the Trieste Italian community, called by Mayor Pagnini to the town hall on April 10, 1945, Coceani, emphasizing the glorious Irredentist tradition, outlined his program of defense:

> Confronted with the danger which knocks at our door, we cannot permit ourselves the luxury of an internal political struggle. . . . Today, when once more they [the Slovenes] try to impair our nationality, we must be one single idea, one single soul, an Italian bloc.[15]

According to Coceani, all Italian forces should unite in defense of the city. He and the mayor would rally them and prepare for the time when the Germans had left or were ready to transfer power to Italian representatives. No diversionary attacks should be made against the Germans, for this would weaken the German forces fighting a ferocious battle in the face of the advancing Yugoslav Fourth Army and so undermine the defense of Trieste against the Slavs. Once the Germans had signified their intent to transfer power to Italian representatives, or had left Trieste, present administration heads would at once acknowledge the leaders of the CLN to be in supreme command of all regular and volunteer troops in the territory.

14. Coceani, pp. 288–89; Cesare Pagnini, *Storie e storia della occupazione tedesca* (Milan, 1959), p. 5; *Trieste nella lotta,* p. 76.
15. Coceani, p. 296.

LIBERATION OF TRIESTE

If the Germans turned over control directly to the CLN, or retreated without harming the port installations or other public or private facilities, they should be left to retire from Trieste in peace. If not, the Italians should fight to prevent damage. After the German evacuation, all Italian forces would join to halt Yugoslav occupation until Anglo-American troops arrived in Trieste.[16] In case the Germans did not depart before the coming of the Anglo-Americans, the Italians should wait, and not hinder the Germans in their fight against the advancing Yugoslavs.[17] The main task of Coceani was to organize a peaceful transition of power and to prepare a military force able to resist Yugoslav pressure and prevent a local Partisan uprising.

The most trusted unit under the direct command of Mayor Pagnini was the Guardia Civica, organized as a police force eighteen hundred strong, during the German occupation. It had no specific political orientation and was resented especially by the Republican Fascists because it did not fall under their command. Composed of trusted Italian patriots, it was to have the important role of keeping order and preventing looting in the city during the transition period. At a meeting of the Guardia Civica held April 26, 1945, the commander, in the mayor's presence, explained that the future duties of the Guard would be to protect Italian property and defend the city of Trieste against any Partisan uprising. The Guard would act under command of the CLN as soon as the latter took power.[18]

Disturbances broke out in the center of the city all during the day of April 27 as the young people became convinced that the end of the war was near. Italian Fascist police were concentrated at their headquarters, in case intervention was necessary against the demonstrations. The questor (police inspector) decided that the police should keep order up to the time of German withdrawal, and only then join the CLN volunteers. Succumbing to the general excitement, however, the police put on Italian armbands on April 28, only to find themselves immediately disarmed by the German Schutzpolizei. All during this period clashes ensued between German soldiers and the demonstrators, between German

16. Edo Funaioli, *Atti, meriti, sacrifici della Guardia Civica di Trieste* (Trieste, 1953), p. 14.
17. Coceani, p. 303.
18. Funaioli, pp. 13–14.

soldiers and the Italian police, and, in the suburbs, between German soldiers and the local Partisans. At the same time Coceani was trying to persuade the local Fascist Republican forces to participate in the liberation of Trieste. Later in the day Mayor Pagnini accepted arms from former Fascist units which were disbanding.[19]

Alarmed by these events, the German General Schäffer, commander of the S.S. and police troops, sent word that he would like to talk with the prefect, the mayor, the questor, and other representatives of the people of Trieste at 6:00 P.M. on April 28. Believing the invitation to mean the Germans were about to transfer power to Italian authorities, especially as news had just arrived that in Milan the CLNAI had negotiated with the Germans, Coceani sent Mayor Pagnini to bring members of the CLN to the prefecture to discuss the invitation. For this meeting Coceani urged the CLN to have its representatives present to receive power directly from German hands; he and the mayor would then resign.[20]

The members of the CLN, however, were suspicious. They felt the S.S. in reality wanted to make them hostages to assure that the city stayed calm. It was finally decided that Antonio Fonda-Savio and Schiffrer of the CLN would accompany the administration leaders only as observers, and that their leadership in the CLN would not be revealed.[21]

The S.S. general was in fact not concerned about a transfer of power at all, but wanted to inform the Italians that he was sending armed cars into the streets and, in case of anti-German manifestations, would order his men to open fire on the people. General Schäffer assured the visitors that the Germans, in the face of Yugoslav attack, would defend the city to the last. Returning from the meeting, Coceani explained to the people waiting in the prefecture:

> Germany is now facing defeat. The downfall is imminent. It is necessary to be patient for a few days or maybe only a few

19. Coceani, pp. 300–301.
20. Ibid., p. 301.
21. Carlo Schiffrer, "Due vie e due costumi," *Trieste,* no. 31 (May–June 1959), pp. 22–23. Coceani's statement in his book, pp. 301-2, seems to be wrong. There he reports that neither Antonio Fonda-Savio (Manfredi) nor Schiffrer accepted his invitation to accompany him to see General Schäffer.

hours. It is only to be hoped that the Germans resist the pressure of Tito's brigades long enough to allow time for the Anglo-American forces to arrive.[22]

While on the next day, Sunday, April 29, relative calm still prevailed, it was indeed clear that the end of German rule was in sight. With the German civil administration beginning to leave, rumor spread that German troops would evacuate the city or surrender, as had occurred in northern Italy. In the evening Bishop Santin, in constant touch with both the administration leaders and heads of the CLN, went on the air to appeal to Trieste's population to remain calm. That very night, at 10:00 P.M., German batteries opened heavy fire against Partisans advancing on the city. The barrage also covered up the retreat of all S.S. and police forces, marking a split between the S.S. and the German army-navy command.[23]

When the German army agreed to capitulate in northern Italy, S.S. General Globocnik refused to lay down his arms and ordered all S.S. and police forces under his command to retreat from the Julian Region toward the Alps, where he hoped to hold a new line against the advancing Allies. Accordingly, during the night of April 29–30, his men, including the Italian Republican Fascists, were ordered to cross the Isonzo River and concentrate around Tolmezzo, the new Globocnik headquarters.[24]

At 4:00 A.M. on April 30, Coceani learned what was going on and informed Ercole Miani of the CLN. Further encouraged by rumors that an Anglo-American flotilla was approaching Trieste, the CLN decided to give the signal for an uprising within the hour. By this revolutionary act the CLN took power and Coceani stepped down as he had agreed.[25]

During the early part of 1945 this third group, the Comitato di Liberazione Nazionale (CLN), had kept in close touch with Prefect Coceani and Mayor Pagnini, both of whom, according to their own accounts, were protecting the leaders of the CLN as far as possible. For example, when Carlo Schiffrer, the Socialist representative, was arrested by Gaetano Collotti's Republican Fascist secret police, Mayor Pagnini intervened and obtained Schiffrer's

22. Coceani, pp. 302–3.
23. Ibid., pp. 303–5.
24. Ibid., p. 305.
25. Coceani, pp. 305–7.

release. Again, when the CLN had no safe place to meet, Pagnini provided a room in the town hall itself and protected the members from the Republican Fascist police and the Germans by stationing his Civil Guards outside. In the end Pagnini put the entire body of the Guardia Civica at the disposition of the CLN, which merged it with the CLN underground force.[26]

The CLN, besides dealing with Coceani, remained in touch with the Slovenian Liberation Front. The leaders of both groups occasionally met each other and talked about the current news. Around April 8, 1945, in just such a private conversation between Rudi Uršič, alias Karl or Carlo, an important member of the Slovenian Liberation Front, and Carlo Schiffrer of the CLN, the former proposed a new era of cooperation between the two organizations. According to Uršič, both undergrounds would send representatives to a mixed committee which would become the supreme political and military authority of all the anti-Fascist forces in Trieste. It would organize and direct a common uprising against the Germans and function as the city's provisional government after the liberation. This mixed committee would be composed according to the ethnic principle, two-thirds of it Italian and one-third Slovene.[27] Schiffrer listened to the Uršič proposal and promised a reply soon. After consulting with members of the CLN Schiffrer let Uršič know that the CLN accepted his proposal and would send representatives to a joint meeting with delegates of the Slovenian Liberation Front to elect the proposed mixed Italo-Slovenian committee. Then Schiffrer made a further proposal that the mixed committee be composed of ten members, of whom seven would be Italians and three Slovenes. Of the seven Italians, two—the chairman and vice-chairman—would not belong to any political party, while each of the other five members would represent a different Italian political party including the Italian Communists.[28] The joint meeting was held during the night of April 12 to April 13 but no agreement was reached.[29]

26. Pagnini, pp. 5–7.
27. Sala, p. 142; Maserati, *L'occupazione jugoslava*, p. 60; *Trieste nella lotta*, p. 77.
28. Sala, p. 143.
29. There were other negotiations between the representatives of the Slovenian Liberation Front and the CLN. However, Yugoslav and Italian writers are quite vague on this point. The Yugoslavs usually

After some other contacts the final negotiations apparently took place on the evening of April 29, 1945, one day after the CLN leaders had met with the German S.S. General Schäffer. Again Tito's Partisan chiefs asked the CLN to state the conditions on which they could cooperate. The CLN leaders replied that the entire Julian Region, including Rijeka and the islands, should be administered jointly by both Slavs and Italians with flags of both nations flying from all public places except on the town halls in Italian cities, where only the Italian flag was to be exposed. Pending acceptance by the Partisans, the CLN agreed to postpone its planned insurrection in Trieste.[30] But no agreement was reached between the CLN and the Slovenian Liberation Front for unified action against the German and Fascist forces.

At the time of planning the insurrection, the directing committee of the CLN was composed of four men, each the leader of an Italian party: Biagio Marin, a Liberal, Marcello Spaccini, a Christian Democrat, Giovanni Paladin, representing the Action party, and Carlo Schiffrer, Socialist.[31] The CLN underground, called the Corpo Volontari della Libertà, or CVL (Corps of Volunteers for Liberty), was under the command of an independent, Colonel Antonio Fonda-Savio, with two divisions: Triestina "Giustizia e Libertà" (Trieste "Justice and Liberty" Division)

---

mention the negotiations of April 12-13 (April 13-14 according to Jeri, p. 67), but only to underline the unwillingness of the CLN to conclude an agreement. For this see *Trieste nella lotta,* p. 77; *Slovensko Primorje in Istra,* p. 467. The Italian authors give different dates for meetings, and Teodoro Sala, the historian of the CLN, further subdivides these negotiations into official and unofficial ones. Based upon the dates given in Italian works, four periods can be established during which the negotiations took place, namely around April 8, and April 12-15, April 20-25, and April 28-29. See, for example: Sala, pp. 142-45, 179; Ercole Miani, "Le giornate triestine dell'aprile-maggio 1945," *Trieste,* no. 1 (May-June 1954), pp. 7-9; "Maggio jugoslavo a Trieste," *Trieste,* no. 7 (May-June 1955), p. 27; Quarantotti-Gambini, pp. 18-37; De Castro, p. 120.

30. Quarantotti-Gambini, pp. 18-37; De Castro, p. 120. The article "Maggio jugoslavo a Trieste" gives the date as April 28.

31. Carlo Schiffrer, "Trieste nazista," *Trieste,* no. 28 (Nov.-Dec., 1958), p. 21.

and Divisione "Domenico Rossetti."[32] Their total strength was estimated at two to three thousand men, evidently including some men of the mayor's Guardia Civica, and some members of other collaborating units.[33]

The meeting with S.S. General Schäffer on April 28 had made it clear that hopes for a peaceful transition of power would have to be abandoned. And, as there was no agreement with Tito's Partisans, the CLN decided to begin its own uprising. Such an insurrection was also preferable to alliance with the Partisans, for the latter course could jeopardize the destiny of the Julian Region. Moreover, the CLN feared, such an agreement could be used against Italy at the peace conference. Therefore, on receipt of news of the evacuation of Trieste by all German S.S. and police units, and accepting the rumor that an Anglo-American naval force was approaching Trieste, the CLN decided quickly on an uprising. Pier Antonio Quarantotti-Gambini, the municipal librarian of Trieste, has described the plan very well: "What we have to do is to hit the Nazis and at the same time hold back the Slavs of Tito until the Anglo-Americans come from the Venetian lowlands."[34] The CLN hoped to be able to disarm the German military and naval troops left behind and thus become the only

32. Miani, *Trieste*, no. 1, p. 9, n. 3. Attached to Colonel Fonda-Savio were two deputy commanders, Ercole Miani, the commander of the underground forces Giustizia e Libertà of the Action party, and E. Carra, commander of the Christian Democratic forces. (Sala, pp. 135–36.) The division "Domenico Rossetti" was named after Trieste's nineteenth-century poet and political thinker.

33. For the numbers of Italian volunteers see: Sala, p. 179; S. S. [Sylvia Sprigge], "Trieste Diary," *The World Today: Chatham House Review*, n.s., 1, no. 4 (Oct. 1945): 172; and Cox, p. 196. About the participation of the Guardia Civica see Quarantotti-Gambini, p. 47. General Esposito, the commander of the Italian military forces in Trieste which had collaborated with the Germans, reported in his book that he had seen, early on the morning of April 30, 1945, many of his men leaving the barracks in plain clothes with Italian tricolor armbands, going toward the center of the city. (Esposito, pp. 199–200.) By this statement General Esposito shows that some of his officers and men participated in the CLN-led uprising.

34. Quarantotti-Gambini, p. 47.

organized authority in Trieste.[35] By the time Allied forces arrived, Trieste would be safe in the Italian hands of the CLN. But these plans were doomed to defeat.

The first disappointment came on the morning of April 30, when it was found that the fleet approaching Trieste was not Anglo-American, but a German-Croatian flotilla rushing to support the German forces in Trieste.[36] After the first shock of the uprising, the German army and navy contingents had retreated to prepared strongholds—the Palace of Justice, the castle of San Giusto, the port fortifications, and several other centers where they continued to resist the CLN fighters.[37] On top of this, the new flotilla opened fire on the city proper, causing substantial damage.[38]

A second unexpected factor arose when the CLN found itself not the sole driving force of the insurrection. The local Partisans, too, became engaged, for they had long prepared for such an event. Soon they were in control of all the suburbs, and were fighting in the very center of the city side by side with the CLN.[39] At the same time the Partisans took the precaution of disarming all the other forces, such as the Customs Guards (Guardia di Finanza) and the former members of the Guardia Civica, as far as they could.

Quarantotti-Gambini well describes this situation in his account of a walk around the city on the afternoon of April 30. He first encountered two guards in the uniform of the municipal Guardia Civica wearing tricolor armbands. These guards said, "We are all fighting for the Committee [CLN]; it is the Committee which is issuing the orders. But why are they disarming us when we are fighting for the same cause?" To the question, "Who is disarming you?" the reply was, "Those with the red star [Partisans]."[40]

The CLN plans went awry also because of the rapid advance of the Slovenian Partisan troops, who arrived, together with the

35. In Trieste there remained about seven thousand German troops composed of the army, navy, and gendarme units. (Sala, p. 147.)
36. Quarantotti-Gambini, pp. 42–43.
37. Ibid., p. 44; Sala, pp. 181, 183–84.
38. Quarantotti-Gambini, p. 46.
39. See Sala, pp. 181–82.
40. Quarantotti-Gambini, p. 48.

armored units of the Yugoslav Fourth Army, in the suburbs of Trieste during the night of April 30 and reached the center of the city at 9:30 A.M. the next day.[41]

The CLN had begun the uprising, but it was never master of the entire city. It dominated only the very center, and even here it had to fight shoulder to shoulder with local Partisans. All this time Mayor Pagnini remained in contact with the CLN. He and Bishop Santin tried several times to get the Germans to surrender to the CLN, but without success.[42]

With the coming of Yugoslav troops into Trieste on May 1, the active role of the CLN ended. Before fleeing, the German ships helped evacuate some of their troops from the port, and then sped in the direction of Venice.[43] Yugoslav soldiers concentrated their fire against the remaining German strongholds, while the CLN, having tasted the results of some clashes between their CVL and the Partisans, decided to cease fighting, since their maneuvers to control the city had come to naught.[44] As Quarantotti-Gambini wrote: "We remained in silence to listen to the battle which now appeared useless, vain, and we did not know why it continued."[45]

During the insurrection, the CLN leaders stayed in session in the palace of the prefecture. Upon arrival of the New Zealand Division of the British Eighth Army on May 2, one day after the Yugoslav troops, the CLN tried to reach the division's commander, General Bernard C. Freyberg, but without success.[46] The next morning they were driven out of the building by Yugoslav military authorities, and met for the last time in a room in the public library offered by the director, Quarantotti-Gambini.[47]

In the meantime Carlo Schiffrer had received a message from the CLNAI, together with a letter from a brother of the famous Giacomo Matteotti (the Socialist deputy murdered by the Fascists

41. See below, end of this section.
42. Coceani, pp. 310–11.
43. Quarantotti-Gambini, pp. 67, 69–72.
44. Miani, *Trieste*, no. 1, p. 9; Sala, pp. 184–85; Maserati, *L'occupazione jugoslava*, p. 54.
45. Quarantotti-Gambini, p. 60.
46. Ibid., pp. 91–93, 99; Maserati, *L'occupazione jugoslava*, pp. 55–57.
47. Quarantotti-Gambini, pp. 97–98.

in 1924), urging the Socialists to leave the CLN and ally themselves with the Italian Communist party in a joint movement similar to that already established in Italy. These missives were delivered to Schiffrer by Nito Boglione, an engineer of the Aquilea fuel refineries in Trieste. Schiffrer, the Socialist representative in the CLN, chose to compromise. The Socialists left the CLN officially, but he remained as an observer.[48]

In a final meeting on May 3, the CLN decided to reject collaboration with the Yugoslav occupation authorities, and instead to send delegates to the Italian government as soon as possible urging intervention through the Allied powers to end the Yugoslav occupation of the Julian Region.[49] The same day, after the meeting, Carlo Schiffrer, Michele Miani—the member designated by the CLN as the new mayor of Trieste, together with Schiffrer's father and four other CLN members, were arrested by the Partisans.[50] The others dispersed, hiding to avoid arrest. The CLN retreated into the underground, from whence it continued its struggle, now aimed against the Yugoslav occupation forces.

The strength of the pro-Communists in Trieste lay in the Slovenian Liberation Front and Unità Operaia (Workers' Unity). The first represented the Slovenes living mostly in Trieste's suburbs, and Workers' Unity the laborers in the factories of Trieste, Monfalcone, and Muggia, the majority of whom were Italians. The task of the Slovenian Communists was to induce these workers to support the unification of Trieste and the Slovenian Littoral with Yugoslavia. Before April 1944 the Slovenian Communists had tried to recruit individual workers. But after the April and July agreements of 1944 with the Italian Communist party and the CLNAI, the Slovenian Communists gained broader support among Italian labor.[51] From the summer of 1944 on, Workers' Unity became an important force, and was used by the Slovenian Communists to help achieve their goals. Constantly referring to Russian directives to organize all progressive elements in a broader anti-Fascist body to fight the German occupation, the Slovenian Communists obtained endorsements from both Italian Commu-

48. Ibid., pp. 101–3.   49. Ibid., p. 103.
50. Ibid., p. 112; S. S. [Sprigge], *The World Today*, 1, no. 4:173.
51. See chapter 5.

nists and the CLNAI. After this first success, the Slovenian Communists convinced the Italian Communists and the local Italian working men that Yugoslavia would be a workers' state, while Italy would probably remain bourgeois and capitalistic, controlled by the Western powers. When called upon to choose between a capitalistic bourgeois Italy or a socialistic Yugoslavia, the workers should not hesitate. Moreover, socialistic Yugoslavia would provide prosperity for Trieste, since the latter had traditionally functioned as a port for its Yugoslav hinterland. This development would secure economic stability for the workers of Trieste. Yugoslavia would also guarantee national minority rights to the Italian ethnic group. Such were the slogans and promises of the Slovenian Communists.[52]

The Trieste Italian workers had, in fact, never felt at home in Italy. No sooner had they come under Italian control after World War I than Fascists began to harass them. Socialist and Communist parties were disbanded, workers' cooperatives taken over by the Fascists, and workers' newspapers banned. All of which kept Italian laborers in Trieste from looking to Italy as a homeland, and prepared fertile ground for Yugoslav propaganda disseminated by Slovenian Communists.[53]

After securing the support of the Slovenes and of Italian workers, the Triestine Communists (Slovenes and Italians) tried to get the CLN to join them in a single anti-Fascist movement, as described above. They did this for two reasons. First, to obtain absolute control over all anti-Fascist forces including the Italian CLN, and second, to prevent an independent uprising of the CLN by which it might take control of Trieste in the name of Italy. The Communists tried to achieve these aims at the meeting on the night of April 12–13, 1945. About twenty-five delegates gathered in a suburb of Trieste, the majority belonging to the Slovenian Liberation Front, the Unità Operaia, and their auxiliary organizations. The CLN sent only two representatives, Carlo Schiffrer and Signore Caracci.[54]

52. See Bulajić, pp. 7–9.
53. Schiffrer, *Trieste*, no. 56, pp. 16–17.
54. For the negotiations of April 12–13 see: *Trieste nella lotta*, pp. 77–78; *Slovensko Primorje in Istra*, pp. 467–68; Sala, pp. 143–44; Maserati, *L'occupazione jugoslava*, p. 61.

Here a pro-Communist delegate proposed formation of an executive committee of three Slovenians and eight Italians, representing all the anti-Fascist organizations. Those attending agreed that the three Slovenians should represent the Slovenian Liberation Front and its two auxiliary organizations, the Union of Slovenian Youth and the Union of Slovenian Anti-Fascist Women. But disagreement arose as to who was to appoint the eight Italians. The Communists demanded that they should appoint five of the eight members who were to represent the Italian Communist party, the Unità Operaia, and the three Italian Communist auxiliary organizations, the Union of Italian Anti-Fascist Women, the Union of Italian Youth, and the Independent Italian Democrats.

Here was a masterpiece of Communist strategy. They had enticed the CLN to participate by offering a two-to-one clause based on the ethnic principle. The CLN had interpreted this to mean that it would appoint two-thirds of the members, leaving one-third to the Communists. But the CLN became a victim of its own nationalistic sentiments. By their clever maneuver the Communists would attain an absolute majority of eight (three Slovenes and five Italians) leaving to the CLN only three Italian members, while still adhering to the ethnic ratio of about two Italians to one Slovene. It is understandable that the CLN turned down this proposal.

There was another disagreement over the Guardia Civica, the city's police force, which had been organized by Mayor Pagnini. The CLN stood for unification of the Guardia Civica with its own military underground. The Communists opposed, arguing that the city police had been organized by German collaborators and had fought together with the Germans against the Partisans.

The discussion lasted the entire night but no agreement was reached. Toward morning the two CLN representatives left and the Communists elected an executive committee as the supreme authority of all anti-Fascist forces. They called it the Comitato Esecutivo Antifascista Italo-Sloveno (Italo-Slovenian Anti-Fascist Executive Committee) or CEAIS. This pro-Yugoslav CEAIS had eight members, three Slovenes and five Italians. Three additional seats remained, reserved for Italian members to be nominated by the CLN.

On April 15, 1945, the CLN made a new compromise proposal. Each side should nominate five members to the joint committee. The chairman should be an Italian Communist, a man known for opposition to the Yugoslav annexation of Trieste. The Communists rejected this proposal and thereafter appointed three more members to the CEAIS, bringing its total to eleven.[55] By the middle of April the CEAIS became the supreme political body of all pro-Communist forces in Trieste.

For the pro-Communist and pro-Yugoslav forces, a CEAIS including members of the CLN would have had strong political significance. It would have represented a united front, not only against the Germans, but also in favor of a pro-Yugoslav solution to the Trieste problem. Such a CEAIS acting as a provisional government could also more easily win acceptance from the Western Allies as an established pro-Yugoslav administration in Trieste. Despite these advantages, the Communists' determination to win absolute control in the joint committee was greater than their desire to cooperate with the CLN. After failing to achieve absolute control in this way, the Communists organized their own CEAIS rather than form a joint committee with the CLN on equal terms. The CLN had good reason to refuse cooperation with a CEAIS in which it would be a minority, forced to work for annexation of the Julian Region to Yugoslavia. This aim was, of course, diametrically opposed to its own goal, reunification of the Julian Region with Italy.

The Slovenian Liberation Front and Unità Operaia had also prepared themselves militarily for an uprising against the Germans, by dividing the city into four sectors and organizing a Partisan unit for each. In the second half of 1944, a city Partisan headquarters was formed to prepare and direct an armed uprising. The detailed plans, finished by the middle of April 1945, were submitted for approval to the superior military authority, the Ninth Slovenian Corps. At that time, according to Yugoslav sources, about 2,500 organized Partisans were in Trieste, to be joined between April 15 and May 1 by another 5,000. Their insignia was the Yugoslav Partisan cap with a red star.[56]

55. Sala, pp. 144–45; *Trieste nella lotta*, p. 78.
56. *Trieste nella lotta*, pp. 81–82; *Slovensko Primorje in Istra*, pp. 465, 466; V. Novak et al., p. 409; Maserati, *L'occupazione jugoslava*, pp. 43–44. The Ninth Corps appointed Martin Greif alias Rudi as com-

LIBERATION OF TRIESTE

The Partisan uprising in Trieste was planned as part of a general drive of the Yugoslav Fourth Army, which began its offensive from Dalmatia in the direction of Trieste on March 20, 1945.[57] Moving along the eastern shore of the Adriatic, by April 20 the Fourth Army reached the Yugoslav-Italian border of 1939. Bypassing Rijeka, the main force fought hard against the Germans and their allies, and on the afternoon of April 28 reached the outer fortifications of Trieste.[58] The same day, April 28, Mar-

---

mander of the city and Vinko Šumrada alias Radoš as political commissar.

57. The Yugoslav account is to be found in the official work: Yugoslavia, Beograd, Vojno-istoriski institut (Belgrade, War-Historical Institute), *Završne operacije za oslobodjenje Jugoslavije, 1944-1945* (The Final Operations for the Liberation of Yugoslavia, 1944-1945), Velimir Terzić, general editor (Belgrade, 1957), pp. 611-57, cited hereafter as *Završne operacije;* and in Pavle Jakšić, *Oslobodilački pohod na Trst četvrte jugoslovenske armije* (The Liberation March on Trieste of the Fourth Yugoslav Army) (Belgrade, 1952), pp. 244-78. General Jakšić was the chief of staff of the Fourth Army. Both works described the actions of the regular Yugoslav army and the Ninth Partisan Corps. Only Jakšić gave a short account of the activities of the Trieste Liberation Front and its city command. While both works are written in an impersonal vein Jakšić gives in his appendix (pp. 344-53) the names of commanders, political commissars, and chiefs of staff for the Fourth Army, its corps, and divisions. Based on the first two works but with more detail about the activity of the Slovenian Ninth Corps is the book by Stanko Petelin, *Osvoboditev Slovenskega Primorja* (The Liberation of the Slovenian Littoral) (Nova Gorica, 1965), pp. 171-241. For the activities of Trieste's Partisans see: *Trieste nella lotta*, pp. 82-87; and *Slovensko Primorje in Istra*, pp. 468-69.

58. In his notes, written at the time of Tito's march on Trieste, Schiffrer—the Socialist representative in the CLN—expressed suspicion that the Germans were deliberately opening the road to Tito so that Partisan forces could reach Trieste before the Anglo-American forces and thus create intense friction between the Allies and Tito. See Schiffrer, *Trieste*, no. 31, p. 23. Such statements were violently denied by the Yugoslavs, who stressed that the Yugoslav Fourth Army had been ferociously fighting with the Germans before it entered Trieste. For this see: *Završne operacije*, pp. 611-68; Jakšić, pp. 244-78; Petelin, pp. 196-223; Jeri, p. 68.

shal Tito ordered the Fourth Army to concentrate all of its efforts on entering Trieste immediately. The Slovenian Ninth Partisan Corps, gathered in Trnovski forest north of Trieste on April 28, received an order to join the Fourth Army in its attack on Trieste. During the next two days, April 29 and 30, the Yugoslav forces tried hard to break through the outer defenses of Trieste. By the evening of April 30 they penetrated the German positions and entered the first suburban villages. The next morning, May 1, about 9:30 the first armed units of the Yugoslav army reached the center of Trieste.[59]

To support a concentrated attack on Trieste from within the city, the Partisan city command had received in the afternoon of April 28 a radio dispatch from the Ninth Corps to begin the uprising. While the Partisans assembled in places previously assigned, the German heavy artillery opened fire against the advancing Yugoslav army. To the city Partisans this was proof that the Yugoslav army was close by to help them. In neighboring villages and suburbs the city Partisans clashed with the Germans and Italian Fascist units and began to disarm them during the night of April 28-29 and the next day.[60]

The morning of the CLN insurrection of April 30 found the Trieste Partisans fighting together with the CLN in the center of the city against the Germans.[61] In the suburbs, by then controlled by the Partisans, they already had begun to disarm such soldiers of the CLN as had been heretofore members of the Guardia Civica or other armed forces such as the Guardia di Finanza, Pubblica Sicurezza, and Carabinieri.

When on May 1, 1945, the Fourth Army and the Slovenian

59. *Slovensko Primorje in Istra,* pp. 468-69; Jeri, pp. 67-68; Pacor, p. 325.

60. *Slovensko Primorje in Istra,* pp. 468-69.

61. Ibid.; Pacor, p. 323. Maserati's statement (*L'occupazione jugoslava,* pp. 51-52), that there had been no clashes between the formations of the Slovenian Liberation Front and the Germans in the center of the city either on April 28, 29, or 30 takes into account only the units of the Ninth Partisan Corps but not the formations of the Partisan city command. Such a participation of the units of the city command in the center of the city was confirmed by the pro-CLN work of Quarantotti-Gambini.

Ninth Corps entered the city, they immediately concentrated against the remaining fortified points held by the Germans—the Palace of Justice and the castle of San Giusto. By then the CLN and Partisan forces had already taken the port, which had been evacuated by the enemy's ships.[62] Following this move, the CLN dropped out of the fight. The Germans in the castle did not surrender until late afternoon of the next day, May 2, when they turned themselves over, not to the Yugoslavs, but to New Zealand units, part of the English Eighth Army which had arrived that day. The Germans in the Palace of Justice did not yield until forced to do so by a combined attack of Yugoslav and New Zealand troops.[63]

Both the British recognition of Tito and the Russian advance toward Yugoslavia had great impact upon anti-Communist movements in Yugoslavia. However, the anti-Communist forces continued to believe that the alliance of the Western democratic powers with the Soviets was a temporary expedient to defeat the Germans. They could thus view British support of Tito as temporary, and believed it their duty to keep their own forces as nearly intact as possible to readily take part in the inevitable war against the Communists.[64] In accordance with these beliefs, the Serbian leaders tried to form a strong united Yugoslav anti-Communist military force out of divergent army units operating in the western part of Yugoslavia and in the Julian Region during March and April 1945.

At that time the territory of Yugoslavia and of the Julian Region was distinctly divided into two parts. In the east Tito had established his legal government and his regular Yugoslav army, supported by British heavy armament, and had launched a great offensive toward the west with Trieste as its main objective. In the western part the Croat state was the largest territorial unit with the greatest degree of independence. The rest of the land remained divided into small provinces under direct German con-

62. Quarantotti-Gambini, pp. 62–63.
63. Cox, pp. 8, 194.
64. When visiting Serbian troops after their surrender to the British Eighth Army, Cox, a senior intelligence officer, found this belief still prevailing. (Cox, p. 219.)

CONTENDING FACTIONS

trol. In each of these provinces separate Slovenian and Serbian military formations existed, lacking a common independent command.[65]

In many respects the plan of the Serbian leaders was similar to that of Prefect Coceani in Trieste. All existing Croatian, Slovenian, and Serbian military formations should agree, according to this plan, to recognize a united military command to take over the heavy armament from the Germans after the latter had surrendered to the Western Allies. Then, with the support of the Western Allies, this new anti-Communist Yugoslav army—some 100,000 strong—would begin an all-out attack against the Partisans and liberate all of Yugoslavia for the king. To gain Croat support, the Serbs agreed to a federal rather than a centralized form of government for the future Yugoslav kingdom.[66]

This plan was never realized. Before an anti-Communist army could be formed, Tito's Fourth Army reached Trieste and separated the Serbian and Slovenian forces in the Julian Region from the Croat army and from the Slovenian Domobranci of Ljubljana Province. The plan in any case had little chance of success. It was conceived under the false assumption that the British would support such a plan, as they had in Greece by backing the anti-Communists against the Communists. But today it is known that Stalin had agreed that Greece belonged to the British sphere of interest, while this was not so for Yugoslavia. Next, there was not much chance for cooperation between the Serbs and Croats because of bitter hostility between them, sharpened enormously by wartime massacres of Serbs by the Ustashi Croats. An important question was whether the Germans would act ac-

65. Slovenian forces numbered approximately as follows: Slovenian Home Guards, 10,000 to 15,000; Slovenian Chetniks, 500; Littoral National Guard, 1,500. The Serbian Volunteer Corps and the Serbian Chetniks numbered between 20,000 and 25,000 men. The Italian forces including Trieste's Guardia Civica numbered around 10,000. For more information on the numerical strength of different military units see: Petelin, pp. 10–33; Esposito, pp. 154–61; Karapandžić, *Grandjanski rat*, p. 403.

66. Markert, p. 112; Karapandžić, *Gradjanski rat*, pp. 401–5, 455–57; Maks Loh, "Bajeslovje v zgodovini" (Myths in History), *Vestnik*, 17, no. 10–11–12 (Oct.–Dec. 1966): 243–46.

cording to the designs of this plan. Would they permit formation of a strong anti-Communist army, and would they surrender their armament to it? However, for the Julian Region the most important factor remained the behavior of the Italian troops. The Italians might take advantage of a civil war in Yugoslavia to secure the Julian Region for themselves. It was to clear this last question that the Serbian leaders approached Prefect Coceani twice, on April 13 and again on April 23, 1945. According to Coceani the Serbs proposed to defend Trieste alongside the Italians against Tito's Partisans. Quite understandably Coceani tried to find out the Serbian position on the Julian Region and on Trieste in particular before making any agreement. The Serbs replied that the first task was to defend the land and the city from the Communist danger and then to leave the matter for the peace conference. When the Serbs refused to recognize the Julian Region as undisputed Italian territory Coceani, in consultation with Bishop Santin, Mayor Pagnini, and other close associates, rejected their help for defense of Trieste.[67]

With the advance of the Fourth Army, the Serbian troops and the majority of the Slovenian Littoral National Guard retreated toward the west, crossing the Isonzo (Soča) River near Gorizia during April 29–May 1, 1945. Here they surrendered to the British Eighth Army on May 3. Later they were transported to Forlì and then to Eboli, Italy, where they found themselves in a camp established for detachments of the Yugoslav royal army. From the Trieste area the Littoral National Guard was evacuated by German-Croatian ships on April 30 and later surrendered to the British Eighth Army at the mouth of the River Tagliamento, whence it was sent by sea to Bari. Many members of the National Guard, however, were not evacuated and were taken prisoners by Tito's troops. The majority were put to death, a fate also suffered by their commander, Colonel Kokalj.[68]

After Trieste had already been taken by the Partisans the Slovenian Alliance, true to its plan, called into session an assembly of erstwhile Slovenian deputies to the Belgrade parliament and cultural, social, and economic representatives from all walks

67. Coceani, pp. 254–57; Karapandžić, *Gradjanski rat*, p. 403.
68. Karapandžić, *Gradjanski rat*, pp. 449–50, 454; Tratnik, *Koledar-Zbornik, 1951*, p. 151.

of life. This underground Slovenian parliament met in Ljubljana on the evening of May 3, 1945, and solemnly proclaimed a United Slovenia whose territory would now embrace all Slovenian lands, including the Slovenian Littoral, Venetian Slovenia, the Kanal Valley, and Slovenian Carinthia, and which would be a member of a federated Yugoslavia with King Peter as ruler. The assembly elected the Narodni odbor za Slovenijo (National Committee for Slovenia) to function as the provisional government vested with supreme administrative authority for all of Slovenia. The assembly pronounced that the Home Guards and the newly organized Slovenian Chetniks should form the Slovenian army. Colonel Krenner, until then commander of the Slovenian Home Guards, was elevated to the rank of general and appointed as the supreme commander of the Slovenian army. In its proclamation the National Committee guaranteed political freedom according to democratic principles for every political party. To end the fratricidal civil war the National Committee urged the Partisans to suspend immediately all their attacks on the Slovenian army.[69]

Using maneuvers similar to those in Trieste, the National Committee met with the German General Erwin Rösener in Ljubljana on May 4, 1945, to ask him to transfer his authority to the National Committee. But Rösener refused to do so, as had General Schäffer in Trieste a few days earlier. Before it could come to a showdown between the National Committee and the Germans, the Partisan forces began to move toward Ljubljana. To avoid Partisan encirclement the National Committee left Ljubljana on May 5 and retreated toward the north to Carinthia in Austria, the only way left for escape. The Slovenian army followed the National Committee a few days later and surrendered to British troops in Austria during May 12 and 13. The soldiers and the many civilians who followed were put in a prison camp at Vetrinje (Viktring) southwest of Klagenfurt in Austria. During the time from May 24 to May 31, 1945, more than ten thousand

69. "Združena Slovenija vstaja" (United Slovenia Is Rising), *Slovenec*, May 4, 1945. The proclamation of the National Council is reprinted in the Serbian language in Karapandžić, *Gradjanski rat*, pp. 452–53. See also Franc Bajlec, "Narodni odbor za Slovenijo in vetrinjska tragedija" (The National Committee for Slovenia and the Tragedy of Vetrinje), *Vestnik*, 13, no. 5–6 (May–June 1962): 136–41.

Slovenian Home Guards and Chetniks were turned over to the Partisans by the British army. Most of them were massacred by the new Yugoslav rulers without a trial, in the Kočevje forests in the southeastern part of Slovenia.[70]

WHO LIBERATED TRIESTE?

The question of exactly who was responsible for the liberation of Trieste became a significant matter at the peace conference and other diplomatic negotiations, and directly affected the future of the city. The arguments that raged were also important to the newly formed neo-Fascist groups vis-à-vis their Italian opponents in the CLN.

From September 1943 on, the new Italian democratic governments had concentrated on persuading the Western Allies to occupy the entire Julian Region. Representatives of the Allies repeatedly assured the Italians that they intended to do so.[71] It was due to these assurances that Tito threw all available forces into the race for Trieste, while still leaving in German hands sections of Slovenian and Croat territory of Yugoslavia. For example, while Yugoslav armies arrived in Trieste on May 1, the Partisans did not reach Ljubljana, the capital of Slovenia, nor Zagreb, the capital of Croatia, until May 9.[72] The CLN also decided to liberate Trieste to show the world that the Julian Region and Trieste were Italian and had been freed by the Italian people.[73] In no city of the Julian Region other than Trieste was there an independent Italian uprising against the Germans.[74]

70. For more detail on the return of the Domobranci see: Bajlec, *Vestnik*, 13, no. 8 (Aug. 1962): 189–90; no. 10–11 (Oct.–Nov. 1962): 258–63; *Vetrinjska tragedija;* and Karapandžić, *Kočevje Titov najkrvaviji zločin*.

71. See chapter 6, "Yugoslavia and Italy."

72. *Završne operacije*, pp. 672–73, 721; Jakšić, pp. 325–29; the *New York Times* (May 9, 1945), however, gives the date for the fall of both cities as May 8, one day before.

73. Maserati, *L'occupazione jugoslava*, pp. 38–40.

74. In Gorizia a mixed Partisan command and a mixed provisional administrative committee were formed from the CLN and the Slovenian Liberation Front. Here the CLN agreed to cooperate with Slovenian Partisans, and hence there was no independent uprising of the CLN

WHO LIBERATED TRIESTE?

Later, at diplomatic conferences on the future status of Trieste, the Yugoslav representatives always stressed that the Julian Region and Trieste had been liberated by local Partisans with the help of the Yugoslav Fourth Army. Though the Corpo Volontari della Libertà of the CLN shared in the joint uprising against the Germans, Yugoslav sources give it little credit—if they mention it at all. Rather, they stress that the Italian uprising was made possible only because of the presence of the local Partisans and the Yugoslav Fourth Army.[75] Before the New Zealand Division—the Western Allied force—had even entered the city, the Yugoslav army had been fighting for more than a day to conquer the German-held strong points. The Germans would have had to capitulate to the Yugoslavs whether the Allied troops had been present or not, just as the Germans had surrendered to the Yugoslavs in Rijeka and in Istria. Furthermore, charged the Yugoslavs, the Germans' knowledge that the Allies were rushing toward Trieste actually encouraged them to hold out longer so as to surrender to the Allies rather than to the Yugoslavs.[76]

The stand taken by Coceani and Pagnini during the postwar controversy with the leaders of the CLN was as follows: It was only because they had decided on legal resistance against the Germans and had taken over the Italian administration during the

---

against the Germans. However, when Tito's troops arrived in Gorizia, the Slovenian Liberation Front took over the entire administration. The CLN leaders were arrested or were forced into the underground. See: Iolanda Pisani, "Gorizia, aprile 1945," *Trieste*, no. 59 (Jan.–Feb. 1964), pp. 22–23. Similar mixed committees were established in Muggia, Monfalcone, Grado, and other towns. The majority of the members of these mixed committees belonged to the pro-Yugoslav Communists, and the CLN was represented in most cases only by three members. (See Pacor, p. 325.)

75. Maserati, *L'Occupazione jugoslava*, pp. 41–44, nn. 13, 14.

76. Petelin, pp. 218–19; Yugoslavia, *Memorandum of the Government of the Democratic Federative Yugoslavia Concerning the Question of the Julian March and Other Yugoslav Territories under Italy* [Belgrade, 1945], pp. 20–21. This was the official Yugoslav Memorandum presented to the Conference of Foreign Ministers in London in September 1945. Hereafter cited as Yugoslavia, *Memorandum* (1945). Cf. also Jeri, pp. 68–69.

German occupation that organization of the CLN had been possible at all. The CLN created its underground force with the knowledge and protection of the administration, which had indeed even agreed to turn over power to the CLN as soon as the Germans had left in order to present a solid Italian front against the Slavs. According to Coceani the CLN did not follow the line agreed upon, but betrayed Italian national interests in the Julian Region. First, the CLN maintained friendly relations with the Slovenian Liberation Front and the Partisans, knowing that the latter claimed all of the Julian Region for Yugoslavia. Second, the CLN committed an act of treason on April 30 by staging an uprising which destroyed Italian unity and opened the door of Trieste to Tito's soldiers.[77] Coceani stressed that "at that time and at that place Fascism had factually meant Italy while Anti-Fascism had practically signified Yugoslavia."[78]

In these polemics Pagnini reminded the CLN leaders that he had maintained friendly relations with them, had helped them, and had protected them in his town hall rooms during the entire insurrection. According to Pagnini, the friction between himself and Schiffrer originated only after June 7, 1945. The CLN would have had no arms to start an insurrection, Pagnini stated, if the CLN had not collaborated with him and Coceani.[79]

Schiffrer, the Socialist delegate to the CLN, has said that the "united front" of Coceani and Pagnini represented primarily the interests of some bourgeois groups desiring a peaceful transition of government in order to protect their interests. According to Schiffrer, the plan of an all-Italian united front was doomed to failure. Had the CLN joined forces with Coceani's Committee for Public Welfare in defense of Trieste against Tito's fighters, it would have made Tito the real liberator of Trieste against a Fascist-CLN-German alliance. Even if this alliance could have resisted Tito's forces for a few days, the Allies would have had to help Tito win and all Italian elements would have been branded as pro-Fascist, while Tito would have posed as the only ally of the

77. Bruno Coceani, *Trieste durante l'occupazione tedesca, 1943–45* (Milan, 1959), pp. 44–46. Coceani's pamphlet is an answer to the article "Trieste nazista" by Carlo Schiffrer.

78. Coceani, *Trieste,* p. 41. Coceani is here quoting Piero Operti.

79. Pagnini, pp. 8–9, 13.

Western powers who fought against Fascism and the Germans in the Julian Region. Such an alliance, Schiffrer said, would have meant suicide for Italian democratic organizations in Trieste.[80]

Furthermore, according to Schiffrer, a CLN-Fascist alliance would have placed all Italian claims to the Julian Region in danger at the peace conference. The Yugoslavs, he asserts, were looking for proof of just such cooperation to bring before the conference. He charged that the Partisans immediately after the uprising claimed that the Fascists and CLN had united in the insurrection, which was directed not against the Germans but against Tito's victory.[81] To prove his point Schiffrer quoted what Pagnini had written in May 1945 about Partisan interrogations:

> They [the Partisans] let me understand that the following was their thesis: The CLN had for its program the rallying of all forces, including the Fascists, to fight not against the Germans but against the Slavs, and holding on until the coming of the English.[82]

With this Partisan thesis undermining the value of the CLN action, Schiffrer went on, how much more damage would have been done had the so-called Coceani plan for an Italian united front against the Slavs been actually carried out?

The result of the bitter discussion between the Coceani group and the CLN illustrates the relationship between them that had existed during the war. The Yugoslav charges on this score had some foundation. But Yugoslav assertions that the CLN had pro-Fascist sympathies went too far. An authentic anti-Fascist sentiment could not be denied the delegates of the CLN. The trouble lay in that this sentiment was secondary to their ardent nationalistic ambitions. It was for this reason that the first aim of the CLN in Trieste was not to fight against Fascism (as it was in Italy proper) but to battle to preserve all of the Julian Region for Italy. Because of this, the right wings of the democratic parties became the spokesmen for virulent nationalism, a feature that lasted all during the period to 1954. As a consequence, the distance between the neo-Fascists and the democratic parties of the center became

80. Schiffrer, *Trieste,* no. 28, pp. 19–20.
81. Ibid., pp. 20–21.
82. Ibid., p. 21.

much less in the Trieste area than in Italy proper, and permitted united action of all Italian parties against Slavic demands.

Because of this same nationalism, the Italian Socialists and Communists in Trieste could never reach a working alliance, entirely unlike the situation in Italy. Only after 1954, when Trieste was returned to Italy, did the nationalist issue lose its primary importance. And only then did the real ideological differences between the parties become exposed, causing, in turn, the acrid debate between the neo-Fascists and the political parties whose leaders had been in the CLN.

8
THE FORTY DAYS (MAY 1– JUNE 12, 1945)

TITO FAILS TO OUST THE ALLIES

When British and Yugoslav troops met in Trieste on May 2, 1945, the great problem became: Who would administer the Julian Region? By that evening the Yugoslavs knew that presence of the New Zealand Division in Trieste, Monfalcone, and Gorizia could jeopardize their control over these cities. The more so as the cities had an Italian majority, half of which opposed Yugoslav occupation hoping the Western Allies would take over. To remain in control the Yugoslavs had to fulfill two vital tasks without delay.

First, Yugoslav troops had to occupy the remaining parts of the Julian Region. According to the prepared plan they were to advance from Monfalcone and Gorizia toward the north, along the Soča (Isonzo) River, to the Austrian border. Second, a Yugoslav military administration had to be organized before the Western Allies could take over on their own. This was the case especially for Trieste.

The center of Yugoslav activity was the headquarters of the Fourth Army. The commander, General Petar Drapšin, was a small intelligent man in his early thirties. Before the war he had been a schoolteacher and later had served in the International Brigade in Spain. At his headquarters were also General Arso Jovanović, Yugoslav chief of staff and second in command after Marshal Tito; Edvard Kardelj, a Slovene and a leading Communist figure in Yugoslavia; and Ivan Ribar, president of the Executive Committee of the Yugoslav National Liberation Movement (AVNOJ). The presence of these men well illustrates the great importance the Yugoslavs assigned to the Fourth Army.[1]

1. Franc Potočnik, *Žice, morje in gozdovi* (Wires, Sea and Forests) (Ljubljana, 1951), p. 124. The headquarters moved along with the advancing Fourth Army. On May 1 or May 2, according to Potočnik's account, the headquarters was in Opatija, a summer resort in the north-

FORTY DAYS

General Josip Černi was chosen as city commander of Trieste and charged with organizing the military administration there.[2] During the night of May 2–3 he set up headquarters in the palace of the prefecture, the seat of the former Italian provincial administration. The city command included, besides General Černi, General Dušan Kveder as vice-commander and Franc Štoka as political commissar. On the morning of May 3, the city command posted its first decrees informing the public that the Yugoslav army had taken over administration of Trieste. The city command reserved all authority for itself as long as military operations continued in the region. Both General Černi and Commissar Štoka signed these first decrees.[3]

The next move of the Yugoslavs would have been their most important, had it been successful. They tried to get the Allied troops out of the Julian Region. Marshal Tito sent a message to Marshal Alexander on May 3, asking for an immediate explanation as to why the Allied forces had entered Trieste, Gorizia, and Monfalcone.[4] The same day the Yugoslav news agency Tanjug issued a communiqué from the supreme headquarters of the Yugoslav army in which an objection was raised against Marshal Alexander's daily report stating that the New Zealand Division had liberated Trieste, Monfalcone, and Gorizia. The communiqué read:

> The seaport Trieste, Monfalcone and Gorizia could not be occupied by the above mentioned division [the New Zealand Division] as these cities had already been liberated after hard and bloody struggles by the Yugoslav army.
>
> Likewise no German garrison could surrender [to the New Zealand Division] in these cities as these cities had been

---

eastern part of Istria, just west of Rijeka. It was then moved to Št. Peter where on May 4 Cox met with Generals Drapšin and Jovanović. (See Cox, pp. 202, 206–7.)

2. Before General Černi took over the military command of the city, this function was performed by the highest-ranking Yugoslav officer present in the city, Colonel Vodopivec. (*Trieste nella lotta*, p. 87.)

3. Ibid., pp. 87–88; Maserati, *L'occupazione jugoslava*, pp. 58–59; Cox, pp. 200–201.

4. Coles and Weinberg, p. 596.

completely cleared of enemy troops by our forces as far back as April 30.

It is true that some Allied forces have without our permission entered into the above mentioned cities which might have undesirable consequences unless this misunderstanding is promptly settled by mutual agreement.[5]

Yugoslav determination to get the Allies out of the region was made plainer still in a message sent to General Freyberg the following day, May 4.[6] To strengthen their case the Yugoslavs boldly asserted that they had liberated Trieste well before Allied troops had entered the area. This Yugoslav behavior put the commander of the Allied forces, General Freyberg, in a precarious position demanding an immediate decision.

The New Zealand Division, part of the British Eighth Army, had entered the Julian Region by crossing the Isonzo (Soča) River some twenty miles west of Trieste in the late afternoon of May 1, 1945. This was the same day that Yugoslav tanks had pushed into the center of Trieste. After advancing for about six miles, the New Zealand Division reached Monfalcone, the first important town of the region. The Partisans of Monfalcone were in a festive mood. They had liberated the town the same morning and were celebrating the victory with great demonstrations.[7]

The New Zealanders had made their first contact with the Partisans on their way toward Monfalcone. These were the Slovenian units of the Ninth Partisan Corps. General Freyberg was anxious to meet with the Yugoslav commander to explain his intention to occupy Trieste, hoping to prevent tension between Allied and Yugoslav troops. The Partisans agreed to bring the commander of the Ninth Corps to the town hall of Monfalcone at 7:30 of the same evening. Later came news that the Partisan commander would not come before the next morning at 8:30. When the Yugoslav commander still failed to appear General Freyberg ordered his troops to proceed to Trieste. Soon thereafter the commander of the Ninth Corps arrived. General Freyberg explained that his orders were to press on to Trieste and open the port as a base for the British armies which were to move into

5. *Slovensko Primorje in Istra,* p. 509; Cox, p. 208.
6. See below, end of this section.
7. Cox, pp. 1–4.

Austria. The Yugoslav commander did not like this news, but said it was beyond his authority to accept or reject the plan. He promised to reach his superior, the commander of the Fourth Army, who would come to Monfalcone at 2:30. But the commander of the Fourth Army never appeared and the New Zealand Division continued to advance toward Trieste. By 4:00 P.M. of the same day, May 2, the New Zealand tanks reached the outskirts of Trieste and were linking up with the Yugoslav infantry.[8]

Considering the short distance, a little more than twenty miles, the New Zealand Division might have gone all the way to Trieste on May 1, the day it crossed the Isonzo River. Italians may be right in stressing that the Yugoslavs, by their negotiations in Monfalcone, were trying to delay the entrance of the Western Allies into Trieste for a period long enough for the Yugoslavs to annihilate the remaining German strongholds. Then the Yugoslavs could claim to be the sole liberators of the Julian Region.

These Yugoslav wishes, however, did not materialize. When the New Zealand Division entered Trieste the Germans were still resisting. Though the New Zealanders helped destroy the German strongholds, the Yugoslavs demanded any German prisoners for themselves on the ground that they had arrived first in Trieste. They continued from this time on to act as if they were the true masters of the Julian Region, an attitude which made the New Zealanders quite uncomfortable. Geoffrey Cox, one of the latter, best describes the situation. Up to the Isonzo (Soča) River, the people had been friendly, greeting the New Zealanders as liberators, decorating their tanks and vehicles with roses and Italian flags. After they crossed the Isonzo the greetings stopped and the people watched with suspicion the Allied vehicles covered with Italian flags. In Monfalcone Italian flags flew side by side with Slovenian and Yugoslav banners, all with a red star in the center. But then, Cox continues:

> Suddenly . . . the atmosphere was completely changed. There was a difference, ill-defined but certain, between these people in these streets, and those whom we had met all the way from Piave. In the weariness, in the rain, the troops rapidly sensed the change. It may have been only that here and there a girl

8. Ibid., pp. 2, 4–7.

to whom they waved would turn aside instead of waving back, it may have been that the men shook their heads at our dog-Italian, but it was unmistakable. We felt like strangers in a strange land, as if at the Isonzo we had passed some unmarked but distinct frontier. As indeed we had. We had driven from Italy into what was to become a No Man's Land between Eastern and Western Europe, and like any No Man's Land it was extremely unpleasant.[9]

The first night, between May 2 and May 3, General Freyberg appointed General Gentry as commander of all British troops in Trieste. General Gentry set up headquarters in the Albergo Grande, also called the Hôtel de la Ville, on the waterfront around the corner from Yugoslav headquarters, and garrisoned the main strongpoints in the city, including the castle of San Giusto.[10]

The Italian population not affiliated with the pro-Yugoslav CEAIS enthusiastically greeted the Allied troops. Allied presence awakened new hope that the British and Americans would administer Trieste and force the Yugoslavs to retreat from all of the Julian Region. But when the leaders of the CLN urged the Allied officers to assume control of the administration in the name of the Italian population, General Freyberg displayed great caution.[11]

The next day the Yugoslav command posted its first decrees, as mentioned above. There was to be a curfew between three in the afternoon and ten the next morning. All civilian vehicles had to be declared within five days and all arms surrendered. Employees of all public concerns such as gas, electricity, and streetcars were to report for work at once. Clocks would be set back one hour to conform to Yugoslav time. More serious, the Yugoslavs began to make widespread arrests.[12]

Italian hopes, so bright the day before, abruptly sank. The Italians began to regard themselves as de facto annexed to Yugoslavia. However, they calculated that the situation might not endure, as long as the Allied troops stayed in Trieste. The flood of Italian delegations to Allied headquarters increased, explaining

9. Cox, p. 192.
10. Ibid., p. 200.
11. Maserati, *L'occupazione jugoslava*, pp. 56–57; Pacor, p. 324.
12. Cox, pp. 200–201; Maserati, *L'occupazione jugoslava*, pp. 58–59.

how Yugoslav decrees had violated basic civil, political, and family rights. Again Cox illustrates well the mood and complaints of these delegations:

> Frantic Italian business men wanted to get protection for their property. The Bishop of Trieste was concerned about the extent of the arrests. Italians who had belonged to the Italian Committee of National Liberation [CLN] protested that not only were ex-Fascists being run in by the Yugoslavs and marched away into the interior, but that also anti-Fascist Italians who were opposed to the city going to Yugoslavia were being held. An Italian demonstration formed up outside the Albergo and started to cry "Trieste to Italy." Yugoslavs fired over their heads. The crowd panicked and tried to storm into the hotel, and some were wounded. Over the whole city fear spread like a miasma.[13]

The willful introduction of the Yugoslav administration took the Allies by surprise. General Freyberg had at once to decide whether to accept it or insist that the Allied Military Government be installed in the Trieste region as it had been in other Italian areas liberated by the Allied forces. He chose the first alternative, thinking it better to allow the Yugoslav administration to function until he received further orders from Caserta, Italy, the headquarters of his superior, Marshal Alexander, the supreme commander of the Mediterranean theater. To prevent further tension the Allies stopped a charabanc full of Italian Carabinieri on the outskirts of Trieste and ordered them back to Monfalcone. British-American officers appointed to organize the Allied Military Government in the Julian Region were, for the same reason, told to wait in Monfalcone until further notice.[14]

The Allied city commander General Gentry visited the Yugoslav city commander and transmitted General Freyberg's decision. But General Gentry also underlined that the Allies "could not stand by if summary arrests were carried out or people removed from the city without trial."[15]

The same message was sent to headquarters of the Fourth Army. Senior Intelligence Officer Cox and Colonel Clarke, a Brit-

13. Cox, p. 201.   14. Ibid.   15. Ibid., pp. 201–2.

ish liaison officer with the Fourth Army, delivered it to Generals Jovanović and Drapšin on the morning of May 4. The Yugoslav generals were not satisfied, but instead advanced demands of their own. According to Cox, General Jovanović said immediately after the introduction:

> "I have a protest to make to your commander, in the name of Marshal Tito, a protest against your troops in crossing into our operational zone." . . . "I must ask your commander to withdraw his troops at once behind the Isonzo [river]. You are getting in the way of operations we are undertaking to the north, and in Gorizia your tanks have broken up a partisan demonstration and protected local Fascists. You are interfering, too, with our civilian administration."[16]

General Drapšin nevertheless accepted General Freyberg's invitation to come next day and see General John Harding, the commander of the Thirteenth Corps of the British Eighth Army, part of which was Freyberg's New Zealand Division.

Meanwhile, on the same day the permanent British liaison officer with the Fourth Army sent in a formal protest from Tito. It contained much the same wording as the oral protest of General Jovanović. To it, however, General Pavle Jakšić, the chief of staff of the Fourth Army, had added a warning that "from now on the Fourth Army would not be responsible for anything that might happen if their request was not met."[17] The Yugoslavs also demanded that all Allied liaison officers and military missions be immediately withdrawn. Later the Allies were again reminded of the communiqué from the supreme headquarters of the Yugoslav army, when it was issued by the Yugoslav press agency Tanjug.

Quite understandably General Freyberg took necessary countermeasures. He summoned a divisional conference to draw up defense plans and sent Colonel Clarke back to headquarters of the Fourth Army with orders to inform General Drapšin

> that Freyberg understood that the whole question of the garrisoning of Trieste was being discussed between Field-Marshal Alexander and Marshal Tito; that we ourselves would ensure that no trouble broke out meanwhile from our side; but that

16. Ibid., p. 206.   17. Ibid., p. 208.

we should certainly defend ourselves with great effect should the forces under his command dare to dispute our presence by force.[18]

General Freyberg again repeated that General Drapšin should come and see General Harding as soon as possible.

This firm Allied position brought positive results. Late the same night, between May 4 and May 5, Colonel Clarke returned and reported that "Drapšin had responded unhesitatingly that no threat was meant. There must be some error in translation."[19] The Yugoslav pressure for the Allied withdrawal had not worked.

General Drapšin met General Harding on May 5 in Monfalcone and approved the established situation. The Yugoslavs were temporarily to administer all of the Julian Region until an agreement could be concluded between marshals Alexander and Tito. The Allied forces were to remain in Trieste and along the roads connecting Trieste with Austria via Monfalcone and Gorizia. This agreement remained in force for five weeks while negotiations were held on higher levels. During this time the Eighty-eighth United States Division and the British 56th London Division joined the New Zealanders in securing the roads from Trieste to Austria.[20]

TEMPORARY YUGOSLAV ADMINISTRATION IN THE JULIAN REGION

The Yugoslav Fourth Army in Trieste formed merely a wedge along the Adriatic extending into enemy territory. Most of Slovenia and Croatia north of this wedge was still under German control. It took some ten days more before Tito's armies occupied the rest of the territory.

By May 7 the Fourth Army had finished operations in the Julian Region. From then until May 15 Tito's forces occupied the rest of Yugoslavia and entered Southern Carinthia in Austria.[21]

18. Cox, p. 209.
19. Ibid.
20. Ibid., p. 210.
21. "Spominski dnevi v maju" (The Days to Be Remembered in May), *Borec,* 5, no. 5 (May 1953): 176; *Završne operacije,* pp. 657–68, 672–73, 721.

Only on May 9 did Partisan units take Ljubljana. The Slovenian government proclaimed by the Partisans on May 5 in Ajdovščina, a small town in the Julian Region taken by the Fourth Army, could enter the Slovenian capital only on May 10.[22]

The liberation of Slovenia and Croatia from German forces was simultaneously a victory for the Communist revolution. It was followed by a bloody persecution of real and potential opponents. Not before the beginning of 1946 did the terror give way to a new legal political order, which was, of course, a Communist dictatorship emulating the Stalinist regime.[23] This lawless, chaotic time may be divided into two periods. During the first, ending around the middle of May 1945, the struggle for Slovenia and Croatia continued and the liberated regions were administered by decrees executed jointly by military authorities and by local National Liberation committees. After the middle of May 1945, when the second period began, the state of war ended and control was transferred to a new civil administration of National Liberation committees and councils, the backbone of which was the Communist party.

By this move, various National Liberation committees and councils were transformed from guerrilla bands into the organs of regular administration. At the bottom of the administrative ladder, in meetings of each village, men and women elected their local (village) National Liberation committee. Delegates from the villages formed district assemblies, each of which in turn elected its district executive committee, the two bodies being known as the District National Liberation Committee. The same pattern of assembly and executive committee was followed for the higher levels of province and region, the assembly of each being chosen by the next lower level and the executive committee chosen by its own assembly. The decision-making power, and hence the true power, in each case lay with the executive committee. Further up were the republican National Liberation councils, selected in the

22. The Partisan Slovenian government was formed two days after the provisional assembly had met in Ljubljana and elected the National Committee for Slovenia to act as a pro-Western Slovenian government. Boris Kidrič, a known Slovenian Communist, headed the Partisan government.

23. For more details see Zalar, pp. 117-49.

same fashion. Thus the people participated directly only in the election of the local (village) National Liberation committees.[24]

The Yugoslav federal state was divided into six republics: Slovenia, Croatia, Bosnia-Herzegovina, Serbia, Montenegro, and Macedonia. The republican executive committee became the republican government. On top was a federal assembly and a federal government for all of Yugoslavia, headed by Marshal Tito. The Russian blueprint is evident. As the Russian revolutionary Soviets (Councils) of Workers', Peasants', and Soldiers' Deputies replaced, after the revolution, the previous Russian administration, so the Yugoslav guerrilla National Liberation committees and councils became, after the liberation, the new Yugoslav administration.

Yugoslav administration of Trieste followed the same pattern though with a few modifications because of the mixed ethnic character of the area and the presence of the Allies. Until May 13 Trieste was ruled by the military command, assisted by the CEAIS, representing the Italo-Slovenian Liberation Movement. After May 13 the new civil administration was introduced. But already before that time preparations were under way for the change. A few days after the "liberation" of Trieste the city command got a new head. General Černi having been promoted to commander of the Yugoslav fleet, his place in Trieste was taken by General Dušan Kveder, the vice-commander, while an Italian, Giorgio Jaksetich (Adriano) became the new vice-commander. Franc Štoka remained the political commissar.[25] This change, whatever the reason behind it, brought an Italian into the city command, whereas before there was none.

The first step in preparation for a civil administration was taken on May 7, 1945, at a meeting of some sixty delegates of pro-Communist organizations, the ones which had set up the CEAIS in the middle of April, in the Casa del Popolo (Home of the People), the former Casa del Fascio (Home of the Fascists). Here the delegates agreed on the future organization of the city admin-

24. *Trieste nella lotta,* pp. 94–95; Makso Šnuderl, *Politični sistem Jugoslavije* (The Yugoslav Political System), vol. 1: *Družbeno-politična in ekonomska ureditev* (Socio-Political and Economic Organization) (Ljubljana, 1965), pp. 11–35.

25. *Trieste nella lotta,* pp. 87–88; Maserati, *L'occupazione jugoslava,* p. 58.

istration. The CEAIS, hitherto functioning as a supreme coordinating committee of all guerrilla pro-Communist organizations, was renamed the Consiglio di Liberazione di Trieste (the Liberation Council of Trieste) or the CLT. By this action its former guerrilla function changed into an administrative one. The CLT was to take over provisional administration from the city military command as soon as military operations were concluded and the war ended. Thenceforth, in the shortest possible time, the CLT was to organize an indirect election for a permanent city administration—a city assembly and executive committee—according to the Yugoslav pattern. To enable the CLT to carry out its newly assigned tasks, the old CEAIS, numbering eleven members, was enlarged to nineteen, of whom twelve were Italians and seven Slovenes. The chairman of the CLT became Umberto Zoratti, an Italian Independent Democrat. Of the two vice-chairmen, one was an Italian Communist, and the other a Slovenian Communist. One secretary was an Italian Independent Democrat, the other a Slovenian Communist.[26]

Events developed as planned. A week later, on May 13, in an official ceremony at the town hall, General Kveder, the Yugoslav commander of the city, transferred the civil administration to the CLT. The city command retained, however, direct supervision over internal affairs, foreign trade, and industry. Present at the ceremony were British, American, and Russian military representatives.[27]

During the next four days, May 13–17, the CLT organized the election of 1,348 delegates to the city's constituent assembly. The elections were conducted in a typical revolutionary manner. The Sindacati Unici (Unitary Trade Union), the legal continuation of the underground Unità Operaia, called meetings of its

26. Maserati, *L'occupazione jugoslava*, pp. 63–65; *Trieste nella lotta*, pp. 91–92. *Slovensko Primorje in Istra* (p. 536) gives the date as May 6, and the number of delegates as "52 leaders of eight anti-Fascist organizations."

27. *Trieste nella lotta*, pp. 92–94; *Slovensko Primorje in Istra*, p. 536; Quarantotti-Gambini, pp. 208, 215; Cox, pp. 226–27. S. S. [Sprigge] (*The World Today*, 1:4, 175) gives the date as May 18, while Maserati's (*L'occupazione jugoslava*, p. 66) date, May 23, is evidently a printing mistake as he cites *Il Nostro Avvenire* dated May 15, 1945.

branches in factories, shipyards, commercial and credit establishments, navigation and insurance companies, and public and private offices, where the members elected their delegates to the constituent assembly. In addition, the Slovenian Liberation Front and other pro-Communist organizations called public electoral meetings or city ward assemblies, which also elected delegates to the constituent assembly.[28] This dual system gave some persons the chance to vote twice, while others who were against the new administration had no way to express their opposition. On the positive side it must be said that women participated in elections for the first time in the history of Trieste.

The 1,348 elected deputies forming the constituent assembly met on May 17, at 6:00 P.M. in the Rossetti Theater, the environs of which were heavily guarded by the Yugoslav army to prevent incidents. The assembly was opened by Giuseppe Gustincich, a Triestine Italian Communist. The inaugural speeches were made by the secretary of the CLT, Rudi Uršič, by the president of the Regional National Liberation Committee, France Bevk, by the Yugoslav city commander, Dušan Kveder, by the vice-city commander Giorgio Jaksetich, and by the commander of the People's Militia, Rudi Greif. Present also were the military representatives of Great Britain, the United States, and the Soviet Union. The assembly then proceeded with elections. It confirmed the nineteen members of the CLT, giving it a permanent character, and elected by acclamation 120 members of the newly created Consulta della Città di Trieste. Both bodies together made up the city's Liberation committee, of which the Consulta was the assembly and the CLT its executive committee.[29] By electing a constituent assembly, the Communists were seemingly departing from the Yugoslav administrative system, but it was felt that such a body might give the appearance of a democracy and thus impress the Western Allies.

In the last part of May, because of an increase in the work load, the CLT was enlarged from nineteen to twenty-seven members of whom eighteen were Italian and nine Slovene. The new

28. *Trieste nella lotta,* p. 94. Maserati (*L'occupazione jugoslava,* p. 69) gives the number of delegates as 1,384.

29. *Trieste nella lotta,* pp. 95, 201–10; Maserati, *L'occupazione jugoslava,* pp. 68–70.

members were chosen by the Consulta. The CLT was subdivided into ten departments, namely: internal affairs, alimentation, transportation, social assistance, agriculture, industry, justice, finance, education, and press–public relations, and two commissions—one for administration of municipal property, and the other for purging of war criminals. When toward the end of May Umberto Zoratti, chairman of the CLT, disappeared from Trieste, the Yugoslav authorities explained his absence by stating that he had been promoted to the first vice-presidency of the Regional National Liberation Committee. The Consulta then appointed Giuseppe Pogassi as the new chairman of the CLT.[30]

The ethnic ratio was observed also in selection of the members of the Consulta. Of the total, eighty-two were Italians and thirty-seven Slovenes. The members came from all walks of life: forty-one laborers, seventeen intellectuals, twenty-seven clerks, eighteen craftsmen, ten shopkeepers, and seven from other occupational groups.[31]

People's courts, militia, and the labor unions provided the usual Communist tools to keep the people under control. The Consulta and the CLT organized during the second half of May three kinds of law courts: a Special People's Court, regular courts, and a court for housing problems. All were subordinated to the department of justice of the CLT.

On May 21, the Consulta constituted the Special People's Court to judge the Fascists and their collaborators who were directly or indirectly guilty of wrongs which the Fascist regime had done to the Trieste community. A chairman and ten members were appointed to form the Special People's Court. The chairman and eight members were Italian, and two members Slovene. None was a judge by profession. The chairman and all ten members were to be present when judging a person accused of crimes for which the punishment could be death. Lesser offenders were to be tried by a group of three judges, selected from the Special People's

30. Maserati, *L'occupazione jugoslava*, p. 70; *Trieste nella lotta*, p. 96. The work done by the ten departments and the two commissions is described in detail in *Trieste nella lotta*, pp. 96–121. For Zoratti's disappearance see below, next section.

31. *Slovensko Primorje in Istra*, p. 536. Note that the ethnic origin was not given for one member.

Court. An Italian, Dr. Adelmo Nedock, was appointed as public prosecutor to the court. The court, however, met only twice, on June 11 and 12, before it was disbanded by the British-American military government. It condemned to death one Slovene and judged not guilty an Italian Fascist.[32]

To help the Special People's Court detect Fascists, the Consulta constituted purging commissions on the same day that the Special People's Court had come into being. The branches of the labor union (Sindacati Unici) were to organize purging commissions in individual factories and offices which would denounce any Fascist to the Special People's Court or to the public prosecutor of that court. The same right to denounce a Fascist or a collaborator was given to every individual.[33]

In its meeting of May 29, the Consulta organized regular courts. It divided the city into six judicial sections, where courts of first instance were to be constituted for judging minor trespasses. To judge more serious crimes the Consulta created one superior court with jurisdiction over the entire city. This court was to function also as an appeals court for the six courts of first instance. For the appeals court, the Consulta elected thirty-six judges, of whom eight had a legal education and twenty-eight were from other walks of life. Of the eight professional judges, seven were Italians and one a Slovene. Of the rest of the twenty-eight, twenty were Italians and eight Slovenes. It was decreed that people of each section of the city were to elect their own judges for courts of first instance. These elections probably never took place. Though the new regular courts never functioned, they reflected a new principle of "people's democracy." Each court judging an accused person or hearing a case of appeal was to be composed of three judges and a secretary. Of the three judges the one acting as chairman was to be a judge by profession, the other two were not. The secretary was to have a legal education but no right to vote. The new system was to be a combination of the old continental practice and the jury system. Both professional judges and

32. *Trieste nella lotta,* pp. 107, 241–42. Maserati (*L'occupazione jugoslava,* p. 73) spells the name Nedoc instead of Nedock.

33. *Trieste nella lotta,* pp. 118–21, 213–14; Maserati, *L'occupazione jugoslava,* p. 74.

nonprofessionals were thus to make decisions of personal guilt or innocence.[34]

At the same meeting of May 29 the Consulta also formed an arbitral court to solve disputes among persons claiming the right to the same apartment. The court had two groups, each composed of three members. Each group had a chairman, who was a judge by profession, and two lay members. In each group the chairman and one layman were Italian, the second layman a Slovene. The decision of the court was to be final, without any appeal.[35]

To keep public order and to prevent looting, a People's Militia (Guardia del Popolo, called also Difesa Popolare) was organized immediately after the war out of the former city Partisan units. Rudi Greif, the former commander of these units, became the head of the new police force, which counted about 2,500 men. Until May 13, it remained under control of the city military command and after that day, when the military command transferred the civil administration to the CLT, the People's Militia was subordinated to the Department of Interior Affairs of the CLT.[36] The People's Militia was an arm of the Communists, not only to keep peace and order, but to persecute their political opponents. In this aim it was helped by the notorious Yugoslav secret police known as OZNA, an abbreviation for Odeljenje za zaštitu naroda (the Department for the Protection of the People).

Another instrument of Communist control was the Sindacati Unici. On May 8, a meeting of factory and head committees of the previously underground Unità Operaia had taken place. There it was decided to form a single labor organization for both Italian and Slovenian workers, with sections for clerks and intellectuals.[37] Like the Yugoslav trade unions, the Sindacati Unici copied the pattern of Soviet unionism. Anyone seeking employment had to belong to the Sindacati Unici. Persons known for anti-Communist sentiments in the past were denied a membership card and could get no employment.

During the first part of May the entire Julian Region was

34. *Trieste nella lotta,* pp. 107, 228–31, 232, 253.
35. Ibid., pp. 108, 233.
36. Ibid., pp. 96–97, 208; Maserati, *L'occupazione jugoslava,* pp. 81–82.
37. Maserati, *L'Occupazione jugoslava,* p. 82.

divided into two regions along the ethnic line separating Slovene and Croat territory. The northern part formed the Slovenian Littoral and the southern part, south of the Dragonja River, constituted Croat Istria.

On May 12 the Slovenian Littoral was divided into two provinces (Gorizia and Trieste) plus the autonomous city of Trieste. The first included the territory of the old Gorizia Province to which were added Venetian Slovenia and the Tarvisio district, both formerly part of Udine Province. Trieste Province comprised all the Slovenian land south of Gorizia Province except the ethnically mixed municipality of Trieste which became the autonomous city of Trieste with status equal to that of both provinces. The two provinces were further divided into six districts. Based upon this territorial division the new Yugoslav administration was composed of many local (village), six district, two provincial, and Trieste's National Liberation committees. On top the Regional National Liberation Committee was the supreme authority for the entire Slovenian Littoral and in its turn was subordinated to the Slovenian government in Ljubljana.[38] Of all these committees the most important were the district, city, and regional, as the true decision-making power rested with them. On June 5, the delegates representing the autonomous city of Trieste and the six districts met in Trieste to elect an enlarged Regional National Liberation Committee for the Slovenian Littoral. The new regional committee counted sixty members of whom two-thirds were Slovenes and one-third Italians. The executive committee of the regional committee, called the Presidium, had fifteen members.[39]

To the south, Croat Istria was divided into eight districts and the autonomous city of Pula. The city of Rijeka was during May 1945 part of the Croat Littoral, and afterwards became an autonomous city directly under control of the Yugoslav military administration. The local and the eight district National Liberation committees were subordinated to the Regional National Liberation Committee, the highest authority for Istria. The Istrian Regional Committee was subordinated to the Croat government in Zagreb.[40]

38. *Slovensko Primorje in Istra*, p. 536; *Trieste nella lotta*, p. 250.
39. *Slovensko Primorje in Istra*, pp. 394, 536.
40. Ibid., p. 537.

The main social, economic, and political decisions were prepared by the executive committees and then put before the city, district, and regional assemblies for approval. Yugoslavs stressed that this new political order was a true democracy, where the assemblies elected from below by the people issued new decrees and laws expressing the will of the people. On the surface this may be true. A closer study, however, reveals that the new laws did not express the will of the people, but instead the will of a small minority, the Communists who held the key positions in the small executive committees.

The decision-making power in the Slovenian Littoral including Trieste was in the hands of the Slovenian Communist party. Only in Trieste did the Italian Communists participate to a great extent, but even here Italian Communists held only subordinate positions. The Italian and Slovenian Communist parties had organized a joint city committee for coordinating the work of the two Communist parties in Trieste. In this joint committee the Slovene Rudi Uršič (alias Karel) was the first, or political secretary, and the Italian Alessandro Destradi (alias Gigi) was the second, or organizational secretary. Important members of this joint committee of both Communist parties were the Slovene Franc Štoka (alias Rado) and the Italian Giuseppe Gustincich (alias Gildo).[41] The same people also held the key positions in the administration of Trieste. Rudi Uršič was the secretary of the CLT and signed all its decisions until the first days of June, while Franc Štoka held the position of vice-chairman of the CLT. Around June 7, they exchanged their positions, Štoka becoming the secretary and Uršič the vice-chairman of the CLT. Giuseppe Gustincich and Giuseppe Piemontese held the key positions in the Consulta.[42]

Moving upward from the local to the regional level, the situation was the same: the leaders of the regional Communist party organization also held the key positions in the regional administration. Branko Babič (alias Vlado) was the secretary of the Regional Communist Party Committee with Dr. Jože Vilfan an important member. Both were Slovenes. The same Babič had been

41. *Trieste nella lotta*, pp. 71–72.
42. Based on an analysis of the decrees issued by the Consulta and the CLT which were published as an appendix in *Trieste nella lotta*, pp. 211–55.

the founder of the Regional National Liberation Committee, and its first secretary. Though in May 1945 Babič was only the vice-chairman of the Regional National Liberation Committee, there was no doubt that he was the most important personality in this committee, receiving orders directly from the central committee of the Slovenian Communist party, which had been during the war and continued to be the highest policy-making body for the entire Slovenian Littoral. Inside this highest committee, Dr. Aleš Bebler (alias Primož) and Lidija Šentjurc (alias Joža) acted as the principal links with the Slovenian Littoral and Trieste, organizing the party and underground, supervising activities, and reporting back to the top committee. Both were Slovenes, trained in Yugoslavia by the Slovenian Communist party.[43]

It is obvious that the military and police power in Trieste was in the hands of trusted Communists. The city commander Dušan Kveder was an old Slovenian Communist who had been a member of the International Brigade in Spain, entered the Partisan units as political commissar as early as 1941, and became during the war the administrative chief of the supreme headquarters of Slovenian Partisan forces.[44] The Italian Giorgio Jaksetich, the vice-commander of the military forces, also had an outstanding record among Trieste Communists. Before the war he was active abroad, and during the war was the liaison officer at Slovenian Partisan headquarters for the Italian Garibaldi units.[45] The commander of the People's Militia, Rudi Greif (alias Martin), was a Slovene who had been the commander of Trieste's Partisan units. He was probably a member of the Communist party. However, the power behind the People's Militia was again Franc Štoka who had been the political commissar of Trieste's Partisan units and later the commissar of the city command and People's Militia.[46]

These were just a few of the well-known Communists holding key positions in Trieste. The same, of course, was true for Gorizia,

43. See *Slovensko Primorje in Istra*, pp. 392, 394, 472, 473, 478; *Jesen 1942: Korespondenca Edvarda Kardelja in Borisa Kidriča* (Autumn 1942: Correspondence of Edvard Kardelj and Boris Kidrič) (Ljubljana, 1963), pp. 351–52, n. 2.
44. Ibid., p. 117, n. 34; *Dokumenti*, 1:64, n. 23; *Zbornik*, pt. 6, 2:88.
45. Pacor, pp. 123, 132, 260.
46. Ibid., p. 321; *Trieste nella lotta*, p. 208.

Pula, and Rijeka, the major cities of the Julian Region, and for the entire "people's democracy." These men faithfully executed the orders of the Slovenian and Yugoslav Central committees of the Communist party. The victory of the National Liberation war was a Communist victory. It introduced a revolutionary Communist regime similar to the so-called war communism introduced in Russia after the Bolshevik victory in the October revolution. Two main characteristics of such a regime can easily be detected also in Trieste's Yugoslav administration: namely, the persecution of their "bourgeois" enemies, and the establishment of Communist control over all phases of public life. The persecutions may have been more violent in Trieste and other major cities of the Julian Region than in the Region as a whole, because it was here that the Partisans had an opportunity to purge their enemies for the first time and they had to do it without delay. In other "liberated territories" the persecutions had begun during the war, but the Partisans had never before controlled the bigger cities. Moreover, during the entire month of May and the first third of June, the Communists were never sure they would retain control over the Trieste and Gorizia areas. Hence they had to hurry. However, the Communist aims had to be camouflaged to a certain degree, so as not to cause protests and countermeasures from the British-American military commanders in Trieste and Gorizia.

The first proclamations issued by the Yugoslav military command between May 3 and 6 created an ideal situation in Trieste for the mass arrest of opponents of the Communist regime. A strict curfew forced the people to stay at home during the night hours. Further, all travel was restricted, so that enemies of communism could not escape. To operate a motor vehicle one had to acquire a special permit. For any travel, from Trieste to the nearest village or from village to village, another special permit was needed. Permits for such travel were issued only several days after an application had been filed, and applications were carefully checked by Communist authorities. To prevent armed resistance, all arms, including hunting guns, had to be handed over to the authorities.[47]

According to Italian statistics, the Communists arrested about

47. See Quarantotti-Gambini, pp. 127–28, 147, 226.

6,000 persons in the Trieste and Gorizia areas.[48] Of these about 1,850 were deported, out of which about 1,150 never returned and are presumed to be dead. The remaining 4,150 were later released. Many of the deported persons were Slovenians. Of the deported Italians only two-fifths were born in the Julian Region, while three-fifths were from other Italian provinces. The same Italian source indicates that data for Istria and Rijeka were harder to obtain. However, about 850 persons were deported from Istria, of whom 670 never returned, and some 280 were missing from Rijeka. Based upon these statistics, about 2,100 persons never returned to their families. The great majority of these people perished without a trial.[49]

Yugoslav authorities and the Yugoslav press explained the strict measures introduced by the Yugoslav military command by pointing out that the war against the Germans and Italian Fascists had not ended for the Yugoslavs until the middle of May. True, they said, there might have been more arrests in this region than in other Italian cities but this too was easy to explain. Trieste, for example, was the last great city of the Apennine and Balkan peninsulas to be liberated after the war. Therefore it had become the last gathering place for many Fascists. The presence of a greater number of Fascists resulted in a greater number of arrests. At the end of the war, continued the Yugoslavs, many Italians changed their black shirts of Fascism for the white shirt of democracy, but this did not deceive the Yugoslav authorities. The arrested, argued the Yugoslavs, might have indeed included persons who never fired a shot against the Partisans. But they might have nonetheless denounced the Partisans to the Fascist and German authorities, who had arrested the denounced persons and sent them to concentration camps where many had died. Finally, the Yugoslavs pointed out that the persecutions were greatly blown up by the Italian press and radio in order to convince the British and American authorities that the bloody persecution of Italians

48. Maserati, *L'occupazione jugoslava,* pp. 122–25.

49. The number of deported persons was greatly exaggerated by the Italian press and by private and semiprivate organizations in the first months after the war, running as high as 10,000 to 12,000. By the end of 1945 the figure was reduced to some 3,000 or 4,000. On this see: De Castro, pp. 176–82; S. S. [Sprigge], *The World Today,* 1:4, 168.

would end only after Allied intervention. The Allies, who pursued the goal of introducing an Allied military administration in the Julian Region, disseminated in a more cautious way the Italian accusations, to win world support for their demand that Yugoslavia evacuate this region. Or so the Yugoslavs concluded.[50]

Italians instead like to underline that the persecutions had been caused by Slovenian and Croat nationalism. To Quarantotti-Gambini and Diego de Castro, for example, Tito's communism was only a mask to win the support of Italian Communists in Trieste, a disguise behind which stood the old Slavic imperialist drive toward the West. The CLN had been disarmed and its leaders arrested because they were Italians. Order Number 7, issued on May 6, prohibiting any manifestation of a national character, the Italians rightly stressed, was primarily directed against an expression of pro-Italian sentiments, while pro-Yugoslav manifestations continued and were supported by the Yugoslav authorities. The deportation of Italians from Trieste, Gorizia, and the small towns of Istria typified Slavic terrorism against an Italian majority. In short, the Italians stressed that their population was persecuted in order to Slovenize Trieste and Gorizia, and to achieve a Croat majority in Western Istria.[51]

Both interpretations of the persecutions were well known to leaders of the British-American forces in Trieste. This is confirmed by Cox, the senior intelligence officer, who knew well the thinking of his superiors with whom he was in close contact. He wrote that Yugoslav rule "was that of the iron hand. Its rigour was exercised in two main directions. Action was taken against Fascism and against the Triestini who were linked with the former Fascist rule. At the same time action was taken against those who opposed the transfer of Trieste and the rest of Venezia Giulia to the Yugoslav flag."[52]

In analyzing the anti-Fascist measures, Cox made a very important observation: that they had attracted little world attention at that time for "the eyes of other countries were fixed more firmly on the other measures taken to check and crush pro-Italian feel-

50. See *Trieste nella lotta,* pp. 121–25.
51. See for example Quarantotti-Gambini, pp. 64–65; and De Castro, pp. 173–75, 176.
52. Cox, pp. 227–28.

ing."[53] But it seemed to Cox that neither the Yugoslav nor the Italian interpretation offered a complete explanation of the persecutions.

> These arrests, though widespread, followed no coherent plan, or if they did follow such a plan they followed it inefficiently. A good portion of Gestapo agents and Fascists of some seniority came unscathed through the Yugoslav clutches to fall into our [British-American] hands later. Other people who were taken were not Fascists by any means, and some may even have been cases of mistaken identity, or people arrested for personal or trivial reasons.[54]

It was not easy for contemporaries to understand the persecutions, because they knew and understood very little of what was going on in Eastern Europe and in Yugoslavia in particular. True, every interpretation made some valuable contribution but explained only one or another aspect of the persecutions. It is equally true that many of the above interpretations were made for political and propagandistic reasons and not with the aim of discovering the truth. With the passing of more than twenty years and with much more knowledge of what was going on during the time in Yugoslavia and in other countries in which Communist rule had been introduced, a better explanation of the persecution can be made. What happened in Trieste and in the rest of the Julian Region was an integral part of Yugoslav events. It was a successful conclusion to the communist revolution. From the beginning of the National Liberation Movement the Communists forced the people to make the critical decision: were they for the Liberation Movement, meaning the Communists, or against it? As illustrated in previous chapters, this Communist policy compelled many pro-Western groups and individuals into collaboration with the enemies as the lesser evil. By this action such groups and individuals made it easy for the Communists to label them as Fascists and collaborators. Also the ones who did not collaborate, but opposed a Communist takeover, were regarded by the Communists as their enemies, which they were. The Communists, in keeping with their slogan, "Who is not with us is against us," proclaimed every political opponent as a Fascist or pro-Fascist.

53. Ibid., p. 229.   54. Ibid., p. 231.

TEMPORARY YUGOSLAV ADMINISTRATION

Already during the war, but especially by its end, the Communists were persecuting all potential enemies of their regime, accusing them of collaboration, of Fascism, or at least of pro-Fascist leanings. During the winter of 1944-45, when Tito had firmly established his rule over the eastern part of Yugoslavia, whole Chetnik units had been shot down. Later, at the end of the war in May and June 1945, entire Ustashi and Domobranci divisions were summarily machine-gunned. Many other opponents who were at no time members of the collaborating units were arrested or had disappeared. The great majority of them were not granted the right to defend themselves before a people's court. The result was that tens of thousands were massacred without any trial.[55]

The same was true for the Julian Region. Italians, Slovenes, and Croats who opposed the Communist rule for whatever reason were proclaimed Fascists and were persecuted. On the other hand known Fascists who allied with the Communists or performed a useful service for them held jobs under the new Communist authorities, or were set free unmolested. Some of the Fascists held key positions in the new Yugoslav administration. Such was the case of Della Motta who became the first editor of *Il Nostro Avvenire*, the Italian-language newspaper published in Trieste by Yugoslav authorities. Only after strong protests by Slovenes and Italians, who pointed to his long career as a Fascist, was Della Motta removed and arrested.[56] Another example was former Mayor Pagnini, who had been set free after the authorities got from him a signed statement that the CLN had collaborated with the Fascists against the Yugoslav occupation of Trieste, a statement which was useful to the Yugoslav Communist authorities for accusing the CLN of pro-Fascist sentiments.[57]

Both East and West used the word fascism but the meaning was different in each case. By accepting the Eastern interpretation, signifying every potential opponent to communism, the Yugoslav persecutions in the Julian Region can be better understood. What seemed to Cox and to other Western observers only incoherent

55. Zalar, pp. 113-15; see also chapter 7, end of "Contending Factions."
56. S. S. [Sprigge], *The World Today*, 1:4, 184; Quarantotti-Gambini, pp. 175, 258.
57. Schiffrer, *Trieste*, no. 28, pp. 20-21.

arrests, becomes a coherent persecution. However, the execution of this plan was less thorough in the Julian Region than in Yugoslavia for obvious reasons. The British-American troops and Western newspapermen were present in the region, the question as to who would administer this region was not yet settled, and Yugoslav rule over the western part of the Julian Region lasted only for about forty days.

Likewise one must refuse such a contemporary Italian interpretation as that which held the persecutions to be directed above all against the Italians in order to give a Slovenian or Croat ethnic character to the cities of the Julian Region. The weak point of this Italian interpretation lies in putting the entire blame for the persecution on Slovenian and Croat nationalism, while overlooking the role played by communism. It is true that Tito had built his Partisan movement on the national feelings of the Slovenes and Croats. Hence the importance of nationalism cannot be denied. Yet the primary goal of Tito's Partisans at that time had been to achieve absolute power in Yugoslavia and an extension of Communist rule as far west as possible. The more so as these Yugoslav goals were only an integral part of similar aims of Soviet Russia. It is noteworthy that Tito's Partisans had also been active in ethnically Italian Friuli, and the Friulian Communists, encouraged by Tito's Partisans, advocated a unification of Friuli with Communist Yugoslavia to achieve the same goal, an extension of communism toward the west.[58]

Another important fact to note is that the people in charge of the persecutions included not only Slovenes and Croats, though they might hold the leading positions, but also Italian Communists, who participated in the administration and were members of the purging commissions. If more Italians than Slovenes and Croats faced persecution in Trieste and other cities and towns it was simply because of the Italian majority there. Besides, the Italians in the cities of Trieste and Gorizia had full opportunity to collect data on these persecutions. The Slovenes and Croats persecuted in the hinterland had no such chance to expose their situation. For the latter no special agency existed to collect the data, there was no place to present it, and no one to publish it.

58. See Berce, p. 138.

Thus, the killings of almost all the Italians are known, while the suffering of only a small proportion of Slovenes and Croats has reached the ears of the general public.

When former non-Communist Partisans protested the persecution of those known for anti-Fascist beliefs who could not be called collaborators of any kind, the objectors also disappeared or were tried before the people's courts and condemned as undercover agents of Western imperialism. No one knows exactly how many former Slovenian and Croat Partisans perished in this way, but their number was by no means low.

The initial steps taken to nationalize the economy were further proof that Yugoslav authorities tried to introduce communism. Such proof exists especially for Trieste, which was the seat of the major financial, commercial, and industrial establishments of the Julian Region.

Order Number 4 issued on May 4 by the Yugoslav military command for Trieste decreed that all banks and insurance companies were to remain closed until a new order was proclaimed. Later the banks were reopened but not the insurance establishments. Every individual was permitted to withdraw from his savings account 3,000 lire. This sum was raised to 5,000 lire toward the end of the Yugoslav administration. Prohibited, however, was any transfer of accounts, and any transaction of bills of exchange, foreign exchange, shares of stock, lands, and other valuables. Each bank was supervised by a commissar, who was appointed by the Financial Institute of Slovenia. A special Financial Commission for the Slovenian Littoral, composed of six experts, was to prepare a money exchange. A new littoral lira was to replace the old Italian lira in circulation.[59] This exchange never did take place but it showed the desire of the new authorities to get the money still in private hands. This kind of exchange did occur in Yugoslavia. Besides being a by-product of nationalization, such exchange strengthened the control of the Communists over the people, who became financially dependent on the new masters.

Orders issued on May 10 and May 11 imposed Communist control over all commercial and industrial establishments, including the shops of craftsmen. Property rights were to remain

---

59. *Trieste nella lotta*, pp. 108–11; Maserati, *L'occupazione jugoslava*, pp. 127–28.

untouched, but no sales or other transfers of property could take place henceforth.[60] Confiscated was all the property of the German government and of its subjects (except that belonging to the Germans who had fought in the Partisan or Allied ranks) and the property belonging to war criminals and collaborators. All the confiscated property and the property of absent persons was to be administered by the authorities.[61]

At the same time, May 10, 1945, an advisory commission was constituted to direct production of the main branches of the economy. It was divided into four subcommissions, chemical, mechanical-metallurgical industries, alimentation, and labor unions. This commission was to prepare all necessary data for a planned economy, a major part of any socialist regime. This commission prepared a list of all factories and artisan shops, with detailed information for each individual enterprise. It concluded that there were in the Trieste region 1,200 businesses and 7,000 artisan shops ready to resume production. These would employ 5,000 clerks and 35,000 workers.[62]

This tendency of the Yugoslav administration to introduce a socialistic economy scared the upper bourgeoisie in Trieste. To win them over the Yugoslav Communist authorities affirmed that Yugoslavia would not adopt the Russian economic system. Instead, Yugoslavia would introduce an economic and political system somewhere between the Russian system and that practiced in the West. But similar promises had been given to the Yugoslav bourgeoisie during the war to gain their support, and later broken by the Communist regime. In the same vein were the efforts of Yugoslav authorities to achieve economic cooperation with representatives of Trieste's industry. *Il Nostro Avvenire* of May 23, 1945, reported that the prime minister of the Slovenian government, Boris Kidrič, received the representatives of Trieste's industry and told them that Yugoslavia needed their products, while Trieste needed Yugoslav raw materials. Hence Trieste was to sell its products to Yugoslavia and Yugoslavia was to sell its raw materials to Trieste. On this occasion Yugoslavia placed orders for recon-

60. Cox, p. 228.
61. *Trieste nella lotta,* p. 234.
62. Ibid., pp. 104–5.

struction of bridges destroyed during the war, for repair of railroad machines, and for trucks and other machinery.[63]

No Communist regime tolerated a free press or radio. Hence, it is not surprising that the Yugoslav authorities sequestered printing establishments, newspapers, and the radio broadcasting station in Trieste.[64] While justification for the seizures was based on Fascist activity and collaboration with the Germans, there is no question that Communists secured by these measures a monopoly over all media of communication, to the benefit of their own propaganda. The Communist authorities permitted only such newspapers to operate as followed their lead: *Il Lavoratore* was the organ of the local Italian Communist party, and *Primorski dnevnik* that of the Slovenian Liberation Front. For the general Italian public, the authorities published *Il Nostro Avvenire,* and for trade unionists, *Unità Operaia*. Besides these principal journals, Italian and Slovenian weekly and biweekly papers were published by various pro-Communist mass organizations formed during the war.[65] Not a single newspaper was now legally issued in Trieste by any party or organization independent of Communist control.

THE UNDERGROUND CLN COMBATS A NEW OPPONENT

With the entry of Yugoslav troops into Trieste on May 1, 1945, the Italian democratic underground, the Comitato di Liberazione Nazionale (CLN), continued its struggle, this time against the new Yugoslav master. The CLN was active in Trieste and sent a special delegation to Italy.

From May 3 to May 7, the leaders of the CLN met secretly

63. Maserati, *L'occupazione jugoslava,* pp. 126–27.
64. Confiscated were Società Editrice Italiana del "Piccolo" (the joint stock company which published the Fascist newspaper *Il Piccolo*), Stabilimento Tipografico Triestino (the printing establishment where *Il Piccolo* was printed), Ente Italiano Audizioni Radiofoniche (Radio Broadcasting Society), and offices and property of the Agenzia Stefani in Trieste (an Italian press agency). The text of the ordinances which decreed the confiscation is reprinted in *Trieste nella lotta,* pp. 218–20, 224.
65. Berce, pp. 146–48.

in the civic library and in the office of the parish of Sant' Antonio Nuovo in the center of the city.[66] The CLN decided to plead with the Allied commander in Trieste against the Yugoslav prosecutions of democratic Italians and to obtain recognition for the CLN as the legitimate representative of the Italian population in Trieste.[67] Failing to obtain an interview with the local Allied commander General Freyberg, who kept to his nonintervention policy, the CLN decided to send its own delegation to Venice and to Rome, to inform the supreme Allied command and the Italian government about the situation in Trieste. A five-member delegation was chosen, composed of two members of the Christian Democratic party, two of the Action party, and one without party affiliation.[68] As three of the delegation were leading members of the CLN, they were replaced in office by other members. The chairman of the newly reconstructed CLN became Vittorio Furlani of the Action party. The new CLN had nine principal members, of which three, including the chairman, belonged to the Action party, two were Socialists, two did not have any party affiliation, one was a Christian Democrat, and one belonged to the Liberal party.[69]

On May 3, 1945, the CLN distributed an illegal manifesto addressed to the citizens of Trieste. In it the leaders refuted the accusations of the pro-Yugoslav forces that the CLN had served as a mask for the Fascists. The manifesto stressed that the CLN was the legitimate representative of the Italian democratic gov-

66. Quarantotti-Gambini, pp. 97–98, 103; Maserati, *L'occupazione jugoslava,* pp. 142–43.

67. Maserati, *L'occupazione jugoslava,* pp. 56–57.

68. The chairman of the delegation was Don Edoardo Marzani (Christian Democrat). The members were Giovanni Paladin (Action party), Antonio de Berti (without party affiliation), Marcello Spaccini (Christian Democrat) and Isidoro Maras (Action party). The last two joined the delegation later. (Ibid., p. 143.)

69. Antonio Fonda-Savio (without party affiliation) was vice-chairman, and Mario M. Midena (without party affiliation) became secretary. Other important members were: Ercole Miani and Carlo G. Ferluga, both members of the Action party; Redento Romano, a Christian Democrat; Giacomo Marega, member of the Liberal party; and Armando Benedetti and Venusto Rossi, both members of the Socialist party. (Ibid.)

ernment, receiving its orders directly from the ministry for unliberated territories in Rome. It listed the underground activities of the CLN against the Germans, and blamed Yugoslav nationalism for persecutions of Italians. It concluded with the significant statement: "Brother Triestines! Have faith in your future, have faith in the wisdom of the Allies, pioneers of justice in our tormented land! . . . Long live a truly democratic Trieste! Long live the Italian civilization!"[70]

The principal goal of the CLN was to oppose the Yugoslav annexation of the Julian Region and to voice the will of democratic Italians, especially those in Trieste, to be reunited with Italy. To achieve this goal all Italians were to rally behind the CLN, forming a united front which was to request the retreat of Yugoslav forces from the Julian Region and demand that the British-American forces take over the administration of the entire region until the question could be settled by the peace conference. No Italian was to collaborate with the Yugoslav administration, and contacts were to be established with the Allied forces in Trieste and Gorizia to explain the Italian point of view.

The CLN organized a pro-Italian manifestation in Trieste on May 5.[71] The demonstrators marched along the Corso, a street in downtown Trieste, bearing Italian flags and shouting, "Italy, Italy!" People living on the Corso opened the windows of their apartments and with Italian flags joined in acclaiming Italy. Yugoslav sentries marching along the Corso opened fire into the mass of demonstrators approaching them. According to Yugoslav authorities, five were killed and some ten wounded; however, there were rumors that more people were killed and hurt.[72]

70. Ibid., p. 95. For the text of the manifesto see ibid., pp. 93-95.
71. Quarantotti-Gambini wrote (pp. 144-45) that the manifestation was a spontaneous expression of Italian will to be reunited with Italy and a protest against Yugoslav efforts to unify Trieste with Yugoslavia. Pacor (p. 330), instead, directly stated that the manifestation had been organized by the CLN, while Maserati (*L'occupazione jugoslava*, p. 97) expressed himself more cautiously: the manifestation was initiated (*iniziata*) by the members of CVL, the CLN underground force.
72. Quarantotti-Gambini reports (pp. 144-45) that there was rumor of about eight being killed and some thirty wounded. See also Maserati, *L'occupazione jugoslava*, p. 98, n. 21.

Il Nostro Avvenire wrote the next day, May 6, that the manifestation had been organized by the remnants of Nazism and Fascism which, joined by reactionary forces, would have liked to exploit the confused situation by inciting disorders directed against the newly established democratic authorities. However, the paper continued, the Yugoslav authorities intervened immediately to protect the liberties gained by the people.[73] On the same day, the Yugoslav military authorities published Order Number 7 prohibiting any manifestation of nationalistic intolerance regardless of its source, an order evidently issued to prevent pro-Italian manifestations in the future.[74]

Members of the New Zealand forces had watched the manifestation and seen the violent end of it but remained silent observers, limiting themselves to taking pictures.[75] There were no public manifestations after May 5. The CLN may well have realized that any such manifestation would prove to be too costly, and that the British-American forces preferred to remain silent witnesses rather than intervene in favor of a pro-Italian policy directed against the Yugoslav occupation of Trieste.

The desire of democratic Italians to be reunited with Italy was voiced also by the underground newspapers, *Osservatorio del C.L.N.*, the official bulletin of the CLN, with a circulation of about a thousand copies, *La Nostra Vigilia*, *La Voce Giuliana*, and *La Rinascita Giuliana*.[76] The last was published in Udine, Italy, and distributed clandestinely in Trieste. These newspapers propagated the overall aims of the CLN: The Yugoslav occupation must terminate and the Allied forces take over administration of the Julian Region. The Italians should not lose hope for a just solution. It was mandatory that they not collaborate with the Yugoslav administration. The press further collected news about the persecutions and gave it the interpretation mentioned above, namely as an expression of barbaric Yugoslav imperialism. The postwar confusion, shortage in foodstuffs, and other malfunctionings of the Yugoslav administration were used to illustrate the

73. Quarantotti-Gambini, p. 156.
74. Ibid., pp. 155–56; Maserati, *L'occupazione jugoslava*, p. 76; Cox, p. 230.
75. Maserati, *L'occupazione jugoslava*, p. 98.
76. Ibid., p. 96, n. 19.

inability of Yugoslavs to administer the region. The same points were stressed in different memoranda prepared by the CLN and handed over to the Allied officers in Trieste. The CLN also established contacts with various newspapermen from Western Europe to whom it explained the Italian point of view.[77]

To discourage and if possible prevent any collaboration of democratic Italians, especially those without party affiliation, with the Yugoslav authorities, persons who had entered the Yugoslav administration were attacked in the underground newspapers, and intimidated by the terroristic activities of Nucleo d'Azione Patriottica (NAP) organized by Claudio Villi.[78] The NAP received help and protection from individual Allied officers. A typical example was the kidnapping of Umberto Zoratti, the chairman of the Consiglio di Liberazione di Trieste, on May 25, 1945, and his transportation to Italy. This was done with the help of British Lieutenant Maugham, a man of Italian descent.[79]

On May 7, 1945, the CLN delegation departed from Trieste, again with Allied help. The delegation stopped first in Venice at the headquarters of the regional CLN. It explained the situation in the Julian Region and asked for help. The delegation established a section of the CLN for the Julian Region in Venice. In the middle of May the delegation came to Rome. Here the members were guests of the Italian Prime Minister Ivanoe Bonomi. On May 16, the group handed its memorandum to Admiral Ellery W. Stone, head of the Allied Military Commission for Italy, asking for occupation of the entire Julian Region by Allied forces. The same kind of memorandum was handed to the embassies of the Western powers in Rome. Giovanni Paladin, the chairman of the CLN delegation, explained the situation in the Julian Region to the Italian public in a broadcast from Radio-Rome. The delegation was also accepted by Pope Pius XII on May 18. Then it departed for Milan, the headquarters of the CLN for northern Italy. Here it formed a special committee for the Julian Region to support Italian claims.[80]

It is noteworthy that the activities of the CLN in the Julian

77. Ibid., pp. 143–47; *Trieste nella lotta,* pp. 122–24.
78. Maserati, *L'occupazione jugoslava,* p. 147.
79. Ibid., pp. 64–65, n. 27.
80. Maserati, *L'occupazione jugoslava,* pp. 147–48.

Region were limited to that part in which the British-American forces were present, that is to Trieste and Gorizia. There is no doubt that the Western Allies looked upon the activities of the CLN with sympathetic eyes, the more so as the CLN demanded the withdrawal of Yugoslav troops from the Julian Region and supported the organization of a British-United States administration in the region. So the aims of the Western Allies happily coincided with the demands of the CLN.

HOSTILITY OF ALLIED TROOPS TO THE YUGOSLAVS

Yugoslav persecutions, coupled with skillful Italian propaganda, quickly transformed the attitude of the Allied soldiers toward Tito's Partisans. When the New Zealand contingents had first met the Yugoslav units and Slovenian Partisans they had a high opinion of the Slavs. During the war they had heard of the Partisans' ferocious fighting against the German invaders, but in the weeks of their stay in Trieste their friendliness began to turn to hostility. Not only did international tension between the Allies and Tito contribute to this, but also the facts of local life.

In the first place, hardly a soldier in the Allied armies spoke a word of a Slavic tongue, and interpreters were rare indeed. On the other hand, the Allied soldiers had come to Trieste through Italy, where they had spent a year and half and had learned Italian well enough to mix with the people in Trieste.[81]

Second, on the Yugoslav side stood a barrier of reserve. Soccer matches and other sports events for the troops, together with formal dinners for the officers, helped to establish mutual relations, but these efforts did not extend to mingling with civilians. To the latter the presence of the Westerners represented a denial of the claims of Yugoslavia. Furthermore, they were afraid to mingle with Allied personnel, for fear of being singled out as pro-British or pro-American and suspected of opposition to Tito's regime.[82]

On the other hand, the Italians went more than halfway to meet the Allied soldiers, whether to get protection, food, a pair of army boots, or a blanket. Cox best explained the effectiveness of Italian propaganda when he wrote:

81. Cox, pp. 232–33.   82. Ibid., pp. 233–34.

HOSTILITY OF ALLIED TROOPS

Before many days were past, our relations with the local Italians were much closer than with the Slovenes. It would have taken a soldier either of puritanical habits or rigid political discipline to resist these approaches, particularly if they were made by a Trieste Italian blonde in a two-piece bathing suit....[83]

As a result the ordinary soldier heard the Italian case from every angle, and heard very little of the Tito case. He had come, moreover, to regard the Italians as full allies, not, as did the Yugoslavs, as very recent enemies who had invaded their country only four years before. The New Zealander saw that there was an Italian majority in Trieste itself, and that there were Italians elsewhere throughout the area. [Trieste-Gorizia railroad junctions were the only places in the Julian Region where the New Zealand soldiers were stationed.] And he argued that the Yugoslavs had, therefore, on the face of it, no final right to run the place.[84]

Two further facts must be added. First, the war was over and the Allied soldiers wanted to go home. They saw Yugoslav insistence on occupying the territory as the cause of their continued stay. Second, the officers became increasingly certain that Yugoslavia represented in fact a pro-Russian rather than pro-Western regime. This impression was confirmed by reports from Yugoslavia itself, where the Tito-Šubašić provisional government had clearly not resulted from a compromise of Partisans and democrats, but was only a screen to blind Western opinion while the Communists fastened their rule upon the whole country.[85]

Aware of these impressions on the Allied officers, the Tito administration in Trieste did everything possible to camouflage its Communist character. The fist salute was discouraged, as was flying the red flag.[86] But these measures proved of no avail. Tension between the Western soldiers and Tito's troops steadily mounted.

Various acts of the Western soldiers were also to blame, as Yugoslavs thought them designed to strengthen Italian resistance in Trieste. For example, many Italian nationalists, ardently op-

83. Ibid., p. 236; a similar description is given by Quarantotti-Gambini, pp. 140, 203.
84. Cox, p. 237.
85. See chapter 5, "Yugoslavia: Tito Triumphant."
86. Quarantotti-Gambini, p. 175.

posed to Yugoslav occupation of any part of the Julian Region, found an easy refuge in apartments turned over to Allied officers. Again, after the Allied command had reserved the open-air public bathing place, Bagno Savoia, solely for their own troops, many Italians who feared persecution by the authorities stayed there during the day and were protected by Allied friends, since the Yugoslav police could not enter. But the greatest irritation arose when Yugoslav sentries stopped Allied cars carrying Italian girls after the curfew hours, and arrested the girls for violation of the curfew laws.[87]

Even more serious was the fact that many individual Allied officers in Trieste helped persons escape to Italy who were being sought by Yugoslav authorities. These people were often not anti-Fascist but real collaborationists with the enemy. For example, former Mayor Pagnini organized an escape for himself and Prefect Coceani with the help of an Allied officer.[88] Many Italian patriots and anti-Fascists also escaped with the help of individual Allied persons. On May 7, 1945, an Allied chaplain transported the delegates of the CLN to Italy, hiding them in a hearse with the dead body of an Allied soldier as it passed the Yugoslav sentries on the Isonzo River. Similarly, Quarantotti-Gambini describes in his book how he and three other persons got away from Trieste on May 27 with the help of an Allied officer.[89] Allied officers not only entertained close contacts with the illegal CLN centers but some of them were also directly involved in the terroristic acts of the CLN's Nucleo d'Azione Patriottica.[90]

Thus already the first Allied-CLN alliance had been constructed against Yugoslav rule. Whether the Yugoslavs knew of the above examples of escape and terrorism is problematic, but they could scarcely fail to note the Allied-CLN friendship directed against their interests.

THE BELGRADE AGREEMENT OF JUNE 9, 1945

As already mentioned, in the first days of May 1945, the definitive line of demarcation between the Allies and Yugoslavs in

87. Ibid., pp. 140, 203.
88. Coceani, *Mussolini, Hitler, Tito*, p. 328.
89. Quarantotti-Gambini, pp. 159, 296–316.
90. See above, this chapter, "The Underground CLN."

the Julian Region had been left to marshals Alexander and Tito. Confusion in the field, partly due to the absence of any written agreement and the lack of a clearly defined line, had its source in differing views held by the British foreign office and the state department of the United States. The former favored drawing a line but the state department opposed and sought an Allied Military Government for all of the Julian Region.[91]

On March 21, 1945, the United States Secretary of State Edward Stettinius had rejected Mr. Eden's dividing line proposed at the Yalta conference, on the assumption that Tito would allow an Allied Military Government over the whole of the Julian Region. This proved to be incorrect. Marshal Alexander, aware of the new situation, then asked the combined chiefs of staff whether both the American and British governments were prepared to use force to establish Allied military control over all of the Julian Region. Receiving no reply, Alexander on April 26 informed the combined chiefs of staff that he would act according to principles agreed on in Belgrade in February. Anglo-American task forces would take those parts of the Julian Region essential to his military operations, including Trieste and its lines of communication to Austria, and also Pula. In this section he would organize an Allied Military Government, inform Marshal Tito of his intentions, and explain to him that any of Tito's forces still in the area would have to come under Allied command.[92]

On April 28, 1945, the combined chiefs of staff instructed Marshal Alexander to occupy all of the Julian Region including Rijeka and the Quarnero islands, and to establish an Allied Military Government. This plan was backed jointly by the American and British governments. Soviet concurrence would be sought to encourage Yugoslav withdrawal from this area. Should Yugoslavia resist, Alexander was to communicate with the combined chiefs of staff before using force. Although the proposal clearly envisaged Soviet and Yugoslav agreement, it is important to note that the instructions allowed Alexander to implement the plan before such accord had been reached "if military necessity so requires."[93]

91. See chapter 6, "Yugoslavia and Italy."
92. Harris, pp. 332–33; Coles and Weinberg, p. 594.
93. Coles and Weinberg, pp. 594–95; Harris, pp. 333–34; Churchill, 6:551–52.

On April 30, 1945, Alexander informed Tito of his intention to establish an Allied Military Government over all of the Julian Region, to function through such local authorities as had effective control, and asked Tito to make known his plans. Tito replied that the situation had appreciably changed since the Belgrade conversations, and, in order to liberate Yugoslavia and round up all enemy troops as quickly as possible, a new plan was being carried out to liberate Istria, Trieste, Monfalcone, and the rest of the territory up to the Isonzo River, and even up that river clear to the Austrian border. Thus Yugoslav troops would operate from the mouth of the Isonzo River via Gorizia and Tolmin to Tarvisio and Villach. Tito also stated that in accordance with the Belgrade understanding the Allied troops could use the ports of Pula and Trieste, as well as the railway line from Trieste to Tarvisio. Tito agreed, too, that his regular units and Partisans operating to the west of the Isonzo River would come under Allied command.[94]

This was the situation when Yugoslav and Allied troops met in Trieste on May 2. A few days later negotiations began between Alexander and Tito. In order to reach an amicable settlement, Alexander was ready to propose a compromise: Tito should recognize the Allied administration now, with the understanding that the area later would be incorporated into Yugoslavia after the Allied retreat. On May 5, Alexander informed Churchill by telegram of his intention, but in his reply on May 6, the latter forbade Alexander to make any such proposal.[95]

For the actual negotiations, General William D. Morgan, Alexander's chief of staff, went to Belgrade on May 8. Morgan proposed a line of demarcation, later called the Morgan line, to separate clearly the Yugoslav and Allied areas of control, the western section coming under the Allies and the eastern under the Yugoslavs. All Yugoslav armed forces west of the line would fall under the Allied command at once, and later withdraw from the area. The Allies would recognize the Yugoslav civil administration of the western part of the Julian Region as long as it worked satisfactorily.[96] With Tito's rejection of this proposal and the return

94. Harris, p. 335; Coles and Weinberg, pp. 595–96.
95. Churchill, 6:553–54.
96. For the text of Morgan's proposals see Harris, p. 337. See also map, p. 243.

of an empty-handed General Morgan, a very tense situation developed between the Anglo-Americans and the Yugoslavs.

This tension was exacerbated by the Partisan terror in Trieste, which greatly heightened the hostility of the Allied soldiers to the Yugoslavs. This, in turn, brought a change in Marshal Alexander's position. On May 1 he had informed Prime Minister Churchill that should he have to use force against the Yugoslavs, it would be hard to explain to his soldiers why they were fighting the Partisans, their former allies against Germany.[97] But after General Morgan's unsuccessful mission to Belgrade, Marshal Alexander expressed his new thinking in a message to the combined chiefs of staff on May 17:

> Jugoslav behaviour both in Austria and Venezia Giulia is making a very unfavourable impression on Allied troops both US and British. Our men are obliged to look on without power to intervene whilst actions which offend their traditional sense of justice are committed. Further, our men feel that by taking no action they are condoning such behaviour. As a result feeling against Jugoslavs is now strong and is getting stronger daily.
> It is now certain that any solution by which we shared an area with Jugoslav troops or Partisans or permitted Jugoslav administration to function would not work.[98]

The tensions were approaching their height when on May 19 Marshal Alexander issued his well-known condemnation of Tito in a message to the Allied troops:

> Our policy publicly proclaimed is that territorial changes should be made only after thorough study and after full consultation and deliberation between the various Governments concerned.
> It is, however, Marshal Tito's apparent intention to establish his claims by force of arms and military occupation. Action of this kind would be all too reminiscent of Hitler, Mussolini and Japan. It is to prevent such actions that we have been fighting this war.[99]

97. Churchill, 6:553.
98. Coles and Weinberg, p. 600.
99. "Message Issued to Allied Armed Forces in the Mediterranean Theater," May 19, 1945, reprinted in *New York Times,* May 20, 1945

To this statement Tito replied on May 21:

> I cannot but express my resentment and surprise at the impossible comparison that the presence of Yugoslav troops in Istria and the Slovene Littoral is similar to Hitler's, Mussolini's and Japanese methods of conquest. Such an accusation can be thrown into the face of an enemy. It cannot be thrown at a tortured Ally who has been bled white and who has until now been recognized by all freedom-loving people as an example of heroism and self-sacrifice in this great war of liberation. The Jugoslav Army expelled the enemy by the might of their arms from the area up to the River Soca [sic] (the Isonzo) and beyond, and no character of conquest can be attributed to its presence in this territory.[100]

Both sides had poured in reinforcements, and for a while it seemed that only armed conflict would settle the controversy.[101] It was Tito who finally yielded, when convinced that the Soviet Union would not support him in any armed struggle with the Allies.[102]

On May 21 Tito notified the British and American ambassadors in Belgrade that he would accept the Morgan line, but he demanded

> that representatives of the Jugoslav army be allowed to take part in Allied Military Government, that Jugoslav units be

---

(© 1945 by The New York Times Company. Reprinted by permission); Cox, p. 224.

100. Cox, p. 224.

101. Quarantotti-Gambini, pp. 247, 255; "Message, Combined Chiefs of Staff to Allied Headquarters, May 21, 1945," Coles and Weinberg, p. 600. The governments of Great Britain and the United States took different attitudes toward this vexing question. Great Britain was for strong action, including the use of arms if necessary, to get Tito's forces out of the region. The United States preferred a show of force but would agree to the use of arms only if the Yugoslavs attacked first. The United States wanted to avoid a conflict in Europe while war with Japan continued. (See Churchill, 6:554–57.)

102. Harris, pp. 340–41; Jeri, pp. 87–88; Mikuž, *Zgodovinski časopis*, 12–13:44–45; De Castro, p. 149. Note that Stalin did not protest against the attitude of the Western Allies toward Yugoslavia until June 21, 1945, a month after the crisis. For this see Churchill, 6:559–60.

permitted to remain in the territory under Allied control and that the Allied command act through civilian authorities already established.[103]

The British and American governments on their part insisted that Tito recall all his armed forces from west of the Morgan line and that Marshal Alexander organize his Allied Military Government there. After further negotiations a compromise was reached in the agreement signed in Belgrade on June 9, 1945.[104]

By this compromise the Julian Region was divided in accordance with the line proposed by General Morgan into two zones, later called A and B. The city of Trieste and its route of communications with Austria became part of Zone A, under direct Allied military administration, while the territory of the Julian Region east of the Morgan line, called Zone B, remained under Yugoslav military control. Originally Pula and the small Italian-populated towns along the Istrian coast were also placed under Zone A, but later only the city of Pula was included in this Allied zone. The regular Yugoslav army would have to retreat east of the Morgan line, while the Partisan detachments would either have to do the same or hand over their arms to the Allied authorities. A small detachment of regular Yugoslav troops, not exceeding two thousand men, could stay in Zone A, but they were to remain stationary in one district chosen by the supreme Allied commander without access to the rest of the area. They would be maintained by the Allies. A small Yugoslav mission could be attached to the headquarters of the Eighth Army in Italy but no participation of Yugoslav officers was permitted in the Allied Military Government of Zone A.

To meet Yugoslav demands that the Allies recognize their civil administration, Article Three of the agreement stated:

> Use will be made of any Yugoslav civil administration which is already set up and which in the view of the Supreme Allied

103. *AC Weekly Bulletin* 2, no. 8 (May 26, 1945): 1; Harris, p. 341.
104. U.S., Department of State, *Provisional Administration of Venezia Giulia: Agreement between the United States of America, the United Kingdom of Great Britain and Northern Ireland, and Yugoslavia, Signed at Belgrade June 9, 1945*, Executive Agreements Series 501, Department of State publication no. 2562 (Washington, D.C., 1946). Cited hereafter as *Belgrade Agreement*.

Commander is working satisfactorily. The Allied Military Government will, however, be empowered to use whatever civil authorities they deem best in any particular place and to change administrative personnel at their discretion.[105]

The agreement also declared that the Yugoslav government should return all residents they had arrested and deported, with the exception of persons possessing "Yugoslav nationality" in 1939. The Yugoslav government was also to make restitution of all property confiscated or removed. It was further stated that the Belgrade agreement in no way prejudiced the ultimate disposal of any part of the Julian Region.

Article Three became the most important and the most controversial part of the agreement. Forced to accept the military retreat from Zone A, the Yugoslavs tried to save their Communist civil administration there. But the Allies were equally determined not to tie their hands in this matter. Consequently the compromise left the Yugoslavs very dissatisfied. In the future they lost no opportunity to demand that the Allies recognize the Yugoslav administration in Zone A.

In obedience to the agreement, the Yugoslav armed forces retreated east of the new line on June 12, 1945, and the Allied Military Government began administration of the western part of the Julian Region, including the municipality of Trieste.

The new Morgan line could have interfered with normal life in both zones by separating the rural areas from their urban centers, Trieste and Gorizia, which were the seats of communication, transportation, commerce, and industry. To prevent this, the Allies and the Yugoslavs agreed to meet at Duino, a town situated on the Adriatic west of Trieste, near Monfalcone in Zone A. Here General Morgan for the Allies and General Arso Jovanović for the Yugoslavs signed amendments to the Belgrade agreement on June 20 which laid down the principles for future cooperation between the Allied Military Government (AMG) and the Yugoslav authorities to assure the continuation of normal life between the two zones. Accordingly the telephone, telegraph, and mail facilities were to be left uncontrolled. Residents of the two zones were to travel across the Morgan line without restriction. Railway communication would continue and a joint operating committee was to

---

105. Ibid., p. 1.

regulate traffic and to assure a fair and balanced use of equipment. Normal economic transactions between the zones were to be uninterrupted. A joint economic committee would devise detailed arrangements for the interchange of electric power, water, and agricultural and industrial resources. Arrangements would be made by the main financial institutions of AMG territory to furnish funds needed by post offices and branch banks east of the Morgan line, in Zone B.[106]

Both sides agreed to the above amendment. However, the Yugoslavs used this occasion to press for acceptance of two more amendments. First, they demanded that Venetian Slovenia, a part of Udine Province, Italy, be included in Zone A, rather than remain a part of Italy. This General Morgan refused to discuss. Still more important was the second demand. It was attached to the Duino agreement as a separate note to Marshal Alexander, and stated that since the people of Zone A had resisted the Italian army before its surrender, and had built up and were still maintaining their own civil administration,

> the old system of Italian civil administration will not be renewed. Instead of that, the new organs of the already existing civil administration will be accepted, if they are working satisfactorily, according to the opinion of the Supreme Allied Commander. In case the A.M.G. is not satisfied with the work of the administrational personnel or any organs of the civil administration, the Regional National Committee, as the first subordinate organ of the civil administration to the A.M.G., is obliged, on request and to the satisfaction of A.M.G., to carry out immediate replacements.[107]

Here the Yugoslavs tried again to acquire Allied recognition for their Communist civil administration in Zone A. But Marshal Alexander never confirmed this note and it did not become part of the Duino agreement. If accepted, the note would have clarified Article Three of the Belgrade agreement in favor of the Yugoslavs. But even so the Yugoslavs did not give up. The struggle continued, though limited to Zone A.

106. "Appendix I of Agreement Between Chief of Staff, Allied Forces Headquarters, and the Yugoslav Chief of Staff, 20 June 1945," reprinted in Coles and Weinberg, pp. 601–2; hereafter referred to as the *Duino Agreement;* see also Harris, pp. 342–43.

107. Harris, p. 343.

9
THE TWO WORLDS OF ALLIED AND YUGOSLAV MILITARY OCCUPATION

ZONE A AND THE AMG

With the retreat of the Yugoslav army from Zone A, the British and American governments achieved part of their primary goal—to stop the Communist advance farther westward—though they were limited to control of Zone A and had not been able to secure the entire Julian Region.[1] The aims of the Allied Military Government (AMG) in Zone A would be to continue this overall strategy, replacing with a civil administration of its own the Communist-controlled administration left by the Yugoslavs. The Communist administrative system was to be destroyed but the Communists were invited to take part in the AMG as long as they cooperated with other political groups.

Quite understandably the Communists defended their own system and were opposed to innovation. As they had been the only well-organized group in the area, it took not only time but a great deal of diplomacy and skillful maneuvering for the AMG to obtain the aid of democratic forces and undermine the Communist supremacy.

According to Allied plans, worked out during March and April 1945, the AMG in the Julian Region was to follow the general pattern laid down by the AMG in Italy, with certain modifications. Great care had to be taken to avoid impairing the ultimate disposition of the territory in the peace treaty. The AMG in

---

1. This common concern was also stated in Churchill's letter to Stalin dated June 23, 1945: "It seems to me that a Russianised frontier running from Lübeck through Eisenach to Trieste and down to Albania is a matter which requires a very great deal of argument conducted between good friends." (Churchill, 6:561.) Compare also ibid., pp. 456–57, 551–60.

the Julian Region had to be completely independent, except for responsibility to the supreme Allied commander, and entirely removed from any connection with the Italian government. No attempt would be made to apply in the Julian Region any legislation passed since the fall of Mussolini by the new Italian government. At the same time any Italian laws and administrative practices directed against the minority rights of the Slovenes must be annulled.[2]

The AMG for the Julian Region set up headquarters at Udine on May 22 and readied provincial teams for Trieste and Gorizia provinces pending the outcome of negotiations with Marshal Tito. The Trieste team entered that city on May 25 under strict orders not to disclose their identity as military government officers.[3]

After the Yugoslav evacuation, the AMG was set up in Trieste on June 12 and in Gorizia on June 14.[4] As planned, the AMG of Zone A separated itself from the Italian AMG (Control Commission) and became a special unit, first called AMG Thirteenth Corps and later AMG Venezia Giulia.[5] The supreme Allied commander for the Mediterranean theater, Marshal Alexander, became the highest military and government authority. He announced this fact to the people of Zone A in his first proclamation:

> All powers of government and jurisdiction in those parts of Venezia Giulia occupied by Allied troops and over its inhabitants, and final administrative responsibility are vested in me as Military Commander and Military Governor, and Allied Military Government of such territory is hereby declared and established to exercise these powers under my direction.[6]

2. Harris, p. 346.
3. Ibid., p. 345.
4. Allied Control Commission Headquarters, "Report for June 1945," in Coles and Weinberg, p. 602.
5. Harris, pp. 345–46. By that time the Italian AMG had merged with the Allied Commission, which was a military unit under the direct supervision of the Allied Forces Headquarters (Italy) and following the instructions of the combined chiefs of staff. (Mary E. Bradshaw, "Military Control of Zone A in Venezia Giulia," *Department of State Bulletin,* 16 [June 29, 1947]: 1257.)
6. "Proclamation No. 1," printed in Allied Military Government, Thirteenth Corps, Venezia Giulia, *The Allied Military Government Ga-*

Alexander's superiors were the combined chiefs of staff and the governments of Great Britain and the United States. As Marshal Alexander had headquarters in Italy, Lieutenant General John Harding, commander of the Thirteenth Corps, became his representative and hence the highest authority in Zone A. The head of the AMG itself was Senior Civil Affairs Officer (SCAO) Colonel Nelson M. Monfort. He was subordinate to General Harding and acted as his principal staff officer and adviser in all matters pertaining to civil administration.[7]

Colonel Monfort commenced by organizing the AMG. This took time and was complicated by constant transfer of military personnel. By the end of June 1945 Colonel Monfort himself had left, and was replaced as SCAO by the American Colonel Alfred C. Bowman. At the end of September 1945 Marshal Alexander departed for Canada to be governor-general, and General William D. Morgan, his chief of staff, took over as supreme Allied commander.[8]

The AMG was a caretaker government for Zone A, composed of divisions, such as those for legal affairs, food, housing, labor and industry, displaced persons, welfare, public health, education, police, port facilities, and internal affairs. The heads of divisions, called chiefs, formed a kind of AMG cabinet with the SCAO as chairman or "prime minister." The supreme Allied commander

---

zette, 1, no. 1 (Sept. 15, 1945): 3, hereafter cited as *AMG Gazette VG*. Proclamation No. 1 was undated. It was posted on June 12 in Trieste and June 14 in Gorizia, when the AMG took control. Similarly, no date is given for Proclamations Nos. 2, 3, 4, and 5. According to the Allied Military Government, British–United States Zone, Free Territory of Trieste, *Official Gazette,* 1, no. 1 (Sept. 16, 1947): 2, Proclamations Nos. 2, 3, and 4 were posted on June 24, 1945. The *Official Gazette,* published two years after the beginning of *AMG Gazette VG*, will hereafter be cited as *AMG-FTT Gazette*.

7. "Proposed Supplementary Directive, Allied Forces Headquarters to Headquarters XIII Corps and Headquarters Allied Commission, July 29, 1945," in Coles and Weinberg, p. 606; *AC Weekly Bulletin,* 2, no. 11 (June 16, 1945): 4; ibid., 2, no. 12 (June 23, 1945): 4.

8. *AC Weekly Bulletin,* 2, no. 13 (June 30, 1945): 4, and no. 26 (Sept. 29, 1945): 2; Alfred C. Bowman, "Venezia Giulia and Trieste," *Military Government Journal* (Washington, D.C.), 1, no. 8 (June 1948): 12.

first issued seven proclamations of broadest application. Then came general orders issued by the head of the AMG, the senior civil affairs officer, dealing with matters of special significance. Further orders and administrative instructions and notices of a more specific nature could be put out by the SCAO or any divisional chief.[9]

Subordinate to this central government were three area commissioners—for Trieste, Gorizia, and Pula. They acted as connecting links between the AMG and the local civil government composed of the native population. From the area commissioners upward, British and American officers divided responsibility equally.

The AMG went immediately to work. In the first days it disbanded the Special People's Court and ordered the People's Militia to cease making arrests and to keep off the streets. Two important institutions of Communist terror thus lost power. Some ten days later, on June 24, the People's Militia was officially dissolved.[10] The AMG also issued proclamations and orders against both the old Fascist and the new Communist regimes. Proclamation No. 1, mentioned above, struck at Communist principles by guaranteeing personal and property rights to the people of Zone A and by reintroducing Italian law. It stated:

> Your existing personal and property rights will be fully respected and the laws of the territory, in effect on the 8th September, 1943 will, remain in force and effect except insofar as it may be necessary for me, in the discharge of my duties as Supreme Allied Commander and as Military Governor, to change or supersede them by proclamation or other order by me or under my direction.[11]

Proclamation No. 2 established property control, settled the legal tender and exchange rates (dollar and sterling) of Allied Military lira, prohibited foreign trade transactions, and continued

---

9. Taken from the description of AMG activities since June 12, 1945, as published in *AC Weekly Bulletin,* 2, no. 49 (Mar. 9, 1946): 4–10, and from the *AMG Gazette VG,* indexes to vol. 1:4–15.

10. *AC Weekly Bulletin,* 2, no. 11 (June 16, 1945): 4–5, and no. 13 (June 30, 1945): 4–5; *Trieste nella lotta,* pp. 151–52.

11. *AMG Gazette VG,* 1, no. 1 (Sept. 15, 1945): 3.

the existing system of rationing of consumer goods, and of controlled wages and prices.

Proclamation No. 3 curbed the activities of pro-Communist organizations by prohibiting meetings and assemblies without special permission from the AMG. It made licenses for publishing newspapers or other printed matter easily obtainable from the AMG. It resulted in the appearance of a non-Communist press freely criticizing Communist actions. The same proclamation also dealt with the regulation of private means of communication (wireless sets), the prohibition of photography, the declaration of cameras, and the display of flags on public buildings. The display of the Stars and Stripes and Union Jack jointly on public buildings was permitted but not that of the Soviet or Yugoslav flags. Proclamation No. 4 enjoined the closing of financial institutions and established the moratorium.

Proclamation No. 5 dealt with "epuration" of former Fascists. The word "epuration," accepted into AMG terminology, came from the Italian word *epurazione* meaning cleansing, purging. The AMG established special military commissions which screened lesser Fascists. If it was proved they did not hold any post of importance in the Fascist party, such civil servants were proclaimed in good standing and could continue in their job. By this act they were cleansed or purified. On the other hand if it were proved that they belonged to the upper ranks of Fascism, such Fascists were sent before a special court of assize for the trials of Fascists and collaborators. Proclamation No. 5 established such special military courts. An appeal from the special court of assize was permitted to the civil court of appeals in Trieste, but no appeal was permitted to the Court of Cassation (the highest Italian court) in Rome. No sentence of death was to be executed unless and until confirmed by the supreme Allied commander or by such other officer, not below the rank of general, to whom this power was delegated by Marshal Alexander.

Proclamation No. 6, issued August 18, 1945, dissolved the Fascist party and organizations affiliated with it and dealt with the disposal of Fascist property, which was to be applied by the AMG for the benefit of the inhabitants of Zone A. The last, Proclamation No. 7, issued August 28, 1945, ordered the publication of all proclamations, general orders, orders, and administrative directives of the AMG in the newly established *Allied Military Government Gazette*.[12]

In the cities with an Italian majority (Trieste, Gorizia, Monfalcone, and Pula) the AMG tried to reintroduce the old Italian administrative system. Both Communists and Italian democrats (CLN) were invited to participate. The Communists opposed violently any such solution and the Italian democrats were still too weak. They had not recovered from the effects of Communist terror, and many lacked the courage to turn against the Communist majority, for they were unsure who the future sovereign of Zone A might be. Thus the political power of the Communist bloc remained unbroken, forcing the AMG to try a temporary solution. It ordered municipal employees to remain at their posts under direct instructions from officers of the AMG. Most municipal personnel had served the previous Italian administration and only a few heads of departments had been replaced by the Yugoslavs. By this policy the AMG sidetracked the Communist National Liberation committees, which still existed but had lost the power to govern.[13]

Quite different was the situation in Slovenian rural areas. Here the Communist administration had been already organized during the war and enjoyed support of the majority of Slovenes. The Slovenian employees obeyed the Communists and not the AMG. Therefore, in its first days the AMG had no way to organ-

12. "Proclamation No. 2," posted June 24, 1945, printed in ibid., pp. 7–9; "Proclamation No. 3," posted June 24, 1945, printed in ibid., pp. 10–11; "Proclamation No. 4," posted June 24, 1945, printed in ibid., pp. 12–13, and revised edition posted July 12, 1945, printed in ibid., pp. 13–15; "Proclamation No. 5," no date given, printed in ibid., pp. 16–18; "Proclamation No. 6," printed in ibid., pp. 19–20; and "Proclamation No. 7," printed in ibid., pp. 20–21. See also Harris, p. 347; and Bradshaw, *Department of State Bulletin*, 16:1261.

13. See "Minutes of SCAO's Meeting at Headquarters AMG, XIII Corps, July 10, 1945," in Coles and Weinberg, p. 607; "Colonel Bowman, SCAO, XIII Corps, Report for July 1945," in ibid., pp. 607–8; "Minutes of SCAO's Meeting at Headquarters AMG, XIII Corps, July 28, 1945," in ibid., p. 608; "Progress, Slow but Sure," *AC Bulletin*, 2, no. 17 (July 28, 1945): 5–6, and no. 49 (Mar. 9, 1946): 5; see also below, this chapter, next section.

ize an administration of its own in rural communes and the National Liberation committees retained their power.[14]

Of all the AMG measures, introduction of Italian law and the Italian administrative system provoked the strongest protests. Both the Communist organizations in Zone A and the Yugoslav government accused the AMG of violating Article Three of the Belgrade agreement.[15] Both renewed their demand that the AMG recognize the existing Yugoslav civil administration.

Because of continuous Yugoslav objections and Communist passive resistance, some AMG officers sought a new solution which would tolerate the dual administrative system. In the cities with an Italian majority the old Italian administrative system would continue. Justification for it was simple. Here the Yugoslav civil administration could not work satisfactorily, and the AMG thus had the right to reintroduce the Italian administration under the provisions of the same Article Three. In the Slovenian rural sections where the Communists remained firmly in control the Yugoslav civil administration would continue but under supervision of the AMG.

Marshal Alexander, who refused to recognize the Yugoslav civil administration in any part of Zone A, disagreed with this AMG interpretation of Article Three. Rather, he advanced his own in his report to the combined chiefs of staff on June 25, 1945, and asked for confirmation of its correctness. Article Three, which provided "that use will be made of any Yugoslav Civil Administration which is already set up and which in the view of

14. Jeri, p. 92.

15. About the Yugoslav note to the Duino agreement (June 20, 1945) see chapter 8, "The Belgrade Agreement." On July 18 the Yugoslav government sent a note to the United States Government, and on July 26 letters from Marshal Tito and Dr. Ivan Šubašić were sent to President Truman and Prime Minister Churchill. (See Coles and Weinberg, p. 606.) The Regional National Liberation Committee for the Slovenian Littoral sent its memorandum to the governments of Great Britain, the United States, Soviet Union, and Yugoslavia on July 28, 1945. The memorandum is reprinted in Jeri, pp. 100–103. For other local protests see below, this chapter, next section.

the Supreme Allied Commander is working satisfactorily," should be interpreted, said Marshal Alexander, in the following way:

> We have maintained that inasmuch as the basic law of this area is and must continue to be Italian the Italian administrative system must in its essentials be continued; that it was the intention of the agreement that our commitment to continue existing administration related to personnel rather than to the system of administration itself; and that the [National Liberation] committee system as an executive instrument of local government cannot be recognized but that [National Liberation] committees where useful will be employed in an advisory capacity as in other parts of Italy.[16]

In the same report Marshal Alexander explicitly refused recognition to those Yugoslav National Liberation committees which might "in the view of the Supreme Allied Commander be working satisfactorily" by arguing that "we might then have the wholly anomalous situation of a committee form of government in one commune and the Italian system functioning in the adjacent locality. This would obviously be unworkable in practice."

The next day, June 26, Marshal Alexander sent to the Thirteenth Corps his directive for the organization of local government in which he expressed the same views but included a provision to make some "adjustments" and "modifications," if needed. This directive read:

> The local government through which you will administer the area will be based on the Italian administrative system which existed and was in effect on 8 September 1943. It is not necessary, however, that all offices and appointments be filled. You may also, if for administrative reasons it appears expedient to do so, make adjustments and modifications in the foregoing administrative system, so long as its essential structure is not changed. You will administer the area as a separate region, under your command but subject to the technical control of the Allied Commission. No civilian govern-

16. Coles and Weinberg, p. 604. The right date is probably June 25 and not July 25 as printed in Coles and Weinberg. (See "Message, Allied Forces Headquarters to Combined Chiefs of Staff, August 25, 1945," in ibid., p. 606.)

ment official will be permitted to refer to or obtain instruction from authorities outside the area.[17]

In his directive, regarding Article Three of the Belgrade agreement, he repeated: "In interpreting the term 'civil administration' you should consider that the term relates to personnel employed rather than the system of administration itself."

The combined chiefs of staff approved these directions in their message to Marshal Alexander on August 25, 1945, by stating:

> You should as far as possible administer the area on the following lines: Jugoslav system of national committees should in general be discontinued in whole area and Italian system reinstalled. In predominantly Jugoslav towns and villages, token Jugoslav administration might be retained and national committee used in advisory capacity.[18]

Without doubt the Allied interpretation of Article Three was legally wrong. To explain this highhanded twist of the text the Allies argued that the AMG had to administer Zone A impartially, and would "take no action which will prejudice the position of either of the disputing parties."[19] The AMG could thus not recognize the Yugoslav civil administration, the argument went on, because the National Liberation committees openly propagated a pro-Yugoslav solution. Though this was true, the argument could be turned around, as it was by the Yugoslavs, to show that reintroduction of the Italian administrative system would favor the Italians. In the long run such proved to be the case.

Consequently the "equal protection" clause was only a cover for Allied actions principally directed against the Communist order. The Allies opposed the National Liberation committees because these committees were Communist controlled. The cover-up was needed in order not to enrage the Soviet Union whose help the Allies still sought for the war against Japan.

As soon as the new SCAO, Colonel Bowman, became familiar with the situation, he carried out the above directives in his General Order No. 11 issued on August 11, 1945.[20] It reinstalled the

17. Ibid., pp. 604–5.   18. Ibid., p. 607.   19. Ibid.
20. "General Order No. 11," issued August 11, 1945, printed in *AMG Gazette VG*, 1, no. 1 (Sept. 15, 1945): 45–48.

old Italian administrative system for all of Zone A, thus ending the dual administration and attempting to remove the chaos which had prevailed. Whatever authority the National Liberation committees had retained until August 11 was now legally ended.

For the purpose of local government, General Order No. 11 divided Zone A into two areas, Gorizia and Trieste, and into the commune of Pula. Each area was to be governed by a president, corresponding to the old Italian prefect, and by an area council. The area council for Trieste would comprise a chairman and seventeen members, and that for Gorizia, a chairman and fourteen members. The area presidents would be appointed by, and subject to removal by, the AMG, as would also members of the area councils. A vice-president would assist the area president. The area council was to be an advisory and consultative body to the area president and was to meet at least once a week.

The Trieste and Gorizia areas (provinces) would be further subdivided into communes and fractions. At the head of each commune was to be a communal president with the powers and duties of a mayor. The communal president of Pula would, in addition, possess all of the powers and duties of an area president. The communal councils were to serve as advisory and consultative bodies to the communal presidents and, in addition to a chairman for each, were to be composed of twelve members in communes with over 250,000 inhabitants, eight members in communes having over 30,000 inhabitants, and four members in the other communes. The AMG would appoint all commune presidents, chairmen, and members of the commune councils. They were to function under the Italian laws in force on September 8, 1943. Communal councils would meet at least once a week, the minutes being transmitted from the communal president to the area president and thence to the AMG area commissioner no more than seven days after each meeting.

Sections 10 and 11 of General Order No. 11 abolished the established administrations of the National Liberation committees throughout all of Zone A. These sections read:

> Section 10. *Other Committees.* No committee, council or group other than those herein created and provided for, except those previously constituted by a Proclamation or Order of the Allied Military Government, shall possess any of

the administrative, legislative, executive or other powers of government.

Section 11. *Control of Allied Military Government.* 1— Allied Military Government is the only government in those parts of Venezia Giulia occupied by the Allied Forces and is the only authority empowered to issue orders and decrees and to make appointment to public or other office.[21]

The AMG then invited both sides, the pro-Communist group and the CLN, to nominate candidates for the newly created administrative positions.[22] It was still the policy of the AMG to seek cooperation between the two groups and to create an Italo-Slovenian administration in the cities. This intention can also be inferred from the wording of General Order No. 11:

Consideration shall be given to the selection of the Chairman and Members from the leading citizens of the Area of the highest moral and political probity who shall be, as far as possible, representative of all racial, political and economic groups and classes in the Area according to their respective local strength.[23]

The negotiations with the Communist bloc proved to be useless. In his monthly report for August 1945 Colonel Bowman well illustrated this situation:

The attitude of the Regional National Liberation Council can be summed up as follows:
"We will willingly cooperate if the Allied Military Government will govern in accordance with our views and through our institutions, but we will not cooperate otherwise, as any other form of government is considered to be Fascist and non-democratic."[24]

21. Ibid., p. 48.
22. Bowman, *Military Government Journal*, 1, no. 8: 13; see also "Bowman, Senior Civil Affairs Officer, XIII Corps, Report for August 1945," Coles and Weinberg, p. 610; "Minutes of Meeting at AMG Headquarters, XIII Corps, September 1, 1945," ibid.; and "Minutes of Meeting at Headquarters AMG, XIII Corps, September 8, 1945," ibid., pp. 610–11.
23. *AMG Gazette VG*, 1, no. 1: 46.
24. Coles and Weinberg, p. 610.

After a month of fruitless discussion with the Communist bloc the AMG decided, at its meeting of September 8, 1945, to go ahead with appointment of officials and formation of area and communal councils.[25] By this move the new area and communal administrations in Trieste, Monfalcone, Gorizia, and Pula came into the hands of representatives of Italian parties, while in communes ethnically Slovenian, a Civil Affairs Officer (British or American) governed, acting as commune president in conjunction with his staff of employees.

In his monthly report for September 1945, Colonel Bowman could state that all area presidents and councils were functioning in accordance with General Order No. 11. Eighteen out of the thirty-seven communes had commune presidents and councils, while the other nineteen had refused to nominate any officials and were either operating under a local civil affairs officer or had retained their original National Liberation committees, which were carrying on under the supervision of the local civil affairs officer. Not all of the latter communes were ethnically Slovenian: in four, the population was over 90 percent Italian, but pro-Communist.[26] On the other hand, among the eighteen cooperating communes were some Slovenian communes, especially in the area of Gorizia, which were mostly anti-Communist. Cooperation with the AMG, therefore, did not entirely follow ethnic lines, but depended also on political and ideological alignments.

Where a pro-Communist majority existed, the population did not cooperate with the AMG. In the cities, where the Italian majority contained a large non-Communist section, the AMG could establish the new administration more easily. Also, in the cities anti-Communists did not fear Communist intimidation to any great degree. In the rural communities, on the other hand, there was no police protection, and any move against Communist authority could easily lead to reprisals. This was an important factor in hindering Slovenian anti-Communists in rural communities from cooperating with the AMG. The civil administration as it was established by the end of September 1945 remained basically unchanged for two years, until the peace treaty with Italy came into effect.

25. Ibid. 26. Ibid., p. 611.

MILITARY OCCUPATION

An important task of the AMG was to secure law and order in Zone A. Proclamation No. 1 established three kinds of Allied military courts with jurisdiction over public and private matters. Highest was the General Military Court which could impose the death penalty. The Superior Military Court had the power to impose lawful punishment, other than death or imprisonment for more than ten years. The lowest were the Summary Military Courts, with authority over crimes punishable by less than one year's imprisonment or a fine of less than fifty thousand lire.[27] Such civil courts as had existed in the territory on September 8, 1943, were reestablished by General Order No. 6 on July 12, 1945, with the proviso, however, that Slovenes had the right to be heard in their own language. Furthermore, no appeals could be made to the Court of Cassation at Rome.[28]

To take the place of the People's Militia the AMG organized a special police force recruited from the local population. This body was rapidly enlarged, as is shown by the monthly reports of the Allied Commission in Rome.[29] Heading the Julian Region police were British and American officers, who patterned their organization after the metropolitan police in London and New York.

British Colonel Gerald Richardson, formerly an officer of the London metropolitan police, should receive the principal credit for raising the Julian Region police force to the point where, by 1948, it was regarded as one of the best organized in all of Europe. It was far ahead in the fields of forensics, scientific crime detection, radio communication, and other aspects of modern police work. It

27. *AMG Gazette VG,* 1, no. 1: 5–6.
28. "General Order No. 6," dated July 12, 1945, printed in ibid., p. 32; Charles M. Munnecke, "Legal Challenge in Trieste," *Military Government Journal,* 2, no. 2 (Summer 2949): 7; Bradshaw, *Department of State Bulletin,* 16:1262.
29. About the decision to organize a special police force see Coles and Weinberg, pp. 605–6, 608. The police force numbered 1,950 in December 1945, 2,788 in February 1946, 3,771 in March, and 4,450 in November 1946. For this see Bradshaw, *Department of State Bulletin,* 16: 1262. By September 1947 the police force was about six thousand strong. See J. D. Lunt, "The Venezia Giulia Police Force," *The Army Quarterly* (London), 58, no. 2 (July, 1949): 215.

also had many specialized branches, such as traffic, mounted police, fire department, and a motorized section. The territorial organization was divided by communal zones, each having police districts in charge of a superintendent, and operating as self-sufficient units.[30] Because of its very efficient methods, it was the most condemned by the Communists of all AMG institutions. Seventy percent of the police recruits came from the Italian population; the rest were Slovene.

The AMG did not aim its policy directly against the Slovenian ethnic group as such. True, it abolished the Communist institutions and the city National Liberation committees in which the Slovenes had played a leading role, but this was done only after the pro-Communist bloc had declined to cooperate with the AMG. This refusal enabled the Italian parties to get the upper hand and to seize the leading positions in the AMG administration. Even then the AMG tried to guarantee certain fundamental rights to the Slovenian population: official decrees were published in the Slovenian tongue; Slovenes could use their own language in the courts; a certain number of Slovenes were recruited into the police force; and Slovenes were permitted to petition the authorities for readoption of their old Slovenian names, formerly forbidden by Fascist law. Most important for the Slovenes was a free press that permitted publication of Slovenian newspapers, and the establishment of Slovenian schools.[31]

The organization of Slovenian elementary and secondary schools in Zone A had to surmount many obstacles, the first of which was the well-organized Communist resistance against AMG schools. Besides, there was a dearth of qualified teachers, thanks to previous Fascist policies. To remedy this defect the AMG issued Order No. 118 on April 21, 1946, setting up a six-months course at the Slovenian Teachers Training School in Gorizia.[32] Here

30. Lunt, pp. 213-18; Bowman, *Military Government Journal*, 1, no. 8: 12.

31. Ibid., pp. 13-14.

32. "Order No. 118," dated April 21, 1946, printed in *AMG Gazette VG*, 1, no. 18 (May 15, 1946): 31. For Croats living in the Pula municipality similar Croat teacher-training courses were given in Pula. For this see "Order No. 245," dated October 17, 1946, printed in ibid., 2, no. 3 (Nov. 1, 1946): 144-45. Special teachers' summer courses were given in

Slovenes with Italian teachers' diplomas could become familiar with Slovenian history and literature in order to teach these subjects to Slovenian children. The AMG also employed many qualified persons who had left Yugoslavia because of their anti-Communist convictions.

The Slovenian schools opened in October 1945.[33] Elementary schools were to be organized in all communes having such schools on June 1, 1914, and in communes where twenty-five children within a radius of four kilometers wished to attend. The school curriculum was to be patterned after the Italian system in existence on September 8, 1943, except that all subjects, including Slovenian history and literature, would be taught in the Slovenian language. The chief education officer heading the educational division of the AMG then appointed an Italian and a Slovenian adviser for their respective schools.

However, both superintendents in each of the two areas (provinces) of Zone A, namely Gorizia and Trieste, were Italians, to whom the Slovenian provincial inspectors for the Slovenian schools were responsible. This failure to create separate Slovenian superintendents for Slovenian schools brought constant complaints by Slovenians.

In the same year Slovenian secondary schools were organized in Gorizia and Trieste, including a Slovenian gymnasium and teacher training school in Gorizia and a gymnasium and commercial academy in Trieste.[34] Similarly, in the Pula area, Croatian

---

Trieste and Gorizia for Slovenian teachers in 1946 according to "Order No. 194," dated July 27, 1946, published in ibid., 1, no. 24 (Aug. 15, 1946): 46–48.

33. For the educational organization see *AC Weekly Bulletin*, 2, no. 18 (Aug. 4, 1945): 6–7; no. 49 (Mar. 9, 1946): 9; 3, no. 2 (Apr. 13, 1946): 6; Bradshaw, *Department of State Bulletin*, 16:1262–65. The Slovenian and Croat elementary schools were established mainly by the following three decrees: the "Administrative Instruction-Education No. 4," dated August 1945, published in *AMG Gazette VG*, 1, no. 12 (Feb. 15, 1946): 18–23; "Administrative Instruction-Education No. 8," dated October 8, 1945, printed in ibid., p. 26; and "Administrative Instruction No. 9," dated October 16, 1945, printed in ibid., 1, no. 6 (Nov. 15, 1945): 5.

34. "Administrative Instruction-Education, No. 7," dated October 8, 1945, published in *AMG Gazette VG*, 1, no. 12 (Feb. 15, 1946): 25.

elementary and secondary schools began to function. Despite all the difficulties, the AMG successfully organized its own school system. Table 1 shows data on schools open and functioning in Zone A of the Julian Region as of December 1945. Note the shortage of Slovenian elementary school teachers. In Italian schools there were 10.4 pupils per teacher, while in Slovenian schools there were 58.1 pupils per teacher.[35]

The preparation of textbooks for Slovenian schools also cre-

TABLE 1

AMG SCHOOLS IN THE JULIAN REGION (DECEMBER 1945)

Slovene and Croat

Kind	Number	Enrollment	Teachers
Kindergarten	2	80	...
Elementary	105	11,802	203
Lower trade	...	......	...
Lower secondary	2	1,003	50
Upper secondary	4	380	32

Italian

Kind	Number	Enrollment	Teachers
Kindergarten	20	1,702	75
Elementary	533	28,027	1,740
Lower trade	27	5,530	348
Lower secondary	14	4,530	313
Upper secondary	20	6,351	504

SOURCE: Bradshaw, *Department of State Bulletin*, 16:1263.

35. For more information on Slovenian schools see: J. V. [Jože Velikonja], "Slovenske šole na Tržaškem" (Slovenian Schools in Trieste Region), *Koledar-Zbornik, 1955*, pp. 179–80; *Izvestje državnih srednjih šol s slovenskim učnim jezikom v Gorici za šolsko leto 1954–55: Jubilejna številka ob desetletnici obstoja* (Report on the State Secondary Schools in Gorizia with Slovenian as Language of Instruction for the School Year 1954–55: A Jubilee Number for the Tenth Anniversary of Existence) (Gorizia, 1955); Maks Šah, "1945–1955: Deset let slovenskih šol na Tržaškem" (1945–1955: Ten Years of Slovenian Schools in Trieste Area), *Izvestje srednjih šol, 1955* (Report on the Secondary Schools, 1955) (Trieste, 1955), pp. 3–7.

ated problems. During the summer of 1945 the AMG decided to use Italian books purged of all pro-Fascist sections in Italian schools and to publish books with pro-Communist propaganda deleted for use in Slovenian schools. The decision to bar pro-Communist schoolbooks evoked strong opposition from the pro-Communist bloc and resulted in many school strikes. Parents belonging to pro-Communist organizations were instructed to refrain from sending their children to AMG schools.[36]

The AMG educational officer, Captain John P. Simoni of the United States, an outstanding supporter of the effort to establish Slovenian schools in Zone A, came under fire from two sides. On the one hand, the Communist bloc attacked him in their daily press. Indeed, his Slovenian adviser, Professor Srečko Baraga, was proclaimed a traitor and condemned to death in absentia by Yugoslav courts. On the other hand, strongly supporting Professor Baraga as he did, Captain Simoni faced denunciation by Italian nationalists for the mere establishment of Slovenian schools in the Gorizia and Trieste areas.

Following its policy of allowing a free press to function, the AMG permitted the continued publication of *Primorski dnevnik* (Littoral Daily), the organ of the Slovenian Liberation Front, but counterbalanced its propaganda by having its Allied Information Service publish both a Slovenian daily, *Glas zaveznikov* (Voice of the Allies), and an Italian daily, *Giornale Alleato* (Allied Journal). Besides, the official AMG *Gazette* was also issued in English, Italian, and Slovenian.[37]

The Italian lira remained the recognized currency in Zone A. Both the prewar money and new bills issued by the AMG for Italy (AMG lire) circulated. The Allied Commission in Rome assigned three hundred million AMG lire to the headquarters of the Thir-

36. See "Administrative Instruction-Education, No. 2," dated August 1945, published in *AMG Gazette VG*, 1, no. 12 (Feb. 15, 1946): 16; "Order No. 89," dated March 20, 1946, published in ibid., 1, no. 16 (Apr. 15, 1946): 29; *AC Weekly Bulletin*, 3, no. 2 (Apr. 13, 1946): 6; "Reading, Writing and Revolution," *Time*, Mar. 25, 1946, p. 35.

37. See "Proclamation No. 3," *AMG Gazette VG*, 1, no. 1 (Sept. 15, 1945): 10–11; "Proclamation No. 7," ibid., pp. 20–21; "Order No. 133," dated May 16, 1946, published in ibid., no. 20 (June 15, 1946), pp. 11–12.

teenth Corps for administrative expenses of Zone A. Italian government bonds of 1945 could also be serviced in the usual manner, and the sale of Italian postal savings bonds and the acceptance of postal savings deposits continued. The local machinery of the Banca d'Italia was used to finance government and commune expenditures, the cash being supplied by AMG finance officers in AMG lire. However, the issue of other Italian government securities was suspended.[38]

A most important concern of the AMG was to put the population to work. A large public works program began with the much-needed repair of damaged industrial, housing, and port facilities. Peak employment in this program was twenty thousand persons. The program came to an end later with the revival of normal business and industry. The United Nations Relief and Rehabilitation Administration never functioned in the Julian Region even though its shipments were passing through the port of Trieste on the way to Austria, Yugoslavia, and Czechoslovakia. It did furnish some employment to Trieste workers, however, in the course of these shipments.[39]

COMMUNIST REACTION TO THE AMG AND ITS CONSEQUENCES

Having seen AMG operations in the Julian Region from the Allied point of view, and with only intimations of Yugoslav displeasure, we must now witness in more detail the Communist reaction to the policies of these "intruders."

As indicated, the Communists knew that Allied occupation of Zone A would endanger the power they had built with their civil administration. This peril increased because the urban centers (Trieste, Gorizia, Monfalcone, and Pula) had an Italian majority, part of which was prepared to cooperate with the Allies. These Italians, represented by the CLN, opposed the Yugoslav administration and policies for two reasons: as Italian nationalists they were against any kind of Yugoslav rule in the Julian Region, and second, as urban middle-class supporters of democracy, they opposed a pro-Communist administration.

38. Harris, p. 346.
39. Bowman, *Military Government Journal*, 1, no. 8: 12.

The Communists of Zone A thus prepared to defend their civil administration and to develop a giant propaganda campaign claiming Zone A for Yugoslavia at the peace conference. Propaganda stressing that Zone A should go to Yugoslavia pursued a dual aim, ideological and nationalistic. The unification of Zone A with Yugoslavia would extend Communist rule farther toward the west, and would at the same time satisfy Slovenian and Croat nationalistic claims.

To achieve these aims the local Communists decided, at a meeting of delegates of all pro-Communist organizations in Trieste on June 4, 1945, to form a united bloc for the Julian Region. This meeting took place, however, only eight days before the Yugoslav forces retreated from Zone A, and it was not until two months later, on August 13, that all the Communist parties—Italian, Slovenian, and Croat—united into a single Communist Party of Venezia Giulia (CPVG). Shortly, a new mass organization of all pro-Communists followed the CPVG into existence under the name of the Italo-Slavic Anti-Fascist Union, abbreviated UAIS-SIAU for Unione Antifascista Italo-Slava—Slovansko-italijanska antifašistična unija. The new UAIS-SIAU did not replace the old organizations, such as the Slovenian Liberation Front or other mass agencies. Rather, it represented only a union of these organizations on central and local levels. It should be underlined that the leading positions in these new groups were held by old Communists. Non-Communist sympathizers filled only unimportant posts. Such was the case in Trieste, where Giuseppe Pogassi, president of the CLT, became the president of the UAIS-SIAU, and the former political commissar Franc Štoka became secretary. Julij Beltram, a known Communist leader, was made secretary of the UAIS-SIAU in Gorizia.[40]

After the signing of the Belgrade agreement the Communists concentrated primarily on Trieste. Other parts of Zone A remained important but Trieste was more and more singled out, for quite evident reasons. It was an important city-port with a numerous working class and an important Italian middle class. The Yugoslavs had a tough ally in the former but a strong enemy in the bourgeoisie.

The first task of the Communists in Trieste was to find out

40. *Slovensko Primorje in Istra,* pp. 553–54.

how far the Allied authorities would go in recognizing the Yugoslav civil administration. A delegation of the Trieste Liberation Committee (CLT) headed by Pogassi met with the Allied commandant in Trieste, General Eve, on June 11, 1945, the day before the Yugoslav forces were to withdraw behind the Morgan line. The delegation declared that the CLT, as an administration which had secured peace and order for Trieste, was prepared to collaborate loyally with the AMG. General Eve in a noncommittal reply assured the men that he would transmit their statement to his superiors.[41]

The following day, when the Allied forces took over administration of Zone A, Major F. G. Pallotti, an AMG officer for municipal affairs, occupied the town hall without giving a sign of recognition to the CLT except to ask the members for a short report on their functioning and organization. The Allies also occupied the Casa del Popolo, the seat of the Sindacati Unici or pro-Communist labor union. The people's court was suspended, and the flag of the city of Trieste removed from the town hall, the headquarters of the CLT.[42]

Thoroughly alarmed, the CLT, on the evening of the same day, wrote to Lt. Colonel Francis J. Armstrong, the new AMG area commissioner for Trieste, protesting these acts as hostile to the Communist administration. They followed the next day, June 13, with a visit to the colonel. Here they learned that they came under his control as a representative of the supreme authority in the region. Colonel Armstrong requested, however, that the CLT members remain at their posts and continue their work. The CLT heads of the various departments were invited to communicate with the respective heads of the AMG government, and Colonel Armstrong promised to send to the latter directions to this effect.[43]

On June 15 a vast manifestation of workers, sixty thousand

41. Consiglio di Liberazione della Città di Trieste, *L'attività svolta dal Consiglio di Liberazione della Città di Trieste, 17 maggio–21 settembre 1945, con una breve premessa storico-politica* (Trieste, 1945), pp. 20–21. This is an abridged version of *Trieste nella lotta* but includes a few new facts, hereafter cited as *L'attività dal CLT*.

42. *Trieste nella lotta*, pp. 136–37.

43. *L'attività dal CLT*, pp. 21–22. For a somewhat different account see *Trieste nella lotta*, pp. 137–39.

strong, took place before the Government House (Prefettura) in the Piazza Unità, at which a special petition was approved for submission to the AMG. The workers demanded that the pro-Communist civil administration remain in force, and stated that they would refuse to recognize any reintroduction of the pro-Fascist Questura or Carabinieri, for many members had been war criminals. They demanded the arrest of all Fascists and collaborators and their arraignment before the people's court. The petition further asked that the Regional National Liberation Committee be recognized as the civil authority in Zone A and the CLT as the legal civil administration in Trieste on the ground that these organs had been "elected by the great majority of the anti-Fascist population of our city."[44]

On June 18 Major Pallotti, who had refused to collaborate with the CLT, issued an order prohibiting municipal employees from having relations with that body. The CLT now sought an interview with Colonel Nelson M. Monfort, senior civil affairs officer. The interview took place on June 21, the day after the signing of the Duino agreement. In Duino, as we know, the Yugoslav delegation had demanded recognition of the Yugoslav civil administration. Colonel Monfort promised the CLT delegation that Pallotti's order would be annulled. At the same time, however, he explained in friendly fashion that institutions such as the Consiglio di Liberazione di Trieste and the municipal Consulta had no counterparts in the Italian system of government, and he had therefore advised the reestablishment of the old Italian administrative units: the province and municipality. Hence, Colonel Monfort suggested that someone should be selected to serve as the future prefect of Trieste Province, and that a mayor (*podestà*) and members of the municipal council should be chosen according to the old Italian system. For this purpose, he argued, the CLT should reach an agreement with the other Italian political parties represented in the CLN.[45]

44. *L'attività dal CLT*, pp. 22–23; *Slovensko Primorje in Istra*, p. 634. *Trieste nella lotta* (p. 140) gave the number of the participants as being over seventy thousand.

45. *L'attività dal CLT*, p. 22; Jeri, p. 92. A similar proposal was made by area commissioner Armstrong on July 9, 1945. For this see "Minutes of SCAO's Meeting at Headquarters AMG, XIII Corps," dated July 10, 1945, printed in Coles and Weinberg, p. 607.

To introduce Italian institutions again, the CLT explained to Colonel Monfort, would only strengthen Italian chauvinism. Moreover, Italian civil service employees known for pro-Fascist sympathies would be brought back into the administration. While Italian institutions reflected the Fascist days gone by, the new policies represented the people who had opposed Fascism all the years before the war and had fought it during the war. Such institutions as the Prefecture, Questura (police), Guardia di Finanza, Carabinieri (gendarmes), and the judicial administration were drenched with the blood of anti-Fascist fighters.[46] These institutions, stressed the CLT, "were so completely Fascist, that a simple epuration would not be sufficient, but a complete abolition of them was rendered necessary, and the creation of completely new institutions instead."[47]

In reply to the advice of Colonel Monfort to arrive at a modus operandi with other parties, the CLT delegates explained that they had in their midst representatives from the Italian Communist and Socialist parties, Slovenian nationalists, democratic Triestini, people without affiliation, and even an Italian priest. Furthermore the CLT members informed Colonel Monfort that they were already negotiating with other Italian parties to enlarge the CLT. But these Italian parties, though representing only a minority, were demanding numerical parity with other groups forming the CLT which had a vastly greater following. Thus a future compromise with these Italian parties was quite dubious in the eyes of the CLT. With this the interview ended.[48]

On June 24, Colonel Monfort put into force his Notice No. 2, dated June 14, 1945, ordering disbandment of the People's Militia.[49] In retaliation a general strike was proclaimed by pro-Communist forces for June 25, and the CLT on June 26 sent a written objection to Marshal Alexander himself.[50] This protest repeated

46. *L'attività dal CLT,* p. 22. The same was repeated in the letter to Marshal Alexander, dated June 26, 1945, and reprinted in ibid., pp. 24–27.

47. Ibid., p. 27.   48. Ibid., p. 22.

49. "Notice No. 2," dated June 14, 1945, published in *AMG Gazette VG,* 1, no. 2 (Oct. 1, 1945): 12; *L'attività dal CLT,* p. 24.

50. *L'attività dal CLT,* p. 24; *Trieste nella lotta* (p. 152) gives June 24 as the date for the strike. *AC Weekly Bulletin* (2, no. 13 [June 30, 1945]: 5) gives June 26 as the date of the strike.

the points explained to Colonel Monfort, and again requested "that the Council of Liberation of Trieste and the municipal Consulta be recognized as the supreme civil legislative and executive authority of the city, which does not exclude a control of its functioning on the part of the Supreme Allied Authorities."

The letter of protest also asked that relations between Allied authorities and the Liberation Council of Trieste be based on mutual respect. Finally, it requested that the Allies consider the particular situation of the Littoral and of Trieste, which could not be met by imitation of the institutions in use in Italy.[51] This letter went unanswered.

On July 9, 1945, the British military police arrested two leading Communists, Giuseppe Pogassi, the president of the CLT, and Giorgio Jaksetich, editor of the Communist paper *Il Lavoratore* and former vice-commander of the city, together with some fire department personnel and former members of the People's Militia, on the grounds that none had turned in their arms. This provoked another protest strike on July 11.[52]

By then the CLT had become an administrative body in name only, for the AMG officers were dealing directly with each separate department of Trieste's municipality. The AMG, however, continued its piecemeal tactics directed against Communist institutions.

General Order No. 6, issued July 12, 1945, abolished the regular people's courts established by the Yugoslavs and restored the regular (Fascist) Italian courts in effect on September 8, 1943. By this move the last of the Communist institutions had been eliminated.[53]

---

51. "CLT's letter to Marshal Alexander," dated June 26, 1945," published in *L'attività dal CLT*, pp. 24–27, and in *Trieste nella lotta*, pp. 153–56. There are a few differences between the texts.

52. *L'attività dal CLT*, pp. 27–28; *Trieste nella lotta* (p. 164) gives July 10 as the date of arrest. The second general strike began July 18, and a third one occurred the day Jaksetich was condemned to an eighteen-month prison term in a legal process beginning August 6, 1945. (Ibid., pp. 166–67.)

53. See "General Order No. 6," dated July 12, 1945, published in *AMG Gazette VG*, 1, no. 1 (Sept. 15, 1945): 32; *Trieste nella lotta*, pp. 175–79.

COMMUNIST REACTION TO THE AMG

On July 29, the AMG made its final compromise proposal to the CLT. The latter would remain a political organization, similar to the Italian CLN, while the city administration would come into the hands of a new committee composed of delegates from both the CLT and CLN. The CLT refused.[54] Convinced that adjustment with the Communist bloc was impossible, the AMG thus decided to organize its own civil administration.

On August 15, 1945, came the final blow, General Order No. 11, which formally abolished the local Communist administration (i.e., the CLT in Trieste). It is probable that this general order would have appeared a month before had it not been that Colonel Monfort was replaced toward the end of June by Colonel Bowman. General Order No. 11, dated August 11, was released to the press on August 15, 1945, together with an official comment which stated that:

> Among the principal duties which the Allied Military Government has to face are the protection of minorities, the protection of those groups of persons who do not know how to react to intimidations or threats on the part of associations well organized by persons belonging to different ethnic groups or parties, and also the maintenance of legality and order.[55]

The following day a manifestation of about eighty thousand people protested the abolition of the "people's administration." The slogans used, such as: "Trieste is not an enemy territory!" "We are waiting for the realization of promises of the Atlantic Charter!" and "We do not accept an administration forced upon us!" did not defend openly the Communist power but typically used democratic ideas of freedom and representation.[56]

On August 25 the CLT presented a new protest against General Order No. 11 to Colonel Bowman, in which it claimed again to be the legal representative of the great majority of the people, while all opposing parties (Italian democratic) represented only a minority. In condemnation of the new order, the CLT stated:

> The Allied Military Government which affirms, through its mouth-piece, to act in the name of the principle of democ-

54. *Trieste nella lotta*, p. 186; *Slovensko Primorje in Istra*, p. 635.
55. *L'attività dal CLT*, p. 36.
56. *Slovensko Primorje in Istra*, pp. 634-35.

racy, and for the protection of [political] minorities, has created this paradoxical situation: in homage to the said democratic principle it has abolished a body elected *from below,* that is to say in the most democratic way and representing the will of the majority of the population, and appoints, in its place, *from above,* that is to say in the most authoritarian way, a body in which *the majority* [power] *will lie with the minority.*

For the above mentioned reasons the Council of Liberation refuses to participate either directly or indirectly in the body about to be formed by offering their own representatives.[57]

The CLT then elaborated its position as follows: First, it should be allowed to continue its administration; second, it would accept an adequate representation of other political parties; and third, new free elections should be held in the shortest possible time.

On August 29 Colonel Bowman replied that the AMG administration was only a temporary military arrangement based on international agreement, and invited CLT members to participate. In hopes that the CLT would do so, he declared he would wait a while before forming a new local administration.[58] The CLT answered on September 6, 1945, repeating its position and again calling for new elections.[59] On September 21 the AMG acted by appointing a new municipal president and communal council for Trieste. The next day the CLT proclaimed its own dissolution.

One factor stands out. The Communists fought for recognition of their administration with a single purpose in mind—to retain their power. They were not prepared to share it with any other group. A compromise to include the Italian political parties of the CLN would weaken Communist power and endanger the gains of the socialist revolution. Rather than accept these terms, the Communist bloc went into opposition.

As in Trieste, so in Gorizia and in all of Zone A, the Com-

57. *L'attività dal CLT,* p. 37.
58. The letter from Colonel Bowman is reprinted in ibid., pp. 39–40.
59. The letter to Colonel Bowman is reprinted in ibid., pp. 40–42.

munist bloc under leadership of the UAIS-SIAU began a militant attack on the AMG and on all its collaborators. September 21, 1945, therefore, marked the end of the AMG hope to achieve cooperation with the Communists. Abolition of Communist administrative institutions did not immediately weaken the Communist forces. On the contrary, it consolidated their bloc.

Before the AMG took over Zone A two tensions had been developing within the pro-Communist bloc. On the one hand, many one-time Partisans condemned the terror and mass execution of "Fascists and collaborationists." The rural Slovenian population became increasingly aware that the Communists' fight was for power and not for national liberation. Also, many resented the so-called Italo-Slovenian brotherhood as a blow to Slovenian nationalist aspirations. Discontent among the Slovenian rural population was quite widespread, especially in the province of Gorizia.

On the other hand, tension existed among the Italian laboring class especially in Monfalcone and Trieste. Faced with Yugoslav occupation, many pro-Communist workers began to doubt the intentions of the new administration, and to ponder whether they were seeking to create a new social order or whether their move was only a screen for Slovenian nationalism to annex the Slovenian Littoral to Yugoslavia.

Because of the authoritarian nature of the Communist organizations, these potential dissensions never reached damaging proportions, though they were to cause trouble in the future. For the present, however, the Communists, when faced with an open fight against the AMG, were able to reunite themselves more solidly and thus diminish the internal friction that had arisen.

The AMG placed a strong argument in the hands of the Communist bloc in deciding to adopt Italian laws and forms of administration. The Communists ably used the occasion to propagandize among the Slovenian peasants, arguing that the AMG was favoring Italian claims to the Julian Region. The Communist bloc pictured itself as the only political force struggling for unification of the Julian Region with Yugoslavia. It thus regained the confidence of the Slovenes, in whose eyes the AMG began to represent the same old anti-Slovenian principles as had the Fascists.

Turning now to the Italian workers, the Communists could explain that by abolishing the Communist institutions established during the struggle against Fascism, the AMG was introducing not only a bourgeois capitalist order, but the old Fascist law in force before September 1943. Only a socialist state like Yugoslavia could sincerely protect the rights of the workers. Thus propaganda was able to rally the Italian masses more closely to communism.

Through such consolidation the Communist bloc became a strong political opposition that could not be counterbalanced by the Italian democratic parties' support of the AMG. With the destiny of the Julian Region not yet settled, many still hesitated to oppose the Communist bloc which might yet win the day. This was an important factor in explaining why the AMG could not organize an administration in nearly half of the communes of Zone A.

During 1945-46 the Communists effectively attacked those accepting posts in the AMG, calling them traitors to Slovenian national interests or to the working class. Because of this opposition, the AMG was able to organize its administration only in the big cities, and in the larger towns where Allied troops and later the police force could protect those who dared accept positions. In these cities and in some towns, as pointed out before, the old administrative machinery had remained almost intact even during the forty days of Yugoslav occupation. Naturally, the AMG had to use the same apparatus. Most of these government employees, though they might have been opposed to Fascism, had been members of the Fascist party, if only in order to hold their jobs. The hiring of these former Fascist employees heightened the effect of Communist propaganda against the AMG. But at the same time it increased Italian influence in that same government. The Italians, indeed, were able to secure a practical monopoly of all positions.

In the rural communes the situation differed sharply. Here the AMG still could not establish a civil administration for quite a time. As a consequence, the AMG had to rule through the civil affairs officers, and did so with great difficulty. A civil affairs officer, with the rank of perhaps captain or major, acting as mayor of a rural commune, needed an interpreter, a secretary, and other assistants to deal with the local population. Owing to the sharp attacks made by the Communists against anyone who took such a post, it was practically impossible for the officers to get local help.

Denounced as a traitor, such an employee together with his family was under constant threat; many were kidnapped and taken across the Morgan line where they disappeared, or were found murdered in the nearby forests of Zone A.[60]

Nevertheless the AMG got cooperation from some Slovenes, especially those opposing communism from the start, who had sympathized with the National Guards during the war. These, mainly Slovenian intellectuals in Zone A, were later joined by those who had fled Slovenia because of Communist persecution or who were otherwise opposed to communism. They were the first Slovene supporters of the AMG and remained loyal despite daily attacks against them in such papers as *Primorski dnevnik* and *Il Lavoratore*.

The people who helped the civil affairs officers could not live in the rural communities because of the danger and had to move to Trieste or Gorizia, where they were relatively more secure, though here too kidnapping was not uncommon during 1946. Each morning the AMG transported these employees to their places of work in the rural communes where they remained in an office guarded by the Julian Region police until brought back to the city at night.

A task of greatest difficulty was the organization of AMG Slovenian elementary schools in those rural communes where Partisan schools had been functioning since the war. At first the people refused to accept any teacher sent by the AMG and stood by their old Partisan instructors. The first breakthrough occurred in those villages or towns which were also the seats of the communal administration and where the teachers could be transported from the cities each day, together with the other communal employees, and be given police protection.

This did not solve the problem, however, since the UAIS-SIAU would then proclaim a school strike and no children would

60. Bowman, *Military Government Journal*, 1, no. 8: 13; "Protest against Yugoslav Obstruction to Allied Military Government," *Department of State Bulletin*, 15 (Sept. 1, 1946): 409–11. The same was expressed in a note delivered September 17, 1946, by Ambassador Patterson to the Yugoslav Ministry of Foreign Affairs. For this see "Reply to Yugoslav Notes Alleging Improper Treatment of Yugoslavs in Venezia Giulia," *Department of State Bulletin*, 15 (Sept. 29, 1946): 579–81.

appear. The AMG countered by ordering that the only recognized diplomas would be those signed by an AMG teacher and only with such a diploma could a pupil apply for higher education. In many instances this order helped, but not in all. More difficult was the case in those villages where the teachers remained unprotected.

A second great dispute about the schools concerned the choice of textbooks. Even when parents wished their children to have a legal elementary school diploma and hence decided to send them to AMG schools, some still demanded that only textbooks published by Partisan authorities be used. To avoid further difficulties, many AMG teachers succumbed and used the Partisan textbooks, especially in villages where no police existed to protect the teacher. The AMG firmly opposed use of the Partisan textbooks, and on March 20, 1946, issued Order No. 89 to end the practice: any AMG teacher so doing would be dismissed from his job.[61]

Finally, during the school year 1946–47 a new practice began. In the communes and villages scheduled to go to Yugoslavia according to the Paris peace negotiations, the civil affairs officers permitted pictures of Tito to hang on the walls of the school rooms; AMG teachers could become members of the Sindacati Unici (Partisan Labor Union); and former Partisan teachers could apply for AMG teaching positions. In return, the UAIS-SIAU ended the campaign against the AMG textbooks, which continued to be used in all the schools.

Upon signing of the peace treaty in February 1947, active opposition to AMG administration from the UAIS-SIAU came to a close in all communes allotted to Italy, and distinctly lessened in those communes forming the Free Territory of Trieste. On the other hand, AMG officers compromised in favor of UAIS-SIAU in those communes which were to be annexed to Yugoslavia.

In the long run, the boycott policy of the UAIS-SIAU became detrimental to the Communist bloc. Italian influence greatly increased within the AMG, and what should have been an Italo-Slovenian administration turned into a purely Italian one, on both the provincial level and in such communes as Trieste and Gorizia. These facts, pointed out in full by the Slovenian anti-

61. *AMG Gazette VG*, 1, no. 16 (Apr. 15, 1946): 29; see also Allied Military Government, Thirteenth Corps, "Daily Press Summary," no. 436 (Dec. 24, 1946) (mimeographed).

Communist press, caused a serious withdrawal of Slovenian peasant support from the Communists.

Moreover, as the sole participants in the local civil administration, the Italians regained their self-confidence, courage, and even strength. The Italians held their first large manifestation in Trieste on November 3, 1945, the holiday of San Giusto, the city patron. The CLN, representing the non-Communist Italians, grew to be a second political power, challenging the Communist bloc and supporting the AMG. By 1946 the CLN felt strong enough to penetrate the workers' ranks, hitherto the exclusive domain of the UAIS-SIAU, and formed its own labor union, Sindacati Giuliani. The AMG welcomed the appearance of this second political bloc, especially as it opposed communism. Among its other support the AMG gave financial help to the Sindacati Giuliani whereas their rivals in the Sindacati Unici were deprived of it.[62]

Pressing their advantage, the CLN hammered home the point that the UAIS-SIAU had failed to follow a policy in the interests of the Italian working class, but, as its main goal, had sought to achieve Yugoslav annexationist claims. The Communist trade union, according to the CLN, was supporting, not Italo-Slovenian workers' interests, as claimed, but Yugoslav nationalism.[63] This propaganda had some effect on Italian Communist fellow-travelers and partially diminished the strength of the UAIS-SIAU, but did not seriously weaken the Italo-Slovenian Communist bloc at the time.

When in September 1945 the Communist bloc decided on militant opposition against the AMG in Zone A, its struggle went hand in hand with the bloc's propaganda that the entire zone should be united to Yugoslavia. During the peace negotiations on a future boundary between Italy and Yugoslavia which went on from September 1945 until February 1947, the Communists sent, through their local UAIS-SIAU committees, hundreds of letters, memoranda, and wires to the Council of Foreign Ministers, to different commissions of the Paris peace conference, and to the peace conference itself. They demanded, in the name of the

62. *AC Weekly Bulletin,* 2, no. 49 (Mar. 9, 1946): 5; Elio Apih, "L'atteggiamento dei partiti a Trieste in rapporto alla situazione attuale," *Il Ponte,* 4, no. 4 (Apr. 1948): 331.

63. Apih, *Il Ponte,* 4, 4:334–35.

majority of the people of Zone A and of the entire Julian Region, which they claimed to represent, that the Julian Region be annexed to Yugoslavia. At the same time the Communist bloc attacked the AMG, accusing it of pro-Italian feelings and of favoring Italian claims to the Julian Region. The UAIS-SIAU organized big demonstrations in Zone A on behalf of Yugoslavia, especially in Trieste and Gorizia. Often during such manifestations they came to bloody clashes with the civil and military police, in which many people were wounded and some killed.

The surprising fact remains that in this campaign the entire Communist bloc of Italians and Slovenes formed a united front in the Julian Region. One cannot ascribe this unity to the Slovenian Communists having won control over all the local Italian Communists, for, when the Cominform condemned Tito in 1948, the pro-Yugoslav Communists in Zone A remained very much a minority. Nor does another argument—that prior to February 1947 the Slovenian Communist position was stronger because the future destiny of the region had not yet been determined—explain this unity either, though the point may be of some value.

The real cause of the unity might have come from a higher directive of the Soviet Union. Unfortunately, a study has not been made to throw light on this question, in the manner of Metod Mikuž's survey of the relations between the Yugoslav (Slovenian) and Italian Communist parties during the war. A pamphlet published by the Serbian Communist party after the Cominform condemnation of the Yugoslav party does, however, give some clues, though it must be studied with caution.[64]

In October 1944 the Italian Communist party had agreed to occupation of the entire Julian Region by Tito's forces. But withdrawal of Tito's Yugoslav army from Zone A and subsequent occupation of the zone by Anglo-American troops may have changed this understanding. If the Communist party of Italy, after Yugoslav withdrawal from Zone A, were to continue to favor union of the entire Julian Region with Yugoslavia, the Italian party would lose followers in Italy. It would be attacked by Italian bourgeois parties for supporting a cause against the interests of the Italian nation. To save the prestige of the Italian Com-

64. The pamphlet *Pitanje Trsta u svjetlosti novih dogadjaja* was written by M. K. Bulajić.

munist party the Soviet Union probably agreed that the Italian party was free to fight for such parts of the Julian Region as had an Italian majority, especially Trieste. Such a position would avoid Italian bourgeois attacks on the Italian party and the latter would retain popular support. On the other hand, Soviet Russia remained interested in extending Communist control as far west as possible. For that reason she continued supporting Yugoslav claims to the entire Julian Region. All Italian, Slovenian, and Croat Communists of the Julian Region followed this Soviet policy even though the Communist party in Italy might seek to claim Trieste and parts of the Julian Region. Hence a wish, if not an order, from Stalin might have been fundamental for the formation of the united front. In this way the Communists of the Julian Region proved that they valued a Communist victory more highly than the defense of their national (ethnic) interests.

The facts described in the above-mentioned pamphlet confirm this theory. Up to the time of the Yugoslav retreat from Zone A there were three Communist parties in the Julian Region, the Slovenian, Croat, and Italian. After the Yugoslav evacuation a new single Communist Party of Venezia Giulia (CPVG) was founded on August 13, 1945. The same year, on September 24, the Central Committee of the new party declared itself in favor of annexation of the entire Julian Region, and especially of Trieste, to Yugoslavia. The Italian Communist party in Rome in a letter of September 30, 1945, condemned this decision. It demanded that disposition of the city of Trieste be left to the Conference of Foreign Ministers, which was meeting at that moment in London.[65]

From this time on the Communist Party of Venezia Giulia supported Yugoslav claims to the entire Julian Region. On an international level the Soviet Union also upheld Yugoslav pretensions. The Italian party, on the other hand, sustained Italian claims to the parts of the Julian Region where Italians were in the majority. Thus a policy was established which supported the extension of Communist rule as far west as possible and at the same time permitted freedom of action for the Italian party in order not to damage its position at home.

65. Ibid., pp. 18–21.

YUGOSLAV ADMINISTRATION OF ZONE B

According to the Belgrade agreement of June 9, 1945, the eastern part of the Julian Region, known as Zone B, remained under Yugoslav occupation. However, it had to be administered as a separate unit until the peace conference could decide on its ultimate disposition.

The Communist administration based on the National Liberation committees continued, and Zone B remained divided into three parts: the Slovenian Littoral, Croat Istria, and the city of Rijeka. The highest civil authority for each continued to be the Regional National Liberation Committee for the Slovenian Littoral, the Regional National Liberation Committee for Istria, and the City National Liberation Committee for Rijeka. But the regional committees for the Slovenian Littoral and Istria ceased to be subordinate to the Slovenian and Croat governments, respectively. Instead, the Military Administration of the Yugoslav Army (Vojaška uprava jugoslovanske armade) became the supreme authority over all of Zone B, supervising and coordinating the work of the National Liberation committees. The head of the Yugoslav military administration, Lt. General Večeslav Holjevec, was directly responsible to and received orders from the Yugoslav government. He also represented Zone B abroad.

The Yugoslav military administration issued orders and decrees for development of the economic and sociopolitical life of the zone. The National Liberation committees executed these directives. But the Yugoslav military administration had direct control over customs, traffic, finances, prices, and over the management of the larger industrial and mining enterprises. It was also the supreme judicial authority.[66]

Whereas the Communist party remained the sole ruler, some seeming concessions were made to other political groups. The Socialist Party of Venezia Giulia and, later, the Independentist Front were allowed to exist. But on the ground that they incited dangerous nationalistic animosities, no other Italian parties were permitted to function.[67]

66. *Slovensko Primorje in Istra*, p. 538.
67. "Annual Report of the Yugoslav Army Military Government on the Administration of the Yugoslav Zone of the Free Territory of

Moreover, because of the Belgrade agreement, Zone B did not participate in the elections for the Yugoslav constituent assembly. When the assembly met on November 29, 1945, on the second anniversary of the formation of AVNOJ, the supreme political body of the Tito movement, some delegates of the National Liberation Movement from Zone B were present, but only as guests. The constituent assembly proclaimed Yugoslavia a socialistic federative republic, and on January 31, 1946, adopted as the new instrument of government a slightly modified version of the Soviet constitution of 1936. None of these measures was introduced in Zone B. Thus, for the time being, the socialization of industry and the collectivization of land was not extended to the zone.

After the first rush of persecutions had subsided, regular people's courts were organized as guardians of the new order. Toward the end of 1945 and in the beginning of 1946 elections were held in different parts of the zone. In the Slovenian Littoral they took place from September 25 onward for those local and district National Liberation committees for which no elections had been held during the war. On November 25, 1945, general elections took place for all of Istria. The voters had only two choices: to vote for a single list, that of the UAIS-SIAU, representing the National Liberation Movement, or to abstain from voting. Out of 137,318 registered voters, 119,830, or 87.26 percent, cast their ballots. This percentage might seem quite high, but not for a Communist-style election, where a 98 to 100 percent turnout is expected. This showed the continued strength of opposition to the new rule. In the municipality of Rijeka elections took place on March 3, 1946. Of 34,625 eligible voters, 32,848 cast ballots, including 2,111 who voted against the candidates of the UAIS-SIAU—again evidence of important opposition in a Communist-led election.[68]

The Yugoslavs, however, used the elections for propaganda purposes, to prove that the Yugoslav military administration was

---

Trieste for the Period 15 September 1947 to 15 September 1948," United Nations, Security Council, Doc. S/1066 (November 4, 1948), pp. 12–13 (mimeographed), hereafter cited as *First Yugoslav Report* (S/1066). The United Nations Security Council documents will be cited as *UNSC*, Doc.

68. *Slovensko Primorje in Istra*, pp. 539–41.

ruling Zone B in accordance with the wishes of the people, while the Allied Military Government in Zone A was going against their desires. Elections were also important as a pro-Yugoslav argument at the peace negotiations. Yugoslavia repeatedly stressed that the majority in Zone B favored a union with her. To support such statements she cited election results in Istria and Rijeka.[69]

Proclaiming the principle of brotherhood of the three nationalities living in Zone B, the new authorities recognized Slovenian, Croatian, and Italian as official languages in the mixed territories, especially in Istria.[70] In no sense, however, did a free press exist; only newspapers supporting the new regime had the right to publish. The government did not formally prohibit religion, but restricted its observance to churches. Moreover, parents who wished to have their children instructed in religion had to sign special application forms. At the same time, school teachers received directives to explain to their pupils that religion, according to Communist theory, was based on mere superstition. The new schoolbooks similarly glorified socialism and explained the struggle for national liberation as a fight for a better social order.[71]

The new authorities entirely reorganized the school system. Previously, during Italian rule, only Italian schools had been allowed in the Julian Region. In the Slovenian Littoral a start toward reopening of Slovenian schools had taken place during the German occupation, and illegal Slovenian schools had flourished in regions under Partisan influence. Now Yugoslav authorities organized Slovenian schools, which developed so rapidly that in 1946 in Zone B of the Slovenian Littoral there were 277 Slovenian elementary schools with 17,986 pupils and 411 teachers, as well as ten secondary schools with 2,432 students and 85 professors.[72] Likewise Croat elementary and secondary schools were organized in Istria and Rijeka. In Istria, during the 1945–46 school year, 259 Croat and 81 Italian elementary schools began instruction. In Rijeka there were, during the same school year, 19 Croat elemen-

69. For this see ibid., p. 543.
70. *First Yugoslav Report* (S/1066), p. 12.
71. "Comments on the Yugoslav Administration in Zone B of the Free Territory of Trieste," *Italian Affairs*, 3, no. 3 (May 1954): 326–28.
72. *Ljudska pravica*, Sept. 21, 1947, p. 5; somewhat different figures are given in *Slovensko Primorje in Istra*, p. 567.

tary schools with 2,778 pupils and 12 Italian schools with 1,998 pupils. Moreover 2,374 Croat and 1,278 Italian students enrolled in the Croat and Italian secondary schools in Rijeka.[73]

In the economic field feverish reconstruction took place to repair damage caused by the war and guerrilla fighting. Work proceeded along lines similar to that in Yugoslavia. On top of efforts of regular authorities to speed recovery in Zone B, youth brigades were organized in the summer of 1946 to build new roads and bridges in place of those destroyed.

Because the Duino agreement had not worked out as planned, many hardships afflicted the economy of Zone B. The Yugoslavs blamed the AMG, with some reason. But the difficulties were also an excuse for the Yugoslav military administration to bring in new measures. For example, the Yugoslav military administration of Zone B introduced a new currency, the Yugoslav lira, or Yugolira, by Order No. 26 of October 18, 1945, on the ground that the AMG was not providing the supply of lire from Trieste as agreed to at Duino. The different currencies in Zone A and Zone B further hindered economic exchange between the two regions.[74] The Morgan line increasingly became a boundary harder to cross than any frontier with Western countries. It was rapidly turning into an iron curtain dividing two systems of life.

The authorities in Zone B abolished the *coloni* system in Istria on November 25, 1945, and by fundamental decisions of July 1 and December 1, 1946, began to partition the land.[75] As a consequence, 3,393 tenants (*coloni*) received 9,621 hectares of land at the expense of 957 landlords, though this amounted to less than three hectares (about seven acres) per family. The abolition of the *coloni* system marked only the end of a feudal institution, long overdue, and not the beginning of collectivization of the land. The land, in fact, was given to the peasant as private property. The step favored Croat and Slovenian peasants against their Italian landlords who resided in the small Istrian towns. Italians laid

---

73. *Slovensko Primorje in Istra*, pp. 564–66. No number of pupils enrolled in the elementary schools is given for Istria, for the 1945–46 school year.

74. Ibid., pp. 571–72; "Comments," *Italian Affairs*, 3, no. 3:324.

75. *First Yugoslav Report* (S/1066), p. 7. The decree of November 25, 1945, is reprinted in *Slovensko Primorje in Istra*, pp. 544–45.

the move to anti-Italian nationalist persecution, but in reality the reform was socioeconomic and tended to benefit the Slavs because they made up the bulk of the lower classes.

Italian complaints are more justified in other instances. The same decree of November 25, 1945, which abolished the *coloni* system voided all the compulsory sales of Croat farms in Istria that had been made at auction after World War I because the owner could not pay state taxes or because of debts to Italian banks. Such land had to be returned to the original owner. The same directive also applied to Italians who had lost their farms, but only if they could prove they had fought in Tito's National Liberation Movement. A second decree returned to the original Slavic form any individual Slavic names that had once been Italianized. Inasmuch as some families had been using Italian names for two or three generations and had begun to regard themselves as Italians the decree might have been unjust to them. But it also corrected the injustice done to so many Slavs, whose family names had been forcibly Italianized by the Fascists.[76]

It is true that introduction of the new social system in Zone B, and especially in Istria, was closely tied to the ethnic question. For centuries the Italian city and town dwellers had presided over the political, economic, and social life of Istria, and the Italian Fascist regime had strengthened this domination. Now the Yugoslav army and the Communist party held the leading roles. As the Italian intelligentsia had been overwhelmingly pro-Fascist or extremely nationalistic, they began to suffer persecution. Without any chance to hold a job, they were forced to leave Zone B. Again, organization of Slav schools left many onetime teachers in Italian schools without employment. These people became embittered enemies of the new order, joined by dispossessed Italian landowners dependent on the *coloni* system.

When Italians did obtain jobs in the administration they had to take secondary posts instead of the places in the top leadership to which they had been accustomed. The Italian press in Zone A

76. Italian authorities Italianized 107,678 Slavic family names with 25,069 decrees. Slavic family names were Italianized even on memorials in cemeteries, according to *Slovensko Primorje in Istra,* p. 564. About Italian complaints see, for example, "Comments," *Italian Affairs,* 3, no. 3:328–29.

and Italy magnified these facts into examples of the persecution of Italians in Istria.

The Italian argument cannot be entirely denied. Indeed, the new social system established in Zone B did not favor Italian privileges and nationalism. The changes, however, resulted primarily from introduction of the new social order, and not only from an anti-Italian policy. Every revolutionary change was directed against the leading class of the old regime, and in Istria the Italians had happened to be that class.

But it was equally true that the new reforms, if not originating in Slavic nationalism, nevertheless strengthened it. In other words, the new reforms and Slavic nationalism were entangled to such a degree that it was, and will be, quite impossible to unravel them.

10

THE PEACE TREATY AND THE FREE TERRITORY OF TRIESTE

At their meeting in Potsdam from July 17 to August 2, 1945, the heads of government of Great Britain, the Soviet Union, and the United States agreed that the first peace treaty after World War II should be concluded with Italy. The Council of Foreign Ministers of these three nations, plus France, began work in September, and by July of the following year had a draft ready for the Paris peace conference.[1] Delegates from the twenty-one states that had been at war with Italy voiced their approval without major change after nearly three months of study.[2] The Council of Foreign Ministers then met again, in New York, during November and December and reaffirmed its satisfaction, whereupon, on February 10, 1947, the delegates of the twenty-one nations officially signed the new peace treaty with Italy. Our attention necessarily turns to the problems they faced in drawing a border between Italy and Yugoslavia. Neither country, to be sure, was happy to accept what some called a *Diktat* of the four Great Powers.

A TREATY IS SIGNED

The first meeting of the Council of Foreign Ministers took place in London from September 11 to October 2, 1945.[3] Both

1. China participated only at the first meeting. Later all the decisions were made solely by the four powers mentioned above.
2. The twenty-one states represented at the Paris peace conference were: Australia, Belgium, Brazil, Canada, China, Czechoslovakia, Ethiopia, France, Great Britain, Greece, Holland, India, New Zealand, Norway, Poland, South Africa, Soviet Union, Ukraine, United States, White Russia, and Yugoslavia.
3. The following section describing the making of the peace treaty is only a summary based, in general, on the Italian work of De Castro, *Il problema di Trieste,* and on the Yugoslav work of Jeri, *Tržaško vprašanje po drugi svetovni vojni.* A good analysis is to be found in Leonard

Italians and Yugoslavs had sent memoranda to the peace conference, and the council resolved to let each explain its views. The vice-president of Yugoslavia and head of its delegation, Edvard Kardelj, presented his country's demands on September 18. The future border, he said, should coincide with the ethnic line between the Italians and the Slovenes. Only for needs of transportation or the economy should there be deviations. As a possible frontier, Kardelj proposed the Austro-Italian border that had existed before the First World War. This line should be altered according to the ethnic principle, in the north in favor of Yugoslavia, and in the south in favor of Italy. Cities and towns of the Julian Region, where Italians were in the majority, were only foreign islands amidst Croat and Slovenian lands. Trieste fitted this description, but Kardelj also claimed the city for economic reasons. The port had grown under the stimulus of its Slovenian hinterland, and should be joined to it. Yugoslavia was prepared, however, to internationalize the port, and to give Trieste a broad autonomy as one of the federal republics of Yugoslavia.[4]

Alcide de Gasperi, the Italian foreign minister, presented the Italian claims on the same day, September 18. Trieste and Gorizia, he stated, were Italian towns acting as the economic and cultural centers of their regions. To safeguard the interests of the cities, their hinterland ought to be under Italian jurisdiction. The Italians proposed as the best solution the Wilson line, dating from the end of World War I. De Gasperi also demanded the basin of the Raša River, in southeastern Istria, east of the Wilson line, in an effort to obtain the region's lignite mines. Yugoslavia, rich in natural resources, would not miss them, he said, while Italy was critically short of coal. Like his Yugoslav counterpart, De Gasperi would accept internationalization of the Trieste port, but with the

---

S. Stein, "The Problem of Trieste since World War II" (unpublished M.A. thesis, University of Chicago, 1949). During the time of the peace negotiations many memoranda, pamphlets, and some books were published by Italian and Yugoslav authorities and by private persons, dealing with Trieste and the Julian Region. An annotated bibliography of both Yugoslav and Italian works was published by Fran Zwitter, *Zgodovinski časopis*, 2–3:259–326.

4. Jeri, pp. 134–35; De Castro, pp. 208–10; Yugoslav demands were elaborated upon in Yugoslavia, *Memorandum* (1945).

city itself remaining under the Italian flag. De Gasperi admitted the sovereignty of Yugoslavia over Rijeka, which had been such a sore point after World War I, but requested that the city be autonomous. He also asked international guarantees for the Italian minority in Zadar.[5]

If Rijeka had declined as a cause of tension, Trieste was ready to take its place, and the Council of Foreign Ministers had a difficult problem to solve. They decided the very next day to unload it onto the shoulders of a commission of experts, composed of members from each of the four Great Powers. The commission was to visit the disputed territory, study the local ethnic and economic conditions, and recommend a border that would leave as few Yugoslavs as possible in Italy, and the minimum number of Italians in Yugoslavia. A deviation from the ethnic principle ought to occur only so far as necessary to assure that all states had equal access to the port for international commercial purposes.

The next meeting of the Council of Foreign Ministers, held in Moscow from December 16 to 26, 1945, primarily dealt with matters of procedure in negotiating treaties, and had little to do with the Julian Region. But East-West tensions, already apparent in the last days of the London meeting, pointed to an end of cooperation among the partners of World War II, and the split had a strong impact on the future of the Julian Region. While Soviet Russia would continue support for Yugoslav claims, the Western powers became reluctant to cede more land to the Communist bloc and were brought to the point of defending their onetime enemy Italy, against their old ally Yugoslavia.

The Council of Foreign Ministers on January 18, 1946, appointed a council of substitutes to remain in session in London and act in their stead, and on March 2 the substitutes announced selection of the commission of experts.[6] The commission began

5. De Castro, pp. 210–13; Jeri, pp. 136–37. For more details on Italian claims see collection of Italian documents in *Frontière Italo-Yugoslave*, pp. 9–32.

6. The heads of the four delegations composing the commission of experts were: Jean Wolfrom for France, C. H. Waldock for Great Britain, V. Gerashenko for the Soviet Union, and Philip Mosely for the United States. (See Jacques Leprette, *Le Statut international de Trieste* [Paris, 1949], p. 40, n. 3.)

0 5 10 15 20 25
miles
AUSTRIA
Villach
Klagenfurt
Tarvisio
KANAL VALLEY
ITALY
VENETIAN SLOVENIA
Soča-Isonzo
Kobarid
Tolmin
Bača
YUGOSLAVIA
Udine
Ljubljana
Idrija
Gorizia
Gradisca
Ajdovščina
Vipava
Vipava
SLOVENIA
Monfalcone
Duino
Postojna
Trieste
Št. Peter
Koper
Piran
Buje
CROATIA
Novigrad
ISTRIA
Opatija
Rijeka
Pazin
QUARNERO
Raša
ADRIATIC
SEA
Pula
Julian Region
Boundary proposals 1946
Austro-Italian boundary 1866-1918
Italo-Yugoslav border 1924
Austrian border 1920
Morgan line
American proposal
British proposal
French proposal
Russian proposal
Italian offer
Yugoslav claims

work in Trieste on March 9 and remained in the Julian Region until April 5. But when it ended its deliberations it could do no more than recommend four different solutions, each reflecting the national bias of the experts who suggested it.

The boundary proposed by the Russian experts was almost identical to that claimed by Yugoslavia. The next line to the east was that set forth by the French—the nearest to the old Austro-Italian border of the days before the First World War. In fact, in the north, along the Soča River, the French line was almost identical to that border. In the south it left ethnically Italian territory to Italy. The Kanal Valley, Venetian Slovenia, and the cities of Gorizia and Trieste would remain in Italy, while almost all of Istria, as well as the city of Rijeka, would go to Yugoslavia.

The British and American experts followed the French line closely between the Austrian border and Trieste, but otherwise tended to award more land to Italy. The British would give her the western shore of Istria; the Americans, whose line was farthest of all to the east, would also allot her the southern tip of the peninsula. Even so, the American solution ran west of the Wilson line demanded by Italy.[7]

Without a doubt the French line fitted most closely with the idea of balanced minorities. This principle, recommended by the Council of Foreign Ministers as a guidepost for setting up future borders, could be easily applied where two national states were concerned. Yugoslavia, however, was multinational. To utilize the principle of equal minorities through the French proposal would favor the Croats and discriminate against the Slovenes. The Croats would gain jurisdiction over a considerable part of the Italian minority in Istria, Rijeka, and Zadar, and there would be no Croats left in Italy. On the other hand, the entire Yugoslav minority remaining in Italy would be Slovenian, with almost no Italians left in Slovenia. In short, the Slovenian minority in Italy would pay for the Croatian gains in Istria. The Russian line would leave no Yugoslav minority at all in Italy. The British and American lines would preserve a small Italian minority in Yugoslavia, but not enough to balance the Yugoslav minority remaining in Italy.

7. The four proposals are reprinted in *Frontière Italo-Yugoslave,* pp. 47–67. See also Jeri, pp. 145–49; De Castro, pp. 231–39.

A TREATY IS SIGNED

The Council of Foreign Ministers studied the experts' report at their third meeting, this time in Paris. The first of two sessions took place from April 25 to May 16, 1946, and during this time the ministers again asked Yugoslavia and Italy to state their positions. Neither expressed satisfaction. Kardelj, the Yugoslav vice-president, pointed out on May 3 that, by the Western solution, both Gorizia and Trieste would go to Italy, thus destroying the economic unity of the Julian Region by cutting the rural sections away from their administrative and economic centers. Besides, Trieste could be connected to Italy only by passing over a strip of land settled entirely by Slovenes. Yugoslavia, said Kardelj, would continue to demand the same line as she had proposed to the London conference.[8]

The Italian foreign minister De Gasperi remarked that none of the proposals accepted the Wilson line desired by Italy. He emphasized, of course, that the American line was closest to Italian wishes, but perceived with sorrow that no attention was paid to the loss by Italy of Rijeka, Zadar, and the islands of Cres and Lošinj. Though officially Italy still clung to the Wilson line, De Gasperi indicated that his country would be prepared to discuss a compromise between the Wilson and American lines.[9]

By the middle of May, at the end of the first session of the Council of Foreign Ministers' meeting in Paris, it became apparent that the French line was the best compromise solution. Even so, it was in principle agreed by the Great Powers only to accept, for the moment, that portion running from the Austrian border to the Adriatic Sea, near Monfalcone. The disputed section to the south, including the most important city of Trieste, remained for decision after a month of recess. The United States insisted that the city go to Italy, and the Soviet Union that it should become a part of Yugoslavia.

The Council of Foreign Ministers resumed operations on June 15, 1946, until the middle of July, and on July 3 publicly announced its solution. Italy would cede to Yugoslavia all territory east of the French line. Land west of that line would remain Italian from the Austrian border to the Adriatic, north of Duino

8. Jeri, pp. 150–51; De Castro, pp. 243–46.
9. De Gasperi's talk is reprinted in De Castro, pp. 247–50.

PEACE TREATY

and near Monfalcone. The entire region south of Duino and west of the French line would form an independent Free Territory of Trieste (FTT), whose integrity and independence would be guaranteed by the Security Council of the United Nations. A special commission of members of the four Great Powers, after conferring with representatives of both the Yugoslav and Italian peoples, would formulate proposals for the peace conference, and send them through the conference to the Security Council and General Assembly of the United Nations, on the administration of the FTT as well as the statute, or fundamental laws, on which the administration would be based. The following procedures were to be maintained: (1) A governor of the FTT would be appointed by the Security Council, after previous consultations with Yugoslavia and Italy; (2) legislative and executive branches of the government would be established according to democratic principles, and in particular through universal suffrage; (3) protection of the rights of citizens, especially the rights of man and his fundamental liberties, would be observed, as would rights regarding religion, language, press, instruction, and free access to public office.[10]

In summary, this decision of the Council of Foreign Ministers assigned most of the Julian Region to Yugoslavia. The Kanal Valley and Venetian Slovenia, claimed by the Yugoslavs, did, however, remain under Italy, and Italy also retained the city of Gorizia, but almost all of the territory of Gorizia Province went to Yugoslavia. Accordingly, Italy lost the Istrian western coast, consisting of many small towns, and three larger cities: Pula, Rijeka, and Zadar, all having an Italian majority. The stormy question of Trieste was to be resolved by creating a small international territory, guaranteed by the United Nations Security Council, thus avoiding assignment of it to either Yugoslavia or Italy.

Neither contender was pleased, the greatest regret on both sides centering about formation of the Free Territory of Trieste. Both Italy and Yugoslavia opposed it vehemently and still hoped to obtain the important city for themselves. But the entire pro-

10. The announcement regarding the creation of the Free Territory of Trieste is reprinted in De Castro, pp. 270–72. See also Jeri, pp. 157–58.

posal had yet to be approved by the peace conference, and it was here that the rivals sought to change the decision of the Council of Foreign Ministers.

The internationalization of Trieste was a typical compromise of the Great Powers—a result of the slow crystallization into Western and Eastern blocs. Giving Trieste to Italy would mean exclusive use by the Western bloc of this important northern Adriatic port, and Russia was thus opposed. To assign Trieste to Yugoslavia would bring it under the domain of the Eastern bloc, to the dismay of the Western powers, especially the United States and Great Britain. Creation of an international territory would give both East and West a chance to use the port. Thus, out of the disputed city and its immediate surroundings emerged a no-man's land.[11]

Representatives of the twenty-one nations of the peace conference met in Paris from July 29 to October 15, 1946. Each had the right to introduce new ideas in regard to the Italo-Yugoslav border. The question was discussed before the plenary sessions and Political Territorial Commission of the peace conference, with both Yugoslavia and Italy trying to secure a correction in the border compromise.

Yugoslavia was ready to reduce her demands to the eastern halves of the Kanal Valley and Venetian Slovenia. However, the Yugoslavs claimed the city of Gorizia, arguing that it should not be separated from the rest of the province by an artificial border. Yugoslavia also objected to a territorial link between the Free Territory and Italy. According to the Yugoslavs, the land between Trieste and the future Italian border near Duino was, ethnically speaking, completely Slovenian and had no Italian minority. Yugoslavia was prepared to recognize Trieste as an international zone, whose territory would be limited to the city and suburbs. This internationally guaranteed autonomous city should, however remain in *l'union réelle* with Yugoslavia. Yugoslav efforts thus went in two directions. First, they sought to limit the Free Territory to the city itself, the rest going to Yugoslavia. Second, they hoped to have the internationally recognized city retain a close

11. The same idea about the Trieste problem was expressed by the British review *Economist* as early as May 11, 1946.

legal and economic tie with Yugoslavia, and be surrounded on all sides by Yugoslav soil.

Italy on the other hand sought a correction of that part of the French line which ran along the Soča (Isonzo) River. The future boundary should pass on the eastern side of the Soča, instead of the western, leaving to Italy an important electric power station on the river. In regard to creation of the Free Territory, Italy likewise had two objectives. First, she tried to postpone the solution for a year. This move, according to Yugoslav sources, was taken in the hope that by that time Italy's international position would be improved, as the result of increased tension between East and West. Second, Italy sought to enlarge the area of the Free Territory to include the entire western coast of Istria as far south as, and including, the city of Pula.[12]

There were many other proposed solutions of this difficult problem.[13] But those of neither Yugoslavia nor Italy, the directly interested states, nor any advanced by other participating states was accepted by the peace conference. On September 28, 1946, the Political Territorial Commission adopted the proposal of the Council of Foreign Ministers with twelve votes in favor, five against, and three abstentions. During the night of October 9 and

12. Jeri, pp. 158-69; De Castro, pp. 283-90, 292-331.

13. Among the many proposals for a new frontier between Yugoslavia and Italy was one made by the Action Committee for a United and Sovereign Slovenian State, a Slovenian anti-Communist group in Rome. This Action Committee submitted, in the summer of 1946, a "Memorandum on the Problem of Trieste and Northern Adriatic to the Allied Governments Concerned" to the ambassadors of the Great Powers in Rome, proposing the creation of a north Adriatic state as the immediate economic hinterland of Trieste. The new state was to include all of the Republic of Slovenia (part of Yugoslavia), all of the Julian Region, Austrian Carinthia, and part of Udine Province (Friuli) which would include the rail and road connections between Trieste and Villach. The state was to be organized on the model of Switzerland's cantons so as to assure all of the five ethnic groups involved (Austrian Germans, Croats, Friulians, Italians, and Slovenes) complete equality. The new territory was estimated to contain about 40,000 square kilometers and about 2,600,000 population—1,600,000 Slovenes, 300,000 Italians, 200,000 Friulians, 200,000 Croats, and 300,000 Austrian Germans.

A TREATY IS SIGNED

10, 1946, the plenary session of the peace conference also ratified the measure, with fourteen votes in favor, five against, and two abstentions. All of the four Great Powers, including the Soviet Union, voted for the proposal agreed upon by the territorial commission.[14]

With regard to a statute for the Free Territory, the Council of Foreign Ministers gave only general directions in its decision of July 2, 1946. Preparation of the statute was to be the duty of a special commission appointed by the Council of Foreign Ministers on July 3, 1946. The Western powers, fearing possible Yugoslav domination of the assembly and consequent forcible annexation of the FTT by Yugoslavia, stood for a strong governor with near dictatorial powers, and a weak assembly. The Soviet Union, on the other hand, upheld a strong assembly with a government responsible to the assembly, and for a weak governor. The special commission could not agree on a single answer. Again, as in the case of the border, every one of the four Great Powers prepared its own proposal. Great Britain gave most of the control to the governor. The United States proposal came closest to that of the British, though the rights of the governor were not so wide as the British would allow. France tried to solve the problem by giving the governor strong powers in time of crises, while in normal times the assembly and governor would share control.

On July 18, 1946, Aleš Bebler submitted a fifth proposal on behalf of the Yugoslavs, conforming to their demands about Trieste. It stated that a smaller territory of Trieste should be represented by Yugoslavia in international affairs, and that it have Yugoslav tariffs, money, and railroads, as well as postal, telephone, and telegraph systems. All the power would rest in an elected assembly, which would also appoint the administrative council.

The five projects were presented to the Political Territorial Commission of the peace conference, which accepted the French proposal on October 3, 1946, with fourteen votes in favor and six opposed. Here the Soviet Union voted against the French plan, not being bound by a previous agreement of the Council of Foreign Ministers. Yugoslavia and Italy gained permission once more to explain their position on the future of the statute, before the final decisions on the peace treaty were made. The plenary session

14. Jeri, pp. 168–69.

of the peace conference of October 9-10, 1946, which accepted the future boundary, also adopted the French proposal on the statute with fifteen votes in favor and six opposed.[15] So, by the end of the Paris peace conference on October 15, 1946, the future Italo-Yugoslav boundary had been decided, as was the statute for the future Free Territory of Trieste. Still pending was confirmation by the Council of Foreign Ministers of the final wording of the proposed peace treaty.

From the end of July 1946 until the beginning of the final meeting of the Council of Foreign Ministers in November 1946, Italy and Yugoslavia sought to reach an agreement directly between themselves. However, neither was willing to come closer to a workable compromise. Besides, the United States and Great Britain opposed such direct dealings. Both were unwilling to change any decision that had been accepted already by the Council of Foreign Ministers, and bilateral Italo-Yugoslav negotiations had begun after July 2, 1946, the date on which the Foreign Ministers had agreed to the new boundary.

Part of the direct Italo-Yugoslav negotiations involved the meeting in Belgrade of the Italian Communist leader, Palmiro Togliatti, with Marshal Tito, between the third and fifth of November 1946, just when the Council of Foreign Ministers had begun its sessions in New York. Togliatti proposed an exchange in which Italy would give up Gorizia for Trieste. Yugoslavia was prepared for such a trade, according to the Slovenian political scientist Janko Jeri, if the Italian government would grant a special statute for Trieste, in which Italy would guarantee economic privileges to Yugoslavia and secure minority rights for the Slovenes. After his return, on November 6, 1946, Togliatti published the substance of his talks with Tito in his newspaper *L'Unità*. But the next day the Italian government issued a statement refusing further discussion of this proposal.[16]

The Council of Foreign Ministers, meeting in New York from November 4 to December 12, 1946, first heard the recommendations of the Yugoslav and Italian delegations on the future of the FTT. Stanoje Simić, head of the Yugoslav deputation, tried again

15. Ibid., pp. 169-73; De Castro, pp. 276-78,.290-92.
16. De Castro, pp. 340-42; Jeri, pp. 180-83.

to narrow the territory of the FTT to the city of Trieste. He also criticized the peace treaty for cutting off the city of Gorizia from its provincial territory. The Italian Foreign Minister Pietro Nenni, leader of the left-wing socialists, demanded a plebiscite for all disputed areas in the Julian Region. If the plebiscite were refused, then the western coast of Istria, up to and including Pula, should be united with the FTT—a demand that had been requested in Paris by the Italian delegation. After hard bargaining, by which the Soviet Union tried to achieve some changes in favor of Yugoslavia, the Council of Foreign Ministers approved the draft of the peace treaty, together with the statute for the Free Territory of Trieste.[17]

On February 10, 1947, the representatives of the twenty-one nations participating in the peace conference met again in Paris and signed the treaty with Italy. Before affixing his signature, Yugoslav Foreign Minister Simić gave an official statement, in the name of his government, that the nations of Yugoslavia did not, by signing the document, renounce the territories they regarded as ethnically theirs, and would continue to claim their right regardless of ethnic changes occurring in the future as a result of foreign domination.[18]

The peace treaty also dissatisfied Italy. Foreign Minister Nenni called in the ambassadors of the four Great Powers in the latter part of January 1947, prior to signing of the peace treaty, and pointed out that not a single Italian request for correction of the Italo-Yugoslav border had been accepted by the Council of Foreign Ministers at its last meeting in New York. He insisted that revision of the peace treaty be made possible through bilateral agreement of Yugoslavia and Italy under the auspices of the United Nations, before Italy would sign the treaty.[19]

Because of the Yugoslav and Italian resistance it was decided that the peace treaty should come into force, regardless of Italian or Yugoslav signature, after the four Great Powers had ratified it and deposited the papers with the French government in Paris. This was done September 15, 1947. Hence, both Italy and Yugoslavia had good reason to claim that the peace treaty was imposed

17. Jeri, pp. 183–84; De Castro, pp. 333–40, 344–49.
18. Jeri, pp. 183–85.   19. De Castro, pp. 349–50.

by the four Great Powers and had not been achieved through free and direct agreement of the two interested neighboring states.

LOBBYING IN SOUND AND FURY

The peace negotations, lasting from September 1945 to February 1947, had an especial impact on the local situation in Zone A, with the Italian political parties of the CLN supporting the Italian claims, and the pro-Communist bloc represented by the UAIS-SIAU backing the Yugoslav demands. Both blocs staged great manifestations whenever important decisions were in the making: when the Council of Foreign Ministers met in London in September 1945, during the visit of the commission of experts in the latter part of March and the first part of April 1946, and during the meeting of the Council of Foreign Ministers in Paris in June and July 1946. Relative calm prevailed, however, during the meeting of the peace conference in August and September of the same year.

In the beginning the initiative seemed to be on the pro-Communist side, but with the passing of time the Italian bloc gained in strength. After July 2, 1946, when creation of the Free Territory of Trieste was accepted by the Council of Foreign Ministers, an independentist movement came into being, favoring internationalization of Trieste, and standing between the two main hostile blocs, the Italians and pro-Communists. Its position was difficult and it never mustered enough strength to play a decisive role in the local (FTT) or international situation. The major battle continued to rage between the Italian and Communist blocs. It was fought mainly in Trieste, the largest and most disputed city, though similar struggles went on in Pula and Gorizia.[20]

The first big pro-Communist manifestation was perfectly timed, for it erupted on the same day, September 11, 1945, that the Council of Foreign Ministers opened discussions in London. In the village of Basovizza, near Trieste, where eighty thousand Slovenes had gathered, the UAIS-SIAU and its mass organizations unveiled a monument to Slovenian victims condemned by Fascist Italy, at the very place where they had been shot. The dedication

20. The origins of the independentist idea and movement are described below, this chapter, next section.

closely coincided with the anniversary of the Italian surrender of 1943 and the proclamation by the Slovenian Liberation Front of unification of the Slovenian Littoral with Yugoslavia. According to Yugoslav accounts, about sixteen hundred telegrams went to the Council of Foreign Ministers that day, reminding it that the people of the Slovenian Littoral had decided two years ago to be united with Yugoslavia; their underground fight on behalf of Yugoslavia from that time until the end of the war was ample testimony to their persistence.[21]

Later in the same month, as the Council of Ministers continued to meet, the Communist bloc proclaimed a two-day strike. Though laid to economic motives, the strike may well be said to have been organized to show the power of the pro-Yugoslav Communist bloc in the center of Trieste. One of the biggest shipbuilding establishments in the city, for want of orders, had discharged 3,400 workers. The Communists claimed that Yugoslavia had placed orders for two years in advance and the dismissal was due to capitalistic intrigue—hence the strike. On the last day of the walkout, September 25, some 200,000 workers are said, by Yugoslav sources, to have paraded through the streets of Trieste.[22]

As mentioned, the first Italian countermanifestation to celebrate the holiday of the city patron, on November 3, 1945, was weak. The pro-Communists answered with a giant demonstration on November 4, demanding unification of the entire Julian Region, including Trieste, with Yugoslavia. This time 150,000 people took part.[23]

The visit of the commission of experts to the Julian Region gave the Italian bloc a chance to let off steam, and fights broke out with the pro-Communists.[24] The commission arrived in Trieste on

21. *Slovensko Primorje in Istra,* p. 639.

22. Ibid., p. 638; *AC Weekly Bulletin,* 2, no. 29 (Oct. 20, 1945): 4–5. The strike took place on September 23 and 24. There was no violence according to the AMG report.

23. *AC Weekly Bulletin,* 2, no. 49 (Mar. 9, 1946): 5; *Slovensko Primorje in Istra,* p. 638. Besides being the holiday of San Giusto, November 3 coincided with the end of World War I and the victorious entry of Italian troops into Trieste.

24. Lunt, *Army Quarterly,* 58, no. 2:215; Bowman, *Military Government Journal,* 1, no. 8:14. *AC Weekly Bulletin,* 3, no. 1 (Apr. 6,

March 7, 1946, and went to both Zones A and B. It received hundreds of memoranda from individual persons, institutions, political parties, and blocs, proposing different solutions. Italians demanding unification with Italy and Communist and pro-Communist organizations seeking unification with Yugoslavia staged huge demonstrations in Trieste, Gorizia, and Pula to show they expressed the will of the people. But the principal source of trouble was Trieste. Because of constant obstruction of the Allied Military Government by the UAIS-SIAU, tension flared often between the police and the pro-Communist masses. During a manifestation on March 10, 1946, in a suburb of Trieste, two persons were killed and about twenty-two wounded in a shooting incident. In protest, the Communist bloc staged another two-day general strike. On the last day, March 12, about 250,000 persons, according to Yugoslav reports, marched in the funeral procession for the victims.[25]

These events were used to show the commission of experts how the Allied Military Government was persecuting the pro-Yugoslav groups in Zone A. Italian political parties countered this evidence by presenting data on the persecution of Italians in Zone B by the Yugoslav administration. Diego de Castro, onetime Italian adviser to the AMG in Trieste, writes that while the commission traveled through Zone B, the Italians did not have a chance to organize manifestations for Italy. However, many Italian women in the town of Piran painted an Italian flag on the palms of their hands, and when the commission passed they opened their fists to show the Italian colors, in order to testify to their pro-Italian sentiments. The greatest Italian manifestations took place toward the end of the commission's stay in Trieste. On March 25–27, almost all of the non-Communist Italian population went into the streets, forming a mass of over 100,000 people to demand that Trieste be unified with Italy.[26]

1946): 7, printed a telephone report of April 4 from Trieste according to which there were twelve demonstrations of a major kind between March 24 and April 1. The AMG police arrested 548 persons; 150 civilians, nine native police officers and one Allied officer were injured. A large store of weapons of all kinds was seized by the police.

25. *Slovensko Primorje in Istra,* pp. 639–40.
26. De Castro, p. 231, n. 1.

Many anecdotes point up the dramatic nature of events during the commission's visit. A pro-Yugoslav account states that the Italians, having announced that their countrymen were fleeing Zone B, especially Istria, in great numbers, had prepared apartments and railroad cars in which to house them. But when the commission came to see these exiles, the apartments and railroad cars were empty.[27]

When the commission visited an ethnically mixed village, the pro-Communist bloc organized manifestations for Yugoslavia. The people were found repeating a slogan in Slovenian: "We want to join Yugoslavia." But the voices were too low, forcing Italian Communist leaders to encourage the people with a "Più forte, più forte" ("Louder, louder") in Italian. The commission immediately inquired about the language of the people. Too great a zeal of the Communists on behalf of Yugoslavia did not always work to their advantage.

After the departure of the commission of experts, the May Day celebration of 1946 provided the occasion for a great turnout of pro-Communist forces. Hundreds of telegrams were sent to the Council of Foreign Ministers, which was now meeting in Paris. Afterwards, a special delegation from the Slovenian Littoral and Istria, headed by France Bevk, former president of the Slovenian Liberation Front, came to Paris to support the Yugoslav claims. The delegation tried to reach the foreign ministers, and publicized the Yugoslav claims to influence French public opinion, before going on to Belgium. It tried to visit Great Britain also, but was refused a visa.[28]

During the second session of the Council of Foreign Ministers' meeting in Paris, at a time when the final compromise was being reached on the Italo-Yugoslav border, great disturbances occurred again in Trieste. The blocs, now equally strong, began to clash with each other. In the latter part of June 1946, Italian right-wing elements attacked Slovenian stores and offices of pro-Communist organizations. The Communist bloc in Trieste retaliated. In one such clash in the Trieste suburb of San Giacomo, police opened fire and one worker was slain and two wounded. The UAIS-SIAU proclaimed a general strike the same day, June 30. While the

---

27. *Slovensko Primorje in Istra*, p. 519.
28. Ibid., pp. 525–27, 641.

strike was still in effect, on July 3, 1946, the Council of Foreign Ministers announced its decision concerning the new Italo-Yugoslav border and the creation of a Free Territory. Now both sides attacked the Allied Military Government which represented Great Britain and the United States. The Italians organized huge demonstrations, while the general strike proclaimed by the Communists continued. The Italian demonstrators shouted such slogans as "Down with the Allied traitors!" "Get out of Italy and let us settle the score!" and "Why don't you go back to America?" However, the Italian political parties continued to cooperate with the AMG. And, while huge manifestations were organized by the Communists in the center of Trieste, protesting police "brutality" and the decision of the Council of Foreign Ministers, the strike came to an end at midnight of July 12.[29]

In fact, after the middle of July the great demonstrations had begun to decline. But rumors spread that Yugoslavia was concentrating her armed forces on the border of Zone B. If Yugoslavia were denied any part of the Julian Region, so it was said, her troops would enter Zone A. Such rumors heightened tension along the line separating Zones A and B, and after many incidents, the border had to be closed, becoming, in effect, the southern extension of the Iron Curtain. During the latter part of July and in August 1946, tension between the Western Allies and Yugoslavia increased still further, leaving the local population of Zone A in a state of extreme insecurity. The rumors that Yugoslavia had concentrated her forces along the border of Zone B were countered by a Yugoslav accusation that Great Britain and the United States had moved the Polish troops of General Anderson, stationed in Italy, toward the Julian Region. These Poles, fighting as part of the Eighth Army against the Germans in Italy during the war, had refused to return home. They were permeated with anti-Communist sentiment and were therefore hated by the Italian and Yugoslav Communists. The Yugoslav government protested that the Polish troops had given support to Yugoslav royalist groups, especially to the Chetniks, who had retreated to Italy after the war.

29. Ibid., pp. 530, 642–44; *AC Weekly Bulletin*, 3, no. 12 (July 6, 1946): 2; no. 13 (July 13, 1946): 3–4; no. 14 (July 20, 1946): 5–6; "Masochists," *Time*, July 15, 1946, p. 33.

THE INDEPENDENCE FRONT

Rumors about concentration of Yugoslav and Allied forces increased Yugoslav sensibility toward the unauthorized flights of American planes over Yugoslav territory. The Yugoslavs regarded this action as an effort to intimidate them and their allies, the Communist forces in Zone A. In a protest note to the American government, Yugoslavia listed 172 such unauthorized flights from July 16 to August 8, 1946. Two incidents finally occurred, the forced landing of an American airplane early in August and the shooting down of another on August 19.[30] These incidents, however, did not help the Yugoslav cause. Western public opinion condemned the Yugoslav action against the planes, and the Italian press in Zone A used the incident to its advantage, pointing out the violent means Yugoslavia was prepared to use to achieve her goals.

From that time through October of 1946, the main struggle for the Julian Region and the city of Trieste was fought in Paris at the peace conference. The population of Zones A and B followed the discussions with great interest in the local newspapers. When it became more and more certain which parts of the Julian Region would go to Yugoslavia, Italy, and the Free Territory, the people calmed down and returned to their everyday tasks. The great demonstrations had abated for the time being.

FORMATION OF THE INDEPENDENCE FRONT

When the foreign ministers agreed on July 2, 1946, to create the Free Territory, the decision brought to life a third bloc in Zone A, favoring independence for Trieste. The idea was not new. It had been proposed by Valentino Pittoni, leader of the Trieste socialists, at the international socialist congress in Trieste as early as 1905. Next, on April 8, 1915, Italy demanded that Austria create a Free Trieste State as a price for Italian neutrality during World War I. Later, in October 1918, Pittoni, in the Austrian Parliament, called for Trieste to be made a neutral state under

---

30. "Protest against Entry of Yugoslav Forces into Zone A," *Department of State Bulletin*, 15 (Sept. 1, 1946): 414–15; "Protest against Yugoslav Attack on American Plane and Detention of American Personnel," ibid., pp. 415–19; "Facts Relating to Flights of American Planes over Yugoslav Territory," ibid., 15 (Sept. 15, 1946): 501–5.

international protection. When the Italian army entered Trieste in November 1918, after World War I, the Trieste socialists still favored an independent Trieste.[31]

The idea was revived during the German occupation in World War II, when creation of the Adriatic Littoral reminded people of the onetime role of Trieste as the main port of central Europe. Again, during the Yugoslav occupation after World War II, certain commercial circles in Trieste foresaw an opening of new markets in Trieste's hinterland.[32] After withdrawal of the Yugoslav troops, these people saw that Trieste could continue its historic role only by remaining neutral and independent.

This viewpoint was held by the independentist movement, composed of two groups, each of which later formed a separate political party, namely Il Fronte dell'Indipendenza (the Independence Front), and Il Blocco Triestino (the Triestino bloc). From 1946 to late 1948, both groups supported the Independence Front which was the first organized.

Teodoro Sporer and Mario Giampiccoli were the leaders of the Independence Front. They expressed their ideas in the newspaper *Il Corriere di Trieste* (the Messenger of Trieste). This loosely organized movement was supported by small shopkeepers and skilled workers, many of whom were former socialists who had supported the independence idea before, during, and after World War I. They cooperated in the Partisan CEAIS and in the CLT. During the period of Yugoslav rule they defended local autonomy. Their presence in the CLT was probably one of the reasons the Yugoslav authorities, at least formally, had granted autonomy to Trieste. After withdrawal of Yugoslav forces from Trieste in June 1945, this group at first favored an autonomous Trieste under Yugoslav sovereignty with an international free port. In March 1946, when the special commission sent by the peace conference visited the Julian Region, *Il Corriere di Trieste* demanded only an autonomous Trieste as part of Yugoslavia. On June 22, 1946, the newspaper published its first article stressing that a Free Territory would be the best solution of the opposing claims and beneficial to the people of Trieste. When the decision of the foreign

31. Silvestri, *Trieste*, no. 21, p. 31, n. 1, and p. 29; see also chapter 2 above.
32. See Quarantotti-Gambini, pp. 103, 169, 216–18.

THE INDEPENDENCE FRONT

ministers to create a Free Territory became known on July 3, 1946, *Il Corriere di Trieste* greeted it with great enthusiasm.

The second group, which later formed the Triestino bloc, was composed of owners of small private stores and industrial and financial establishments. Their leader was Mario Stocca. While the Independence Front represented a leftist trend within the independence movement, the second group was its right wing. Yet this latter faction had supported the Partisans with money during the war. They were, however, now frightened by Partisan totalitarian methods and by economic measures during the forty days of Yugoslav occupation in 1945. In order to preserve the established social order and at the same time retain economic ties with Trieste's hinterland, they favored a Free Territory.

Italians attacked both independence groups. Favoring an independent Trieste, according to the Italians, meant taking an anti-Italian position. The Italians further asserted that Yugoslavia supported *Il Corriere di Trieste* with over one hundred million lire each year in order to strengthen anti-Italian sentiment.

The second group, the Triestino bloc of Mario Stocca, was described by Italians as influenced by the "old Austro-Hungarian nostalgia" and encouraged by "some high English functionaries."[33]

POST-TREATY POLITICAL MANEUVERS

After the signing of the peace treaty on February 10, 1947, preparations were made to divide Zones A and B among Yugoslavia, Italy, and the Free Territory of Trieste. The future border must now be transferred from maps to the terrain itself. Great Britain and the United States invited Italy and Yugoslavia to send representatives to Trieste, where on February 28, 1947, a commission to establish the provisional boundary was formed. In order not to cut individual homes or properties into two parts, the commission could establish the future border within about a one-mile radius.

The new body encountered many obstacles in the face of nationalistic emotions of both Italians and Yugoslavs. As the line

33. De Castro, pp. 600–603; Corrado Belci, "L'indipendentismo a Trieste," *Trieste*, no. 9 (Sept.–Oct. 1955), pp. 6–9; "La storia segreta de *Il Corriere di Trieste*," *Trieste*, no. 36 (Mar.–Apr. 1960), pp. 7–11.

was being established on the west side of the Soča (Isonzo) River, a member of the Italian delegation could not resist weeping, remembering the great battles the Italians had fought to gain this territory, in which he had participated. The work of this commission was especially difficult in that it had to divide the ethnically Slovenian territory of Gorizia Province. During the day the commission agreed on the future border by placing white pillars in the ground. When it returned the next day to continue the work, the pillars had disappeared, or had been transferred during the night toward the west by the local population.[34]

Other commissions were also formed to deal with the transfer of public and private property, and to examine the economic possibilities of the newly created Free Territory of Trieste.

According to the peace treaty, most of Zone B of the Julian Region was to go to Yugoslavia. The only exceptions were two districts of northwestern Istria, which would be part of the Free Territory of Trieste. One, the Koper district, was Slovenian, and the other, the Buje district, was Croat, though each had a strong Italian population centered in the towns and surrounding area. The supreme civil authority for the Koper district had been in the hands of the Regional National Liberation Committee for the Slovenian Littoral; in the Buje district authority had been embodied in the Regional Committee for Istria. Both agreed in the latter part of February 1947, to create, out of the two districts, a new Istrian Region, and to place its supreme civil authority in a Regional People's Executive Committee.[35]

In August 1947, a Regional People's Assembly of thirty-five representatives from the Koper district and twenty-five from the Buje district met and elected the executive committee of fifteen members, including seven Italians, five Slovenes, and three Croats. Six were workers, four peasants, two intellectuals, two shopkeepers, and one a fisherman.[36]

These two districts of Zone B of the Julian Region were to

34. Taken from an interview (Aug. 1949) with Mr. Josip Pavlin, a Yugoslav member of the commission; *Slovensko Primorje in Istra,* p. 534.

35. Note that two years after the war the old terminology was changed from National Liberation committee to People's committee both in Yugoslavia and in Zone B.

36. *Slovensko Primorje in Istra,* p. 651.

Julian Region 1945-1947

Map legend:

- Austro-Italian boundary 1866-1918
- Austrian border 1920
- Italo-Yugoslav border 1924
- Italo-Yugoslav border 1947
- Italo-Yugoslav border since 1954
- Boundary of Free Territory of Trieste (FTT) 1947-1954
- Morgan line
- Slovenian-Croat boundary

- Zone A of Julian Region
- Zone B of Julian Region
- Zone A of Free Territory of Trieste (FTT)
- Zone B of Free Territory of Trieste (FTT)

Locations: Villach, Klagenfurt, Tarvisio, Kanal Valley, Venetian Slovenia, Udine, Gorizia, Gradisca, Monfalcone, Trieste, Koper, Piran, Umag, Buje, Istria, Pula, Rijeka, Quarnero

Regions: Italy, Austria, Yugoslavia, Slovenia, Croatia, Adriatic Sea

form in the future the Yugoslav Zone (B) of the Free Territory of Trieste, and would remain under Yugoslav military administration. The Yugoslav authorities thus tried to assure continuation of the newly established Communist order in the future Yugoslav Zone of the FTT.

The rest of Zone B of the Julian Region, already under Yugoslav military administration, preserved the Communist civil government that had been introduced during the war. Hence, no important transformation was needed to prepare the territory for annexation to Yugoslavia. The official introduction of Yugoslav law, and the incorporation of the zone into the Yugoslav Five Year Plan were more a formality than a real change in the established economic and social structure. But at least now the Communist regime and the socialist order became internationally recognized facts.

Zone A of the Julian Region was divided into three parts according to the peace treaty. All territory east of the French line was to go to Yugoslavia. Land west of this line was allotted to Italy or the British-American Zone (A) of the Free Territory of Trieste. Though no one knew exactly when the peace treaty would take effect, preparations started for the evacuation of people and movable private property from such territory of Zone A as was to be annexed to Yugoslavia. Many Italians in Pula preferred to go to Italy, or to the British-American Zone of the Free Territory of Trieste, rather than come under Yugoslav rule. Here nationalism played the important role, though many Italians also left for fear of Communist rule. In the same fashion, in the north along the Soča River, many Slovenes also decided to leave their homes. Their decision mostly stemmed from ideological and economic motives—a refusal to live under Communist rule and a socialistic economy. Many went to Italy and later migrated overseas.

The evacuation of Pula began in August 1946. As soon as it became known that the Council of Foreign Ministers had accepted the French line, Italian propaganda urged the Italians to leave Pula, trying to impress on world opinion that Pula was Italian and should go to Italy, or else the entire population would leave the city.[37] The UAIS-SIAU tried to stop this trend, especially the

37. After ten years of Italian exodus from Pula and Istria, for the first time critical voices were heard. Many Italian writers asked them-

removal of machines from the factories, causing many clashes between the UAIS-SIAU and the civil police when the latter protected individual owners in their efforts to move their property. On January 3, 1947, before the peace treaty was ratified, three workers were slain and eight wounded in just such a scuffle. Then, when the peace treaty was actually signed, Italian nationalistic emotions reached such a peak in Pula that a former Fascist, Maria Pasquinelli, assassinated Brigadier General Robin De Winton, commander of the British garrison. But this act did not alter the treaty and the Yugoslav troops entered Pula on September 15, 1947.[38]

When the peace treaty came into force, the Slovenian émigré group which had helped the AMG to organize the Slovenian administration and schools in Zone A lost their jobs in all parts of the zone which went to either Yugoslavia or Italy. Because they opposed the Yugoslav Communist regime, these émigrés refused to submit to Yugoslav jurisdiction. Nor could they stay in Italy, not being Italian citizens, for only the latter could retain the employment given them by the AMG. Many retreated to the British-American Zone of the Free Territory, which still remained under AMG administration. Others, unable to obtain new jobs, migrated to Argentina, Canada, Australia, and later to the United States.

After the signing of the peace treaty, the different political groups in Zone A, knowing now where they stood and no longer fearing reprisals, prepared themselves for action, especially in those parts of the zone going to Italy or the Free Territory of Trieste.

The UAIS-SIAU decided to change its policy, and belatedly offered to cooperate with the AMG in Trieste. The AMG rejected the move, as it would help the Communists to regain positions already lost. The next step of the UAIS-SIAU was to seek

---

selves if it had been a wise policy, in the long run, to encourage the evacuation of Italian towns in Istria. See, for example, "10 febbraio 1947," *Trieste,* no. 18 (Mar.–Apr. 1957), pp. 16–17; Nicolò Ramani, "E' stato un errore fermare i profughi a Trieste?" *Trieste,* no. 19 (May–June 1957), pp. 24–25.

38. Bowman, *Military Government Journal,* 1, no. 8:14; Robert Law, "Trieste Close-up," *Time,* Aug. 5, 1946; *Slovensko Primorje in Istra,* pp. 561, 630–33.

administrative elections. The AMG again refused, afraid the Communists would still be able to win. The UAIS-SIAU then offered to form a leftist bloc with the Socialist and Action parties to protect the interests of the working people, but here too they were rebuffed.[39]

On August 31, 1947, fifteen days before the peace treaty came into force, a Communist Party of the Free Territory of Trieste (CPFTT) was formed. At the same time, the founding congress of the new party decided that members of the Communist Party of Venezia Giulia would join the Slovenian Communist party for the portions of the Slovenian Littoral assigned to Yugoslavia, while for Istria, Rijeka, and the Adriatic islands the members would join the Croat Communist party. In the parts of the territory assigned to Italy the Slovenian and Italian members would join the Italian Communist party. The founding congress also underlined that Yugoslavia had signed the peace treaty to contribute to world peace, but in so doing had not achieved the ultimate solution for which the "democratic masses" had fought. The gains of the national democratic revolution could be preserved only by annexation of this territory to Yugoslavia. Though the CPFTT recognized the FTT as a fact, creation of the Free Territory represented a sacrifice and a setback from positions earlier reached by the democratic masses. The congress hoped the retreat was not a permanent one, and stressed the need to begin a new fight in accordance with the changed situation.[40]

In his report on the founding congress, M. K. Bulajić stressed that the CPFTT would continue its fight to introduce a socialist order in the new territory, but failed to make clear whether the party, if it should come into power in the FTT, would favor annexation to Yugoslavia. The Italian nationalists were justified in fearing that the CPFTT and its pro-Communist supporters would pursue this goal. But the Communist bloc officially recognized the FTT, and defended it in press and public pronouncements.

Until the signing of the peace treaty, the Comitato di Liberazione Nazionale continued to battle for unification of Trieste with Italy. In that aim the CLN represented all the Italian democratic

39. Apih, *Il Ponte*, 4, no. 4:332–33.
40. Bulajić, p. 42.

parties. But after February 10, 1947, the CLN was dissolved and each party began to build its own political organization. Even so, the leaders of the Italian parties formed the Giunta d'Intesa, a council to coordinate the defense of Italian interests in the future Free Territory. Between February and September 1947, four Italian parties began to strengthen themselves. These were: Democrazia Cristiana, Partito Liberale Italiano, Partito Repubblicano, and Partito Socialista Venezia Giulia. The first two were organized according to the political tenets of the parties of the same name in Italy. The Partito Repubblicano was formed by a union of the former Partito d'Azione (a liberal party with a social program) and the republicans. The Partito Socialista Venezia Giulia (PSVG) was made up of two socialist groups. The reformist or right-wing socialists were the majority.[41] They were also called the Saragat Socialists after their ideological leader Giuseppe Saragat, who was active in Italy and known for his refusal to join the left bloc formed by the left-wing (Nenni) Socialists and Communists. The second group made up the left-wing or Nenni (after Pietro Nenni) Socialists, which in Trieste did not ally with the Communist party as was the case in Italy. Because the local Communists (CPVG) favored a pro-Yugoslav foreign policy, the left-wing Socialists united with their right-wing foes forming the Venezia Giulia Socialist party. Hence for the leftist socialists in Trieste, Italian nationalism without doubt was stronger than ideological opposition to the right-wing socialists.

The neo-Fascist right was also present but, due to AMG opposition, could not legally form its own political organization.[42] The neo-Fascists nevertheless actively participated in all manifestations that defended the Italian character of Trieste, Pula, and Gorizia.

Until the signing of the peace treaty, the Slovenian anti-Communists did not have their own political party. In August 1945 a Catholic group in Gorizia had begun to publish a weekly, *Slovenski Primorec* (the Slovene from the Littoral). Somewhat later *Nedelja* (Sunday), a religious paper for the Trieste region, appeared. During 1946 the Catholic Cultural Organization in Gorizia and a university student group, Jadran (Adriatic), in Tri-

41. Apih, *Il Ponte*, 4, no. 4:334–37.
42. Ibid., p. 337.

este, were also formed. After February 1947, events pressed the anti-Communist Slovenes toward a more active political life. In March 1947, the AMG decided to discontinue its Slovenian daily, *Glas zaveznikov* (Voice of the Allies). The non-Communist Slovenes consequently had to organize their own party and publish a new political newspaper. Toward the end of March the Catholic group in Gorizia and liberals in Trieste decided to form a new political party, Slovenska demokratska zveza (Slovenian Democratic Union), under the leadership of Dr. Josip Agneletto and Dr. Franc Vesel. On April 15, 1947, the Slovenska demokratska zveza began to publish the weekly *Demokracija* (Democracy) edited by Slavko Uršič.[43]

The first articles of *Demokracija* condemned Communist policy toward the AMG. They pointed out that Slovenes were not represented in the central AMG administration because the UAIS-SIAU had refused to cooperate with the AMG. Indeed, the new journal maintained that had it not been for the stubborn work of the local anti-Communist Slovenes and the Slovenian émigré group, there would have been no Slovenian school system and no local Slovenian administration.

In reply, the Communists, in their daily *Primorski dnevnik*, attacked the Slovenska demokratska zveza as a pro-Fascist and collaborationist organization. They threatened dire punishment of the leaders and members of the new party. That these were not empty threats was soon evident when the editor of *Demokracija*, Slavko Uršič, was kidnapped and transported to Zone B where he disappeared. But no threats by the Communists could turn the clock back. The new party grew and continued its work.

Thus by September 15, 1947, all political groups that were to play a role in the future of the Free Territory had come formally onto the stage. The Communist bloc was still strong, although challenged now by Italian and Slovenian democratic parties. But the Slovenian and Italian nationalists could never unite against their Communist foe, while the Communists were able to forge an Italo-Slovenian unity. Apart from this major struggle stood the Independence Front.

On September 15 and 16 Yugoslav authorities entered the

43. Arnež, pp. 175, 182; Guido Botteri, "Catalogo-Dizionario degli Sloveni nella regione," *Trieste*, no. 38 (July–Aug. 1960), pp. 4, 5.

parts of Zone A of the Julian Region which had been assigned to Yugoslavia, thereby gaining 7,183 square kilometers of new territory with 495,104 inhabitants. According to Yugoslav sources 210,034 Yugoslav nationals remained outside her borders. Of this group, 85,300 were Slovenes in Italy, and 111,676 Slovenes and 13,058 Croats in the Free Territory of Trieste.[44]

The Italians estimated that there remained 325,000 Italians (according to the 1910 census), or 447,000 (according to figures of 1921) outside her borders. Of this number, 125,000 Italians (according to the 1910 census), or 181,000 (according to the 1921 count) were left in Yugoslavia, and 200,000 (census 1910) or 266,000 (census 1921) in the Free Territory of Trieste. Italian sources recognized only 10,500 Slovenes (according to the 1921 census) or 21,000 Slovenes (the figure of 1910) as left in Italy.[45]

Yugoslavia annexed the Slovenian Littoral to the Slovenian Republic. Istria, Rijeka, Zadar, and the Adriatic islands were added to the Croatian Republic. Italian troops, followed by the Italian administration, entered Gorizia and the territory assigned to her by the peace treaty. Thus the struggle for the Julian Region had ended for all territory coming under Italian or Yugoslav sovereignty. However, the battle for the newly created Free Territory of Trieste continued, and would disturb world peace for seven more years.

44. *Slovensko Primorje in Istra,* p. 535, n. 1.
45. De Castro, p. 279.

11

THE ASCENDANCY OF ITALY IN ZONE A

THE PROVISIONAL AND PERMANENT STATUTES

The Free Territory of Trieste began life with the bifurcation of a miniature Julian Region. Zone A, strongly Italian in complexion, and run by the Allied Military Government, had the smaller area, only 86 square miles, but included the city of Trieste and was thus far ahead in population. A narrow belt linked Trieste with the new Italian border. Zone B, to the south of the city, and under the Yugoslav Military Government, encompassed 199 square miles, but had only one-fourth the population of its rival zone. Both zones shared borders at the Morgan line and touched the French line and the Adriatic Sea.[1]

In actual figures, Zone A had about 309,000 inhabitants, 200,000 in the city of Trieste alone, according to AMG statistics of 1950, while the Yugoslav census of 1945 showed only 68,500 for the entire Zone B. The AMG reported some 246,000 Italians and 63,000 Slovenes in Zone A. The Yugoslavs, in control of Zone B, were far from matching the Italians of Zone A, not only in total population, but in ethnic percentage as well. The census of 1945 tallied 37,000 Slovenes and Croats in Zone B, but almost as many (30,000) Italians. The Italians in both zones were city dwellers, while the Slavs dominated the rural sections.[2]

The Free Territory had come into being as a compromise between East and West to solve the problem of an ethnically mixed region, and to assure revival of the historically significant

    1. One must distinguish between Zones A and B of the Julian Region (Venezia Giulia) in existence from June 12, 1945, to September 15, 1947, and the smaller Zones A and B of the Free Territory of Trieste in existence from September 16, 1947, to October 26, 1954.

    2. Information is based on Allied Military Government, *Trieste Handbook* (Trieste, 1950), p. 18; cited hereafter as *Trieste Handbook;* and on *Who Should Have Trieste?* (Ljubljana, 1953), p. 26.

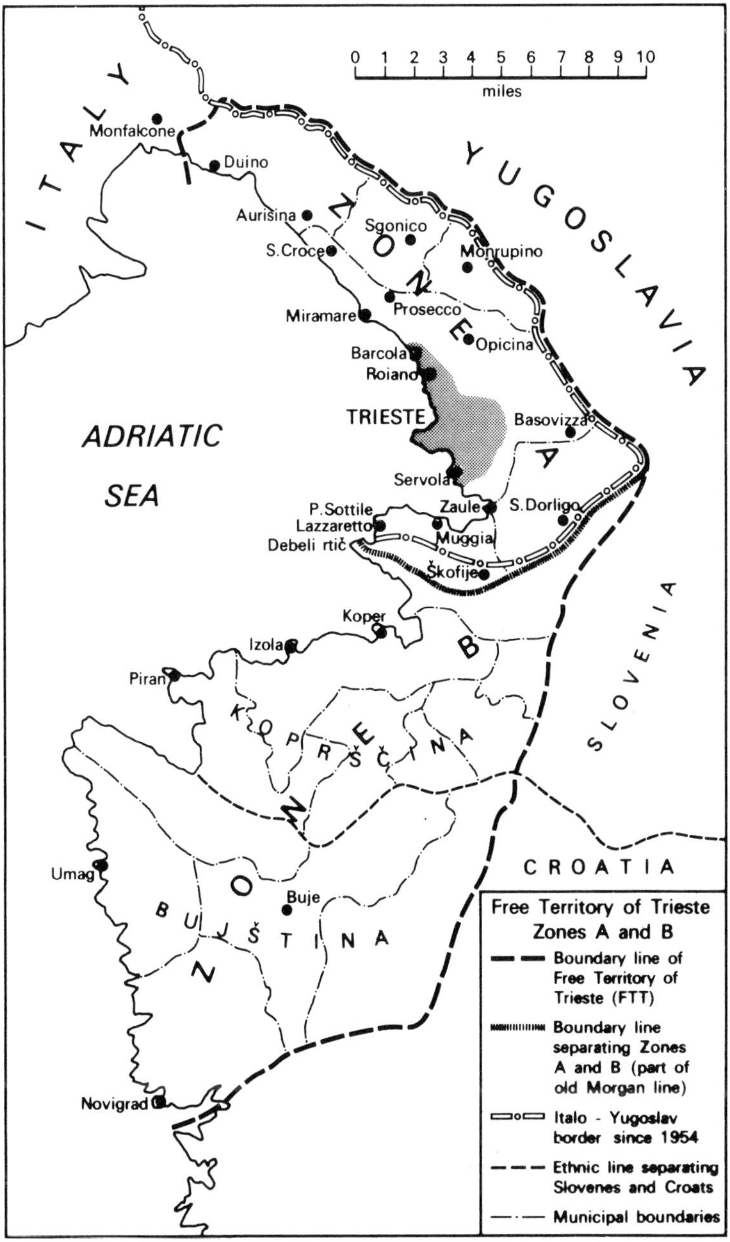

0 1 2 3 4 5 6 7 8 9 10
miles
ITALY
YUGOSLAVIA
ZONE A
ZONE B
SLOVENIA
CROATIA
ADRIATIC SEA
Monfalcone
Duino
Aurisina
Sgonico
S.Croce
Monrupino
Prosecco
Miramare
Opicina
Barcola
Roiano
TRIESTE
Basovizza
Servola
Zaule
S.Dorligo
P.Sottile
Lazzaretto
Muggia
Debeli rtič
Škofije
Koper
Izola
Piran
KOPRŠČINA
Umag
Buje
BUJŠTINA
Novigrad
Free Territory of Trieste Zones A and B
Boundary line of Free Territory of Trieste (FTT)
Boundary line separating Zones A and B (part of old Morgan line)
Italo - Yugoslav border since 1954
Ethnic line separating Slovenes and Croats
Municipal boundaries

role of the port of Trieste as a center of foreign trade for the states of its hinterland, namely Yugoslavia, Hungary, Austria, Czechoslovakia, Poland, Switzerland, and Italy. Only the last two and sections of Austria belonged to the West. All the others were a part of the Eastern bloc.

When the Council of Foreign Ministers agreed to create the Free Territory of Trieste in the early summer of 1946, they assumed that future disputes would be solved by the United Nations Security Council, internationally respected as the highest judge. In accordance with that policy they negotiated the Permanent Statute and the Instrument for the Provisional Regime of the Free Territory of Trieste (or Provisional Statute, for short) and included them in the Italian peace treaty as Annexes VI and VII, respectively.[3]

The foreign ministers envisioned three stages in the transfer from military control to a permanent civil administration: first, continuance of military stewardship until a governor could come into office—a short period, or so it was thought; second, an interim in which the governor would rule under the Provisional Statute, and before introduction of permanent civil institutions; finally, embodiment of fixed legislative, administrative, and judicial institutions under the supreme law of the Permanent Statute.

But, contrary to expectations, the governor was never appointed. As time went by, a question arose as to whether the Free Territory should still be ruled by the old military commands— Allied and Yugoslav—or whether the Provisional Statute and the general principles of the Permanent Statute should be applied instead. The Italian parties preferred continuation of the existing military arrangement, based on Italian law, for quite evident reasons. They opposed introduction of any portion of the Provisional or Permanent Statutes which would transform the FTT into an individual state and give equal rights to Slovenes. The Slovenian democrats, the independentists, and the Communists, on the other hand, pressed for adoption of the Statutes to achieve exactly these things.

3. U.S., Department of State, *Treaty of Peace with Italy* (Treaties and Other International Acts Series no. 1648, Department of State Publication no. 2960; Washington, D.C., 1947), pp. 185–99. Hereafter cited as *Italian Peace Treaty*.

The Provisional Statute laid down very few rules for the first stage of transition to civil administration. The anticipated brevity of the period was revealed in Article 1 which said that "the Governor shall assume office . . . at the earliest possible moment after the coming into force of the present Treaty," that is, September 15, 1947. It continued: "Pending assumption of office by the Governor, the Free Territory shall continue to be administered by the Allied military commands within their respective zones."

Article 10 confirmed the validity of existing laws, and Article 11, dealing with the subject of currency, stated:

> Pending the establishment of a separate currency regime for the Free Territory, the Italian lira shall continue to be the legal tender within the Free Territory. The Italian Government shall supply the foreign exchange and currency needs of the Free Territory under conditions no less favorable than those applying in Italy.
>
> Italy and the Free Territory shall enter into an agreement to give effect to the above provisions as well as to provide for any settlement between the two Governments which may be required.[4]

Article 5 limited occupation troops to fifteen thousand men, five thousand each from Great Britain, the United States, and Yugoslavia.

The other articles in the Provisional Statute applied to the second period after the governor had assumed office. In consultation with Italy and Yugoslavia, he was to select a provisional council of government, composed of members domiciled in the Free Territory. The rights and duties of the governor and provisional council were to be the same as those provided for their counterparts in the Permanent Statute. "Likewise all other provisions of the Permanent Statute shall be applicable during the period of the Provisional Regime . . . in so far as they are not suspended by the present Instrument."

The governor, according to the Provisional Statute, was to report directly, from headquarters in Trieste, to the chairman of the United Nations Security Council. To take care of his principal function, the preservation of public order, the governor was to

---

4. Ibid., p. 199.

appoint a provisional director of public security to reorganize and preside over the police and security service. The occupation troops of all three powers were placed at the governor's disposal for a total of ninety days after his assumption of office, after which time they would be evacuated in no more than forty-five days, "unless the Governor advises the Security Council that, in the interests of the Territory, some or all of them should not, in his view, be withdrawn." In this latter event the soldiers would have to leave not later than forty-five days after the governor had told the Security Council he would no longer need foreign troops. Should the size of the military force be diminished, the equal ratio of British, American, and Yugoslav troops was to be maintained.

Though conditions were never fulfilled for installation of the Permanent Statute, its provisions deserve to be stated, for it laid down the fundamental rights guaranteed to the people of the Free Territory. Moreover, it gives us a picture of how the foreign ministers proposed to solve a complex situation.

The Permanent Statute, in order to allay national anxieties, guaranteed equal rights for Italians and Slovenes. Article 7 stated: "The official languages of the Free Territory shall be Italian and Slovene. The Constitution shall determine in what circumstances Croat may be used as a third official language." Article 8 confirmed as the Free Territory's official flag and coat of arms the traditional ones of the city of Trieste, namely a silver halberd on a blood-red background.

Its independence and integrity assured by the Security Council of the United Nations, the Free Territory was to have no military or paramilitary formations except a regular police force. Human rights and fundamental freedoms, defined in Article 4 as "freedom of religious worship, language, speech and publication, education, assembly and association," were to be guaranteed to all persons under Free Territory jurisdiction without distinction as to ethnic origin, sex, language, or religion. All citizens were also assured of equal chance to qualify for public office.

In regard to citizenship, Article 6 declared:

> Italian citizens who were domiciled on June 10, 1940, in the area comprised within the boundaries of the Free Territory, and their children born after that date, shall become original citizens of the Free Territory with full civil and polit-

ical rights. Upon becoming citizens of the Free Territory they shall lose their Italian citizenship.[5]

Rules for becoming a citizen, for those not already qualified, would be determined by the assembly that was to draft a constitution.

The Free Territory was to be run by a governor, a popular assembly, a council of government, an independent judiciary, a director of public safety, and a director of the free port. The governor, who was to be appointed or reappointed for a term of five years "by the Security Council after consultation with the Governments of Yugoslavia and Italy," could not be a citizen of either of these nations or of the Free Territory. He was to share executive authority, except the power of pardon and reprieve, with the council of government. The Security Council would settle disputes between the governor and the council of government, or between him and the popular assembly. The governor, as representative of the Security Council, was to see that no legislation or administrative measures were adopted contrary to the terms of the Permanent Statute. In case of violation the governor was empowered to use his veto, and failing concurrence by local authorities could refer the conflict to the Security Council for final decision. His salary would be borne by the United Nations. Very important was Article 22 of the Permanent Statute, which gave the governor special powers "in cases which in his opinion permit of no delay, threatening the independence or integrity of the Free Territory, public order or respect of human rights." In such instances the governor was empowered to issue decrees and assume control of the security services, subject to an immediate report to the Security Council.

Within four months of the governor's assumption of office, he was to arrange for election of a constituent assembly to draft a constitution for the Free Territory which could not contravene any of the general provisions laid down in the Permanent Statute. Legislative authority would be vested in a single-chambered popular assembly elected by citizens of both sexes on the basis of proportional representation. Suffrage was to be universal, equal, direct, and secret. Legislative initiative could be exercised by the

5. Ibid., p. 186.

governor, by members of the popular assembly, and by the council of government. Before promulgation of any legislation, the governor was required to review it for possible violations of the Permanent Statute.

The council of government was to be elected by the assembly and was responsible to it. The council was charged with preparing the budget of the Free Territory, which was then to be brought to the assembly for vote.

Article 15 of the Permanent Statute stated that "the Constitution of the Free Territory shall guarantee the complete freedom and independence of the Judiciary and shall provide for appellate jurisdiction." Details of establishment and organization of the tribunals, and provisions of the law codes, were to be left to the constituent assembly.

Next to the governor, the most important single officer was the director of public security. He was to be appointed by the governor from a list of candidates submitted by the council of government. Like the governor, he could be a citizen of neither Italy nor Yugoslavia. He had command of the entire police force, and could recruit members or dismiss them. In normal circumstances he would be under the "immediate authority" of the council of government, but in times of emergency, as indicated above, when the governor assumed special powers, the police force might come directly under the governor's personal command.

A director was also to be placed in charge of the free port, an incorporated juridical entity embracing all the establishments bounded by the port of the city of Trieste. This Free Port of Trieste was established by Annex VIII to the Italian peace treaty. As a state corporation, it administered its own autonomous budget. The director, in the same manner as the director of public security, was to be appointed by the governor from a list of qualified candidates submitted by the council of government, and could not be a citizen of either Yugoslavia or Italy. An international commission, consisting of one representative each from the Free Territory, France, Great Britain, the United States, the Soviet Union, Yugoslavia, Italy, Czechoslovakia, Poland, Switzerland, Austria, and Hungary could investigate all matters relating to the operation, use, and administration of the free port. The representative of the Free Territory was to be the permanent chairman of this international commission.

The Permanent Statute could be amended only by the Security Council. The popular assembly, however, could petition the Security Council for an amendment, provided two-thirds of the votes cast in the assembly so ordered.

THE FUTILE SEARCH FOR A GOVERNOR

Inasmuch as the Great Powers dominating the Security Council could not agree on who should become the governor, the military governments of the Allies and Yugoslavia continued to administer Zones A and B, respectively, as provided in Article 1 of the Provisional Statute.

Pending the appointment of a governor, the commander of the British–United States forces, Major General T. S. Airey, issued his "Proclamation No. 1" to residents of Zone A, and had it posted on September 16, 1947, in the streets of Trieste and in rural communes. The proclamation stated, among other things:

> 1. . . . all powers of government and administration . . . , as well as jurisdiction over its inhabitants, shall continue to be vested in me in my capacity as Commander of the said British–United States Forces.
>
> 2. An Allied Military Government . . . is hereby continued.
>
> 3. . . . all administrative and judicial officials and all other Government and Municipal Functionaries and employees and all officers and employees of Public, Municipal or other services, shall continue in the performance of their duties. . . .
>
> 4. All existing laws, decrees and orders in force . . . shall remain in force and effect. . . . "Allied Forces" . . . shall be interpreted as referring to the British and United States Forces stationed in the Zone.[6]

6. *AMG-FTT Gazette,* 1, no. 1 (Sept. 16, 1947): 1; see also "Report on the Administration of the British–U.S. Zone of the Free Territory of Trieste for the Period 15 September to 31 December 1947 by Major General T. S. Airey . . . ," *UNSC,* Doc. S/679 (Feb. 18, 1948), pp. 39–40. (Mimeographed.) The report will hereafter be cited as *First AMG Report (S/679).*

This proclamation made clear that the AMG administration, as introduced by General Order No. 11 on August 11, 1945, was to continue in force in Zone A of the Free Territory of Trieste until the governor took office.

The issuance of Proclamation No. 1 started a new controversy on how to interpret Article 1 of the Provisional Statute. That article stated that "the Free Territory shall continue to be administered by the Allied military commands within their respective zones."[7] The Yugoslavs held this to mean that all of the Free Territory was to be administered jointly by the "Allied military commands"; the two other powers, to the contrary, insisted the key word was "continue"—the status quo must be maintained. The Western view thus justified a separate Anglo-American administration in Zone A and another by Yugoslavia in Zone B, a practice already in operation.[8]

Nor was this the only trouble that marked the days near to September 15, 1947, when the Italian peace treaty went into effect. At that time, in accordance with the treaty, the Allied forces withdrew from certain areas in Zone A of the Julian Region, part of which, including Gorizia and Monfalcone, were to be turned over to Italy. But between the time of Allied troop evacuation and the entrance of Italian soldiers into the areas under their jurisdiction, a night passed when no troops were present whatsoever. Extreme Italian nationalists seized this opportunity to attack and demolish many Slovenian stores and private houses, especially in Gorizia.

On September 21, 1947, *Ljudska pravica* (People's Right), organ of the Slovenian Communist party, published a special number celebrating unification of the Slovenian Littoral with the Slovenian Republic. In this issue the paper condemned the attacks of the Italian neo-Fascists on the Slovenian minority left in Italy. It charged Italy with violating Articles 15, 16, and 17 of the peace treaty, which guaranteed human rights and fundamental freedoms to all persons under Italian jurisdiction without regard to race, religion, or language, and prohibited molestation of anyone who had fought on the Allied side.[9] According to Article 17,

7. *Italian Peace Treaty*, p. 196.
8. Munnecke, *Military Government Journal*, 2, no. 2:7.
9. *Ljudska pravica*, Sept. 21, 1947, pp. 1, 2, 4.

Italy was not to permit any resurgence of Fascist organizations or similar groups that would deprive the people of their democratic rights.[10] The Slovenian press in Yugoslavia reiterated the fear that Italian persecutions of the Slovenian minority in Italy would follow the pattern of 1919.

The Italians saw September 15, 1947, as a day of mourning. They had lost not only most of the Julian Region, but, more importantly, the city of Trieste, separated from Italy by a *Diktat* of the Great Powers. In Trieste Italian patriots organized wild demonstrations, which reached a climax in sharp clashes with adherents of the pro-Communist bloc in which five people were reported killed and hundreds wounded.[11]

A second great source of friction stemmed from the continued division of the Free Territory into two zones, one representing the Western democratic political and economic order, the other introducing a socialistic system. The Italian press, both in Italy and in Zone A, charged the pro-Communist bloc with aspirations to introduce a socialistic order in all of the Free Territory, especially if the zones were unified. Countering this, the pro-Communist papers within the area and in Yugoslavia constantly made the point that Italy would never sincerely support an independent Free Territory, but would try to sabotage the nomination of a governor in order to prove that a Free Territory could not exist. Should Italian tactics prevail, Italy would begin to demand annexation of the Free Territory just as was done in the case of Rijeka after World War I.

Month after month the situation worsened as the appointment of a governor continued to be delayed. This failure to nominate a governor was due not only to the specific disagreement between Italy and Yugoslavia, but also to the heightened general tensions between the Western democracies and the Soviet Union. Signs of this disagreement had been expressed during negotiations over the peace treaty with Italy in general, and the future Statute of Trieste in particular. Tensions increased early in 1947 when President Truman decided to take a firmer stand toward the Soviet Union, and General George C. Marshall replaced James E.

10. For the text of Articles 15, 16, and 17, see *Italian Peace Treaty*, p. 134.
11. "Hot Curve," *Time*, Sept. 29, 1947, p. 32.

Byrnes as secretary of state. The turning point came March 12, 1947, when Truman, in a speech promising help to Greece in her fight against Communist guerrillas, laid down the new political course known as the Truman Doctrine. In line with this policy, Secretary of State Marshall, in his speech at Harvard University, June 5, 1947, outlined a plan for extending American economic help to European countries, later known as the Marshall Plan.

The United States had now joined Great Britain and France in opposing Russian expansion toward the west. As a consequence, a strong Western economic, military, and political bloc came into existence. Countering the Marshall Plan, the Soviet Union organized, toward the end of September 1947, a closer political unity among her satellites through a newly-created Cominform having its seat in Yugoslavia, the country directly supporting the Greek Communist guerrillas.[12]

It is only in light of this general increase in world tensions that the failure to nominate a governor for the Free Territory can be understood. Neither the Great Powers forming the Security Council, on the one hand, nor Yugoslavia and Italy on the other, could agree on whom to appoint. The candidates proposed by the Western powers and Italy were rejected by the Soviet Union and Yugoslavia, who, in turn, proposed candidates sympathetic to a socialist order and not acceptable to the West.[13] Furthermore, the creation of these two opposing blocs brought into question the role of the United Nations itself. The Statute of the Free Territory depended for enforcement on the Security Council. A paralyzed Security Council would make the statute unworkable. The failure to nominate a governor was thus an early sign that the whole existence of the Free Territory, as defined in the Italian peace treaty, had become dubious, since it was premised on a harmony in the Security Council which was never realized.

Italy had accepted the peace treaty as a *Diktat* and had begun to work for revision before it was signed in February 1947.[14] She

12. See J. B. Duroselle, *Histoire diplomatique de 1919 à nos jours* (Paris, 1957), pp. 535–39, 541.
13. For the negotiations to nominate a governor see De Castro, pp. 353–78, for the Italian and Jeri, pp. 195–202, for the Yugoslav version.
14. On February 11, 1947, Sforza sent a message in behalf of this idea to all the governments which had participated in the Paris peace

believed that creation of the Free Territory was only a compromise to meet Yugoslav demands claiming the entire region. Given, therefore, the division of the world powers, and with Yugoslavia as one of the Soviet allies opposed to the West, Italy hoped for Western support to achieve a revision of the peace treaty which would return the Free Territory to her. Italy's argument now ran that the Statute of the Free Territory could not be applied since the governor could not be agreed upon. Furthermore, it would be dangerous to decide on a governor, since in a Free Territory there was a threat that the Communist system would expand from Zone B into Zone A, thus exposing the port of Trieste to Communist control.

The Yugoslavs never renounced their claims over all of the Free Territory. They regarded its creation as a compromise in favor of Italy imposed on Yugoslavia. Yugoslavia believed that if the Statute became unworkable her old claims would be revived and the whole territory might then come under her sovereignty as part of a new Federal Republic of Yugoslavia. Though hinting at this basic policy as early as the signing of the peace treaty, Yugoslavs nonetheless persistently tried to claim that while Yugoslavia sincerely desired to cooperate with Italy in the nomination of a governor, it was Italy that rejected all proposed candidates. To prove that Italy never really tried to cooperate, the Yugoslavs quoted the statement of the Italian foreign minister Carlo Sforza that he was afraid Belgrade would accept one of the candidates proposed by Italy.[15] However, the truth is that Yugoslavia also refused to agree to any candidate suggested by Italy.

The respective Italian and Yugoslav positions naturally influenced the major political parties in the Free Territory. The pro-Italian parties adopted an Irredentist view that Trieste and the Free Territory should be returned to Italy. The pro-Commu-

---

conference. See Carlo Sforza, *Cinque anni a palazzo Chigi: La politica estera italiana dal 1947 al 1951* (Rome, 1952), pp. 16–17. The same idea to revise the terms of the peace treaty was expressed in Sforza's speech to the Constituent Assembly on July 24, 1947 (see ibid., pp. 18–39, and 326).

15. Jeri, pp. 197–200. For Sforza's statement see his *Cinque anni a palazzo Chigi,* p. 340.

nist bloc charged the Irredentists with illegally working against the peace treaty and against the Free Territory. The Italians countered with accusations that the Communists wanted to introduce socialism into Zone A and hence represented a vanguard of Russian expansion toward the west.

Hemmed in by these two blocs, the independentists had little chance to grow. With the future destiny of the Free Territory in question, many people found it wise to proceed with caution in support of a Free Territory. Unlike the strong Italian parties and the pro-Yugoslav Communist bloc, both of which received financial help for their newspapers and propaganda, the independentists and the Slovenian democrats were limited to their own resources.[16]

The Security Council attempted to establish direct dealings between Italy and Yugoslavia on the governorship of the Free Territory, but the negotiations broke down in January 1948, and solution of the problem seemed hopeless. By this time not only had friction increased between Italy and Yugoslavia, but throughout the world East-West relations had markedly worsened. The Western powers were beginning the formation of the Atlantic Pact, and the Soviet Union was starting the Berlin Blockade, both aspects of the Cold War.

The line separating the Eastern and Western blocs ran from Stettin to Trieste. Disjoining Europe into two separate economic, political, and ideological systems, the borders truly became an Iron Curtain. This line, running directly through the Free Territory, became fatal to any hope for its independence. The city and port of Trieste which remained in Western hands could not resume the former role of import-export center for adjacent countries because those countries, including the Russian zone in Austria, which had given Trieste its main flow of commerce, were in the Eastern bloc. Without traffic through Yugoslavia, Trieste could not exist economically as an independent state. Thus the

16. A different opinion was stressed by the Italians. They claimed that Yugoslavia was financially aiding the Fronte dell'Indipendenza and its journal *Il Corriere di Trieste* for the purpose of breaking up Italian solidarity. See, for example, De Castro, pp. 600–601; "Il Corriere di Trieste," *Trieste*, no. 9 (Sept.–Oct. 1955), pp. 30–31; and "La storia segreta," *Trieste*, no. 36, pp. 7–11.

inability to establish a normal East-West economic relationship became a further obstacle preventing the formation of the Free Territory.

THE TRIPARTITE PROPOSAL

This was the situation when the Western powers announced the so-called Tripartite Proposal on March 20, 1948, promising to return the Free Territory to Italy. The announcement came soon after the Communist coup d'état in Czechoslovakia in February and was apparently designed as part of the general Cold War effort to help obtain a pro-Western victory in the Italian elections to be held that year in April.

According to the announcement, because of the hopeless situation,

> the Governments of the United States, Great Britain, and France proposed to the Governments of the Soviet Union and Italy that those Governments join in agreement on an additional protocol to the treaty of peace with Italy which would place the Free Territory of Trieste once more under Italian sovereignty.

The statement explained that the proposition was decided upon because it was impossible to agree on a governor and

> because they [the three Western governments] have received abundant evidence to show that the Yugoslav Zone has been completely transformed in character and has been virtually incorporated into Yugoslavia by procedures which do not respect the desire expressed by the Powers to give an independent and democratic statute to the Territory.[17]

The document concluded by saying that the Western powers at the peace conference had felt that "Trieste, which has an overwhelmingly Italian population, must remain an Italian city." But, in order to find a middle ground, the West had agreed to the Free Territory, believing all parties would work together. Cooperation having failed, the Western powers now felt the best solution was

17. "Statement by the Governments of the United States, United Kingdom and France, March 20, 1948," reprinted in *Department of State Bulletin,* 18 (Mar. 28, 1948): 425.

return of the Free Territory to Italy. Inasmuch as the Security Council had "assumed responsibility for the independence and territorial integrity" of the Free Territory, the Western powers would "submit to the Security Council for approval the arrangements to be jointly agreed upon."

The fact that the Tripartite Proposal was released on March 20, 1948, only a month before the Italian elections of April 18, caused a bitter quarrel. Opposition newspapers called it electoral propaganda, a charge the pro-government Italian papers of course denied.

The label of propaganda has been substantiated in the memoirs of Alberto Tarchiani, who was at the time the Italian ambassador in Washington. Tarchiani states that with the elections of April 18 approaching, an "act of friendship" by the West was needed for fear that the East was preparing a similar "action" of its own.[18]

Of the same opinion was Anthony Eden, who says in his memoirs that the Tripartite Proposal did not mean much in juridical terms because Russian agreement was needed, and it was certain to be denied. According to Eden, the proposal was not designed as an immediate signal for action, but only a recommendation for consideration by both sides.[19]

Contemporary progovernment Italian newspapers rejected the charge of "election propaganda," and insisted that the Tripartite Proposal presented the sincere viewpoint of the Western powers.[20] It is true that the proposal did help the Christian Democrats in Italy to win a significant electoral victory, but in the long run it bound the hands of the Western powers and became an important obstacle to an agreement between Italy and Yugoslavia over Trieste.

The Tripartite Proposal had a telling effect on internal affairs in the Free Territory. Naturally the Italian parties greeted it with fervor, while the pro-Communist bloc, following the line taken by Yugoslavia and the Soviet Union, condemned it as op-

18. Tarchiani, p. 143.
19. Anthony Eden, *Full Circle: The Memoirs of Anthony Eden* (Boston, 1960), pp. 198–99.
20. See De Castro, pp. 410–11.

portunistic election propaganda. They charged that since the Italian peace treaty committed the Western powers to evacuate their troops as soon as a regular administration could be set up in Trieste, these powers were blocking nomination of a governor in order to prolong their stay and transform Trieste into a military and naval base.[21] The Communists of the Free Territory therefore demanded that a governor be agreed upon in the shortest possible time. Yugoslavia and the Soviet Union supported them in this move.

The Tripartite Proposal greatly influenced Allied military administration in Zone A. The economy of the zone became a part of the Italian economy. Moreover, pro-Italian influence also increased in the civil administration of the zone.

ITALIAN INFLUENCE OVER TRIESTE'S ECONOMY

The increase of Italian influence over Trieste's economy resulted from a series of financial and economic agreements between Italy and the Allied Military Government. Most important were the financial agreement of March 9, 1948, and the financial-economic accords of April 16 and September 22 of the same year, all justified by the AMG on the basis of Article 11 of Annex VII of the peace treaty with Italy.

Technically, the financial agreement of March 9, 1948, did not transcend the framework of the peace treaty, although stating that the command of the zone would "apply in the Territory under its jurisdiction all regulations of the Italian Republic concerning monetary circulation" and "avoid taking any contrary measures."[22] This provision gave rise to an argument that the

---

21. Ibid., pp. 423–25; "Report on the Administration of the British–U.S. Zone of the Free Territory of Trieste for the Period 1 April to 30 June 1948 by Major General T. S. Airey . . . ," *UNSC*, Doc. S/953 (August 6, 1948), pp. 6, 13–14. (Mimeographed.) Hereafter cited as the *Third AMG Report* (S/953).

22. "Agreements on Finances and Provisions of Foreign Exchange between British–United States Zone, Free Territory of Trieste, and the Government of Italian Republic," concluded March 9, 1948, reproduced in "Report on the Administration of the British–U.S. Zone of the Free Territory of Trieste for the Period 1 January to 31 March 1948 by Major General T. S. Airey . . . ," *UNSC*, Doc. S/781 (May 25, 1948), pp. 38–

AMG was limiting its freedom of action and introducing Italian laws in Zone A in contradiction to the peace treaty guarantee of independence to the Free Territory.

Liable to attack in a similar fashion was a statement that the AMG would limit its expenditures to the reasonable economic needs of the zone. Thanks to this short statement, Italian control was introduced over the Zone A budget which was to be approved in advance every six months by the Italian government. Italy also secured for itself the "current foreign exchange earnings accruing to the Command of the Zone under the exchange regulations in force." The AMG could, however, retain "any special dollar or sterling grants or advances which it may receive as international aid."

The real end to an independent economy in the Free Territory came with a second agreement, April 16, 1948, by which the Italian ministry of foreign trade took control of all import and export activities in Zone A.[23] Licenses were to be granted only by the Italian ministry of foreign trade and all payments to or from Zone A had to be made through that ministry.

During this time, basic consumer goods such as food, fuel, and medical supplies were being furnished to Zone A by the United States foreign relief program. Shortly before the end of this program, scheduled for June 30, 1948, the Italian delegation to the Organization for European Economic Cooperation (OEEC) proposed on June 13 to the Council of the OEEC that Zone A be admitted to membership so that the zone could receive aid from the European Recovery Program (ERP). On September 25, 1948, the OEEC allocated eighteen million dollars for the first year of the zone's recovery plan. Of this sum, twelve million was to be used to purchase basic economic supplies, and the remaining six million invested in new industrial equipment and raw materials.

---

42. (Mimeographed.) The Report will hereafter be cited as *Second AMG Report* (S/781).

23. "Agreement between the Allied Military Government of the British–United States Zone of the Free Territory of Trieste and the Italian Ministry of Foreign Trade Defining the Procedure for Implementing the Financial Agreement of 9 March 1948," concluded April 16, 1948, reproduced in *Third AMG Report* (S/953), pp. 33–36.

On October 14, 1948, the OEEC formally admitted Zone A into full membership.[24]

In connection with Zone A's participation in the European Recovery Plan, a third agreement was signed on September 22, 1948, whereby the Italian government became the only agency through which the Allied Military Government could exchange its dollar grants into lire for import and export purposes.[25] Thus ended the policy, stated in the March 9, 1948, agreement, that the AMG could freely use the exchange received from foreign aid programs. Now, not only did the Italian government have the privilege of exchanging AMG dollars received from ERP into lire but the AMG had to take care that

> no dollars or sterling are made available for specific purchases in cases where it can be determined that as a means of reducing the drain on Italian dollar and sterling currency resources, procurement can be made in the Italian market or through Italian trade agreements under equally favourable conditions.[26]

Italian control over the economy of Zone A increased still further by creation of a mixed commission in Rome to discuss

24. "Report on the Administration of the British–U.S. Zone of the Free Territory of Trieste for the Period 1 July to 30 September 1948 by Major General T. S. Airey . . . ," *UNSC*, Doc. S/1174 (January 5, 1949), pp. 4–5 (mimeographed), hereafter cited as *Fourth AMG Report* (S/1174); and "Report on the Administration of the British–U.S. Zone of the Free Territory of Trieste for the Period 1 October to 31 December 1948 by Major General T. S. Airey . . . ," *UNSC*, Doc. S/1242 (February 3, 1949), p. 1. (Mimeographed.) Hereafter cited as *Fifth AMG Report* (S/1242).

25. "Agreements Reached at the Meetings Held in Rome during the Period 20 to 31 July 1948 for the Purpose of Implementing the Agreements Signed on 9 March 1948 between the Government of the Italian Republic and the British–United States Military Command of the Relevant Zone of the Free Territory of Trieste on Finance and Foreign Exchange with Particular Reference to the Command of the Zone's Plan for the Participation of the Zone in European Recovery Programme (Trieste, September 22, 1948)," reproduced in *Fourth AMG Report* (S/1174), pp. 23–26.

26. Ibid., p. 25.

monthly all financial and economic matters of mutual interest, and coordinate the ERP programs for Italy and Zone A. The financial-economic agreements that followed only strengthened the already established Italian influence over Trieste's economy, especially over the budget of Zone A. For example, an accord of September 29, 1949, expressly stated that the zone's command was to notify the Italian government of any variations "which may take place in the items of the budget."[27]

As a net result, Zone A became a part of the Italian economy directly controlled from Rome. All parties favoring independence of the Free Territory naturally opposed these measures and accused the AMG of acting against the interests of the territory. Equally opposed were the Communists, the Yugoslav government, the Independence Front, the Blocco Triestino, and the Slovenian Democratic Union.

The Yugoslav government, in a note to the Security Council dated July 28, 1948, lodged an official protest against the March 9, 1948, agreement and repeated it in a memorandum to the same body on October 24, 1948.[28] These complaints were based on the texts found in Paragraphs 2 and 4 of Article 24 of the Permanent Statute, which stated:

> 2. Treaties and agreements, as well as exequaturs and consular commissions, shall be signed jointly by the Governor and a representative of the Council of Government. . . .
>
> 4. Economic union or associations of an exclusive character with any State are incompatible with the status of the Free Territory.[29]

27. "Agreement on Finances and Foreign Exchange," concluded September 29, 1949, reproduced in "Report on the Administration of the British-U.S. Zone of the Free Territory of Trieste for the Period 1 July to 30 September 1949 by Major General T. S. Airey . . . ," *UNSC*, Doc. S/1424 (November 30, 1949), pp. 35–38. (Mimeographed.) The report will be cited as *Eighth AMG Report* (S/1424).

28. "Yugoslav Note to the Security Council of the U.N.," *UNSC*, Doc. S/927 (July 28, 1948) (mimeographed); "Memorandum from the Ministry of Foreign Affairs of Yugoslavia Transmitted to the President of the Security Council by Telegram on October 24, 1948," *UNSC*, Doc. S/1054 (November 2, 1948). (Mimeographed.) The memorandum will be cited as *Yugoslav Memorandum* (S/1054).

29. See *Italian Peace Treaty*, p. 192.

According to the Yugoslav memorandum, the Allied Military Government had violated Paragraph 4 by entering into an economic and customs union with the Italian state. Secondly, the AMG had appointed a mixed commission in Rome without consent of an elected government—the sequel to an old Communist charge that the AMG had not established an elected government in Zone A. Communist opposition to the Marshall Plan in general was also behind these complaints.

But a more important fault of the AMG was its failure to include under its control Italian state and para-statal property existing in Zone A. This property, which was helping to increase Italian influence in the zone, was supposed, according to the peace treaty, to be turned over to the Free Territory. Paragraph 1 of Annex X of the peace treaty with Italy declared:

> 1. The Free Territory of Trieste shall receive, without payment, Italian State and para-statal property within the Free Territory.
> The following are considered as State or para-statal property for the purposes of this Annex: movable and immovable property of the Italian State, of local authorities and of public institutions and publicly owned companies and associations, as well as movable and immovable property formerly belonging to the Fascist Party or its auxiliary organizations.[30]

The Yugoslav memorandum of October 24, 1948, called the Security Council's attention to the fact that, in direct violation of the express decision contained in Paragraph 1, the Italian government was still managing from Rome all of Trieste's para-statal property belonging to the Istituto Ricostruzioni Industriali (IRI).

The IRI had been founded on January 23, 1933, by Mussolini's government as a means to save Italy's big industry, mercantile enterprises, and financial institutions from collapse in the worldwide depression. As a first installment, the IRI had received from the government a grant of five billion lire, with which it bought the stock of three great banks that had been financing industry, namely, Banca Commerciale Italiana, Banco di Roma, and Credito Italiano. Very soon thereafter, state intervention expanded so that the IRI came to control about 75 percent of Italian industry, and almost all the maritime enterprises.

30. Ibid., pp. 208–9.

These moves under Mussolini did not represent full-scale nationalization or socialization of the Italian economy, but stood halfway between private capitalism and nationalization. Formally, the previous owners remained; the IRI merely placed its representatives on the administrative boards of the controlled companies. In return for state credits or subsidies granted by the IRI to a certain enterprise, the IRI received stock of that establishment equivalent in value. This stock in the hands of the IRI, however, could be bought back by the formal owners of the establishment and when a substantial amount of such stock had been repurchased the owners could become represented in the administrative council of the IRI itself.

The IRI was divided into different branches according to its chief economic functions. Finsider (Società Finanziaria Siderurgica), for example, was a branch supporting the iron industry; Finmare (Società Finanziaria Marittima) controlled maritime enterprises; Finmeccanica subsidized shipbuilding and other mechanical industries. Banks and the electrical and chemical industries, however, remained under direct control of the IRI.

In Trieste, Finsider controlled Ilva, a metallurgical establishment having 1,276 employees in 1951.[31] Finmeccanica dominated Cantieri Riuniti dell'Adriatico, a large shipbuilding works employing about ten thousand persons. Also under the IRI in Trieste were the shipbuilding plants San Marco, with four thousand, and San Rocco, with fifteen hundred employees, the machinery plant San Andrea, with four thousand, L'Arsenale Triestino, a plant for repair of ships, and OMSA, a factory making varied types of machines. Finmare controlled almost all the stock of Trieste's greatest enterprises, Lloyd Triestino, which, during the Austrian domina-

31. Data on Italian para-statal institutions in Trieste are based on the following works: Ive Mihovilović, *Trst problem dana* (Trieste, the Problem of the Day) (Zagreb, 1951), pp. 112–14; Stanislav Vilhar, "Državno-monopolistički kapitalizam u Italiji: Stvaranje državnog sektora u privredi" (State-Monopolistic Capitalism in Italy: Formation of a State Sector in the Economy), *Medjunarodni problemi* (International Problems), 3, no. 2–3 (Mar.–June 1951): 36–67; Italy, Presidenza del consiglio dei ministri, Servizio informazioni, *Trieste nella sua realtà* (Rome, 1958), pp. 48–49, 59–63, 78–80. The last work will hereafter be cited as *Trieste nella sua realtà*.

tion, had handled 75 percent of Trieste's passenger and freight sea traffic. Besides Lloyd Triestino, Finmare controlled other steamship lines such as Italia, Società Adriatica, and Società Tirrenia in Trieste.

The IRI directly governed branches of the Banca d'Italia, Banca Commerciale Italiana, Banco di Roma, and Credito Italiano in Trieste and thus monopolized credit to industry and commerce. Besides all this, the IRI supervised many smaller Trieste enterprises such as TELVE (a radio broadcasting station), Forestal Triestina, an agency for forestation of the territory, and many others. In short, almost all important aspects of economic life in Trieste were, in one way or another, controlled by para-statal institutions of the IRI.

Thus, all during the AMG administration, Italy, through the IRI, dominated Trieste's economic life. The Yugoslav memorandum of October 1948 further revealed that already in the second half of 1948 Italy had given close to three billion lire credit to the AMG, earmarked for the sole purpose of improving IRI establishments. This meant, according to the Yugoslavs, that Italy was in effect lending money to improve her own (IRI) property in Zone A, which would in time have to be repaid by the citizens of the Free Territory. The AMG was thus agreeing, said the Yugoslavs, to saddle the citizens of the Free Territory with a large debt without their consent.

In accepting the loans for improvement of IRI property, the AMG, according to the Yugoslav memorandum, was acting in distinct violation of the peace treaty and the Permanent Statute. Approval of the loans was beyond the competence of a temporary military occupation authority, as the AMG claimed to be, especially since the loans would create a heavy long-term burden upon the people of the entire Free Territory, including Zone B. Further, inhabitants of the Free Territory had no chance to express themselves about the loans.[32]

Nor was this all. The Yugoslav memorandum pointed out that the help given Trieste by the ERP was also invested in Italian

32. In fact, the loan mentioned in the Yugoslav memorandum was not the only one of its kind. An analysis of Zone A budgets, as given in AMG reports, confirms the existence of other Italian loans earmarked for improvement of IRI property in Trieste.

para-statal property. Besides the quota assigned her directly by the ERP, Italy thus benefited also from ERP help to Zone A.

In the light of these facts, should the Free Territory ever really become independent Italy would suffer a damaging economic blow. This was one of the reasons why, according to the Yugoslav viewpoint, Italy opposed creation of the Free Territory.

Thanks to the AMG, Italy maintained her control from Rome, not only over all important economic activities in Zone A of the Free Territory, but also many aspects of public life. For example, when the cultural organization of the Slovenian Democratic Union, a non-Communist body, asked to rent the big hall of the Excelsior, one of the largest hotels in Trieste, for a Slovenian dance, the administration of the hotel replied that it first needed approval from Rome. Out of three such applications, only once was permission granted to rent the hall.

The same situation arose when Yugoslavia tried to open its own bank in Trieste. Permission was refused on the ground that all financial operations had to be decided by the Roman headquarters of the Banco di Roma, which in turn stated that it saw no need for a new bank in Trieste. Again, when Yugoslavia asked to rent part of a warehouse in the free port, the para-statal Magazzini Generali rejected the application after a long wait, on the ground that only private firms, but not a state, could rent rooms in warehouses.[33]

Similar rebuffs met all independentist groups, including foreign companies, seeking to begin any kind of economic activity in the Free Territory. Only firm intervention of the AMG compelled the Italian government to allow a Swiss travel agency to open an office in Trieste. It happened, incidentally, only after General Airey had left Trieste, and when the AMG had begun to pursue a more independent policy in conjunction with a change in official attitude on the part of Great Britain and the United States, a topic to be discussed in a subsequent chapter.

The first consequence of the Tripartite Proposal was thus to reinforce Italian control over Trieste's economy, and to slow the development of an independent economy that might have strengthened the independentist movement in Trieste.

33. *Third AMG Report* (S/953), p. 12.

ITALIAN INFLUENCE IN ADMINISTRATION

After September 15, 1947, Zone A of the Free Territory of Trieste was of course smaller than the former Trieste area, and comprised now only Trieste and five other municipalities (communes). It continued to be administered in accordance with General Order No. 11 until April 1948. True, there were some minor changes but these were in titles rather than substance. For example, in January 1948, the title of the senior civil affairs officer was altered to that of director general of civil affairs. But the director general retained the same authority. His function continued to be comparable to that of a prime minister.[34] Similarly the title of area commissioner was changed to zone commissioner but the officer performed the same functions as before. He supervised the local civil administration and remained the link between the British-American central government and the local administration.[35]

However, after the Tripartite declaration the AMG changed its policy. On April 12, 1948, it abolished the office of the zone commissioner and decided to limit itself to the function of a central government, giving greater autonomy and authority to the local civil administration. For that purpose, on June 25, 1948, the AMG substituted for the old General Order No. 11 a new Order No. 259.[36] The order nonetheless made it clear that the AMG was to remain the supreme authority over Zone A. Thus the right to

34. In the latter part of June 1947 Colonel Alfred C. Bowman had been replaced by Colonel James J. Carnes as senior civil affairs officer. After September 15, 1947, Colonel Carnes continued as SCAO of Zone A of the Free Territory of Trieste, until October 23, 1947, when U.S. General Ridgely Gaither took over as SCAO. (See "Notice No. 3," dated in Trieste, October 24, 1947, in *AMG-FTT Gazette*, 1, no. 5 [Nov. 1, 1947]: 71.) General Gaither's title changed from SCAO to Director General of Civil Affairs in January 1948. (See "Order No. 55," dated January 10, 1948, *AMG-FTT Gazette*, 1, no. 12 [Jan. 11, 1948]: 197.)

35. "Order No. 229," dated in Trieste, April 12, 1948, *AMG-FTT Gazette*, 1, no. 22 (Apr. 21, 1948): 369; *Second AMG Report* (S/781), p. 8.

36. "Order No. 259," dated in Trieste, June 25, 1948, issued by General Ridgely Gaither, director general of civil affairs, *AMG-FTT Gazette*, 1, no. 29 (July 1, 1948): 463–68. The order is reproduced also in *Third AMG Report* (S/953), pp. 18–23.

reverse, amend, or substitute any order, decree, decision or deliberation to be issued by officers of local administration was expressly reserved to the director general, acting in the name of the AMG. Likewise, exclusive authority over all police and security services remained under direct control of the AMG.

The new order also repeated the clause in the former General Order No. 11 annulling the authority of the National Liberation committees: "No committee, council or group other than those herein created and provided for, shall possess any administrative, legislative, executive or other powers of government unless otherwise provided for by Order of the Allied Military Government."[37]

Order No. 259 created three levels of local civil authority, namely the zone, the province, and the municipality:

> For the purpose of local government that part of the Free Territory of Trieste administered by the British–United States Forces shall constitute one single Zone composed of the Communes comprised within its boundaries and including the autonomous body "Provincia di Trieste."[38]

The zone remained subdivided into the traditional six communes: Duino-Aurisina, Sgonico, Monrupino, Trieste, San Dorligo, and Muggia. Besides the local administration, the zone, province, and commune authorities supervised the departments of public health, public utilities, agriculture and fisheries, and civil transport.[39]

A zone president, appointed by the AMG, with powers similar to those of an Italian prefect, was to head the zone administration.[40] The AMG also named a zone vice-president. The president was aided by a zone administrative board (Giunta Amministrativa di Zona) composed of nine members, of which the president appointed the first four and the provincial council the other five.[41]

37. *AMG-FTT Gazette,* 1, no. 29: 467.
38. Ibid., p. 464.   39. *Fourth AMG Report* (S/1174), p. 2.
40. The zone president had the same functions as the area president had had according to General Order No. 11: the more so as the same man (Gino Palutan) who had been area president was now appointed as the new zone president.
41. Appointed by the zone president were the provincial inspector (Ispettore Provinciale), the superintendent of finance (Sovraintendente

ITALIAN INFLUENCE IN ADMINISTRATION

The zone president appointed the president of the province, as well as the provincial council (Deputazione Provinciale, called also Consiglio Provinciale). The provincial president could select from the members of the provincial council his provincial vice-president. The provincial authorities were responsible, among other functions, for administration of welfare services and maintenance of roads on the provincial level.

Of the six communes only Trieste and Muggia had Italian majorities; the other four were Slovenian in complexion. The heads of communes were still to be appointed by the Allied Military Government. They were given the old Italian title of *sindaco* (mayor) instead of the previously used "communal president." The Sindaco was to be assisted by a communal board (Giunta Municipale). The members of the communal board, instead of being appointed by the AMG as before, were now appointed and removed by the zone president. In case of such removal, no appeal could be lodged before the judicial or administrative authorities.

Changes made in personnel substantially increased the influence of the Italian parties in the local administration.[42] Professor Gino Palutan, a Christian Democrat, became zone president, and Professor Carlo Schiffrer, a Socialist, was appointed as zone vice-president; Michele Miani of the Action party became mayor of Trieste. Thus, all leading positions remained exclusively in Italian hands. On the zone administration board there was only one Independentist against nine pro-Italians; on the Trieste provincial committee of five members, the two independentists were in a minority; on Trieste's communal board of ten members, eight were pro-Italian and two independentist. No representative of the Communist bloc or of the democratic Slovenes was placed on the zone or provincial boards or on the commune boards of Trieste and Muggia. Only in the Slovenian communes were Slovenian

---

di Finanza), and two prefecture councilors (Consiglieri di Prefettura). The other five members, to be appointed by the provincial council, consisted of the accountant general (Capo Ragioniere della Prefettura) and four regular members "to be chosen from persons who are expert in legal, administrative, and technical branches."

42. "Italian" is used to describe a member of a pro-Italian political party advocating the return of the FTT to Italy.

mayors and communal boards nominated, except in the Duino-Aurisina commune, where the mayor was Slovenian and the board of four members evenly divided between Italians and Slovenes. The increase of Italian influence in Slovenian communes was due to the members of the boards being appointed by and responsible to the zone president.[43]

Next, the AMG limited its own function to that of a central government as previously planned. To readjust to this new situation the AMG was reorganized according to Order No. 308 which came into full force on August 1, 1948.[44] The director general of civil affairs remained the head of the government, with the functions of a prime minister. The central government, headed by the director general, was made up of three directorates: directorate general, directorate of interior, and directorate of finance and economics. The directorate general was subdivided into one department and two offices, namely, the office of the executive director, the department of legal affairs, and the public information office. The directorate of interior had three departments: interior, public safety, and labor. The largest was the third, the directorate of finance and economics with seven departments: finance, industry, commerce, public works, transportation, port authority, and posts and telecommunication. (For greater detail see table 2.) All the departments and offices of the central government remained in the hands of British–United States military officers.

Orders Nos. 259 and 308 enlarged the autonomy of the local civil administration, in turn benefiting the Italian parties; finding themselves in firm control of the local administration, the Italians tried to transform Zone A administratively into an Italian province. Italian pressure manifested itself first in the Vital Statistics Office (Ufficio Anagrafico), which, under the Italian system, maintained the records of all residents in a given commune. It issued certificates affirming which persons were considered permanent residents and which were only provisional, and furnished appropriate identification cards.

During the war many Italians had moved from rural sections

43. For a list of local government appointments from the zone to communal level see *Fourth AMG Report* (S/1174), pp. 19–21.

44. "Order No. 308," dated July 26, 1948, *AMG-FTT Gazette*, 1, no. 32 (Aug. 1, 1948): 517–21.

TABLE 2
ORGANIZATION OF THE AMG

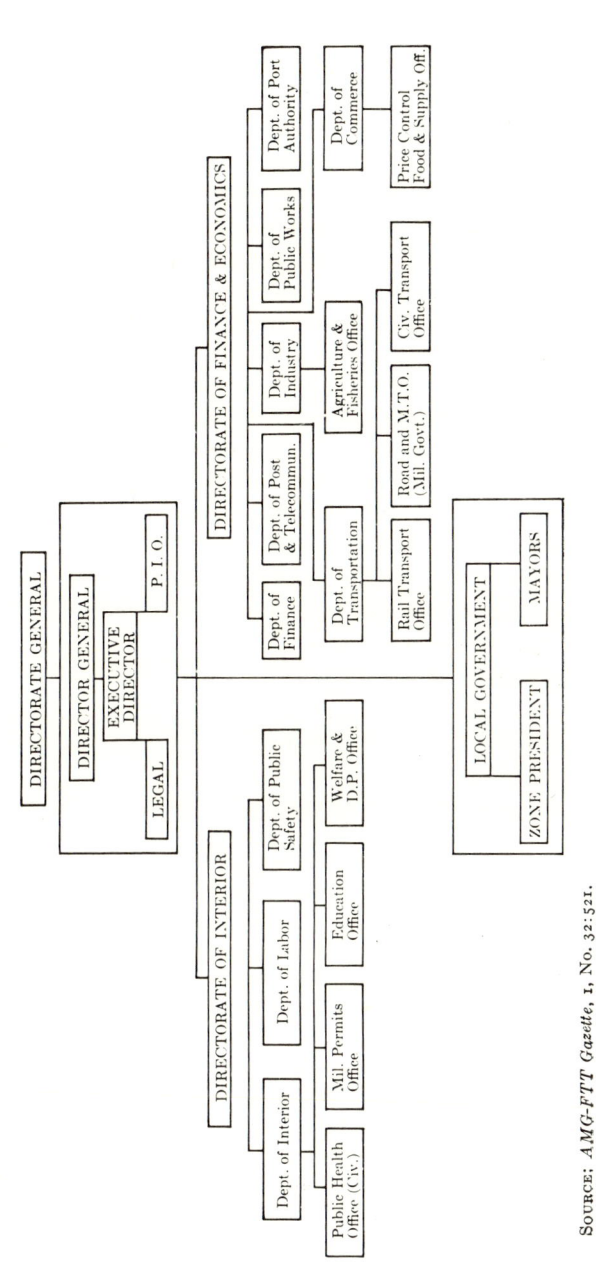

DIRECTORATE GENERAL

DIRECTOR GENERAL
EXECUTIVE DIRECTOR
LEGAL
P.I.O.

DIRECTORATE OF INTERIOR

- Dept. of Interior
  - Public Health Office (Civ.)
- Mil. Permits Office
- Dept. of Labor
  - Education Office
- Dept. of Public Safety
  - Welfare & D.P. Office

DIRECTORATE OF FINANCE & ECONOMICS

- Dept. of Finance
- Dept. of Transportation
  - Rail Transport Office
  - Road and M.T.O. (Mil. Govt.)
  - Civ. Transport Office
- Dept. of Post & Telecommun.
- Dept. of Industry
  - Agriculture & Fisheries Office
- Dept. of Public Works
- Dept. of Port Authority
- Dept. of Commerce
- Price Control Food & Supply Off.

LOCAL GOVERNMENT

- ZONE PRESIDENT
- MAYORS

SOURCE: *AMG-FTT Gazette*, 1, No. 32: 521.

ASCENDANCY OF ITALY IN ZONE A

of the Julian Region to get out of the Slavic area and into Trieste. After the war and also after the peace treaty with Italy came into force, more Italian refugees, who had lived in sections of the Julian Region now given to Yugoslavia, increased the number of Italians in Trieste. At the start, the Vital Statistics Office registered them as provisional residents, but soon recognized them as permanent, and when the office issued new identification cards in 1948, the majority received permanent status. The situation was quite different for non-Communist Slovenes and Croats who had also been Italian citizens, but residents of the parts of the Julian Region given to Yugoslavia, and who, having moved into Zone A of the Free Territory, now claimed the same status as the Italian refugees. These people were given merely provisional resident cards. The number of Italian refugees who received the status of permanent residents has been variously estimated as between twenty-five thousand and thirty-four thousand persons.[45] The Slovenian émigré group employed by the AMG received only the status of provisional residents. The question of permanent residence would naturally become important in elections.

The distribution of new identity cards during 1948 further aided the Italian cause.[46] While the previous cards for Zone A had been in three languages, English, Italian, and Slovenian, the new ones were issued only in the Italian language for the municipality of Trieste and in Italian and Slovenian in the Slovenian rural communes. Further, the new identity cards indicated the citizenship the holder had enjoyed prior to creation of the FTT. As the AMG

---

45. Mihovilović in his work *Trst problem dana* (p. 94) estimated that there were in Trieste over 34,000 such Italian refugees. AMG in its report for 1950 estimated about 25,000 Italian refugees coming into Trieste after the war. For the latter see "Report on the Administration of the British–U.S. Zone of the Free Territory of Trieste for the Period 1 January to 31 December 1950 by Major General T. S. Airey . . . ," *UNSC*, Doc. S/2062 (Mar. 29, 1951), p. 7. (Mimeographed.) Hereafter cited as *Tenth AMG Report* (S/2062). *Yugoslav Memorandum* (S/1054) from October 1948 stated that 30,000 to 40,000 refugees from Istria entered Trieste after June 10, 1940.

46. The issue of the new identity cards was decreed by "Order No. 193," dated April 9, 1948, *AMG-FTT Gazette,* 1, no. 22 (Apr. 21, 1948): 365–67; see also *Fifth AMG Report* (S/1242), p. 4.

failed to recognize the FTT citizenship, the majority of the inhabitants of Zone A were identified as citizens of Italy instead of the FTT.

The Yugoslav government, in a note of December 25, 1948, pointed out that the use of only the Italian language in Trieste was a violation of Article 7, Annex VI of the peace treaty with Italy, which clearly stated that the official languages were to be both Italian and Slovenian. This failure to recognize the Slovenian tongue was also condemned as a violation of Slovenian ethnic rights guaranteed in the Permanent Statute. The Yugoslav note also stressed that refusal to recognize Trieste citizenship while continuing to recognize Italian was a violation of Article 6, Annex VI of the treaty, and represented an attack on the integrity of the Free Territory itself. Mario Stocca, leader of the independentist Blocco Triestino, in a speech of February 21, 1950, summed up the matter by stating that the Free Territory had been established as an independent state with a flag and coat of arms, recognized by the AMG, but had no citizens.[47] This denial of citizenship was a successful move to dim enthusiasm for a Free Territory.

The AMG took its stand on the language dispute in September 1949. Italian was to be the official language of Zone A. Slovenian could be used in addition to the Italian language only in Slovenian communes. However, official communications of the transactions of the communal councils with authorities outside the communes had to be either in the Italian language or in both Italian and Slovenian.[48] By this policy Slovenian came to be restricted to the status of a secondary language, and even that only in the Slovenian communes.

Connections between Zone A and the Italian Republic were

47. "Note Regarding the Administration of the Free Territory of Trieste," signed in Belgrade, December 25, 1948, *UNSC*, Doc. S/1183 (January 5, 1949) (mimeographed), hereafter cited as *Yugoslav Note* (S/1183); Mario Stocca, *Discussioni sul T.L.T. al consiglio comunale di Trieste* (Trieste, n.d. [1950]), p. 7.

48. See "Order No. 183," dated September 2, 1949, *AMG-FTT Gazette*, 2, no. 25 (Sept. 11, 1949): 449. The order was signed by the new director general of civil affairs, U.S. Brigadier General Clyde D. Eddleman, who replaced General Gaither in June 1949.

made still closer during the summer of 1949 when the AMG abolished all restrictions on travel between Zone A and Italy for all citizens of the Italian Republic in possession of a valid identification card.[49]

In the course of time Italian influence also increased over the controversial and important department of education. At the start the department head was an Allied officer, first American, later English. He had two advisers, with equal status, one for Slovenian and the other for Italian schools. The situation changed, however, as soon as the Italian adviser became head of the department, for then the Slovenian adviser became subordinate to an Italian head, which meant in practice the subjection of Slovenian schools to the Italians. Not long afterward the position of Slovenian adviser was abolished.

Alarmed by this growing trend in favor of the Italians, and fearful that Slovenian fundamental rights would again be denied, as they had been during the time between the two world wars, the Slovenes conducted a campaign of vigorous protest against these violations of the peace treaty. In his reports to the United Nations, General Airey tried to cover up these violations by accusing the Communists of having

> used every device and much violence of language in attempts to revive racial bitterness and to this end they have not failed to raise the standard of nationalism and exploit the problem of bilingualism wherever they have seen an opportunity to do so.[50]

No one could deny that the Communists exploited the situation. Nevertheless it was also true that the AMG gave the Communists ample "opportunity to do so."

49. *Eighth AMG Report* (S/1424), p. 5. Previously every citizen of the Italian Republic had to possess an entry permit, issued by the AMG, according to "Order No. 140," dated February 14, 1948, *AMG-FTT Gazette,* 1, no. 16 (Feb. 21, 1948): 279–84; and "Order No. 202," dated March 17, 1948, in ibid., 1, no. 19 (Mar. 21, 1948): 334–36.

50. *Eighth AMG Report* (S/1424), p. 5; see also *Fifth AMG Report,* (S/1242), p. 4.

TITO'S SCHISM

Only a little over three months after the Tripartite Proposal had been made, another important international event profoundly influenced the political scene in Zone A. This was Tito's expulsion from the Cominform. On June 28, 1948, the Cominform published its resolution which condemned the Central Committee of the Yugoslav Communist party and particularly "Comrades Tito, Kardelj, Djilas, and Ranković."[51] The Central Committee of the Yugoslav Communist party countered the accusations on June 29, 1948, with its own statement.[52] *Borba*, the official organ of the Yugoslav Communist party, published both the Cominform Resolution and the Yugoslav answer on June 30, 1948.

On July 3 and 4, 1948, the ten members of the Executive Committee, the highest body of the Communist party in the Free Territory, came together to discuss the Cominform Resolution. Six members were in favor of it, with a minority of four defending the Yugoslav position.[53] With this meeting the split of the Communist bloc began in Zone A. The six members headed by Vittorio Vidali represented the leadership of the pro-Stalinist or pro-Cominform group from that time on.[54] The other four, under

51. "Resolution of the Information Bureau Concerning the Situation in the Communist Party of Yugoslavia," printed in *The Soviet-Yugoslav Dispute: Text of the Published Correspondence*, ed. by the Royal Institute of International Affairs (London, 1948), pp. 61–70. Here is to be found the complete text of the Cominform Resolution. For an abbreviated text with commentary see Robert Bass and Elizabeth Marbury, eds., *The Soviet-Yugoslav Controversy, 1948–58: A Documentary Record*, introduction by Hans Kohn (New York, 1959), 40–46.

52. "Statement of the Central Committee of the Communist Party of Yugoslavia on the Resolution of the Information Bureau of Communist Parties on the Situation in the Communist Party of Yugoslavia," reprinted in *The Soviet-Yugoslav Dispute*, pp. 71–79.

53. See Bulajić, pp. 23–26.

54. Vittorio Vidali, a loyal agent of Stalin's will, was a Communist of international significance. For his activities in North and South America see "Tito and the Executioner," *Time*, Sept. 6, 1948, p. 22; and Isaac Don Levine, *The Mind of an Assassin* (New York, 1959), pp. 70–71. See also Giorgio Cesare, "Vidali sotto accusa," *Trieste*, no. 35 (Jan.–Feb. 1960), p. 18.

Branko Babič, took charge of the pro-Tito or pro-Yugoslav forces.

After July 4, 1948, the Babič group called a plenary session of the Central Committee, and expelled the pro-Vidali Cominformists. Cleared of the latter, the Central Committee held its second plenary meeting on July 20, 1948. Five new members were elected to the Executive Committee from the Babič party, bringing its total to nine.

On August 21 and 22, 1948, the Vidali group held a congress of the Cominformist party. Here they elected a new Executive Committee and a new Central Committee for their party. A few days later, on August 28, a conference of the Babič party met. The Cominform Resolution was condemned again, as was creation of a Cominform party in Zone A, for this would weaken the fight of the working class against the imperialistic powers administering the zone.

By the end of August there were two Communist parties in Zone A—the CPFTT (Vidali), and CPFTT (Babič). In Zone B, the Yugoslav authorities prohibited any activity of the Vidali group. Whoever was suspected of pro-Cominform leanings was arrested. Many pro-Cominform members fled from Zone B to Zone A.

Following the break at the top came a split of the entire Communist bloc including all mass organizations such as the Sindacati Unici, the UAIS-SIAU, the anti-Fascist women, and the youth organization. The Cominformists took over *Il Lavoratore,* while *Primorski dnevnik* remained under Babič's control. The Cominformists published a newspaper, *Delo* (Work), for the Slovenes. With the passing of time, the struggle between the Cominformists and pro-Titoists increased. It was as a result of this fight that many obscure events that had happened during the war now came to light.

The Italian Socialist party used the struggle between the Communist groups for its own propaganda, urging the workers to abandon the Communist-controlled labor unions and to join the socialists.

In the beginning, however, the Cominform Resolution had little effect on the international situation, for two main reasons. First, future development within the Yugoslav Communist party was not yet clear. Conceivably, the Cominform followers, with Russian help, might overthrow Tito and become the real rulers in

Yugoslavia. Stalin himself was quite convinced that events would turn out this way.[55] Second, even when it became clear that Tito would keep control, some doubt remained as to whether the episode was not a trap, a clever maneuver to create, through Tito's apparent defection, a Communist Trojan horse.[56] Italian newspapers devoted many pages to this theory. Thus, not until the end of 1949 did the Western powers publicly acknowledge that Tito's break with Moscow was real, and that Tito's control in Yugoslavia was firm.

But by September 1948, it was already apparent that the split in the Communist bloc of Zone A was serious. No one could predict how many members would follow Vidali, and how many Babič. The rift affected both Italians and Slovenes. For the time being, both Communist parties still stood for a Free Territory and continued to fight the AMG. But the attacks were no longer dangerous, as the once powerful Communist opposition broke into two hostile groups.

FIRST ELECTIONS

With Italian parties greatly strengthened and Communist opposition significantly weakened, the AMG decided it was at last safe to hold municipal elections, something long demanded by the Yugoslav government and Communist bloc. Consequently, on September 24, 1948, the AMG issued Order No. 345 for the compilation of electoral rolls.[57] Article II established who was to be a voter—a most controversial provision:

> In the first compilation of the Electoral Rolls there shall be inscribed all male and female persons—to whom the right of voting is hereby expressly extended—who on 15 September 1947 were Italian citizens and have reached or will reach the age of 21 within December 31, 1948 and are lawfully inscribed

55. Eden, p. 199.
56. The idea that the split between Tito and Moscow was a fake was also spread among Yugoslav émigré circles. See for example Slobodan M. Draskovich [Drašković], *Tito, Moscow's Trojan Horse* (Chicago, 1957).
57. "Order No. 345," dated September 24, 1948, *AMG-FTT Gazette*, 1, no. 38 (Oct. 1, 1948): 383–98. (There is a printing mistake. Pages should be 583–98.)

in the Register of the Permanent Population of one of the Communes of the Zone.[58]

According to the same order each commune had to prepare its own electoral rolls under the supervision of the zone president. Only Fascists who had held the highest positions in the party or state administration were excluded from the right to vote. Persons who had lost or were to lose their Italian citizenship were to be cancelled from the electoral rolls. Any person could at any time inspect all documents concerning the rolls. Anyone could copy, print, or sell copies of these rolls. Rolls contained in alphabetical order the following data on each voter: the surname and name, the father's name, the place and date of birth, and the address.[59]

The Yugoslav government in the memorandum to the Security Council a month later, on October 24, 1948, protested the above vital decision of Article II as a direct violation of Article 6, Annex VI, of the peace treaty with Italy.[60] As pointed out in the memorandum, moving the base date of residence from 1940 to 1947 meant giving the right to vote to all Italian refugees who had settled in Trieste during or after the war and would inevitably influence the election in favor of pro-Italian parties.

The second main objection to Order No. 345 raised by the Yugoslav memorandum was that, according to the new regulations, the electoral rolls of the Trieste municipality would be prepared in the Vital Statistics Office by Italian employees. The memorandum demanded that all recognized political parties be allowed to aid in drawing up these rolls. Local Trieste pro-independentist newspapers also raised objections, but without success.

On February 21, 1949, the AMG published Order No. 33 laying down rules for the coming election.[61] The newly elected com-

58. Ibid., p. 383 [583].
59. See also "Order No. 61," dated March 29, 1949, *AMG-FTT Gazette,* 2, no. 10 (Apr. 11, 1949): 164, which amended Order No. 345.
60. *Yugoslav Memorandum* (S/1054), pp. 1–2, 8.
61. "Order No. 33," dated February 21, 1949, *AMG-FTT Gazette,* 2, no. 5 (Feb. 21, 1949): 72–95. The order was reproduced also in "Report on the Administration of the British–U.S. Zone of the Free Territory of Trieste for the Period 1 January to 31 March 1949 by Major General T. S. Airey . . . ," *UNSC,* Doc. S/1318 (May 6, 1949), pp. 21–51. (Mimeographed.) The report will be cited as the *Sixth AMG Report* (S/1318).

munal administration would be composed of a communal council (Consiglio Comunale), a communal board (Giunta Municipale) and a mayor (Sindaco). The communal council would have

 a. 60 members for the commune of Trieste
 b. 30 members for the commune of Muggia
 c. 20 members for the communes of Duino-Aurisina and San Dorligo della Valle
 d. 15 members for the communes of Sgonico and Monrupino.

The communal board would be composed of the mayor as chairman and of

 a. 12 assessors and 3 substitutes for the commune of Trieste
 b. 4 assessors and 2 substitutes for the communes of Muggia, Duino-Aurisina, and San Dorligo della Valle
 c. 2 assessors and 2 substitutes for the communes of Sgonico and Monrupino.

The voters were to elect the members of the communal council for a term of two years. The communal council would then elect among its members the mayor and the members of the communal board.

Each person entered on the electoral rolls had the right to vote and the right to be elected. Elections were to be conducted by lists of candidates. Each political party or a group of electors could present a list of candidates, the number of which had to be not less than one-fifth of and not greater than the number of councillors to be elected for a particular commune. Such a list must be signed by at least

 a. 300 voters in the commune of Trieste
 b. 100 voters in the commune of Muggia
 c. 30 voters in the communes of Duino-Aurisina and San Dorligo della Valle
 d. 10 voters in the communes of Monrupino and Sgonico.

The voters were to vote for an entire list. The number of candidates elected on a list was to be in proportion to votes cast for the list. A paper ballot was to be used. Complete freedom was assured for election propaganda. Other detailed provisions of the order described the preparations for voting, the voting process itself, the counting of votes, the proclamation of elected candidates, and the penal provisions for violators of the rules set down in this order. The laws regulating the election and the date of the elections came from the AMG. The organization of the election was left to the zone president. The elections, as described in Order No. 33, were to be based on a universal, direct, free, and secret vote for lists of candidates, and on the principle of proportional representation.

The election campaign started after the AMG announced on April 21, 1949, that the elections would be held Sunday, June 12, in Trieste and the following Sunday, June 19, in the rural communes.[62] The Italian parties tried to turn the communal elections into a plebiscite for Italy, in the belief that their overwhelming victory would bring the Tripartite Proposal into effect. The Italian government and also the parties in Italy supported their adherents in Trieste with large sums of money. Election propaganda became intense. Practically no wall on the streets in the center of Trieste was without a poster, and propagandists could scarcely find an empty space in which to post their latest appeal. During the last days the leaders of the respective parties in Italy came to Trieste to aid their embattled Italian comrades.

All other parties and blocs counteracted the Italian propaganda by defending the continued existence of the Free Territory. Such a position was taken by the Independence Front, the Blocco Triestino, the Slovenian Democratic Union, the Cominform Communist party, and the Titoist Communist party.

So far as the Communists were concerned, since the elections would reveal the relative strength of Titoists and Cominformists each attacked the other more bitterly than it did the non-Communist democratic parties. While the Cominformists were supported by the Italian Communist party, the Titoists were aided financially from Yugoslavia. Thus all major parties received substantial monetary help from abroad, except the independence parties and the Slovenian democrats. Each of the independence parties—the Independence Front and the Triestino bloc—presented its own list. The Slovenian democrats, on the other hand, went into the

62. "Order No. 81," dated April 18, 1949, *AMG-FTT Gazette*, 2, no. 11 (Apr. 21, 1949): 218. The order came into effect upon publication in the *Gazette*.

election with one list supported by the liberal Slovenian Democratic Union and the newly created Catholic Slovenian Christian Social Union (Slovenska krščansko–socialna zveza).

The Trieste elections reflected the complicated struggle that raged among the Italian parties of the Left, Right, and Center, between the two Communist parties, between Italian and Slovenian parties, and between pro- and anti-Communists. The most important immediate issue, however, was the union of Trieste with Italy versus the existence of an independent Free Territory of Trieste.[63]

The elections were held on June 12 for the commune of Trieste and on June 19 for the five rural communes. In Zone A, 212,658 voters had been inscribed on the electoral rolls, but only 196,526 received the electoral certificate needed for voting. The latter figure therefore represented the factual electorate. According to the AMG report 94.2 percent of the electorate or 185,127 went to the polls, and of these, 181,820 ballots were declared valid (see table 3).[64] Table 4 gives detailed results for all six communes.

Regarding the main issue, the independence of Trieste, 112,684 votes (or 62 percent) were cast for the return of Trieste to

63. For the issues among the pro-Italian parties see for example Apih, *Il Ponte*, 4, no. 4; 329–38. The following are pro-Titoist pamphlets: Branko Babič, *Tržaško demokratično gibanje in KPI* (Trieste's Democratic Movement and the CPI) (Trieste, 1949); Boris Mrak, *Il fronte popolare italo-slavo e le elezioni* (Trieste, 1949); Giovanni [Ivan] Regent, *Sulla difesa della rivoluzione democratica* (Trieste, 1949). The Slovenian Democratic Union published *Program Slovenske demokratske zveze za Svobodno tržaško ozemlje v Trstu* (Program of the Slovenian Democratic Union for the Free Territory of Trieste in Trieste) (Trieste, 1949). A short analysis of the political parties is to be found in *Trieste Handbook 1950*, pp. 26–32.

64. The data on the election results are based on the "Report on the Administration of the British–U.S. Zone of the Free Territory of Trieste for the Period 1 April to 30 June 1949 by Major General T. S. Airey . . . ," *UNSC*, Doc. S/1374 (August 11, 1949). (Mimeographed.) Hereafter cited as the *Seventh AMG Report* (S/1374). Other works give slightly different figures, as, for example, *Risultati elettorali e analisi cartografica delle elezioni amministrative dal 1949 al 1952 nel comune di Trieste e negli altri comuni del territorio* (Trieste, n.d.) or Mihovilović, *Trst problem dana*.

TABLE 3
ELECTORATE AND VOTES IN ZONE A, FTT (1949)

	Inscribed in Electoral Rolls	Received Electoral Certificates	Undelivered Certificates	Valid Votes	Abstentions and Invalid Votes
Trieste	197,266	181,971	15,295	168,108	13,863
Rural communes	15,392	14,555	837	13,712	843
Total	212,658	196,526	16,132	181,820	14,706

SOURCE: *Seventh AMG Report* (S/1374), pp. 6-7, 20-21.

TABLE 4
FIRST ADMINISTRATIVE ELECTIONS IN ZONE A (JUNE 1949)

Commune of Trieste

Party	Votes	Percent	Councillors
Christian Democrats	65,627	39.04	25
FTT Communist party (Cominformists)	35,548	21.14	13
Italian Republican party (Republicans and Partito d'Azione)	9,081	5.41	3
Venezia Giulia Socialist party	10,747	6.39	4
Italian Liberal party	3,094	1.84	1
Italian Slovene Popular Front (Titoists)	3,957	2.35	1
Italian bloc (Qualunquists and Monarchists)	8,252	4.91	3
Independence Front	11,476	6.83	4
Slovene Democratic Union	3,004	1.79	1
Italian Republican Movement	2,291	1.36	...
Trieste bloc	4,860	2.89	1
Italian Social Movement (MSI—Neo-Fascists)	10,171	6.05	4
Total	168,108	100.00	60

Commune of Muggia

Party	Votes	Percent	Councillors
FTT Communist party (Cominformists)	4,182	56.86	17
Christian Democrats	2,046	27.81	9
Italian Slovene Popular Front (Titoists)	323	4.39	1
Italian Republican party	242	3.28	1
Venezia Giulia Socialist party	564	7.66	2
Total	7,357	100.00	30

SOURCE: *Seventh AMG Report* (S/1374), pp. 20-21.

TABLE 4—*Continued*

Commune of Duino-Aurisina

Party	Votes	Percent	Councillors
Slovene National list (Slovenian democrats)	752	27.75	5
Workers and Farmers League (Slovenian independentists)	51	1.81	..
Italian Slovene Anti-Fascist Union (Cominformists)	949	34.97	7
Slovene Italian Popular Front (Titoists)	395	14.54	3
Italian democrats (Christian Democrats and Socialists)	569	20.93	4
Total	2,716	100.00	20 (*sic*)

Commune of San Dorligo della Valle

Party	Votes	Percent	Councillors
Independent list (Slovenian democrats)	772	29.25	6
Italian Slovene Anti-Fascist Union (Cominformists)	1,466	55.56	11
Slovene Italian Popular Front (Titoists)	401	15.19	3
Total	2,639	100.00	20

Commune of Sgonico

Party	Votes	Percent	Councillors
Italian Slovene Anti-Fascist Union (Cominformists)	345	51.12	8
Slovene Italian Popular Front (Titoists)	148	21.92	3
Slovene National list (Slovenian democrats)	182	26.96	4
Total	675	100.00	15

Commune of Monrupino

Party	Votes	Percent	Councillors
Italian Slovene Anti-Fascist Union (Cominformists)	97	29.84	4
Independent Economic Union (Slovenian democrats)	142	43.70	7
Slovene Italian Popular Front (Titoists)	86	26.46	4
Total	325	100.00	15

Italy, of which 109,263 came in Trieste itself (65 percent of Trieste's vote); and 69,136 votes (or 38 percent) for continuation of the Free Territory of Trieste, of which 10,291 were cast in the surrounding communes.

The total Communist vote amounted to 47,931, a reduction from previous estimates. Of this total the Cominformists mustered 42,587 and the Titoists only 5,344. It is significant that the Cominformists led not only in the city of Trieste, but also in the other communes, where the totals cast were 8,039 for the Cominformists to 1,387 for the Titoists. Taking only the four Slovenian communes, the Cominformists received 2,857 votes, to 1,064 for the Titoists. The total strength of the Communists remained superior in all communes to that of the Slovenian democratic bloc. Thus, the election results showed that the Communists favored the Cominformists rather than the Titoists. Ethnic differences seemed to play no significant role in this decision. Before the Cominform Resolution the Italian Communists had favored Tito's program in Zone A; afterwards the great majority of Slovenian Communists supported the line of the Italian Communist party and the Russians. Thus the solidarity manifested between Italian and Slovenian Communists during the entire period from the end of World War I was not seriously damaged by Tito's schism.

The final question of importance to be analyzed in these returns is the proportion of votes cast by Slovenes. With safety, it might be considered that the entire vote for the Slovenian democratic list was Slovenian, as was practically the whole vote for the Titoists. Many Slovenes, however, did vote for the Cominformists and in Trieste for the Independence Front. Furthermore, many deeply religious Slovenian women gave their votes to the Italian Christian Democratic party as the only Catholic party they could approve, since the Slovenian Catholics were allied with the Slovenian Liberal party, an organization not favored by these women.

A statistical study to ascertain the size of the Slovenian vote was made by Professor Carlo Schiffrer. He based his analysis on the percentage of votes received by Cominformists and by independentists in the Slovenian villages forming the Trieste commune, and then extended his average percentage to the entire vote. On this basis Schiffrer calculated that from 6,563 to 10,380 Slovenian votes were cast for the Cominform list and from 3,030 to 4,700 such votes went to the Independence Front.[65] Using average figures, according to Schiffrer, this would mean about 21,000 Slovenian votes in the Trieste commune. With the addition of the Slovenian votes in the other communes the approximate Slovenian vote was 28,500.[66]

The election results showed that the strongest of the Italian parties was the Christian Democratic party. The Italian Liberals, once the leading party, won only a little over 3,000 votes. The rightists and Fascists received over 18,000 votes. They had two lists, those of the Italian bloc and the Italian Social Movement. The latter was a neo-Fascist group. The Italian bloc was composed of monarchists and Qualunquists, who were pro-royalist Fascists named after their journal *Il Uomo Qualunque* (The Common Man). The Socialist party received 10,747 votes. In this election, however, many former Socialists voted for the Independence Front.

The Italian press, both in Italy and in Trieste, was jubilant over the election. The newspapers pointed out the great majority the Italian parties had received, and appealed to the Western powers to return the Free Territory to Italy, a step evidently favored by the majority of voters. The AMG was also satisfied with the election returns, although AMG officials had expected the Italians to get about 75 percent of the vote instead of the 65 percent they actually received in the commune of Trieste.[67]

65. Actor Spectator [Carlo Schiffrer], "Orientamenti politici degli elettori sloveni," *Trieste,* no. 10 (Nov.–Dec. 1955), pp. 11–12. See also the continuation of "Orientamenti politici," *Trieste,* no. 14 (July–Aug. 1956), pp. 12–13, signed by Carlo Schiffrer.

66. The figure 28,500 (or 28,493) was reached by taking as the base the mean between Schiffrer's maximum and minimum estimates of the Slovenian votes of the commune of Trieste (20,833). To this number was added the number of votes received by Slovenian lists, and half of the votes received by the Cominform list in the communes Muggia (Milje) and Duino-Aurisina (Devin-Nabrežina). To this amount was added the entire vote of the Slovenian communes where no Italian lists were presented, namely the communes San Dorligo della Valle (Dolina), Sgonico (Zgonik) and Monrupino (Repentabor).

67. Guido Sabini, "Trieste 1949," *Trieste,* no. 13 (May–June 1956), p. 38.

ASCENDANCY OF ITALY IN ZONE A

On the other side, the independentist, pro-Yugoslav, Cominform, and Slovenian press underlined various factors that tended to minimize the Italian victory. As summarized by Ive Mihovilović, these were three:[68] first, people were given the right to vote who were not entitled to do so under the peace treaty; second, the electoral registers were prepared exclusively by pro-Italian officials in the Trieste commune, without participation by representatives of all recognized parties, the request for such participation never having been accepted by the AMG; third, 16,132 registered persons had not received voting certificates, a matter officially recognized in the *Seventh AMG Report*.

TABLE 5

PERCENTAGE OF VOTES FOR OR AGAINST ITALY IN 1949 ELECTIONS

FTT Commune	Percentage of Votes against Italy	Percentage of Votes for Italy
Trieste	36.36	63.64
Sgonico	100.00	.....
Duino-Aurisina	79.07	20.93
Monrupino	100.00	.....
San Dorligo della Valle	100.00	.....
Muggia	61.25	38.75

SOURCE: Mihovilović, *Trst problem dana*, p. 93.

The Slovenian national press (for example, *Demokracija* and *Katoliški glas*) drew the conclusion that the elections in reality proved that Trieste represented an Italian island in a Slovenian region, without any connection with Italian ethnic territory. Only in the commune of Trieste did the Italian parties advocating a return of the Free Territory to Italy receive a majority. In all other communes surrounding Trieste not a single election majority was found for the Italians; in three of these communes not even one Italian list was presented. Of the same opinion was Mihovilović, who prepared the statistics in table 5. It should be noted that, except for Trieste and Muggia, each of the communes had an absolute Slovenian majority in population. In Muggia, while the Italians had a majority in population, the

68. Mihovilović, *Trst problem dana*, pp. 92–94.

majority of voters endorsed the Free Territory, the decisive group being the Cominformists.

The 65 percent of the votes cast in favor of Italy in the commune of Trieste was also challenged on the ground that only a little more than half of the voters were born in Trieste, the other votes being from persons born in Italy who settled in Trieste after World War I or who had fled from the part of the Julian Region ceded to Yugoslavia or from Zone B of the Free Territory. Ive Mihovilović prepared the figures which give the birthplaces of the voters registered in the commune of Trieste. Table 6 is based

TABLE 6

PLACES OF BIRTH OF VOTERS REGISTERED IN TRIESTE FOR 1949 ELECTIONS

Place of Birth	Number of Voters
Trieste Commune	95,001
Other communes in Zone A	3,482
Italy	42,220
Other states	8,928
Zone B of FTT	14,076
Yugoslav part of Venezia Giulia	33,538
Total	197,245

SOURCE: Mihovilović, *Trst problem dana*, p. 93.

on data taken from the electoral rolls, which had been displayed for public inspection before the election.

The vote for the independentists, although relatively small (11,476), nonetheless showed them to be the third strongest party in the Trieste commune, after the Christian Democrats and the Cominformists. This raised their confidence, which had been badly hurt by the Tripartite Proposal. General Airey, who had constantly emphasized in his previous reports to the Security Council the overwhelming Italian majority in Zone A, and his opinion that there was no important Triestine consciousness, gave the following reason for the independentist vote in his report to the Security Council following the elections:

> The most significant aspect of the result of these elections, will be clearly seen in the large Italian majority of the

electorate and in the small percentage of the pro-Yugoslav and the Independence groups, although the latter inevitably receives support from those elements of the population who are personally interested in the continuance of A.M.G. and who have been led to confuse existing conditions with those which would obtain in a free territory deprived of Italian economic support and protection.[69]

This and similar statements of General Airey were a surprise to no one. They merely reflected the AMG policy which had been distinctly pro-Italian during the years 1948 and 1949. The AMG had been favoring the return of the FTT to Italy and for that purpose had incorporated the economy of Zone A into that of the Italian Republic and had given the pro-Italian parties a greater share in the administration of Zone A. By laying down the rules for municipal elections the AMG had aided the pro-Italian parties to gain a majority. It is questionable if the pro-Italian parties could have obtained a majority at all had the AMG respected the rules prescribed in the Permanent Statute.

On the other hand the AMG policy had remained hostile to both Communist groups and detrimental toward the independentists and Slovenian democrats, all of whom stood for the establishment of the Free Territory as prescribed by the peace treaty.

From a historical perspective the AMG policy in Zone A during the years 1948 and 1949 was an outgrowth of the international situation. The split of the world into two hostile blocs prompted the Tripartite Proposal, by which the Western powers expressed their intention to return the FTT to Italy. This solution would make the entire FTT a part of the West. The pro-Italian policy of the AMG in Zone A was therefore in accordance with the Tripartite Proposal, and unquestionably the AMG contributed its share in preparing Zone A for such a return.

Something quite different was the question of how to force Yugoslavia to abandon Zone B and to unite it with Italy. As long as Yugoslavia remained a member of the Eastern bloc this could be accomplished only by force, and such action might transform the cold war into a hot one. Were the Western powers prepared to go so far is today, of course, a purely hypothetical question. The

69. *Seventh AMG Report* (S/1374), p. 7.

Cominform Resolution, instead, altered Yugoslav-Russian relations and created a new international situation in the Balkans, which demanded in turn a reevaluation of the relationship between Yugoslavia and the Western powers. The old Tripartite declaration became outdated and a new approach to the FTT had to be found corresponding to this new situation.

12
CONSEQUENCES OF THE COMINFORM RESOLUTION

THE IMPACT ON INTERNATIONAL RELATIONS

During 1949 Soviet-Yugoslav relations went from bad to worse. In the second half of 1948, after the Cominform Resolution, Tito arrested or liquidated the pro-Cominform faction inside Yugoslavia. By early 1949 Stalin realized that Yugoslav Communists would not overthrow Tito from the inside, whereupon Soviet propaganda turned against Yugoslavia and the Yugoslav Communist party, in an effort to terminate Tito's regime from the outside. In May and June of 1949 economic pressure was applied, when the Soviet bloc countries abrogated their commercial agreements with Yugoslavia. In June the Soviet Union in a note to Yugoslavia said that Tito's terroristic and anti-Communist regime had gone over to the camp of the enemy. In the same month, Russia decided no longer to support Yugoslav claims to Southern Carinthia in Austria. This policy was communicated to the Yugoslav government in a Soviet note of August 11, 1949, which further suggested that Tito could ask his new friends, the imperialists, to support his case in Carinthia. The note ended with a statement that the Soviet government regarded Yugoslavia not as friend and ally but as an enemy.[1]

Yugoslavia retaliated against the Greek Communist guerrillas. On July 10, 1949, Tito in a speech in Pula announced that Yugoslavia was closing the Greek frontier to the guerrillas and withdrawing all support. This decision led to defeat of the guerrillas and the end of the Greek civil war in October of the same year, marking a great setback for the Soviet bloc. In the same speech Tito declared that Yugoslavia had requested a loan from the West-

---

1. Hamilton F. Armstrong, *Tito and Goliath* (New York, 1951), pp. 102–3, 106; Markert, pp. 165, 240; Zalar, pp. 167, 169; Jeri, p. 253.

IMPACT ON INTERNATIONAL RELATIONS

ern powers.[2] On September 29, 1949, Soviet Russia renounced the Soviet-Yugoslav treaty of friendship, mutual assistance, and postwar cooperation. Her satellites faithfully followed suit, denouncing similar treaties with Yugoslavia. The split between Yugoslavia and her Cominform neighbors had become final.[3]

The end of the Greek civil war and the break between Yugoslavia and the Soviet bloc were welcome gains for the West. The cold war frontiers moved toward the east and Western influence increased in the Balkans. The Western powers, by then convinced that Tito was unquestionably the ruler of Yugoslavia, decided to support his resistance to the Soviet bloc. Toward the end of 1949 Tito received aid from the United States and Great Britain in the form of loans, gifts, credits, and the opening of new markets, thus improving Yugoslavia's economic situation and making her independent of Soviet pressures.[4] In December 1949 the United States government let it be known that it opposed any aggression including that against Yugoslavia.[5] In giving economic support, the Western powers avoided pressure on Tito to bring a change of regime inside Yugoslavia. Communism still prevailed. Neither did the Western powers urge Tito to join them. The West was interested primarily in keeping Yugoslavia outside the Soviet bloc.

2. For the full text of Tito's speech see Josip Broz-Tito, *Govori i članci* (Speeches and Articles), 12 vols. (Zagreb, 1959), 4:202-17; see also Zalar, p. 169; Armstrong, pp. 192-93; Markert, p. 168.

3. Markert, p. 165; Armstrong, p. 108. Poland and Hungary denounced their respective treaties with Yugoslavia on September 30, followed by Bulgaria and Rumania on October 1, and Czechoslovakia on October 4, 1949.

4. In September 1949 the Export-Import Bank gave a loan of $20,000,000; in October followed a currency loan of $3,000,000 by the International Monetary Fund, and the International Bank supplied $2,300,000. In November 1949 the United States modified its ban on shipment of potential war materials to Yugoslavia. In December of the same year Great Britain signed a trade agreement with Yugoslavia providing a credit of £8,000,000 sterling. Other loans followed. By the middle of 1950 Yugoslavia had received from the United States and Great Britain a sum of $89,100,000. (See Armstrong, pp. 125-26.)

5. Such a statement was made by the new American ambassador to Yugoslavia before he left for Belgrade. See *New York Times*, Dec. 8, 1949.

This situation remained unchanged until November 1951. Tito on his part claimed to be neutral in the struggle between East and West.

Because of the changed international scene the Western powers slightly modified their attitude toward the problem of Trieste. The United States, Great Britain, and France, which had signed the Tripartite Proposal in 1948, continued in principle to uphold the view that the FTT should be returned to Italy. However, by the end of 1949, the Western powers had agreed to accept any solution that might emerge from direct bilateral talks between Italy and Yugoslavia. This new approach did not change until March 1951.

Soviet Russia held to her previous position and demanded establishment of the Free Territory as prescribed in the Italian peace treaty. In April 1948 she had refused to accept the Tripartite Proposal. Then in February 1949 she recommended a Swiss, Hermann Flückiger, as future governor of Trieste, a shrewd move, inasmuch as Flückiger had been a candidate for governor previously proposed by the Western powers. In April 1950 Soviet Russia again demanded the nomination of a governor, and at the same time urged the end of Anglo-American and Yugoslav military occupation of Zones A and B. She especially condemned the occupation of Zone A as in effect preserving a naval and military base in the interests of the Atlantic Pact countries. The Soviets stressed that according to the Italian peace treaty, the Free Territory should be neutral and demilitarized. For the same reason Soviet Russia opposed any partition of the FTT between Italy and Yugoslavia. The Western powers having declined all her proposals, the Soviet Union declared in May 1950 that she would not sign a peace treaty with Austria until the FTT had been established and a governor nominated in accordance with the Italian peace treaty.[6]

Before the break with the Soviet Union, Yugoslavia had favored a Free Territory and the nomination of a governor. During the summer of 1949 she changed her policy and demanded partition of the FTT. There are two explanations for Yugoslavia's altered position. She may have been advised (or forced) to make

6. Jeri, pp. 252, 268, n. 1.

the switch by the Western powers, or may have decided on her own. The first alternative should not be overlooked, but up to the present there is no evidence available to support it. Therefore only the second alternative will be taken into consideration.

Two important events of June 1949, the elections in Zone A and the new Soviet attitude toward the Austrian peace treaty, essentially contributed to the change of Yugoslav behavior toward the FTT. When on June 19, 1949, Soviet Foreign Minister Andrei Vyshinsky accepted the Austrian borders of 1938, this meant that Soviet Russia would cease to support Yugoslav claims in Southern Carinthia. Yugoslavia had good reason to fear that Soviet Russia might go further in hurting Yugoslavia, namely by accepting the Tripartite Proposal, in which case Yugoslavia would lose Zone B.

Elections in Zone A (June 12 and June 19) were harmful to the Yugoslav cause in two ways. In the city of Trieste the majority of voters preferred Italy to an FTT or to any other solution. Second, the Titoists (Babič faction) emerged as a small minority compared to the pro-Cominform Communists (Vidali faction). Until then Yugoslavia might have believed that, given a democratic Free Territory, Communist forces would be able to take over its administration. This did not necessarily mean that a Communist majority would unify the Free Territory with Yugoslavia, though such a possibility existed. But Italian Irredentists exaggerated the peril, claiming that a union with Italy was the only way to save the Free Territory from Yugoslav conquest. After the elections, it became apparent to Yugoslavia that establishment of the Free Territory would extend the control of the pro-Italians and Cominformists over the entire territory including Zone B. Such a united FTT could become a center for Cominformist propaganda on the western border of Yugoslavia. In order to keep control over Zone B, Yugoslavia had opposed the Tripartite Proposal and turned now also against the FTT, favoring partition.

The first signs of such a change came in the beginning of July 1949. The Yugoslavs introduced their own dinar currency in Zone B on July 4 and 5. A few days later, on July 10, 1949, Marshal Tito delivered a speech in Pula, the one in which he announced his break with the Greek guerrillas and made it known that Yugoslavia had asked the Western countries for financial aid. For more than a year Tito had been silent on Trieste. Now, on July 10, he again condemned the Tripartite Proposal as a one-sided decision reached without Yugoslav participation. He demanded that Yugoslavia be asked to express her opinion about the FTT.[7] Here was the first, though mild, indication that Yugoslavia had changed her position toward the FTT and was prepared for bilateral talks with Italy. It was significant that Tito had not repeated his demand for establishment of the FTT or for nomination of a governor.

In the first days of October 1949 the idea of partition assumed definitive shape as evidenced by the diametrically opposite positions taken by the Cominformist and Titoist factions of the FTT.

From September 16 to 18, 1949, the congress of the Cominformist faction (Vidali) met in Trieste to condemn Titoists and Yugoslavia. Echoing Soviet phrases, the congress accused Yugoslavia of supporting the interests of the imperialistic powers in their struggle against socialism and the Soviet Union. In regard to the FTT, the congress urged the nomination of a governor, unification of both zones, the introduction of the Permanent Statute, and the withdrawal of all troops, Anglo-American and Yugoslav, from the FTT. The congress further stressed that neither Trieste nor any part of the FTT should go to Yugoslavia, because Yugoslavia had ceased to be a socialistic state and instead had become an ally of the imperialistic powers. According to the congress, it should be the duty of the Cominformist party to continue its struggle for the socialistic goals endangered by imperialistic pretensions in Zone A and by Yugoslav administration of Zone B.

The congress of the Titoist faction of the CPFTT (Babič) met three weeks later from October 8 to 11, 1949, in Izola in Zone B to evaluate the decisions made by the Cominformists and to decide its own policy. The Babič faction repeated that the Cominform Resolution had split the Communist forces and caused great damage to socialism in general. The Cominformist faction of the FTT had changed from a militant to a reformist and evolutionary party. It cooperated with bourgeois parties in the municipal council of Trieste. But while the Cominformists were on friendly terms with the bourgeois parties in the Anglo-American Zone A, they struggled against the true socialistic authorities in the Yugoslav Zone B. In their desire to undermine socialism in the Yugoslav

---

7. Tito, 4:212–13; Jeri, pp. 223, 244, n. 38.

IMPACT ON INTERNATIONAL RELATIONS

zone the Cominformists had demanded unification of the two zones and withdrawal of the Yugoslav army. The Trieste problem, according to the Babič congress, should not be solved by bargaining between the Western powers and the Soviet Union. Instead, a final agreement should be achieved between the two directly interested states, Italy and Yugoslavia, and with the consent of the democratic masses of the FTT. The Tito-Togliatti proposal of November 1946 could serve as a basis for such an agreement, according to the congress.[8] Of course Trieste's Titoists did not make these statements on their own but rather were voicing the point of view of the Yugoslav Communist party and government.

After Yugoslavia changed her policy toward Trieste, she had to discover whether the Western powers would agree to partition. In December 1949 the Yugoslav representative, Aleš Bebler, discussed the possibility with the United States secretary of state, Dean Acheson, who made it clear that all depended on Italy. If the latter agreed, the United States and the other Western powers would happily approve a permanent solution to the Trieste problem. Was Italy prepared for a new compromise or would she still demand return of the entire Free Territory? In February 1950, Mladen Iveković, the Yugoslav ambassador in Rome, discussed the issue with the Italian foreign minister, Count Carlo Sforza.[9]

After this conversation, the Yugoslav diplomat saw that Italy still regarded the Tripartite Proposal as the base for direct negotiations. Italy would not compromise her claims to the entire Free Territory, except for minor border corrections. The negative outcome of these first unofficial Italo-Yugoslav talks had bad results for Italians in Zone B. During 1950 Yugoslavia introduced new measures to strengthen the ties between Zone B and Yugoslavia, partly to convince the Italian government that Yugoslavia had no intention of giving up the zone.[10]

Yugoslavia saw her new policy as bounded by two extremes. Her maximal demands would be to allow the city of Trieste to go to Italy, exchanged if possible for the city of Gorizia; the rest of the Free Territory would be assigned to Yugoslavia (Tito-Togliatti agreement of November 1946). Her minimal demands would be

8. Bulajić, pp. 26–32, 35–42.
9. Sforza, *Cinque anni a palazzo Chigi*, pp. 366, 367–70.
10. See below, this chapter, next section.

that Yugoslavia must retain the zone already under her administration, though she would talk about Zone A. It must be noted, however, that from 1949 to 1954 Yugoslavia pursued a dual policy in regard to Trieste. While the Yugoslav government favored partition, the pro-Yugoslav organizations in Zone A continued to defend establishment of the Free Territory.

Italy attentively followed details of Tito's break with the Soviet bloc and the Yugoslav rapprochement with the West. The Italian statesmen knew that the Western powers might now retreat from the Tripartite Proposal. In the past, these powers had supported Italian claims to the entire Free Territory as the only way to prevent extension of Soviet influence there. But after Tito's break with Moscow, Italy was not likely to obtain the entire Free Territory. Moreover, Italian statesmen felt that Yugoslavia would try to exploit her rapprochement with the West. For this reason, Italian diplomats in the Western capitals repeatedly pressed for confirmation of the "Tripartite Declaration" to remind the West that it had "promised" to return the entire Free Territory to Italy and that abrogation of this pledge would have serious repercussions in Italy.

But with establishment of closer relations between Yugoslavia and the West, the Italians were forced to reexamine their views. Should they still demand the entire Free Territory as promised in the Tripartite Proposal, or should they agree to direct Italo-Yugoslav negotiations, which would mean a compromise, a division of the territory? The Italian foreign minister, Count Carlo Sforza, clearly expressed this dilemma in a letter to the Italian ambassador to the United States, Alberto Tarchiani, who had informed Sforza about the above-mentioned Acheson-Bebler conversation of December 1949:

> It depends on us to decide if we prefer to maintain the present *status quo* with its inconveniences but also with its guarantees, and demand that it be maintained or if we desire to explore instead the possible ways of arriving at a final solution of the problem of the Free Territory of Trieste, a solution which could not but be a compromise.[11]

11. Sforza, *Cinque anni a palazzo Chigi,* p. 366.

Although the United States left Italy to make her own decision, Sforza knew that Italian refusal to negotiate with Yugoslavia might lead to alienation of Yugoslavia from the Western camp, an estrangement the Western powers would not take lightly. Accordingly, Sforza, one of the ablest of Italian diplomats, chose the new tack revealed in his unofficial conversations with Mladen Iveković, the Yugoslav ambassador in Rome, in February 1950. Italy would not formally reject mediation with Yugoslavia, but would insist that the basis for future negotiation remain the Tripartite Proposal. As we know Italy had requested the entire Free Territory, but would now consider minor changes along the border in favor of Yugoslavia.[12]

But further Italian conditions made direct Italo-Yugoslav agreement more difficult. Alarmed by new Yugoslav measures in Zone B during 1950, the Italian government demanded that all steps tying Zone B closer to Yugoslavia be annulled before direct Italo-Yugoslav negotiations could take place.[13]

Though Sforza's new line envisaged only some minor border corrections, the Italian right wing bitterly attacked it, demanding firm refusal to enter into direct negotiations, and return of the entire Free Territory to Italy. This assault forced Sforza to assure the rightists that Italy "will never accept a transaction which would sacrifice new Italians."[14] Sforza was also criticized by the Communists, who demanded nomination of a governor for the Free Territory. Following the Moscow line, the Communists stood for an independent Free Territory and resisted direct negotiations with their new foe, Yugoslavia. Sforza, however, paid little attention to the Communists, considering them opposed to Italian interests.[15]

The Cominform Resolution not only brought need for reorientation of Italian and Yugoslav foreign policy but also exercised its impact on the local political life of both zones of the FTT.

12. Ibid., pp. 367–70.
13. Ibid., pp. 371–96.
14. Ibid., p. 402.
15. Ibid., pp. 365, 399; see also Jeri, pp. 221–25; De Castro, pp. 443–49.

ADMINISTRATION OF ZONE B

When the peace treaty with Italy took effect on September 15, 1947, it made no change in the established Communist regime of the Yugoslav Zone B. By virtue of the first order issued on September 16, 1947, the supreme authority remained in the hands of the military commander of the Yugoslav forces occupying the zone, as with the AMG in Zone A. Subordinated to the military commander, Colonel Mirko Lenac, was the local civil administration composed of different people's committees. An order issued on September 22, 1947, confirmed the previous division of Zone B into two parts: the Slovenian-Italian district of Koper (Capodistria), also called Koprščina, and the Croat-Italian district known as Bujština. Koper, a small city on the Adriatic coast, became the seat of the military and civil authorities of the zone.[16]

The Executive Committee of the Regional People's Committee remained the highest civil authority directly subordinated to the Yugoslav Military Government (YMG). Subjected to the regional committee were the two district committees, and below them were the local (village and city) People's committees. This administrative organization, by now familiar to us, remained essentially the same during all of the period under consideration. Though on November 14, 1948, the membership of the regional committee increased from 60 to 145, and again after the elections in 1950, to 183, these changes did not alter the structure of the regime.[17] The YMG and the regional executive committee published their orders, decrees, ordinances, and notices in the official gazette (*Uradni list, Bollettino ufficiale, Službeni list*) in each of

16. *First Yugoslav Report* (S/1066), pp. 3, 8–12.

17. "Decree No. 88," dated in Koper on November 14, 1948, published in *Uradni list vojne uprave JA jugoslovanske cone na STO in istrskega okrožnega ljudskega odbora* (Official Gazette of the Military Administration of the Yugoslav Army for the Yugoslav Zone of the FTT and of the Istrian Regional People's Committee), 2, no. 6 (Nov. 30, 1948): 91; "Annual Report of the Yugoslav Army Military Government on the Administration of the Yugoslav Zone of the Free Territory of Trieste for the Period from 15 September 1948 to 15 September 1949," UNSC, Doc. S/1467 (March 9, 1950), p. 8. (Mimeographed.) The Yugoslav official gazette will be cited as *Uradni list,* and the above Yugoslav annual report as *Second Yugoslav Report* (S/1467). See also *Slovensko Primorje in Istra,* pp. 650–51.

the three official languages of Zone B, Slovenian, Italian, and Croat.

The first two Yugoslav reports on administration of the zone, covering the period to September 1949, did not mention the Cominform Resolution or its consequences. No further reports were ever sent to the Security Council. Although the Yugoslavs still transmitted many notes of protest over affairs in Trieste, these did not deal with the administration of Zone B.

The first report of the Yugoslav Military Government of Zone B outlined the bases of authority and principles guiding the YMG. The entire administration, the report stated, was an outgrowth of the people's resistance movement expressed through the People's committees, a new name for the former National Liberation committees. The civil administration, elected by the people in 1945, had its base in principles of "self-government of the people," "friendship between different nationalities," and "social justice."[18]

The second Yugoslav annual report stated that the YMG administration had been founded on rules and provisions outlined in the peace treaty with Italy, including the Permanent Statute; administration had been transferred to civil authorities; and only a very small number, fifty to be exact, of Yugoslav Military Government staff members held positions in the administration. "Peace and order" prevailed in Zone B, there was "full equality of the three nationalities in political, economic, and cultural spheres," "individual civil rights [were] guaranteed," and cooperation had been established between civil authorities and the political parties and organizations. The Yugoslavs sought, by this statement, to contrast as sharply as possible the situation in Zone B with that in Zone A, where, according to the second Yugoslav report, the people had still to fight to achieve these principles.[19]

Closely connected with any political administration are polit-

18. *First Yugoslav Report* (S/1066), pp. 4, 45.

19. *Second Yugoslav Report* (S/1467), pp. 4–5, 7. The need for an attentive analysis of Yugoslav statements can be illustrated by the example given in the report that the death penalty had been abolished in Zone B by the Regional Committee. In fact the death penalty had been abolished only "for criminal acts coming under the jurisdiction of the civil courts" (ibid., p. 8), while the death penalty could still be enforced by YMG authorities or by civil courts in cases involving political crimes.

ical parties and cultural and religious associations, and their newspapers and journals. The first and second Yugoslav reports listed the following political parties and organizations registered with the authorities: the Slavic-Italian Anti-Fascist Union (UAIS-SIAU) of the FTT, the Liberation Front of the FTT, the Communist party of the FTT, the Anti-Fascist Slavic-Italian Women's Front of the FTT, the Anti-Fascist Youth Union of the FTT, the Socialist party of the FTT, and the Independence Front for the Free State of the Littoral (Venezia Giulia).[20]

Aside from the pro-Communist organizations, only two parties were recognized in both zones: the Independence Front and the Socialist party. The Slovenian democratic and all pro-Italian political parties of Zone A were prohibited in Zone B on grounds of obstructing implementation of the peace treaty, issuing warmongering propaganda, or inciting nationalist hatreds.[21]

As for cultural, religious, and gymnastic organizations in Zone B, most prominent were the Slovensko-hrvatska prosvetna zveza (Slovene-Croat Cultural Union) and the Italian Centro di Cultura Popolare. The Slovenian daily *Primorski dnevnik* and the Italian daily *Il Lavoratore,* both printed in Trieste, circulated also in Zone B until the Cominform split, after which *Il Lavoratore* was banned. In September 1948 Babič began a new Titoist weekly, *La Nostra Lotta,* in the Italian language and printed in Koper, the capital of Zone B. *Istarski tednik* (Istrian Weekly) and *Hrvatski glas* (Croat Voice) were the two periodicals printed in the Croatian language. Italian and Slovenian democratic newspapers published in Zone A were barred in Zone B on the same grounds as those given for keeping out political parties. Furthermore, all papers publishing articles defamatory to the honor of the Yugoslav army were also barred from Zone B[22]—an excuse to halt influence of the Slovenian and Italian democratic and Cominformist press.

On February 27, 1950, the Regional People's Committee published rules for elections in Zone B.[23] Taking into consideration

20. Ibid., p. 11; *First Yugoslav Report* (S/1066), p. 13.
21. *First Yugoslav Report* (S/1066), p. 4.
22. Ibid., pp. 13, 14; *Slovensko Primorje in Istra,* p. 652.
23. "Odlok št. 26" (Decree No. 26), dated in Koper, February 26, 1950, *Uradni list,* 4, no. 4 (Feb. 27, 1950): 51–58.

the existence of the two different administrative systems (Communist and People's committees) of both zones, the prescribed procedures for elections were very similar to those in Order No. 33 for Zone A, which had been published almost exactly a year before (February 21, 1949) by the AMG.

According to Decree No. 26 the elections of the members of the two district People's committees in Zone B were to be based on general, equal, and direct suffrage by secret ballot and on the principle of proportional representation. The date of the elections would be announced by the regional executive committee. Every citizen entered on the electoral rolls would have the right to vote in his electoral unit or be elected as a member of the district committee. The number of district committee members was to be based on population: one for every four hundred inhabitants. Elections were to be held according to the electoral lists, which could be presented by either a political or social organization, or by a prescribed number of voters. Every citizen was to have the right to vote for any lists of candidates or to abstain from voting.

The elections of members for the two district committees took place on April 16, 1950. There were 123 members to be elected to the district committee of Koper, and 60 for Buje. Three parties presented their lists. The UAIS-SIAU, the pro-Communist party, was supported by the YMG. The two opposition parties, the Socialists and the Christian Socialists, were parties in name only, without their own party machinery. As they both stood for preservation of the FTT and for the nomination of a governor, they lacked recognition and support from the Socialists and Christian Democrats of Zone A.[24] M. S. Handler, correspondent for the *New York Times,* who was present in Zone B on Sunday, April 16, 1950, reported that by noon, after the polling stations had been open for five hours, about 50 percent of the registered voters had cast their votes in Koper and about 45 percent in the two other towns (Izola and Piran) of the Koper district at an average ratio of one Italian to four Slavic votes. Broadcasting vehicles of UAIS-SIAU circulated among the towns urging the people to go to the polls, denouncing abstainers as pusillanimous and cowardly, but

24. *Keesing's Contemporary Archives: Weekly Diary of Important World Events,* 7 (London, 1948–50): 10662; *New York Times,* Apr. 17, 1950.

otherwise there was no visible evidence of intimidation. Among the foreign journalists present were a large number of correspondents from Italy. It was said that one of them, the correspondent of the Cominformist *L'Unità,* had been assaulted in Buje. "American correspondents visited Buie [Buje]," reported Handler, "and sought further details. Officials in Buie said the Italian correspondent had made provocative remarks that had led to arguments."[25]

Out of 42,064 registered voters, 37,963 or 90.39 percent went to the polls. The official party (UAIS-SIAU) received 33,951 or 89.29 percent of the votes. The Socialist party got a mere 414 votes or 1.29 percent, and the Christian Socialists, 278 or 0.76 percent. A total of 3,320 ballots, or 8.75 percent, were declared invalid—a relatively large number. Abstention (4,101) and invalid votes (3,320) added up to 7,421 out of 42,064 registered votes, rather remarkable opposition for a Communist-style election, and a sign of Italian and Cominformist resistance.[26]

Without question the balloting had been held in the usual Communist style, under which the official party automatically receives a great majority of the votes. The Irredentist and Cominform press in Zone A criticized the election and expressed fear that Yugoslavia would use the results as an excuse to annex Zone B.[27]

Out of the 123 elected members of the district committee for Koper, 76 were Slovenes and 47 Italians, and of 60 elected members of the Buje district committee, 47 were Croats and 13 Italians. The members of each district committee elected among themselves an executive committee, the highest executive authority for each district. Joint sessions of both district committees formed the Regional People's Committee numbering 183 members. Its executive committee remained the supreme civil authority of Zone B directly subordinate to the YMG.[28]

The Yugoslav Military Government proudly announced that

25. Ibid. (© 1950 by The New York Times Company; reprinted by permission).

26. *Slovensko Primorje in Istra,* p. 652.

27. *Italian Affairs,* 3, no. 3:336; Committee of National Liberation of Istria [CLN for Istria], *Trieste: Zone "B" Land without Liberty* (Trieste, August 1954), pp. 29–30, cited hereafter as *Trieste: Zone B.*

28. *Slovensko Primorje in Istra,* pp. 651–52.

ADMINISTRATION OF ZONE B

friendly cooperation existed among all three ethnic groups, Slovenian, Croat, and Italian. Old Fascist racial laws that had Italianized Slavic names were revoked, together with all other pieces of Fascist legislation. Unlike the situation in Zone A, where the second Yugoslav report found ethnic discrimination still in effect, the people in Zone B at public demonstrations condemned all efforts of the Irredentists to incite racial antagonism. The report further asserted that Irredentist propaganda had shown no positive results in Zone B, despite efforts of the Irredentists to make a case for racial persecution by falsely transforming ordinary criminals, condemned by the people's authorities, into political victims.[29]

Unlike Zone A, the Yugoslav zone of the Free Territory was mainly rural in character, and the reports treated agriculture as the most important branch of the economy. Truck farming was predominant. The report noted the formation of peasant cooperatives to increase agricultural output and to introduce modern techniques of cultivation.[30]

Against Italian economic pressures manifested in Zone A, as described above, Yugoslavia took sharp countermeasures in Zone B. According to the terms of the peace treaty, Italy was to supply lire until separate money currency could be established for the Free Territory.[31] Under these provisions Yugoslavia applied for Italian currency in her verbal note of November 25, 1947.[32] The Italian government rejected this request on December 10, 1947, on the basis

> that in the Free Territory of Trieste under Yugoslav Administration a currency different from the Italian lira is in circulation, which is contrary to the provisions of Article 11. It is considered that under such circumstances all the prerequisites for the implementation of the other parts of Article 11 have become void.[33]

29. *First Yugoslav Report* (S/1066), p. 12; *Who Should Have Trieste?* pp. 26–27; *Second Yugoslav Report* (S/1467), p. 7.
30. *Second Yugoslav Report* (S/1467), p. 5.
31. See chapter 11, first section.
32. "Verbal Note," issued November 25, 1947, by Yugoslav Legation in Rome, reproduced in the *First Yugoslav Report* (S/1066), p. 50.
33. "Verbal Note Answering Yugoslav Note," issued December 10, 1947, by the Italian government, reproduced in ibid., p. 51.

In its reply, sent January 7, 1948, Yugoslavia pointed out that no currency changes had occurred in the Yugoslav zone after signing of the peace treaty in February 1947. Already at that time the currency in use in Zone B was the Yugo-lira, issued by the Yugoslav occupation forces in 1945. The Italian government had recognized this currency and had assumed responsibility for it under Paragraph 4 of Article 76 of the peace treaty.[34] Therefore, concluded the Yugoslav note, the rejection "could not be considered otherwise than an illegal refusal to carry out an obligation assumed by Italy under the terms of the Peace Treaty."[35]

The answer of the Italian government, contained in its note of February 21, 1948, simply stated that the exchange rate of lira B, or Yugo-lira, was pegged at 1:2 with respect to the metropolitan lira, while lira A, issued by the AMG, always circulated in Italy at par with the metropolitan lira. The Yugo-lira was thus in effect a new currency.[36]

In a new note of March 20, 1948, Yugoslavia pointed out that the Italian government was avoiding the main issue. This note affirmed that lira B had already been pegged at the rate of 1:2 when the peace treaty was signed and when Italy assumed responsibility for it. Thus the excuse that lira B represented a new currency was irrelevant.[37] This note remained unanswered and Italy refused to supply any lira currency to Zone B.

The same fate met a Yugoslav note of May 10, 1948, asking for payments of civil and military pensions owing to persons now

34. Paragraph 4 of Article 76 of the Italian peace treaty stated: "The Italian Government shall assume full responsibility for all Allied military currency issued in Italy by the Allied military authorities, including all such currency in circulation at the coming into force of the present Treaty." (See *Italian Peace Treaty*, p. 158.) It should be mentioned that Italy interpreted the term "Allied military authorities" as applying only to the British-American administration, while the Yugoslav interpretation included also Yugoslavia.

35. "Verbal Note to Italian Government," issued January 7, 1948, by the Yugoslav Legation in Rome, reproduced in the *First Yugoslav Report* (S/1066), p. 52.

36. "Verbal Note," issued February 21, 1948, by Italian Ministry of Foreign Affairs, reproduced in ibid., p. 53.

37. "Verbal Note," issued March 20, 1948, by the Yugoslav Legation in Rome, reproduced in ibid., p. 54.

citizens of the Free Territory.[38] Italy had assumed liability for such payments under Paragraph 8, Annex X, of the peace treaty, which stated:

> Italy shall continue to be liable for the payment of civil or military pensions earned, as of the coming into force of the present Treaty, for services under the Italian State, municipal or other local government authorities, by persons who under the Treaty acquire the nationality of the Free Territory, including pension rights not yet matured. Arrangements shall be concluded between Italy and the Free Territory providing for the method by which this liability shall be discharged.[39]

Faced with these difficulties, Yugoslavia decided to introduce its own dinar as currency in Zone B. The change was decreed by Order No. 44 of July 3, 1949, and took effect July 4–5 of the same year. The exchange rate was 30 dinars for 100 Yugo-liras.[40] In a "Letter from the Yugoslav Government Concerning the Free Territory of Trieste," dated Belgrade, July 2, 1949, and transmitted to the Security Council on July 5, the Yugoslav government explained its introduction of the dinar as currency in Zone B.[41] The letter listed especially the refusal of the Italian government to supply lira currency, the AMG-Italian agreements of March 9 and September 22, 1948, by which a monetary, economic, and customs union was created between Zone A and Italy, and the obstacles placed by the AMG in the way of free circulation of goods between the two zones. The conclusion followed that because the amount of Yugo-lira currency was not enough to develop a healthy economy in Zone B, the YMG had been compelled to ask Yugoslavia for a loan of five hundred million dinars, which took place on July 1, 1949. It is worthwhile to note that the Yugoslav currency was introduced less than two weeks after the elections in the British–United States zone, the results of which had signified a great defeat of the pro-Yugoslav (Babič) Communists.

38. "Verbal Note," issued May 10, 1948, by the Yugoslav Legation in Rome, reproduced in ibid., p. 55.
39. *Italian Peace Treaty,* p. 210.
40. Order No. 14, issued by Colonel Mirko Lenac in Koper, July 3, 1949, *Uradni list,* 3, no. 2 (July 3, 1949); see also *Second Yugoslav Report* (S/1464), pp. 26–27.
41. UNSC, Doc. S/1348 (July 5, 1949). (Mimeographed.)

The introduction of the Yugoslav dinar as the currency of Zone B was therefore an early sign of fundamental change in Yugoslav policy toward the Free Territory. Whereas all the reasons listed in the above Yugoslav letter for introducing the new dinar currency were in existence in the fall of 1948, only after the June elections in Zone A did Yugoslavia take action.

Relations between the Allied and Yugoslav military administrative authorities had always been tense. The Yugoslavs, however, presented these tensions in a darker light than the AMG, and explained them in a more one-sided fashion. Within a few days after the peace treaty had come into force, the YMG proposed to the AMG that a permanent joint commission be set up to deal with all questions of common interest. The AMG declined, but agreed to a separate economic mission attached to each military government to represent its own zone in relation to interests of the other zone. The Yugoslav economic mission then advocated freedom of movement, circulation of goods, and employment between the two zones. All these proposals, according to the first Yugoslav report, had been blocked by the AMG, which instead began to identify Zone A with Italy and Zone B with a foreign country.[42]

When the Yugoslav economic mission pressed the AMG to at least agree to a list of goods that could be imported into Zone B from Zone A, a representative of the AMG replied on May 6, 1948:

> The AMG cannot submit such a list. The AMG cannot export anything beyond that which is allowed by the Italian Government, because the Anglo-American Zone obtains raw materials and other commodities from Italy and the Italian Government is not prepared to supply the Anglo-American Zone with commodities in excess to those actually required by the population. The AMG cannot therefore submit a list, because in practice it has nothing to export into the Yugoslav Zone. All it might possibly export would be marble, cement and lime-stone.[43]

Zone B, the Yugoslavs said, had a plentiful supply of these materials and no need to import them.

42. *First Yugoslav Report* (S/1066), p. 41.
43. Ibid., p. 42.

The same day, May 6, 1948, the YMG reached agreement with the AMG on a system of payments, but shortly thereafter all exports from Zone A were prohibited, as the first Yugoslav report stated. It should be noted that Zone A was now part of the Marshall Plan, participation in which Yugoslavia had rejected.

The relations became worse when Yugoslavia introduced its dinar currency into Zone B in July 1949. Finally, in March 1950 the YMG announced that Zone B had been incorporated into the Yugoslav economy and that all customs barriers between Yugoslavia and Zone B were abolished. This move gave rise to violent Italian protests in Zone A and in the Italian Republic.[44]

From the above one gets the impression that practically no trading went on between the zones. However, *Slovensko Primorje in Istra,* a Yugoslav work, lists exports from the Yugoslav zone to the Anglo-American zone in the amount of 299 million lire in 1949, and 383 million lire in 1950. While the Yugoslav source does not give figures for imports from the Anglo-American zone, it states that imports increased during the same years. Zone B traded also with Yugoslavia. Exports to Yugoslavia amounted to 576 million dinars in 1949 and increased to 731 million dinars in 1950. During the same years the imports from Yugoslavia were in the value of 566 million and 595 million dinars, respectively. Zone A and Yugoslavia were the only two places with which Zone B established foreign trade relations of any importance.[45]

From this condensed analysis of political, social, and economic life it is evident that the Yugoslav Communist regime, based on the People's committee system, continued in Zone B after the Italian peace treaty. With a democratic regime in Zone A and with a socialistic order in Zone B it became highly problematic whether a Free Territory as envisioned in the peace treaty could ever be established. Though the Yugoslav government formally favored and defended the establishment of the FTT until the middle of 1949, it had factually assisted in undermining a chance to establish the FTT by continuation of the Communist rule in Zone B. The Western powers in control of Zone A would not allow, on their part, a Communist regime to take over all of the FTT. They expressed this opinion quite clearly in the Tripartite Proposal.

44. *Keesing's Contemporary Archives,* 7:10598.
45. *Slovensko Primorje in Istra,* p. 657.

But in the second part of 1949 Yugoslavia changed its policy and publicly abandoned the idea of the FTT. The pro-Italian parties in Zone A as well as the Italian government had been opposed to the FTT from the beginning. The problem from this time on was not how to establish the FTT but rather how to divide it. Based on the Tripartite Proposal the Italian government claimed all or almost all of the FTT for Italy. The AMG had supported the Italian claims and introduced measures which had tied Zone A, under its administration, closer to Italy. But this was all the AMG and the Western powers could do. During 1949–50 the Yugoslav government made it clear time and again that it would never give up the zone under its control. To prove that they meant what they said, the Yugoslavs took steps, similar to those of the AMG in Zone A, to tie Zone B closer to Yugoslavia. The introduction of the Yugoslav dinar as legal currency, the establishment of a customs union between Zone B and Yugoslavia, and the holding of elections for district people's committees were all measures similar to those previously taken in Zone A. The purpose was clear. Yugoslavia was tightening its hold over Zone B.

Quite understandably these Yugoslav actions caused violent objections from the pro-Italian parties in Zone A and from the Italian government itself. But the Italian protests were not raised to protect the FTT. They were rather the expression of Italian fears that the Tripartite Proposal would become a dead letter through Yugoslav incorporation of Zone B.

INDEPENDENTISM, IRREDENTISM, AND ZONE A

During the years 1949 and 1950 the economy of Zone A prospered. Shortage of consumer goods, a common occurrence for Triestines during the war and postwar years, disappeared. War damage to industry and shipyards was repaired, and Trieste enjoyed economic prosperity as never before. In 1949 imports and exports by sea reached 3,482,490 tons, surpassing by 32,761 tons the previous record set in 1913. In the next year, 1950, combined maritime and railway import and export traffic totaled 5,933,934 tons, far above the 5,378,674 tons recorded in 1938, the highest level under Italian rule.[46] True, this increase can be ascribed

46. Compare data given in: "Report on the Administration of the British–U.S. Zone of the Free Territory of Trieste for the Period 1

mainly to aid given Zone A by the European Recovery Plan and the shipping of ERP supplies to Austria via Trieste.[47] Nevertheless, so important a rise in economic well-being was bound to produce in Trieste a desire to keep the status quo. It became a significant proposition, though not the only one, in rousing support for independentism. The changed international situation and conditions in Zone B were other factors used by the independentists to propagate their ideas.

The Cominformist (Vidali) faction of the CPFTT, in line with Russian policy, continued to demand unification of both zones and establishment of the FTT in accordance with the Italian peace treaty. The same was publicly demanded by the Slovenian democrats, the Titoist (Babič) faction of the CPFTT, and both independentist political parties, Fronte dell'Indipendenza and Blocco Triestino. The independentist political parties pursued a propaganda campaign to weaken the pro-Italian parties by pointing out that the only way the Italians of Zone B could escape being incorporated into Yugoslavia was by establishment of the FTT.[48] Otherwise, the independentists said, Italy might gain Zone A but would lose Zone B. Because of Tito's break with Moscow, they reasoned, the Western powers would avoid forcing Tito to abandon Zone B.

The pro-Italian parties, holding slightly less than a 65 percent majority in the city of Trieste, became rightfully alarmed by such a turn of events. After the election victory in June 1949 they were jubilant and were convinced the Western powers would return all of the Free Territory to Italy. Yugoslavia, according to the pro-Italian parties, was in no condition to oppose such action, being without Russian support and in need of economic aid from the

---

October to 31 December 1949 by Major General T. S. Airey . . . ," *UNSC*, Doc. S/1473 (March 22, 1950), p. 5 (mimeographed), hereafter cited as the *Ninth AMG Report* (S/1473); *Tenth AMG Report* (S/2062), pp. 2, 32–33; Pertot, p. 52; Roletto, *Il porto di Trieste*, pp. 245–46.

47. For a more detailed economic analysis see the two studies previously mentioned: *Trieste ed i suoi problemi: Situazione, tendenze, prospettive* by Roletto, and *Trst medjunarodni privredni problem* by Pertot.

48. Mario Stocca, *Segnalazioni dalla stampa triestina* (Trieste, 1950), pp. 2–3, 5.

West. But very soon the annexationists noticed that events had begun to unfold differently. Disillusionment drew them closer together. Disregarding party differences the pro-Italians concentrated on achieving the return of the FTT to Italy. Any action against this aim gave rise to newspaper protests in Zone A and Italy. Yugoslav measures in Zone B twice caused such newspaper campaigns, first during July of 1949 and then again in 1950 from the middle of March to the end of May.

The July campaign was a reaction against Yugoslav introduction of the dinar as legal currency in Zone B. The press in Zone A and in Italy pointed out that the Yugoslav measure violated the Italian peace treaty. Newspapers accused the governments of Great Britain, the United States, and France of conspiring with Marshal Tito and promising him Zone B in compensation for giving Zone A to Italy. Hence, the Italian government should demand that the Western powers withhold economic aid to Yugoslavia until she agreed to annexation of the entire FTT to Italy as promised in the Tripartite Proposal of 1948.[49] At this point the Italian government made known its position. De Gasperi's government assured the Italian parliament that Italy would press for return of the entire FTT, and Foreign Minister Count Sforza asked the governments of Great Britain, the United States, and France to prevent a possible Yugoslav incorporation of Zone B within Yugoslavia.[50]

By the end of July the excitement calmed down, and relations between Italy and Yugoslavia improved to such a degree that in August a trade agreement was concluded between them, which left the pro-Italian parties of Zone A quite unhappy.[51] In their newspapers they constantly reminded the public in Italy about Yugoslav persecutions of Italians living in Zone B. For example, they pointed out that the Yugoslavs had prevented the clergy in Zone B from announcing that the Catholic church had excommunicated all the Communist functionaries and prohibited the reading of Communist newspapers. Toward the end of August, the press reported that arrests and expulsions of Italians were continuing in Zone B. Special targets of police action at that time were the workers living in Zone B and employed in the city of

49. *New York Times,* July 4, 8, 10, 22, 1949.
50. Ibid., July 7, 8, 1949.   51. Zalar, p. 170.

Trieste. Moreover, several well-known local professional men were expelled from Koper. The Italian government again protested to Yugoslavia, stating that it would put the issue before the United Nations as a violation of the Italian peace treaty.[52]

At the beginning of 1950, Italy and Yugoslavia unofficially discussed means to solve the Trieste problem. Very soon it became apparent that no agreement could be achieved, as both participants claimed most of the FTT. Nevertheless, the sole fact that the Italian government had discussed the question with Yugoslavia caused uneasiness among the pro-Italian parties of Zone A.

A new emotional eruption came in March 1950, reaching its highest degree in April and then slowly decreasing in May. The outbursts of Italian sentiment came, as a half-year before, because of Yugoslav actions in Zone B. On March 14, 1950, the Yugoslavs, as we know, announced establishment of a customs union between Zone B and Yugoslavia, and on April 16 elections were held in the Yugoslav zone.

Italian Foreign Minister Count Sforza protested against the customs union in a memorandum handed to Mladen Iveković, the Yugoslav ambassador in Rome, on March 21, 1950. The interesting fact is that the Italian government recognized that it had incorporated Zone A into the Italian economy. Moreover, the Italian government now declared that it was ready to remedy this situation by reestablishing the economic, financial, and customs unity of the Free Territory provided Yugoslavia was willing to do the same for Zone B.[53] The Italian government realized that Yugoslav measures in Zone B were harmful to Italian interests and had made the Tripartite Proposal obsolete.

The Yugoslav foreign minister answered on March 29 by explaining that actions taken in Zone B were necessary because of previous acts of the Italian government that had brought about the de facto incorporation of Zone A into Italy. He made it clear that Yugoslavia would under no circumstances surrender Zone B to Italy and he warned Italy that Italian Irredentist demands against Yugoslavia's legitimate interests in the Free Territory would only cause serious harm to relationships between the two countries.[54]

52. *New York Times,* July 22, Aug. 10, 24, 27, 1949.
53. Ibid., Mar. 22, 1950.   54. Ibid., Mar. 30, 1950.

The pro-Italian parties in Zone A became aware of the grave situation. They sent a special petition to the United Nations to prevent Yugoslav annexation of Zone B.[55] As the elections in Zone B approached, the pro-Italians of Zone A became convinced that Yugoslavia would use the elections as a plebiscite for annexation. The CLN for Istria reported arrests and intimidation of Italians before the elections took place.[56] Afterwards the Italian press in Zone A and Italy with unanimity denounced the elections as a political move to bolster Yugoslav nationalism, and dispatches from Trieste gave lengthy descriptions of what they said were episodes of intimidation and terror carried out by Yugoslav authorities.[57]

The Italians described the elections quite differently than did *New York Times* correspondent M. S. Handler. Whereas the latter, basing his report on a portion of the day's activity, had indicated only minor irregularities, the Italians said that their own and foreign correspondents had been expelled from Zone B. The urns, they said, were kept open past the official time, until 10 P.M., and young Yugoslav Partisans had knocked on house doors forcing Italian voters, with the usual threats, to come out and vote.[58]

On April 18, 1950, the Italian government let it be known that it would protest in Belgrade the beating of several Italian journalists when they visited Zone B during the election. The next day great student demonstrations arose in Rome and other Italian cities against violence suffered by Italians in Zone B. All groups of students, from Communists to neo-Fascists, cooperated in the demonstrations.[59]

The same opinion was voiced in the Italian parliament. On April 22 and later on May 3, 1950, the former premier and one of the Big Four at the Paris peace conference after World War I, Senator Vittorio E. Orlando, an ardent nationalist, urged the Italian government and specifically Foreign Minister Count Sforza

55. Ibid., Apr. 8, 1950.
56. Ibid., Apr. 15, 16, 1950.   57. Ibid., Apr. 17, 1950.
58. *Trieste: Zone B,* pp. 29–30. The above information was taken from an article published in the *Manchester Guardian* on May 4, 1953, by a correspondent of the same newspaper, who had been present in Zone B during election day.
59. *New York Times,* Apr. 19, 20, 1950.

to follow a more forceful foreign policy. "History is made not by bleating like sheep but by roaring like lions," exclaimed the ninety-year-old Orlando. Socialist Senator Labriola pointed out that emotions were so excited "that even war could be popular in Italy if it were waged against Yugoslavia to save Trieste."[60]

On April 28, 1950, Count Sforza explained to parliament the government's foreign policy by stating that the Tripartite Proposal was still the base for any negotiations with Yugoslavia. However, Italy was prepared for small border corrections along the FTT-Yugoslav frontier, by ceding to Yugoslavia some ethnically Slovenian and Croatian villages. Sforza assured parliament that no further ethnically Italian territory was to be sacrificed. On May 1, 1950, Prime Minister de Gasperi in his speech to the Senate confirmed that he was in full agreement with his foreign minister.[61]

The sensitivity of national emotions was best illustrated by Italian reaction to an editorial published in the *New York Times* on April 20, 1950, which had said that the Tripartite Proposal of March 20, 1948, was only an expression of hope and was devoid of legality in terms of the Italian peace treaty. The editorial was a great shock to public and press. In Rome the *Giornale d'Italia* asserted that "the Three Power Declaration is a commitment, a solemn commitment confirmed on several occasions, and Italy is in the habit of trusting the word of men of honor, especially when these men of honor represent great countries which boast of being defenders of international morality." "We believe," *Giornale d'Italia* continued, "that *The New York Times* prefers to be classed among men of honor and to cause its great country also to be classed among men of honor."[62]

To make emotions still more excited Soviet Russia in her note of April 20, 1950, demanded organization of the FTT, and nomination of a governor. At the conference of Western foreign

60. Ibid., May 3, 1950 (© 1950 by The New York Times Company; reprinted by permission).

61. Italy, Presidenza del consiglio dei ministri, Centro di documentazione, *Documenti di vita italiana*, 3 (Rome, November 1953): 1852; Jeri, pp. 224–25. The first work will be cited as *Documenti di vita italiana*.

62. *New York Times*, Apr. 21, 1950 (© 1950 by The New York Times Company; reprinted by permission).

ministers in London, Dean Acheson for the United States, Ernest Bevin for Great Britain, and Robert Schuman for France urged on May 23, 1950, that Italian Foreign Minister Count Sforza continue with direct Italo-Yugoslav negotiations to solve the Trieste problem.[63] All these developments convinced the pro-Italians in Zone A that Italy might not get the entire FTT. The more so as Yugoslavia had repeatedly stressed that it would not give up Zone B. As recently as April 28, 1950, Marshal Tito made it clear in an interview that Yugoslavia was demanding the entire Free Territory, but would exchange the city of Trieste for the Italian city of Gorizia.[64] Discouraged by these facts, the pro-Italian groups in Trieste turned to terroristic acts.

The newspapers reported on May 12 and 13 that the Yugoslav police had seized Trieste's passenger steamer serving Trieste and ports of Zone B. Belgrade radio reported on May 13 that the ship had been seized because arms found on board were being smuggled from Trieste for terroristic activities planned by Italian Irredentists.[65] Then on November 3, 1950, the newspapers reported bombings of three buildings occupied by the Yugoslav newspaper and press agency in Trieste. AMG police said that the bombs were set by unknown persons. On February 15, 1951, another bomb exploded in Trieste, this time near the entrance to the Allied Military Government, and yet another near a printing plant.[66]

The Yugoslavs closely followed the pro-Italian press in Zone A, comparing its writings with newspaper articles published in Italy, speeches of Italian deputies and senators, and statements made by the Italian government. In the eyes of the Yugoslavs these articles and pronouncements all disclosed the rise of anti-Yugoslav sentiment, claiming not only the entire Free Territory and the land Yugoslavia had received under the recent peace treaty, but also Dalmatia, which had been unsuccessfully claimed by Italy after World War I. Fearing these recurrent symptoms of Italian nationalism could lead to the kind of adventurism personified after World War I in Gabriele d'Annunzio, the Yugoslav

63. Ibid., May 24, 1950.
64. Ibid., Apr. 29, 1950; Jeri, pp. 224–25.
65. *New York Times,* May 13, 15, 1950.
66. Ibid., Nov. 3, 1950, Feb. 16, 1951.

writers, especially Ive Mihovilović, analyzed all such Italian articles and statements and concluded that the anti-Yugoslav propaganda was to a large degree the result of a well-coordinated conspiracy organized by Italian Irredentist circles.

In describing Italian Irredentism the Yugoslav writers committed some errors of their own by exaggerating for propaganda effect. They asserted that Italian foreign policy had been subordinated to Irredentist goals aiming to regain for Italy the entire FTT, and if possible, also the other land ceded to Yugoslavia. Moreover, said the Yugoslavs, all Italian parties agreed upon and supported these aims.

Irredentist demands for return of the FTT to Italy must be separated from a general concern for the well-being of the Italian minority in Yugoslavia. It was true that all Italian political parties, from extreme right to left, condemned the Yugoslav actions in Zone B, but here the seemingly coordinated action ended and each political group pursued its own goals. The Italian right, neo-Fascists and nationalists, demanded return of the FTT to Italy. It opposed and ridiculed direct Italo-Yugoslav negotiations, which could only be harmful to the Italian national interest. The Right asked that the Italian government press the Western powers to fulfill their Tripartite Proposal of March 1948. Should the Western powers show any reluctance to carry out their promise, Italy should abandon NATO. The Left, especially the Communists, also condemned Yugoslav measures in Zone B, but for different reasons. The Italian Communists, like the Soviet Union, stood for establishment of the FTT, while Yugoslavs tried to tighten the links of Zone B to Yugoslavia. Second, the Italian Communists tried to condemn the Yugoslav Titoists whenever possible. They regarded them as ideological heretics who for their own narrow nationalistic interests had split the ranks of world communism.

The Italian government, representing the Christian Democratic center, followed a middle course. It stood for Italian participation in NATO, hoping the Western powers would support their ally Italy in her claims to the FTT. While it used the Tripartite Proposal as the base for direct Italo-Yugoslav negotiations, the Italian government was prepared to agree to some minor border corrections, but felt that the majority of Zone B should go to Italy. For this reason the Yugoslav measures in Zone B were emphatically condemned. Attacks from the Right had a greater impact on the Italian government than criticism from the Left. They aroused Italian national sentiment, which in turn affected many Christian Democrats. How much the government was forced to act because of nationalistic propaganda of the Right or to what degree instead the government used this propaganda and the criticism of the Left to press the Western Allies for a favorable solution will remain open to speculation.

With the above reservations, the Yugoslav writers, especially Ive Mihovilović, provided some useful data about Irredentists, who certainly played an important role in arousing Italian nationalistic emotions after World War II.

Mihovilović introduced his description of Irredentism by the following quotation which well described both the aims of Italian Irredentism and Yugoslav apprehensions:

"We will provoke a wave of Irredentism so that there will be no peace in Europe!"

So declared the Christian Democratic Deputy Bettiol in the [Italian] parliament during the time when the peace conference was searching for a solution for Trieste. An Italian newspaper which published this statement added:

"Trieste had broken up the Austrian Empire, which was mightier than the organization of the United Nations!" [The United Nations Security Council was to watch over the independence of the FTT.]

In such a way had Irredentist Italy threatened during that time. Although this "threat" comprises a lot of known Italian exuberant rhetoric there is nevertheless some truth in it. The Italian Irredentism truly represents a danger for peace in the world.[67]

All pro-Italian political parties in Zone A were Irredentist in Yugoslav eyes, working for return of the FTT to Italy. Their newspapers, especially the daily *Giornale di Trieste,* strove to keep the Trieste problem alive. Trieste was the true battleground, the first line of attack for all Irredentist organizations, but most important were the two local organizations: The Comitato di Liberazione Nazionale dell' Istria and the old Irredentist group, Lega

67. Mihovilović, *Trst problem dana,* p. 144.

INDEPENDENTISM, IRREDENTISM, AND ZONE A

Nazionale, which had functioned in the Julian Region before World War I.[68]

The CLN for Istria was composed of émigré political leaders who left Istria or Zone B of the FTT and found refuge in Trieste. It defended the Italian character of Istria, and prepared memoranda for the United Nations Security Council and the Western powers, describing the persecution of Italians in Yugoslav Istria, and in Yugoslav Zone B. The CLN for Istria, besides collecting information about the situation in Istria, specialized in founding terrorist groups, a fact unearthed in the trials held in Koper in Zone B in September 1949 and again in July 1951, according to Yugoslav reports.

The Lega Nazionale, in the past mainly concerned with the support of Italian schools, now stated that its aim was

> to promote in Venezia Giulia the study, the love, and defense of the Italian language, tradition and culture.
> To this end the association will primarily develop cultural, educational, relief and recreation activities, independently of any political party or party organization.[69]

Behind these harmless cultural and social aims were hidden the real activities of the Lega Nazionale. By being above all political parties it became a true rallying point for Italians regardless of political affiliation. Great Italian manifestations in Trieste were usually organized by the Lega. It gathered data about Yugoslav persecutions of Italians in Zone B and about the economic, cultural, and social position of the Italian minority in Yugoslavia. Based upon these materials the Lega Nazionale sent reports and petitions to the Italian government and to the United Nations.

Both the CLN for Istria and the Lega Nazionale also undertook relief services for Italian refugees and received support through large grants of money from the Italian government. The trial of Gino Monaco, financial secretary of the Lega Nazionale, held in Venice in April 1950, revealed that the Italian government had allocated thirty-five million lire to the Lega. Out of this

68. Ibid., pp. 150–52; Ive Mihovilović, *Italian Expansionist Policy toward Istria, Rijeka and Dalmatia, 1945–1953: Documents* (Belgrade, 1954), pp. 53–70, 81–97.
69. *Statuto della Lega Nazionale* (Trieste, 1949), p. 5.

sum over seven million lire were allegedly spent to buy arms for terrorist groups in Istria and Zone B.

However, according to Yugoslav authors, the true center of organized Irredentism was Rome. The Italian government and Irredentist groups in the Italian parliament provided secret monetary allocations and ideological leadership to a well organized network of Irredentist organizations which was spread over all of Italy.

In October 1947, a few weeks after the Free Territory came into being, a Christian Democratic deputy, Fausto Pecorari, stimulated formation among members of parliament of the Gruppo Parlamentare pro Trieste, to help bring Trieste back to Italy. Another group, the Gruppo Parlamentare Giuliano-Dalmata, composed of well-known veteran Irredentists, had a broader aim, namely to keep alive the idea that one day all of the territories ceded to Yugoslavia by the peace treaty would be recovered by Italy. Both groups combined forces in parliament to further the return of the Free Territory to Italy. They prepared resolutions supporting Italian claims and pressed through secret allocations from the budget to the foreign ministry to be used in support of Irredentism.[70]

The leader of the Italian majority party and prime minister, Alcide de Gasperi, himself a veteran Irredentist from the Southern Tyrol, followed with the greatest interest the work of the Irredentist parliamentary groups and kept closely in touch with Pecorari, the Irredentist expert in his party. This same Pecorari organized in 1947 the first Irredentist organization in Italy, the Comitato per la Venezia Giulia e Zara, later renamed Associazione Nazionale per la Venezia Giulia e Dalmazia (ANVGD).[71] ANVGD was a union of many Irredentist organizations which existed in different Italian cities. These city organizations had their own names, usually called Lega Dalmata, Lega Fiumana, or Lega Istriana. The provincial communities tied together the city organizations. At the top was the ANVGD in Rome. Among other activi-

---

70. Mihovilović, *Trst problem dana,* pp. 144–46; V. Sedmak and J. Mejak, *Trieste: The Problem Which Agitates the World* (Belgrade, 1953), pp. 55–56.

71. Mihovilović, *Trst problem dana,* pp. 146, 148; same author, *Italian Expansionist Policy,* pp. 44–46.

ties the branch organizations of ANVGD kept alive the idea that many Italians were left in Yugoslavia. One of the first activities of the ANVGD was a movement to rename the principal streets in Italian cities after cities in the Julian Region and Dalmatia, such as Viale Fiume "in honor of the lost but not forgotten city," Viale Trieste, and so on.

Two other important Irredentist organizations, not affiliated with the ANVGD, were Associazione Nazionale Dalmata and the Movimento Istriano Revisionista. The first, with its seat in Rome, was primarily interested in Dalmatia. Antonio Tacconi, the president of the Associazione Nazionale Dalmata, had been the leader of Dalmatian Irredentists between the wars, and returned to Dalmatia after the Italians occupied it in 1941.[72] The second, the Movimento Istriano Revisionista (MIR), had its seat in Gorizia in order to be closer to the unredeemed lands. It accused the ANVGD of being under the influence of the Roman bureaucracy and hence lacking radicalism. MIR was composed mostly of Istrian refugees. It had special offices for Istrian refugees in other Italian cities which were to provide for lodging and food and to find employment for jobless Istrians. Besides these three main groups, there existed some ten other smaller organizations which used Venezia Giulia or Dalmatia in their names.

All the major Irredentist organizations supported the Centro Studi Adriatici, which was to promote research on the history of all lands ceded to Yugoslavia. The aims of the Centro Studi Adriatici may be seen in more detail in this excerpt from its *Bollettino d'informazione* of June 30, 1950:

> to defend the Italian character of the eastern shore of the Adriatic, to collect data, material, documentation, and the evidence of its Italian character, to spread among the Italians—by means of pamphlets, leaflets, conferences, and exhibits—the understanding of the problems arising from acceptance of an unjust peace treaty and from the military occupation of Dalmatia and almost all of the Julian Region by Yugoslav troops.[73]

72. Mihovilović, *Italian Expansionist Policy*, pp. 28–31, 52–53; Mihovilović, *Trst problem dana*, pp. 148, 149.
73. Mihovilović, *Trst problem dana*, p. 147.

Among the executive members of the Centro Studi Adriatici were the former minister of education and justice, secretary of the Christian Democratic party, Guido Gonella, the former prefect of Trieste, Bruno Coceani, and leaders of various Irredentist societies, such as Professor Luigi Dragicchio, vice-president of the ANVGD; Anteo Lenzoni, vice-president of the Movimento Istriano Revisionista (MIR); Antonio Tacconi, president of the Associazione Nazionale Dalmata; and others.[74] The Centro Studi Adriatici was housed in the building belonging to the state-supported historical institution known as the Istituto per la Storia del Risorgimento, and also received subventions from the Italian government for its research.

The Irredentist organizations all published their own journals and bulletins. The weekly organ of ANVGD was *La Difesa Adriatica,* first published in Rome, September 4, 1947. Its founder and first editor was Fausto Pecorari, later succeeded by Silvano Drago. *L'Arena di Pola* was the weekly organ of the MIR, published first in Pula and then moved to Gorizia after Pula came under Yugoslavia in September 1947. Its editors were Pasquale de Simone and Corrado Belci. Besides these two principal weeklies, other journals of lesser importance appeared, such as *Voce di Fiume* (Venice), *La Favilla* (Milan), *La Vedetta d'Italia* (Padua), and others.[75]

The annual commemorations of the Tripartite Proposal of March 20, 1948, became special occasions for a flood of articles stressing that it was time for the Western powers to fulfill their promise. The dates, November 3 and 4, celebrating the days the Italian army first entered the Julian Region after World War I also attained special importance for Irredentist propaganda. Up to the end of 1950 the propaganda in Zone A was limited to articles and demonstrations except for a few terroristic acts. Beginning with 1951, however, the March and November days became more violent, leading to direct clashes with the AMG civil police and British troops. Hence the alarm of Yugoslavs proved to be justified, though they may have evaluated Irredentism as a much greater force than it really was.

74. Ibid., pp. 116–48; Mihovilović, *Italian Expansionist Policy,* pp. 28–31.

75. Mihovilović, *Trst problem dana,* p. 149.

INDEPENDENTISM, IRREDENTISM, AND ZONE A

Little has been published about Yugoslav institutes and individuals who defended the rights of Slovenes in Zone A and the Slovenian minority left in Italy.

Yugoslav Foreign Minister Edvard Kardelj played a leading role during the war and at the time of the peace negotiations in 1945-47. Himself a Slovene, he exercised a great influence on Tito and the leaders of the Yugoslav Communist party. That Yugoslavia claimed Trieste so stubbornly was partly a result of Kardelj's influence.

The new Yugoslav leaders also supported institutions devoted to defense of the Slovenian and Croat Littoral. Most well-known was the Jadranski institut (Adriatic Institute) in Sušak, which published its *Anali jadranskog instituta* (Annals of the Adriatic Institute). The Adriatic Institute was concerned with the study of Croat history in Istria and Dalmatia. The outstanding workers in this field were Professor J. Roglić, an expert in the cultural geography of Istria, and Ive Mihovilović, a journalist specializing in the problem of Italian colonization of the Julian Region between the world wars. Mihovilović also closely followed the Italian Irredentist movement and in 1951 published *Trst problem dana* (Trieste, the Problem of the Day), in which he dealt with Italian policy toward the Free Territory and toward Zone A in particular.

Inštitut za narodna vprašanja (The Institute for National Questions) concerned with the Slovenian Littoral, was another institution supported by the government of the Slovenian Republic. The Institute published pamphlets and articles in different newspapers and reviews defending Slovenian rights and interests in Zone A. The Institute closely cooperated with the University of Ljubljana in Slovenia.

Other federal and local institutions and journals also took up the task of defending Slovenian and Croat interests. The Institute for International Politics and Economics in Belgrade, for example, in 1954 published in English *The Italian Genocide Policy against the Slovenes and the Croats,* to inform the world that Italian discrimination against Slovenes continued in Zone A of the Free Territory. Selected documents about Italian persecution of Slovenes and Croats between the world wars preceded documentary material about harassment of Slovenes in Zone A by the

Allied Military Government and by the local Italian authorities after World War II.

Many articles describing Italian Irredentist aims toward Trieste and the persecution of Slovenes in Zone A of the Free Territory appeared also in *Medjunarodni problemi* (International Problems) and in the *Review of International Affairs*, both published in Belgrade. The first review began its life in 1949; the second, which started in 1950, was intended to reach the public abroad and was therefore written in English. In Trieste, the Študijska knjižnica (Research Library), organized and supported by the pro-Tito group, dedicated its work to collecting material published about Trieste and about Slovenes in Trieste.

An important problem advanced by Italian Irredentism and contradicted by Yugoslav and independentist jurists was the question of Italian sovereignty over the Free Territory. The question first arose in the course of a speech by Professor Angelo E. Cammarata, rector of Trieste University, December 4, 1949, opening the new academic year. Cammarata advanced the thesis that, juridically speaking, Italian sovereignty over the Free Territory had never terminated because no governor had been appointed. Italian sovereignty, he said, was only dormant or ineffective. The entire Italian press in Trieste and Italy hailed this theory with such headlines as "Trieste is Italy," "The Diktat of Paris Did Not Sanction the Cessation of Sovereignty over Trieste," "The FTT Does Not Exist," and so on. The same theory was later espoused by Professor Manlio Udina.[76]

On the other side, Ivan Tomšič, professor of international public law at the University of Ljubljana, Mario Stocca, lawyer and leader of the Blocco Triestino, and other jurists in favor of the FTT declined to accept Cammarata's thesis.[77] The matter was

76. See G. Tanasco, *La posizione giuridica di Trieste* (Rome, 1951); R. Accerboni, "La situazione giuridica del territorio libero de Trieste," *Rivista di studi politici internazionali,* 18, no. 3 (July–Sept. 1951): 477–83.

77. For the antiannexationist viewpoint see: Ivan Tomšič, "Da li suverenitet nad STT zaista još pripada Italiji?" (Does the Sovereignty over the Free Territory of Trieste Really Still Belong to Italy?), *Medjunarodni problemi,* 2, no. 2–3 (Apr.–June 1950): 8–21; Antun Dabinović, "Državnopravni položaj STO-ja" (The Situation of the Free

important, since the independentists had consistently demanded that the Allied Military Government put the Permanent Statute into effect, even without a governor. Opposed to this, the AMG maintained that, as a mere regime of military occupation, it could not properly apply the articles of the Permanent Statute until a governor had been appointed for the Free Territory. At first, therefore, the AMG welcomed the theory that Italian sovereignty over Trieste had never terminated, for this justified the claim that the AMG had not violated the peace treaty in arranging for a financial, economic, and customs union between Zone A and Italy.

GENERAL AIREY'S REPORTS: ANTI-COMMUNISM CUM IRREDENTISM

Strengthening the Free Territory entailed first the development of a Triestine consciousness that would lead to friendly cooperation between Italians and Slovenes, based on reciprocal renunciation of all claims for a future union with Italy or Yugoslavia. Given such a foundation, the Free Territory would represent, not a compromise between Yugoslavia and Italy enforced by the Great Powers, but a settlement freely arrived at between the two ethnic groups and approved by the two countries directly involved. It would mean renouncing any attempt to impose the social and political system of either of these nations. Moreover, the Free Territory could develop its own consciousness only with an independent economy based on traditional trade with its hinterland.

The Irredentists fought any tendency toward an independent

Territory of Trieste According to the Public Law), *Stvarnost: Neodvisna slovenska revija*, 1, no. 4–5 (Sept. 1951): 81–92; Stocca, *Discussioni sul T.L.T.*, pp. 5–6. Josef L. Kunz, professor emeritus of international law at the University of Toledo, in his article "The Free Territory of Trieste," *Western Political Quarterly*, 1, no. 2 (June 1948): 99–112, similarly agreed that Italian sovereignty over the FTT was terminated with the coming into effect of the Italian peace treaty on September 15, 1947. But he added a new concept. While the failure to appoint a governor prolonged the military occupation, "this occupation is no longer an *occupatio bellica,* but constitutes an *occupatio pacifica,* the legal title of which stems from the Italian Peace Treaty."

Triestine consciousness, a strong independent Trieste economy, or peaceful cooperation between the ethnic groups. Here the Irredentists found a great supporter in the commander of Zone A, General Airey.

From the beginning, he denied the existence in Zone A of signs favoring the Free Territory. Later, when confronted with proof of increasing independentist activity and economic recovery, he continued to deprecate the weight of evidence that worked against his views.

He wrote in his first report, handed to the secretary general of the United Nations on February 18, 1948:

> The period reviewed by this report has disclosed no evidence of a real, disinterested and ready disposition to build up a local Triestine political consciousness distinct from, but not necessarily antagonistic to, Italian or Yugoslav national and racial ideology. The hopes and ambitions of the two groups must be expected, in the main, to continue to be centered on restoration to Italy or incorporation into Yugoslavia.
>
> Both racial and political motives are closely interwoven and on the whole those whose sympathies are Italian tend to look to the democratic ideas of the West, while the Slav elements, supported by a body of Italian adherents to the "party line," rally round the standard of communist totalitarianism. A Slovene democratic and nationalist movement, independent of U.A.I.S. and its satellite organs, has recently been created but its numbers are small and it has already been subjected to scarcely veiled threats of retaliation in the Slav-communist press.[78]

Faced with failure to agree on a governor for the Free Territory, General Airey in the same report underlined the need for a new solution. When the answer came in the form of the Tripartite Proposal in March 1948, he warmly recommended its implementation in his report for the first quarter of that year, transmitted to the secretary general of the United Nations on May 25, 1948:

> I believe that a natural and robust economic recovery can only begin when the territory is regrafted on to the body of Italy, which alone is likely to restore life to its shipyards and

78. *First AMG Report* (S/679), p. 37.

kindred industries. . . . I conclude, therefore, that the solution to the problem of Trieste lies in the implementation of the tripartite proposal of 20 March 1948 as soon as this is possible.[79]

In his third AMG report, for the second quarter of 1948, General Airey justified his financial agreement with Italy by pointing out that Trieste's economy was dislocated and cut off from Italian resources, and had no other avenue by which to achieve prosperity. Then, speaking of the administrative reforms introduced by Order No. 259, he stated that they followed closely the Italian pattern "which is in accordance with the wishes of the majority of the local population."[80] Again he stressed: "It has become increasingly apparent that the Free Territory settlement established as a compromise by the Treaty of Peace with Italy is neither politically nor economically viable."[81] The Italian Irredentists and the Italian government could not have wished for a better report.

Such words could scarcely strengthen an independentist consciousness. But when the movement still showed signs of life, it received a new blow in General Airey's report for the fourth quarter of 1948 in which he linked it to the Communist bloc:

> There existed no evidence of a real, disinterested and ready disposition to build up a local Triestine political consciousness. . . . There exist, it is true, independence parties and fronts but the more prominent of these are clearly discernible as the familiar appurtenances of international communism, whence they derive their inspiration, their instructions and their funds.[82]

During the time of the Tito-Cominform split and the concomitant division of the Communist ranks in Zone A, General Airey continued to maintain that only two blocs existed, one pro-Italian and pro-Western, and the other pro-Communist. Again he connected the independentist bloc with the Communists. He agreed with the policy expressed in Italian Irredentist papers which accused the Independence Front of receiving support from

79. *Second AMG Report* (S/781), p. 28.
80. *Third AMG Report* (S/953), p. 5.
81. Ibid., p. 17.   82. *Fifth AMG Report* (S/1242), p. 2.

Yugoslavia, but failed to foresee political consequences deriving from the split between Tito and Soviet Russia. As in all his other reports General Airey called for restitution of the FTT to Italy, but added a new point that the return "will be in the interests not only of the people of this Zone, but of future peace in this sensitive part of Europe."[83]

In his report for the first quarter of 1949 General Airey hastened to recognize the new economic prosperity prevailing, but denied any relationship of this achievement to Trieste's independence:

> It would be vain and indeed dangerous to expect . . . a full return of that remarkable volume of transit and entrepot trade which reached its peak before the first world war . . . It is not on the conditions of the past that the economic future of Trieste can be rebuilt.
>
>   I have repeatedly pointed out that Trieste, separated as it is from Italy, is no longer a viable entity.[84]

For the second quarter of 1949, General Airey, noting the June election results, argued that the independentist vote came from employees of the AMG.[85] At the same time, forgetting about ERP aid, he declared that the people in Zone A had voted to return the Free Territory to Italy "as the natural home of the majority of its people and the source of their prosperity when Allied Administration is withdrawn."[86]

Despite evidence that import-export activities in Trieste were approaching the levels reached in 1938 and later even those of 1913, General Airey continued, in his eighth report, for the third quarter of 1949, to repeat that the FTT could not live by its own economy:

> I am convinced that any other solution will not only sever the ethnic and cultural roots of the majority of the population, but would lead the territory through economic collapse into the orbit of communist totalitarianism.[87]

83. Ibid., p. 3.
84. *Sixth AMG Report* (S/1318), pp. 5–6.
85. See chapter 11, "First Elections."
86. *Seventh AMG Report* (S/1374), p. 7.
87. *Eighth AMG Report* (S/1424), p. 6.

In his eighth report he again recommended return of the FTT to Italy, and repeated it in his ninth report, for the last quarter of 1949, where he wrote:

> I am further convinced that any attempt to construct a separate economy will not be in the interests of the inhabitants of the area and will be contrary to the trend of Western Europe towards a closer economic integration and political unity.[88]

Comparing these reports with the viewpoints expressed in the Irredentist press, it is apparent that the arguments of both for return of the FTT to Italy ran in parallel lines. They can be summarized as follows: the majority of the people want this return; the continued existence of the FTT endangers world peace; the FTT is economically unable to live; the FTT will eventually fall prey to the Communist bloc; there is no genuine independentist movement in Trieste; the independentist movement is paid for by Yugoslavia; the independentist movement receives mainly the votes of Italians employed by the AMG, and so on.

As the international situation changed, and the Western powers began to seek a new solution for the Trieste problem, General Airey did try to adapt himself to the shift, though leaving the appearance that he had not departed from his previous views. In his tenth and last report, for the year 1950, he wrote:

> I believe that the economy of Trieste cannot be separated from that of Italy and that dislocation of the existing integrated economic structure would cause a sharp fall in employment and a collapse of the standard of living.... Conversely, it will be equally essential for the Italian economy to take into account Trieste's special position as an outlet for the trade with the Danubian countries which she needs to keep her maritime connections alive and to sustain her relatively large population. There seems to be no reason why these two cardinal factors should not be balanced though the process will need the exercise of some vision.
>
> As I have so often reiterated in my previous reports, I believe that a permanent and peaceful settlement of the Trieste question, based on the needs and well-being of the inhabitants in the area, could best be achieved within the frame-

---

88. *Ninth AMG Report* (S/1473), p. 8.

work of the Tripartite proposal of 20 March 1948. I am, moreover, convinced that such a settlement could best be realized by agreement among the parties primarily concerned.[89]

A final question may be asked: To what degree did General Airey merely follow directions of the British and American governments, and to what extent were the views he expressed his own? It is true that Airey never contradicted the general line of British-American policy toward Trieste, but within this framework he favored the Italian position more than necessary. As a soldier and anti-Communist, he saw only two sides: one, Communist, Slavic, pro-Yugoslav; the other, Italian, democratic, pro-Western. When he had to choose between them, he chose the latter. His analysis failed to reveal the true and much more complex situation.

89. *Tenth AMG Report* (S/2062), pp. 8–9.

13
ITALO-YUGOSLAV NEGOTIATIONS: A SOLUTION FRUSTRATED (MARCH 1951–MARCH 1952)

When Great Britain recalled General Airey and appointed General John Winterton as commander of Zone A in March 1951, the act signified a break with the past, the beginning of a new AMG policy in Zone A, and a new Allied attitude toward the entire Trieste problem. Until that time Great Britain had recognized the Tripartite Proposal of March 20, 1948, as the basis for Italian-Yugoslav agreement on the FTT. In March 1951, however, Britain subordinated the Tripartite Proposal to direct Italian-Yugoslav negotiations. Still later, in September, the Western Big Three, the United States, Great Britain, and France, urged a direct Italian-Yugoslav accord without mentioning the Tripartite Proposal. This new policy toward the FTT and Zone A was, in turn, only a logical consequence of the changed international situation.

THE NEW INTERNATIONAL SCENE

From the beginning of the Korean War the Western powers debated the possibility that the Soviet bloc might start a new incident to release Western pressure on the Communist forces of North Korea. It was also possible that any new conflict might start a general war between the Western powers and Soviet Russia.[1] To be prepared for such a turn of events the West, under the leadership of the United States, began rearming and building a network of security alliances. Part of this global program in Europe sought to strengthen NATO and extend it to the eastern Mediterranean by including Greece and Turkey, to rearm Italy, and to give military aid to Yugoslavia.

In the eyes of the Western powers, Yugoslavia was one of the

1. Harry S. Truman, *Memoirs,* vol. 2: *Years of Trial and Hope* (Garden City, N.Y., 1956), pp. 420–21.

danger areas where conflict might ignite a new war. When in the beginning of 1951 rumors of an impending Stalinist attack on Yugoslavia spread, the three Western powers issued in February separate public warnings to potential aggressors. Marshal Tito, on his part, declared on February 17, 1951, that Yugoslavia would resist any aggression and defend her independence. Consequently in the first days of April Tito requested military equipment from the United States, Great Britain, and France. On April 14, 1951, France promised to supply small arms and military equipment under a new trade agreement. Two days later President Truman set aside up to 39 million dollars in military aid for the Yugoslav forces. Similar promises were made by Great Britain. In June the Yugoslav chief of staff, Koča Popović, came to the United States to procure more arms. After lengthy negotiations a military aid agreement was signed on November 14, 1951, between the United States and Yugoslavia, by which Yugoslavia became a regular recipient of arms under the Mutual Security Act.[2]

Parallel with Yugoslav armament, negotiations began for revision of the Italian peace treaty. In the treaty, Italy had been characterized as an ex-enemy state. Her armed forces were to remain limited and she was forbidden to manufacture war materials in excess of those needed for self-defense. From the beginning of 1951 Italian statesmen had vigorously urged the three Western powers to revise the peace treaty. Thus on April 13, Italian Foreign Minister Count Sforza in a letter to his French colleague asked for such a revision. Then on July 13 the Italian government presented its formal request to the governments of the three Western powers. Four days later Secretary of State Dean Acheson, in a conversation in Washington with Italian chargé d'affaires Mario Luciolli, indicated that the United States was ready to confer with other governments on revision.[3]

But the question was complex, for revision needed the consent of all signatories to the Italian peace treaty, including the countries of the Soviet bloc. And Yugoslavia stressed that revision would whet the appetites of Italian Irredentists for more Yugoslav

2. *The United States in World Affairs, 1951,* published by the Council on Foreign Relations (New York, 1952), pp. 340–41; *New York Times,* Apr. 9, 12, 15, 17, June 9, 12, 19, Oct. 27, Nov. 15, 1951.

3. *New York Times,* Apr. 14, May 21, July 14, 18, 1951.

lands. Hence she opposed any changes in the treaty prior to settlement of the Trieste question. Britain was of the same opinion though she had not made it a condition for support.[4]

At the meeting of the North Atlantic Council (NATO) in Ottawa, Canada, in September 1951, Italian Premier de Gasperi explained to the foreign ministers of the three Western powers that Italy was distinguishing between the Trieste dispute and treaty revision, hoping that revision might facilitate solution of the Trieste problem. The three Western powers, yielding to Premier de Gasperi, informed the Soviet Union on September 26, 1951, that they favored removal of the military restrictions and discrimination embodied in the treaty. Soviet Russia in her note of October 11, 1951, replied that she would accept such revision, if Italy would leave NATO and if the peace treaties of her satellite countries were similarly modified. At this point the Western powers decided to act on their own. The United States rejected the Soviet note on October 12, and on December 21, 1951, notified Italy that "since the military clauses [of the peace treaty] are not consistent with Italy's position as an equal member of the democratic and freedom-loving family of nations, Italy is released from its obligations to the United States."[5] Following the United States' lead other Western countries accepted the revision, enabling Italy to rearm according to the needs of NATO.[6]

FUTILE ITALO-YUGOSLAV ATTEMPTS AT NEGOTIATION

Italian Irredentists and the Italian government followed with deep anxiety the rapprochement between Yugoslavia and the Western powers. In Italian calculations any cooperation between the West and Yugoslavia would lessen Italian opportunities to regain the Free Territory. When in March 1951 it became known that Italian Premier de Gasperi and Foreign Minister Count Sforza

4. Mihovilović, *Trst problem dana,* pp. 69–76, 180–83; *New York Times,* July 8, Aug. 11, Sept. 3, 17, 1951.
5. *Department of State Bulletin,* 25 (Dec. 31, 1951): 1050.
6. *The United States in World Affairs, 1951,* pp. 342–44; *Documents on International Affairs, 1951,* a publication of the Royal Institute of International Affairs (London, 1954), pp. 83–89; *New York Times,* Sept. 20, 27, Oct. 12, 13, Dec. 22, 1951.

would visit London for a round of talks with British Prime Minister Clement Attlee and new Foreign Secretary Herbert Morrison, the Italian press urged its government to defend Italian rights to the entire Free Territory. When rumor spread that the Italian government would make a deal with the Yugoslavs in London to solve the Trieste problem, the Irredentists and Communists organized demonstrations in Rome, again demanding that the government defend Italian rights to the entire FTT.[7]

De Gasperi and Count Sforza made good use of these pressures when they met with the British on March 13, 1951, by asking for reaffirmation of the Tripartite Proposal of 1948. The British continued to assert the validity of the proposal but at the same time subordinated it to direct negotiations. In its original meaning according to the British, the Tripartite Proposal had not promised the Free Territory to Italy, but rather had been a proposal to the Soviet Union to agree that the territory should be returned to Italy. As the Soviet Union did not seem ready to approve, the Tripartite Proposal had lost much of its practical meaning. Hence, the only realistic way to find an answer appeared to be through direct Italo-Yugoslav agreement, meaning naturally a partition of the territory between the two countries.

This British view was expressed in the official statement of the foreign office on the London meeting, issued March 15, 1951, and confirmed at a press conference held by the Italians, De Gasperi and Sforza, on the same day. The official statement of the British foreign office announced:

> The British Ministers confirmed that they maintain the tripartite declaration on Trieste of March 20, 1948, with a view to settlement by conciliation; and the Italian Ministers declared that it was their desire to reach a friendly agreement with the Yugoslav Government on this question.[8]

The statements made by De Gasperi and Sforza to the news correspondents were reported by the press as follows:

> Emphasizing their satisfaction with the understanding on Trieste, they [De Gasperi and Count Sforza] pointed out that the tripartite declaration of 1948 had been not a promise to

7. *New York Times,* Mar. 12, 13, 14, 1951.
8. *Documents on International Affairs, 1951,* p. 89.

return the Free Territory to Italy, but an attempt to obtain Soviet consent to its return.[9] The practical importance of the declaration was accordingly small at the present stage, though it was "a point of departure," and the only practical course open to Italy was to seek a settlement with Yugoslavia by conciliation.[10]

Great Britain further confirmed this new course by removing General T. S. Airey as supreme commander of the British–United States forces in Zone A and replacing him with Sir John Winterton. It is significant that the ministry of defense in London announced the appointment of General Winterton on March 14, 1951, the very time when De Gasperi and Sforza were conferring with the English ministers.[11]

Encouraged by this new course, the Yugoslavs began talks toward settlement of the Trieste problem. In the last part of May 1951 contacts were made between the Yugoslav and Italian ambassadors in London, followed by talks among Italian and Yugoslav representatives in Rome between July 18 and 30, 1951.[12]

9. Note that until this time the Italian government had defended the viewpoint that the Tripartite Proposal had been a promise to return the Free Territory to Italy.

10. *Keesing's Contemporary Archives,* 8 (1950–52): 11363.

11. Ibid., p. 11338.

12. Jože Brilej was the Yugoslav and Tommaso Gallarati-Scotti the Italian ambassador in London. The most detailed account of the negotiations in Rome (July 18 to July 30, 1951) is given in Sforza, *Cinque anni a palazzo Chigi,* pp. 417–29. However, Yugoslavs Vlado Sedmak ("Survey of Progress," *Review of International Affairs,* 5, no. 109 [Oct. 16, 1954]: 7–8) and Jeri (p. 230) pointed out that Sforza's description was not exact and complete. The negotiations in Rome took place between the former Yugoslav ambassador in France, Marko Ristić, and the Italian ambassador to the Vatican, Antonio Meli Lupi di Soragna. During the negotiations Italian Prime Minister de Gasperi replaced Count Sforza by taking over also the ministry of foreign affairs on July 26, 1951. Moreover, the Italian Giulio Bettasa in his article "L'ultima fase della questione di Trieste: 1951–1954," *Rivista di studi politici internazionali,* 22, no. 1 (Jan.–Mar. 1955): 21, mentions Italian Ambassador to the Vatican Di Soragna, and Yugoslav Minister of the Interior Aleksandar Ranković, as the negotiators in Rome. This is evidently a mistake as no other work refers to Ranković.

In general, two solutions were offered: first, a division along the Morgan line, Zone A going to Italy, Zone B to Yugoslavia; second, the construction of a new line from north to south by which almost the entire coast would go to Italy and the interior to Yugoslavia. The discussions were informal and no conclusion was reached.

During the talks it became clear to the Italian statesmen that any agreement would mean partition of the Trieste territory, leaving Yugoslavia at least half of the land. Though Italy agreed to direct negotiations, she still defended the Tripartite Proposal as the starting point of any accord. Italy would permit some modifications in favor of Yugoslavia, but the greater part of the Free Territory including all of its coast would be returned to Italy. Seeing that the British policy of direct negotiations would not favor Italian demands, Italian statesmen tried to win the support of the United States and other NATO countries against the British idea. Accordingly, during the summer of 1951 the entire Italian political and press campaign was directed toward preparing world opinion for demands to be made by De Gasperi, during a planned autumn visit to America, that the United States should support Italian claims to the Trieste territory.

The Italian press campaign of 1951 mainly blamed Great Britain for initiating a new policy so unfavorable to Italy. The articles demanded not only return of the entire Free Territory to Italy, but also claimed the Yugoslav part of Istria whenever the Italian peace treaty should be revised. Such articles appeared not only in the right-wing press but in pro-government newspapers such as *Il Nuovo Corriere della Sera;* they contributed not at all to Italo-Yugoslav agreement but instead worsened relations between the two countries, for they were matched by violent reaction in Yugoslavia.

In the beginning of September, before De Gasperi's departure for the United States and Canada, Augusto de Marsanich, secretary general of the Italian Social Movement, expressing the views of the right wing, stressed that De Gasperi could not ask for anything less than return of the entire FTT to Italy or he would be committing political suicide.[13]

Premier de Gasperi, who had also taken over the ministry of

13. *New York Times,* Sept. 1, 1951.

foreign affairs on July 26, came to America to press for a pro-Italian solution of the Trieste problem. He pointed out that the problem was limited not merely to Yugoslavia and Italy, but was of vital interest to the Western powers in their efforts to preserve world peace. Hence the West, and especially the United States, should take the initiative in urging upon Yugoslavia a solution based on the Tripartite Proposal, with some minor corrections in favor of Yugoslavia.

This position of the Italian government was defended by De Gasperi at the conversations he had with the foreign ministers of the Western Big Three on the occasion of the meeting of the North Atlantic Council at Ottawa from September 15 to September 20, 1951. Here De Gasperi was successful in obtaining separation of the two important issues discussed: Italian rearmament and the Trieste problem.

As we know, the Western powers agreed to revision of the Italian peace treaty and allowed Italy to rearm, but evidently refused to endorse Italian demands regarding the FTT.

De Gasperi tried also to get American support for a pro-Italian solution of the Trieste problem in his conversations of September 24–26, 1951, with President Truman and Secretary of State Acheson. The results of these talks were given in a joint communiqué on September 26: the United States government was to solicit the admission of Italy to the United Nations, had already asked the Soviet Union to accept revision of the Italian peace treaty, and promised to continue military and economic aid to Italy. About Trieste the communiqué stated:

> Both the Prime Minister [De Gasperi] and the Secretary of State [Acheson] agreed that a solution to this question would greatly strengthen unity of Western Europe. As stated in the conversation between the Prime Minister and the President; the policies of both Governments on this question are well known. The solution should take into account the legitimate aspirations of the Italian people.[14]

Evidently, as in the British communiqué of March 15, 1951, the United States favored direct Italian-Yugoslav negotiations. It

14. Ibid., Sept. 27, 1951 (© 1951 by The New York Times Company; reprinted by permission).

was significant that the British had still explicitly mentioned the Tripartite Proposal of March 20, 1948, while the United States communiqué did not. Moreover, the communiqué referred only in general to Trieste but avoided the term Free Territory of Trieste.

This factor was noticed at once by the Italian public and press. The *New York Times* correspondent Arnaldo Cortesi reported from Rome on September 26:

> Public opinion had been so thoroughly exercised over the Trieste problem of late that when the communiqué became known all that many readers saw in it was what it said about Trieste. A large number were horrified to note that it did not even clearly reaffirm the validity of the three-power declaration of March 20, 1948, which advocated the return of the Free Territory to Italy.
>
> The phrase to the effect that the solution should take into account the legitimate aspirations of the Italian people was judged to be couched in weak and debilitative terms.[15]

The pro-government weekly *Relazioni internazionali* reflected this same attitude in its analysis of De Gasperi's visit to the United States. It pointed out how the premier could observe the changed international position of Yugoslavia in the eyes of Washington, which up to this point had been in favor of adhering to the Tripartite Proposal, and how Yugoslavia had gained by being inserted into the system of Western defenses.[16]

The Irredentists looked upon De Gasperi's visit in the United States as a complete failure. Their dissatisfaction was especially high in Trieste, and was expressed by a bomb hurled on the night of September 27 against the AMG building. The explosion blew out window panes for several blocks around, but no casualties were reported.[17]

From the accessible evidence it seems very probable that by the end of September 1951, all three Western powers had agreed

15. Ibid.
16. *Relazioni internazionali: Settimanale di politica estera* (published by Istituto per gli studi di politica internazionale in Milan), 15, no. 39 (Sept. 29, 1951): 748.
17. *New York Times*, Sept. 28, 1951.

to abandon the Tripartite Proposal as the basis for a solution of the Trieste problem.

A speech delivered by the Yugoslav Foreign Minister Edvard Kardelj, three days after the issue of the communiqué in Washington, further confirmed this supposition. Kardelj explained to the Federal Assembly in Belgrade on September 29 that no agreement between Italy and Yugoslavia could be reached as long as it was based on old demands. Italy had to abandon the Tripartite Proposal and Yugoslavia her old claims to the entire Free Territory as put forward at the peace conference. After both states had given up their demands, Kardelj stressed, a third, and more realistic, solution could be sought. It would show the existence of two zones: Zone B in Yugoslav hands, and Zone A presided over by an Allied administration favoring Italy. Only by departing from the present situation, concluded Kardelj, could a permanent solution be reached between Italy and Yugoslavia.[18] Further available evidence indicates that the Western powers had not only abandoned the Tripartite Proposal but were also urging, if not actually pressuring, Italy and Yugoslavia to reach a final settlement on the Trieste question.[19] The usually well informed *New York Times* published November 20, 1951, a short note from Belgrade, dated November 19, which stated:

> Responsible sources said today that Yugoslavia and Italy would negotiate, probably in a matter of weeks, on a division of the Free Territory of Trieste.
>
> A big part of the foundation for agreement was said to have been worked out in September and October in Washington conferences. Representatives of the Western powers worked separately with Yugoslav and Italian diplomats there. The prospective agreement was reported to hinge on these points:
>
> 1. Trieste would become Italian. However, it would be kept open to free trade privileges for Yugoslavia and Austria.
> 2. Through special arrangements with Italy, the Big

---

18. For an extract in English of Kardelj's speech see *Documents on International Affairs, 1951*, pp. 92–93; *Keesing's Contemporary Archives*, 8: 12146; the entire text of Kardelj's speech is reprinted in Mihovilović, *Trst problem dana*, pp. 180–83.

19. See Jeri, p. 234.

Three Western powers would maintain defensive bases at Trieste.

4. [*sic*] The Free Territory would be split roughly along the present occupation line, with Yugoslavia keeping Zone B, and Italy getting Zone A, now held by a British–United States occupation force.

5. Yugoslavia would get some additional territory, including a port, in return for renouncing claims to other parts of Zone A.

6. Both Italy and Yugoslavia might receive additional financial aid from the West. [© 1951 by The New York Times Company; reprinted by permission.]

Two days later, on November 21, 1951, negotiations started in earnest between Italy and Yugoslavia. They took place in Paris during the sixth regular session of the United Nations, between Aleš Bebler, Yugoslav ambassador to the United Nations, and Gastone Guidotti, the Italian observer at the United Nations. The negotiations lasted with various interruptions until January 8, 1952. Guidotti demanded the entire coast of the Free Territory for Italy, leaving Slovenian and Croat villages of the interior to Yugoslavia. Italy called this the continuous ethnic line. The Yugoslavs pointed out that no such line existed. The ethnic line, according to the Yugoslavs, ended at Monfalcone. From Monfalcone on, was continuous Slavic land with isolated Italian islands such as Trieste and other smaller Istrian towns in Zone B.

Bebler proposed three main solutions, each with some variations. The first was to divide the territory along the zonal border, Zone A going to Italy and Zone B to Yugoslavia, with a free port in Trieste and protection guarantees for the Slovenian minority of Zone A. The second plan would give Yugoslavia a corridor to the Adriatic, south of Trieste, to build a new port for Slovenia. In return Italy would get a small part of the coast in Zone B including the town of Koper. The third proposal asked that Italy and Yugoslavia jointly administer the entire Free Territory through nomination of an Italian governor and a Yugoslav vice-governor, who would exchange their posts every three years. This new idea of an Italian-Yugoslav condominium was to be based on principles accepted in the Permanent Statute.

The Italian government refused the above proposals, but contacts between Italian and Yugoslav diplomats nevertheless continued. On March 11, 1952, the Italian government proposed a plebiscite to take place at once under international supervision by disinterested states. Yugoslavia on March 28, 1952, refused a plebiscite under such conditions, explaining that she could agree only after correction of wrongs done to the Slovenes and Croats by forced Italianization between the two wars. Hence Yugoslavia demanded a condominium with Italy over the FTT for fifteen years, during which time the injustice could be rectified, before she would agree to a plebiscite.[20]

By March 1952 it was evident that Italian-Yugoslav negotiations were not a success.

ITALIAN OPPOSITION TO THE AMG

The changed British–United States policy in the administration of Zone A was formally inaugurated in March 1951 when the new commander of the Allied forces, General John Winterton, arrived in Trieste. The exchange of commanders only served to emphasize the new line, whose beginnings could be traced back to the latter part of 1950. While the old policy, identified with General Airey's administration, favored pro-Italian political parties in Zone A, the new one tried to remain neutral toward all groups. General Winterton also tried to establish better relations with the Yugoslav Military Government of Zone B. On April 18, 1951, he was host to the new Yugoslav commander of Zone B, Colonel Miloš Stamatović, an event which had never taken place during General Airey's administration.[21]

Previously the AMG had favored or tacitly tolerated such reforms and innovations as would facilitate the zone's unification with Italy. The new AMG policy, on the contrary, assumed that Zone A formed a part of the Free Territory, which was an international entity separate from Italian sovereignty.

During Airey's administration civil servants had several times applied judicial and administrative legislation of the Italian Re-

20. Ibid., pp. 228–34; Bettasa, *Rivista di studi politici internazionali*, 22, no. 5:21–22.

21. *New York Times*, Apr. 19, 1951. In the spring of 1951 Colonel Stamatović replaced Colonel Lenac as Yugoslav commander of Zone B.

public to Zone A. It had become customary for Trieste's courts to appeal to the Court of Cassation in Rome, the highest court in the Italian judicial system. Beginning in March 1951, the AMG forbade any such application or recognition of Italian legislation. The AMG made it clear that it was the supreme and sole authority for Zone A according to proclamations and orders in effect since 1947. In April 1951, the AMG particularly prohibited the courts in Trieste from recognizing the jurisdiction of any court outside Zone A, and insisted that violations be reported immediately to the justice department of the AMG.

This new policy greatly alarmed the Italian Irredentists. In their opinion the AMG attitude conflicted with the Tripartite Proposal and the repeated assurances that Zone A would be considered economically and administratively a part of Italy.[22] To align Italian opinion behind their cause, they started a huge press campaign in Zone A and in Italy. In July 1951 the leading Italian daily of Milan, *Il Nuovo Corriere della Sera*, began a series of articles entitled "What Is Happening in Trieste," written by Enzo Grazzini, its special correspondent there. The articles described in detail the complaints of the pro-Italian parties against the new administrative policy of the Allied Military Government in Zone A. Furthermore, the articles emphatically informed the Italian people that the Allied powers had changed their attitude toward the Trieste problem and now favored Yugoslavia.

On July 2, 1951, Grazzini informed the Italian public that the AMG had forbidden the courts in Trieste to have any connection with the Court of Cassation in Rome.[23] In the article, "The Prohibition of the Italian Flag and the Absurd Limitations of Broadcasting," he complained that the AMG forbade the flying of the Italian flag on the town hall on November 3, 1950, when the Italian minister of education visited Trieste for the opening ceremony of a new university building. The article also asserted that the Trieste radio station devoted more time to Slovenian than to Italian programs (which of course was not true). The correspondent asserted that this new anti-Italian policy was further evident at the celebration of the American Independence Day in Trieste.

22. See *New York Times,* July 7, 1951.
23. Articles of *Il Nuovo Corriere della Sera* were quoted and analyzed in Mihovilović, *Trst problem dana,* pp. 45–48.

Previously, the American general had invited only the Italian generals from Padua and Udine and no Yugoslav officers. But in the current year the American general invited only the commander of the Yugoslav Zone B. In addition, the American general and the Yugoslav colonel had been photographed together as good friends.

In the July 10 issue, another article entitled "The Italian Flag Also Disappeared from Vessels" complained that the AMG had ordered all ships registered in Trieste to display only the flag of the Free Territory of Trieste. The article then outlined the argument that such a flag had never been internationally recognized because the Free Territory had never come into being. This action, the article stressed, was another anti-Italian measure of the Allied government in Trieste.

Il Nuovo Corriere della Sera was followed by other Italian newspapers, which added still other complaints. A speech delivered by the director of the Trieste fair had been censored ahead of time by AMG authorities; besides, an official representative of the Italian government had not been allowed to speak at the opening ceremony of the fair. Trieste's coat of arms had been introduced on tobacco kiosks, cigarette packs, railroad cars, and police badges.[24]

The Irredentists had again succeeded in generating a press campaign, this time directed against the AMG, and urging the Italian government to defend Italian claims to Trieste. Senators and deputies from all political parties submitted numerous interpellations demanding to know what the government had done and was doing to defend Italian rights to the FTT. Some senators demanded that Italy denounce the peace treaty unless the AMG rescinded its order about the courts. In a speech delivered to the Senate on July 11, 1951, Prime Minister de Gasperi recognized the gravity of the step taken by the AMG when it cut off the Trieste law courts from contact with Italy, but he minimized other complaints by stating that "nothing irreparable has happened in Trieste." If ordinary diplomatic means proved ineffective, he asserted, the Italian government would appeal to The Hague International

24. *New York Times*, July 11, 1951; see also De Castro, pp. 460–66; and S. Vukušić, "What Is Happening in Trieste?" *Review of International Affairs*, 2, no. 15 (July 18, 1951): 12.

Court for a decision regarding the jurisdiction of the Court of Cassation in Rome over the Trieste law courts. He hinted that Italy's continued adherence to the Atlantic Pact might become doubtful if Italian hopes about the FTT were to be disappointed.[25]

Foreign Minister Carlo Sforza meanwhile delivered a memorandum to the United States and British ambassadors in Rome, underlining the difficulties that might arise for the government if Italian hopes in Trieste were rebuffed.[26]

As usual, the United States hastened to reassure Italy that nothing had changed. The State Department said on July 11, 1951:

> The American Ambassador at Rome has been authorized to inform Prime Minister de Gasperi that the United States has noticed that there has recently been speculation in the Italian press about United States policy regarding Trieste.
>
> Accordingly, the United States desires to assure the Prime Minister that United States policy in this respect remains unchanged. That policy continues to be guided by the spirit of the March 20, 1948, declaration and by the belief that a permanent and peaceful settlement of the Trieste question can best be realized by agreement between the parties directly concerned—Italy and Yugoslavia.[27]

This note was similar to the British-Italian statement of March 1951, but did not subordinate the Italian-Yugoslav talks to the Tripartite Proposal, though it referred only to "the spirit of" rather than directly to the Tripartite Proposal of 1948. This might have caused some hopes among Italians that the United States policy toward Trieste was more favorable to Italy than the British one.

In reply to Irredentist press propaganda, the independentists in Trieste pointed out that in reality no fundamental change had taken place in AMG administration which would separate Zone A from Italy and transform it into an independent state. Zone A was still part of the Italian tariff area and integrated with the

---

25. Vukušić, pp. 12–13; *New York Times*, July 12, 1951; for extracts from De Gasperi's speech see *Documents on International Affairs, 1951*, pp. 89–92; De Castro, p. 466.

26. *New York Times*, July 11, 1951.

27. Ibid., July 12, 1951 (© 1951 by The New York Times Company; reprinted by permission).

Italian financial and currency system. Moreover, the Italian government still possessed IRI property in Zone A. Italy still had not returned merchant ships registered in Trieste, amounting to 550,000 tons. Italian Fascist legislation, the independentists added, was still in force in Trieste and separate Trieste citizenship had not yet been established by the AMG. The Slovenian press in Trieste added that Slovenes in Zone A still did not enjoy equality with Italians as guaranteed by the Permanent Statute and Slovenian property destroyed or confiscated during Fascism had not yet been restored.[28]

According to the independentists the Irredentist propaganda was pursuing but one goal: to convince all pro-Italian parties to join in a single list for the coming elections in Zone A.

In 1951 all the political parties were preparing for new communal elections. The communal councils had been elected in June 1949 for a two-year term, expiring in June 1951. On February 20, 1951, the AMG issued new provisions concerning communal elections, a sign that elections were approaching. On May 28, 1951, the AMG announced that elections would take place on Sunday, October 7, for the commune of Trieste and on the following Sunday, October 14, 1951, for all other communes. The next day the AMG extended the tenure of office of the communal councils, which was to expire in June, until elections could be held.[29]

By the middle of May the pro-Titoist group had published its electoral program, demanding application of the Italian peace treaty and unification of both zones. This came as a surprise, because it had been known that the Yugoslav government favored direct Italian-Yugoslav negotiations to settle the problem. In addition the Titoist program called for election of a zonal council which together with the district assemblies of Koper and Buje in Zone B would form a constituent assembly for the entire Free Territory. Other demands included the institution of separate FTT citizenship, the return of the Italian para-statal (IRI) prop-

28. Vukušić, *Review of International Affairs*, 2, no. 15:13; Mihovilović, *Trst problem dana*, p. 48.

29. "Order No. 38," signed in Trieste, February 20, 1951, *AMG-FTT Gazette*, 4, no. 6 (Mar. 1, 1951): 111–36; "Order No. 86," signed in Trieste, May 28, 1951, ibid., no. 15 (June 1, 1951): 32; "Order No. 88," signed in Trieste, May 29, 1951, ibid., no. 16 (June 11, 1951): 327.

erty of Zone A to the FTT, especially the restitution to Trieste of its shipyards, steelworks, and other key enterprises, and the banning of Italian Irredentist organizations and their anti-FTT propaganda.[30]

The Cominform party, which continuously followed the Soviet policy toward Trieste, used the election propaganda to demand unification of both zones, establishment of the FTT according to provisions of the Italian peace treaty, and withdrawal of all military forces, British-American and Yugoslav, from the territory.

Though representing opposing ideologies, in their electoral propaganda the Titoists, Cominform Communists, Independence Front, Blocco Triestino, and Slovenian democrats demanded establishment of the Free Territory and opposed any division of the FTT between Italy and Yugoslavia. Taking advantage of the new international situation and the impartial position of the AMG the independentist newspapers asserted that the Tripartite Proposal of 1948 was no longer of importance. Hence what pro-Italian political parties could achieve was reunification with Italy of Trieste and with luck, possibly the entire Zone A, but the annexationists would have to abandon the Italian minority in Zone B. The only way to save the Italians of Zone B, the independentists stressed, was to demand unification of both zones and establishment of the Free Territory.

Continuation of economic prosperity due to the European Recovery Program also worked in favor of the independentists. About 130,000 Triestines worked in local industry. From October 1948, when economic aid had started to come to Trieste, until March 1951, the shipyards, which were Trieste's major industry, had built 120,000 tons of new ships with an additional 76,000 tons scheduled to be completed in the coming few months. Under the ERP, construction of apartment houses with a total of 3,000 rooms had helped to relieve the housing shortage.[31] Based upon this evidence of prosperity the independentists affirmed that the living standards in Zone A were higher than in neighboring Italy.[32]

The pro-Italian or annexationist political parties were con-

30. *New York Times,* May 16, 1951.
31. Ibid., Mar. 18, 1951.
32. Mihovilović, *Trst problem dana,* p. 94.

scious of these changes. Moreover, a great number of Istrian refugees, who had voted in previous elections for pro-Italian parties, were leaving Trieste in great numbers, emigrating to Australia, Canada, the United States, and South America. In short, time and circumstances were detrimental to a pro-Italian victory. It was not surprising that the annexationists began propaganda for postponement of the election. The independentists might have had a point when asserting that Irredentist newspaper propaganda against the AMG had been only part of the annexationist effort to postpone the elections in Zone A.

In an article dated July 15, 1951, *Il Nuovo Corriere della Sera* of Milan frankly expressed fear that the majority party, the Christian Democrats, might suffer a setback in the coming communal elections in Trieste. On one hand the independentists would obtain a much greater vote and, on the other, the right-wing parties would try to profit from the new situation, proclaiming their uncompromising fight for return of the entire Free Territory to Italy. To remedy this new situation, the article stressed that the Allies must take two steps: the new Italian electoral law of linked lists should be applied in Zone A.[33] Second, the Allies must renew their pledge on the original meaning of the Tripartite Proposal (omitting recommendation of a direct Italian-Yugoslav agreement). A refusal to accept these proposals would weaken Italian democratic forces at home and in Trieste and, at the same time, strengthen the independentist movement. The article concluded that continuation of the status quo would be proof that the Allied powers favored Yugoslavia and had broken the promise given earlier to Italy.[34]

Italian Premier de Gasperi was equally alarmed. He sent to Trieste Giuseppe Bettiol, the leader of the Christian Democrats in the Italian parliament, to convince the pro-Italian political par-

33. The new electoral law of the linked lists (*apparentamento*) was used in the communal elections in Italy during the same year, 1951. Political parties could form coalitions by agreeing on one set of candidates entered on one election list. The list with a majority vote got two-thirds of all the seats of the new communal council regardless of the number of votes received. The other lists divided among themselves proportionally the remaining one-third of the seats.

34. Quoted in Mihovilović, *Trst problem dana*, p. 95.

ties to form a single list for the elections. It was to be called the San Giusto list after the patron saint of Trieste. But though the annexationist political parties feared they might suffer a decline in the coming elections, they refused to agree on a single coalition list. At this point De Gasperi, supported by the press, began a great campaign to postpone the elections. He also appealed to the governments of Great Britain and the United States toward the same end.[35]

When on September 6, 1951, an official announcement of the AMG stated that the elections had been deferred to a later date in 1951, the independentist *Il Corriere di Trieste* published the next day an article speculating that the step had been taken because the British government, in agreement with the United States, had decided to urge direct Italian-Yugoslav negotiations. The elections were therefore postponed to avoid complications and to create friendlier surroundings for an agreement. Though a spokesman for the foreign office immediately denied this assertion he acknowledged that the elections had been postponed to satisfy the wishes expressed in London and Washington by the Italian government.[36]

It is important to note that the deferment of elections coincided with the eve of De Gasperi's departure for the United States. It was very probable that postponement of elections in Zone A signified a new policy toward the Trieste question by the governments of Great Britain and the United States. Both governments agreed to discontinue affirming the validity of the Tripartite Proposal and instead to press for division of the FTT between Italy and Yugoslavia. The above article of *Il Corriere di Trieste* might, after all, be right in asserting that the elections were deferred to create a calmer atmosphere for such Italian-Yugoslav negotiations. Moreover, should it come to a division of the FTT, it was by then evident that Italy would gain the city of Trieste, where the majority of the FTT population lived and where both annexationists and independentists had their base. When Trieste became united with Italy, the explosive annexationist-independentist controversy

35. Ibid., pp. 96–97.
36. Ibid., pp. 98, 100, 102; *Relazioni internazionali*, 15, no. 37 (Sept. 15, 1951): 716; see also "Order No. 145," signed in Trieste, September 7, 1951, *AMG-FTT Gazette*, 4, no. 25 (Sept. 11, 1951): 457–58.

would be removed and the municipal elections could be conducted in a more peaceful manner.

The pro-Italian press in Zone A and in Italy naturally expressed satisfaction with the deferment of elections.[37] The independentists, on the other hand, violently protested. The Titoist *Primorski dnevnik* wrote on September 8, 1951, that the annexationists had realized that they would be defeated at the polls; this defeat would have grave consequences for them, especially in the international field, because no international forum could seriously support Italian claims to Trieste should the elections indicate that the majority of Trieste's population opposed such a solution. *Il Corriere di Trieste* wrote in the same vein on September 7, 1951.[38]

Later, on October 6, 1951, the AMG postponed the elections once more, until sometime in 1952, a retreat from the previously neutral AMG policy.[39] This trend was seen also in the regulations set for crossing the border between Zone A and Italy. On April 12, 1951, the AMG had issued Order No. 63, which demanded that every person entering Zone A must have a crossing permit issued by the AMG. On November 12, 1951, this order was repealed. Citizens of the Italian Republic could according to the new regulation cross the border with only a valid identification card issued by the Italian Republic. An AMG crossing permit was no longer necessary.[40]

After De Gasperi's return from the United States at the end of September 1951, the tensions and press campaigns slowly abated. During November 1951 a census of population, industry, and commerce was taken in Zone A. To avoid new emotional upheavals, the AMG, with the concurrence of the Slovenian parties, determined that the census should omit any questions about ethnic origin.[41]

37. See, for example, the article "Revisione a Trieste," *Relazioni internazionali*, 15, no. 37 (Sept. 15, 1951): 707–8.
38. Mihovilović, *Trst problem dana*, pp. 99–100.
39. *New York Times*, Oct. 7, 1951.
40. For Order No. 63 see *AMG-FTT Gazette*, 4, no. 11 (Apr. 21, 1951): 218–19; "Order No. 179," signed November 12, 1951, ibid., no. 32 (Nov. 21, 1951): 611–14.
41. "Order No. 141," signed in Trieste, August 27, 1951, ibid., no. 24 (Sept. 1, 1951): 448–52; "Tržaško ljudsko štetje" (Trieste's Population

The life of the five thousand American troops stationed in Zone A was well depicted by Camille M. Cianfarra, the *New York Times* correspondent in Rome, who visited Trieste at the end of February 1951:

> The food is good, the barracks are airy and clean. There are well-equipped indoor gymnasiums and the PX's are stocked with anything a G.I.'s wife may want for her overseas home, from perambulators to vacuum cleaners, from scarlet nail polish to sheer nylon stockings.
>
> There is a good educational program under the direction of Lieut. Col. Allison Conrad, with courses taught by University of Maryland professors, so that a degree received here is equal to one in the United States. There are libraries, billiard and ping-pong tables and snack bars in enlisted men's clubs. There are bus tours for soldiers on furlough and there are the movies.[42]

The soldiers were reading the *Blue Devil Daily,* which was a one page sheet containing mostly TRUST (Trieste United States Troops) news, but a lesser number were buying the *Stars and Stripes,* a newspaper published for American troops in Europe.

Cianfarra, however, complained that there was no program which would inform the soldiers about what the United States government was doing in the field of domestic and foreign policy.

> No one here makes a determined effort to explain to them [the soldiers] why, for instance, they have been undergoing intense training for the nine months since the outbreak of the Korean War, and why it is so hard to get a furlough. Because of this, there has been a lot of beefing, which could be minimized if it were explained to the G.I.'s that the officers are not a bunch of sadists who enjoy seeing soldiers sweat and puff, but that the duty of the Army is to be ready for any eventuality, especially when there is a danger of a Soviet attack on Western Europe.[43]

Census), from special correspondent in Trieste, *Klic Triglava* (The Call of Triglav) (London), 4, no. 81 (Nov. 19, 1951): 3–4. (Mimeographed.)

42. *New York Times,* Mar. 17, 1951 (© 1951 by The New York Times Company; reprinted by permission).

43. Ibid.

Because of much higher United States pay and lavish stocks in the United States PX's, the relations between American and British troops were strained. Regarded as well-to-do, the American soldiers were easily accepted by the local Italian community and many of them married Italian girls. The British, on the other hand, could not compete socially with the Americans and resented their status. In this way Trieste contributed to the awareness of the Allied powers that differences in living standards were detrimental to friendly relations and military morale of the Allied troops in such strategic areas, where American forces were to cooperate with the British and native soldiers. This lesson was of special value at a time when General Eisenhower was organizing the NATO forces.[44]

THE HOSTILITY IN ZONE B

While the Irredentists were primarily occupied with Zone A during 1951, they nevertheless attentively observed the conditions under which the Italian population was living in Zone B. Injustices done to Italians were promptly registered by the CLN for Istria, and described often in an inflated form in the annexationist newspapers in Trieste. The news was then relayed to their Irredentist friends in the Italian parliament.

From March to the middle of November 1951, the annexationist press reported Yugoslav police brutalities, impediments by the Yugoslav authorities to border crossing between the two zones, and physical attacks on individual Italians. Other articles were of a more general nature, but to the same effect—that the Yugoslav administration was detrimental and unjust to Italians in Zone B.

In the beginning of March it was reported that Yugoslav police were involved in the killing of a farmer, Pietro Minca, who had been arrested on a charge of stealing goods. Although the Yugoslav authorities announced that Minca had hanged himself in prison on March 6, 1951, the Irredentists asserted that they had witnesses to testify he died as a result of ill treatment by the Yugoslav police.[45]

44. See, for example, the article by Arthur Krock on the editorial page of the *New York Times,* Apr. 12, 1951.
45. *Trieste: Zone B,* p. 28.

In the same month young Communist activists molested people who returned to Buje after a shopping trip to Trieste. Evidently such practices were aimed at discouraging the inhabitants of Zone B from doing their buying in Zone A.[46]

In April news spread that Yugoslav authorities were forcing people to wait in long lines before being allowed to pass into Zone A. Moreover, the Yugoslav authorities rendered it more difficult for youths under eighteen to cross the border. For crossing, an identity card was required, but no cards had been issued to those under eighteen. To cross the border these persons had to get a special permit from local people's committees.[47]

During the great press campaign of July, which was mainly directed against the AMG in Zone A, the Irredentists pointed out also that the regime in Zone B was a Communist one as in Yugoslavia, and that this Communist police regime was detrimental to Italians living there. When in July the Italian parliament discussed the situation in Zone A, special references were made to Zone B. In the beginning of August the Christian Democratic deputy Attilio Bartole, himself born in Istria, urged in the Italian parliament that British and United States troops take over administration of Zone B. Giuseppe Saragat, the right-wing socialist, supported him and added that if the first alternative were not workable, troops of neutral nations should assume control of the administration. After De Gasperi's return from the United States on October 10, 1951, Bartole again discussed in the Italian parliament the situation of Italians in Zone B and affirmed Italy's right to Zone B according to the Tripartite Proposal.[48]

An assault on an Italian priest stirred up probably the greatest excitement of 1951 in the annexationist press in Trieste, leading to another interpellation in the Italian parliament. The parish priest of Koper, Giorgio Bruni, who had gone to administer First Communion to the children of a nearby Slovenian village, was attacked by thirty hoodlums. The attack occurred in the open countryside on November 12. The aggressors left the priest unconscious, believing they had killed him. After an hour he regained consciousness and returned to Koper, from where he was

46. *New York Times,* Mar. 9, 1951.
47. *Trieste: Zone B,* p. 20.
48. De Castro, p. 558; *New York Times,* Aug. 5, 1951.

taken by ambulance to a Trieste hospital. He remained there for two months recuperating from fractured ribs and numerous bruises covering his body.[49]

Though the annexationist press published relatively many articles describing the suffering of Italians in Zone B, they could affirm few facts as concrete as the incident illustrated above. All other cases were old or could be applied to the Slavs as well as to the Italians. Among grievances which had been previously voiced belong assertions that the Italians were discriminated against in elementary and secondary schools, that a Slavic element was in overwhelming preponderance in all organs of government, and that the Communist economic system was used to confiscate Italian property. To the second category belonged complaints that there were no political and religious freedoms, that Zone B had a police regime, and that the Yugoslav authorities were obstructing the crossing into Zone A.

The Italian writer Diego de Castro was quite conscious of the limited number of concrete facts available to prove the persecution of Italians. He tried to explain by maintaining that the Yugoslavs had introduced a new policy in Zone B. The previous rudimentary, violent, and open persecution was replaced by a new and more sophisticated system. By constant minor harassment, he affirmed, the Yugoslav authorities tired out the Italians and so indirectly forced them to abandon Zone B for a calmer life in Zone A or Italy.[50]

In May 1951 the Yugoslavs pointed out that the progress of Slovenes and Croats in cultural, political, social, and economic fields might seem the result of privileges, but in reality Slovenes and Croatians were only catching up with Italians. The Slovenes and Croats were backward, they said, because of the policy of ethnic inequality imposed upon them by the Fascist regime. The YMG contended that cooperation between the Italian, Slovenian, and Croat populations in Zone B had been successful and profitable to all because it was based on equality of legal and cultural rights. The Italians, according to the Yugoslavs, not only were employed in local administration but formed the majority in the administration of the coastal towns. Italians were also employed

49. *Trieste: Zone B*, pp. 25–26; De Castro, p. 588.
50. See De Castro, p. 557.

on the local police force and many held officer rank. Italians had their own schools, elementary and secondary, where Italian was used for instruction. The Yugoslavs again averred that the Italian language enjoyed equality with the Slovenian and Croat languages not only in schools but also in the courts and people's committees.

In connection with agrarian reform, the Yugoslavs pointed out that the only persons who had been dissatisfied were the landowning families that had fled to Trieste and Italy after the war. According to the Yugoslavs, Italian, Slovenian, and Croatian peasants worked jointly on the new cooperative farms. Efforts to improve social insurance, the health service, the development of industry, crafts, mining, electrification, wine growing, vegetable gardening, and fishing benefited the entire population, said the Yugoslavs. They listed the following gains in 1951: New dispensaries had been set up as well as consultation centers for pregnant women; free medical examination was made available to children, and fifty-five hectares of arable land had been reclaimed through the melioration programs along the rivers of Mirna and Dragonja. Wine production went up in one year five hundred railroad tank cars, and wine cellars to preserve wine were built in Koper and Umag. New orchards had been planted, and milk production increased seven percent compared to production in 1949. Three nurseries had been built for 700,000 saplings and fishing ponds for procreation had been increased in number.[51]

In July 1951 the Yugoslavs went from defense to attack. In the middle of the month they accused the Irredentists, and the CLN for Istria in particular, of intelligence operations against Yugoslavia. The CLN agents were, according to the Yugoslavs, photographing Yugoslav military installations not only in Zone B but in Yugoslav Istria as well. The CLN for Istria, it was charged, also indulged in large-scale bribery of Italian teachers and local officials in Zone B and Istria to subvert the civil administration and obtain intelligence information. The Yugoslav authorities in Zone B disclosed that Irredentist agents, who had been intercepted by the Yugoslav security police, would soon be put on trial. According to the Yugoslavs the violent press campaign in Italy and

---

51. I. K., "Cultural and Material Progress in Zone B of the Free Trieste Territory," *Review of International Affairs*, 2, no. 11 (May 23, 1951): 14–15.

the Irredentist activities in Zone B pursued the definite goal of disrupting rapprochement between Yugoslavia and the United States, by creating such a tense situation between Belgrade and Rome that Washington would find it impossible or embarrassing to pursue its support for Yugoslavia.[52]

It also happened that in the middle of July 1951 the YMG opened the frontier between Zone B and Zone A to the United States and British military and civilian personnel. This was done for two purposes: to establish normal relations with the Allied command of Zone A, and to prove to American and British officials that the accusations of Irredentists and the Italian government against the Yugoslav administration of Zone B were untrue.

M. S. Handler, who reported from Zone B, well characterized the action, its meaning, and the period. He wrote:

> Parties of United States and British military and civilian personnel already have begun to visit Zone B and utilize its many beaches. The visits are unimpeded and Yugoslav officials hope that the Allies will be able to see for themselves that conditions in the zone are normal for this part of the world. It is noteworthy that the authorities of the Free Territory have been discreet about these visits to minimize any violent reaction by the irredentists, who become aroused whenever they hear of new forms of cooperation between the Allies and the Yugoslavs.[53]

On July 22, 1951, the Yugoslavs reacted to Italian Irredentist propaganda, which had reached its climax by this time. In the name of the population of Zone B, Ivan Regent, the vice-chairman of the Slovenian People's Assembly, condemned Irredentist aspirations to the Free Territory and especially to the Yugoslav zone, in a speech delivered to the people who gathered in Koper for celebration of the tenth anniversary of the formation of the Slovenian Liberation Front. Regent recalled how all democratic people of Zone B, the Slovenes, Croats, and Italians, had fought together against Fascism during the war, to achieve liberty and social justice. But the Italian Irredentists were trying to take away these gains. The Cominformists, said Regent, supported the claims

52. *New York Times*, July 15, 1951.
53. Ibid., July 16, 1951 (© 1951 by The New York Times Company; reprinted by permission).

of the Irredentists to Zone B and other parts of Yugoslavia because the Cominformists supported everyone who was against Yugoslavia. Nevertheless, the people of Zone B, emphasized Regent, realized who their true friend was, and condemned Irredentist as well as Cominform propaganda directed against Yugoslavia. From the meeting the pro-Titoist organizations sent telegrams to Marshal Tito thanking him for his protection and asking for a union of Zone B with Yugoslavia.[54]

During 1951 new economic measures were introduced in Zone B, a reflection of the changing economic situation in Yugoslavia. The expulsion from the Cominform created a serious problem for the Yugoslav economy. To recover from the economic crisis, the Yugoslavs abandoned the Soviet pattern of a centralized economy and introduced a new type of socialistic decentralized economy by which the management of industrial enterprises was entrusted to the workers' council. The result was a return to a freer economy in which prices were set by supply and demand rather than imposed from the center. During 1951, the Yugoslavs had discussed this reform and finally decided to try it out in Zone B. A pilot experiment was introduced in the Yugoslav zone during the summer of 1951. Besides being an experiment for the Yugoslav economy the new economic reform was an attempt to close the gap between the standard of living of the people in Zone B and that of Zone A. It was also a move to counter the Irredentist accusation.

The decentralization measures in Zone B included decontrolling all crops, abolition of the entire rationing system for food and other consumer goods, transfer of industrial management to workers' councils, and the abolition of the state monopoly over foreign trade. The relative uniformity of wages for skilled and unskilled workers was abandoned, resulting in greater wage differentiation. Minimum monthly wages were to be 6,000 dinars (about $120) and the maximum wage for highly skilled workers was not to exceed the theoretical limit of 38,000 dinars. Some other side gains included the increase of social insurance benefits for all employed persons and their families. Parents of a newborn child received payments totaling 20,000 dinars instead of 2,000 as

54. *Relazioni internazionali,* 15, no. 30 (July 28, 1951): 602; De Castro, p. 454.

previously. The monthly food supplement for pregnant women was increased from 600 to 2,000 dinars, and monthly allowances for children were raised from 240 to 350 dinars. The decontrolling of crops ended compulsory deliveries to the authorities, and instead introduced an income tax on average yields.[55]

While the reform was without doubt a step toward economic liberalization, political control nonetheless remained in the hands of the Communist party and its secret police in Zone B as well as in Yugoslavia.

The period of relative calm beginning with the middle of November 1951 ended in the middle of February 1952 with new Irredentist activities. On February 15, 1952, the Bishop of Trieste and Koper, Antonio Santin, made public a detailed list of religious persecutions against the faithful in Zone B. Later, on March 12, he appealed for help and support in a cable to the Archbishop of New York, Cardinal F. J. Spellman, stating among other things:

> I beseech Your Eminence to bring to the attention of the American Government and American Catholics the raging, pitiless religious persecution, especially at the present time, in Zone B of the Free Territory, my diocese, where clergy and laity are being terrorized and deprived of religious rights.[56]

On March 4, Gianni Bartoli, the Christian Democratic mayor of Trieste, formed a new annexationist group, the Comitato di Difesa per l'Italianità di Trieste e dell'Istria. The committee was to represent all Italian political parties and groups, and as such buttress the activities of the CLN for Istria which represented mainly the refugees from Zone B and Istria. The CLN for Istria meanwhile developed new activities of its own. It accused the Yugoslav administration of Zone B of new irregularities and persecutions: traffic between the two zones was blocked, circulation of the lira was prohibited in Zone B, police began nocturnal visits and searches of private homes, many Italians were arrested and tortured, people were brought before courts for obviously political

55. *New York Times,* Aug. 4, 1951. Note that on January 1, 1952, the exchange rate increased from 50 to 300 dinars for a dollar.

56. "Yugoslavia's Efforts to Denationalize Zone B and Italy's Desire for Peace," *Italian Affairs,* 2, no. 6 (Nov. 1953): 132; see also De Castro, p. 561.

reasons, and the church was persecuted. On March 15, 1952, the CLN for Istria informed General Winterton about the condition of Italians in Zone B and asked for AMG intervention. On March 20, the CLN for Istria published new detailed data about the persecutions in Zone B, listing 8 murders, 300 arrests, and 150 cases of torture. To escape persecution 4,652 persons fled from Zone B, according to the same source.[57]

On March 17 the Italian government reacted to this new propaganda campaign and sent a note to the governments of the United States, Great Britain, and France regarding the situation in Zone B. By introducing a series of reforms modeled upon the Yugoslav Communist system, the note asserted, Yugoslav authorities had changed the old Italian judicial, administrative, and economic system of Zone B to such an extent that it seemed justifiable to suppose that the Yugoslav authorities were pursuing a plan according to which Zone B was to be separated from Zone A and then incorporated into Yugoslav territory. To substantiate this general assertion the note then systematically analyzed the events which had occurred in Zone B since 1947.[58]

What caused the new Irredentist campaign in February 1952? De Castro blamed the Yugoslavs. According to him the Yugoslavs realized by February that direct Italian-Yugoslav negotiations had ended in failure, and consequently initiated a new regime of terror against the Italians in Zone B to force them to leave and so prepare the zone for incorporation into Yugoslavia.

The Yugoslav explanation was probably closer to the truth. According to it, the new Irredentist propaganda was only the harbinger of a new period that would be ushered in by violent clashes between the annexationists and the AMG.[59]

57. Jeri, p. 235; De Castro, pp. 561–62.
58. "L'azione del governo italiano per Trieste dopo il trattato di pace," *Documenti di vita italiana*, 3, no. 24 Nov. 1953): 1854–56.
59. See De Castro, p. 561; Jeri, pp. 234–35.

14

STEPS TOWARD A FINAL SOLUTION (MARCH 1952–JUNE 1953)

Riots in Trieste by Italian Irredentists against the AMG, and especially against the British, on March 20, 1952, introduced a new phase of the Trieste question which would last until Italian parliamentary elections took place in June 1953. The most important consequence of the riots was the London Agreement of May 9, 1952, which gave the Italian government the right to share in administering Zone A. The Yugoslavs protested without success, but countered by introducing similar measures in their own zone, tying it still closer to Yugoslavia. This move in turn caused consternation among the Italians, who began to press for a final solution.

THE GENERAL SITUATION

International conditions were still propitious for Yugoslavia during this period. The Korean War continued and so did East-West tensions. The Western powers, in order to close a gap in their NATO defenses in the eastern Mediterranean, sought a military alliance between Yugoslavia, Greece, and Turkey. After lengthy negotiations the Balkan Pact of Friendship and Cooperation was signed at Ankara on February 28, 1953. Though not a military pact, it did associate Yugoslavia with two members of NATO. The following month (March 16–20, 1953), Tito visited Great Britain. With the increase in Yugoslavia's prestige, she had strong reason to expect that time would work for her in Trieste. Ever since direct dealings with Italy had broken down in the middle of February 1952, Yugoslavia had waited, still insisting on the proposals advanced in the Guidotti-Bebler talks, and prepared to accept only two solutions. The first, as we know, would divide the FTT along the border separating the zones, with some minor corrections. The second advocated a condominium with Italy. Only when Italian parliamentary elections were about to take place did Yugoslavia, in May 1953, initiate new talks.[1]

This continuous improvement in the position of Yugoslavia prompted changes in the Italian attitude toward Trieste. Since the end of World War II De Gasperi had likewise followed a waiting policy. He was convinced that the passage of time would improve Italy's weak position and that ultimately she could negotiate from a position of strength. This policy had indeed worked well in the past. There was a question now, however, as to how much longer it would be well for Italy to wait. Even so De Gasperi continued to uphold the Tripartite Proposal. For him, it was the vital document from which the Italian claim to the entire FTT was derived, and he still saw it as the basis for any future agreement with Yugoslavia. He realized, of course, that Italy could not gain all of the FTT, and was prepared to cede Slovenian and Croat villages along the Yugoslav border to Yugoslavia, but would insist that the major Italian centers go to Italy together with Slovenian land along the Adriatic coast. Out of this desire had been born the so-called "continuous ethnic line." For De Gasperi this had been a maximum concession to the Yugoslavs, who, according to the Tripartite Proposal, had no right to this territory. He had rightly suspected that Yugoslavia would never agree to Italy's demands and had foreseen that the Western powers would have to exert pressure on Yugoslavia to reach a final solution. Moreover, De Gasperi had tried to convince the Western powers that they were morally obligated to support these reduced Italian claims because of the Tripartite Proposal. This also explains why De Gasperi referred in his speeches time and again to the Tripartite Proposal. From the very beginning he had little faith in direct negotiations. Only because the West had urged him to do so had De Gasperi consented to undertake direct talks with Yugoslavia. By February 1952 he became convinced that events had proven him right. At the NATO meeting in Lisbon at the end of that month he explained to Eden and Acheson, the foreign ministers of Great Britain and the United States, that direct Italo-Yugoslav negotiations had failed because of excessive Yugoslav demands. On the same occasion he reiterated his old belief that without a firm

1. *The United States in World Affairs, 1953* (New York, 1955), pp. 206, 422–23.

intervention by the Western powers, Yugoslavia would never agree to a compromise that Italy could accept.[2]

After the March rioting Italian policy added a further principle. Italy should achieve fulfillment of her demands by progression. The first step, accomplished with the London Agreement, was association of the Italian government in the administration of Zone A. Later Italy would take over Zone A. Neither of these two steps should prejudice Italian rights to Zone B.[3] While gradualism presented a new element it was still based on the Tripartite Proposal.[4] To De Gasperi the London Agreement was only a partial fulfillment of the promises, and the Italian right to participate in the administration of Zone A derived directly from the Tripartite Proposal. Moreover, because of the Tripartite Proposal Yugoslavia had no right to introduce similar measures in Zone B. When Yugoslavia proclaimed new decrees tying Zone B closer to her, De Gasperi appealed to the Western powers to prevent it.

After signing the London Agreement the Italian diplomats, but not De Gasperi, became convinced that time had ceased to work for Italy. There were many signs pointing that way. The Yugoslav position continued to improve. Friendly contacts were established between Yugoslavia and her neighbors, Greece and Turkey. Yugoslav countermeasures in Zone B were detrimental to Italian interests, and the Western powers failed to make a serious protest against them. These developments convinced the Italian diplomats that the Trieste problem must be settled as soon as possible. To achieve this end, Manlio Brosio and Alberto Tarchiani, Italian ambassadors in London and Washington, became very active. They proposed new, more realistic solutions, but De Gasperi refused every proposal.

Of the big powers, Great Britain was the only one primarily concerned with a quick solution, but she would not act without

2. Andreotti, p. 319.
3. This idea was clearly expressed in the article "Nuova crisi a Trieste," written by B. C. in *Relazioni internazionali,* 16, no. 13 (Mar. 29, 1952): 325–26.
4. A more realistic evaluation of the Tripartite Proposal was given in a letter sent by Gallarati-Scotti, former Italian ambassador in London, to *Relazioni internazionali.* For it see ibid., 16, no. 14 (Apr. 5, 1952): 349–50.

the concurrence of the United States.[5] The latter was in the middle of a presidential election and put off any action. France, which had not been a partner in the administration of Zone A, was occupied with her European community plan more than with Trieste. She nevertheless continued friendly relations with Italy. The Soviet Union kept to her original stand on Trieste, and continued to demand that the Free Territory be established as provided in the Italian peace treaty.

MARCH RIOTING AND THE FIRST LONDON AGREEMENT

Irredentist activities, which began in February 1952, reached their culmination in the March rioting. With the beginning of 1952 a number of factors had alarmed the annexationist political parties and Irredentist groups in Trieste. Failure of direct Italian-Yugoslav negotiations had made it clear that Yugoslavia would refuse to accept the Italian proposal of a continuous ethnic line. The Irredentists of Zone A, who favored annexation of the entire Free Territory to Italy, regarded the continuous ethnic line as the ultimate concession still acceptable to Italy. But direct negotiations had indicated that Yugoslavia was not prepared to renounce Zone B. The administration of General Winterton, in the eyes of the Irredentists, still favored independence. Moreover, the independentists increased their efforts to establish the FTT and sought to interest Austria in their cause. In addition, the municipal elections, which had been postponed in the fall of 1951, were to take place in the near future. The possibility of an independentist victory still alarmed the Irredentists.

The Irredentists thought the situation worse than it had been in the previous July. Encouraged by the success their propaganda had registered the year before, the annexationist political parties and Irredentist organizations rallied around Gianni Bartoli, the Christian Democratic mayor of Trieste, and decided to stage a similar protest. The fourth anniversary of the Tripartite Proposal was regarded as an opportune moment to remind the Western

---

5. According to Foreign Minister Eden, Great Britain was interested in ending the costly military occupation and recalling her 5,000 men. (Eden, p. 200.)

Allies that four years earlier they had promised to return the entire FTT to Italy, and that the majority of Trieste's population demanded the Allied pledge be kept.

Mayor Bartoli had petitioned the AMG for permission to hold an outdoor rally on March 20, 1952. The AMG, however, permitted only an indoor meeting, sponsored by the Comitato di Difesa per l'Italianità di Trieste e dell'Istria (Committee for Defense of the Italianity of Trieste and Istria). The meeting took place on Thursday, March 20, in the late afternoon in the Giuseppe Verdi Theater. It was presided over by Count Renzo di Carrobio, the chief of the Italian mission in Trieste.[6] Amidst patriotic enthusiasm, Mayor Bartoli in his speech accused the Western Allies of double dealing and demanded return of the entire FTT to Italy.[7] After the meeting the participants and the crowd waiting outside the theater formed a procession to march to the city's main square, the Piazza Unità. On their way the marchers shouted anti-British slogans, demanded return of the entire FTT to Italy, and chanted acclamation of Italian Istria, Rijeka, and Dalmatia. The demonstrators broke windows, smashed a British club, and attacked the headquarters of the Independentist Front. When the crowd of some twenty thousand disobeyed a police order to disperse, the civil police used tear gas and fire hoses to break up the unauthorized rally. According to an AMG communiqué issued the following day, thirty civilians and a few policemen needed medical care as the result of the riot, and sixty demonstrators were arrested.

6. When the FTT was created Italy did not open a consulate but instead the foreign ministry sent its first representative, Alberico Casardi, to Trieste. He was replaced by Gastone Guidotti. When the latter became Italian observer at the United Nations, his substitute Augusto Castellani took over. Under his tenure the office of the Italian representative was changed into an Italian mission. One of the central tasks of the mission was to keep in contact with the annexationist political parties and coordinate their activities. In 1951 Di Carrobio replaced Castellani. (See Giorgio Cesare, "Gli otto predecessori di Confalonieri," *Trieste*, no. 29 [Jan.–Feb. 1959], pp. 6–7.)

7. For the text of the mayor's speech see Paolo Berti, ed., *Italia ritorna: Dieci anni di storia triestina nei documenti scritti e discorsi del sindaco Gianni Bartoli* (Rocca San Casciano, 1959), pp. 91–100.

On Friday, March 21, Mayor Bartoli condemned the brutal behavior of the police and demanded that those responsible be dismissed. The annexationist labor union (Camera del Lavoro) proclaimed a general strike in protest against alleged police brutality, and the Italian representative in Trieste, Count Carrobio, handed a formal protest to General Winterton. Attacks against the British cinema, officers' clubs, and cars continued. The police again used fire hoses to disperse the rioters. On Saturday, March 22, a general strike paralyzed Trieste until noon, and many stores and shops remained closed even during the afternoon. The representatives of the annexationist political parties visited General Winterton, protesting against police brutalities, but Winterton explained that the police were only doing their duty, which was to keep peace and order. Mayor Bartoli then announced that the municipal government would suspend collaboration with the AMG "until local civil authorities are given satisfaction." In the afternoon the riots reached their most violent stage. Groups of young extremists stoned British soldiers, attacked the British cinema, the Y.M.C.A. building, the officers' clubs, and hotels which housed families of soldiers, overturned military vehicles, and demonstrated outside the offices of the Independentist Front. During this day of rioting 106 civilians and 51 policemen were injured. The riots continued through Sunday, March 23, with some 20 more being sent to the hospital, but then began to diminish. On March 26 the city returned to normal. On the same day the city council met and condemned the police actions, demanded dismissal of Allied functionaries responsible for police brutalities, expressed sympathy for Italians persecuted in the Yugoslav zone, and then officially suspended its sittings as a token of noncooperation with the AMG.

During all of the rioting from March 20 through 25, British–United States troops did not intervene but remained confined to their barracks, and no one was killed. The demonstrators' anger was directed against the British, independentists, AMG, and Yugoslavia. The British were singled out because the Irredentists had blamed principally Great Britain for urging direct Italian-Yugoslav negotiations and thus denying return of the entire FTT to Italy. No counterdemonstration was organized by the Communist or independentist forces as had been done from 1945 to 1948.[8]

The Yugoslav newspaper *Borba* on March 23, 1952, accused the Italian government and specifically the foreign ministry of responsibility for the disorders in Trieste. *Borba* asserted that the Trieste riots were simply another maneuver to gain success through blackmail. Instead of solving the Trieste question on a basis of mutual interest, the Italian government had refused all Yugoslav suggestions and now had tried to press the Western Allies for new concessions.

Though Italian Prime Minister de Gasperi, in a speech to the Senate on March 25, 1952, denied that the Trieste incidents were staged by the Italian government to blackmail the Western powers, he nonetheless recognized that he was involved in preparing the manifestation.[9] Be that as it may, the Italian government was quick to make common cause with the rioters and pressed the Allies for more concessions. When it had come to a clash with police, De Gasperi in a speech to parliament on March 21 assured the citizens of Trieste "that their cause is the cause of all Italians," and that he was confident of final victory. The Italian defense minister, Randolfo Pacciardi, sent a message to the patriotic associations in Trieste on March 24 exhorting them "not to give up hope" and declaring that "where the cunning and powerful Austrian emperors failed, neither Marshal Tito nor General Winterton will succeed."[10]

On March 24 and 25 the Italian ambassador in London, Manlio Brosio, met with the British foreign minister, Anthony Eden. During these talks Brosio stressed the necessity of eliminating the causes which had engendered the riots. The Italian electoral law should be accepted for the coming elections in Zone A, he said, and Italy should participate in administration of the zone. To agree on these demands a conference should be called to include Great Britain, the United States, and Italy. Brosio and Eden

8. *Keesing's Contemporary Archives*, 8:12146–47; *New York Times*, Mar. 21, 22, 23, 24, 25, 1952; *Relazioni internazionali*, 16, no. 13 (Mar. 29, 1952): 333–35; Jeri, p. 235.

9. *Relazioni internazionali*, 16, no. 13 (Mar. 29, 1952): 335; *New York Times*, Mar. 25, 1952.

10. *Relazioni internazionali*, 16, no. 13 (Mar. 29, 1952): 333; *Keesing's Contemporary Archives*, 8:12147.

also conversed about the possibility of bringing Italian troops to Zone A, perhaps within the framework of NATO. But this topic was later abandoned.[11]

From March 24 to 27 great demonstrations took place in major Italian cities in support of the demands voiced by the Trieste annexationists. They ended after new negotiations on Trieste were announced in London. On March 27, the British foreign office made it known that the British, United States, and Italian governments had decided

> to examine jointly arrangements in Zone A of the Free Territory of Trieste with a view to reaching a closer collaboration in the zone among themselves and with the local authorities there in the spirit of friendly relations which unite them in the Atlantic alliance.[12]

The above announcement of the London talks caused a violent reaction among Yugoslavs. On March 29 and 30 great mass demonstrations took place in Belgrade, Zagreb, Ljubljana, and other cities, and on March 31 in the Yugoslav Zone B. The Yugoslav viewpoint was expressed in a speech of Leo Mates, the deputy foreign minister, on March 29, and in Tito's address on March 31, both delivered to the federal assembly in Belgrade. The two speakers stressed the following facts: Yugoslavia had not been consulted in 1948 before the Tripartite Proposal was made—a big mistake. Now another error had been committed by the Allied powers. Again Yugoslavia was not asked to be a party to negotiations, nor was the Yugoslav government consulted about the London talks. Therefore, no decision made at the conference could have binding force upon Yugoslavia. A solution to the Trieste question could be reached only by direct Yugoslav-Italian negotiations. Consequently Yugoslavia opposed Italian occupation of Zone A and any division of Zone B. She still desired a joint condominium of the entire Free Territory, and would not oppose a plebiscite, when the wrongs done to Slovenes in Zone A were remedied after a period of

11. *Relazioni internazionali,* 16, no. 20 (May 17, 1952): 483.
12. *Keesing's Contemporary Archives,* 8:12148; see also *Relazioni internazionali,* 16, no. 14 (Apr. 5, 1952): 358. For a similar statement made by the American Secretary of State Dean Acheson see *Department of State Bulletin,* 26 (Apr. 14, 1952): 585.

such condominium. Until now Italy had sabotaged all direct negotiations by demanding the entire Free Territory. Italy had tried to pressure the Allied powers, by using the Atlantic Alliance as a pretext, first to gain control of Zone A; later she would also demand Zone B and other Yugoslav territory. It should be remembered that Italian claims extended not only to both zones of the Free Territory but also to Istria, Pula, Dalmatia, and even Montenegro, as was shown by the recent Irredentist demonstrations in Trieste and Italy. Yugoslavia was still in favor of direct negotiations, but she did not want any bargaining behind her back and at her expense.[13]

On March 31, the British foreign office issued a statement concerning the London conference to the effect that the talks would be confined to the internal administration of Zone A and would try to find ways of associating Italy more closely with it. No final settlement of the Trieste question was contemplated. Final responsibility for law and order would still rest with the Allied Military Government. The Yugoslav government should be left in no doubt that the rights of Slovenes in Zone A would continue to receive proper safeguards.

Two days later, on April 2, Foreign Minister Eden repeated the above statements in the House of Commons and added:

> As regards the wider issue, H.M. Government are most anxious to see a solution of the whole Trieste problem. It is our view that this can best be brought about by direct conversations between the Italian and Yugoslav Governments. We have done our best to encourage such conversations for some months past.[14]

The London discussions took place between April 3 and May 9, 1952. Pierson Dixon, deputy undersecretary at the foreign office; Julius C. Holmes, the American minister in London; and Brosio, the Italian ambassador, participated. The negotiations terminated with the signing on May 9 of the Memorandum of Understanding, subsequently called the First London Agreement.[15]

13. *Relazioni internazionali*, 16, no. 14 (Apr. 5, 1952): 358–59. For the complete text of Tito's speech see Tito, 7:28–38.
14. *Keesing's Contemporary Archives*, 8:12148.
15. For the text of the "Memorandum of Understanding between the Governments of Italy, the United Kingdom, and the United States

According to the agreement the supreme authority would remain vested in the zone commander, General Winterton. At his side were to be three political advisers, representing the governments of the United States, Great Britain, and Italy. The Italian political adviser would be appointed by the Italian government "to represent it in all matters affecting Italy in regard to the zone."

All British–United States forces and some important branches of the civil administration, such as the departments of public security (police force), legal affairs, public information, post office and communications, free port, and traveling permits would remain under direct control of the zone commander. The rest of the civil administration would be divided into two directorates: one for interior, and the other for finance and economics. Both directorates would come under Italian administration with the senior director of administration at their head. He "will be proposed by the Italian government and will be appointed by the zone commander. The senior director of administration will be responsible to the zone commander and under the latter's direction will administer, by means of two directorates, the functions of civil government."

The Italian government would participate in the control of the administration not only by choosing the senior director, but also by proposing all officers to staff directorates, departments, and offices under the administration of the senior director. However, the zone commander would retain the right to appoint these officers proposed by the Italian government. He could replace them and ask the Italian government to propose their successors. But the Italian government would also preserve the right to recall persons proposed by it "on due notification to the zone commander." All officers proposed by the Italian government were to be responsible to the zone commander through the Italian senior director of administration.

Members of the local population employed by the Allied

Regarding Administration in Zone A of the Free Territory of Trieste," signed in London on May 9, 1952; and for the text of the United States, United Kingdom, and Italian "Communiqué" issued the same day, May 9, 1952, see *Department of State Bulletin,* 26 (May 19, 1952): 779–80.

Military Government until that time were given the following assurance that they would not lose their positions:

> Employees who have been recruited locally and who are now exercising civil functions in the Military Government will be retained to the maximum practicable extent; any dismissal shall be effected with the prior approval of the zone commander.[16]

It is clear that this was only a relative, not an absolute assurance. The same was true regarding the protection of Slovenian rights in Zone A. These were supposed to be guaranteed by a general clause, stating that the new arrangements should be of such nature "as to continue to ensure to all inhabitants of the zone the enjoyment of human rights and fundamental freedoms without distinction as to race, sex, language or religion."

The Italian statesmen accepted the London Agreement only as the first step toward solution of the Trieste question. This viewpoint was clearly expressed in the remarks De Gasperi made to the press conference held in Rome on May 9. He asserted also that the new agreement in no way prejudiced the Tripartite Proposal of 1948, which was to remain the basis for any final settlement with Yugoslavia. With this agreement, asserted De Gasperi, Italy did not renounce her rights to Zone B.[17] When evaluating the London Agreement, the weekly for foreign affairs, *Relazioni internazionali* added a further important fact: the agreement would deliver a mortal blow to the independentist movement in Trieste.[18]

Tito voiced Yugoslavia's reaction to the London Agreement in his speech in Zrenjanin on May 11, 1952, denouncing it as a "gross violation of the Italian Peace Treaty" and a "shameful injustice to Yugoslavia." The new arrangements in Zone A constituted an "ambush against Yugoslavia" whereby De Gasperi would "find it easier to fight for the incorporation of the whole Trieste Free Territory, Istria, and Dalmatia." Tito also denied Eden's statement that the Yugoslav government had been kept informed about the London discussion.[19]

16. Ibid., p. 780.
17. *Relazioni internazionali*, 16, no. 20 (May 17, 1952): 491–93.
18. Ibid., p. 483.
19. *Keesing's Contemporary Archives*, 8:12234; Tito, 7:75–79; see also D. Janičijević and B. Babović, "Londonska konferencija: Ohra-

A Yugoslav aide-mémoire issued on May 13 expressed similar views. Particular concern was paid to the joint communiqué issued on May 9, 1952, stressing that the London Agreement was "designed to give greater practical recognition to the predominantly Italian character" of Zone A. The Yugoslav aide-mémoire declared that this statement signified abandonment of the hitherto recognized principle of equality of the Italian and Slovenian population, guaranteed by the Italian peace treaty.[20]

The London Agreement was therefore very differently interpreted. To the British foreign minister it meant a step toward final division of the Free Territory, assigning Zone A to Italy and Zone B to Yugoslavia. For the Italian prime minister the London Agreement was also a first step toward the ultimate solution of the Trieste problem, but the difference lay in the final aims. De Gasperi did not mean that the division should be along the zone line but, on the contrary, that the majority of the Free Territory should go to Italy. Yugoslavia, prepared for partition of the Free Territory, saw her bargaining position diminished. In the future she would try to gain definite renunciation of all Italian claims to Zone B and assurance of Slovenian national rights in Zone A before she would accept a division along the zonal border.

The consequences of the First London Agreement were as follows: it introduced administrative changes in Zone A and indirectly caused administrative changes in Zone B; it raised the question of Slovenian minority rights in Zone A and Italian rights in Zone B; and it exacerbated direct Italo-Yugoslav negotiations during the period under discussion.

ADMINISTRATIVE CHANGES IN ZONE A

The pro-Italian political parties gained their first victory immediately after the riots. On March 26, 1952, the AMG issued

---

brenje fašizma u Italiji" (London Conference: The Encouragement to Fascism in Italy), *Medjunarodni problemi*, 4, no. 3-4 (May–Aug. 1952): 27-38.

20. *Keesing's Contemporary Archives*, 8:12234; *Relazioni internazionali*, 16, no. 21 (May 24, 1952): 516. The Soviet Union also protested against the London Agreement in her note of June 24, 1952, accusing the Western powers of further violation of the Italian peace treaty. The United States and Great Britain rejected the Soviet note on September 20, 1952. See *Department of State Bulletin*, 17 (Oct. 6, 1952): 521-22.

Order No. 51, which satisfied annexationist demands that the Italian electoral law be adopted for administrative elections in Zone A.[21] The elections were set for May 25, 1952, for all communes of the zone. Elections were also held in Italy on the same Sunday.[22]

Order No. 51 laid down two types of procedures: one for the communes of Trieste and Muggia, and the other for the four rural communes. For the first two communes two-thirds of the seats of the communal council (forty in Trieste and twenty in Muggia) would go to the group of linked lists or to whichever nonlinked list obtained the greatest number of votes. The remaining one-third of the seats would be distributed to other groups of linked lists and to nonlinked lists according to the principle of proportional representation. Voters were to cast ballots for only one list but could manifest their preference for up to two candidates on their list.

In the four rural communes each elector was entitled to vote for sixteen out of twenty councillors in the communes of San Dorligo della Valle and Duino-Aurisina, and for twelve out of fourteen in Sgonico and Monrupino. The voter could also vote for candidates on different lists. The twenty candidates in San Dorligo and Duino-Aurisina and the fifteen in Sgonico and Monrupino who obtained the greatest number of votes, were to be declared elected. In practice this meant that the winning list would automatically obtain four-fifths of the seats in the communal council. The number of seats for each commune was to remain the same as before. The same was true for the communal government, which would still be composed of the communal council, communal board, and a mayor.

The announcement of the London Agreement on May 9, in the midst of the electoral campaign, was a great boost for the annexationist political parties. The pro-Italian political parties used the agreement as proof that sooner or later the FTT would be unified with Italy. The Italian government also exercised certain pressures on the voters. On May 12, 1952, the Italian parliament voted into law a proposal that all civil servants employed by the

21. For Order No. 51 see *AMG-FTT Gazette*, 5, no. 9 (Apr. 1, 1952): 155–85.
22. "Order No. 54," issued April 2, 1952, *AMG-FTT Gazette*, 5, no. 10 (Apr. 11, 1952): 205.

AMG be taken over by the Italian government as its civil servants. However, persons engaged in activities directed against annexation of the FTT to Italy would be denied the benefits of this law. The new law was obviously directed against the independentists. The Yugoslavs pointed out that many new refugees were entered on the electoral rolls.[23]

In general, the election results did not differ markedly from those obtained in 1949. In the commune of Trieste, out of 200,486 registered electors, 178,984 ballots were declared valid. There were two groups of linked lists and eight nonlinked lists. The results are shown in table 7.[24]

It was significant that the Independence Front almost doubled its vote (from 11,476 in 1949 to 22,415) although it went to the polls under very unfavorable conditions. Also noteworthy was the great increase of votes for the neo-Fascist Italian Social Movement (from 10,171 in 1949 to 20,570) which had played the most aggressive role in the March riots and condemned direct Italo-Yugoslav negotiations. The four Italian center parties (Liberals, Republicans, Christian Democrats, and right-wing Socialists) forming the first group of linked lists, received 46.79 percent of the votes and obtained the forty seats of the communal council. The monarchists and neo-Fascists united in the second group of linked lists and received 13.12 percent of the votes. Other monarchists and right-wing elements had their own nonlinked list and received 0.88 percent. As all the above groups and lists favored the unification of Trieste with Italy, the pro-Italian parties obtained 62.25 percent of the votes. This meant a loss of 2.75 percent (compared to the 1949 results) to the benefit of the independentists. In general it could be said that a good third of the Trieste population remained opposed to annexation to Italy.

The Christian Democrats and Cominformists suffered some

23. Jeri, pp. 239–40.
24. "Report on the Administration of the British–United States Zone of the Free Territory of Trieste for the Period 1 January to 31 December 1952 by Major General Sir John Winterton, . . ." *UNSC*, Doc. S/3156 (December 23, 1953), p. 7. (Mimeographed.) Hereafter cited as the *Twelfth AMG Report* (S/3156). The report, but without appendixes, is reprinted also in *Department of State Bulletin*, 30 (Jan. 25, 1954): 124–30.

losses. The first probably lost the votes of those who opposed direct negotiations with Yugoslavia. Some of these votes went to the more radical neo-Fascists. Some Cominform votes went to Nenni's Socialists who presented their own list for the first time in 1952. The total vote cast in the Trieste commune was also greater by about 10,000 in 1952 (178,984) than it had been in 1949 (168,108).

The electoral principle in the commune of Muggia was the same as for Trieste. The results are given in table 8.

The three annexationist parties (Republicans, right-wing Socialists and Christian Democrats) presented the only linked list but were defeated by the Cominformist list. The latter obtained an absolute majority (58.30 percent) and the twenty seats.

TABLE 7

ADMINISTRATIVE ELECTIONS, MAY 25, 1952

(Results in the Commune of Trieste)

Party	Votes	Percent	Seats Assigned
Italian Liberal party (PLI)	5,768	3.22	3
Italian Republican party (PRI)	8,407	4.70	4
Christian Democrat party (DC)	59,133	33.04	28
Venezia Giulia Socialist party (PSVG) (Saragat Socialists)	10,445	5.83	5
Total (1st group of linked lists)	83,753	46.79	40
Italian Social Movement (MSI)	20,570	11.49	4
Monarchist National party (PNM)	2,915	1.63	1
Total (2d group of linked lists)	23,485	13.12	5
Communist party of FTT (PCTLT) (Cominformists)	30,978	17.31	6
Julian Autonomous Movement (MAG)	1,209	0.67	...
Italo-Slovene Popular Front (FPIS) (Titoists)	4,924	2.75	1
Independence Front (FI)	22,415	12.52	5
Monarchists and Common Men Front (FMQ)	1,560	0.88	...
Italian Socialist party (PSI) (Nenni Socialists)	2,609	1.46	1
Triestine bloc (BT)	4,492	2.51	1
Slovene Democratic League (LDS)	3,559	1.99	1
Grand Total	178,984	100.00	60

SOURCE: *Twelfth AMG Report* (S/3156), pp. 42–43.

In the other four Slovenian rural communes the Titoists and Slovenian democrats united and presented a single list of the Slovene Union. Their most powerful opponents were the Cominformists. The results are shown in table 9.

The Cominformists won a close race in San Dorligo, while the Slovene Union received the greatest number of votes in the other three communes. The pro-Italian parties presented their list, as the Italo-Slovene Democratic Union, only in the commune of Duino-Aurisina and obtained 21.4 percent of the votes. In their

TABLE 8

ADMINISTRATIVE ELECTIONS, MAY 25, 1952

(Results in the Commune of Muggia)

Party	Votes	Percent	Seats Assigned
Italian Republican party (PRI)	387	4.81	1
V. G. Socialist party (PSVG)	768	9.54	3
Christian Democrat party (DC)	1,701	21.12	5
Total (Linked lists)	2,856	35.47	9
Communist party of FTT (PCTLT) (Cominformists)	4,695	58.30	20
Popular Union for Independence	502	6.23	1
Grand Total	8,053	100.00	30

SOURCE: *Twelfth AMG Report* (S/3156), pp. 42–43.

electoral campaign the Titoists defended the independence of the FTT although the Yugoslav government had already negotiated for its partition. As in previous elections the pro-independentist political parties again received an absolute majority in all the communes except Trieste.

After the elections, preparations began for reorganization of the AMG in compliance with the London Agreement. On July 6, 1952, General Winterton approved the nomination of Gian A. Vitelli, former prefect of Genoa Province, as the future senior director of administration, and ten days later confirmed Diego de Castro as Italian political adviser to the AMG.[25]

The nomination of De Castro, who was a prominent defender

25. *Keesing's Contemporary Archives*, 9 (1952–54): 12348.

TABLE 9

ADMINISTRATIVE ELECTIONS, MAY 25, 1952

(Results in the Rural Communes)

San Dorligo della Valle

Party	Votes	Percent	Seats Assigned
Communist party of FTT (Cominformists)	1,362	49.31	16
Slovene Union	1,239	44.86	4
Independent list	161	5.83	...
Total	2,762	100.00	20

Duino-Aurisina

Party	Votes	Percent	Seats Assigned
Communist party of FTT (Cominformists)	856	29.30	4
Slovene Union	1,253	42.90	16
Italo-Slovene Democratic Union (pro-Italian)	625	21.40	...
Triestine bloc	187	6.40	...
Total	2,921	100.00	20

Sgonico

Party	Votes	Percent	Seats Assigned
Communist party of FTT (Cominformists)	375	49.02	3
Slovene Union	390	50.98	12
Total	765	100.00	15

Monrupino

Party	Votes	Percent	Seats Assigned
Communist party of FTT (Cominformists)	82	24.77	2
Slovene Union	177	53.48	12
Independent Economic Union	72	21.75	1
Total	331	100.00	15

SOURCE: *Twelfth AMG Report* (S/3156), pp. 42–43.

of Italian claims to the FTT, caused loud protests from the Slovenes in Zone A.[26] They were supported by the Yugoslav government, which expressed its complaints to Great Britain and the United States. The British and American ambassadors in Rome tried to persuade De Gasperi to nominate another man, because De Castro had been so much involved in the Irredentist movement. But De Gasperi would not yield.[27]

Finally the new AMG organization came into existence with Order No. 165, signed by General Winterton on September 13 and retroactively effective as of September 1, 1952.[28] Until then the AMG administration had remained substantially the same as established by Orders No. 259 and No. 308 in 1948.[29] According to the old system, already described above, the military commander had been the highest authority, and the general director for civil affairs the next in rank. His directorate general had been the highest office for the entire civil administration. Subordinated to it

26. F. A., "The Arbitrary Acts of the Italian Administration in Trieste," *Review of International Affairs*, 3, no. 14 (July 16, 1952): 3.

27. Andreotti, p. 321, n. 1.

28. Order No. 165 was published in *AMG-FTT Gazette*, 5, no. 26 (Sept. 21, 1952): 497–501.

29. Order No. 398, issued December 14, 1948 (*AMG-FTT Gazette*, 1, no. 46 [Dec. 21, 1948]: 713–14) consolidated the department of public works and the department of post and telecommunications into one department of public service. It also created a new department of production replacing the department of industry, which became an office of the new department. Both changes took place inside the directorate of finance and economics. Order No. 51, issued March 8, 1949 (ibid., 2, no. 7 [Mar. 11, 1949]: 136–37) added to the directorate of the interior a new department of social assistance including the offices of public assistance, social insurance, child welfare, displaced persons, and office of research, statistics, and accounts. The old office of welfare and displaced persons, part of the department of the interior, was herewith discontinued. According to Order No. 229, issued December 14, 1950 (ibid., 3, no. 35 [Dec. 21, 1950]: 596–97) the office of post and telecommunications was transferred from the department of public service in the directorate of finance and economics and became an independent office of the directorate of the interior. Order No. 6, issued January 10, 1951 (ibid., 4, no. 1 [Jan. 11, 1951]: 12–13) changed the department of public services back into that of the department of public works and utilities.

had been the two directorates (for interior, and for finance and economics) and the local government (zone president and the mayors). Order No. 165 abolished the position of the director general for civil affairs together with his office. All the prerogatives of the director general reverted to the zone commander, who retained supreme authority over all offices regardless of whether they remained in Allied hands or were transferred to the Italians according to the London Agreement. Viewed from this aspect, the AMG was composed of two parts: one continued to be administered by the British-American personnel, the other by Italian functionaries.

All the offices remaining in British-American hands were divided into three main branches consisting of the office of the zone commander, the directorate of legal affairs, and the special directorate for security.

The office of the zone commander included four major positions. The AMG chief of staff acted as vice commander of the zone and performed such functions as were assigned by the zone commander. The comptroller supervised budgetary and fiscal matters and performed auditing functions. He provided for payment of current AMG expenses for wages and rents, and settled claims advanced against the AMG. The public information officer had control and supervision of all publications and films published or circulated within the zone. He operated and controlled AMG broadcasting stations and was responsible for all press releases and public announcements made by the AMG. The real estate officer was responsible for all housing and construction programs for British and United States troops.

The directorate of legal affairs was headed by a director who was the legal adviser to the zone commander. He had supervision and control over the military and civil courts, and exercised all powers, duties, and functions of a minister of grace and justice. Besides, the director of legal affairs was responsible for the legal form of all legislation submitted for promulgation. He was also in charge of publishing the official gazette.

Head of the third branch was the special director for security. Responsible to him were six British-American chief officers. The first, the director of public safety, was responsible for public order in the zone. He was also the inspector general of the AMG civil police. It was significant that British Colonel Gerald Richardson, the organizer and veteran head of the civil police, retained his position. He had been blamed by Irredentists and the Italian government for police brutality during the March riots. The other five officers were: the director of the port of Trieste, chief of postal services and telecommunications, shipping control officer, military permit officer, and displaced persons officer.

All AMG Italian functionaries were subordinated to the senior director of administration, G. A. Vitelli, who had been proposed by the Italian government and appointed by the zone commander. The senior director was the supreme authority for all administrative offices taken over by Italians according to the London Agreement, and directly responsible to the zone commander. The senior director coordinated the activities of the directorates of interior and of finance and economics. The first consisted of the following branches: local government (zone presidency and communes), department of labor, department of social assistance, office of public health, office of education, office of census and survey, and fire service. The directorate of finance and economics was subdivided into the department of commerce, department of production, department of finance (including finance guards and customs), department of transportation, department of public works and utilities, office of agriculture and fisheries, and loans section.

Not including the heads of local government the reorganized AMG consisted of fifteen British-American and seventeen Italian higher functionaries. Italian senior officers increased in number from four to seventeen. Prior to the reorganization the Italians had held only the department of labor, public health office, education office, and office of agriculture and fisheries.[30]

30. During his press conference on May 9, 1952, De Gasperi had distributed a prospect for the future reorganization of the AMG in line with the London Agreement. According to this prospect the important AMG positions (including the zonal president) would be divided among 6 British, 7 Americans, and 21 Italians. This would establish a ratio of 13 to 21, or 13 to 20 without the zonal president. (See *Relazioni internazionali*, 16, no. 20 [May 17, 1952]: 492.) The number of Italian high positions was three short of De Gasperi's prediction. Administrative Order No. 60, issued December 9, 1952 (*AMG-FTT Gazette*, 5, no. 35 [Dec. 21, 1952]: 593) appointed three more Italians: one became deputy

ADMINISTRATIVE CHANGES IN ZONE B

The London Agreement also brought administrative changes in Zone B. To counter association of the Italian government with the administration of Zone A the Yugoslavs introduced almost identical measures in their zone.

On May 15, 1952, Colonel Miloš Stamatović, the commander of the Yugoslav zone, issued three decrees.[31] The first facilitated travel between Zone B and Yugoslavia: special passes, hitherto required for Yugoslav citizens entering Zone B, were abolished. Permanent residents of Zone B possessing an identity card were permitted to enter Yugoslavia without any other document. Hereafter the boundary between Yugoslavia and Zone B could be crossed without restriction, as was the case with the frontier between Zone A and Italy. Residents of Zone B traveling abroad were henceforth furnished with Yugoslav passports. This meant that an Italian resident of Zone B must have a Yugoslav passport for his visit to Italy. The second was the most important of the three, and reorganized the administration of Zone B. The Regional People's Committee, the highest civil authority of the zone, was abolished, and its powers transferred to the two district committees. The Slovenian district committee of Koper became supreme for the Slovenian part of Zone B called Koprščina, and in the same way the Croat district committee of Buje became the highest civil authority for the Croat part called Bujština. The Yugoslav commander of the zone appointed a political adviser for each of the two district committees. The adviser to the Koper district committee was nominated by the Slovenian government and the adviser for Buje district by the Croatian government. Without doubt this indicated that Yugoslavs regarded the Koper district as part of Slovenia and the Buje district as part of Croatia. The second

---

chief of the department of labor, the second, deputy chief of the department of social assistance, and the third, deputy director of finance and economics. This brought the number of Italian officers to 20, or 21 when including the zonal president, as predicted by De Gasperi.

31. *New York Times,* May 16, 1952; *Keesing's Contemporary Archives,* 8:12234; *Relazioni internazionali,* 16, no. 21 (May 24, 1952): 509, 516–17.

decree also provided for appointment by the Yugoslav government of a political adviser to the zone commander. This representative of the Yugoslav government was empowered to make decisions concerning economic matters and on problems of civil administration. He also coordinated his activities with those of Slovenian and Croat advisers. The Yugoslav military government retained direct control only over the administration of justice, internal security, police, the status of residents, regulation of foreigners, and representation abroad. The YMG turned all other civil administration over to the district committees. The second decree also confirmed the principle of national (ethnic) equality for all inhabitants of the zone. Each person was guaranteed the right to use his mother tongue in public and private life and the rights of each national group to its own cultural development were to be respected. The third decree provided that the National Bank of Yugoslavia would take over all principal banking operations in Zone B. It opened branches at Koper and Buje which had the exclusive right to conduct all operations of public finance and foreign exchange. Other banks could continue operation only with permission of the National Bank of Yugoslavia.

This was only the beginning. On July 31, and again on August 28, 1952, Colonel Stamatović published other decrees introducing more laws and administrative changes modeled after the Yugoslav system.[32]

On July 31, 1952, the Yugoslav criminal code and the law governing misdemeanors were applied to Zone B. The law courts and the office of the public prosecutor were reorganized to conform with the Yugoslav blueprint. New Yugoslav laws regarding economic decentralization were also introduced in the zone. These included rules governing the distribution of the wage fund, wage scales in state enterprises, wage scales for privately employed persons, import and export trade, taxation, and rates of interest. Then on August 28, 1952, provisions of the Yugoslav civil code dealing with family law (marriage, relationship of parents and children, guardianship, adoption, and proof of death) were also applied to Zone B. Most important, however, was the introduction of the Yugoslav electoral law.

32. *New York Times,* Aug. 3, 31, 1952; *Keesing's Contemporary Archives,* 9:13195.

The Italian government violently protested these changes. The Italian minister in Belgrade, Enrico Martino, on May 20, 1952, delivered a sharply worded note to the Yugoslav government protesting the changes brought about by the May 15 decrees. Besides, the Italian note accused the Yugoslav government of police intimidation and prosecution against Italians residing in Zone B.[33] On August 8, 1952, the Italian government called the attention of the governments of Great Britain, France, and the United States to the arbitrary measures illegally adopted in Zone B by the Yugoslav government on July 31, and urged the Western powers to intervene.[34] Finally on October 30, 1952, Italy proposed in a note to Yugoslavia that the whole matter be submitted to judgment of the International Court of Justice at The Hague. On December 23, 1952, Yugoslavia rejected this idea.[35]

The elections in Zone A had their counterpart in Zone B. On Sunday, December 7, 1952, they were held according to the new Yugoslav electoral law the same day as in Yugoslavia. All registered men and women over eighteen who were permanent residents of the zone were permitted to vote. While in the elections of 1950 two opposition parties had been allowed to nominate candidates in a few constituencies, in 1952, according to the new law, only the officially recognized People's Front presented its electoral list.

The Yugoslav government announced that 97 percent of the 42,000 registered voters went to the polls. About 1 percent of the votes were declared invalid. Yugoslav Communists were jubilant over the heavy turnout despite cold weather, sleet, and the inimical propaganda campaign coming from Zone A. One day before the elections, on Saturday, December 6, the Trieste workers had proclaimed a strike for fifteen minutes in protest of the one-party elections in Zone B. The Irredentists and the Catholic church, said the Yugoslavs, had urged the population to abstain from voting. All propaganda efforts of Cominformists, Irredentists, and the

33. *New York Times,* May 21, 1952; *Relazioni internazionali,* 16, no. 21 (May 24, 1952): 517.
34. *Documenti di vita italiana,* 3, no. 24 (Nov. 1953): 1856–61.
35. *Relazioni internazionali,* 16, no. 45 (Nov. 8, 1952): 1169–70; ibid., 17, no. 1 (Jan. 3, 1953): 13; *New York Times,* Oct. 31, Nov. 1, Dec. 24, 1952.

Catholic church had failed, the Yugoslavs asserted, because the residents of Zone B were overwhelmingly in favor of remaining permanently under Yugoslav jurisdiction.[36]

MINORITY RIGHTS

The London Agreement changed the administration in both zones. These changes in turn were protested by both Italians and Slovenes. Each charged violation of its minority rights. These accusations were not new. The administrative changes in both zones merely multiplied these complaints and made minority rights an issue of press campaigns in Italy, Yugoslavia, and the Free Territory.

The Slovenian charges may be divided into two groups. The first demanded elimination of old injustices done to the Slovenian minority by the Fascist regime and still not corrected. The second group of complaints protested new discrimination against the Slovenes in Zone A during the administration of the Allied Military Government, especially after the London Agreement.

Among the first group may be listed the following: Slovenes, who had left the Trieste territory after the First World War because of losing administrative jobs to the new Italian bureaucracy, or because of having to escape the Fascist persecutions, had not been able to return to Zone A from Yugoslavia. No decree prohibited reentry of these Slovenes or their descendants, but the economic-administrative organization of Zone A hindered such a return. Slovenes pointed out that if they went back, no jobs were available and no political rights granted.[37] Though this complaint was true, it was raised by pro-Tito newspapers only after 1947. Until that time, the Tito authorities themselves did not allow such persons to return to Trieste unless they were party members.

Another complaint held that the old Fascist law decreeing the change of first and last names from Slovenian to Italian had never been annulled in Zone A. Persons whose names had been changed

36. *Keesing's Contemporary Archives*, 9:13195; *New York Times*, Dec. 7, 8, 9, 1952.
37. Lavo Čermelj, "The Denationalization of Slovenes in the Anglo-American Zone of FTT," *Review of International Affairs*, 3, no. 1 (Jan. 1952): 11–13.

could apply for permission to use the original form, but many did not do so because they were employed by an Italian enterprise or individual.[38] Such an application could result in loss of their jobs.

The pro-Tito UAIS-SIAU fought for abrogation of the Fascist law which had forced alteration of Slovenian names, but at the same time prohibited its members from petitioning the Allied Military Government for such a change. This group argued that Slovenian names had been changed by a law from above and therefore this law should be repealed by another law from above, applying to all cases without the need of individual petitions.

The fight for local Slovenian geographical names was more violent. About 1950, Slovenian communes adjacent to the Yugoslav border introduced bilingual names for their communes. The Allied Military Government did not object. These bilingual inscriptions were mainly in sections far from the principal traffic lines between Trieste and Italy. But when the municipal council of Duino-Aurisina made the same decision in January 1952 and by November had erected about seventeen bilingual signs, trouble began. This commune included territory through which passed the main lines connecting Trieste with Italy. The pro-Italian political parties objected to the signs, which demonstrated that Slovenian villages existed between Trieste and the Italian border. On November 26, the president of the zone requested the mayor to remove the signs, because they had been erected in defiance of the old Italian Law No. 800 of March 29, 1923. Against this demand the mayor appealed to the zone commander, General Winterton. The latter received the Slovenian mayor in a special audience but repeated the order to remove the bilingual signs as being a violation of existing law.[39]

38. Provisions for the restitution of surnames were given in Order No. 75, issued December 10, 1947, in *AMG-FTT Gazette,* 1, no. 9 (Dec. 11, 1947): 129–31.

39. For a letter from Dr. Josip Agneletto, president of the Slovenian Democratic Union, to General Winterton, and a letter of Slovenian mayors of Zone A to the United Nations Security Council, signed in Nabrežina (Aurisina), December 21, 1952, see *Demokracija* (Democracy), Dec. 23, 1952; see also "Boj slovenske občine" (The Struggle of a Slovenian Municipality), *Stvarnost in svoboda* (Reality and Liberty), 2 (Trieste, 1953): 3–7.

The mayor of Duino-Aurisina was supported in his fight for Slovenian rights by all the mayors of Slovenian communes and by all Slovenian organizations, including Slovenian liberal and clerical political parties and cultural organizations and all independentist groups. The only parties opposed were the pro-Italian parties of the Trieste municipality.

Fascist Law No. 800, applied to prohibit Slovenian geographic names, had been one of the first steps of the denationalization policy in the Julian Region. The Slovenian press stressed that the Allied Military Government was confirming this law in demanding the removal of these signs. When the mayor refused to obey, the Allied Military Government appointed a special police detachment to remove the signs. Protests to the British and American governments and to the United Nations brought no results.[40]

Through all the years of the Allied military administration came constant complaints that the Slovenian economic and cultural institutions confiscated by the Fascist authorities had not been returned to Slovenes, who were not allowed to organize new economic institutions either. To all demands for return to Slovenes of the former national homes, cooperatives, and banks, the AMG answered that it had neither the legal basis nor the funds to pay for compensation. Regarding the legal question, the Slovenes pointed out that the same situation had existed in Germany, where the confiscated property was returned to persons persecuted by

40. "In the Footsteps of Mussolini's Laws," *Review of International Affairs*, 4, no. 1 (Jan. 1, 1953): 6–7.

Similarly, an attempt was made to uphold the Fascist laws in the case of Dr. August Sviligoj, the president of the Slovenian Democratic Union in Gorizia (Italy). Dr. Sviligoj had been condemned before 1945 by the Fascist Special Tribunal and sentenced to twenty years' imprisonment for his work among the Slovenes in Italy. After 1947, when Gorizia was united with Italy, the Italian government of the new democratic republic issued an order to Dr. Sviligoj requiring his imprisonment because he had not served his entire term. An appeal against this decision saved Dr. Sviligoj from a second imprisonment. However, the final decision in the case was still not known at that time. Such practice in the Republic of Italy was watched by Slovenes in Zone A with great anxiety, as they wondered what would be their destiny should Zone A be annexed by Italy. (For more detail see: Lavo Čermelj, "Slovenes in Italy," *Review of International Affairs*, 4, no. 17 [Sept. 1, 1953]: 14–15.)

the Nazi regime, although the Allied forces were also only the military occupation there. Secondly, the Slovenes stressed that the AMG in Zone A of the Julian Region had abolished all anti-Jewish laws as far back as 1945 and had decreed in 1946 that all property belonging to Jews must be restored to them, even if it was in the hands of a third person.[41] The same policy was not applied to Slovenes, who stressed that the denationalization laws had not been abolished nor property returned to Slovenian individuals or institutions.[42]

As for complaints of new discrimination against Slovenes in Zone A after the Second World War, these were many. First, the Slovenes protested against Italian refugees in Zone A. While the Slovenes born in Zone A had no chance to settle in the Trieste territory under the British-American administration, this was not the case for Italian refugees. Italian refugees from the part of the Julian Region which came under Yugoslav control by the Italian peace treaty and others from Zone B of the Free Territory numbered about 24,000, according to the census of 1951. By Order No. 219 of November 29, 1950, they were registered as permanent residents, which gave them the right to vote.[43] Due to Italian influence on the local administration of Zone A, these Italian refugees

41. The main decrees dealing with the repeal of anti-Jewish laws were General Order No. 3, issued July 3, 1945 (*AMG Gazette VG*, 1, no. 1 [Sept. 15, 1945]: 25–27); General Order No. 44, issued February 11, 1946 (ibid., no. 17 [May 1, 1946]: 4–9); and Order No. 174, issued July 15, 1946 (ibid., no. 24 [Aug. 15, 1946]: 40–41). For the restoration of Jewish property see General Order No. 18, issued October 13, 1945 (ibid., no. 5 [Nov. 1, 1945]: 6–7); and General Order No. 58, issued May 27, 1946 (ibid., no. 22 [July 15, 1946]: 12–19).

42. Vladimir Sedmak, "The Trieste Issue and Restitution of Slovene Property," *Review of International Affairs*, 5, no. 100 (June 1, 1954): 9–10.

43. For Order No. 219 see *AMG-FTT Gazette*, 3, no. 33 (Dec. 1, 1950): 577–78. This order permitted any person who on November 1, 1950, had been registered for at least a year as a temporary resident to be inscribed in the register of permanent population. But only Italian refugees got the right to vote, because they were Italian citizens. For voting there were three demands, as we know: a person had to be twenty-one years old, an Italian citizen, and had to be inscribed as a permanent resident.

enjoyed a privileged position in regard to housing and employment opportunities. This was discrimination against the native Slovene and Triestine population.

A second phenomenon, closely connected with the first, was the effort of the pro-Italian administration in Zone A to denationalize Slovenian land. Slovenian sources stressed that this attempt was centered especially on the Slovenian corridor separating Trieste from ethnically Italian territory.[44]

The Slovenes argued that their land was expropriated. New apartment houses for Italian refugees were built not only in the Trieste suburbs but in completely Slovenian villages separated from the city of Trieste although belonging to the Trieste municipality. In Duino, close to the Italian border, a new fishing settlement was built for Italian refugees and again Slovenian land was expropriated. Close to Opicina a children's village (Villaggio del Fanciullo) was founded for orphans. Along the coast between Trieste and Duino new hotels and summer resorts appeared, causing further expropriation of Slovenian land. South of Trieste a new industrial port was constructed at Zaule by Ente per il Porto Industriale di Zaule supported by European Recovery Program funds. Close to Opicina a new village was built for the families of Allied officials in Trieste. For this project, also, Slovenian land was expropriated.

The consequence of these expropriations was the Italianization of some Slovenian villages. Italian families settled there and new Italian elementary schools were opened for their children, followed shortly by Italian stores. There was now a good excuse to employ only Italians in the police force and railway stations of such villages. Slovenes stressed that slowly, but following a premeditated pattern, the Slovenian corridor between Trieste and Duino was being Italianized.

To Slovenian protests against denationalization of Slovenian

44. See, for example: Stane Lenardič, "Od Trsta do Devina" (From Trieste to Duino), *Slovenski poročevalec* (Slovenian Reporter) (Ljubljana), July 17, 1953; "Italianization of the Slovene Coast," *Review of International Affairs,* 4, no. 8 (Apr. 16, 1953): 6; "Razlastitev se nadaljuje" (The Expropriation Continues), *Demokracija,* Aug. 8, 1952; V. Sedmak, "The Ethnic Character of the Slovene Coast," *Review of International Affairs,* 4, no. 19 (Oct. 1, 1953): 6.

land, Italians replied that the expropriations were not a consequence of premeditated denationalization but rather a result of modern ways of life. Trieste had been transformed into a great urban center based on a modern economy; hence, Trieste's expansion was organic, conditioned by economic factors. Ethnic considerations were involved only because the Trieste suburbs were settled by Slovenes. The new policy was caused by economic needs and not by a denationalization policy.[45]

The validity of this Italian explanation was undeniable when applied to the building of new apartment houses in Trieste's suburbs, new industrial establishments, or new highways connecting Trieste with Italy. But no organic extension of the city necessitated the building of apartment houses for Italian refugees in completely Slovenian villages outside the suburbs. No economic factors dictated the building of an Italian fishing village in Duino. The creation of the village for orphan children had a humanitarian character, but it should be remembered that institutions for orphan children had also in the past represented a means of Italianizing the territory. It was hard to convince the Slovenes that the new village for orphan children would not follow the same policy, especially as it was entirely in Italian hands though accepting Slovenian children.

The Slovenes pointed out that the process of Italian economic and political expansion in Zone A was the more dangerous for Slovenes since they neither participated in the local European Recovery Program nor were represented in the zonal administration. In the bureaucracy Slovenes held only subordinate positions, small in number and of a temporary character. After the London Agreement of 1952, some Slovenes employed by the railroads were again transferred to Italy by the Italian ministry of transportation. The Slovenes protested that the discriminatory practices of the Fascist period were again being used by the Italian government. The same situation was evident in the economic field. Slovenes were not allowed to organize new economic and financial establishments, though they petitioned the local Italian and Allied authorities for permission to do so.[46]

45. Il Comitato di Liberazione Nazionale dell'Istria, *Il problema di Trieste: Realtà storica, politica, economica* (Trieste, 1954), pp. 14–15.
46. *Italian Genocide Policy*, pp. 188–93.

A further Slovenian complaint concerned Slovenian schools. They were of a temporary character, not legally protected by law, and could be closed at any time. The administration of Slovenian schools was not independent, but instead a part of the education office headed by the Italian Giuseppe Fadda, who even before the London Agreement followed directions received from the Italian ministry of education in Rome. After the London Agreement this dependence on Rome became still greater. The Slovenian demands for new schools or other administrative changes were further hindered by Rome's typical policy of delay. Slovenian teachers, after eight years of employment, had only temporary status, and had to apply annually for their jobs. Consequently, Slovenian teachers were deprived of employment benefits such as pensions and social security. While new Italian schools were built in Slovenian villages, the Slovenian elementary and secondary schools still had to use outmoded buildings and private houses for their classes. Furthermore, economic and political pressure was now put on Slovenian parents to enroll their children in Italian schools. Since the Italians represented the economically dominant social group, they were able to exert considerable pressure on their Slovenian employees. In addition, students with Slovenian diplomas were refused jobs by Italian employers, who made the excuse that they had no vacancies while at the same time appointing Italian refugees to new positions.[47] Table 10 shows the decrease in enrollment in Slovenian schools as contrasted with an increase in the Italian, a fact which worried the Slovenes greatly. It might be added that, in addition to the above explanations for the decline, emigration and a natural decrease in the number of school age children ought to be taken into consideration.

Political pressure against Slovenes was not applied in Zone A, but only in Italy. Therefore Slovenes were afraid that the same policy would be adopted should Zone A unite with Italy. Under the peace treaty, Italian nationals in Yugoslavia could opt for Italy. Many Slovenes of the former Julian Region seized the opportunity to migrate as Italians from Communist Yugoslavia. If they settled in Gorizia (Italy), they could not send their children

---

47. "Slovene Memorandum to the Military Administration: A Letter from Trieste," *Review of International Affairs*, 4, no. 12 (June 16, 1953): 20.

to Slovenian schools but only to Italian. Many such persons preferred to settle in Zone A, where this new Italian policy was not yet in force.

Although during the period under consideration all Slovenian parties supported Slovenian claims for the betterment of Slovenian schools, it should be remembered that the Communist bloc had opposed any collaboration with the Allied Military Government during 1945–47, an opposition which hurt the development of Slovenian schools.[48]

TABLE 10

PUPILS IN SLOVENIAN AND ITALIAN SCHOOLS IN ZONE A, FTT

Year	Slovenian Schools	Italian Schools
1945–46	5,969	26,294
1946–47	6,317	26,151
1947–48	5,544	27,395
1948–49	5,247	27,875
1949–50	4,993	28,072
1950–51	4,454	28,023
1951–52	4,115	27,836
1952–53	4,164	28,159
1953–54	3,972	29,408
1954–55	3,733	29,790

SOURCE: Šah, *Izvestje srednjih šol, 1955*, pp. 4–5, for Slovenian schools; and *Trieste nella sua realtà*, p. 94, for Italian. The table includes the number of students in elementary and secondary schools.

Italian complaints against the Yugoslav administration in Zone B can be divided into three kinds. Yugoslav measures introduced in Zone B represented first a violation of international law, second a violation of basic human rights and freedoms, and lastly they introduced a denationalization policy against Italians.

The introduction of the new Yugoslav system in Zone B caused a radical change in the zone's economy, social conditions, and administration. The new system was introduced and preserved only by terrorist police measures. According to the Italians, the initiation of such a new system was a violation of Article 10 of the Provisional Statute (Annex VII) of the Italian peace treaty stating

48. J. V. [Velikonja], *Koledar-Zbornik, 1955*, pp. 179–80.

that "existing laws and regulations shall remain valid unless and until revoked or suspended by the Governor."[49] Here the Italian grievance went back to the old controversy on the nature of the "existing laws and regulations" in force in the Julian Region after World War II. In Zone A the AMG recognized the Italian legislation and laws enacted before September 1943, when it replaced the Partisan administration after June 12, 1945. The Italian point therefore supported the assumption that Italian legislation and law should be recognized for the entire Free Territory. Italian participation in the administration of Zone A was only a logical development of this assumption and therefore did not violate the peace treaty.

The Yugoslav explanation was different. The new economic, social, and administrative order had already been introduced during the war in the territory liberated by Partisan forces and was recognized by people throughout the Free Territory prior to the beginning of the Allied administration in Zone A. The new order was in force in Zone B at the time the Italian peace treaty was negotiated and signed. Therefore, the "existing laws and regulations" in Zone B were the ones introduced by the people's authorities and not the old Italian law. This Yugoslav viewpoint seemed to be confirmed by the fact that Article 10 of Annex VII did not mention Italian laws but only "existing laws and regulations." The Italian protest against the Yugoslav administration of Zone B, based on the assumption of the violation of international law, was therefore debatable.

However, the second Italian complaint was accurate. Yugoslav authorities had violated the basic human rights and freedoms guaranteed by the Italian peace treaty in the Permanent Statute to all inhabitants of the Free Territory. The Italians accused the Yugoslav authorities of quenching freedom of the press, religious freedom, freedom of movement, and free expression of opinion by free elections, and replacing them with a regime of police terror directed against the Italian ethnic group.[50]

Closely connected with the first two complaints was a third Italian grievance concerning the Yugoslav denationalization pol-

49. *Italian Peace Treaty*, pp. 198–99; *Documenti di vita italiana*, 3, no. 24 (Nov. 1953): 1854–61.
50. "Comments," *Italian Affairs*, 3, no. 3:326–36.

icy in Zone B. The Italians stated that between May 1945 and September 1953 over twelve thousand Italians were compelled to leave Zone B. They were replaced by an equal number of Slovenes and Croats emigrating from Yugoslavia and from Zone A to Zone B. With this shift of population, Slavs became far more numerous in the local administration than Italians.

The Yugoslav school system also discriminated against Italians in Zone B. School programs were radically changed and bore the stamp of Leninist and Titoist Communism. All students having a Slavic name were forced to go to Slav schools, though their parents might express Italian national consciousness. To increase the number of Slav schools the Yugoslav authorities sent students from Yugoslavia and Zone A into Zone B and these pupils were housed free in special "Student Homes." In 1945, there were 61 Italian elementary schools and 9 secondary schools in Zone B. New Slav schools were founded during 1946–47, by which time there were 117 schools in Zone B, including only 40 Italian ones. During 1950–51 Italian schools were reduced to 38, with 250 teachers and 3,651 pupils. The Slovenian and Croatian element had, at the same time, 65 schools, with 173 teachers and 3,910 pupils. Many Italian teachers left Zone B to escape police persecution, and others left for personal reasons, due to the insupportable political and economic situation. During 1952 and 1953, the Italians claimed that the Yugoslavs closed an additional 9 Italian schools in rural centers.[51]

A further Italian complaint was directed against introduction of the Slovenian form of family names by the Yugoslav authorities. While in Zone A the Slovenes had to petition to obtain their old Slavic names, in Zone B the change was decreed by the Yugoslav authorities. Consequently, the Italians complained that many people who were Italian "in language, customs, and sentiments" found themselves classified as Slavs.[52]

51. For a Yugoslav description of the school system in Zone B see I. K., *Review of International Affairs*, 2, no. 11 : 14–15. Here the number of Italian schools is greater than given above.

52. "Comments," *Italian Affairs*, 3, no. 3:328. The Slavic form had been changed by Fascist decree in 1926 in two ways. The first one was a direct translation from Slavic into Italian, for example, from Slavic *Vodopivec* to Italian *Beviaqua*. The second way was to change only the

A further discrimination against Italians was contained in housing legislation in Zone B. Under the pretext of a housing shortage, the Yugoslav authorities could demand evacuation of a house or apartment, assigning the owner or tenant "another adequate habitation." By this practice Italian owners or tenants were dislodged from many houses in Istrian towns. Italians stated that their places were taken in many cases by Slavs coming to Zone B from Yugoslavia.

SEARCHING FOR A NEW SOLUTION

Promulgation of the new decrees which tied Zone B closer to Yugoslavia and the increase of independentist votes at the municipal elections in Zone A strengthened the belief of Italian diplomats that a continuation of the status quo had become detrimental to Italian interests. During the summer of 1952 the Italians engaged in great diplomatic activity in London and Washington to solicit support for Italian claims and to put pressure on Yugoslavia to accept them.[53]

The Western powers relented and on August 18, 1952, the French, British, and American ambassadors in Belgrade went to Brioni and told Tito that Italy and Yugoslavia should renew their talks to obtain a final solution based on the principle of a continuous ethnic line. The identical message was transmitted to the Italian government. As the principle of a continuous ethnic line clearly favored Italy, it is not surprising that Yugoslavia politely declined direct negotiation.[54]

Afterwards, British Foreign Minister Eden abandoned the principle of a continuous ethnic line and came up with his own quite realistic proposal, the essence of which would assign Zone A to Italy and Zone B to Yugoslavia with eventual minor corrections.[55] Eden tried to reach such a solution when he visited Yugoslavia from September 17 to 23, 1952.

---

transliteration, for example, the old Slavic form *Dušič* was changed to the Italian form *Dussich*.

53. See Tarchiani, pp. 211–14; and the article "Le reazioni jugoslave nella zona B," by B. C. in *Relazioni internazionali,* 16, no. 21 (May 24, 1952): 509.

54. Jeri, pp. 255–56; Tarchiani, pp. 214–15.

55. Eden, pp. 200–203.

SEARCHING FOR A NEW SOLUTION

Prior to flying to Belgrade, Eden explained his plan to American Secretary of State Acheson and to De Gasperi. The latter made clear that he opposed continuance of the present situation, and refused the Yugoslav idea of a condominium. Then Eden asked De Gasperi "whether a division on zonal lines, Zone A to Italy, Zone B to Yugoslavia, with certain adjustments, would be acceptable. On this he [De Gasperi] was cautious and noncommittal, though he did not rule it out as a solution."

During his conversations with Tito and Edvard Kardelj, Eden formed the following picture. The Yugoslavs were for condominium or for status quo, but they "would acquiesce in the permanency of the present division between zones, provided that it was pressed upon them by others." If such a permanent division were to follow, the Yugoslavs would refuse to discuss Italian demands for coastal towns (Koper, Izola, Piran) in Zone B.

After his return from Belgrade, Eden was convinced that the only way to resolve the problem was for both the United Kingdom and the United States to impose a solution on Italy and Yugoslavia. Eden therefore proposed to Washington that Zone A be given to Italy and Zone B to Yugoslavia. Such a solution should be presented to both countries as final and having the full backing of Great Britain and the United States.

Eden's proposal was not accepted by the United States, which was unwilling to put pressure on De Gasperi for two reasons. First, Italian parliamentary elections were coming up in 1953, and second, the United States was aware that the Italian parliament had yet to ratify the European Defense Community agreement signed in May 1952. The ratification might fail if the United States pressed for a Trieste solution contrary to Italian demands. As soon as he was informed of the content of Eden's proposal, De Gasperi declared that Italy could never give up the coastal towns in Zone B.

Hence the Americans were not in favor of Eden's proposal, but continued to support Italian demands, the so-called continuous ethnic line. For its part, the Italian government regarded the new English proposal as dangerous to Italian claims in Zone B. Italy therefore tried to better her position by urging her ambassador in Washington to press for a new proposal more favorable to Italian interests. This new proposal should be advanced by the

United States. To make sure that Tito would not refuse it, the United States should put pressure on the Yugoslav government by threatening to discontinue economic and military aid.

The United States government decided to prepare a new proposal to end the Trieste dispute, and at the beginning of December 1952 Secretary of State Dean Acheson informed Great Britain and Italy about its contents. It assigned Zone A and the commune of Koper in Zone B to Italy, while Zone B and some villages along the Yugoslav border of Zone A would go to Yugoslavia. But the proposal failed to satisfy De Gasperi, who demanded also other coastal towns in Zone B, and on December 8, 1952, Italy announced that the new American plan was unacceptable. This was the last proposal prepared by the American Democratic administration. In the future the new Republican administration would have to deal with the Trieste question.[56]

Consequently the Italian ambassador in Washington immediately tried to establish contact with the next secretary of state, John Foster Dulles, in hopes of interesting him in a new proposal for solution of the Trieste question.

The American Republican administration prepared a new proposal, in February 1953, more favorable to Italy than the former one. It offered Italy all the coast of Zone A plus the communes of Koper, Izola, and Piran in Zone B. Yugoslavia would receive the rest of Zone B and the Slovenian communes of Sgonico and Monrupino, the village of Basovizza, and the commune of San Dorligo della Valle in Zone A, with a corridor to the Bay of Piran. Furthermore, the United States promised to put pressure on Yugoslavia to accept the entire proposal without change (*ne varietur* clause), if Italy accepted. The new proposal divided the Free Territory by a north-south line, giving Italy most of the coast and Yugoslavia the interior parts of the territory.

In the view of the Italian ambassador, Tarchiani, this was the best solution Italy could achieve under the circumstances. But De Gasperi refused to accept it, stating that only if the coastal territory in Zone B were extended from Piran to Umag could Italy agree to the American offer. During the second half of March 1953 in a special conference at Rome, the Italian ambassadors

56. For the Italian viewpoint see Tarchiani, pp. 215–83; for a Yugoslav description of events see Jeri, pp. 257–60.

SEARCHING FOR A NEW SOLUTION

tried to convince De Gasperi to accept the American proposal. However, he stood firm.

During April 1953 the Americans tried unsuccessfully to convince De Gasperi to accept some minor changes. The latter, who was in the midst of an electoral campaign, insisted that any agreement not including the coast of Zone B as far as Umag would mean defeat for the Christian Democrats in the coming elections on June 7, 1953. The American statesmen were disappointed that Italy did not accept their original plan. They included the Italian demands in a new proposal, and presented it to the Yugoslav foreign minister, Koča Popović, on May 7, 1953. But it was offered only as a possibility for future agreement, and no pressure was exerted on Yugoslavia to accept. Popović informed the American government that Yugoslavia could not agree to any such proposal, because she had already begun direct negotiations with Italy.

The Italo-American negotiations were secret and took place from February until the beginning of May, when Yugoslavia learned of them. The Yugoslavs were afraid that the United States might grant Italy new concessions to help the Christian Democrats win the elections on June 7. As a result, the Yugoslav government abandoned its policy of waiting and again initiated direct negotiations with Italy at the beginning of May 1953. The talks took place in Rome. The Yugoslavs were prepared to give Italy a strip of coast in Zone B from Koper to Piran. This isolated coastal area would be connected to Zone A by a corridor, including a highway. In exchange, Italy would give to Yugoslavia Slovenian villages in Zone A along the Yugoslav border. This Yugoslav proposal was refused by Italy because it was worse than both American plans. But the Yugoslavs had achieved their purpose; no new Allied proposal was advanced in Italy's favor before the elections. The pre-election period was the most dangerous for the Yugoslavs, because they suspected that Italy would press for new concessions, and that the Allies would then be inclined to grant special favors as a means of affecting the outcome.

Moreover, the Italian ambassador in Washington actually tried to achieve a new American declaration in Italy's favor before the elections. But the State Department, disillusioned by the Italian refusal of the previous American proposals, became more cautious. The Americans declined to promise any additional concessions.

15
FROM VIOLENCE TO COMPROMISE (JUNE 1953–OCTOBER 1954)

AUTUMN CATACLYSM

Italian parliamentary elections in June 1953 gave rise to a chain of events that contributed, one year and four months later, on October 5, 1954, to a compromise solution to the Trieste problem acceptable to both Italy and Yugoslavia.

After the elections a political crisis broke out in Italy. De Gasperi formed his eighth and last government, but on July 28, 1953, he failed to receive a vote of confidence and had to resign. On August 15, Giuseppe Pella, a leader of the right wing of the Christian Democratic party, set up a caretaker government, which was to function only until disagreement among the center coalition parties (Christian Democrats, Liberals, Republicans, Saragat Socialists) could be resolved.[1]

Meanwhile Yugoslavia further strengthened her international position. Since the death of Stalin in March 1953, relations between Yugoslavia and the Soviet Union had been improving and during the summer the two nations had their first direct contacts. Marshal Tito acknowledged in a speech in Pazin, Istria, on June 14, 1953, that the Soviet Union had expressed the desire to send an ambassador to Belgrade, and Belgrade had given consent. But while Yugoslavia welcomed normal relations with Russia, Tito asserted, her policy toward the West and especially toward the Balkan Pact countries would not change.[2] The end of her feud with the Soviets gave Yugoslavia greater maneuvering possibilities with regard to Trieste. The Yugoslavs presupposed rightly that the West wanted to keep Yugoslavia outside the Soviet bloc. Hence, the Yugoslavs reasoned that the Western powers would refrain from pressing Yugoslavia into an agreement on Trieste un-

---

1. Walter Hildebrandt, *Der Triest-Konflikt und die italienisch-jugoslawische Frage* (Göttingen, 1953), p. 81; Jeri, p. 261.
2. Tito, 8:124–25, 128–29. For an extract in English see *Documents on International Affairs, 1953* (London, 1956), p. 280.

AUTUMN CATACLYSM

acceptable to the Yugoslavs. Any such coercion might draw Yugoslavia closer to Russia. During the summer of 1953 talks also took place among the Balkan Pact countries to extend the treaty of friendship and cooperation into a military alliance.[3] Moreover, the United States informed Italy on July 14, 1953, that Yugoslavia had been invited to a military conference in Washington.[4]

Italian statesmen observed these developments with great concern. In their eyes, the Balkan Pact could not only be directed against Soviet aggression but could also be detrimental to Italian interests, because it included Yugoslavia, Greece, and Turkey. Each had had quarrels with Italy in the past. Yugoslavia and Greece fought against Italy during World War II, and Turkey during World War I. But most important, a military alliance would strengthen Yugoslavia's position and make her more reluctant to accept Italian demands for Trieste.

Hence before giving a vote of confidence to the new government, Italian senators and deputies inquired as to what Pella's foreign policy would be. Both the Right and Left opposition attacked Italian participation in NATO. The Right furthermore demanded a firmer position on the Trieste question. To gain a majority Pella needed some votes from the opposition. There was no chance the left-wing opposition would vote for him, and he had therefore to make concessions to the Right. When Pella presented his program to a joint session of both houses on August 19 and again in his debate in the senate on August 22 and in the lower house on August 24, he stressed that Italy would remain a member of NATO but would hold firm in demanding that the NATO powers also support Italian national interests. Pella was most clear-cut in the house of deputies, where he assured the Right that the government would firmly demand that the Allies keep the promises given Italy in the Tripartite Proposal. With this stand Pella gained the support of the Right. The National Monarchists voted for his government and the neo-Fascists abstained. The senate gave him its vote of confidence on August 22, and the lower house on August 24, 1953.[5]

The position of Pella's government was obviously weak. It

3. *Documents on International Affairs, 1953*, p. 281.
4. Tarchiani, p. 282.
5. See *Relazioni internazionali*, 17, no. 35 (Aug. 29, 1953): 815–16, 822–23, 824–25.

depended on right-wing support that would last only so long as Pella could satisfy their nationalistic ambitions. Trieste became a crucial issue. Pella was aware that all previous Italian demands had ended in failure because the Western powers had refused to put pressure on Yugoslavia. Something more potent than diplomatic action was needed. By making Trieste an international issue of first rank he might force the West into granting more concessions to Italy. What Pella needed was a pretext. His opportunity came on August 28, 1953, when the Yugoslav semiofficial agency Yugopress released a statement commenting upon Pella's speech in the Italian parliament in support of the Tripartite Proposal:

> According to information obtained by Yugopress, Belgrade's political circles consider Pella's latest speech as proof that Yugoslavia's conciliatory and peaceable attitude leads nowhere in view of Rome's negative attitude to the solution of the Trieste problem. These circles affirm that the Trieste problem arose as result of Italy's expansionistic aims and the big powers' acquiescence to these aims, by which the big powers revealed that they are ready to sacrifice Yugoslavia's vital interests in this problem. The new proof of Italy's negative attitude in this question, given in the new Italian Premier's speech, convinced many personalities in Belgrade that it is necessary to seriously reconsider Yugoslavia's attitude toward this problem. The opinion prevails that this re-consideration will bring results which impose themselves by the circumstances created in the Trieste question, in view of the situation brought about by the process of cold annexation of Trieste by Italy. . . .[6]

Yugopress distributed the above statement to its subscribers on the evening of August 28. The American United Press agency, one of Yugopress's subscribers, diffused the news the next day, August 29. The United Press dispatch from Belgrade was dated August 28,

6. Donald C. Dunham, "Political Aspects of Press Reporting of Crisis of November, 1953, Trieste, F.T.T." (Trieste, 1954), p. 67. (Mimeographed.) This is a valuable collection of official pronouncements, lengthy quotations from the newspapers published in Trieste, Italy, Yugoslavia and other countries, to which Mr. Dunham added timetables of events and his explanations. The author takes this opportunity to thank Mr. Dunham for his generosity in lending the above work.

1953: "It was stated today that Yugoslavia lost patience with Italy in matters regarding the Trieste question and is said to be thinking of changing her 'moderate and tolerant' attitude, possibly by annexing Zone B, in reply to Italy's 'cold annexation' of Zone A."[7] When communicating the Yugopress statement the United Press evidently added its own opinion, "possibly by annexing Zone B," which had not been in the Yugopress release.

Pella received the United Press dispatch on August 29 and took it at its face value. To him it represented the official opinion of the Yugoslav government. He did not wait for the text of the Yugopress statement, nor did he ask the Yugoslav embassy for an explanation. The same day, August 29, Pella convoked a meeting with Emilio Taviani, the defense minister; General Efisio Marras, the chief of staff; and Vittorio Zoppi, secretary general of the foreign ministry. They decided to move Italian troops to the Yugoslav border. Pella immediately explained to the Western powers that Italy would remain faithful to NATO, but at the same time he expected the West to refuse to recognize the annexation of Zone B. Should Yugoslavia proceed with her plans Italy would be compelled to occupy Zone A. In such case Italy hoped, said Pella, that the Western powers would give tacit or explicit approval.[8]

On August 31, 1953, the ambassadors of the three Western powers in Rome saw Pella and explained that according to their governments Yugoslavia did not intend to annex Zone B. Pella expressed satisfaction with the good news. He promised the ambassadors to avoid any border incidents, and then came to his main point: Italy should be put on an equal level with Yugoslavia, by being permitted to occupy Zone A.[9]

Pella obviously had succeeded in reopening the Trieste problem, and he pressed for new concessions. The Western Allies should leave Zone A to Italy without prejudicing Italian rights to Zone B, the second step in satisfying Italian demands according to the progression principle first expressed after the March 1952 revolts.

The Yugoslavs were quick to denounce Pella's actions. On August 30, 1953, the government press agency Tanjug stated that

7. Ibid.
8. Duroselle, *Le Conflit de Trieste,* pp. 379–80.
9. Tarchiani, pp. 284–85.

official Yugoslav circles considered the information and comments of the Italian press about Yugoslav intentions to annex Zone B as a calculated provocation.[10] During the next few days Yugoslavia sent the Italian government a series of notes objecting to Pella's actions. In the first of two transmitted on September 1, Yugoslavia protested an Italian military demonstration along the Yugoslav-Italian border as a brutal violation of the rules of normal behavior among nations, and as the culmination of a long-term policy of hostility against Yugoslavia. The second note protested border violations by the Italian army. North of Gorizia, said the Yugoslavs, Italian soldiers had crossed the Yugoslav border and gone a distance of about one hundred yards into Yugoslav territory. A note of September 4 specifically criticized Pella's interpretation of the United Press dispatch. The arbitrary interpretation of certain pronouncements, stated the note, could not have been sufficient motive for a military demonstration, especially when normal diplomatic channels existed for obtaining an explanation. Only by extreme tolerance had the Belgrade government restrained itself from taking countermeasures. But if the Italian government continued the abnormal situation along the Yugoslav border, the note concluded, Yugoslavia would be forced to take similar measures.[11]

In Yugoslavia at the same time, preparations went on for a great celebration of the tenth anniversary of the proclaimed annexation of the Slovenian Littoral to Yugoslavia, which had followed the Italian armistice in September 1943. As part of the commemoration, Tito spoke to the former Partisans at Okroglica near the Italian border on September 6, 1953.[12] Addressing a crowd of a quarter of a million people, Tito strongly condemned Pella's policy. His speech touched three important issues. As an introduction, he enumerated the Fascist persecutions. He reminded the world that the Fascists had deported, from Slovenia alone, 67,230 persons, of whom 11,606 had died in concentration

10. For the Tanjug statement see *Relazioni internazionali*, 17, no. 36 (Sept. 5, 1953): 845.

11. For the text of the Yugoslav notes see ibid., no. 37 (Sept. 12, 1953): 869–70.

12. Tito, 8:183–202. For extracts in English see *Keesing's Contemporary Archives*, 9:13191; and *Documents on International Affairs, 1953*, pp. 286–88.

camps. For all of Yugoslavia, said Tito, the figures of Fascist brutalities were much greater. There had been 437,956 persons killed, 84,512 had been sent to do forced labor, and 109,437 to concentration camps. In condemning Pella's recent actions Tito was at the same time sarcastic and threatening. "Why is he [Pella] . . . pretending to move his troops in case we should annex Zone B? Why should we, comrades, annex Zone B? We are there already!" Yugoslavia, said Tito, would be very stupid to act in this way. The entire world would condemn Yugoslavia for a quite unnecessary action. The press notice stating that Yugoslavia intended to annex Zone B was just a pretext, continued Tito.

> Signor Pella . . . apparently wanted to launch against us a policy of the strong hand. He mounted his steed and is now sweeping through the air flourishing his wooden sabre. . . . We know well enough that it was nothing but a circus show. . . . But if this whole affair is a serious matter—as they themselves say it is—then we too shall have to look at the matter in a different way, and tell them in all seriousness: Do not keep producing circus shows, because quite a few unexpected things could result from it. . . . We had already seen their divisions—not merely one or two—armed and disarmed. This is why we don't fear their threats.[13]

Turning to the Trieste question, Tito condemned Pella's reaffirmation of the Tripartite Proposal and added that what Pella really wanted was to take Zone A and thereafter to talk about Zone B. This policy would not succeed, Tito said. "We are interested in the entire Free Territory of Trieste, not only in Zone B but also in Zone A because our co-nationals are there also." Tito rejected all past proposals, Italian and Yugoslav alike, and advanced a new solution: "You have led the affair into such a blind alley that in reality you, and we together with you, can get out of it in no other way than by making Trieste an international city and annexing the entire Slovenian hinterland to Yugoslavia. This is the solution and nothing else."

The Italian press immediately attacked Tito's speech, characterizing it as coarse and insolent, and expressive of typical Yugoslav megalomania. The Italian democratic annexationist parties in Trieste and the CLN for Istria sent a memorandum to Prime

13. Tito, 8:195, 196.

Minister Pella on September 11, urging the Italian government not to abandon the Italians of Zone B. They expressed their opposition to a de facto partition of the FTT along the zonal border. Instead the annexationists proposed that the future of the two zones be decided by a free plebiscite under international control. To eliminate Yugoslav arguments about denationalization of the territory, the memorandum proposed that the vote be limited to persons or descendants of persons born in the FTT before November 4, 1918, that is, before the Italian occupation. The annexationists also asked the Italian government to accept a plebiscite taken by communes, to counter the Yugoslav assertion that Italy wanted to decide the fate of other communes with the votes of the Italian majority in Trieste.[14]

Pella decided to reply to Tito's speech.[15] Like Tito, he chose a nationalistic occasion, the celebration of the tenth anniversary of Italian resistance to the German occupation of Rome. In the presence of General Cadorna, leader of the Italian resistance, Pella remembered with gratitude those who had fought on the side of the Allies against the Germans. With regard to Trieste, Pella again affirmed that the Tripartite Proposal should be the basis for any future solution. Because all Italian efforts to find a solution had ended in failure, Pella proposed a plebiscite. He assured his listeners that it would be at "the same time an assent to the desires of the involved population and a practical realization of the Tripartite Proposal." However, Pella accepted only the idea of a plebiscite, not the rest of the proposal advanced by the Trieste annexationists:

> We are therefore for a plebiscite on the whole of the territory on the basis of the democratic principle of the ascertained wish of the majority and for a choice between Italy and Yugoslavia, of course without troops of the two involved parties being present.[16]

While proposing a plebiscite, Pella also asserted that it was time that the United States and Great Britain recognize that their occupation of Zone A had become an "anachronism."

14. *Trieste: Zone B*, p. 5; Duroselle, *Le Conflit de Trieste*, p. 384.
15. Pella's speech is reprinted in *Relazioni internazionali*, 17, no. 38 (Sept. 19, 1953): 890–92.
16. Ibid., p. 892.

For Pella the plebiscite was only a tactical maneuver; his real goal was the Italian occupation of Zone A. Pella made this clear when he saw Ambassador Tarchiani on September 15, 1953, before the latter's return to Washington. In accordance with Pella's instructions Tarchiani explained on September 23, 1953, to the United States Department of State the following points: The rejection of the plebiscite without any alternative would make a very bad impression on the Italian public. The next possibility would be a division of the FTT along the zonal border, but such a solution must be only provisional. To internationalize the city of Trieste or to give Yugoslavia an outlet to the sea in Zone A would be disastrous. The Great Powers should not hesitate to turn Zone A over to Italy without Yugoslav consent, and any decision on the question whatsoever should be made known to Italy beforehand.[17]

Italian pressure continued. On October 1 and 4, Pella urged Tarchiani anew to make sure the Americans would not permit Yugoslavia to annex Zone B. On October 2, Pella further declared that assuredly the Italian parliament would not ratify the European Defense Community treaty if Italy could not annex Zone A—an obvious attempt to put pressure on American Secretary of State John Foster Dulles who regarded the EDC as one of his major projects and had already had trouble in persuading France to ratify the treaty.[18]

The pro-Italian press in Trieste hailed Pella's proposal for a plebiscite. The independentists, including the Cominformists, protested not against the plebiscite but against having only two choices. They demanded three alternatives: for Italy, for the FTT, or for Yugoslavia. Both the secretary general of the Independence Front, Giampiccoli, and the leader of the Triestino bloc, Mario Stocca, stressed that before any plebiscite could take place voting registers should be corrected. If tens of thousands of persons who had been illegally registered should retain their votes, there could be no democratic plebiscite to find out the wishes of the real inhabitants of the FTT.[19] The Slovenian democrats went further by pointing out that a plebiscite with only two alternatives could not

17. Tarchiani, pp. 287–88.
18. *Keesing's Contemporary Archives*, 9:13193.
19. Jeri, pp. 270–71, n. 63.

be based on the national consciousness of the inhabitants of the FTT under present circumstances. It would be merely a choice between a democratic and a Communist way of life. The people, Italians and Slovenes, of the FTT had experienced Communist rule and had no desire to return to Tito's Communism. Furthermore, the Cominformists, former allies of Tito, were now also opposed to Yugoslavia. Pella knew, according to the Slovenes, that under such conditions not only the independentists but most of the Slovenes and Croats would vote in favor of Italy or would abstain, thus contributing to an overwhelming Italian victory.

Italian Irredentists therefore deliberately exploited the difficult Slovenian and Croat political situation in trying to force them to opt for Italy. This attitude had been clearly expressed in a proposal previously advanced by De Castro, the Italian political adviser in Trieste. According to him, Italy and Yugoslavia should agree to accept the partition of the FTT based on an ethnic line to be determined by an international commission composed of members from three neutral states. The commission should define the ethnic line by means of an inquiry of all the people born in the FTT. It should be announced beforehand that after the accord the minorities would be exchanged. Faced with an obligatory exchange "almost all Slavs will declare themselves as Italians," De Castro concluded.[20] While refusing a plebiscite after World War I, the Irredentists pressed for it at this time because they knew the circumstances favored Italy. However, it is true that Pella himself was not favorably disposed toward the plebiscite. He was aware that Austria might also demand a plebiscite for the South Tyrol (Alto Adige), where the situation would not favor Italy. There the choice would be between two democratic states, and the ethnic factor would play a decisive role. It may be that for the same reason Pella intentionally remained vague when speaking about a plebiscite. He neglected to mention that only persons born in the FTT before 1918 (and their descendants) would have the right to vote and that the plebiscite would be decided by communes as proposed by Trieste's pro-Italian political parties.

Yugoslavia naturally rejected the plebiscite in a note of September 28, 1953, knowing that the people would prefer liberty to a Communist system regardless of national origin. But the Yugo-

20. Duroselle, *Le Conflit de Trieste,* p. 376.

slav government could not voice this true reason for rejecting the plebiscite. Hence the note asserted that the point of view of Yugoslavia regarding a plebiscite was already known to the Italian government, having been exposed in detail in the Yugoslav memorandum handed to the Italian representative in Belgrade, Enrico Martino, on March 28, 1952. Thus Yugoslavia refused the plebiscite with the same arguments as in 1952. "The plebiscite," said the note, "could be justified only on condition that the injustices and results of the policy of denationalization followed by Italy since 1918 were repaired." The note then listed all Yugoslav grievances.[21]

By his actions Pella succeeded in creating a new international crisis. Trieste again made front-page news in the West. The governments of Great Britain and the United States became convinced that continuing inaction on their part could become dangerous. To end the critical situation the United States decided to act. On September 14, 1953, the American ambassador in London handed Lord Robert Salisbury, acting foreign minister, proposals from Washington. They were almost the same as the plan prepared by Anthony Eden at the end of 1952. The two governments should inform Yugoslavia and Italy, without further consultation with either, that they had decided to withdraw their troops and to hand over the administration of Zone A to Italy. Both governments would also agree that this solution was final. Great Britain and the United States would not object if Yugoslavia or Italy later decided to annex their zone, provided Italy gave assurances for free port facilities and both Italy and Yugoslavia guaranteed fair treatment for minorities. But Washington and London disagreed on the extent to which a public declaration should be made that the solution was to be final. The British government felt that the public declaration should state clearly that the decision was final. Otherwise the Italian government would have a pretext to maintain its claims on Zone B. Moreover the Yugoslav government would accept the partition by zones only if this were a final settlement. But the United States opposed. The American secretary of state would agree to make public only the following clause: "The two governments expect that the measures being taken will lead to

21. For full text in English see *Documents on International Affairs, 1953*, pp. 288–90.

a final peaceful solution." However, he consented that it should be explained privately to the Italian government that the United States and Great Britain considered the Trieste problem solved, except for some minor corrections that Italy and Yugoslavia might agree upon. There is no question that Tarchiani, the Italian ambassador in Washington, had convinced John Foster Dulles that any final solution might jeopardize the ratification of the European Defense Community treaty. Great Britain finally agreed to the United States plan, but the lack of finality in the public declaration became fatal.[22]

On October 8, 1953, the American and British ambassadors in Rome handed Prime Minister Pella the public announcement and the secret annex. Simultaneously the public announcement was communicated to the Yugoslav government. France was informed the previous evening, October 7. Georges Bidault, French foreign minister, protested because France was not consulted and expressed his doubts over success of the plan.

The public announcement said that the governments of the United States and Great Britain had decided to terminate the Allied Military Government, to withdraw their troops, and to relinquish the administration of Zone A to the Italian government. It concluded: "The withdrawal of troops and the simultaneous transfer of administrative authority will take place at the earliest practical date, which will be announced in due course." In a secret annex the two powers stated that they were aware that their decision would create a de facto situation but their intention was that this de facto solution be considered as final. The two powers would not oppose bilateral negotiations for further frontier corrections, but they would not intervene in favor of either of the two parties. Moreover the two powers would be opposed to a Yugoslav military intervention against Italy or Zone A but would not protest if Yugoslavia should annex Zone B.[23] This secret annex was made known only to Italy. Yugoslavia received only the public statement.

Confusion inevitably ensued. Each country could interpret

22. Eden, pp. 204–5.
23. For the text of the October 8, 1953, announcement see *Department of State Bulletin*, 19 (Oct. 19, 1953): 529; see also Duroselle, *Le Conflit de Trieste*, p. 388.

the announcement in its own way. The reaction was therefore quite different in Italy, Yugoslavia, and Zone A.

Pella gave his official view in a speech to the Italian parliament on October 9. The October 8 announcement, he said, must be looked upon as a provisional solution and a partial fulfillment of the Tripartite Proposal, which had definitely not been abrogated:

> Particularly I could declare in the most formal way that the fact of accepting the administration of Zone A in no way implies an abandonment of the revindications concerning Zone B on the Italian side.[24]

In the same manner the pro-government press interpreted and evaluated the October announcement. *Il Corriere della Sera* wrote, on October 9, 1953:

> The Allies have accepted Italy's point of view. This is the triumph of justice and it is also a success for Pella. . . . This is merely a "de facto" solution, and its aim is just this: to re-establish equality between the two de facto positions—ours and the Yugoslavs'. . . . Today we have obtained the utmost of what we could obtain under present circumstances. . . . Of course, if we wanted the moon, this solution is not the one we wished for. But it is time we faced reality. . . .[25]

The Right was also satisfied with the announcement, but urged the government to take vigorous action to secure Italian claims to Zone B. The most outspoken criticism came from the Left opposition. The Communist leader Palmiro Togliatti declared in parliament on October 9 that the announcement modified the peace treaty and annulled the Tripartite Proposal. It accepted a pure and simple partition of zones. Though this partition was to be de facto, in time de facto would become a permanent solution. This meant the abandonment of the Italians living in Zone B. The only positive aspect, said Togliatti, was that British-American troops would evacuate Zone A, but this was counterbalanced by further enslavement of Italy by the Atlantic Pact.[26]

24. For the text of Pella's speech see: *Relazioni internazionali,* 17, no. 42 (Oct. 17, 1953): 995.
25. Dunham, p. 84.
26. *Relazioni internazionali,* 17, no. 42 (Oct. 17, 1953): 996, 998.

FROM VIOLENCE TO COMPROMISE

The October 8 announcement came as a great surprise to Yugoslavia, and was received with anger and dismay. Large-scale demonstrations against Great Britain and the United States took place in major Yugoslav cities, and units of the Yugoslav army were sent to Zone B and to the Italian frontier. Yugoslav grievances were well expressed in the note of protest handed to the British ambassador Sir Ivo Mallet and to the American chargé d'affaires Woodruff Wallner on October 9, 1953.

The note stated that the decision of October 8 was a unilateral violation of the peace treaty with Italy, benefiting a power which in 1941 had committed aggression against Yugoslavia and waged war on the side of the Axis powers. The handing over of Zone A to Italy was an unjust act, continued the note, because the zone was a mixed area with an Italian majority only in the cities of Trieste and Muggia while the remaining territory was entirely Slovene. Thus "the Slovenes in Zone A are being handed over . . . to the mercy of Italy for, in getting Zone A, Italy neither takes any real obligations nor gives any guarantee that she will honor their human and minority rights." Moreover, Trieste would be doomed to economic ruin by being cut off from its natural hinterland. But the handing over of Zone A to Italy was also endangering peace, asserted the note. This unilateral decision was a partial implementation of the Tripartite Proposal, "to which the Yugoslav government never has, nor will ever, agree." Inasmuch as this proposal had not been explicitly revoked, "the Italian government will inevitably keep on invoking it." Because of the known Italian imperialistic tendencies, Zone A will become only a bridgehead for further unjustified claims. The Yugoslav government therefore "energetically declares," said the note, "that it is under no circumstances prepared . . . to renounce the justified Yugoslav claims on this territory," and "demands [that] the above-mentioned decision should not be carried out."[27]

In his speech in Leskovac on October 10, 1953, Tito analyzed the background of the Trieste problem, condemned the British-American decision, and enumerated the consequences.[28] He as-

27. For the text of the identical notes see *Documents on International Affairs, 1953*, pp. 291–93; see also *Keesing's Contemporary Archives*, 9 : 13193.

28. Tito, 8:266–80; for extracts in English see *Documents on International Affairs, 1953*, pp. 293–95.

serted that it should not be forgotten that the Yugoslav army had liberated Trieste and Zone A but had abandoned it to prevent a clash with "those who were our allies." Later Yugoslavia had signed the peace treaty to preserve peace in that part of the world, and had never recognized the Tripartite Proposal. Turning to the announcement of October 8, Tito stated that he had told the representatives of Great Britain and the United States "that no one has the right to put us and Italy on the same level. We have fought against Italy, against Fascism." The Yugoslavs recognized the right of the Allies to occupy Zone A and to remain there in the future. But the Allies had no right to let Italy, which had been an enemy of both the Yugoslavs and the Allies during the past war, occupy the smallest part of Yugoslav land. "No one asked us for our opinion," stated Tito. "Suddenly we have been faced with a *fait accompli*. But we do not consider it a *fait accompli*." Speaking "in the name of 17 millions of proud citizens of a socialist state," Tito then pointed out what Yugoslavia would do to prevent fulfillment of the October decision.

> Our patience has come to an end.... We would consider the entry of Italian troops into Zone A as an act of aggression against our country.... We have decided to defend our interests in accordance with the spirit of the United Nations Charter and we have the right to have recourse to all means provided for in the Charter, including armed force if necessary.... They have violated the peace treaty and we have the right to rise up against that violation, and against the harm to our interests.... We will not permit Italian imperialism to advance against us so easily and tear our land from us piece by piece.[29]

Tito also pointed out that the Yugoslavs were thankful for economic and military help coming from the Western powers, "but we cannot sell our land for that help." Moreover, Tito made it clear that if recognition of the British-American announcement was a condition for continuation of such aid, the Yugoslavs would decline any further help.

In his speech Tito proposed a new solution: Zone B and that part of Zone A exclusively inhabited by Slovenes should become an autonomous unit under Yugoslav sovereignty, and the city of

29. Tito, 8:269, 270, 271.

Trieste by itself should become another autonomous unity under Italian sovereignty. And Tito concluded:

> If they [the Western powers] will also pass over this proposal as they did over all previous ones, then it means that they do not want peace in this part of Europe, it means that they do not want our friendship, it means that they do not want to respect our interests, but on the contrary, that they are making every effort to satisfy the imperialistic appetites of Italian imperialism. Well, this is my answer to this problem.[30]

The next day, October 11, 1953, in his speech in Skopje, Tito further affirmed that "the moment the first Italian soldier enters Zone A we shall also enter it," and again appealed to Great Britain and the United States to revoke their decision.[31]

On October 12 Yugoslavia transmitted another note to Great Britain and the United States proposing a four-power conference on Trieste. The note underlined that the peace treaty with Italy recognized for Yugoslavia a special interest in Trieste, as well as in the whole FTT, and nominated Yugoslavia as a mandatory power over this territory. The British-American decision of October 8 was a one-sided disposition of Yugoslav rights and national interests and therefore constituted a violation of the peace treaty. It was also a breach of the principle of the sovereign equality of states laid down by the charter of the United Nations. The note asserted further that the Anglo-American decision had been directly connected with the Italian military demonstration along the Italian-Yugoslav border. Hence, acceptance of that decision by Italy on October 9, and statements made by the Italian government that the decision was only the first step for further demands on Yugoslav territory represented a new danger for Yugoslavia. Thus, "for its part, the Yugoslav Government would see in the carrying out of the said decision the passing over to open aggressive action by the Republic of Italy." The duty and the right of Yugoslavia, continued the note, was to resort to self-defense. However, to prevent a military clash the Yugoslav government proposed direct talks to the governments of Great Britain, America, and Italy. The note concluded "that the proposed conference would be objectless, in case the decision . . . of

30. Ibid., pp. 276–77.   31. Ibid., 8:290.

October 8, would be meanwhile carried into effect."[32] On the same day, October 12, 1953, Yugoslavia conveyed a similar note to Italy, and a memorandum to the United Nations secretary general. The last was more elaborate, informing him about the events in Trieste and the dangers involved. The Yugoslav government again pointed out that it would consider entry of the Italian army into Zone A as an act of aggression. However, to avoid armed self-defense the Yugoslav government had proposed a conference of four interested powers to find a peaceful solution.[33]

The main causes for such violent Yugoslav reaction were the following: Marshal Tito's pride and the pride of the Yugoslav people were deeply hurt by the unilateral decision. Yugoslavia was not a party to the October 8 decision, as she had not been to the Tripartite Proposal of March 1948 nor to the London Agreement of May 1952. The Yugoslavs regarded these decisions as an inheritance of the imperialistic policy of the Great Powers, who had been determining the destiny of smaller nations without consulting them.[34] Moreover, the Yugoslavs protested because the October 8 decision did not state that the settlement was to be final. In the eyes of the Yugoslavs nothing was said about the future of Zone B, the protection of the Slovenian minority in Zone A, and the safeguarding of Yugoslav economic interests in Trieste. Thus the October 8 announcement fell short of talks that British Foreign Minister Eden had had with Tito in September 1952. Eden himself blamed American Secretary of State Dulles for this discrepancy.[35]

On October 12, 1953, the Soviet Union also protested against the October 8 decision in a note transmitted to the governments of Great Britain and the United States. According to the note, the October 8 decision "constitutes a flagrant violation of the terms of the Peace Treaty with Italy." The partition of the FTT "is incompatible with the task of maintaining peace and security and

32. The note is reprinted in the *New York Times,* Oct. 13, 1953 (© 1953 by The New York Times Company; reprinted by permission), and in *Documents on International Affairs, 1953,* pp. 297–98.

33. *Relazioni internazionali,* 17, no. 42 (Oct. 17, 1953): 1002–3; Duroselle, *Le Conflit de Trieste,* pp. 390–91.

34. See, for example, Jeri, pp. 266–68.

35. Eden, pp. 204–5.

is only capable of causing fresh complications." The facts showed that the decision of October 8 led "to an intensification of friction in the relations between states, and in the first place between countries bordering on the Free Territory of Trieste."[36]

Instead of solving the problem the October 8 announcement created a new crisis. The Italian and Yugoslav armies were facing each other, with about fifty thousand soldiers lined up along the border. The danger of armed conflict was real. The British and American governments anticipated some Yugoslav protests but were taken by surprise by such a vehement reaction. Both did their utmost to prevent an outbreak of hostilities. France conveniently played an intermediary role, as she had not been a party to the October 8 decision. The Great Powers assured Yugoslavia that the British-American troops intended to remain in Trieste for some time. Moreover, the powers would take into account justifiable Yugoslav grievances. Yugoslavia should get a pledge that the Great Powers would not support any further Italian claims. Yugoslav rights to a free port in Trieste should be confirmed and a special guarantee should be given to the Slovenian minority. The Western powers were pleased with the Yugoslav proposal to call a four-power conference but Yugoslavia insisted that she would participate only if the decision of October 8 was not carried out.

Italy meanwhile accepted the proposal to participate in a conference but added two conditions. It should be a conference of five, instead of four, including also France, and second, the October 8 decision should be put into effect before the conference met. The British, French, and American diplomats were trying their best to achieve a compromise between the opposing Yugoslav and Italian requirements. This demanded a lot of work, and the passing of time made the Italians suspicious that the decision of October 8 would remain another unfulfilled promise similar to that given in the Tripartite Proposal of March 1948. During the meeting of the Organization for European Economic Cooperation in Paris on October 29 and October 30 Pella met French Foreign Minister Georges Bidault from whom he learned that Great Britain and the United States might give in to Yugoslav demands and

36. For text see *Documents on International Affairs, 1953*, pp. 295–96.

call a conference without previously carrying out the plan of October 8. Italian Prime Minister Pella became nervous. On October 30, 1953, he sent a telegram to his ambassadors in London and Washington urging them to repeat to the governments of the United States and Great Britain that Italy would not participate in any conference before the announcement of October 8 was carried out. Moreover, the ambassadors should explain that the hesitation of the British and American governments to implement the above decision had created an impression among Italians that the two Great Powers had no real intention of putting the announcement into force. Hence, the Italians must ask themselves how far they could still trust the word of the American and British governments. Tarchiani, the Italian ambassador in Washington, transmitted Pella's message to John Foster Dulles on November 3, 1953. The action greatly irritated Dulles, and Tarchiani questioned if the "harsh and nervous attitude of the Italian government" served to improve such a difficult and confused situation. Tarchiani therefore advised Pella to take a more conciliatory attitude.[37]

BLOODY DAYS IN TRIESTE

The British-American decision was announced in Zone A on the day of its issuance, October 8, 1953. At 6:00 P.M., Trieste radio broadcast the two-power statement together with a special message by the zone commander General Winterton, which read:

> The statement is clear and concise and it is not necessary for me to enlarge upon it. I would, however, like especially to draw your attention to the final sentence. The date on which the changes provided for in the statement will come into effect has not yet been fixed. But it is certain that it will not be long-delayed. In the meantime the administration of Zone A will remain exactly as it is now.
>
> I call upon all the citizens of the Zone to remain tranquil and to continue at their daily tasks during this period. Many uncertainties may be felt, but I am confident that with the good-will of all concerned they can be overcome. This is not the first time that we have been called upon to face a changed

37. Tarchiani, pp. 291–96; see also *Relazioni internazionali,* 17, no. 46 (Nov. 14, 1953): 1081–82; and Duroselle, *Le Conflit de Trieste,* pp. 396, 398–402.

situation at short notice, and I rely on the people of Trieste and all Zone A with their traditional understanding and long history to give me their loyal cooperation during this period of transition.[38]

The October 8 decision caused shock, perplexity, and nervousness to all the inhabitants of Zone A. It was bad news for the independentists and especially for the Slovenes. But not even the pro-Italian political parties rejoiced. Many Triestines worried about their economic future. The next few days, when Yugoslavia moved troops into Zone B, closed the border between the two zones, and encircled Zone A with her military units, brought still greater tension and worries.

The October 8 statement not only failed to produce any pro-Italian manifestation but split, at least for a few days, Trieste's pro-Italian political parties. All annexationists were greatly concerned for the Italians living in Zone B. The pro-Italian Right was of the opinion that Italy should accept the offer and later press for Zone B. The center coalition (Christian Democrats, Liberals, Republicans, and Saragat Socialists) instead asked the Italian government to refuse the two-power decision. Of the same opinion were the CLN for Istria and De Castro, the Italian political adviser to the AMG. In a special declaration sent to Pella, the above groups argued that acceptance of the two-power decision would mean burial of the Tripartite Proposal of March 1948 and renunciation of Zone B.

Pella explained that the Italian government was in no position to reject the October 8 decision. He assured the Trieste center political parties that by accepting the two-power declaration Italy would retain her right to Zone B and promised to continue demanding a plebiscite for the entire FTT limited to the inhabitants born before 1918, as proposed by the Trieste annexationists.

De Castro was dissatisfied and decided to resign from his post. Later, however, he was persuaded to remain. The annexationist parties were more or less content with Pella's promises. They accepted Italy's occupation of Zone A as long as Italy did not renounce Italian territory in Zone B.[39]

38. Dunham, p. 74.
39. Cesare, *Trieste*, no. 29, p. 8; *Relazioni internazionali*, 17, no. 42 (Oct. 17, 1953): 995, 996, 998.

In the beginning a similar lack of enthusiasm was reflected in the writings of annexationist newspapers. *Giornale di Trieste* stated on October 9:

> The Allied decision to hand over Zone A to Italy does not solve the problem of Trieste ... It may almost be termed a tactical surprise, levelled above all at Belgrade. ... The Italian Government ... does not give up its right to Zone B ... and maintains its demand for an equal and direct plebiscite to be held in the entire FTT ... Independentism will inevitably meet the end it deserves. . . .[40]

On October 10, the tone changed and the *Giornale di Trieste* came out in favor of the October 8 decision. Reporting on Pella's speech to the Italian parliament on October 9, the newspaper asserted that "this was one of the most memorable days." During Pella's speech Trieste's Mayor Bartoli was sitting in the Italian parliament where "the long awaited return of Trieste to the motherland was announced." From that time on the pro-Italian press stressed that Trieste was legally already part of Italy.[41]

Though pro-Italian newspapers began to praise the October 8 statement there were still no spontaneous public manifestations. Only on October 12 could there be seen occasional bands of students singing pro-Italian songs, but the rest of the city remained quiet and almost gloomy. Many Triestines knew that their economic well-being came directly or indirectly from the presence of the Allied troops and the AMG. About six thousand AMG civil policemen were receiving comparatively high wages. They might be kept in service by the Italian government but for less pay or they might not be kept at all. Apart from the people directly employed by the AMG, merchants, dock workers, food shops, and the entertainment industry profited from the presence of the Allies. Combined British and American expenditures amounted to fifteen million dollars annually. Moreover, everyone in Trieste knew that there was a critical unemployment problem in other Italian cities and everyone was also aware that the Italian government would not spend as much money as the Allied governments had been doing.[42]

40. Dunham, p. 75.   41. Ibid., p. 76.
42. *New York Times,* Oct. 10, 11, 13, 1953.

FROM VIOLENCE TO COMPROMISE

The independentist political parties and groups all vehemently protested the October 8 decision. The Triestino Bloc and the Independence Front especially pointed to the economic ruin which would paralyze Trieste's life. The Slovenian democrats feared Italians would hinder their cultural and economic development. The Titoists used arguments similar to those of Yugoslavia. The October statement was, according to the Titoists, a unilateral breach of commitments and a transfer to Italy of rights which the British and Americans could not dispose of. The Cominformists stressed that "the great majority of the population begins to realise that the Communists were right" when asserting that only the establishment of the FTT could save the Italians of Zone B. The result of the October decision, the Cominformists continued, was that the nationalist leaders in Italy stressed satisfaction, while the pro-Italian nationalist leaders in Zone A declared themselves opposed "to the Anglo-American decision because it spells doom for the population of Zone B."[43]

The democratic Slovenes and pro-Titoists formed a "committee for the FTT," and held protest meetings in the Slovenian communes on October 13. For the next day all the independentist political parties planned a great protest meeting in the center of Trieste. However, at 8:00 P.M. on October 13, General Winterton let his message be broadcast prohibiting all public meetings, in order to prevent disorders. Some two thousand Slovenes disobeyed the ban and protested against the October 8 decision in the center of Trieste on October 14. The next day Slovenian students continued with demonstrations for a free Trieste. Italian youths enraged by Slovenian protests invaded the offices of the Yugoslav economic delegation and broke windows and hurled out furniture.[44]

All kinds of rumors spread among the Trieste population from the middle of October until November 3, 1953, the first of the four most tragic days of the entire AMG administration. The independentist press reported that Italian soldiers in civilian clothes were secretly coming to Trieste and that leaflets were being prepared for distribution urging the Italians to come out on the streets to take part in the patriotic action, for which arms were

43. Dunham, pp. 78–83.
44. Ibid., pp. 100–105; *New York Times,* Oct. 14, 15, 16, 1953.

about to arrive. The annexationist *Giornale di Trieste* informed the public of the infiltration of extraneous Yugoslav elements, preparing to take over Zone A for Yugoslavia. On October 22 the same newspaper reported that Cominformist leader Vidali had said that if the Yugoslavs entered Zone A, Trieste's Communists would fight against Yugoslavia because the "Italian army has never threatened to hang us." On November 3 both independentist newspapers, *Il Corriere di Trieste* and *Primorski dnevnik*, warned the AMG to be alert because Italian extremists were preparing a coup d'état.[45]

November 3 would be the right day for such a coup. It was the traditional feast of San Giusto, the patron saint of Trieste, and thirty-five years earlier on this day the first Italian soldiers had disembarked in the city. Mayor Bartoli was preparing a great celebration of this anniversary, as in March 1952. He expressed to the AMG his intention to fly the Italian flag from the city hall for that occasion. When General Winterton explicitly prohibited such action on any public building, the Italian foreign ministry intervened and contacted the British embassy in Rome on November 2, pointing out that the banning of Italian flags might cause incidents. But neither General Winterton nor the British government changed their minds. Both were well aware that the Yugoslavs might interpret the flying of Italian flags from public buildings as a sign that Italy had taken over the administration of Zone A. Only ten days earlier Tito had said in an interview with a correspondent of Agence France Presse: "If Italy obtains the administration of Zone A this would be the same as military occupation. In this case our decision to let our troops march into Zone A does not change."[46] Hence General Winterton and the British government determined to remain firm to prevent any further international conflagration.

In spite of the explicit prohibition Mayor Bartoli hoisted the Italian flag on the city hall tower on the morning of November 3, but shortly afterwards American police officer Colonel Villanti removed the flag. During the late morning, Bishop Santin celebrated a mass at San Giusto Cathedral observing the feast of the city patron. At the end of the mass some two hundred people formed a procession acclaiming Italy. They were immedi-

45. Dunham, pp. 106–20.   46. Ibid., p. 108.

ately disbanded by the police. Around 5:00 P.M. another procession was formed marching toward the monument dedicated to Trieste's Italian poet Rossetti. A young man climbed to the top of the statue and placed the Italian flag around the neck of Rossetti. The police disbanded the crowd and removed the flag from the statue's neck. With these small-scale manifestations, the first day ended with the demonstrators gaining no significant popular support.[47]

On November 4, 1953, the Committee for the Defense of the Italianity of Trieste and Istria, under the leadership of Mayor Bartoli, organized a convoy consisting of some 50 busses, 150 cars, and 50 motorscooters, which left Trieste about 8:00 A.M. for the military cemetery in Redipuglia, Italy, just across the border of Zone A, to attend the armistice ceremonies. Inflamed by patriotic speeches, emotions reached a high pitch. After the commemoration many Irredentists and neo-Fascists from Italy mingled with Italians from Trieste and entered Zone A. In the early afternoon some one thousand people gathered at the railway station after their return from Redipuglia. From here they marched to the main square, the Piazza Unità, carrying Italian flags at their head and singing patriotic songs. The crowd stopped before the city hall and tried to raise the Italian flag on the building. The civil police under command of British Major M. H. R. Carragher dispersed the demonstrators and seized the flag. During the early evening hours groups of one to two hundred persons gathered at different places of the city and threw stones at the civil police. The police had to use clubs to disperse them. One British cinema was stoned, and a Slovenian printing house and the seat of the Independence Front were attacked. Nine demonstrators received injuries requiring hospital treatment, and one policeman was injured by a stone. Seventeen persons were arrested.[48]

Next day, November 5, 1953, the first victims fell. It all began quite innocently with students playing truant, roaming the streets and compelling other students to go on strike. However, it was noticed that dispatch cars were used for liaison among student groups demonstrating in different parts of the city. It was evident

47. A timetable of the events of November 3, 1953, is in ibid., p. 122, and local (Trieste) press reaction in ibid., pp. 130–35.

48. For a timetable of the events of November 4, 1953, and AMG press releases no. 2620 and no. 2621 see ibid., pp. 137–40.

that some older people, known for their nationalist fanaticism, were directing the student demonstrators. About 11:00 A.M. the students, with some older people, gathered before police headquarters next to the church of Sant'Antonio. The group of some three to five hundred demonstrators collected cobblestones being readied for the pavement of a roadway and stoned the police. Police charged the demonstrators and some rioters retreated into the church, and from there they continued to throw stones at the police. A few policemen pursued the demonstrators inside the church and evicted them. Bishop Santin regarded the act as a deconsecration of the church and ordered a reconsecration ceremony for the same afternoon at 4:30 P.M. Some five or six hundred persons came with the obvious purpose of attending the ceremonies. They were joined by a considerable number of the youths who had participated in the morning demonstrations. After the ceremonies had begun a large number of demonstrators remained on the steps of the church. With the arrival of the police these demonstrators began again to throw stones at the police. The attack assumed serious proportions and extended to police headquarters. The commanding British Major Williams gave the order to fire a volley over the heads of the crowd to disperse them. However, some policemen aimed into the crowd. Two persons were killed and fifteen injured. By five o'clock the clash was over and the demonstrators were disbanded. Nevertheless small groups continued to attack British and police vehicles. Special targets were British establishments. Demonstrators threw stones at hotels housing British forces and their dependents, at a British cinema and two NAAFI (Navy, Army and Air Force Institutes) premises. They also smashed display windows of the Allied reading room, and attacked the Independence Front headquarters, the city hall, and zonal headquarters.

In protest against police brutalities the Italian labor union called a twenty-four-hour general strike for the next day, while Trieste's industrialists proclaimed a lockout.[49] The Allied communiqué, issued at 8:30 P.M., stated:

> General Winterton greatly regrets that the activities of irresponsible elements in Trieste to-day should have led to

---

49. For a timetable of the incidents of November 5, 1953, and for the AMG communiqué (press release no. 2622) see ibid., pp. 163–66.

a number of casualties. He wishes to assure the population of Trieste that he will take every measure needed to ensure that order is maintained. He is confident that the responsible members of the community will help in this task by remaining calm and exercising the utmost restraint."[50]

On November 6, the rioting reached its climax. The general strike and lockout which had become effective in the early morning hours aggravated the situation, as many people had had time to come into the streets. Early in the morning the AMG broadcast a special message from the zone commander: "General Winterton warns the people of Trieste not to allow themselves and their children to be exploited by irresponsible elements. In particular he asks them to keep their children off the streets."[51]

The first serious incident took place in the center of the city at about 9:30 A.M. when a group of demonstrators disarmed police personnel on guard at the Titoist printing press. They captured a carbine and two pistols and fired them into the premises. About an hour later a large mob gathered in front of the headquarters of the Independence Front. Demonstrators broke into the building, smashed the offices, threw the furniture out of the window and set it on fire. The building itself was saved by the arrival of the fire brigade. British and United States troops were then called out to protect the AMG buildings and to support the police but they were held in reserve.

When their resentment against independentism was satisfied the rioters moved along Corso Street to the Piazza Unità where the two centers of civil administration were located. At the city hall the Italian flag was flying and Mayor Bartoli with his pro-Italian municipal board was in the building, thus satisfying the rioters. But the other building, the prefecture and seat of zonal administration, was guarded by civil police and no Italian flag was visible on it. Thus it attracted the mob's attention.

Rioters began to throw stones at the police, who attempted to charge and disband them but were compelled to withraw under a heavy hail of stones. This encouraged the rioters. They attacked the police with hand grenades. The police returned the fire. Two persons were killed and some thirty injured. The demonstrators

50. Ibid., p. 166.   51. Ibid., p. 203.

were pushed into the side streets but not disbanded. One hour later, about 12:30 P.M., the rioters returned to the Piazza Unità and attacked the police again in front of the prefecture with hand grenades. A short but violent clash resulted in two more deaths and some forty wounded. British and American troops then moved to the Piazza Unità, and relative calm was restored. Meanwhile a British major accompanied by fourteen civil policemen entered the municipal building and removed the Italian flags from the balcony and the tower. Mayor Bartoli and the board members protested but the major would not discuss the matter.

Shortly after 3:00 P.M. demonstrators began to reassemble in the Piazza Unità. At 4:00 P.M. came a new clash between the rioters and police. The demonstrators threw more hand grenades at policemen and burned two police trucks. Police fired warning shots and dispersed the demonstrators. Wire horses were put around AMG buildings and the prefecture, and Allied authorities made it clear that the troops would open fire if rioters tried to cross the wire horses. In the afternoon police raided the neo-Fascists' headquarters and seized their documents. During the evening small groups of demonstrators still circulated through the town but the rioting was dying out. By 8:00 P.M. the city was quiet, and the riots had ended.[52]

The next day, November 7, remained peaceful and the AMG could release the following communiqué:

> Today is calm and the responsible people of the city have shown their determination that all members of the community must resume their normal lives.
>
> Gen. Winterton hopes that calm will continue to prevail and in this he is joined by a message from the Department of State in Washington which says: "We hope that the Trieste people will recognize their responsibility fully to cooperate with the Zone Commander in the discharge of his responsibilities to maintain order."[53]

52. A timetable of the incidents of November 6, 1953, the special message of the zone commander (press release no. 2623), and the press release no. 2624 about events are in *ibid.*, pp. 201–4.

53. Press release no. 2625 (November 7, 1953), *ibid.*, p. 257. On November rioting see also *Keesing's Contemporary Archives,* 9:13292–94; Berti, ed., pp. 111–36.

The Italian government protested to Great Britain and the United States against the use of firearms and demanded the immediate recall of General Winterton. The Trieste riots caused anti-British demonstrations in major Italian cities on November 6 and 7. The mobs demanded the ouster of General Winterton and the immediate execution of the October 8 decision.[54]

To the question of responsibility for the Trieste riots the Italians, British, independentists, and Yugoslavs gave different answers. The Italian government directly blamed the AMG, especially General Winterton, and indirectly the British government. The Italian report of the official investigation of events, issued on November 8, 1953, underlined that the "student manifestations" were a spontaneous expression of resentment and not organized in advance. The prohibition against displaying the Italian flag on the city hall to celebrate a patriotic anniversary especially sacred to the Trieste population, caused this resentment. The profanation of the church, and the subsequent police disturbance of the reconsecration were other factors which added to the resentment and brought feelings to a boiling point. The resulting incidents took place only because of the brutal intervention of the riot police, always too quick to use firearms when it was not necessary. There would have been no victims, for there would have been no cause for riots, if the British government had listened to Italian warnings and had permitted the Italian flag to be hoisted on the city hall. So concluded the Italian official report.[55]

On the other side British Foreign Minister Eden blamed the Italians exclusively for the riots in his statement to the House of Commons on November 9, 1953. He expressed full support for General Winterton, who had faithfully carried out his responsibilities, and praised the police for showing admirable discipline and restraint in the face of extreme provocation. According to Eden the riots were organized, at least partly, from outside of Zone A. On November 3 and 4 the AMG turned back about three thousand persons attempting to enter Zone A from Italy in organized parties. But in spite of this, large numbers succeeded in entering the zone and took part in the riots. Irresponsible elements ex-

54. *New York Times,* Nov. 7, 8, 1953.
55. The report is reprinted in *Relazioni internazionali,* 17, no. 46 (Nov. 14, 1953): 1097–99.

ploited Italian national anniversaries to provoke incidents. They aimed at causing the breakdown of law and order and the disruption of local security forces. Hence the riot was not a spontaneous expression of emotions but an organized action. When the students came out on strike their activities were organized by older men, members of the neo-Fascist party. The British government, asserted Eden, made it clear to the Italian government that the latter should do all in its power to curb these irresponsible elements. Therefore, Eden concluded, "the sole responsibility for these tragic results must rest with those extremist elements who deliberately provoked and organized these disorders."[56]

The Yugoslavs interpreted the riots in a broader context. Vehement Yugoslav opposition to the October 8 decision had resulted in postponement of the Italian occupation of Zone A, the Yugoslavs asserted. This move had caused great dissatisfaction among the right-wing supporters of Pella. Moreover, the lack of enthusiasm in Trieste for Italian occupation had produced a need for tangible proof that the majority of the inhabitants of Trieste wanted annexation to Italy. To remedy this situation the Italian government, with the cooperation of Trieste's nationalists, resorted to the old precedent of March 1952, hoping it would work again. The armistice anniversary was a convenient occasion to organize demonstrations to prove that Triestines were in the majority pro-Italian, and to impress the Allies with the argument that peace would be retained only by an immediate transfer of Zone A to Italy.[57]

For the independentists the riots were an attempted coup d'état which had failed. They asserted that the Italian government and Trieste's Mayor Bartoli had carefully prepared a plan, according to which the Irredentists would take over the administration of Zone A by seizing police headquarters and the building of the prefecture—the seat of zonal government—the city hall being already in the hands of the mayor. By this action the Allies would face an accomplished fact. Following their basic concept, the independentists gave a unique interpretation to the events of November 3 to 6. The purpose of the flag-raising on the city hall and of the armistice anniversary celebration was to stir up na-

56. *Documents on International Affairs, 1953*, pp. 298–300.
57. See Jeri, p. 278.

tional emotions and get mass support for future actions. On November 5, well-organized small groups of fanatic nationalists, many belonging to the neo-Fascist movement, were operating among the demonstrating students, causing small clashes and keeping the police engaged in different parts of the city. Meanwhile the main body approached police headquarters and tried to storm it. They had been assured that there would be no serious resistance. However, the vigilance of British police officers prevented the plot. The reconsecration services in the afternoon, whether planned or not, gave the conspirators a second chance to attack police headquarters but they were again firmly repulsed.

Proclamation of the general strike and the still more effective lockout brought many more people into the streets. The next day the Irredentists centered their attack on the prefecture, hoping it would be easier to take than the well-garrisoned police headquarters. But the prefecture was also guarded by reinforced police units and all three attacks were repulsed.

According to the independentists the coup failed because the people did not give mass support to the Irredentists. The greatest crowds they could gather were five to six thousand and not twenty thousand or more as had been reported by the foreign press. The energetic protest of the British government, and the support given to General Winterton by the British with the concurrence of the United States, forced the Italian government to call off further disturbances. The Trieste Irredentists obeyed immediately. The abrupt end of the rioting was the best proof that it had been organized, whereas a spontaneous uprising could not be called off, the independentists asserted.

Each of the above interpretations was to a certain degree partial to its own cause and prejudicial to the others. The events had natural dynamics of their own. Mayor Bartoli organized with his "Committee for the Defense of Italianity" the armistice celebration, but later the events might well have gone out of his control, with the right-wing nationalists taking over. As admirers of D'Annunzio's strong hand policy the latter could have tried to perform a coup d'état. The Italian government might have gone through the same change. By its own statement, the Italian government knew of Bartoli's plans and there were good reasons Pella might desire some peaceful manifestation in Trieste in support of his demand of October 30 that the Western powers hand over administration of Zone A to Italy before the meeting of the five-power conference. However, when the manifestations went out of control and became bloody, the Italian government condemned the excesses.

Whenever emotions replace reason, foolish actions take place. One such was the reconsecration ceremony. Bishop Santin could easily have postponed for a few days the reconsecration of Sant' Antonio church, until a time when emotions had calmed down. By failing to do so he exposed himself to accusations that he had intentionally supported the riots.

It was true that the police used harsh methods and were trigger-happy, but times were tense. It should be remembered that Italian and Yugoslav military forces were patrolling the border and any small incident might ignite a war. Hence the police needed to keep order at any price. It has to be recognized that a much greater disaster could have occurred if General Winterton had been less firm and the police had used milder methods. Because both the commander of the zone and the head of police were English, the rioters blamed Great Britain for harshness and brutality, while the United States was regarded more as a bystander though it had backed General Winterton's actions.

Regarding the spontaneity, it should be noted that in the beginning the people joined the manifestations because they had been organized, but later many participated because their national emotions were offended, and some fought because they were paid for it. The following episode proves the last point.

Some ten days after the rioting six or seven men in their early twenties surrounded a well-dressed man in his forties behind the Portici di Chiozza, in the center of the city, and protested because they still had not received the money promised for their participation in the riots. The discussion became very heated and the young men threatened to disclose the entire story to AMG authorities if they did not get the money in the next few days. The older man tried to calm them by explaining that the committee had not yet received the money from Italy. He neither specified the committee nor from whom in Italy the money was to come.

But not all pro-Italian groups in Trieste favored the manifestations which had turned into riots. De Castro, the Italian political adviser to the AMG, did his utmost to prevent disorders and disagreements with the British-American administration. How could we face Tito, De Castro argued, if we quarreled with our allies? He also warned Pella of the dangers involved in planned armistice celebrations, but Pella paid no attention to De Castro's admonitions, at least in the beginning.

The riots caused a split among the pro-Italian political parties and groups in Trieste. The progovernmental or center political parties continued to demand that the Italian government defend Italian rights to Zone B during any future negotiations. The right-wing political parties instead changed their policy. Discouraged and frightened by recent events, they were prepared to accept any compromise as long as it would bring Italian soldiers to the Piazza Unità.[58]

If the purpose of the riots was to achieve the transfer of Zone A to Italy before the conference on the Trieste question met, the disturbances failed to attain their goal. Nevertheless the riots convinced the Western Allies that the Trieste problem needed an urgent solution.

THE LONG NEGOTIATIONS

In order to obtain a durable solution the Western powers had to solve three problems during the remaining months of 1953. They had to normalize Italo-Yugoslav relations, refuse a Soviet proposal in the United Nations, and bring both Italy and Yugoslavia to the conference table.

During November 1953 the Western powers succeeded in lessening tensions between Italy and Yugoslavia and at the beginning of December both states agreed to recall their troops from the border. The withdrawal was completed by December 20.[59]

As I mentioned, on October 12, 1953, Yugoslavia notified the secretary general of the United Nations that she would bring the Trieste problem before the Security Council if her proposal for a four-power conference were refused. The same day the Soviet Union sent a letter of protest against the October 8 decision to

58. Cesare, *Trieste,* no. 29, p. 8.
59. *New York Times,* Dec. 6 and 21, 1953; *Keesing's Contemporary Archives,* 9:13295, 13328.

Great Britain and the United States. On October 13, the Soviet Union demanded that the Security Council discuss the Trieste question. In her note the Soviet Union demanded that the Security Council elect Trieste's governor and put the FTT on a permanent basis, as prescribed in the Italian peace treaty, within three months. The Soviet Union proposed as governor Colonel Hermann Flückiger from Switzerland, who had been suggested for this position by Great Britain in 1947. Though Italy and Yugoslavia faced each other with great hostility they had one thing in common: they both opposed the establishment of an FTT. Hence the Western powers could talk in the name of both interested states, Italy and Yugoslavia, by refusing the Soviet proposal.

The Security Council discussed the issue on October 20, when it decided to postpone the debate for two weeks to provide time for direct negotiations. The Soviet delegate, Andrei Vyshinsky, protested, as he saw urgent need for discussion to prevent a threatening war in Europe. The debate on Trieste was again postponed on November 2, and also on November 23. Finally on December 14 it was postponed ad infinitum.[60]

The most difficult of the three tasks was the organization of Italian-Yugoslav negotiations. As Italy had agreed to participate in a five-power conference only if the October 8 decision were to be carried out and Yugoslavia had insisted she would attend only on condition that the decision not be put into effect, Great Britain, the United States, and France had to search for a compromise. On November 13, 1953, the three powers submitted a new suggestion to Belgrade and Rome. During the conference some AMG positions would be taken over by Italian officials, while the supreme authority would remain vested in the allied commander of the zone. Italy accepted the new proposition but Yugoslavia rejected it. On December 6 the three powers advanced a new but similar compromise, which was again refused by Yugoslavia. Afterwards, during the second half of December, Great Britain and the United States abandoned the plan for a five-power conference, convinced that French-Italian connivance was hindering an agreement with

60. *Keesing's Contemporary Archives,* 9:13195, 13295; *New York Times,* Oct. 14, 15, 16, 21, Nov. 3, 24, Dec. 15, 1953; *Department of State Bulletin,* 29 (Nov. 2, 1953): 609–10, and 30 (January 11, 1954): 70.

FROM VIOLENCE TO COMPROMISE

Yugoslavia. In addition France and Italy were quite reluctant to ratify the EDC treaty.[61]

Because of the above reasons the United States and Great Britain prepared a new plan, according to which negotiations would be conducted in three consecutive stages on an ambassadorial level in London or Washington. The representatives of Great Britain, the United States, and Yugoslavia, the states which were administering the FTT, would meet first. Here the Western powers would seek a reasonable solution with Yugoslavia. Then the two powers would present the results to Italy and negotiate with her. Finally the British and Americans would be intermediaries between Italy and Yugoslavia to remove any remaining differences. The negotiations would remain strictly secret or, as the British foreign minister put it, "I hoped we might reach open covenants secretly arrived at."[62]

On January 4, 1954, the American and British ambassadors in Paris visited French Foreign Minister Georges Bidault to let him know that the Western powers had abandoned the five-power conference. Instead they would ask Italy to send a representative to one of the Western capitals, but beforehand they would sound out the Yugoslavs. Bidault protested because the decision had been made without French participation and decided that France would abstain for the time being. The two Western powers were looking for just such an answer. From this time until the very end of negotiations France did not play a role. But she was also preoccupied with her own troubles, especially the war in Indochina. In the middle of June 1954, France got a new prime minister, Pierre Mendès-France, who was also foreign minister. While Bidault had favored Italian claims to Trieste, Mendès-France was unconcerned about the problem.

The same day, January 4, 1954, the British and Americans notified Italy about their new plan, and on January 9 the two powers made it known to Yugoslavia. Both Italians and Yugoslavs accepted, and preferred London to Washington for the negotiations because it was closer to their own capitals, making it easier to keep the talks secret. Vladimir Velebit and Manlio Brosio, the

61. Jeri, pp. 279–80; Tarchiani, pp. 296–97; Duroselle, *Le Conflit de Trieste,* pp. 402–6.
62. Eden, p. 195.

Yugoslav and Italian ambassadors in London, represented their respective countries. The United States decided to appoint as its representative Llewellyn E. Thompson, American high commissioner in Vienna. The American ambassador in London, Julius Holmes, would have attracted too much attention and made it difficult to keep negotiations secret. The English representative was Geoffrey W. Harrison, assistant undersecretary of state in the British foreign office.[63]

By the end of January everything was prepared for the negotiations.[64] The talks between the Anglo-Americans and Yugoslavs began on February 2, and lasted until May 31, 1954. Neither side had much room for alternatives. The British-American position was well stated by British Foreign Minister Eden, who kept in close touch with the negotiators: "Our purpose was to persuade Yugoslavia to accept a frontier corresponding as closely as possible to the zonal boundaries. We had not much power of manoeuvre, because we could not present to the Italians anything that appeared less favourable than our proposals of October 8."[65] Tito on his part made it clear that any solution changing the status quo to the disadvantage of Yugoslavia would be unacceptable to her.[66]

During the first talks Velebit asserted Yugoslav rights to the entire FTT except for the city of Trieste, which could go together with rail and road connections to Italy. While not disputing the Yugoslav rights to this territory, Thompson and Harrison reminded Velebit that they all had come together to find a solution acceptable to both Yugoslavia and Italy. During the lengthy negotiations which followed the three representatives discussed a solution by reciprocal concessions in both zones. Velebit went as far as to cede to Italy the three towns in Zone B, Koper, Izola, and Piran, but only as enclaves inside Yugoslav territory without connection to Italy. For this concession the Yugoslavs demanded the hinterland of Zone A and an exit to the sea immediately south of Trieste, including Zaule, Servola, and Muggia. Thompson and Harrison would not go that far. Their major concession was to give the hinterland of Zone A to Yugoslavia for an Italian enclave

63. Duroselle, *Le Conflit de Trieste*, pp. 408-9.
64. For London negotiations see Tarchiani, pp. 299-317; Jeri, pp. 283-88; Duroselle, *Le Conflit de Trieste*, pp. 409-20.
65. Eden, p. 207.   66. Jeri, p. 284.

of the three towns in Zone B (Koper, Izola, Piran). They definitely refused an outlet to the sea south of Trieste in Zone A. The Yugoslavs did not regard this as an equal exchange and abandoned the idea of reciprocal concessions.

The second alternative was a division along the zonal boundary. Velebit proposed it with a small correction of the line in Yugoslavia's favor so that the Slovenes could build a new railroad connecting Koper with Slovenia. After some minor corrections the British-American negotiators accepted the new line. It would move the boundary for about a mile and a half of air distance from Cape Debeli rtič to Cape Punta Sottile on the seashore. For it the Yugoslavs would recompense Italy with a small triangle of land in Zone B in the interior along the zonal line. This was a realistic compromise between the British-American and Yugoslav positions. In the beginning of May the agreement was reached on all the points except the legal aspect. Yugoslavia demanded that the solution be regarded as final while the British and Americans wanted only a de facto agreement, knowing that Italy would otherwise refuse to accept. The United States and British governments finally persuaded Yugoslavia to accept a de facto solution by assuring her that the agreement would be a final one as far as the Great Powers were concerned because in the future they would not support any claims by either Italy or Yugoslavia. Decisive in the Yugoslav change of heart was the promise of twenty million dollars by the United States to which the British added two million pounds. This sum was allotted to help pay for construction of a Slovenian port in Zone B and for other necessities.[67]

After four months of negotiations an agreement was finally concluded among Great Britain, the United States, and Yugoslavia ending the first stage of negotiations. The two Great Powers had next to persuade Italy to accept the plan.

Meanwhile Italy went through a two-month-long internal crisis. On January 5, 1954, Prime Minister Pella resigned. Amintore Fanfani formed a new government on January 18 but lost a vote of confidence on January 30, whereupon Mario Scelba constituted another new government which was approved by the senate on February 26 and by the lower house on March 10. The new

---

67. Eden, pp. 207–8.

prime minister, who belonged to the center of his Christian Democratic party, concentrated on solving internal problems. His government was supported by the other three center parties, the Liberals, Republicans, and Saragat Socialists. In his program, presented to the Italian parliament on February 18, Scelba took a moderate stand toward the Trieste problem. He was for a just solution acceptable to both parties which would bring an end to the old controversy and open new possibilities for friendly cooperation between Italy and Yugoslavia. Then the economies of both countries could complement each other for the benefit of both.[68] By this means De Gasperi's obsession with the Tripartite Proposal and Pella's military pressures were replaced with a new realistic approach. In addition Scelba chose Attilio Piccioni, a Christian Democrat, as his foreign minister, the first time since Count Sforza had resigned in 1951 that the positions of prime minister and foreign minister had been separated.

The Italian political adviser to the AMG, Diego de Castro, disagreed with the new official policy and resigned on March 29, 1954. This time the government accepted his resignation and on April 10 appointed Marquis Cristoforo Fracassi as the new political adviser to the AMG.[69]

On June 1, 1954, Harrison and Thompson handed the plan to Italian Ambassador Manlio Brosio and informed a French diplomat about the results of the three-power talks. So began the second stage, the negotiations among Great Britain, the United States, and Italy, which went on until July 14 when Yugoslavia again rejoined the talks.

The plan presented to Brosio had seven points.

1. Military government in both zones to be replaced by Italian and Yugoslav civil administration in Zones A and B respectively.

2. A minor correction of the zonal border in favor of Yugoslavia.

3. The preservation of the free port in Trieste.

---

68. *Relazioni internazionali,* 18, no. 9 (Feb. 27, 1954): 211–14, and no. 11 (Mar. 13, 1954): 272.

69. Cesare, *Trieste,* no. 29, p. 8; Duroselle, *Le Conflit de Trieste,* p. 415. Jeri (p. 286) gives April 3, 1954, as the date of De Castro's resignation.

4. Reciprocal guarantees for national minorities.

5. No person to be persecuted for his efforts in regard to the establishment of the FTT.

6. Resolution of all pending financial questions between the two states.

7. Measures to better the atmosphere and facilitate cooperation between Italy and Yugoslavia.

The Allies stressed that all seven points were mutually interdependent.

Brosio communicated these conditions to his government. Italian Foreign Minister Piccioni called a meeting on June 9, 1954, to draft instructions to be sent to Brosio. On June 12, Brosio explained to Harrison and Thompson the position of his government. He pointed out Italian rights to the entire FTT, as Velebit had done during his first talks with British and American representatives. According to Brosio, prior to the peace conference the Western Allies had recognized the Italian right to a part of the Julian Region greater than the FTT. With the Tripartite Proposal the Western powers acknowledged the Italian right to the entire FTT. The October 8 statement promised the return of the entire Zone A to Italy. In all these instances the Western Allies had retreated from their prior promises because of Yugoslav pressures. Finally they proposed less than promised in the October 8 statement. Brosio underlined that no Italian government could accept this plan without jeopardizing its own existence as well as free democracy in Italy and her support for NATO and the European Community. Nevertheless the British and Americans persuaded Italy to accept the plan. The discussions which followed were limited to minor details, such as the statute for a free port in Trieste, minority guarantees, and territorial settlement. On July 7, 1954, Brosio made his territorial counterproposal. Italy was not much interested in the triangle of almost empty land of Zone B but instead demanded that the Punta Sottile on the Adriatic coast remain in Zone A.

On July 14, Harrison and Thompson explained to Velebit the Italian counterproposals. From this time on until October 5, the British and American representatives acted as intermediaries between Velebit and Brosio. This was the last or third stage of negotiations. By September 3, Yugoslavia and Italy agreed on all points except for the territorial issue. Neither of the two states was prepared to renounce its claims to Cape Punta Sottile, an area of about two square miles. To end the impasse President Eisenhower of the United States sent Undersecretary of State Robert Murphy to Belgrade with his personal letter for Tito, in which the president appealed to Tito for a small territorial concession in order to bring the Trieste problem to a desired solution. Murphy left for Belgrade on September 14, 1954, accompanied by Robert G. Hooker, a foreign service officer with special knowledge of Yugoslavia. During the talks Yugoslavs abandoned their claim to Punta Sottile and offered two alternative solutions. According to the first the border would be moved immediately south of Punta Sottile so as to leave the village of Lazzaretto (Lazaret), situated on the coast between the two capes, to Yugoslavia, and Italy would obtain the triangle of Zone B. The second alternative would move the border farther to the south, somewhere in the middle between the Punta Sottile and Debeli rtič, leaving Lazzaretto to Italy but without compensation with land from Zone B. Because Yugoslavia had a very bad harvest Murphy had been authorized to offer assistance, if circumstances justified. Hence, after the Trieste issue was settled he informed the Yugoslav Deputy Foreign Minister Aleš Bebler that the United States would be willing to deliver 400,000 tons of wheat to Yugoslavia. On September 18, 1954, Murphy flew to Rome where he presented the two alternatives. He talked with Prime Minister Scelba, the new Foreign Minister Gaetano Martino, who had just taken over the position after Piccioni's resignation, and with the secretary general of the foreign ministry, Vittorio Zoppi. Scelba promised to present both alternatives to his cabinet.[70] A few days later the Italian council of ministers chose the second alternative. By the first days of October the agreement was put into its final wording and communicated to France. On October 5, 1954, the Yugoslav, Italian, British, and American representatives initialed the so-called Memorandum of Understanding in London.

70. Robert Murphy, *Diplomat among Warriors* (New York, 1965), pp. 470–73; Eden, pp. 208–9.

FROM VIOLENCE TO COMPROMISE

THE SECOND LONDON AGREEMENT

The Memorandum of Understanding had nine articles and two annexes.[71] The first article gave the reason for the agreement in an introductory statement. Because "it has proved impossible to put into effect the provisions of the Italian Peace Treaty relating to the Free Territory of Trieste," Great Britain, the United States, and Yugoslavia had occupied and administered Zones A and B since the end of the war. As the military administration was intended to be only temporary the four principal governments concerned (British, American, Yugoslav, and Italian) had consulted together on "how best to bring the present unsatisfactory situation to an end."

Articles 2 and 3 referred to the territorial settlement. Within three weeks from the initialing of this agreement the representatives of the AMG and YMG were to carry out a preliminary demarcation of the new border separating the two zones. The Italian and Yugoslav governments were immediately to appoint a boundary commission to effect a more precise border demarcation. As mentioned above, Yugoslavia got a strip of land in Zone A about half a mile to a mile and a half wide and a bit under five miles long. The new border was drawn on the map which formed Annex I.

As soon as the preliminary demarcation of the new border had been carried out the three occupying powers "will terminate military government in Zones A and B." Great Britain and the United States would withdraw their armed forces from Zone A, north of the new boundary, and "will relinquish the administration of that area to the Italian government. The Italian and Yugoslav governments will forthwith extend civil administration over the area for which they will have responsibility."

Article 4 stated that Italian and Yugoslav governments agreed to enforce the Special Statute contained in Annex II. The statute tried to safeguard the minorities by a detailed description of minority rights.

To assure Trieste's continuation as the port for its historical hinterland Article 5 stated that the Italian government would

71. For the text of the Memorandum of Understanding see *Department of State Bulletin*, 31 (Oct. 18, 1954): 556–61.

"maintain the Free Port at Trieste in general accordance with the provisions of Articles 1–20 of Annex VIII of the Italian Peace Treaty."

According to Article 6 the Italian and Yugoslav governments agreed that they would not prosecute or discriminate against persons for their past political activities in connection with the solution of the FTT problem.

Within a period of two months, Article 7 stated, the Italian and Yugoslav governments were to enter into negotiations for an agreement facilitating and regulating the local border traffic.

Article 8 provided that persons formerly resident in the areas coming under administration of either Italy or Yugoslavia would be free to return to their old homes during one year, that is until October 5, 1955. Residents who decided to leave would be permitted to take their movable property and transfer their credit received for immovable property for a period of two years.

Article 9 made it known that "the Memorandum of Understanding will be communicated to the Security Council of the United Nations."

The Special Statute, forming Annex II, had eight articles and was signed by Brosio and Velebit. The introductory paragraph asserted that "it is the common intention of the Italian and Yugoslav Governments to ensure human rights and fundamental freedoms without discrimination of race, sex, language and religion in the areas coming under their administration." Article 1 asserted that fundamental rights and freedoms were to be interpreted as defined in the Universal Declaration of Human Rights adopted by the General Assembly of the United Nations on December 10, 1948. Article 2 stated that the Yugoslav minority in the Italian zone and the Italian minority in the Yugoslav zone "shall enjoy equality of rights and treatment with the other inhabitants of the two areas." This meant equal access to public and administrative offices and "a fair representation in administrative positions, and especially in those fields, such as the inspectorate of schools, where the interests of such inhabitants are particularly involved." Each minority was also to enjoy equal treatment with regard to a trade or profession in agriculture, commerce, industry, or any other field, and equal opportunity to organize and operate economic associations and organizations for this purpose. The minorities were to enjoy the same kind of social assistance and pensions as other citizens, including sickness benefits, old age and disability pensions, pensions for disabilities resulting from war, and pensions to the dependents of those killed in war.

To bring peaceful coexistence between the Italians and Yugoslavs, Article 3 stated that "incitement to national and racial hatred in the two areas is forbidden and any such act shall be punished."

Article 4 dealt with the safeguarding of "the ethnic character and the unhampered cultural development" of Yugoslav and Italian minorities. Each ethnic group would have the right to its own press in its mother tongue, and to its "educational, cultural, social and sport organizations." Special attention was given to schools and to the use of minority languages. The Yugoslav and Italian governments agreed to maintain the existing kindergartens, primary, secondary, and professional schools teaching in the minority tongue. Attached to the Special Statute was a list of all Slovenian schools functioning in the area coming under Italian administration and a list of Italian schools existing in the area coming under the Yugoslav administration. These minority schools were to enjoy equality of treatment with other schools as regards provision of textbooks, buildings, and other material means, the number and position of teachers, and the recognition of diplomas. The teaching was to be performed by teachers of the same mother tongue as the pupils.

Articles 5 and 7 stated that both minority groups should "be free to use their language in their personal and official relations with the administrative and judicial authorities," and they were to have the right to receive from the authorities a reply in the same language. Public documents, official announcements, public proclamations, and publications were to be accompanied by a translation in the minority tongue. "Inscriptions on public institutions and the names of localities and streets" would be in both languages (in the language of the administering authority and the ethnic minority) in those electoral districts of the commune of Trieste and in other communes where the minority group constituted at least one-quarter of the population. Furthermore, "no change should be made in the boundaries of the basic administrative units . . . with a view to prejudicing the ethnic composition of the units concerned." Article 6 asserted that the economic development of each ethnic group "shall be secured without discrimination and with a fair distribution of the available financial means."

The last article of the Special Statute provided for the establishment of a special Mixed Yugoslav-Italian Committee to deal with minority problems. "The Committee shall also examine complaints and questions raised by individuals belonging to the respective ethnic groups concerning the implementation of this Statute." The Yugoslav and Italian governments would grant the committee every facility for carrying out its responsibilities. Both governments also agreed to prepare detailed regulations for the functioning of the above committee.[72]

While the Memorandum of Understanding and its two annexes were published, some confidential statements in the form of letters exchanged between the two Yugoslav and Italian ambassadors in London were kept concealed.

In his letter the Italian ambassador informed Velebit that the Italian government "will provide a house in Roiano or another suburb to be used as a cultural home for the Trieste Slovene Community, and will also make available funds for the construction and equipment of a new cultural home on Via Petronio. It is confirmed that the Narodni Dom at San Giovanni is also available for use as a cultural home." By it the Italian government restored to the Slovenes two national homes in Trieste's suburbs and promised to build a new one in the center of the city as compensation for the one burned down in July 1920. The Yugoslav ambassador in his letter informed Brosio that the Yugoslav government was also "prepared to give sympathetic consideration to requests of Italian cultural organizations for additional premises" in Zone B.[73]

A second Italo-Yugoslav exchange of letters established an Italian consular office in Koper and a Yugoslav consulate general in Trieste.[74] A third exchange of letters provided that Italy would pay to Yugoslavia in three-year installments the amount of thirty million dollars as settlement for reciprocal claims deriving from

72. For the text of regulations see Jeri, pp. 375–79.
73. The text of the two letters is given in ibid., pp. 371–73.
74. For the text of the two letters see ibid., pp. 373–74.

the Italian peace treaty.[75] The final financial settlement was signed in Belgrade on December 18, 1954.[76]

The Second London Agreement resolved three basic problems. It brought a territorial division of the FTT, assured that Trieste would remain a free port for its hinterland, and gave elaborate guarantees to the ethnic minorities. The clauses of the Special Statute regarding human rights and fundamental freedoms were primarily inserted to satisfy Italian complaints about conditions of their minority in Zone B. The detailed outline of the meaning of the principles of "equality of rights and treatment" and of the "safeguards of ethnic character and unhampered cultural development" aimed to calm Slovenian fears and to give them assurance that the national persecutions experienced so bitterly in the past would not be repeated.

Neither Italy nor Yugoslavia formally renounced its claims to the Free Territory. However, for the Great Powers the territorial settlement was final. When the official wording of the agreement was communicated to France, Prime Minister Mendès-France declared that the French government was pleased with the solution and would give its full support. London, Paris, and Washington issued separate official statements saying that in the future Great Britain, France, and the United States "will give no support to claims of either Yugoslavia or Italy to territory under the sovereignty or administration of the other." But they also added that the Great Powers were confident it would be possible for Yugoslavia and Italy "to resolve any outstanding problems by friendly negotiations in a spirit of mutual understanding."[77]

Soviet Russia also recognized the accord, which was a sharp policy shift from her previous opposition to a division of the FTT. The representative of the Soviet Union, Andrei Vyshinsky, sent a letter dated October 12, 1954, to the president of the United Nations Security Council saying that his government accepted the Memorandum of Understanding because it believed that the agreement would restore normal relations between Yugoslavia and

75. Duroselle, *Le Conflit de Trieste,* p. 422.
76. Jeri, p. 296.
77. Duroselle, *Le Conflit de Trieste,* p. 423; *Department of State Bulletin,* 31 (Oct. 18, 1954): 555; *Keesing's Contemporary Archives,* 9:13822.

Italy and contribute to the lessening of tensions in that part of Europe. Without doubt this was also a sign of a new Soviet foreign policy which had begun to develop after Stalin's death.[78]

Yugoslav official circles were content with the accords. In his speech at a meeting of the Communist League in Sarajevo on October 6, 1954, Marshal Tito pointed out that Yugoslavia had to make sacrifices in order to reach the agreement. But even so, Tito continued, the Yugoslav government was satisfied, because the agreement contributed to consolidation of peace and stability in Europe. This was not a dictate put upon Yugoslavia by other powers, he asserted, but an agreement in which Yugoslavia participated as an equal member.[79] The positive points of the agreement were further elaborated in Tito's speech to the joint session of both houses of the federal assembly in Belgrade on October 25, 1954. The Slovenes would have an outlet to the sea and Koper would be developed into a center for the whole southern part of the Slovenian Littoral, which had been cut off from its urban centers of Gorizia and Trieste. Yugoslavia would devote special attention to guaranteeing minority rights, continued Tito, and the Special Statute on Minorities "will serve to ensure the basic rights and status of our minority in the Trieste territory, if it is implemented according to its clauses." The Special Statute was "an important and very progressive document in the annals of international relations," he asserted. The obligation of Italy to maintain a free port in Trieste meant "a recognition of the international character of the port and its significance for the hinterland countries." Tito also hoped that the accord would lead toward further economic, cultural, and political cooperation between Yugoslavia and Italy.[80]

Moreover, the Yugoslavs regarded the accord as having a final character. The fact that the Western powers had announced that they would not support any future Italian claims to Zone B or to Istria made it impossible for Italy to achieve a change of borders by herself. Milan Bartoš, professor of international law and legal adviser to the Yugoslav ministry of foreign affairs, further pointed

78. *Keesing's Contemporary Archives*, 9:13822; *New York Times*, Oct. 14, 1954.
79. Tito, 9:268–69; see also *New York Times*, Oct. 7, 1954.
80. Tito, 9:295–97; for extracts in English see *Documents on International Affairs, 1954* (London, 1957), pp. 224–27.

out that the Second London Agreement was final because it had been accepted by all the Great Powers, which were the permanent members of the United Nations Security Council with the right of veto. When the Memorandum of Understanding had been communicated to the Security Council and distributed to the members of the United Nations no country had asked for a discussion of the problem. Hence the highest international body by tacit consent recognized the new accord, Bartoš asserted.[81]

In Italy Prime Minister Scelba presented the London Agreement to the senate on the same day that it had been initialed. The next day, October 6, 1954, the Right and Left opposition assailed Scelba's cabinet in a stormy senate debate, by denouncing the Trieste accord as a sellout. The government had gravely damaged the national interest by agreeing to the partition of the FTT, the opposition speakers asserted. Emotions reached a high pitch. Senator Emilio Lussu, a left-wing socialist, shook his fist at the government bench, shouting "you are slaves of American millionaires and of false friends like Cardinal Spellman." The neo-Fascist Senator Lando Ferretti scoffed at Senator Lussu, "You are weeping crocodile tears about the loss of Italian territory to Yugoslavia." A great tumult followed and ushers had to form a barrier between the left-wing and right-wing senators to prevent clashes.[82]

In his speech to the senate on October 8, 1954, Prime Minister Scelba refuted the criticism voiced by the Right and Left opposition and therewith asserted the conviction of the Italian government that Italy had obtained the best possible solution under the circumstances. Scelba emphasized that almost all of Zone A would return to Italy, comprising "four-fifths of the population and the most important economic part of the Free Territory." In addition the Italians remaining under Yugoslav administration were given broad minority guarantees. Scelba recognized that this was less than promised to Italy by the Tripartite Proposal in 1948 but reminded the opposition of some sober facts. The Tripartite Pro-

81. See the two articles by Bartoš: "Some Legal Problems of the FTT Memorandum," *Review of International Affairs*, 5, no. 111 (Nov. 15, 1954): 3–5; and "The Trieste Problem from a Legal Point of View," ibid., no. 109 (Oct. 16, 1954), pp. 2–4.

82. *New York Times*, Oct. 7, 1954 (© 1954 by The New York Times Company; reprinted by permission).

posal had great moral value in support of the Italian claim to the FTT but it "could never have had any value in law because the U.S.S.R. refused to accept it." Moreover, as the Western powers did not pledge themselves to drive out the Yugoslavs by force, the only alternative was a compromise with Yugoslavia. The same was true for the other Italian proposals. Yugoslavia's consent would have been necessary for the reconstitution of the FTT or for a plebiscite. In reference to the finality of the accord Scelba assured the senate that Italy did not renounce its claims to Zone B. The truth is, stressed Scelba, that "the allies have limited themselves to saying that they will not uphold future territorial claims advanced by either side, and they hope for direct agreements to be made between Yugoslavia and Italy." Reminding the senators again that "the Memorandum of Understanding restores Trieste and almost all of Zone A to Italy, which were lost by the Peace Treaty," Scelba asked for a vote of confidence.[83]

While the Yugoslavs preferred to look at the London Agreement as a final accord, the Italian legal experts underlined its provisional character: it avoided mentioning that Italy and Yugoslavia extended their sovereignty over Zones A and B, but instead provided only for an "extension of civil administration." Some Italian jurists went further and asserted that Italy's sovereignty over the entire FTT did not end but was only dormant. Such assertions had an exclusively theoretical significance. The Italian ambassador in Washington, Tarchiani, expressed a different opinion: the accord "had merely a resemblance of being provisional while in reality it was final."[84] But this provisional appearance was important because it helped the Italian public to accept a less glittering solution than the one proposed in March 1948.[85]

Following the discussions of the London Agreement the Italian senate gave a vote of confidence to Scelba's government on October 8, 1954, with 122 votes for and 99 against. On October 19 the chamber of deputies also gave a vote of confidence, with 295 votes for, 265 against, and 7 abstentions. The chamber also ap-

83. *Documents on International Affairs, 1954*, pp. 220-24; see also Gaetano Martino, "I positivi risultati dell'accordo per Trieste," *Trieste*, no. 64 (Nov.-Dec. 1964), pp. 4-5.
84. Tarchiani, p. 309.
85. Jeri, pp. 299-300, n. 16; Duroselle, *Le Conflit de Trieste*, p. 424.

proved a loan of forty-eight million dollars to help Trieste's economy.[86]

The Yugoslav federal executive council approved the agreement on October 7, 1954, and also decided that the Slovenian republic would extend its civil administration over the Koper district, and the Croat republic over the Buje district. The federal assembly accepted the accord on October 25.[87]

How did Trieste react to the London Agreement? From October 1, 1954, on, rumors were spreading that an accord between Italy and Yugoslavia was imminent. The pro-Italian majority was preparing itself for the reception of Italian troops and for a great celebration. In the early afternoon of October 5, 1954, General Winterton announced the Memorandum of Understanding in his proclamation to the people of Zone A. He reminded them that until the administration was handed over to Italy it would continue to be his responsibility to enforce the laws and maintain order. But he permitted the Italians to fly as many flags as they wished. Shortly after, an enormous Italian flag, thirty by sixty-five feet, was hoisted to the top of a high pole in the Piazza Unità, to symbolize the reunion of Trieste with Italy. Italian flags were also flown at the city hall and other public buildings, and the church bells were rung. Then Italian flags appeared in most windows and crowds poured into the streets and gathered in the Piazza Unità. They were gay and excited, and sang Italian patriotic songs in unison with those issuing from loudspeakers placed around the main square. All schools were declared closed for the rest of the day and for the next day also. Crowds milled around most of the afternoon. The civil police kept order as unobtrusively as possible. The policemen themselves were in a happy mood because they had learned that the Italian government had decided against disbanding them. At night a fireworks display was held.

However, not everyone was happy. The independentists knew that the agreement meant the end of any hope for an FTT, and they were concerned for their economic future. The Slovenian minority was troubled because of ruinous experience with past

86. Tarchiani, p. 317; *New York Times,* Oct. 9, 20, 1954. Note that the *New York Times* (Oct. 9, 1954) gave the results of the vote in the senate as 129 for and 89 against.

87. Jeri, p. 300, n. 20; *New York Times,* Oct. 8, 26, 1954.

Italian promises. The Istrian patriots were also dissatisfied. They knew that the human rights and freedoms guaranteed to Italians in Zone B meant very little under a Communist regime. Mayor Bartoli, who was in a hospital recovering from an operation, addressed a message to the populace in which he stressed that the Triestines were not reconciled to leaving Italians under Yugoslav rule forever. Nevertheless he was restraining his usually militant tone when he asserted:

> The foreigner is still in Istria, that land of martyrdom and faithfulness. But Italy on returning to Trieste will be in a better position to hear the voice of that most noble people that still awaits a solution of justice and peace. The second phase will be won by patient work in a united Europe and a pacified Adriatic.[88]

Slovenian dissent was also voiced in Zone B. Julij Beltram, a leading Communist of the Slovenian Littoral, spoke at a rally in Koper on the morning of October 6, 1954, and asserted that Slovenes had the right to almost all of Zone A, which was ethnically Slovenian. He assured the Slovenes that Yugoslavia would see to it that the minority rights granted to Slovenes were put into force by the Italian government. His statement was broadcast by Belgrade radio at 3:00 P.M., but was not repeated in later broadcasts. It was not included in the report of the rally carried by the official press agency Tanjug the same day. The Slovenes were still more disappointed when Aleš Bebler, deputy secretary for foreign affairs, stated on October 8, 1954, that Yugoslavia probably would not attempt to expand the services of the harbor in Koper. He said that Koper would be modernized for the commercial purposes of the district, but that it would not be built up as a bigger port to be able to compete with Trieste or Rijeka.[89]

Meanwhile preparations went on for implementation of the London Agreement. To prevent any new frustration of Italian national sentiment, the American and British governments had informed the Italian government that they hoped to be able to

88. *New York Times,* Oct. 6, 1954 (© 1954 by The New York Times Company; reprinted by permission).
89. Ibid., Oct. 7, 9, 1954.

carry out all the steps provided in the Memorandum of Understanding within one month. On October 5, 1954, the Italian cabinet appointed General Edmondo de Renzi as its representative to meet with General Winterton to arrange for the transfer of power. The same day the Italian government also appointed Giovanni Palamara as future commissioner general for the Trieste area. The next day General de Renzi arrived in Trieste at the invitation of General Winterton. On October 8, the AMG-YMG border commission began its work of preliminary demarcation as provided in the Memorandum. The American and British troops began their evacuation on October 7 and 14, respectively. On October 25, one day before the transfer of Zone A to Italy, Yugoslav troops moved into the small part of Zone A which came under Yugoslav administration. No one had known when the Yugoslavs would occupy this area although the time had been secretly agreed upon between General Winterton and the Yugoslav commander, Stamatović. A few British troops acted as a kind of buffer between Trieste border police and the Yugoslav forces to prevent any incidents. The same day, Yugoslavia formally extended her civil administration over Zone B.[90]

The next day, October 26, 1954, Italian troops entered Trieste and the British-American occupation came to an end after nine years and four months.[91] It was Tuesday and the weather was bad. A gale known as a *bora* "buffeted the city" and "upset the arrangements for ceremonies." It drenched the crowds and strewed the streets with "tattered bunting and ruined umbrellas."

At 10:00 A.M., General Winterton read over the radio a short proclamation stating:

> 1. The Allied Military government of the British–United States Zone of the Free Territory of Trieste is hereby terminated.
> 2. All powers of government and administration in the British–United States Zone of the Free Territory of Trieste as well as jurisdiction over its inhabitants, so far vested in me in

---

90. *Department of State Bulletin,* 31 (Oct. 18, 1954): 555–56; *New York Times,* Oct. 6, 8, 9, 15, 26, 1954.

91. The description of the events of October 26 is based on Michael L. Hoffman's report in the *New York Times* (Oct. 27, 1954), the author's interviews, and Duroselle's *Le Conflit de Trieste* (p. 427).

my capacity as Commander of the British and United States Forces stationed in the said Zone, are hereby relinquished.[92]

General de Renzi then read his proclamation saying that he was assuming the administration of the Trieste area in the name of the Italian government. According to the plan General Winterton, his deputy, American General John A. Dabney, and General de Renzi, would then watch a parade of British, United States, and Italian honor guards, listen to bands playing their national anthems, observe the lowering of the British and United States flags and the raising of the Italian one, have a drink to one another's health, and say goodbye. But something went wrong. General Winterton did not arrive at the farewell ceremonies. He sent a message to General de Renzi that the Italian escort to take him to the ceremonies had not been able to get through the crowds, "so he wished everyone goodbye and good luck," whereupon the ceremonies were canceled. In Trieste, however, the rumor spread that the real cause was quite different. The Istrian national extremists were attempting to kill General Winterton in protest because the Western powers had abandoned Zone B to Yugoslavia, even as Maria Pasquinelli had killed General Robin De Winton in 1947. Allied Military Police learned about the plot and advised General Winterton to leave Trieste immediately. He probably embarked unobserved on the British aircraft carrier Centaur, which sailed away with the last detachment of British troops.

General de Renzi spoke to the crowds from a balcony overlooking the Piazza Unità shortly after noon. From then on the celebration was an all-Italian affair. The crowds observed twenty-four Italian jets zooming over the city at low altitudes, the arrival of the Italian destroyer *Grecalle*, the cruiser *Duca degli Abruzzi*, and the truckloads of Bersaglieri (the Italian crack division). All the honors went to the Bersaglieri, whose division had first disembarked in Trieste on November 3, 1918. Squads of special state police, the Celere, rolled into the city on the heels of the soldiers.

92. "Proclamation No. 3," dated in Trieste, 10 A.M. on October 26, 1954, *AMG-FTT Gazette*, 7, no. 29B (Oct. 26, 1954): 325. The proclamation was published in a special number (29B) which was the last of the AMG official gazette.

Riding tank-like riot cars and heavy armored trucks, the Celere dashed through all sections of the city.

The weather cleared up about 4:00 P.M., and the Italian crowds gave an enthusiastic send-off when the United States troopship *General V. G. Haan* sailed. There were now no British or United States troops left in Trieste.

No serious incidents occurred. But some Istrian refugees from Zone B tried to force Italian banners onto the houses of the Slovenian suburb of Opicina. The Slovenes encircled them and fighting broke out. Police had to restore order.

Three days later, on October 29, 1954, General de Renzi transferred administration to Commissioner General Giovanni Palamara, who was to be directly responsible to the Italian prime minister. Thus a civilian official took over authority. Before coming to Trieste, Commissioner Palamara had been prefect of Leghorn province.[93] On November 4, the Triestines celebrated the anniversary of the 1918 armistice in grand style. Prime Minister Scelba and the president of the Italian Republic, Luigi Einaudi, were the distinguished guests. In his speech Scelba stressed that the London Agreement should "signify not a point of arrival but a point of departure for an active and productive collaboration, in all sectors, between the two neighboring nations." But the past was not yet forgotten. The neo-Fascists and nationalistic fanatics interrupted Premier Scelba several times by whistling and booing, and with cries of "Istria, Istria."[94]

Tito visited the former Zone B on November 21, 1954, to participate in the official celebration of the unification of this land to Yugoslavia. In his speech in Koper he welcomed the Slovenes, Croats, and Italians to the new Yugoslavia and to a new socialist system that would lead them on the road to a better and happier future. Tito promised the people of the former Zone B that Yugoslavia would send further financial help to complete the reconstruction and to enable them to participate in the industrialization already underway in Yugoslavia. He again expressed his belief that the London Agreement would bring better political and economic cooperation with Italy.[95]

93. *New York Times,* Oct. 30, 1954.
94. Ibid., Nov. 5, 1954 (© 1954 by The New York Times Company; reprinted by permission).
95. Tito, 9: 312–16.

The Italian and Yugoslav governments remained determined to live up to the London Agreement. They discontinued their support of dissident groups on the border and carefully avoided acts which might lead to new tensions. This policy had positive results. Though nationalistic hatred could not be rooted out over night, the new conciliatory policy helped to establish better relations between Yugoslav and Italian ethnic groups. As part of this new program, the two governments carried out the provisions planned for in the Memorandum of Understanding. They appointed a mixed Italo-Yugoslav commission which effected a precise demarcation of the new border between the two states. Both governments prepared the regulations for the Mixed Italo-Yugoslav Committee provided for in Article 8 of the Special Statute on minorities. These regulations, consisting of fourteen articles, were agreed upon in Rome on February 16, 1955.[96] Border traffic was regulated with the agreements concluded in Rome on March 31, 1955, and in Udine, Italy, on August 20, 1955.[97] Aside from the good will of both governments, however, things did not look good in the former FTT region for the first two years. During 1955 and 1956 over 21,000 inhabitants left Zone B. Most of them were Italians, but many Slovenes and Croats also preferred to live in the democratic West. In Trieste the economic situation was bad. There was an increase in unemployment and great numbers of persons were forced to leave for Australia. In 1956 the emigration figure reached 12,126. "Madre e tornata, i figli partono" (Mother [Italy] returned, but the sons are leaving), was written on a poster attached to a ship full of emigrants which sailed for Australia.[98] Government financial aid helped to revive Trieste's economy. Though the port activities slowly declined, the Italian government subsidized the development of new industries and the enlargement of established ones. The free border traffic between Italy and Yugoslavia also benefited Trieste's economy. But this crisis disclosed Trieste's weaknesses. Should the Italian government cease to allocate financial aid, Trieste would be plagued by a new crisis which could strengthen the independentist aspirations, or might bring forward Trieste's demands for closer ties with its hinterland.

96. For the text of the regulations see Jeri, pp. 375–79.
97. Ibid., pp. 294–95.
98. Pacor, pp. 360–61; see also *Trieste nella sua realtà*, p. 14; Duroselle, *Le Conflit de Trieste*, p. 427.

In conclusion it might be said that the settlement was a sacrifice for Slovenes and Italians alike. Both lost part of their land. However, the accord also profited both Italy and Yugoslavia. It brought closer political, economic, and cultural collaboration. The new cooperation served especially both countries' economies, which complemented each other. Janko Jeri rightly stresses that the agreement was a prime example of friendly coexistence between two countries with different political and ideological concepts and social structures.[99] In general the solution seemed to work well. Nevertheless there are dangers which might in the future threaten the established compromise. A war might revive the old claims which neither state renounced, especially if Yugoslavia and Italy happened to be on opposing sides. A great economic crisis in Italy could be another threat and would produce two quite different alternatives. A democratic government would have to suspend its subsidies to Trieste, which in turn might bring great unemployment in Trieste. Trieste's Italians could begin to look back toward its hinterland for a solution and demand an international Trieste with economic ties with Yugoslavia, Austria, and other central European states. Or the economic crisis might strengthen Italian right-wing parties and help them to power. Danger would be great that a right-wing government might propagate an international expedition to recover the lost Istrian lands with intention to avert public attention from internal crises. It did happen once and could happen again.

A political crisis in Yugoslavia, for example after Tito's death, might also reopen the Trieste question. Again two possibilities exist. The people might rise against the domination of the Communist party and demand greater political freedom, and this would cause an internal crisis and weaken the Yugoslav international position. Or the Communist party might be unable to restrain rising nationalistic antagonisms and aspirations of different Yugoslav nationalities demanding greater autonomy or independence, which could lead to a civil war or dismemberment of Yugoslavia.

In short, any serious crisis in Yugoslavia might be a temptation for Italy to regain at least the lost territory of the former Zone B to which she had never renounced her claims, if not the

---

99. Jeri, p. 297.

entire western part of Istria. On such an occasion would a democratic Italian government have the strength to resist the nationalistic forces, which would demand that the opportune moment not be lost?

All people of good will look toward broader cooperation and hope that the ideas of a united Europe, of peaceful cooperation among all nations, and of universalism will prevail over narrow nationalism for the benefit of all mankind. But we have also to recognize that nationalism in its worst aspect—imperialism—still persists and might again bring the Trieste question to world attention.

BIBLIOGRAPHY

Accerboni, R. "La situazione giuridica del territorio libero de Trieste," *Rivista di studi politici internazionali*, 18, no. 3 (July–Sept. 1951): 477–83.
Action Committee for the United and Sovereign Slovenian State. "Memorandum on the Problem of Trieste and Northern Adriatic to the Allied Governments Concerned." Rome, 1946. (Mimeographed.)
Actor Spectator [Carlo Schiffrer]. "Orientamenti politici degli elettori sloveni," *Trieste*, no. 10 (Nov.–Dec. 1955), pp. 11–12.
AC Weekly Bulletin, see Allied Control Commission.
Alatri, Paolo. *Nitti, d'Annunzio e la questione adriatica, 1919–1920*. Milan, 1959.
Alberti, Mario. *L'irredentismo senza romanticismi*. Como, 1936.
Albrecht-Carrié, René. *Italy and the Paris Peace Conference*. New York, 1938.
Alexander, Harold. *The Alexander Memoirs, 1940–1945*. Ed. John North. New York, 1962.
Allied Control Commission. Headquarters, Public Relations Branch. *ACC Weekly Bulletin*. 3 vols. Published in Italy from April 1, 1944, to June 20, 1947. With vol. 2 the name of the Allied Control Commission changed to Allied Commission. Mimeographed until March 23, 1946 (vol. 2, no. 51), and from that date on it was printed. Cited as *AC Weekly Bulletin*.
Allied Military Government. British–United States Zone, Free Territory of Trieste. *Official Gazette*. 7 vols. Trieste, September 16, 1947–October 26, 1954. Cited as *AMG-FTT Gazette*.
———. *Trieste Handbook*. Trieste, 1950. Cited as *Trieste Handbook*.
Allied Military Government. 13 Corps, Venezia Giulia. *The Allied Military Government Gazette*. 2 vols. Trieste, September 1945–September 1947. Cited as *AMG Gazette VG*.
———. "Daily Press Summary." Trieste, 1946. (Mimeographed.)
Amendola, Giovanni, et al. *Il patto di Roma*. Rome, n.d. [ca. 1919].
AMG-FTT Gazette, see Allied Military Government. British–United States Zone, Free Territory of Trieste. *Official Gazette*.
AMG Gazette VG, see Allied Military Government. 13 Corps, Venezia Giulia.
Anali jadranskog instituta (Annals of the Adriatic Institute). Vol. 1. Published by the Yugoslav Academy of Arts and Sciences in Zagreb. Zagreb, 1956.

BIBLIOGRAPHY

Andreotti, Giulio. *De Gasperi e il suo tempo: Trento, Vienna, Roma.* Milan, 1956.
Apih, Elio. "L'atteggiamento dei partiti a Trieste in rapporto alla situazione attuale," *Il Ponte,* 4, no. 4 (Apr. 1948): 329–38.
———."Il fascismo a Trieste," *Trieste,* no. 7 (May–June 1955), pp. 38–43.
———."La stampa nazista a Trieste," *Trieste,* no. 9 (Sept.–Oct. 1955), pp. 25–27.
Armstrong, Hamilton F. *Tito and Goliath.* New York, 1951.
Army Quarterly. Vol. 58. London, 1949.
Arnež, John A. *Slovenia in European Affairs: Reflections on Slovenian Political History.* New York, 1958.
L'attività dal CLT, see Consiglio di Liberazione della Città di Trieste.
Austria. Statistische Zentralkommission. *Österreichische Statistik.* New Series, vol. 1, no. 2: *Die Ergebnisse der Volkszählung vom 31. Dezember 1910 in den im Reichsrate vertretenen Königreichen und Ländern: Die Bevölkerung nach der Gebürtigkeit, Religion und Umgangssprache in Verbindung mit dem Geschlechte, nach dem Bildungsgrade und Familienstande; die Körperlichen Gebrechen; die soziale Gliederung der Haushaltungen.* Vienna, 1914. Cited as *Census 1910.*
———. *Österreichische Statistik.* New Series, vol. 2, no. 2: *Die Ergebnisse der Volkszählung vom 31. Dezember 1910 in den im Reichsrate vertretenen Königreichen und Ländern: Die Ausländer in den im Reichsrate vertretenen Königreichen und Ländern.* Vienna, 1913. (*Census 1910: Foreigners.*)
"L'azione del governo italiano per Trieste dopo il trattato di pace," *Documenti di vita italiana,* 3, no. 24 (Nov. 1953): 1847–61.
Babič, Branko. *Tržaško demokratično gibanje in KPI* (Trieste's Democratic Movement and the CPI). Trieste, 1949.
"Background Statement on Alexander-Tito Talks," released by Allied Military Headquarters, Rome, May 19, 1945, reprinted in *New York Times,* May 20, 1945.
Bajlec, Franc. "Narodni odbor za Slovenijo in vetrinjska tragedija" (The National Committee for Slovenia and the Tragedy of Vetrinje), *Vestnik,* vol. 13, no. 1–2 to no. 12 (Jan.–Feb. to Dec. 1962).
Bartoš, Milan. "Some Legal Problems of the FTT Memorandum," *Review of International Affairs,* 5, no. 111 (Nov. 15, 1954): 3–5.
———. "The Trieste Problem from a Legal Point of View," *Review of International Affairs,* 5, no. 109 (Oct. 16, 1954): 2–4.
Bass, Robert, and Marbury, Elizabeth, eds. *The Soviet-Yugoslav Controversy, 1948–58: A Documentary Record.* New York, 1959.

Battaglia, Roberto. *The Story of the Italian Resistance*. Translated and edited by P. D. Cummins. London, 1957.
B. C. "Le reazioni jugoslave nella zona B," *Relazioni internazionali*, 16, no. 21 (May 24, 1952): 509.
———. "Nuova crisi a Trieste," *Relazioni internazionali*, 16, no. 13 (Mar. 29, 1952): 325–26.
Belci, Corrado. "L'indipendentismo a Trieste," *Trieste*, no. 9 (Sept.–Oct. 1955), pp. 6–9.
Belgrade Agreement, see U.S. Dept. of State. *Provisional Administration*.
Benedetti, Giulio. *La pace di Fiume: Dalla conferenza di Parigi al trattato di Roma*. Bologna, 1924.
Berce, Lojze. *Budućnost Trsta u svetlu njegove prošlosti: Tragedija jedne luke i jednog naroda pod Italijom* (The Future of Trieste in the Light of Its Past: The Tragedy of a Port and of a Nation under Italy). Belgrade, 1948.
Berti, Paolo, ed. *Italia ritorna: Dieci anni di storia triestina nei documenti, scritti e discorsi del sindaco Gianni Bartoli*. Rocca San Casciano, 1959.
Bettasa, Giulio. "L'ultima fase della questione di Trieste: 1951–1954," *Rivista di studi politici internazionali*, 22, no. 1 (Jan.–Mar. 1955): 9–30.
Bevc, Lado. *Na braniku za sokolske ideale* (In Defense of Sokol [Falcon] Ideals). London, 1965.
"Boj slovenske občine" (The Struggle of a Slovenian Municipality), *Stvarnost in svoboda*, 2 (Trieste, 1953): 3–7.
Borec (Combatant). Vol. 5. Glasilo Zveze borcev narodno-osvobodilne vojne Slovenije (Organ of the Union of Combatants of the Slovenian National Liberation War). Monthly. Ljubljana, 1953.
Botteri, Guido. "Catalogo-Dizionario degli Sloveni nella regione," *Trieste*, no. 38 (July–Aug. 1960), pp. 1–9.
Bowman, Alfred C. "Venezia Giulia and Trieste," *Military Government Journal*, 1, no. 8 (June 1948): 9–15.
Bradshaw, Mary E. "Military Control of Zone A in Venezia Giulia," *Department of State Bulletin*, 16 (June 29, 1947): 1257–72.
Bulajić, M. K. *Pitanje Trsta u svjetlosti novih dogadjaja* (The Question of Trieste in the Light of the New Happenings). Belgrade, 1950.
Cadastre national de l'Istrie, see L'Institut Adriatique.
Cadorna, Raffaele. *La riscossa: Dal 25 luglio alla liberazione*. Milan, 1948.
Censimento della popolazione, see Italy. Ministero dell'economia nazionale.
Census 1910, see Austria. Statistische Zentralkommission. ... vol. 1.

BIBLIOGRAPHY

Census 1910: Foreigners, see Austria. Statistische Zentralkommission. . . . vol. 2.

Census 1921, see Italy. Ministero dell'economia nazionale.

Census 1945, see L'Institut Adriatique. *Cadastre national* . . .

Čermelj, Lavo. "The Denationalization of Slovenes in the Anglo-American Zone of FTT," *Review of International Affairs*, 3, no. 1 (Jan. 1952): 11–13.

———. *Life-and-Death Struggle of a National Minority: The Yugoslavs in Italy.* Trans. F. C. Copeland. 2d ed. Ljubljana, 1945.

———. *Ob tržaškem procesu 1941: Spomini in beležke* (About the Trieste Trial in 1941: Recollections and Notes). Ljubljana, 1962.

———. "Slovenes in Italy," *Review of International Affairs*, 4, no. 17 (Sept. 1, 1953): 14–15.

Cesare, Giorgio. "Gli otto predecessori di Confalonieri," *Trieste*, no. 29 (Jan.–Feb. 1959), pp. 6–9.

———. "Vidali sotto accusa," *Trieste*, no. 35 (Jan.–Feb. 1960), p. 18.

Churchill, Winston S. *The Second World War.* 6 vols. Boston: Houghton Mifflin Company, 1948–53.

———. *The Second World War.* Vols. 3, 5, 6. London: Cassell & Co., 1950–54. When used, cited as Churchill (Cassell).

Ciacchi, Aurelio. "Cavour e la Venezia Giulia," *Trieste*, no. 13 (May–June 1956), pp. 47–49.

Clissold, Joseph. *The Slovenes Want to Live.* New York, n.d. [1943].

Coceani, Bruno. *Mussolini, Hitler, Tito alle porte orientali d'Italia.* Bologna, 1948.

———. *Trieste durante l'occupazione tedesca, 1943–45.* Milan, 1959.

Čok, Ivan M. *Memorandum of the Committee of the Yugo-Slavs from Italy: About the Yugoslavs, That Is Slovenes and Croats, under Italy, and Their Aspirations and Claims.* New York, 1942.

Čok, Ivan M., see also Tchok, Ivan M.

Coles and Weinberg, see U.S. Department of the Army.

Cominform Resolution, see *The Soviet-Yugoslav Dispute.*

Comitato cittadino dell'U.A.I.S. *Trieste nella lotta per la democrazia.* Trieste, 1945. Cited as *Trieste nella lotta.*

Il Comitato di Liberazione Nazionale dell'Istria [the CLN for Istria]. *Il problema di Trieste: Realtà storica, politica, economica.* Trieste, 1954.

"Comments on the Yugoslav Administration in Zone B of the Free Territory of Trieste," *Italian Affairs*, 3, no. 3 (May, 1954): 321–37.

Committee of National Liberation of Istria [CLN for Istria]. *Trieste: Zone "B" Land without Liberty.* Trieste, August 1954. Cited as *Trieste: Zone B.*

BIBLIOGRAPHY

Conferences at Malta and Yalta, see U.S. Department of State.
Consiglio di Liberazione della Città di Trieste. *L'attività svolta dal Consiglio di Liberazione della Città di Trieste: 17 maggio–21 settembre 1945, con una breve premessa storico-politica.* Trieste, 1945. Cited as *L'attività dal CLT.*
"Il Corriere di Trieste," Trieste, no. 9 (Sept.–Oct. 1955), pp. 30–31.
Cox, Geoffrey. *The Road to Trieste.* London, 1947.
Čulinović, Ferdo. *Riječka država: Od londonskog pakta i danuncijade do Rapalla i aneksije Italiji* (The State of Rijeka from the London Pact and [the Period of] D'Annunzio to Rapallo and the Annexation to Italy). Zagreb, 1953.
Dabinović, Antun. "Državnopravni položaj STO-ja" (The Situation of the Free Territory of Trieste According to the Public Law), *Stvarnost,* 1, no. 4–5 (Sept. 1951): 81–92.
Deakin, F. W. *The Brutal Friendship: Mussolini, Hitler, and the Fall of Italian Fascism.* New York, 1962.
De Castro, Diego. *Il problema di Trieste: Genesi e sviluppi della questione giuliana in relazione agli avvenimenti internazionali, 1943–1952.* 2d ed. Bologna, 1953.
Dedijer, Vladimir. *Tito.* New York, 1953.
———. *With Tito through the War: Partisan Diary, 1941–1944.* London, 1951.
Demokracija (Democracy). Weekly published by *Slovenska demokratska zveza* (Slovenian Democratic Union). Trieste, 1952.
Department of State Bulletin. Vols. 15–31. Washington, D.C., 1946–54.
De Simone, Pasquale. "I comunisti italiani a Pola di fronte al problema nazionale," *Trieste,* no. 57 (Sept.–Oct. 1963), pp. 16–18.
"10 febbraio 1947," *Trieste,* no. 18 (Mar.–Apr. 1957), pp. 16–17.
Digović, Pero. *La Dalmatie et les problèmes de l'Adriatique.* Introduction by Ivan Meštrović. Lausanne, 1944.
———, and Goranić, Frano. *La Haute Adriatique et les problèmes politiques actuels: Fiume, Istrie, Goritie, Trieste.* Lausanne, 1944.
Djilas, Milovan. *Conversations with Stalin.* New York, 1962.
Documenti di vita italiana, see Italy. Presidenza del consiglio dei ministri.
Documents on International Affairs. For the years 1951, 1953–54. A publication of the Royal Institute of International Affairs. London, 1954, 1956–57.
Dokumenti, see Inštitut za zgodovino delavskega gibanja v Ljubljani.
Draskovich [Drašković], Slobodan M. *Tito, Moscow's Trojan Horse.* Chicago, 1959.
Dulles, Allen. *The Secret Surrender.* New York, 1965.

BIBLIOGRAPHY

Dunham, Donald C. "Political Aspects of Press Reporting of Crisis of November, 1953, Trieste, F.T.T." Trieste, 1954. (Mimeographed.)

Duroselle, Jean-Baptiste. *Le Conflit de Trieste, 1943–1954.* Vol. 3 of *Etudes de cas de conflits internationaux* of the Centre européen de la dotation Carnegie pour la paix internationale. Brussels, 1966.

———. *Histoire diplomatique de 1919 à nos jours.* Paris, 1957.

Economist. London, 1946.

Eden, Anthony. *Full Circle: The Memoirs of Anthony Eden.* Boston, 1960.

Eighth AMG Report (S/1424), see United Nations, Security Council. Doc. S/1424.

Enciclopedia italiana di scienze, lettere ed arti. With Appendixes I and II. Rome, 1937, 1938, 1949.

Esposito, Giovanni. *Trieste e la sua odissea: Contributo alla storia di Trieste e del "Litorale Adriatico" dal 25 luglio 1943, al maggio 1945.* Rome, 1952.

Ethnography of the North-West Frontier of Yugoslavia with Germany on the North and Italy on the West. Ed. G. M. S. Leader. London, 1942.

F. A. "The Arbitrary Acts of the Italian Administration in Trieste," *Review of International Affairs,* 3, no. 14 (July 16, 1952): 3.

Fauro, Ruggero. *Trieste: Italiani e Slavi; il governo austriaco; l'irredentismo.* Rome, 1914.

Feis, Herbert. *Churchill, Roosevelt, Stalin: The War They Waged, and the Peace They Sought.* Princeton, 1957.

Fifth AMG Report (S/1242), see United Nations, Security Council. Doc. S/1242.

First AMG Report (S/679), see United Nations, Security Council. Doc. S/679.

First Yugoslav Report (S/1066), see United Nations, Security Council. Doc. S/1066.

Fogar, Galliano, see G. F.

Fotitch [Fotić], Constantine. *The War We Lost: Yugoslavia's Tragedy and the Failure of the West.* New York, 1948.

Fourth AMG Report (S/1174), see United Nations, Security Council. Doc. S/1174.

Free Italy. Vol. 1. Monthly supplement in English of *L'Italia Libera.* Published by Italian Peoples Union. New York, 1945.

Frontière Italo-Yougoslave, see Italy.

Frontiers between . . . , see Yugoslavia.

Funaioli, Edo. *Atti, meriti, sacrifici della Guardia Civica di Trieste.* Trieste, 1953.

BIBLIOGRAPHY

Gabrovšek, Francis. *Jugoslavia's Frontiers with Italy: Trieste and Its Hinterland.* New York, n.d. [during World War II].

Gaeta, Giuliano. "Chi a tradito la fratellanza," *La Voce Libera,* July 16, 1947.

———. "La posizione di Luigi Frausin," *Trieste,* no. 7 (May–June 1955), pp. 15–16.

Gayda, Virginio. *La Jugoslavia contro l'Italia: Documenti e rivelazioni.* 2d ed. Rome, 1941.

Gestrin, Ferdo, and Melik, Vasilij. *Slovenska zgodovina, 1813–1914* (Slovenian History, 1813–1914). Ljubljana, 1950.

G. F. [Galliano Fogar.] "La politica tedesca nel Litorale Adriatico," *Trieste,* no. 3 (Sept.–Oct. 1954), pp. 19–21, and no. 4 (Nov.–Dec. 1954), pp. 23–26.

Giannini, Amadeo, and Tomajuoli, Gino, eds. *Il trattato di pace con l'Italia.* Milan, 1948.

Great Britain. *Parliamentary Papers.* Vol. 43 *(Accounts and Papers,* vol. 25: State Papers). Cmd. 1239. Miscellaneous, no. 12 (1921). "Recognition by His Britannic Majesty's Government of the Treaty of Rapallo of November 12, 1920, between the Kingdom of Italy and the Kingdom of the Serbs, Croats and Slovenes." London, 1921. (Treaty of Rapallo.)

———. *Parliamentary Papers.* Vol. 51 *(Accounts and Papers,* vol. 25: State Papers). Cmd. 671. Miscellaneous, no. 7 (1920). "Agreement between France, Russia, Great Britain and Italy, Signed at London, April 26, 1915." London, 1920. (London Pact.)

Grum, France, and Pleško, Stane, eds. *Svoboda v razvalinah: Grčarice, Turjak, Kočevje* (The Wreck of Liberty: Grčarice, Turjak, Kočevje). Cleveland, 1961.

Harris, C. R. S. *Allied Military Administration of Italy, 1943–1945.* A volume in *History of the Second World War.* Edited by J. R. M. Butler. United Kingdom Military Series. London, 1957.

Hildebrandt, Walter. *Der Triest-Konflikt und die italienisch-jugoslawische Frage.* Göttingen, 1953.

Hočevar, Toussaint. *The Structure of the Slovenian Economy: 1848–1963.* Vol. 5 of Studia Slovenica. New York, 1965.

"Hot Curve," *Time,* September 29, 1947, p. 32.

I. K. "Cultural and Material Progress in Zone B of the Free Trieste Territory," *Review of International Affairs,* 2, no. 11 (May 23, 1951): 14–15.

L'Institut Adriatique. *Cadastre national de l'Istrie d'après le recensement du 1er octobre 1945.* Zagreb, 1946. Cited as *Census 1945.*

BIBLIOGRAPHY

L'Institut Adriatique. *La Marche Julienne: Etude de géographie politique.* Sušak, 1945. Cited as *Marche Julienne.*

Institute for International Politics and Economics. *Italian Genocide Policy against the Slovenes and Croats: A Selection of Documents.* Belgrade, 1954. Cited as *Italian Genocide Policy.*

Inštitut za zgodovino delavskega gibanja v Ljubljani (Institute for the History of the Labor Movement in Ljubljana). *Dokumenti ljudske revolucije v Sloveniji* (Documents of the People's Revolution in Slovenia). 2 vols. Ljubljana, 1962–64. Cited as *Dokumenti.*

"In the Footsteps of Mussolini's Laws," *Review of International Affairs*, 4, no. 1 (Jan. 1, 1953): 6–7.

Italian Affairs, see Italy. Council of Ministers.

Italian Genocide Policy, see Institute for International Politics and Economics.

Italian Green Book, see Italy. Chamber of Deputies.

"Italianization of the Slovene Coast," *Review of International Affairs*, 4, no. 8 (Apr. 16, 1953): 6.

Italian Peace Treaty, see U.S. Department of State.

Italy. *La Frontière Italo-Yougoslave: Déclarations officielles et autres documents presentés par le Gouvernement Italien au Conseil des Ministres des Affaires Etrangères, Septembre 1945–Juillet 1946, avec une preface.* Rome, 1946. Cited as *Frontière Italo-Yougoslave.*

———. Camera dei deputati. Atti parlamentari. Legislatura XXIV, Sessione 1913–1915. *Documenti diplomatici presentati al parlamento italiano dal ministro degli affari esteri (Sonnino): Seduta dal 20 maggio 1915: Austria-Ungheria*, Rome, 1915. (Il libro verde.)

———. Chamber of Deputies. Acts of Parliament. Legislature XXIV, Sessions 1913–15. *Diplomatic Documents Submitted to the Italian Parliament by the Minister for Foreign Affairs (Sonnino). Session of the 20th May, 1915: Austria-Hungary—The Italian Green Book.* London, n.d.

———. Council of Ministers. Documentary Center. *Italian Affairs: Documents and Notes.* Vols. 2–3. Rome, 1953–54. Cited as *Italian Affairs.*

———. Ministero dell'economia nazionale. Direzione generale della statistica, Ufficio del censimento. *Censimento della popolazione del regno d'Italia al 1° dicembre 1921.* Vol. 3: *Venezia Giulia.* Rome, 1926. Cited as *Census 1921.*

———. Presidenza del consiglio dei ministri. Centro di documentazione. *Documenti di vita italiana.* Vols. 2–5. Rome, 1952–55. Cited as *Documenti di vita italiana.*

———. Presidenza del consiglio dei ministri. Servizio informazioni. *Trieste nella sua realtà.* Rome, 1958. Cited as *Trieste nella sua realtà.*

BIBLIOGRAPHY

Izvestje državnih srednjih šol s slovenskim učnim jezikom v Gorici za šolsko leto 1954–55: Jubilejna številka ob desetletnici obstoja (Report on the State Secondary Schools in Gorizia with Slovenian as Language of Instruction for the School Year 1954–55: A Jubilee Number for the Tenth Anniversary of Existence). Gorizia, 1955.

Izvestje srednjih šol (Report on the Secondary Schools). Annual reports published by the Slovenian Secondary Schools. Trieste, 1950–55.

Jakšić, Pavle. *Oslobodilački pohod na Trst četvrte jugoslovenske armije* (The Liberation March on Trieste of the Fourth Yugoslav Army). Belgrade, 1952.

Janičijević, D., and Babović, B. "Londonska konferencija: Ohrabrenje fašizma u Italiji" (London Conference: The Encouragement to Fascism in Italy), *Medjunarodni problemi*, 4, no. 3–4 (May–Aug. 1952): 27–38.

Jeri, Janko. *Tržaško uprašanje po drugi svetovni vojni: Tri faze diplomatskega boja* (The Trieste Question after the Second World War: Three Phases of the Diplomatic Struggle). Ljubljana, 1961.

Jesen 1942: Korespondenca Edvarda Kardelja in Borisa Kidriča (Autumn 1942: Correspondence of Edvard Kardelj and Boris Kidrič). Ljubljana, 1963.

Jones, William. *Twelve Months with Tito's Partisans*. Bedford, Eng., 1946.

Jugoslav Committee in London. *The Southern Slav Programme*. London, 1915.

The Julian March, Iuliĭskaia Kraïna, la Marche Julienne. Ljubljana, n.d. [1946].

J. V. [Jože Velikonja]. "Slovenske šole na Tržaškem" (Slovenian Schools in the Trieste Region), *Koledar-Zbornik, 1955,* pp. 179–80.

Karapandžić, Bor. M. *Gradjanski rat u Srbiji, 1941–1945* (The Civil War in Serbia, 1941–1945). Cleveland, 1958.

———. *Kočevje Titov najkrvaviji zločin* (Kočevje, the Bloodiest Crime of Tito). Cleveland, 1959.

Keesing's Contemporary Archives: Weekly Diary of Important World Events. Vols. 7–9. London, 1948–54.

Klic Triglava (The Call of Triglav). Published by Slovenian émigré organization Slovenska pravda (Slovenian Right) in London. Vol. 4. London, 1951. (Mimeographed.)

Knežević, Radoje L., ed. *Knjiga o Draži* (A Book about Draža). 2 vols. Windsor, Ont., 1956.

Knjiga o Draži, see Knežević.

Koledar Svobodne Slovenije (Calendar of Free Slovenia). Published yearly by the newspaper *Svobodna Slovenija.* Buenos Aries, 1949–

BIBLIOGRAPHY

67. Subsequently the title changed as follows: *Koledar in Zbornik Svobodne Slovenije* (Calendar and Collection of Free Slovenia) (1952-54); *Zbornik-Koledar Svobodne Slovenije* (Collection-Calendar of Free Slovenia) (1955-62); and *Zbornik Svobodne Slovenije* (Collection of Free Slovenia. Cited as *Koledar-Zbornik*.

Koledar-Zbornik, see *Koledar Svobodne Slovenije*.

Komel, Franta. *Narodno-osvobodilna borba v Sloveniji* (The National Liberation Struggle in Slovenia). Maribor, 1960.

Kozina, Vladimir. *Communism as I Know It*. Piedmont, Calif., 1966.

Krek, Miha, see Letter from Dr. Miha Krek.

Kunz, Josef L. "The Free Territory of Trieste," *Western Political Quarterly*, 1, no. 2 (June 1948): 99-112.

Law, Robert. "Trieste Close-up," *Time*, August 5, 1946.

Lazić, Branko. *Titov pokret i režim u Jugoslaviji: 1941-1946* (Tito's Movement and Government in Yugoslavia: 1941-1946). Munich, 1946.

Lederer, Ivo J. *Yugoslavia at the Paris Peace Conference: A Study in Frontiermaking*. New Haven, 1963.

Lenardič, Stane. "Od Trsta do Devina" (From Trieste to Duino), *Slovenski poročevalec*, July 17, 1953.

Leprette, Jacques. *Le Statut international de Trieste*. Paris, 1949.

Letter from Dr. Miha Krek, Former Minister of the Yugoslav Government-in-Exile. Cleveland, May 19, 1960.

Levine, Isaac Don. *The Mind of an Assassin*. New York, 1959.

Il libro verde, see Italy. Camera dei deputati.

Ljudska pravica (People's Right). Official organ of the Slovenian Communist Party. Ljubljana, 1947. Daily. Ceased publication.

Loh, Maks. "Bajeslovje v zgodovini" (Myths in History), *Vestnik*, 17, no. 10-11-12 (Oct.-Dec. 1966): 243-46.

London Agreement, 1952, see "Memorandum of Understanding . . . ," *Department of State Bulletin*, 26: 779-80.

London Agreement, 1954, see "Memorandum of Understanding . . . ," *Department of State Bulletin*, 31: 556-61.

London Pact, see Great Britain. *Parliamentary Papers*. Vol. 51.

Longo, Luigi. *I comunisti italiani e il problema triestino*. Rome, 1954.

———. *Un popolo alla macchia*. 2d ed. Verona, 1952.

Lunt, J. D. "The Venezia Giulia Police Force," *The Army Quarterly* (London), 58, no. 2 (July 1949): 213-18.

Luzzatto-Fegiz, Pierpaolo, et al. *L'economia della Venezia Giulia*. Prepared under the auspices of the Statistical Institute of the University of Trieste. Trieste, 1946.

Maclean, Fitzroy. *The Heretic: The Life and Times of Josip Broz-Tito*. New York, 1957.

McNeill, William H. *America, Britain, and Russia: Their Cooperation and Conflict, 1941–1946.* A volume of the *Survey of International Affairs: 1939–1946.* Edited for the Royal Institute of International Affairs by Arnold Toynbee. London, 1953.

"Maggio jugoslavo a Trieste," *Trieste,* no. 7 (May–June 1955), pp. 27–29.

Mal, Josip. *Zgodovina slovenskega naroda: Najnovejša doba* (The History of the Slovenian Nation: The Recent Period). Celje, 1928.

Marche Julienne, see L'Institut Adriatique.

March Proposal or Declaration, 1948, see "Statement by the Governments..."

Marin, Biagio. "Coscienza nazionale," *Trieste,* no. 2 (July–Aug. 1954), pp. 14–15.

Marjanović, Milan. *Borba za Jadran 1914–1946: Iredenta i imperijalizam* (The Struggle for the Adriatic, 1914–1946: Irredentism and Imperialism). Split, 1953.

Markert, Werner, ed. *Jugoslawien.* Cologne, 1954.

Martin, David. *Ally Betrayed: The Uncensored Story of Tito and Mihailovich.* New York, 1946.

Martino, Gaetano. "I positivi risultati dell'accordo per Trieste," *Trieste,* no. 64 (Nov.–Dec. 1964), pp. 4–5.

März, Joseph. *Die Adriafrage.* Berlin, 1933.

Maserati, Ennio. *L'occupazione jugoslava di Trieste, maggio-giugno 1945.* Udine, 1963.

———. "Il socialismo triestino durante la grande guerra," *Trieste,* no. 64 (Nov.–Dec. 1964), pp. 8–10.

"Masochists," *Time,* July 15, 1946, p. 33.

Mazzini, Giuseppe. *Scritti editi e inediti di Giuseppe Mazzini: Edizione nazionale.* Vols. 59, 69, and 92. Imola, 1931–41.

Medjunarodni problemi (International Problems). Vols. 2–4. Published by Institut za medjunarodnu politiku i privredu pri ministarstvu inostranih poslova (Institute for International Politics and Economics of the Ministry for Foreign Affairs). Belgrade, 1950–52.

Melik, Vasilij. "Volitve v Trstu, 1907–1913" (Elections in Trieste, 1907–1913), *Zgodovinski časopis,* 1 (1947): 70–122.

"Memorandum of Understanding between the Governments of Italy, the United Kingdom, and the United States Regarding Administration in Zone A of the Free Territory of Trieste," signed in London on May 9, 1952, *Department of State Bulletin,* 26 (May 19, 1952): 779–80. (London Agreement, 1952.)

"Memorandum of Understanding between the Governments of Italy, the United Kingdom, the United States and Yugoslavia Regarding

BIBLIOGRAPHY

the Free Territory of Trieste." Dated at London, October 5, 1954. Printed in *Department of State Bulletin*, 31 (Oct. 18, 1954), 556–61. (London Agreement, 1954.)

Memorandum Presented (1919), see Yugoslavia.

Miani, Ercole. "Le giornate triestine dell'aprile-maggio 1945," *Trieste*, no. 1 (May–June 1954), pp. 7–10.

——. "La resistenza nella Venezia Giulia," *Il Ponte*, 4, no. 4 (Apr. 1948), 339–45.

Mihovilović, Ive. *Italian Expansionist Policy toward Istria, Rijeka, and Dalmatia, 1945–1953: Documents*. Belgrade, 1954.

——. "Talijanska kolonizacija Julijske Krajine: Dokumenti" (Italian Colonization of the Julian March: Documents), *Anali jadranskog instituta*, 1 (1956): 117–56.

——. *Trst problem dana* (Trieste, the Problem of the Day). Zagreb, 1951.

Mikuž, Metod. "Boji Komunistične partije Jugoslavije za zahodne meje od 1941 do 1945" (The Struggles of the Communist Party of Yugoslavia for the Western Boundaries from 1941 to 1945), *Zgodovinski časopis*, 12–13 (1958–59): 7–24.

——. *Pregled zgodovine narodno-osvobodilne borbe v Sloveniji* (Survey of the History of the National Liberation Struggle in Slovenia). 2 vols. Ljubljana, 1960–61.

Military Government Journal. The Military Government Association Magazine. Vols. 1–2. Washington, D.C., 1948–49.

Milone, Ferdinando. *Il confine orientale*. Naples, 1945.

"Mobilizacija in oborožitev primorskega ljudstva ob kapitulaciji Italije" (The Mobilization and the Arming of the People of the Littoral at the Time of the Italian Capitulation), *Ljudska pravica*, Sept. 21, 1947.

Moodie, A. E. *The Italo-Yugoslav Boundary: A Study in Political Geography*. London, 1945.

——. *Slovenia: An Area of Strain*. Yugoslav Document no. 4. London, n.d. [1943].

Mrak, Boris. *Il fronte popolare italo-slavo e le elezioni*. Trieste, 1949.

Munnecke, Charles M. "Legal Challenge in Trieste," *Military Government Journal*, 2, no. 2 (Summer 1949): 6–10.

Murphy, Robert. *Diplomat among Warriors*. New York, 1965.

New York Times, 1945–54.

Ninth AMG Report (S/1473), see United Nations, Security Council. Doc. S/1473.

Novak, Bogdan C. "The Ethnic and Political Struggle in Trieste, 1943–1954." Unpublished Ph.D. dissertation, University of Chicago, 1961.

BIBLIOGRAPHY

Novak, Karl. "Pokret otpora u Slovenačkoj" (The Resistance Movement in Slovenia), *Knjiga o Draži*, 1: 317–32.

Novak, Viktor, et al. *Oko Trsta* (Around Trieste). Belgrade, 1945.

"Ob dvajsetletnici: Iz zapiskov zareškega župnika" (For the Twentieth Anniversary: From the Notes of the Parish Priest of Zarečje), serialized in *Vestnik*, 15, no. 8 (Aug. 1964)–17, no. 6–7 (June–July 1966).

October 8, 1953, Announcement, see "U.S., U.K. to Cease Administering Zone A of Trieste."

Pacor, Mario. *Confine orientale: Questione nazionale e resistenza nel Friuli-Venezia Giulia*. Milan, 1964.

Pagnini, Cesare. *Storie e storia della occupazione tedesca*. Milan, 1959.

Paladin, Giovanni. "L'inizio della 'Porzus' giuliana," *Trieste*, no. 7 (May–June 1955), pp. 21–22.

Paresce, Gabriele. *Italia e Jugoslavia dal 1915 al 1929*. Florence, 1935.

"Il patto del 9 dicembre 1944," *Trieste*, no. 7 (May–June 1955), pp. 11–12.

Paulova, Milada. *Jugoslavenski odbor: Povijest jugoslavenske emigracije za svjetskog rata od 1914–1918* (Yugoslav Committee: History of Yugoslav Emigration during the World War, 1914–1918). Zagreb, 1925.

Pertot, Vladimir V. *Trst: Medjunarodni privredni problem* (Trieste: An International Economic Problem). Belgrade, 1954.

Petelin, Stanko. *Osvoboditev Slovenskega Primorja* (The Liberation of the Slovenian Littoral). Nova Gorica, 1965.

Piemontese, Giuseppe. *Il movimento operaio a Trieste dalla fondazione alla fine della prima guerra mondiale*. Udine, 1961.

Pisani, Iolanda. "Gorizia, aprile 1945," *Trieste*, no. 59 (Jan.–Feb. 1964), pp. 22–23.

Il Ponte: Rivista mensile di politica e letteratura. Vol. 4. Florence, 1948.

Potočnik, Franc. *Žice, morje in gozdovi* (Wires, Sea and Forests). Ljubljana, 1951.

Program Slovenske demokratske zveze za Svobodno tržaško ozemlje v Trstu (Program of the Slovenian Democratic Union for the Free Territory of Trieste in Trieste). Trieste, 1949.

Quarantotti-Gambini, P. A. *Primavèra a Trieste: Ricordi del '45*. Milan, 1951.

Ramani, Nicolò. "E' stato un errore fermare i profughi a Trieste?" *Trieste*, no. 19 (May–June 1957), pp. 24–25.

"Razlastitev se nadaljuje" (The Expropriation Continues), *Demokracija*, Aug. 8, 1952.

"Reading, Writing, and Revolution," *Time*, March 25, 1946.

Regent, Giovanni, see Regent, Ivan.

BIBLIOGRAPHY

Regent, Ivan. *Poglavja iz boja za socializem* (Chapters from the Struggle for Socialism). 3 vols. Ljubljana, 1958–61.

———. *Sulla difesa della rivoluzione democratica.* Trieste, 1949.

———, et al., eds. *Slovensko Primorje in Istra: Boj za svobodo skozi stoletja* (Slovenian Littoral and Istria: The Struggle for Liberty through the Centuries). Prepared under the direction of Juraj Hrženjak. Belgrade, 1953. Cited as *Slovensko Primorje in Istra*.

Relazioni internazionali: Settimanale di politica estera. Vols. 15–18. Published by Istituto per gli studi di politica internazionale. Milan, 1951–54.

"Resolution of the Information Bureau Concerning the Situation in the Communist Party of Yugoslavia," printed in *The Soviet-Yugoslav Dispute,* pp. 61–70. (The Cominform Resolution.)

Review of International Affairs. Vols. 2–5. Published by the Federation of Yugoslav Journalists. Belgrade, 1951–54.

Risolo, Michele. *Il fascismo nella Venezia Giulia: Dalle origini alla marcia su Roma.* Intro. Rino Allessi. Trieste, 1932.

Risultati elettorali e analisi cartografica delle elezioni amministrative dal 1949 al 1952 nel comune di Trieste e negli altri comuni del territorio. Trieste, n.d.

Rivista di studi politici internazionali. Vols. 18, 22. Published by Studio florentino di politica estera. Florence, 1951, 1955.

Roletto, Giorgio. *Il porto di Trieste.* Bologna, 1941.

———. *Trieste ed i suoi problemi: Situazione, tendenze, prospettive.* Trieste, 1952.

Royal Yugoslav Government-in-Exile. *Memorandum on the Slovene Territorial Claims at the Moment of the Establishment of the New Boundaries of the Yugo-Slav State* (At the Seat of the Royal Yugo-Slav Government, May 1, 1941).

Sabini, Guido. "Trieste 1949," *Trieste,* no. 13 (May–June 1956), pp. 38–39.

Šah, Maks. "1945–1955: Deset let slovenskih šol na Tržaškem" (1945–1955: Ten Years of Slovenian Schools in Trieste Area), *Izvestje srednjih šol, 1955* (Trieste, 1955), pp. 3–7.

Saje, Franček. *Belogardizem* (The White Guardism). Ljubljana, 1951.

Sala, Teodoro. *La crisi finale nel Litorale Adriatico, 1944–1945.* Udine, 1962.

Salvadori, Massimo. *Storia della resistenza italiana.* Venice, 1955.

Salvemini, Gaetano. *Racial Minorities under Fascism in Italy.* Chicago, 1934.

———. "Trieste and Trst," *Free Italy,* 1, no. 4 (Apr. 1945): 6–9.

Santin, Antonio. *Trieste 1943–1945: Scritti, discorsi, appunti, lettere,* presentate, raccolte e commentate a cura di Guido Botteri. Udine, 1963.

Sator. *La popolazione della Venezia Giulia.* Foreword by Count Carlo Sforza. Rome, 1945.

Schiffrer, Carlo. "Chiesa e stato a Trieste durante il periodo fascista," *Trieste,* no. 58 (Nov.–Dec. 1963), pp. 4–8.

———. "Due vie e due costumi," *Trieste,* no. 31 (May–June 1959), pp. 21–27.

———. "Il fascismo al termine della parabola," *Trieste,* no. 56 (July–Aug. 1963), p. 15.

———. "Fascisti e militari nel incendio del Balkan," *Trieste,* no. 55 (May–June 1963), pp. 15–18.

———. "La missione storica del C.L.N. giuliano," *Trieste,* no. 7 (May–June 1955), pp. 13–15.

———. "Orientamenti politici degli elettori sloveni," *Trieste,* no. 14 (July–Aug. 1956), pp. 12–13.

———. "La resistenza a Trieste nel panorama europeo," *Trieste,* no. 66 (Mar.–April, 1965), pp. 14–19.

———. *Sguardo storico sui rapporti fra Italiani e Slavi nella Venezia Giulia.* 2d rev. ed. Trieste, 1946.

———. "Trieste nazista," *Trieste,* no. 28 (Nov.–Dec. 1958), pp. 13–21.

———. *La Venezia Giulia: Saggio di una carta dei limiti nazionali italo-jugoslavi con la carta annessa.* Rome, 1946.

———, see also Actor Spectator.

Second AMG Report (S/781), see United Nations, Security Council. Doc. S/781.

Second Yugoslav Report (S/1467), see United Nations, Security Council. Doc. S/1467.

Sedmak, Vladimir. "The Ethnic Character of the Slovene Coast," *Review of International Affairs,* 4, no. 19 (Oct. 1, 1953): 6.

———. "Survey of Progress," *Review of International Affairs,* 5, no. 109 (Oct. 16, 1954): 7–8.

———. "The Trieste Issue and Restitution of Slovene Property," *Review of International Affairs,* 5, no. 100 (June 1, 1954): 9–10.

———, and Mejak, J. *Trieste: The Problem Which Agitates the World.* Belgrade, 1953.

Sedmak, Vlado, see Sedmak, Vladimir.

Šepić, Dragovan. *Supilo diplomat: Rad Frana Supila u emigraciji, 1914–1917 godina* (Supilo the Diplomat: The Work of Frano Supilo in Exile during the Years 1914–1917). Zagreb, 1961.

BIBLIOGRAPHY

Seventh AMG Report (S/1374), see United Nations, Security Council. Doc. S/1374.

Sforza, Carlo. *Cinque anni a palazzo Chigi: La politica estera italiana dal 1947 al 1951.* Rome, 1952.

──. *Jugoslavia: Storia e ricordi.* Milan, 1948.

──. *Pensiero e azione di una politica estera: Discorsi e scritti con studio e note di Alb. Cappa.* Bari, 1924.

Silvestri, Claudio. "Mons. Bartolomasi e il problema slavo," *Trieste*, no. 57 (Sept.–Oct. 1963), pp. 14–15.

──. "Una repubblica delle Tre Venezie con presidente il Duca d'Aosta," *Trieste*, no. 35 (Jan.–Feb. 1960), pp. 25–27.

──. "Il socialismo a Trieste dopo la prima guerra mondiale," *Trieste*, no. 21 (Sept.–Oct. 1957), pp. 29–32.

Sixth AMG Report (S/1318), see United Nations, Security Council. Doc. S/1318.

Škerbec, Matija. *Krivda rdeče fronte* (The Guild of the Red Front). Cleveland, 1961.

Škerl, France. *La battaglia delle popolazioni del litorale per il potere popolare.* Ljubljana, 1945.

──. "Politični tokovi v osvobodilni fronti v prvem letu njenega razvoja" (Political Trends inside the Liberation Front during the First Year of Its Development), *Zgodovinski časopis*, 5 (1951): 7–86.

Slovenec (Slovene). Ljubljana, 1945. Daily newspaper. Ceased publication in May, 1945.

"Slovene Memorandum to the Military Administration: A Letter from Trieste," *Review of International Affairs*, 4, no. 12 (June 16, 1953): 20.

Slovenski poročevalec (Slovenian Reporter). Ljubljana, 1953. Daily, published first by the Slovenian Liberation Front, and later by the Socialistična zveza delovnega ljudstva Slovenije (Socialist Alliance of Working People of Slovenia). Ceased publication.

Slovensko Primorje in Istra, see Regent, Ivan, et al.

Šnuderl, Makso. *Politični sistem Jugoslavije* (The Yugoslav Political System). Vol. 1: *Družbeno-politična in ekonomska ureditev* (Socio-Political and Economic Organization). Ljubljana, 1965.

The Soviet-Yugoslav Dispute: Text of the Published Correspondence. Ed. Royal Institute of International Affairs. London, 1948.

"Spominski dnevi v maju" (The Days to Be Remembered in May), *Borec*, 5, no. 5 (May 1953): 174–76.

S. S. [Sylvia Sprigge]. "Trieste Diary," *The World Today: Chatham House Review*, New Series, 1, no. 4 (Oct. 1945), 159–86.

"Statement by the Governments of the United States, United Kingdom and France, March 20, 1948," *Department of State Bulletin*, 18 (Mar. 28, 1948): 425. (March Proposal.)

"Statement of the Central Committee of the Communist Party of Yugoslavia on the Resolution of the Information Bureau of Communist Parties on the Situation in the Communist Party of Yugoslavia," printed in *The Soviet-Yugoslav Dispute*, pp. 71–79.

Statuto della Lega Nazionale. Trieste, 1949.

Steffè, Bruno. "Le formazioni partigiane a Trieste e nella Venezia Giulia," *Trieste*, no. 66 (Mar.–Apr. 1965), pp. 19–21.

Stein, Leonard S. "The Problem of Trieste since World War II." Unpublished M.A. thesis, University of Chicago, 1949.

Stocca, Mario. *Discussioni sul T.L.T. al consiglio comunale di Trieste*. Trieste, n.d. [1950].

———. *Segnalazioni dalla stampa triestina*. Trieste, 1950.

"La storia segreta de *Il Corriere di Trieste*," *Trieste*, no. 36 (Mar.–Apr. 1960), pp. 7–11.

Stvarnost: Neodvisna slovenska revija (Reality: The Independent Slovenian Review). Vol. 1. Trieste, 1951.

Stvarnost in svoboda (Reality and Liberty). Vol. 2. Trieste, 1953.

Svobodna Slovenija, see *Svobodna Slovenija-Eslovenia libre*.

Svobodna Slovenija-Eslovenia libre. Buenos Aires, 1967. Weekly newspaper published by Slovenian émigrés in Argentina, since 1948. Cited as *Svobodna Slovenija*.

Tamaro, Attilio. *Trieste: Storia di una città e di una fede*. 2d ed. Milan, 1946.

Tanasco, G. *La posizione giuridica di Trieste*. Rome, 1951.

Tarchiani, Alberto. *Dieci anni tra Roma e Washington*. Verona, 1955.

Tchok [Čok], Ivan M. *The Problem of Trieste*. Ridgefield, Conn., 1943.

Temperley, H. W. V., ed. *A History of the Peace Conference of Paris*. 6 vols. London, 1920–24.

Tenth AMG Report (S/2062), see United Nations, Security Council. Doc. S/2062.

Third AMG Report (S/953), see United Nations, Security Council. Doc. S/953.

Time. New York, 1946–48.

Tito, Josip Broz. *Govori i članci* (Speeches and Articles). 12 vols. Zagreb, 1959.

"Tito and the Executioner," *Time*, September 6, 1948.

Tomšič, Ivan. "Da li suverenitet nad STT zaista još pripada Italiji?" (Does the Sovereignty over the Free Territory of Trieste Really Still Belong to Italy?), *Medjunarodni problemi*, 2, no. 2–3 (Apr.–June 1950): 8–21.

Tratnik, Matija (pseud.). "Temna zarja na Primorskem" (Gloomy Dawn over the Littoral), *Koledar-Zbornik, 1951,* pp. 142–51.
Treaty of Rapallo, see Great Britain. *Parliamentary Papers.* Vol. 43.
Trieste Handbook, see Allied Military Government.
Trieste nella lotta, see Comitato cittadino.
Trieste nella sua realtà, see Italy. Presidenza del consiglio dei ministri.
Trieste: Rivista politica giuliana. Trieste, 1954–66. With no. 29 (Jan.–Feb. 1959) the subtitle changed to *Rivista politica della regione.* The review is published six times a year. It follows a right-wing socialistic tendency. Cited as *Trieste.*
Trieste: Zone B, see Committee of National Liberation of Istria.
Truman, Harry S. *Memoirs.* Vol. II: *Years of Trial and Hope.* Garden City, N.Y., 1956.
"Tržaško ljudsko štetje" (Trieste's Population Census), in *Klic Triglava,* 4, no. 81 (November 19, 1951), 3–4. (Mimeographed.)
Twelfth AMG Report (S/3156), see United Nations, Security Council. Doc. S/3156.
United Nations, Security Council. Document S/679 (February 18, 1948): "Report on the Administration of the British–U.S. Zone of the Free Territory of Trieste for the Period 15 September to 31 December 1947 by Major General T. S. Airey . . ." (Mimeographed.) Cited as *First AMG Report* (S/679).

———. Doc. S/781 (May 25, 1948): "Report on the Administration of the British–U.S. Zone of the Free Territory of Trieste for the Period 1 January to 31 March 1948 by Major General T. S. Airey . . ." (Mimeographed.) Cited as *Second AMG Report* (S/781).

———. Doc. S/927 (July 28, 1948): "Yugoslav Note to the Security Council . . ." (Mimeographed.) Cited as *Yugoslav Note* (S/927).

———. Doc. S/953 (August 6, 1948): "Report on the Administration of the British–U.S. Zone of the Free Territory of Trieste for the Period 1 April to 30 June 1948 by Major General T. S. Airey . . ." (Mimeographed.) Cited as *Third AMG Report* (S/953).

———. Doc. S/1054 (November 2, 1948): "Memorandum from the Ministry of Foreign Affairs of Yugoslavia Transmitted to the President of the Security Council by Telegram on October 24, 1948." (Mimeographed.) Cited as *Yugoslav Memorandum* (S/1054).

———. Doc. S/1066 (November 4, 1948): "Annual Report of the Yugoslav Army Military Government on the Administration of the Yugoslav Zone of the Free Territory of Trieste for the Period 15 September 1947 to 15 September 1948." (Mimeographed.) Cited as *First Yugoslav Report* (S/1066).

———. Doc. S/1174 (January 5, 1949): "Report on the Administration

BIBLIOGRAPHY

of the British-U.S. Zone of the Free Territory of Trieste for the Period 1 July to 30 September 1948 by Major General T. S. Airey ..." (Mimeographed.) Cited as *Fourth AMG Report* (S/1174).

———. Doc. S/1183 (January 5, 1949): "Note Regarding the Administration of the Free Territory," signed in Belgrade, December 25, 1948. (Mimeographed.) Cited as *Yugoslav Note* (S/1183).

———. Doc. S/1242 (February 3, 1949): "Report on the Administration of the British-U.S. Zone of the Free Territory of Trieste for the Period 1 October to 31 December 1948 by Major General T. S. Airey ..." (Mimeographed.) Cited as *Fifth AMG Report* (S/1242).

———. Doc. S/1318 (May 6, 1949): "Report on the Administration of the British-U.S. Zone of the Free Territory of Trieste for the Period 1 January to 31 March 1949 by Major General T. S. Airey ..." (Mimeographed.) Cited as *Sixth AMG Report* (S/1318).

———. Doc. S/1348 (July 5, 1949): "Letter from the Yugoslav Government Concerning the Free Territory of Trieste," dated Belgrade, July 2, 1949. (Mimeographed.)

———. Doc. S/1374 (August 11, 1949): "Report on the Administration of the British-U.S. Zone of the Free Territory of Trieste for the Period 1 April to 30 June 1949 by Major General T. S. Airey ..." (Mimeographed.) Cited as *Seventh AMG Report* (S/1374).

———. Doc. S/1424 (November 30, 1949): "Report on the Administration of the British-U.S. Zone of the Free Territory of Trieste for the Period 1 July to 30 September 1949 by Major General T. S. Airey ..." (Mimeographed.) Cited as *Eighth AMG Report* (S/1424).

———. Doc. S/1467 (March 9, 1950): "Annual Report of the Yugoslav Army Military Government on the Administration of the Yugoslav Zone of the Free Territory of Trieste for the Period from 15 September 1948 to 15 September 1949." (Mimeographed.) Cited as *Second Yugoslav Report* (S/1467).

———. Doc. S/1473 (March 22, 1950): "Report on the Administration of the British-U.S. Zone of the Free Territory of Trieste for the Period 1 October to 31 December 1949 by Major General T. S. Airey ..." (Mimeographed.) Cited as *Ninth AMG Report* (S/1473).

———. Doc. S/2062 (March 29, 1951): "Report on the Administration of the British-U.S. Zone of the Free Territory of Trieste for the Period 1 January to 31 December 1950 by Major General T. S. Airey ..." (Mimeographed.) Cited as *Tenth AMG Report* (S/2062).

———. Doc. S/3156 (December 23, 1953): "Report on the Administration of the British-United States Zone of the Free Territory of Trieste for the Period 1 January to 31 December 1952 by Major General Sir

BIBLIOGRAPHY

John Winterton . . ." (Mimeographed.) Cited as *Twelfth AMG Report* (S/3156).

U.S. Department of State. *Provisional Administration of Venezia Giulia: Agreement between the United States of America, the United Kingdom of Great Britain and Northern Ireland, and Yugoslavia, Signed at Belgrade June 9, 1945.* Executive Agreements Series 501. Department of State Publication no. 2562. Washington, D.C., 1946. Cited as *Belgrade Agreement*.

———. *Treaty of Peace with Italy*. Treaties and Other International Acts Series no. 1648. Department of State Publication no. 2960. Washington, D.C., 1947. Cited as *Italian Peace Treaty*.

———. Foreign Relations of the United States, Diplomatic Papers. *The Conferences at Malta and Yalta, 1945*. Washington, D.C., 1955. Cited as *Conferences at Malta and Yalta*.

U.S. Department of the Army. Office of the Chief of Military History. *United States Army in World War II*. Special Studies: Harry L. Coles and Albert K. Weinberg. *Civil Affairs: Soldiers Become Governors*. Washington, D.C., 1964. Cited as Coles and Weinberg.

"U.S., U.K. to Cease Administering Zone A of Trieste." Announcement made simultaneously at Washington and London on October 8, 1953. Printed in *Department of State Bulletin*, 29 (Oct. 19, 1953), 529. (October 8, 1953, Announcement.)

The United States in World Affairs. Years 1951–53. Published by the Council on Foreign Relations. New York, 1952–55.

UNSC, Doc., see United Nations, Security Council. Document.

Uradni list, see Yugoslav Military Administration.

Valiani, Leo. *Tutte le strade conducono a Roma*. Florence, 1947.

Velikonja, Jože, see J. V.

"Venezie, Tre," *Enciclopedia italiana*, 35 (1937): 78, 90.

Ventura, Carlo. "Goebbels e il Litorale Adriatico," *Trieste*, no. 27 (Sept.–Oct. 1958), pp. 26–30.

———. *La stampa a Trieste 1943–1945*. Udine, 1958.

Vestnik, see *Vestnik-Noticiero*.

Vestnik-Noticiero. Glasilo Zveze Slovenskih protikomunističnih borcev (Organ of the Union of Slovenian Anti-Communist Combatants). Buenos Aires, Argentina, 1952–1967. Monthly since 1949.

The title, subtitle and the place of publication changed. Up to September 1953 the monthly was called *Šmartinski vestnik-Noticiero de San Martin*. The subtitle was Glasilo domobrancev in drugih protikomunističnih borcev (The Organ of the Home Guards and Other Anti-Communist Combatants) until 1959. It was published in San Martin, Argentina up to 1960. Cited as *Vestnik*.

BIBLIOGRAPHY

Vetrinjska tragedija, see Zveza Slovenskih protikomunističnih borcev.

Vilhar, Stanislav. "Državno-monopolistički kapitalizam u Italiji: Stvaranje državnog sektora u privredi" (State-Monopolistic Capitalism in Italy: Formation of a State Sector in the Economy), *Medjunarodni problemi,* 3, no. 2–3 (Mar.–June 1951): 36–67.

Vivante, Angelo. *Irredentismo adriatico: Contributo alla discussione sui rapporti austro-italiani.* Florence, 1912.

La Voce Libera. Quotidiano politico d'informazioni. Trieste, 1946.

Vukušić, S. "What Is Happening in Trieste?" *Review of International Affairs,* 2, no. 15 (July 18, 1951): 12–13.

Western Political Quarterly. Vol. 1. Published quarterly by the Institute of Government, University of Utah. Salt Lake City, 1948.

Who Should Have Trieste? Ljubljana, 1953.

The World Today: Chatham House Review. Published by the Royal Institute of International Affairs. New Series. Vol. 1. Oxford, 1945.

Yugoslav Government-in-Exile. Information Department. *The Yugoslav-Italian Frontier: Trieste and Hinterland.* Foreword by John Parker, M.P. Yugoslav Document no. 3. London, n.d. [1943].

Yugoslav Memorandum (S/1054), see United Nations, Security Council. Doc./1054.

Yugoslav Military Administration. Yugoslav Zone, Free Territory of Trieste. *Uradni list vojne uprave JA jugoslovanske cone na STO in istrskega okrožnega ljudskega odbora* (Official Gazette of the Military Administration of the Yugoslav Army for the Yugoslav Zone of the FTT and of the Istrian Regional People's Committee). Koper, 1948, 1949, 1950. Cited as *Uradni list.*

Yugoslav Note (S/927), see United Nations, Security Council. Doc. S/927.

Yugoslav Note (S/1183), see United Nations, Security Council. Doc. S/1183.

Yugoslavia. *Frontiers between the Kingdom of the Serbians, Croatians and Slovenes, and the Kingdom of Italy.* Paris, 1919.

———. *Memorandum of the Government of the Democratic Federative Yugoslavia Concerning the Question of the Julian March and Other Yugoslav Territories under Italy.* [Belgrade, 1945.] Cited as Yugoslavia, *Memorandum* (1945).

———. *Memorandum Presented to the Peace Conference, in Paris, Concerning the Claims of the Kingdom of the Serbians, Croatians and Slovenes.* Paris, 1919.

———. Beograd. Vojno-istoriski institut (War-Historical Institute). *Završne operacije za oslobodjenje Jugoslavije, 1944–1945* (The Final Operations for the Liberation of Yugoslavia, 1944–1945). Velimir Terzić, general editor. Belgrade, 1957. Cited as *Završne operacije.*

BIBLIOGRAPHY

Yugoslavia. Beograd. Vojno-istoriski institut (War-Historical Institute). *Zbornik dokumenata i podataka o narodno-oslobodilačkom ratu jugoslovenskih naroda* (Collection of Documents and Data of the National Liberation War of Yugoslav Nations). 7 parts. Belgrade, 1949–57. Published in Serbo-Croat language. Cited as *Zbornik* (Belgrade).

———. Vojnozgodovinski inštitut jugoslovanske ljudske armade (War-Historical Institute of the Yugoslav People's Army). *Zbornik dokumentov in podatkov o narodno-osvobodilni vojni jugoslovanskih narodov* (Collection of Documents and Data of the National Liberation War of Yugoslav Nations). Part 6: *Borbe v Sloveniji* (The Struggles in Slovenia). 12 vols. Ljubljana, 1953–65. Published in Slovenian language. Cited as *Zbornik*.

"Yugoslavia's Efforts to Denationalize Zone B and Italy's Desire for Peace," *Italian Affairs*, 2, no. 6 (Nov. 1953): 116–44.

Zakrajšek, Kazimir. *Ko smo šli v morje bridkosti* (When We Entered the Ocean of Sorrows). Washington, D.C., 1942.

Zalar, Charles. *Yugoslav Communism: A Critical Study*. Prepared for the U.S. Senate, Subcommittee of the Committee on the Judiciary, 87th Cong., 1st Sess. Washington, D.C., 1961.

Završne operacije, see Yugoslavia. Beograd. Vojno-istoriski institut.

Zbornik, see Yugoslavia. Vojnozgodovinski inštitut jugoslovanske ljudske armade.

Zbornik (Belgrade), see Yugoslavia. Beograd. Vojno-istoriski institut.

"Zružena Slovenija vstaja" (United Slovenia Is Rising), *Slovenec*, May 4, 1945.

"Že leta 1943 so naša narodna predstavništva pravno izvedla priključitev Slovenskega Primorja in Istre k Jugoslaviji" (Already in the Year 1943 our National Representatives Had Legally Accomplished the Annexation of the Slovenian Littoral and Istria to Yugoslavia), *Ljudska pravica*, Sept. 21, 1947.

Zgodovinski časopis (Historical Review). Vols. 1–13. Ljubljana, 1947–59.

Zorec-Kocelj, Franc. "Pogodba med Nemci in slovenskimi partizani" (Agreement between the Germans and the Slovenian Partisans), *Vestnik*, 16 (June 1965): 143–45.

Zveza Slovenskih protikomunističnih borcev (The Union of Slovenian Anti-Communist Combatants). *Vetrinjska tragedija* (The Tragedy of Vetrinje). Cleveland, 1960. Cited as *Vetrinjska tragedija*.

Zwitter, Fran. "Bibliografija o problemu Julijske krajine in Trsta: 1942–1947" (Bibliography on the Problem of the Julian March and Trieste: 1942–1947), *Zgodovinski časopis*, 2–3 (1948–49): 259–326.

———. "Narodnost in politika pri Slovencih" (The Nationality [Problem] and the Politics of the Slovenes). *Zgodovinski časopis*, 1 (1947): 31–69.

INDEX

Acheson, Dean, 319, 320, 338, 354, 359, 382, 415, 416
Action Committee for a United and Sovereign Slovenian State, 248 n. 13
Action Committee of the National Front, 63, 65
Action party: in Italy, 96, 97; in Julian Region, 112, 265
Adriatic islands, 71–72, 121, 267
Adriatic Littoral (Adriatisches Küstenland), 70, 89–119 passim; and Coceani's group, 74–76; German administration of, 71–74; and independentism, 258; and Istria, 87–88; and Ljubljana Province, 72, 77–84; and Mussolini's Fascist Republic, 72–73; Republican Fascist party in, 76–77; Slovenian collaboration in, 84–88. *See also* Istria; Ljubljana Province
Agneletto, Dr. Josip, 266, 405 n.39
Airey, General Terence S., 133, 290, 351, 363; as commander of Zone A, FTT, 275; and independentist votes, 311–12; and Proclamation No. 1, 275–76; recalled, 353, 357; reports to UN, 298, 347–52
Ajdovščina, 124, 169
Albania, 24 n.6, 46, 202
Alexander I, 43
Alexander, Field Marshal Harold, 132, 166, 168, 199–200 passim, 122, 124–25, 132, 223–24
Alexander line, 125 n.16
Allied Control Commission for Italy, 127, 131
Allied forces: enter Milan, 134; and Italian government, 97–98; and Italian resistance, 97, 98–99; liberate Italy, 95; and persecutions in Julian Region, 180–81; and Yugoslavs in Julian Region, 162–67, 192–94. *See also* New Zealand Division

Allied Military Government (AMG)
—in Zone A, FTT: financial and economic agreements with Italy, 283–86, 349; and increase of Italian influence, 283–90, 294–96, 297–98, 335; Italian participation in, 390, 398–408; and local government, 291–94, 302–3; and Mar. 1952 riots, 384–87; and 1949 elections, 301–12, 309 n.66; and 1951 (planned for) elections, 367, 370, 371; and 1952 elections, 392–97; and Nov. 1953 riots, 439–43; and Oct. 8, 1953, announcement, 435–36; organization of, 275–76, 291–94; policy of, before Mar. 1951, 312, 347–52; policy of, after Mar. 1951, 357, 363–65, 366–67, 371; termination of, 465–68
—in Zone A, Julian Region: Communist opposition to, 207–8, 210, 212–13, 221–30; and finances and economic recovery, 218–19; and law courts, 214; and local government, 207–13, 228–30, 291; organization of, 202–5; police force, 214–15; and press, 218; and public works, 219; and schools, 215–18, 229–30; and Slovenian rights, 215–18
Allied military troops, 386, 437, 442, 443
American line, 243–44, 245
AMG. *See* Allied Military Government
Anali jadranskog instituta (Annals of the Adriatic Institute), 345
Annex VIII. *See* Italian peace treaty
Annex X. *See* Italian peace treaty
Anti-Fascist Coordinating Committee, 116–17
Anti-Fascist Council for the National Liberation of Yugoslavia. *See* AVNOJ
Anti-Imperialist Front, 52

495

INDEX

ANVGD (Associazione Nazionale per la Venezia Giulia e Dalmazia), 342–43
April 1934 agreement, 58
April 1944 agreement, 103, 146
April 12–13, 1945, meeting, 141, 147–48, 149
Arena di Pola, L', 344
Armistice, Italian. *See* Italian armistice of 1943
Armstrong, Colonel Francis J., 221, 222 n.45
Arsenale Triestino, 288
Artusi, Ludovico, 88
Ascoli, Graziadio, 3
Association of St. Cyril and Methodius, 18–19, 86
Associazione Nazionale Dalmata, 343
Associazione Nazionale per la Venezia Giulia e Dalmazia (ANVGD), 342–43
Atlantic Pact, 280, 316, 366, 429
Attlee, Clement, 356–57
Aurisina. *See* Duino-Aurisina
Austrian Communist party, 58
Austrian empire, 6, 16, 340; censuses by, 7–9; and 1918 disorders in Prague and Ljubljana, 27; and elections in Julian Region, 19; and Italy, 1915, 23–24; and 1917 offensive against Italy, 25; and proposal for independent Trieste, 257; policy toward Slavs in Julian Region, 17, 18, 19; and provinces of Julian Region, 4
Austrian-Italian Social Democratic party, 39
Austrian Republic, 113, 123, 124, 161, 196, 426; communication with, 168, 199; and ERP supplies, 333; and independentists in Trieste, 384; occupied by Hitler, 44, 46; and signing of peace treaty, 316, 317; and Slovenian Home Guards, 125
Austrian Social Democratic party, 20, 21, 39
Austrian-Yugoslav Social Democratic party, 39
Austro-Italian border, 1866, 241, 244

Avarna, Giuseppe, 23–24
AVNOJ, 48–49, 53, 101, 114, 115

Babič, Branko, 177–78, 300. *See also* CPFTT (Babič)
Bača valley, 106
Badoglio, Marshal Pietro, 34 n.28, 70, 95–97
Bajt, Anton, 108
Balkan Pact, 381, 418, 419
Banca Commerciale Italiana, 287, 289
Banca di Roma, 287, 289, 290
Banca d'Italia, 218–19
Baraga, Srečko, 218
Bari, Italy, 92, 154
Baroš pier, and Treaty of Rome, 34
Bartole, Attilio, 374
Bartoli, Gianni, 379, 384–85, 386, 437–46 passim, 456
Bartoš, Milan, 461–62
Basovizza, 252–53, 416
Basovizza victims, 38
Bazovica. *See* Basovizza
Bebler, Dr. Aleš, 107, 178, 249, 319, 362, 455, 465
Bela garda (White Guard). *See* Village Guards
Belci, Corrado, 344
Belgrade, 94, 124–25, 195, 250
Belgrade agreement, 199–200, 208–10, 234
Beltram, Julij, 220, 465
Benedetti, Armando, 188 n.69
Bersaglieri, 467
Bettiol, Giuseppe, 340, 369
Bevin, Ernest, 338
Bevk, France, 107, 108, 172, 255
Bidault, Georges, 428, 434–35, 450
Bidovec, Ferdinand, 38 n.33
Bihać, first AVNOJ meeting in, 48
Blocco Triestino. *See* Triestino bloc
Blue Devil Daily, 372
Blue Guard. *See* Slovenian Chetniks
Boglione, Nito, 146
Bollettino (Bulletin), 110
Bollettino d'informazione, 343
Bolshevik revolution, and left-wing radicalism in Trieste, 40
Bonomi, Ivanoe, 32 n.23, 96, 97, 117, 137–38, 191
Borba, 299, 387

INDEX

Border commission, 1947, 259, 260
Bosnia, 46, 48, 89, 92, 170
Bowman, Colonel Alfred C., 291 n.34, and General Order No. 11, 210-11, 213, 225-26
Brigata d'Assalto Garibaldi-Trieste, 109, 110
Brigata Fontanot, 109, 110
Brigata Garibaldi-Natisone, 109, 110
Brigata Proletaria, 109
Brigata Triestina, 109, 110
Brilej, Jože, 357 n.12
Brioni, 414
British-American Zone of FTT. *See* FTT, Zone A
British Eighth Army. *See* New Zealand Division
British 56th, London Division, 168
British line, 243-44
British navy, guards Vis, 92
British troops, 155, 373. *See also* Great Britain
Broscio, Manlio: and letter to Velebit, 459; and new ideas on FTT dispute, 383; at 1952 London talks, 387-88, 389; at 1954 London talks, 450-51, 453, 454, 457-58
Broz, Josip-Tito. *See* Tito, Marshal Josip Broz
Bruni, Giorgio, 374-75
Budicin, Pino, 111
Buje, 325, 326, 374
Buje district, 260, 322, 401, 464
Bujština. *See* Buje district
Bulajić, M. K., 264
Bulgaria, 44, 46, 94, 315 n.3

Cadorna Raffaelle, 98, 99, 424
Camera del Lavoro (Labor Union), 386
Cammarata, Angelo E., 346
Cantieri Riuniti dell'Adriatico, 288
Capodistria. *See* Koper
Carabinieri, 151, 166
Caracci, Signore, 147
Carinthia, Austria, 4, 7, 24, 27, 72 n.4; and Association of St. Cyril and Methodius, 19 n.22; Slovenian claims to, 314, 317; and Slovenian Home Guards, 155

Carnaro. *See* Quarnero
Carnes, Colonel James J., 291 n.34
Carniola, 4, 24, 27, 75 n.11
Carra, E., 143 n.32
Carragher, Major M. H. R., 440
Carrobio di Carrobio, Count Renzo, 385 and n.6, 386
Casa del Fascio (Home of the Fascists), 170
Casa del Popolo (Home of the People), 170
Casardi, Alberico, 385 n.6
Cassino, 95
Castellani, Augusto, 385 n. 6
Catholic church in Zone B, FTT, 334
Catholic party. *See* Slovenian People's party
Cavour, Count Camillo di, 14 n.16
CEAIS (Comitato Esecutivo Antifascista Italo-Sloveno) (Italo-Slovenian Anti-Fascist Executive Committee), 148, 149, 171, 258
Celje, 50
Celovec (Klagenfurt), 72 n.4, 155
Census, 1910 (Austrian), 6-9 and n.9
Census, 1921 (Italian), 6, 10
Census, 1945 (Yugoslav), 10-11
Census, 1951, Zone A, FTT, 371
Central Committee for National Liberation in Rome, 96
Centro di Cultura Popolare, in Zone B, FTT, 324
Centro Studi Adriatici, 343-44
Cerknica district, 27
Čermelj, Dr. Lavo, 35 n.29, 38 n.33
Černi, General Josip, 162, 170
Charles, Sir Noel, 131
Chetniks: liquidated in Serbia, 183; organization and aims of, 47-48 and n.5; supported by Polish troops in Italy 256; and Western Allies, 70 and n.1, 89-90, 91, 92-93, 113. *See also* Slovenian Chetniks; Serbian Chetniks
Christian Democratic party (Italy), 96, 97, 282
Christian Democratic party (Trieste): and elections, 308, 309, 311, 394-95; and Irredentism, 339; as

497

INDEX

member of CLN, Julian Region, 112, 265
Christian Socialists, in Zone B, FTT, 325, 326
Churchill, Winston S.: and Istrian landing, 131–32; on occupation of Julian Region, 132; and Partisans, 90, 91, 93; and spheres of interest, 94, 129, 202 n.1; supports Badoglio government, 96; and Yugoslav border claims, 117, 130, 131, 196
Cianfarra, Camille M., 372
Citizenship, of FTT, 272–73
Clarke, Colonel, 166–67, 167–68
Clerical party. *See* Slovenian People's party
CLN (Comitato di Liberazione Nazionale) (Committee of National Liberation), for Julian Region, 76, 96; activities during Yugoslav occupations of Trieste, 146, 187–92; and Apr. 12–13, 1945, meeting, 147–48; contacts with Coceani's group, 112, 113, 117, 119, 136, 137–38, 139, 140–41, 141, 157–58; delegation sent to Italy, May 1945, 191; dissolved, 265; first manifestation under AMG, 253; and forming of joint committees with Slovenian Liberation Front, 156–57; and Italian Communists, 118; and manifestation of May 5, 1945, 189–90; and negotiations with Slovenian Liberation Front, 113–17, 141–42, 148–49; organization of, 112–13; relations with Western Allies, 145, 165, 194, 219, 231; at second Milan meeting, 115–16; supports Italian claims to Julian Region, 118–19, 252; and uprising in Trieste, 135, 140–46, 147, 151 and n.61, 156–57
CLNAI (Comitato di Liberazione Nazionale Alta Italia) (Committee of National Liberation for Upper Italy), 127, 139; formed, 98; and German surrender, 134; and negotiations with Slovenian Liberation Front, 113–17; and relations with Western Allies, 99. *See also* Italy, Italian, Italians, resistance
CLN for Istria (Comitato di Liberazione Nazionale dell'Istria) (Committee of National Liberation for Istria): accused by Yugoslavs, July 1951, 340–41, 376; and data of persecutions in Zone B, 336, 379–80; and memorandum for Pella, Sept. 1953, 423–24
CLT (Consiglio di Liberazione di Trieste) (Liberation Council of Trieste): and AMG, 221, 225–26; departments of, 173; dissolution of, 226; formation of, 171, 172; and independentists, 258
Coceani, Bruno: and CLN, 112, 113, 117, 119, 135, 137–38, 140, 157–58; connections of, with Mussolini, 72, 87; escapes to Italy, May 1945, 194; as executive member of Centro Studi Adriatici, 344; and meeting with Schäffer, 139–40; and collaboration with Germans, 74–75, 76, 137; and Republican Fascists, 76–77, 135, 139; and Slovenes, 86–87, 136; talks with Serbs, 136, 154
Coceani's group, 75–76, 112, 135, 136–40, 158–59
Collotti, Gaetano, 140
Coloni system, 237–38
Combined chiefs of staff, 195, 204, 210
Cominform, 278
Cominformists. *See* CPFTT (Vidali)
Cominform Resolution, 299–301, 314–21, 323, 349–50
Comintern, 58–60, 63, 67, 103
Comitato Antifascista di Coordinamento (Anti-Fascist Coordinating Committee), 116–17
Comitato di Collegamento (liaison committee), 103
Comitato di Difesa per l'Italianità di Trieste e dell'Istria (Committee for Defense of the Italianity of Trieste and Istria), 379, 385, 440, 446
Comitato di Liberazione Nazionale. *See* CLN

498

INDEX

Comitato di Liberazione Nazionale Alta Italia. *See* CLNAI
Comitato di Liberazione Nazionale dell'Istria. *See* CLN for Istria
Comitato di Salute Pubblica. *See* Coceani's group
Comitato Esecutivo Antifascista Italo-Sloveno (CEAIS) (Italo-Slovenian Anti-Fascist Executive Committee), 148, 149, 171, 258
Comitato Fronte Nazionale d'Azione (Action Committee of the National Front), 63, 65
Comitato Giuliano (Julian Committee), 127, 128
Comitato Litorale di Trieste PCI (Littoral Committee for Trieste of of the Italian Communist party), 62–63, 65
Comitato per la Venezia Giulia e Zara, 342
Commission of experts, 242, 258; reports of, 244; visit of, to Julian Region, 253–55
Committee for Defense of the Italianity of Trieste and Istria, 379, 385, 440, 446
Committee for Public Welfare. *See* Coceani's group
Committee for the FTT, 438
Committee of National Liberation. *See* CLN
Committee of National Liberation for Upper Italy. *See* CLNAI
Communist Party of Croatia. *See* Croat Communist party
Communist Party of the Free Territory of Trieste. *See* CPFTT
Communist Party of the Free Territory of Trieste (Babič). *See* CPFTT (Babič)
Communist Party of the Free Territory of Trieste (Vidali). *See* CPFTT (Vidali)
Communist Party of Italy. *See* Italian Communist party
Communist Party of Slovenia. *See* Slovenian Communist party
Communist Party of Venezia Giulia. *See* CPVG
Communist Party of Yugoslavia. *See* Croat Communist party; Slovenian Communist party; Yugoslav Communist party
Communist underground, in Julian Region 1943–45, 100–12
Condominium, 361, 388–89
Congress of Oppressed Nationalities, Apr. 1918, 26
Conrad, Allison, 372
Consiglio di Liberazione di Trieste. *See* CLT
Constituent assembly, Trieste, 172
Consulta della Città di Trieste, 172
Continuous ethnic line, 362, 382, 414
Cormons, 28
Corpo Volontari della Libertà. *See* CVL
Corps of Volunteers of Liberty. *See* CVL
Corriere di Trieste, Il (the Messenger of Trieste): and commission of experts, 258; on Nov. 1953 coup d'état in Trieste, 439; on Oct. 8, 1953, announcement, 429; and postponement of 1951 elections in Zone A, 370–71; and Yugoslav money, 259, 280 n.16
Cortesi, Arnaldo, 360
Council of Foreign Ministers, 240–51 passim. *See also* Italian peace treaty
Court of Cassation, 206, 214, 364
Cox, Geoffrey: on Italian propaganda, 192–93; and persecutions in Trieste, 166, 181–82, 183–84; on Serbian troops, 152 n.64; on Yugoslavs in Julian Region, 164–65, 166–67
Cox, James, 31
CPFTT (Communist Party of the Free Territory of Trieste): and Cominform Resolution, 299–301; formed, 264; opposes AMG economic agreements with Italian government, 286; policy toward FTT, 264, 270, 279–80; and representation in local government, Zone A, FTT, 293; and Slovenian schools in Zone A, FTT, 411; and Zone B, FTT, 324, 331
CPFTT (Babič): and Cominformists, 377–78; and 1949 congress,

499

INDEX

318–19; and 1949 elections, 304, 308, 317; and 1952 elections, 396; and Oct. 8, 1953, announcement, 438; policy of, in Zone A, FTT, 320; and program for 1951 elections, 367–68
CPFTT (Vidali): defends FTT, 33, 368, 426, 438; and 1949 congress, 318; and 1949 elections, 304, 308, 311; and 1952 elections, 394–95, 396; and Zone B, FTT, 324, 326
CPVG (Communist Party of Venezia Giulia): and AMG, 207–8, 210, 212–13, 218, 222, 225–30; dissolution of, 264; formation and aims of, 220; and Italo-Slovenian unity, 227, 232–33; and peace conference, 231–32, 233; and terroristic attacks on AMG local government, 228–29; and Zone B, Julian Region, 234. *See also* UAIS-SIAU
Credito Italiano, 287, 289
Crimean conference, 123, 127, 132
Croat Communist party, 66, 67–69, 264. *See also* CPFTT; CPFTT (Babič); CPFTT (Vivaldi); CPVG; UAIS-SIAU; ZAVNOH
Croatia, Croatian, Croats: as independent state, 44, 46, 50, 66–69, 152, 153; in Istria, 69, 73–74, 88, 119; under Italy, 1918–41, 30, 34–38, 42–43; land, people, historical background of, 4, 7, 14, 18–19, 22, 26–27; and Partisans in Istria, 66–69, 92, 101, 111–12, 113, 179; in Pula, 1945–47, 216–17; and World War I and peace treaty, 26–27, 28–29, 31–32; in Zone B, FTT, 267, 268, 323, 375, 401, 464; in Zone B, Julian Region, 120–21, 176, 184, 234, 236–37, 267. *See also* Buje district; Croat—FTT, Zone B; Istria; Julian Region, Zone B; UAIS-SIAU
Croat National Liberation Committee (—Council; —Movement), 48, 66, 101
Croce, Benedetto, 127
Curiae, 19

Currency: dinar, 317, 329, 379 n.55; Yugo-lira, 237, 327–28
Customs Guards, 144
Customs union, between Yugoslavia and Zone B, 331, 332, 335
CVL (Corpo Volontari della Libertà) (Corps of Volunteers of Liberty): in Italy, 98–99; in Trieste, 142–43, 157
Czechoslovakia, 44, 46, 240 n.2, 281, 315

Dabney, General John A., 467
Dalmatia: historical background of, 3–4, 15, 18; Italians in, 128 n.24; and World War I, 24, 30–31, 32; and World War II, 46, 69, 71–72, 127–28, 150
D'Annunzio, Gabriele, 16, 32, 33, 125, 338–39
Debeli rtič, 452
De Berti, Antonio, 188 n.68
De Castro, Diego: ethnic line of, 426; and fall 1953 events, 436, 447–48; as Italian political adviser to AMG, 396–98; and Italians in Zone B, 181, 254, 375, 380; resigns, 453
De Courten, Raffaele, 136
Ded (George Dimitrov), 58, 103
Dedijer, Vladimir, 113 n.65
De Gasperi, Alcide: appointed foreign minister, 357 n.12, 358–59; and direct negotiations, 382–83; and Eden and American proposals, 415, 416–17; last government of, 418; and Irredentists, 342; and Italian peace treaty, 241–42, 245; at London meeting, Mar. 1951, 355–56, 356–57; Mar. 1952 riots and 1952 London agreement, 387, 391, 392, 398; and postponement of 1951 elections, Zone A, 369–70; and Tripartite Proposal, 334, 337, 382–83, 453; visit of, to Canada and U.S., Sept. 1951, 358, 359, 360, 365–66
Delavska enotnost. *See* Unità Operaia
Della Motta, 183
Delo (Work): Cominformist news-

500

INDEX

paper, 300; Partisan newspaper, 109
De Marsanich, Augusto, 358
Democrazia Cristiana. *See* Christian Democratic party
Demokracija (Democracy), 265, 266, 310
Depolli, Attilio, 34
Depretis, Agostino, 16
De Renzi, General Edmondo, 466, 467, 468
De Simone, Pasquale, 344
Destradi, Alessandro (alias Gigi), 177
Deutsche Adria Zeitung, Die (the German Adriatic Newspaper), 73
Devin-Nabrežina. *See* Duino-Aurisina
De Winton, General Robin, 263, 467
Dežman, Colonel Josip, 82
Di Carrobio, Count Renzo Carrobio, 385 and n.6, 386
Difesa Adriatica, 344
Difesa Popolare (People's Militia), 175, 205, 223-24
Dimitrov, George, 58, 103
Dinar currency, 317, 329, 379 n.55
Di Soragna, Antonio Meli Lupi, 357 n.12
Divisione "Domenico Rossetti," 143
Divisione Giulia, 62
Dixon, Pierson, 389
Djilas, Milovan, 89-90, 91, 299
Doenitz, Admiral, 133, 134
Dolina. *See* San Dorligo della Valle
Domobranci (Home Guards), 83-84, 85-86, 153 n.65, 155-56
Dragicchio, Luigi, 344
Drago, Silvano, 344
Dragonja River, 176, 376
Drapšin, General Petar, 161, 167, 168
Drvar, Bosnia, 92
Duino, fishing settlement of, 408
Duino agreement, 200-201, 237, 245-46
Duino-Aurisina (Devin-Nabrežina), 292, 303; and 1949 elections, 306, 309 n.66; and 1952 elections, 393, 396, 397; and Slovenian geographical names, 405-6
Dulles, Allen, 133

Dulles, John Foster, 416, 425, 428, 433, 435

East-West tensions, 242, 247, 277-81, 381
Eboli, 154
Eddleman, General Clyde D., 297 n.48
Eden, Anthony: answers Stalin on Yugoslav territorial claims, 130; on failure of Oct. 8, 1953, announcement, 427-28, 433; on final negotiations on FTT, 450, 451; and 1952 London agreement, 384 n.5, 387-88, 389, 392; proposal of, at Crimean conference, 123-24 and n.13, 132, 195; 1952 proposal of, 414-15, 415-16; on Nov. 1953 riots, 444-45; on Tripartite Proposal, 282
Eden's line, 123-24, 124 n.13, 132, 195
Eighty-eighth Division, U.S., 168
Einaudi, Luigi, 468
Eisenhower, Dwight D., 373, 455
Elections. *See under names of localities*
Eneo (Rečina), 34
Ente per il Porto Industriale di Zaule, 408
Entente powers, 24
Epuration, 206
ERP (European Recovery Program), 284-85, 333, 408, 409
Esposito, Giovanni, 143 n.33
Ethnic line, FTT, 362, 382, 414
Ethnic mixed territory, 59, 116-17
Ethnic principle, 30, 115, 116, 148, 241-42, 382
Ethnic rights, 215-18, 238, 458-59. *See also* Minority rights
European Defense Community, 415, 425, 428, 454
European Recovery Program (ERP), 284-85, 333, 408, 409
Eve, General, 221
Excelsior hotel, 290
Extraordinary (Military) Tribunal, 38, 57

Fadda, Giuseppe, 410
Falcon Legion, 56-57, 78 and n.18
Fanfani, Amintore, 452

501

INDEX

Fascism, Fascist: Communist interpretation of, 183; fall of, 70; first units of, 35–36; laws of, in Zone A, FTT, 405–6, 406 n.40, 407; laws of, in Zone B, FTT, 327; and persecutions, 35–41, 61, 64, 422–23; after July 1943, 76, 106, 135–36, 151, 173–74, 186, 206
Fascist Law No. 800, 405–6
Fascist Republican party. *See* Republican Fascist party
Favilla, 344
Ferfolja, Dr. Jože, 64, 87
Ferluga, Carlo G., 188 n.69
Ferretti, Lando, 462
Financial Institute of Slovenia and Trieste, 185
Finmare, 288–89
Finmeccanica, 288
Finsider, 288
First London Agreement, 383, 387–94 passim
Fiume. *See* Rijeka
Flags, display of, 206, 439
Flückiger, Colonel Hermann, 316, 449
Fonda-Savio, Antonio (alias Manfredi), 137, 139 and n.21, 142, 188 n.69
Forestal Triestina, 289
Forlì, 154
Forty-third (Istrian) Division, 111
Fotić, Konstantin, 47 n.2, 130–31
Fotitch, Constantine. *See* Fotić, Konstantin
Fourth Army, and Julian Region, 145, 150–52, 153, 157, 161, 166–68, 199, 200
Fracassi, Marquis Cristoforo, 453
France: after Cominform Resolution, 334, 353, 354, 384; French line, 243–44, 245, 248, 262; and final negotiations, 428, 449–50, 455, 460; and Italian peace treaty, 1947, 243–44, 245, 248, 249; and Tripartite Proposal, 281; World War I, 24 and nn.5 and 6, 28–31, 29 n.17
Francis Joseph, 15
Frausin, Luigi, 117, 118
Free port of Trieste, 274–75, 460, 461

Free Territory of Trieste. *See* FTT
French Line, 243–44, 245, 248, 262. *See also* France
Freyberg, General Bernard C., 145, 163–68, 188
Friuli, Friulian, Friulians: and Adriatic Littoral, 71–72; and Partisans, 62, 103, 109, 110, 116; people, 11 n.12; and Yugoslav claims, 28, 100, 128, 184
Fronte dell'Indipendenza. *See* Independence Front
FTT (Free Territory of Trieste): creation of, and Italian peace treaty, 240–56; and events of June 1953–Oct. 1954, 414–17; final negotiations on, 448–55; and General Airey's reports, 347–52; and independentism and irredentism, 332–47 passim; and Italo-Yugoslav negotiations on, 353–80; land and people of, 268; minority rights in, 404–14; and need for new solution, 1952, 414–17; and 1952 administrative changes in Zones A and B, 392–404; and 1952 London Agreement, 381–91; and 1954 London Agreement, 456–71; post-Italian treaty maneuvers concerning, 259–67; and Provisional and Permanent statutes, 268–75; in transitional period, 270–77. *See also* Condominium; Continuous ethnic line; Eden, Anthony, 1952 proposal of; Governor; October 8, 1953, announcement; Plebiscite; Tripartite Proposal
—, Zone A: economy of, 280–81, 283–90, 330, 332–33, 350, 351, 368; and Italian Irredentism, 339–44; political parties in (*see* CPFTT; CPFTT [Babič]; CPFTT [Vidali]; Independence Front; Italian political parties; Slovenian political parties; Triestino bloc); and Slovene rights, 294–97, 298, 404–11
—, Zone A, Allied Military Government: financial and economic agreements of, with Italy, 283–86, 349; increase of Italian in-

502

INDEX

fluence in, 283–90, 294–96, 297–98, 335; Italian participation in (Order No. 165), 390, 398–408; local government of (Orders Nos. 259 and 33), 291–94, 302–3; and March 1952 riots, '384–87; and 1949 elections, 301–12, 309 n.66; and 1951 (planned for) elections, 367, 370, 371; and 1952 elections, 392–97; and Nov. 1953 riots, 439–43; and Oct. 8, 1953, announcement, 435–36; organization of, 275–76, 291–94; policy of, after Mar. 1951, 357, 363–65, 366–67, 371; policy of, before Mar. 1951, 312, 347–52; relations of, with Yugoslavs in Zone B, 330–31, 363, 377; termination of, 465–68
—, Zone B: and customs union, 331; decentralization of economy of, 378–79; and dinar currency, 329; economy of, 327–31, 378–79, 402; extension of Yugoslav control over, 401–2; formation of, 260–62; and 1950 elections, 324–26; 335, 336–37; and 1952 elections, 403–4; and People's committees, 260–62, 322–23, 401–2; Yugoslav administration of, after May 1952, 401–4; Yugoslav administration of, before 1951, 322–32; Yugoslav administration of, Mar. 1951–Mar. 1952, 373–80
Furlani, Vittorio, 188

Gaither, General Ridgely, 291 n.36
Gallarati-Scotti, Tommaso, 357 n.12, 383 n.4
Gammell, General James, 122
Garibaldi formations in Slovenian Littoral, 109
Garibaldi-Natisone, 110
Garibaldi-Osoppo division, 110
Garibaldi units (Communist guerrilla), 97
General Order No. 11, 207–13, 228–30, 291
Gentry, General, 165, 166
German-Partisan agreement, 106
Germany, German, Germans: attack and divide Yugoslavia, 46, 47; occupy Northern Slovenia, 50–51; and property in Trieste confiscated by Yugoslavs, 186; and struggle with Partisans, 92, 105, 106, 109, 111; surrender in Italy, 1945, 133–34; in Trieste, May 1945, 138, 140, 144 and n.35, 145, 151–52, 157, 162, 164. *See also* Adriatic Littoral
Giampiccoli, Mario, 258, 425
Gigante, Vicenzo (alias Ugo), 112
Giolitti, Giovanni, 31, 32 n.23, 33
Giornale Alleato (Allied Journal), 218
Giornale d'Italia, 337
Giornale di Trieste, 340, 437, 439
Giunta, Francesco, 36
Giunta d'Intesa, 265
Giustizia e Libertà (Justice and Liberty), 97
Glas Istre (Voice of Istria), 68, 112
Glas zaveznikov (Voice of the Allies), 218, 266
Globocnik, Odilo, 73, 140
Gonella, Guido, 344
Goriški list (Gorizia's Paper), 86
Gorizia: Allied occupation of, 123, 124, 161; AMG administration of, 203, 207, 211, 213, 229, 275–77; and CLN and Slovenian Liberation Front, 156–57 n.74; and Italian peace treaty, 241, 244, 245, 246, 247, 250; Partisan persecutions in, 179–85; population of, 6, 11 n.12; and Slovenes, 1943–45, 86, 87; and Slovenes under AMG, 216, 265, 266; and Slovenes under Italy, 410–11; and Trieste negotiations, 319, 338, 343, 422; and UAIS-SIAU, 230, 232; and Wilson line, 30; and World War I Italian demands, 23–24, 27; and Yugoslav army, 162, 167, 168, 176, 196; Yugoslav claims in, 1919, 28
Gortan, Vladimir, 38
Gothic line, 95
Governor, 277–81, 283, 337, 449
Grazioli, Emilio, 51
Grazzini, Enzo, 364
Grčarice, 81
Great Britain, 129, 172; and aid to Yugoslavia, 315 and n.4, 354; British personnel in FTT, 377;

503

INDEX

and final negotiations on FTT, 450–55; on Italian flags in Trieste, 439; and Italy's diplomatic status, 125–26; and Julian Region, 1943–45, 132, 194–96, 198 n.101; and Mar. 1951 London meeting, 356–57; and 1952 London Agreement, 387–88, 389, 392; and 1953 riots in Trieste, 444–45, 447; and Oct. 8, 1953, announcement, 427–28; and official statement on 1954 London Agreement, 460; and revision of Italian peace treaty, 355; and Tripartite proposal, 281; and World War I and 1919 peace conference, 24 and nn.5 and 6, 28–31, 29 n.17; and Yugoslav Partisans, 63, 90, 91, 93; and Yugoslav territorial demands 1941–45, 117, 130, 131, 196. *See also* Italian peace treaty; British—

Greece: 44, 353; attacked by Italy, 1940, 46; and Balkan Pact, 381, 418, 419; German evacuation of, 91–92; Greek civil war, 153, 314–15

Greif, Martin (alias Rudi), 149 n.56, 172, 175, 178

Gruppo Parlamentare Giuliano-Dalmata, 342

Gruppo Parlamentare pro Trieste, 342

Guardia Civica, 76, 138, 141, 143, 144, 148, 151

Guardia del Popolo (People's Militia), 175, 205, 223–24

Guardia di Finanza (Customs Guards), 144, 151

Guidotti, Gastone, 362, 381, 385 n.6

Gustincich, Giuseppe (alias Gildo), 172, 177

Habsburg Empire. *See* Austrian empire

Hague International Court, The, 365–66, 403

Handler, M. S., 325–26, 336, 377

Harding, General John, 167, 168, 204

Harding, Warren G., 31

Harrison, Geoffrey W., 451–52, 453–55

Hinterregger, Dr. Rudolf, 72 and n.6

Hitler, 46, 50 n.10, 134, 197, 198

Holjevec, General Večeslav, 234

Holmes, Julius C., 389–91, 451

Home Guards, 83–84, 85–86, 153 n.65, 155–56, 183

Home of the People, 170

Hooker, Robert G., 455

Hotel Balkan (Slovenian National Home), 36

Hrvatski glas (Croat Voice), 324

Hungary, 18, 43, 46, 50, 315 n.3

Hybrids in Istria, 11 n.13

Identity cards, 296–97

Ideology: of CLN and Coceani's group, 112, 119, 159–60; of Coceani and an anti-Communist alliance, 135, 136; of Cominform Resolution, 299–301, 308; and Communist persecutions, 181, 182–84; and Communist propaganda in Zone A, Julian Region, 220, 227–28, 232–33; and cooperation between Slovene and Italian Communists, 266, 308; and De Castro plan, 426; and migration from Yugoslav part of Julian Region, 262–63; and Pella's proposal for plebiscite, 425–26; in Zone B, Julian Region, 236

Idrija district, 4, 30

Ilva, 288

Imperiali, Marquis Guglielmo, 24 n.5

Independence Front: formation of, 258; headquarters of, attacked, 385, 440, 441, 442; and 1949 elections, 304, 308–9 and n.66, 311–12; and 1952 elections, 394; and Oct. 8, 1953, announcement, 438; oppose economic agreements between AMG and Italian government, 286; and Pella's plebiscite proposal, 425; recognized in Zone B, 234, 324. *See also* Independentists

Independent Democratic party in Slovenia, 49

Independentists: and AMG, 270, 280, 293, 312, 333, 366–67; and

504

INDEX

Austrian Republic, 384; formation of, 252, 257–58; and General Airey's reports, 311–12, 349, 350; interpretation by, of 1953 riots, 445–46; and 1949 elections, 305, 310; and 1951 elections, reaction to postponement of, 371; and 1952 elections, 394; and 1952 London Agreement, 385–86, 391; and 1954 London Agreement, 464; and Oct. 8, 1953, announcement, 438; on plebiscite, 425–26; and pro-Italians, 259, 280 n.16; rumors about, and 1953 riots, 438–39, 440, 441, 442. *See also* Independence Front; Triestino bloc

Independent Italian Democrats, 148

Independent Slovenian-Croat Socialist party, 39

Inštitut za narodna vprašanja (Institute for National Questions), 345

Instrument for the Provisional Regime of the Free Territory of Trieste, 270–75, 283, 411–12

International Brigade, Spain, 178

International Court at The Hague, 365–66, 403

IRI (Istituto Ricostruzioni Industriali), 287–89

Iron Curtain, 280–81

Irredentists, 351, 354–55, 360; after World War II, 339–44; in Austrian empire, 15–17; and D'Annunzio, 33; reaction of, to AMG policy after 1951, 364–65; and Zone B, 326, 327, 373–75, 376–77

Isonzo. *See* Soča (Isonzo) River

Istarski tednik (Istrian Weekly), 324

Istarski vjesnik (Istrian Herald), 112

Istituto Ricostruzioni Industriali (IRI), 287–89

Istria, Istrian, Istrians: and Belgrade agreement, 199; and British-American landing in, 80, 113, 131–32; and Croat Communists, 67–69, 102, 104; and Croat claims, 121; and Croat Partisans, 111–16 passim; German administration of, 87–88; and German surrender, 157; and Italian democrats, 69, 112; and Italian Partisans, 111–12; land and people, 4, 7, 9–12 passim; and 1954 London Agreement, 465; and Partisan persecutions, 180, 181; and Pazin agreement, 101; and peace negotiations, 241, 244, 246, 260, 267; rise of nationalism in, 14 n.16, 16, 18; Yugoslav administration of, after May 1945, 176, 234, 235, 236; and Yugoslav claims, 24, 28, 30, 31

Istro-Rumanians (Istrorumeni), 11-12

Italian bloc. *See* Coceani's group

Italian Communist party, 42, 132, 135, 147; agreements with Slovenian Communists, 1941–43, 58–60, 64–65; and Apr. 1934 agreement, 58; and Apr. 1944 agreement, 103; and Apr. 12–13, 1945, meeting, 148; and Central Committee for National Liberation in Rome, 96; and CLN, Julian Region, 112; and Cominform Resolution and Yugoslav answer, 299; and Comintern, 58–60, 63; and Croat Communists, 67–69; and declaration of Jan. 1942, 60; and dissolution of CPVG, 264; forms joint city committee in Trieste with Slovenian Communists, 177; and FTT, 321, 339, 356; and Garibaldi units, 97; letters from, 102; and Littoral Committee for Trieste, and Action Committee of the National Front formed, 62–63; and negotiations with Slovenian and Croat Communists, 1943–45, 102–5; and Oct. 1944 agreement, 104; and persecutions in Trieste, 184; policy of, after Tito's retreat from Zone A, Julian Region, 232–33; and Unità Operaia, 65. *See also* CPFTT; CPFTT (Babič); CPFTT (Vidali); CPVG

Italian Liberal party, 96, 112, 309, 394

Italian peace treaty: Annex VI of (*see* Permanent Statute); Annex VII of (*see* Provisional Statute); Annex VIII of, 274–75, 456–57; Annex X of, 287, 329; Article 76

505

of, 328 n.34; complaints against, 251–52; negotiations for, 240–52; revision of, 251, 278–79, 354–55, 359; signed, 251
Italian Republican party, 96, 98, 394
Italian Socialist party, 42, 96, 97, 145–46, 339; and Austrian Social Democratic party, 20–21; in Julian Region, 112; in Zone A, FTT, 300, 309, 394–95
Italian Social Movement, in Trieste, 309, 394
Italo-Austrian border, 1866, 3, 4, 24, 62
Italo-Slavic Anti-Fascist Union. *See* UAIS-SIAU
Italo-Slovene Democratic Union, 396
Italo-Slovenian Anti-Fascist Executive Committee (CEAIS), 148, 149, 171, 258
Italo-Slovenian brotherhood, 109, 232
Italo-Yugoslav negotiation, 250, 316, 319–21, 335, 337–38, 356–57, 358, 362, 381, 382–83, 417, 454–55
Italo-Yugoslav non-aggression pact, 44
Italy, Italian, Italians: administrative system of, accepted by AMG, 210–11; and American proposal, Dec. 1952, 416; and American proposal, Feb. 1953, 416–17; armistice of 1943, 70–71, 81–85, 89, 100–102; and Balkan Pact, 419; claims to Julian Region, 115–16, 125–29; cobelligerent status of, 125–26; and Cominform Resolution, 301, 320–21; Court of Cassation, 206, 214, 364; democratic government, 1943–45, 95–98; demonstrations in support of Trieste, Mar. 1952, 388; and economic aid to Yugoslavia, 334; and Eden-Brosio talks, 387–88; and Eden's proposal, 414–16; and Fascist Law No. 88, 205, 406; final demands and Austrian answer, April 1915, 23–24; flag, 364, 365, 439–40, 464; and German surrender, 113–34; and governmental crisis, 1954, 452–53; and London meeting, Mar. 1951, 356–57; and London Pact, 24 and n.5; and Mar. 1952 riots, 387–88; nationalism (*see* Nationalism, Italian); and Nov. 1953 riots, 439, 444; number of, outside Italian borders, 267–68; 1918 occupation of, 27; 1941 occupation of, 44, 46; 1951 press campaign, 334, 358, 364–65; and 1952 London Agreement, 387–92; and 1953 elections, 417; and 1954 London Agreement, 453–64 passim; occupation of Yugoslavia, 1941–43, 44, 46; and Oct. 8, 1953, announcement, 427–33; Partisans, 109–10, 111; Pella's actions prior to Oct. 1953, 418, 419–27; persecutions, 34–42; police and military actions in Slovenian Littoral, 1941–43, 57, 61–62; proposal for five-power conference, 434; proposes plebiscite for FTT, Mar. 11, 1952, 363; and province of Ljubljana, 1941–43, 50, 51; and Rapallo treaty, 30–32; and rearmament and Ottawa meeting of NATO, 359; Regency of Quarnero, 33; relations of, with Yugoslavia between wars, 42–45; removal of troops from Yugoslav border, Dec. 1953, 448; refugees, 296, 407, 413; representatives in Trieste, 385 n.6; resistance, 96, 97, 112–19 (*see also* CLN, CLNAI, CVL); and Rijeka events, 30, 31, 32–34; sovereignty over FTT, 346–47, 463; trade agreement with Yugoslavia, Aug. 1949, 334; treaty of Rome, 34; Tripartite Proposal, 281–83, 320; troops moved to Yugoslav border, Aug. 1953, 421; and World War I, 24, 25; in Yugoslavia, 32; Yugoslav Committee, 25–27; and Yugoslav note proposing four-power conference, 433; and Yugoslav proposal, May 1953, 417; and Zone A, FTT, 205, 283–86, 288–89, 330, 369, 387, 392–94; and Zone

INDEX

A, Julian Region, 218, 387–88, 390, 396, 400; and Zone B, FTT, 324, 327–29, 336–37, 368, 375–76, 380, 403, 411–14; and Zone B, Julian Region, 236–37, 238, 368. *See also* Coceani's group; Italian—; Italo—

Iveković, Mladen, 319, 320–21, 335
Izola, 59, 63, 117, 318–19, 325, 415, 416, 451–52

Jadran (Adriatic), 265-66
Jadranski institut (Adriatic Institute), 345
Jajce, 49
Jaksetich, Giorgio, 170, 172, 178, 224 and n.52
Jakšić, General Pavle, 150 n.57, 167
Jeri, Janko, 250, 470
Jerusalem, 47, 120, 130
Jews, 406–7, 407 n.41
Jones, Major William, 81 n.21
Jovanović, General Arso, 161, 167, 200
Jugoslovanski odbor (Yugoslav Committee), 25–27, 25 n.9
Julian Committee, 127, 128
Julian March (Julijska Krajina). *See* Julian Region
Julian Region: and Adriatic Littoral German administration, 71–74; and Alexander-Tito negotiations May–June 1945, 196–200; Allied troops' attitude to Yugoslavs in, 192–94; and armistice of 1943, 70–71, 84–85, 100–102; Austrian policy toward Slavs in, 19, 20; and Belgrade agreement, 199–200; censuses in, 6, 7–12; and CLN, 65, 69, 112–19, 140–46, 147–48; CLNAI negotiations with Slovenian Liberation Front in, 114–18; and Coceani's group, 74–76, 135–40; Communist negotiations on, 1941–45, 58–60, 102–5; and Communist persecutions, 1945, 179–85; and Communist underground, 1941–45, 60–62, 64, 67, 68–69, 84–85, 100–112; and cooperatives, beginnings of, 18; and Croat Chetniks, 69; and Croat Communists, 67, 68, 69, 100–102; and Croat democrats, 69; and Croat nationalism, beginnings of, 18, 22; and Croat Partisans, 67, 68–69, 100–102, 111–12; division of, according to peace treaty 1947 statistical data, 266–67; and Duino agreement, June 20, 1945, 200–201; economy of, under Yugoslav administration, 185–87; election in, under Austrian empire, 19; ethnic groups of, 7–12; Extraordinary Military Tribunal in, 38, 57; Fascist troops for defense of, 76, 136–37; and Fascist rise and victory, 35–38, 40–41; futile search for military demarcation line in, 194–96; geography of, 3–7; German occupation of, 1943–45, 70–88; and Istria, 1941–43, 66–69; and Istria, 1943–45, 87–88, 110–12; and Istria, Yugoslav administration of, 1945, 175; Italian claims in, 1943–45, 125–29; and Italian Communists, 1941–45, 58–60, 62–63, 64–65, 67, 68, 69, 102–5; and Italian democratic resistance (CLN), 65, 69, 112–19, 140–46, 147–48; and Italian military actions against Partisans in 1942, 61–62; and Italian Partisans, 109–10, 111, 112; and Italian nationalism, history of, 14–17, 18–19, 22; land of, 3–7; and Littoral National Guard, 85–87, 105–6, 135, 153 n.65, 154; and Morgan line, 196, 198; name of, 3–4; and peace negotiations, 1919–24, 27–34; and peace negotiations, 1945–47 (*see* Commission of experts; Italian peace treaty); people of, 7–12; in period 1918–41, 34–42; in period 1941–43, 57–69; in period 1943–45, 70–77, 84–88, 100–102, 105–19, 135–54; persecution in, 1918–41, 34–38, 40–41; population figures of, 6–7; provinces and districts of, 3–6; and Rapallo treaty, 1920, 31–32; and Republican Fascists, 76–77, 135–36; and Rome treaty, 1924, 34; and Serbian troops, 88, 154; size, 6–7; and Slovenian Chetniks, 63, 65–66;

507

INDEX

and Slovenian Communists, 1941–45, 58–60, 102–5; and Slovenian democrats, 1941–45, 64, 65, 87; and Slovenian Littoral, 57–66, 84–87, 100–102, 105–10, 175–76; and Slovenian nationalism, history of, 17–18, 18–19, 22; and Slovenian Partisans, 60–62, 64, 84–85, 100–102, 105–9, 113–18, 146–52; and socialism, history of, 20–21, 38–42; and Trieste economy, history of, 12–14; and Trieste, 64–66, 135–54, 156–60, 161–63, 165, 170–87; and Ustashi, 88; Western powers, policy toward, 1943–45, 129–32; and World War I, 24–25, 27; and Yugoslav administration and economy of Trieste, 185–87; and Yugoslav administration, May–June 1945, 161–63, 165, 170–87; Yugoslav claims in, during World War II, 120–25, 132; and Yugoslav Fourth Army and Partisan units, occupation by, 161, 168; Yugoslav provinces of, 175–76; Yugoslavs try to get Allied troops out of, 162–63

—, Zone A: and border commission 1947, 259–60; commission of experts visits, 244; and Communist struggle for recognition of committee system, 220–26; CPFTT formed, CPVG disbanded in, Aug. 1947, 264; CPVG formed in, Aug. 1945, 220; and De Winton, assassination of, 263; during peace treaty negotiations, 252–57; and Italian democratic parties, 231–32, 264–65; Pula evacuation, 262–63; and Sindacati Giuliani, formation of, 231; and Slovenian anti-Communist organization, 265–66; and UAIS-SIAU, 220, 226–30, 263–64

—, Zone A, Allied Military Government: Communist opposition to, 207–8, 210, 212–13, 221–30; finances and economic recovery of, 218–19; law courts of, 214; local government of, 207–13, 228–30, 291; police force in, 214–15; preparation for and organization of, 202–5; press in, 218; and public works, 219; and schools, 215–18, 229–30; and Slovenian rights, 215–18

—, Zone B: and CLN disbanded, 264–65; and colonial system abolished, 237–38; economy of, 237; elections in, 235; and new administration for Koper and Buje districts, 260, 262; organization of administration of, 234; persecutions in, 238–39; political parties in, 234; schools in, 236–37; Yugolira introduced in, 237; Yugoslav military administration of, 234–39, 260, 262

Justice and Liberty, 97

Kalafatović, General Danilo, 47
Kanal Valley, 4, 11, 23, 28, 32, 120, 244, 246, 247
Kardelj, Edvard, 102 n.49, 104, 161, 188, 241, 245, 299, 345, 361, 415
Karst, 6
Katoliški glas, 310
Keitel, Fieldmarshal Wilhelm, 50
Kesselring, Field Marshal Albert, 133
Kidrič, Boris, 169 and n.22, 186–87
Kingdom of Serbs, Croats, and Slovenes. *See* Yugoslavia
Klagenfurt (Celovec), 72 n.4, 155
Kmečki glas (Peasant's Voice), 109
Kobarid, 124
Kočevje, 51, 82–83, 156
Kokalj, Colonel Tone, 86, 105–6, 154
Koper (Capodistria), 59, 63, 117, 260, 322, 325, 326, 335, 341, 362, 376, 377–78, 401, 415, 416, 417, 451–52, 459, 461, 464, 465, 468
Koprščina, Koper district. *See* Koper
Korean war, 353, 381
Krek, Dr. Miha, 126, 130
Krenner, Colonel Franc, 83, 155
Kunz, Joseph L., 347 n.77
Kvarner (Quarnero), 5, 33, 195, 243, 261
Kveder, General Dušan, 162, 170, 171, 172, 178

INDEX

Labriola, Senator, 337
Lake Bolsena line, 122
Lake Bolsena meeting, 122
Language: decision of AMG, 297; identity cards in Zone A, FTT, 1948, 296; rights in Special Statute, 1954, 458
Languages officially recognized in Zone B, 236
Lantz, General (German), 50
Il Lavoratore (The Worker), 41, 110, 187, 229, 300, 324
Lazzaretto (Lazaret), 455
Lega Dalmata, 342
Lega Fiumana, 342
Lega Istriana, 342
Lega Nazionale, 16, 340–41
Legion of Death (Legija smrti). See Village Guards
Lemnitzer, General Lyman L., 133
Lenac, Colonel Mirko, 322
Lenzoni, Anteo, 344
Leskovac, 430–32
Liberation Council of Trieste. See CLT
Liberation Front. See Slovenian Liberation Front
Lipari Islands, 37
Lira currency, and Zone B, 237, 271, 327–28
Lisbon meeting, of NATO, 382–83
Little Entente, 44
Littoral Committee for Trieste of the Italian Communist party, 62–63, 65
Littoral National Guard, 85–87, 105–6, 135, 153 n.65
Livorno congress, 42
Ljotić, Dimitrije, 88
Ljubljana, 27, 30, 83, 156, 169, 176
Ljubljana Province: German occupation of, 71–72, 75 n.11, 77–84 passim, 109–10, 119 n.82, 154–56; Italian occupation of, 51–57 passim
Ljudska pravica (People's Right), 108–9, 276
Lloyd Triestino, 288
London: Agreement, 1952, 383, 387–94 passim, 401; Agreement, 1954, 456–71; announcement in, of talks with Italy, Mar. 1952, 388; conference of Western foreign ministers, May 1950, 337–38; Council of Foreign Ministers meeting, 1945, 240–44; Division, British 56th, 168; line, 27 and n.13, 30, 32; meeting, Mar. 1951, 356–57; Pact, 24 and nn.5 and 6, 29–30; as seat of Yugoslav government-in-exile, 47; talks, 1954, 450–55
Longo, Luigi, 98, 99
Loreto square, Milan, 134
Lošinj (Lussino), 245
Luciolli, Mario, 354
Lussino (Lošinj), 245
Lussu, Emilio, 462

Macchio, Karl, 23–24
Macedonian National Liberation Committee, 48
Magazzini Generali, 290
Mallet, Sir Ivo, 430
Manchester Guardian, 336 n.58
Manifesto alle popolazioni italiane della Venezia Giulia (Manifesto to the Italian People of Venezia Giulia), 114–15
Maras, Isidoro, 188 n.68
March 1951 demonstrations in Rome, 356
March 1952 riots in Trieste, 384–87
Marega, Giacomo, 188 n.69
Marin, Biagio, 137, 142
Marras, General Efisio, 421
Marshall, General George C., 277
Marshall Plan, 278, 331
Martino, Enrico, 403, 427
Martino, Gaetano, 455
Marušič, Fran, 38 n.33
Marzani, Don Edoardo, 188 n.68
Maserati, Ennio, 151 n.61, 189 n.71
Massola, Umberto (alias Quinto), 59, 67, 102 n.49
Massola-Quinto. See Massola, Umberto
Mates, Leo, 388–89
Matteotti, Giacomo, 97, 145–46
Matteotti guerrilla units, 97
Maugham, Lieutenant (British), 191
Mazzini, Giuseppe, 14 n.16, 15

509

INDEX

Memorandum of Understanding (London Agreement): 1952, 383, 387–94 passim; 1954, 456–71
Mendès-France, Pierre, 450, 460
Miani, Ercole, 137, 140, 143 n.32, 188 n.69
Miani, Michele, 146, 293
Midena, Mario M., 188 n.69
Mihajlović, Draža, 47, 48, 57, 77–78, 79, 84, 89, 93
Mihovilović, Ive, 310, 311, 339–40, 345
Mikuž, Metod, 58–60, 232
Milan, Italy, 114, 115–16, 117, 134, 139, 191
Military Administration of the Yugoslav Army, 234–39, 260, 262, 373–80, 401–4, 322–32
Milizia Volontaria Anti-Comunista (MVAC). *See* Village Guards
Milje. *See* Muggia
Miloš, Zvonimir, 38 n.33
Minca, Pietro, 373
Minority rights: and Italian complaints in Zone B, 411–14; and Italians, Slovenes, and Croats, 32; in Scelba's speech, Oct. 1954, 462; and Slovenes in Zone A, 203, 363, 404–11, 433; Special Statute of 1954 London Agreement, 456, 457–59, 460; in Tito's speech, Oct. 1954, 461; and Yugoslav note, Oct. 9, 1953, 430
MIR (Movimento Istriano Revisionista), 343
Mirna River, 376
Mixed Italo-Yugoslav Committee for minority problems, 459, 469
Mogorović, Bogdan, 88
Monaco, Gino, 341–42
Monfalcone, 200, 207, 246; and agreements between Italian and Slovenian Communists, 59, 60, 63, 117; and AMG personnel, May 1945, 166; Drapšin-Harding meeting, 168; and end of Allied occupation, 276; and New Zealand Division, 161, 162, 163–64; and Partisan organizations, 109, 146, 156–57 n.74
Monfort, Colonel Nelson M., 204, 222–23, 225

Monrupino (Repentabor), 292, 303; and American proposal, Feb. 1953, 416; and 1949 elections, 307, 309 n.66; and 1952 elections, 393, 397
Montenegro, 44, 46, 48, 89, 170
Morgan, General William D., 196–97, 200–201, 204
Morgan line, 124 n.13, 237, 243, 261, 268, 358; and Belgrade agreement, 196–97, 198, 199
Morrison, Herbert, 356–57
Moscow: Apr. 1934 agreement in, 58; Churchill-Stalin agreement in, Oct. 1944, 94, 105; Stalin-Eden talks in, Dec. 1941, 130; Tito's visit to, Apr. 1945, 132
Mosely, Philip, 242 n.6
Movimento Istriano Revisionista (MIR), 343
Muggia (Milje), 292, 293, 303, 310, 430, 451; and 1949 elections, 306, 309 n.66; and 1952 elections, 393, 395, 396; Partisan organizations in, 63, 109, 146, 156–57 n.74; and piecemeal accords between Slovenian and Italian Communists, 59, 117
Murphy, Robert, 455
Mussolini, Benito: and Adriatic Littoral, 72–73, 74, 88; connections of, with Coceani, 72, 75–76, 87, 136; death of, 134; on Italo-Yugoslav relations, 1924, 42; and organization of IRI, 287, 288; plot to murder, 57; and Rijeka question, 34; speech of, in Gorizia, July 1942, 61
Mutual Security Act and Yugoslavia, 354
MVAC (Milizia Volontaria Anti-Comunista). *See* Village Guards

NAAFI (Navy Army and Air Force Institutes), 441
Nabrežina (Aurisina). *See* Duino-Aurisina
NAP (Nucleo d'Azione Patriottica), 191
Naples, 95
Narodna legija (National Legion), 57, 78

INDEX

Narodni odbor za Slovenijo. *See* National Committee for Slovenia
Narodno-osvobodilni odbori (NOO). *See* Slovenian National Liberation committees
Narodno-osvobodilni svet (NOS), 107 n.50
National Committee for Slovenia, 119 n.82, 155, 169 n.22
National Council for Slovenia, 49, 50, 56
National home. *See* Slovenian national homes
National Legion, 57, 78
National Liberation committee(s). *See* Slovenian National Liberation Committee; Slovenian National Liberation committees
National Liberation Council for Slovenian Littoral (NOS), 107 n.50
National Liberation Movement in Slovenia. *See* Slovenian Liberation Front; Slovenian Partisans
National Liberation Movement in Yugoslavia, 48–49
Nationalism: and Apr. 12–13, 1945, meeting, 148; and continuous ethnic line, 382; liberation of Trieste and role of, 159–60; and Pella's proposal for plebiscite and, 425–26; and persecutions, 181, 184; and Slavic family and geographical names, 238; and Slovenian rights in Zone A, 404–11; and Trieste's future, 470–71
—, Croat: and Croat national rebirth in Istria, 18–19; and Croat Partisans in Istria and, 66–69; and discrimination against Italians in Zone B, FTT, 375
—, Italian: and assassination of General De Winton, 263; and CLN policy during 1944–45, 112, 119; and cooperation between Nenni and Saragat socialists in Trieste, 265; and D'Annunzio-Rijeka problem, 32–33; and De Castro plan, 426; and discrimination against Italians in Zone B, FTT, 375; impact of, on Italian political parties, 266, 340; and Italian Communists in Istria, 1941–45, 67–69; and Italian defense of Julian Region, 135, 136; and Italian democrats in Istria, 1941–45, 69; and Italian migration from Yugoslav parts of Julian Region, 262–63; and Italians in Zone B, 411–14; rise of, 14–17, 18–19; and Risorgimento, 14–15, 14–15, 14 n.16; and socialists, 20, 21
—, Slovenian: and AMG introduction of Italian laws in Julian Region, 227; and communist persecutions in Julian Region, 184; history of, 17–19; and Partisan propaganda, 60–61; and claims to Julian Region, 59–60; and socialists, 20, 21; and terrorist groups in Slovenian Littoral, 1940, 57; and UAIS-SIAU propaganda in Zone A, Julian Region, 220
Natisone-Garibaldi division, 110
Natlačen, Marko, 50, 54
NATO: Italian political parties' relationship to, 339, 419, 454; Lisbon meeting of, 382–83; Ottawa meeting of, 355, 359
Nedelja (Sunday), 265
Nedić, General Milan, 46, 88
Nedock, Dr. Adelmo, 174, and n.32
Nenni, Pietro, 251, 265
Neo-Fascists, in Trieste, 265, 309, 394–95, 443, 468
New York Times, 325–26, 337, 360, 361–62, 372
New Zealand Division, 145, 152, 157, 161, 163–68, 164, 190
Newspapers, Partisan, in Julian Region, 108–9, 112, 187
Nino incident, 36
Ninth Corps, Slovenian, 110, 149, 151
Nitti, Francesco, 31
North Atlantic Treaty Organization. *See* NATO
Nostra Lotta, La, 324
Nostra Vigilia, La, 190
Nostro Avvenire, Il, 183, 186–87, 190
Nostro Giornale, Il (Our Newspaper), 112

511

INDEX

Novak, Major Karl, 78 nn.16 and 18, 79, 84
Nucleo d'Azione Patriottica (NAP), 191
Nuovo Corriere della Sera, Il, 358, 364–65, 369

Oberdan (Oberdank), Guglielmo, 15
Occupatio bellica, occupatio pacifica, 347 n.77
October 6, 1943, letter from Italian Communist party, 102
October 1944 agreement, 104–5, 232
October 8, 1953, announcement, 427–28, 434–35, 454
Okroglica, 422–23
Opčine (Opicina), 408, 468
Operti, Piero, 158 and n.78
Opicina (Villa Opicina), 408, 468
Organization for European Economic Cooperation (OEEC), 284–85, 434
Organization of Friends of the Soviet Union, 52
Orlando, Vittorio, 26–27, 31, 32–33, 34 n.28, 336–37
Osoppo brigade, 110
Osservatorio del C.L.N., 190
Osvobodilna fronta (OF). *See* Slovenian Liberation Front
Ottawa meeting of NATO, 1951, 359
OZNA (Odeljenje za zaštitu naroda) (Department for the Protection of the People), 175

Pacciardi, Randolfo, 387–92
Pace, Count Marino, 86
Pacor, Mario, 189 n.71
Pact of Rome, 26–27
Pagnini, Cesare, 72, 139, 148; and CLN, 119, 140–41, 145, 157–58; on Coceani's talks with Serbs, 154; escapes to Italy, 194; and Guardia Civica, 76, 138; and meeting, April 10, 1945, 137; on Partisan interrogations, 159, 183; receives arms from Republican Fascists, 135, 139
Palace of Justice, Trieste, 144, 152

Paladin, Giovanni, 142, 188 n.68, 191
Palamara, Giovanni, 466, 468
Pallotti, Major F. G., 221, 222
Palutan, Gino, 292 n.40, 293
Para-statal property. *See* IRI
Paris peace conference, 1919, 27–34
Paris peace conference, 1946, 247–51. *See also* Italian peace treaty
Parri, Ferruccio (alias Maurizio), 98, 99, 128
Partisans, 48 and n.5, 63, 89–90, 91–93, 94. *See also* Croats; Italian Partisans; Slovenian Liberation Front; Slovenian National Liberation committees; Slovenian Partisans
Partito Fascista Republicano (PFR) (Republican Fascist party), 76–77, 112, 113, 135–36
Partizanski dnevnik (Partisan Daily), 109
Pasquinelli, Maria, 263, 467
Pavelić, Ante, 43, 46, 66, 69, 88
Pavlin, Josip, 260 n.34
Pazin, 88
Pazin agreement, Sept. 1943, 101
Pazin speech, June 1953, 418
Peace conference, 1919, 27–34
Pecorari, Fausto, 342, 344
Pella, Giuseppe, 418–19 passim, 434–35, 436, 448, 452, 453
Pensions, 328–29
People's committees, 323
People's courts, 108, 111, 173–75, 205
People's Front, 403
People's Militia, 175, 205, 223–24
Permanent joint commission, 330
Permanent Statute: as Annex VI of Italian peace treaty, 270, 318, 347, 362; Articles 6 and 7 of, 297; Article 24 of, 286; outlined, 272–75
Persecutions: Communist, 179–85, 192; German, 50–51; Italian, 34–38; of Socialists, 40–41
Petelin, Stanko, 150 n.57
Peter II, King, 84, 91, 92, 93, 155
Peterlin, Colonel Ernest, 80, 82
Piave River, 25, 164

512

INDEX

Piazza Unità, 36, 385, 440, 442–43, 464
Piccioni, Attilio, 453, 454, 455
Piemontese, Giuseppe, 177
Pino Budicin battalion, 111
Piran (Pirano), 117, 254, 325, 415, 416, 451–52
Pittoni, Valentino, 39 n.34, 41 n.39, 257
Pius XII, 191
Pizzoni, Alfredo (alias Longhi), 98
Planned economy, 186
Plebiscite, for FTT, 35, 251, 363, 388, 424–27, 436–37, 463
Pogassi, Giuseppe, 173, 200, 221, 224
Pokrajinski narodno-osvobodilni odbor (PNOO) (Provincial National Liberation Committee), for Slovenian Littoral, 107
Pokrajinski odbor osvobodilne fronte (POOF) (Provincial Committee of the Liberation Front), for Slovenian Littoral, 62, 107 n.50
Pola. *See* Pula
Police force, Julian Region, 214–15
Political advisers, 390
POOF (Pokrajinski odbor osvobodilne fronte) (Provincial Committee of the Liberation Front), for Slovenian Littoral, 62, 107 n.50
Popolo units, Il, 97
Popović, Koča, 354, 417
Portici di Chiozza episode, Nov. 1953, 447
Postojna district, 4, 27, 30, 122
Potočnik, Franc, 161 n.1
Potsdam, 240
Prague, 27
Prekmurje, 50
Prezelj, Colonel Ivan, 84
Primorje. *See* Slovenian Littoral
Primorska. *See* Slovenian Littoral
Primorska narodna straža. *See* Littoral National Guard
Primorski dnevnik (Littoral Daily), 187, 218, 300, 334; on Nov. 1953 coup d'état, 439; on postponement of 1951 elections, 371; attacks Slovenes cooperating with AMG, 229, 266
Primorski poročevalec (Littoral Reporter), 109

Principle of balanced minorities, 244
Proclamation(s): on annexation of Istria, Sept. 1943, 101; on annexation of Slovenian Littoral, Sept. 1943, 100–101; No. 1, 205, 275–76; Nos. 2–7, 205–7; of United Slovenia, 155
Provincia di Lubiana. *See* Ljubljana Province
Provincial Anti-Fascist Council of National Liberation of Croatia (ZAVNOH), 48, 66, 101
Provincial Committee of the Liberation Front (POOF) for Slovenian Littoral, 62, 107 n.50
Provincial National Liberation Committee for Slovenian Littoral (PNOO), 107
Provisional Statute: as Annex VII of Italian peace treaty, 270–72; Article 10 of, 411–12; Article 11 of, 271, 283
Pubblica Sicurezza, 151
Puecher, Edmondo, 39 n.34, 41 n.39
Pula (Pola), 70, 88, 131, 196; AMG administration of, 207, 211, 213; and assassination of De Winton, 263; and Belgrade agreement, 1945, 199; Croatian schools in, 216–17; evacuation of, 1946–47, 262–63; German troops disembark in, 92; and peace conference, 1919, 27, 28; population of, 6–7; and Tito's speech, July 1949, 314, 317–18; and UAIS-SIAU clash with AMG police Jan. 1947, 263; and Yugoslav administration, May 1945, 176
Punta Sottile, 452, 454, 455
Purging commissions, 174
Purging law courts, 206
Purić, Dr. Božidar, 92
PX (post exchange), U.S., 372

Qualunquists, 309
Quarantotti-Gambini, Pier Antonio, 143, 144, 145, 151 n.61, 181, 189 n.72, 194

Rainer, Dr. Friedrich, 72
Ranković, Aleksandar, 299, 357 n.12
Rapallo line, 3, 5, 243, 261

513

INDEX

Rapallo treaty, and Yugoslavia, 31–32
Raša River, 241, 243
Ravna gora, 47
Rečina (Eneo), 34
Red star, 132
Redipuglia, 440
Refugees: from Zone B, 469; Italian, 296, 407, 413
Regent, Ivan, 21 n.27, 39 n.34, 41 n.39, 377–78
Reggenzia Italiana del Carnaro (Italian Regency of Quarnero), 33
Regional National Liberation Committee for Istria, 176, 234, 260
Regional National Liberation Committee for Slovenian Littoral, 176, 208 n.15, 234, 260
Regional People's Committee, Zone B, FTT, 260, 322, 325, 401
Relazioni internazionali, 360, 391
Repentabor. *See* Monrupino (Repentabor)
Republican Fascist party, 76–77, 112, 113, 135–36
Rhaeto-Romanic language group, 11 n.12
Ribar, Ivan, 161
Richardson, Colonel Gerald, 214–15, 400
Rijeka (Fiume): annexed to Croatian republic, 267; city council elections in, Mar. 1946, 235; and Communist persecutions, 180 and n.49; Croatian claims to, 121; Croat Communist party in, 66; Croat and Italian schools in, 236–37; D'Annunzio and, 33; and German surrender, 150, 157; German troops disembark in, 92; historical background of, 3–4, 6, 14 n.16; and Italian armistice, 70; Italian army takes over rule of, Jan. 1921, 33–34; and Koper's competitions, 465; as lesson for Trieste, 34, 125; and London Pact, 24; and Italian peace treaty, 242, 244, 245, 246; Mussolini's emissary takes over, Sept. 1923, 34; and peace conference, 1919, 27–32 passim; and Treaty of Rapallo, 32–34; and Treaty of Rome, 34; L'Unione degli Italiani dell'Istria e di Fiume organized for, 111; Western Allies on, 122, 131, 195; Yugoslav administration of, 1945–47, 176, 234, 235, 236–37
Rinascita Giuliana, La, 190
Riots, in Trieste: Mar. 1952, 386, 387; Nov. 1953, 439–48
Risorgimento, 14–15, 14 n.16
Ristić, Marko, 357 n.12
Roesener, General Erwin, 155
Roglić, Josip, 345
Romano, Redento, 188 n.69
Rome: Allied forces enter, 95; as center of organized Irredentism, 342, 343; Central Committee for National Liberation formed in, 96; CLN proclamation broadcast from, Dec. 9, 1944, 118–19; CLN delegation from Trieste visits, 191; conference of Italian ambassadors in, Mar. 1953, 416–17; demonstrations in, Mar.–Apr. 1945, 128; demonstrations in, Mar. 1951, 356; student demonstrations in, Apr. 1950, 336
Roosevelt, Franklin D., 91, 96, 129, 130–32
Rossetti, Domenico, 143 n.32
Rossetti monument, and Nov. 1953 riots, 440
Rossi, Venusto, 188 n.69
Rumania, 44, 94, 315 n.3
Rupnik, General Leon, 72, 75 n.11, 83
Russia: and London Pact, 24 and nn.5 and 6; White Guard of, 56. *See also* Soviet Union
Russian line, 242–44

St. Cyril and Methodius, Association of, 18–19, 86
Št. Peter, 30, 162 n.1, 243
Salandra, Antonio, 23–24
Salisbury, Lord Robert, 427
Salvemini, Gaetano, 127, 128
Sambo, Bruno, 135
San Andrea machinery plant, 288
San Dorligo della Valle (Dolina), 309 n.66, 416; and communal administration, 292, 303; and 1949

INDEX

elections, 307; and 1952 elections, 393, 396, 397
San Giacomo, 40–41, 255
San Giusto, 439; castel, as German stronghold, 1945, 144, 152; list, 370
San Marco shipbuilding plant, 288
San Rocco shipbuilding plant, 288
Sant' Antonio church, 188, 441, 447
Santin, Bishop Antonio: appeals for calm, Apr. 1945, 140; celebrates mass in San Giusto Cathedral, Nov. 3, 1953, 439; and Coceani's talks with Serbs, 154; negotiates for German surrender to CLN, 145; protests Yugoslav arrests in Trieste, in May 1945, 166; and reconsecration ceremonies for Sant' Antonio church, 441, 447; on religious persecutions in Zone B, 379
Saragat, Giuseppe, 265, 374
Sardinia, 62
SCAO (Senior Civil Affairs Officer), 204
Scelba, Mario, 452, 453, 455, 462–63, 468
Schäffer, General, 139–40, 142, 143, 155
Schiffrer, Carlo, 11 n.13, 137, 139 and n.21, 140–41, 142, 145–46, 147, 150 n.58, 158–59, 293, 308–9 n.66
Schranzhofer, German adviser, 72
Schuman, Robert, 338
Schutzpolizei, 138
Second London Agreement, 456–71
Second Milan meeting, July 1944, 115–16
Security Council. *See* United Nations, Security Council
Self-determination: and second Milan meeting, 115; and Wilson line, 30
Senior Civil Affairs Officer (SCAO), 204
Šentjurc, Lidija (alias Joža), 178
Serb, Croat, and Slovenian Kingdom. *See* Yugoslavia
Serbia, Serbian, Serbians, 170; Chetniks, 47, 48, 88, 89, 153 n.65; in Croatia, 66; liberated by Tito troops, Oct. 1944, 94; Nedić government formed in, Aug. 1941, 46-Slovenes expatriated to, 51; Tito; Stalin agreement and liberation of, 94, 103; troops, and Coceani's group, 136; troops, on eve of Trieste liberation, 135; troops, final fate of, 154; troops, in Istria and Slovenian Littoral, 88. *See also* Serbian—
Serbian National Liberation Committee, 48
Serbian Volunteer Corps, numerical strength of, 153 n.65
Servola, 269, 451
Sforza, Count Carlo: asks for revision of Italian peace treaty, 354; and claims to Julian Region 1943–45, 127; conversations of, with Iveković, 319, 320–21; favors revision of peace treaty, in 1947, 278–79 n.14; memorandum by, on new AMG policy in Zone A, 366; and nomination of governor for Trieste, 279; protests Yugoslav measures in Zone B, 1950, 334, 335; resigns as foreign minister, 337, 453; signs Rapallo treaty, 32 n.23; talks to Italian parliament on FTT, 1950, 336–37; visits London, Mar. 1951, 355–57
Sgonico (Zgonik), 292, 303, 307, 309 n.66, 393, 397, 416
Sicily, 62
Sikorski, General Wladyslaw, 91
Silesia, 51
Simić, Stanoje, 250–51
Simoni, Captain John P., 218
Sindacati Giuliani, 231
Sindacati Unici (Unitary Trade Union), 171–72, 175, 230, 231, 300
Skopje, 432
Slavic family, and geographic names, 37, 238, 327, 404–6, 413 and n.52
Slovene-Croat Cultural Union, 324
Slovene Union, 396, 397
Slovenia, Slovenian, Slovenes: AMG and ethnic rights of, in Julian Region, 215–18; anti-Communist military formations, 153 n.65; an-

515

INDEX

ti-Communist organizations in Zone A, Julian Region, 265–66; Catholic group in Gorizia, 265, 266; collaborators, 54–56, 81–84, 85–87; cultural centers in Austrian empire, 17; and De Castro's ethnic line, 426; divided and occupied, 1941, 49–51; government in Ljubljana, 176, 234; Irredentism, and Italo-Yugoslav relations, 42–43; Italian occupation of, 1941–43, 44, 49–57; in Julian Region under Austrian empire, 5–12, 17–22; land, and denationalization of, 408–9; liberals in Slovenian Littoral, 87, 266; and Ljubljana Province under German occupation, 1943–45, 77–84, 119 n.82, 154–56; nationalism (*see* Nationalism, Slovenian); newspapers in Zone A, Julian Region, 218, 265; and 1952 London Agreement, 389, 391; number of, in FTT and Italy after 1947, 267, 268; Oct. 15, 1953, demonstrations in Trieste, 438; and Partisans and armistice of 1943, 80–83; and peace negotiations, 1919, 27–32; persecutions of, in Italy, 1919–41, 34–38; political parties in Zone A, FTT (*see* Slovenian Democratic Union; Slovenian Christian Social Union); rights of, in court, 214; rights of, in Zone A, FTT, 203, 298, 363, 404–11, 433; sacrifices of, in 1954, 470; schools in Italy, after 1947, 410–11; section of Yugoslav Socialist party, 49. *See also* Italian peace treaty; Slavic family, and geographic names; Slovene—; Slovenian—
Slovenian Alliance, 56–57, 78–79, 84
Slovenian Catholic party. *See* Slovenian People's party
Slovenian Chetniks: formation of, 56–57; new commander of, 84; numerical strength of, 78, 79, 153 n.65; and Slovenian army, 1945, 155–56; in Slovenian Littoral, 63, 65–66, 85, 87; surrender to Partisans at Grčarice, 81

Slovenian Christian Socialist party, 52
Slovenian Christian Social Union, 304
Slovenian Communist party, 50, 114, 118; activities in Trieste, 1941–43, 64–65; agreements with Italian Communists on Slovenian Littoral, 1941–43, 58–60; aims and goals in Slovenian Littoral and Trieste, 1945, 146, 147; forms joint city committee for Trieste, 177; and Italian armistice in Ljubljana Province, 80–81; *Ljudska pravica*, organ of, 108–9; negotiations with Italian Communists about Slovenian Littoral, 1943–45, 102–5; and organization of CPVG, 220; and organization of Partisans in Ljubljana Province, 1941, 52; as real power behind Partisan organization, 1943–45, 108; and Slovenian Littoral, 1941–43, 60–63
Slovenian Democratic Union, (SDZ), 266, 286, 290, 304
Slovenian democrats: activities in Trieste, 1941–43, 64, 65–66; AMG policy toward, 1948–49, 312; defend FTT, 333, 368; and elections in Zone A, FTT, 304, 305–7, 395, 396–97; and General Airey's report, 348; and Oct. 8, 1953, announcement, 438; organized in Zone A, Julian Region, 1947, 265–66; and Pella's proposal for plebiscite, 425–26; and Slovenian Littoral, 1943–45, 87
Slovenian Home Guards. *See* Home Guards
Slovenian Independent Democratic party, 49
Slovenian Legion, 56, 78, 79, 80
Slovenian Liberal party (Yugoslav National party in Slovenia), 49, 52, 55–56, 57, 78, 79
Slovenian Liberation Front, 108, 172, 324; annexation proclamations of, in Sept. 1943, 100–102; and Apr. 12–13, 1945, meeting with CLN, 147–48; and British-American landing in Istria, 80,

INDEX

113, 131–32; contacts with CLN in Apr. 1945, 112, 141–42; and formation of joint committees with CLN, 156–57 n.74; founded, 52; and Kokalj's administration, 105–6; and liberation of Trieste, 146–52; negotiations with CLNAI in Milan, 1944, 113–18; in Slovenian Littoral, 1941–43, 58, 59–60, 60–63, 64; and UAIS-SIAU, 220

Slovenian Littoral (Slovenska Primorska, Slovensko Primorje, Primorje, or Primorska): and AMG administration of Zone A, Julian Region, 202–30; annexed to Slovenian Republic, 267; under Austrian rule, 4, 11–12, 17–18, 18–19, 20; Chetniks, 63, 65–66; claimed by Slovenes, 1941–45, 120–25; Communists, 58–63, 102–5, 177–87, 220, 264; and CPVG for all Communists, 220, 264; divided according to Belgrade agreement, June 9, 1945, 192–94; during first part of war, 1940–43, 57–66; German occupation of, 1943–45, 71–74, 84–87, 100–110, 113–18; Italian claims to, 125–29; and Italian collaborators, 74–77, 135–40; and Italian Communists, 58–60, 62–63, 64–65; and Italian democrats (CLN), 65, 112–19, 187–92, 231–32, 264–65; and Italian Partisans, 109–10; and Littoral National Guard, 85–87, 154; and negotiations between Slovenian and Italian Communists, 1943–45, 102–5; and negotiations between Slovenian Liberation Front and CLNAI, 1944, 113–18; and organization of Slovenian Partisan administration, May–June, 1945, 176, 177–87; and peace negotiations after World War I, 27–34 passim; and peace negotiations after World War II (*see* Italian peace treaty); and proclamations of annexation to Slovenia and Yugoslavia, 100–101, and Serbian troops, 88, 154, and Slovenian collaboration, 1943–45, 85–87, and Slovenian democrats, 64, 65, 87, 265–66, and Slovenian Partisans, 59–63, 64, 105–10, 113–18, 146–52, 175–76; and UAIS-SIAU, 220–30, 232–33, 234–35, 263–64; between the wars, 34–42; Yugoslav occupation of, May 1945, 161–63, 168–69; and Zone A, Julian Region, 1945–47, 202–33, 259–67; and Zone B, Julian Region, 1945–47, 234–39

Slovenian National Council in Trieste, 64, 65, 87

Slovenian national (or cultural) homes, 36, 86, 459

Slovenian National Liberation Committee (SNOO), 53 and n.15, 101, 107

Slovenian National Liberation committees: abolished by General Order No. 11, 211–12; formation and organization of, 48, 52, 53, 60–62, 64, 107–8; in Zone A, Julian Region, 207–13

Slovenian National Liberation Council (SNOS), 53 n.15, 107

Slovenian National Radical party, 49

Slovenian Ninth Corps, 110, 149, 151

Slovenian Partisans: and administration of Julian Region, May–June 1945, 161–63, 165, 170–87; and armistice of 1943, 71, 80–83; and annexation proclamations, 1943, 100–101; beginnings of, 52–54, 55 n.19; and Belgrade agreement, 196–200; claims during World War II, 121–25; and liberation of Trieste, 146–52; and negotiations with CLN and CLNAI, 113–18; and persecutions in Julian Region, 179–85; in Slovenian Littoral, 1941–43, 59–63, 64, 67; in Slovenian Littoral, 1943–45, 105–7, 108–10

Slovenian People's party (also referred to as Catholic or clerical party), 49, 55–56, 57, 78–80, 87

Slovenian schools: and AMG, Zone A, Julian Region, 216–18, 229–30;

517

INDEX

under German administration in Slovenian Littoral, 86–87; and 1954 London Agreement, 458; Partisan, in Slovenian Littoral, 108; in Zone A, FTT, 298, 410–11; in Zone B, Julian Region, 236–37

Slovenian socialists, 20–21, 27, 57, 78, 79, 87

Slovenska Benečija. *See* Venetian Slovenia

Slovenska demokratska zveza (SDZ) (Slovenian Democratic Union), 266, 286, 290, 304

Slovenska krščansko-socialna zveza (Slovenian Christian Social Union), 304

Slovenska legija (Slovenian Legion), 56, 78, 79, 80

Slovenska ljudska stranka. *See* Slovenian People's party

Slovenska Primorska. *See* Slovenian Littoral

Slovenska zaveza (Slovenian Alliance), 56–57, 78–79, 84

Slovenski narodni dom (Slovenian national homes), 36, 86, 459

Slovenski narodno-osvobodilni odbor (SNOO) (Slovenian National Liberation Committee), 53 and n.15, 101, 107

Slovenski narodno-osvobodilni svet (SNOS) (Slovenian National Liberation Council), 53 n.15, 107

Slovenski poročevalec (Slovenian Reporter), 108–9

Slovenski Primorec (Slovene from the Littoral), 265

Slovensko-hrvatska prosvetna zveza (Slovene-Croat Cultural Union), 324

Slovensko Primorje. *See* Slovenian Littoral

Soča (Isonzo) River, 75 n.11, 136, 154, 161, 167, 196, 198, and Cox description, 164, 165; and dissolution of Italian army, 1943, 71; and eastern Italian border, 14 n.16; and French line, 244; and Italian demands for border correction, 248; and Parri, 128

Socialists: in Julian Region under Austrian rule, 20–21, 257–58; Saragat and Nenni, in Trieste, 1945–47, 265; in Trieste, between the wars, under Italian rule, 38–42, 147; in Zone A, FTT, 300, 306, 309, 394, 395, 396; in Zone B, FFT, 324, 325, 326; in Zone B, Julian Region, 234

Sokolska legija (Falcon Legion), 56–57, 78 and n.18

Sonnino, Baron Sidney, 23, 27, 34 n.28

South Tyrol (Alto Adige), 14 n.16, 15, 23–24, 29, 131, 426

Soviet Union: aims during World War II, 113, 129, 131; attacked by Germans, June 1941, 48 n.5; and Cominform Resolution, 299; and East-West split, 277–78, 314–15, 316, 353; and Eden's proposal, 1945, 123–24, 132; and FTT, 316, 337–38, 384; improved relations of, with Yugoslavia, 1953, 418; and Italy during the war, 70, 126, 127, 133–34; and Julian Region during the war, 58–60, 113 (*see also* Stalin; Comintern); and the making of Italian peace treaty, 242, 244, 249, 251; and organization of Cominform, 278; policy toward Julian Region, after Yugoslav retreat from Zone A, 1945, 232, 233; protests 1952 London Agreement, 392 n.20; protests Oct. 8, 1953, announcement, 433–34, 448–49; recognizes 1954 London Agreement, 460–61; relations with Yugoslavia after Cominform Resolution, 1948–53, 314–15, 316; and revision of Italian peace treaty, 1951, 354, 355; and signing of Austrian peace treaty and FTT, 316; and spheres of interest, 100; and Tito in Trieste dispute, May 1945, 198 and n.102; and Tito's Yugoslavia during war, 90–91, 94, 123, 132; and Tripartite Proposal, 282–83, 316, 317; and Yugoslav claims in Carinthia, Austria, 314

Spaccini, Marcello, 142, 188 n.68

Special Statute (Annex II) of 1954 London Agreement, 456, 457–59

INDEX

Spellman, Cardinal Francis J., 379, 462
Spheres of interest, 100, 129, 153
Split incident, July 1920, 36
Sporer, Theodoro, 258
Squadre d'azione, 35–36
Stabilimento Tipografico Triestino, 187 n.64
Stalin: agreement of, with Churchill on Yugoslavia, 1944, 94; agreement of, with Tito, Sept. 1944, 94, 103; and Cominform Resolution, 301; death of, 418; and Eden's line, 132; and German surrender in Italy, 133–34; and Slovenian Littoral, 58–60, 60, 130; and spheres of interest, 129; urges Yugoslav Communists to compromise, 90–91; and Teheran conference, 90; and Tito and Yugoslavia in Trieste dispute, May 1945, 198 and n.102; and Yugoslavia after Cominform Resolution, 314–15
Stamatović, Colonel Miloš, 363 and n.21, 401
Stars and Stripes, 372
Stettinius, Edward, 195
Stocca, Mario, 259, 297, 346, 425
Stoianovitch, Costa (Stojanović, Kosta), 32 n.23
Štoka, Franc (alias Rado), 114, 162, 170, 177, 178, 220
Stone, Admiral Ellery W., 131, 191
Študijska knjižnica (Research Library), in Trieste, 346
Styria, Southern, 19 n.22, 75 n.11
Šubašić, Dr. Ivan, 91, 92–93, 94, 122–23, 131, 208
Suez Canal, 13
Šumrada, Vinko (alias Radoš), 150 n.56
Supilo, Frano, 25 n.9
Sviligoj, Dr. August, 406 n.40
Swiss travel agency, in Trieste, 290

Tabori, 17
Tacconi, Antonio, 343, 344
Tagliamento River, 154
Tamaro, Attilio, 136–37
Tanjug, 421–26, 465
Tanjug communiqué, 162–63
Tarchiani, Alberto: on American proposal, Feb. 1953, 416; appointed Italian ambassador to the United States, 126 n.19; and fall 1953 crisis, 425, 428, 435; and new ideas on FTT, 383; and 1954 London Agreement, 463; and Sforza, 320; on Tripartite Proposal, 282
Tarvisio (Trbiž), 5, 11, 243, 261; after World War I, 27, 28, 32; after World War II, 124, 176, 196
Taviani, Emilio, 421
Teheran conference, 89–90
TELVE, 289
Tenki rtič (Punta Sottile), 452, 454, 455
Thompson, Llewellyn E., 451–52, 453
Three Venices (Tre Venezie), 3
Tito, Marshal Josip Broz: agreement of, with Stalin, Sept. 1944, 94; agreement of, with Šubašić, 92–93, 94, 193; and Cominform Resolution, 299; declares Yugoslavia will resist aggression, Feb. 17, 1951, 354; Eden presents his proposal to, 415; establishes headquarters in Belgrade, Oct. 1944, 94; on FTT, 317–18, 338, 388–89, 391, 415, 422–23, 430–32, 433, 439; and German attack on Drvar, 1944, 92; on Greek guerrillas, July 1949, 314; as head of federal government, 170; as leader of Partisans, 48, 49; on London talks, 451; meets with Togliatti, Nov. 1946, 250; message of, to Alexander, May 3, 1945, 162; and negotiations with Alexander, May–June 1945, 196–200; and 1952 London Agreement, 388–89, 391; about 1954 London Agreement, 461; and Oct. 8, 1953, announcement, 430–32, 433, 439; and order to Fourth Army, Apr. 1945, 150–51; protests to the Allies in Julian Region, May 4, 1945, 167; on renewed relations with Russia, 418; speech of, at Okroglica, Sept. 6, 1953, 422–23; talks with Churchill, Aug. 1944, 93,

519

INDEX

122-23, 131; visits former Zone B, Nov. 21, 1954, 468; visits Moscow, Apr. 1945, 132; visits Great Britain, Mar. 1953, 381
Titoists. *See* CPFTT (Babič)
Tito-Togliatti agreement, and Yugoslav demands on FTT, 250, 319
Togliatti, Palmiro, 104, 129, 250, 319, 429
Tolbukhin, Marshal Feodor, 94
Tolmezzo, 140
Tomšič, Ivan, 346
Torre, Andrea, 26
Trbiž. *See* Tarvisio
Tre Venezie (Three Venices), 3
Treaty of Rapallo, 31-32, 127-28 n.24
Treaty of Rome, 34
Trentino (South Tyrol), 15, 23, 29, 131
Trento Province. *See* Trentino
Trieste (Trst), as international problem, 1945-54: De Gasperi's American visit to, Sept. 1951, 359-61; and direct Italo-Yugoslav talks, 1950-53 (*see* Italo-Yugoslav negotiations); and Eden proposal, Sept. 1952, 414-16; and London meeting, Mar. 1951, 356-57; and London talks, 1954, 451-52, 453-55; and 1952 London Agreement, 387-92; and 1954 London Agreement, 456-60; and Oct. 8, 1953, announcement, 427-28; and peace negotiations, 1945-47, 240-51 (*see also* Italian peace treaty); and Pella's actions prior to Oct. 8, 1953, 418, 419-27; and Tito's new proposal, Oct. 10, 1953, 431-32; and Tito's proposal, Apr. 1950, 338; and Tito's proposal, Sept. 6, 1953, 423; and Tito-Togliatti meeting, Nov. 1946, 250; and Tripartite Proposal, 281; and U.S. proposal, Dec. 1952, 416; and U.S. proposal, Feb. 1953, 416-17; and Yugoslav proposal, May 1953, 417; and Yugoslav reaction to Oct. 8, 1953, announcement, 430-33

—, to June 1945: and Adriatic Littoral, 71-74; and Alexander line, 124-25; and Allied soldiers' attitude toward Yugoslavs, May 1945, 192-94; AMG takes over, June 12, 1945, 203; Apr. 27-29, 1945, events in, 138-40; and Belgrade agreement, 199; burning of Slovenian National Home in, 36; Chetniks and Slovenes in, 65-66; and Churchill's letter to Stalin, June 1945, 202 n.1; and CLN activities under Yugoslav administration, 187-92; and CLN proclamation of Dec. 9, 1944, 118-19; and CLN proposal, Apr. 15, 1945, 148-49; and CLN refusal of CLNAI *Manifesto*, 1944, 115; and CLN-Slovenian Liberation Front meeting, Apr. 12-13, 1945, 147-48; and CLN uprising, Apr. 30, 1945, 140-46; CLT takes over civil administration of, May 13, 1945, 171; as Coceani's group, 74-76, 136-40; Communist control in, 185-87; constituent assembly in, 171-72; economy, historical background of, 12-14; and Eden's line, 123; and elections under Austria, 19, 20; and formation of Anti-Fascist Coordinating Committee, 116-17; Fascist persecutions of socialists in, 40-41; and German surrender, 152; and Guardia Civica, 76, 138, 144; independentism in, 1918-19, 39, 252, 257-58; and Irredentists, 16; Italian Communists in, 1941-45, 64-65, 102-3, 118, 117; and Italian delegations to the Allied headquarters, 165-66; and Italian demands from Austria, 1915, 23; and Italian democrats (CLN), 1941-45, 65, 112-19, 140-46, 147-49, 187-92; and Italian demonstrations, May 5, 1945, 189-90; Italian and Yugoslav claims to, 1919, 27, 28, 29-30; and Italo-Slovenian Partisans (CEAIS), 144, 146-52, 157; and joint city committee of Italian and Slovenian Communist party, 177; and joint

520

INDEX

meeting, Slovenian and Italian Communists, Dec. 1942, 64–65; liberation of, Apr. 1945, 134–60; and Littoral Committee for Trieste, 62–63, 65; and London Pact, 24; and negotiations between Italian and Slovenian Communists, 59, 60, 102–3; New Zealand Division in, 145, 152, 161, 164, 165–66; and Oct. 1944 agreement, 104; and organization of CEAIS, 148, 157; Pagnini appointed mayor of, 72; and Partisan persecutions, 174, 179–85; Partisan victory in, as Communist victory, 179–87; people's courts organized in, 174–75; population of, 6, 9; press and radio under Yugoslav authorities, 187; and Republican Fascists, 76–77, 135–36; and Schäffer-Coceani meeting, 139–40 and n.21; and Slovenian collaborators, 1943–45, 86–87, 154; Slovenian Communists in, 1941–45, 64–65, 177; and Slovenian Democrats, 1941–45, 64, 65–66, 87; Slovenian National Council in, 64, 87; Slovenian Partisans in, 1941–45, 64–65, 109, 110, 144, 146–52; Slovenian radio program in, 1943–45, 87; and Slovenian rights, 1943–45, 86–87; and Socialists (Italian and Slovenian), 20–21, 38–42, 147, 257–58; and Tito-Alexander talks, Feb. 1945, 124; and Unità Operaia, 65, 146; who liberated, 156–60; Yugoslav administration of, 170–87; Yugoslav city command, 162, 170; Yugoslav troops enter, 145, 150, 152; Yugoslavs try to get Allied troops out of, 162–63
—, Zone A, FTT, 1947–54: Allied troops and economic well-being of, 437; American troops and their life in, 372; and AMG (*see* FTT, Zone A, Allied Military Government); AMG administration continued in, 275–76; economy of, 280–81, 283–90, 330, 332–33, 350, 351, 368, 469; and free port, 274, 456–57; and increase of Italy's influence (*see* FTT, Zone A, Allied Military Government); IRI property in, 288–89; Irredentism in, 340–41, 364–65; Irredentist terrorist activities in, 338, 360; Italian control over economy of, 283–90; Italian troops enter, Oct. 26, 1954, 466–68; and Mar. 1952 riots, 384–87; and 1949 elections, 302–12; and 1951 (planned for) elections, 367–68, 370, 371; 1954 London Agreement and feeling in, 464–65; and Nov. 1953 riots, 439–47; Oct. 8, 1953, announcement and feeling in, 436–48; political parties in (*see* Christian Democratic party; CLN for Istria; Committee for the Defense of the Italianity of Trieste and Istria; CPFTT; CPFTT [Babič]; CPFTT [Vidali]; Independence Front; Italian Liberal party; Italian Republican party; Italian Social Movement; Qualunquists; Slovenian Christian-Social Union; Slovenian Democratic Union; Socialists; Triestino bloc); and pro-Trieste demonstrations, Oct. 14–15, 1953, 438; rumors about cancelled ceremonies in, 1954, 467; rumors in, Oct. 15–Nov. 3, 1953, 438–39; Sept. 1947 clashes in, 277; Yugoslav consulate general established in, 459. *See also* FTT, Zone A, *for 1947–54 period*
—, Zone A, Julian Region, 1945–47: AMG appointed pro-Italian municipal government in, Sept. 21, 1945, 226 (*see also* Julian Region, Zone A, Allied Military Government); and CLN clash with UAIS-SIAU, 252, 255; CLN dissolved, Giunta d'Intesa formed, 265; CLT dissolves itself, Sept. 1945, 226; CLT, manifestations and strikes in support of, 223, 252–53; CLT struggle for recognition of the committee system by AMG, 220–26; commission of experts comes to, Mar. 1946, 253–54; CPFTT, formed, Aug. 1947, 264; CPVG, formed, Aug. 1945, 220; formation of political parties

521

INDEX

in, 263–66; Free Territory announced, July 3, 1946, and disorders in, 246, 256; Independence Front organized in, 258–59; independentism precedences in, 257–58; Italian gains in, 230; and Italian manifestations, 231, 254; and Italian political parties, spring 1947, 265; and organization of Slovenian Democratic Union, 266; and rumors of Yugoslav concentration of troops, 256; and Slovenian democratic political and cultural organizations, 265–66; Slovenian secondary schools organized in, 216; socialists (Saragat and Nenni) in, 265; and UAIS-SIAU continuation of CLT's struggle against AMG, 226–27, 228–30; and UAIS-SIAU demonstrations, 232, 253, 254, 255–56

Trieste area, 211, 291

Trieste memorandum for plebiscite, Sept. 1953, 423–24, 426

Triestino bloc: defends FTT, 286, 333, 368, 425, 438; formed, 258–59; and 1949 elections, 304; and 1952 elections, 395

Tripartite Proposal: announcement of, and consequences of, 281–83; and De Gasperi, 359, 382–83, 453; and direct Italo-Yugoslav negotiations, 319, 358, 361, 382; and elections in Zone A, 1951, 369; and General Airey's reports, 348–49, 351–52; and Irredentists, 344, 364, 368; and Italy, 320, 332, 334, 337, 339, 374; Mar. riots, 1952 London Agreement, and, 384–85, 388, 391; and Oct. 8, 1953, announcement, 429, 430, 431, 436; and Pella, 419, 420, 424; and Scelba's speech, Oct. 1954, 462–63; and Soviet Russia, 316; and Western powers, 316, 337, 353, 356–57, 360–61, 366; and Zone B, 312–13, 335, 383

Trnovski forest (Trnovski gozd), 151

Trst. *See* Trieste

Truman, President Harry S., 208 n.15, 277–78, 354, 359

Trumbić, Dr. Ante, 25 n.9, 32 n.23

TRUST (Trieste United States Troops), 372

Tržič. *See* Monfalcone

Tuma, Dr. Henrik, 39 n. 34, 41 n. 39, 42 n.42

Turjak, 80, 81–82

Turkey, 24 n.6, 44, 353, 381, 419

Tyrol. *See* South Tyrol

UAIS-SIAU (Unione Antifascista Italo-Slava–Slovansko-italijanska antifašistična unija) (Italo-Slavic Anti-Fascist Union): AMG administration attacked by, 226–27, 228–30; and attacks on *Demokracija* and Slavko Uršič, 266; clashes with police, and strikes, 253, 254, 255–56; and Cominform Resolution, 300; consequences of AMG boycott by, 230–31; formation and leaders of, 220; new policy of, after Feb. 1947, 230, 263–64; organizes manifestations for Yugoslavia, 231–32, 252; and Slovene family names, 405; strikes against AMG Slovenian schools in rural communes, 229–30; and Zone B, FTT, 235, 324, 325, 326

Udina, Manlio, 346

Udine, 203

Udine Province, 6, 60, 71–72, 75 n.11, 100

Ufficio Anagafico (Vital Statistics Office), 294–96, 302

Umag (Umago), 376, 416

Umberto, heir to Italian throne, 96, 97

Unione Antifascista Italo-Slava–Slovansko-italijanska antifašistična unija. *See* UAIS-SIAU

Unione degli Italiani dell' Istria e di Fiume, L', 111

Union of Italian Anti-Fascist Women, 148

Union of Italian Youth, 148

Union of Slovenian Anti-Fascist Women, 148

Union of Slovenian Youth, 148

Unità, L', 250, 326

Unità Operaia (Workers' Unity), 65, 110, 146, 147–48, 149

INDEX

Unità Operaia-Delavska enotnost (Workers' Unity), 110
Unitary Trade Union. *See* Sindacati Unici
United Nations, Security Council: and the 1953 fall crisis, 449; General Airey's reports to, 298, 347–52; Irredentists on, 340; Italian peace treaty and protection of FTT by, 270, 275; and letter from Slovenian mayors of Zone A on Slovenian geographical names, 405 n.39; and 1954 London Agreement, 457; and nomination of governor, 278, 280; and petition of pro-Italian political parties of Zone A, 1950, on 1950 elections in Zone B, 336; and Soviet demand to discuss FTT question, Oct. 1953, 449; and Soviet letter recognizing 1954 London Agreement, 460–61; and Tripartite Proposal, 282; Yugoslav communications to, 286–87, 329, 433
United Nations Relief and Rehabilitation Administration (UNRRA), 219
United Press, 420–21
United Slovenia, 18, 155
United States, 120, 204, 334; airplane incidents with Yugoslavia, 1946, 257; asked by De Gasperi to postpone elections in Zone A, 1951, 370; and Belgrade agreement, 199–200; Dec. 1952 proposal by, 416; De Gasperi's visit to, Sept. 1951, 359–60; diplomatic relations with Italy since Sept. 1943, 125, 126; and Eden proposal, 415; Feb. 1953 proposal by, 416, 417; and FTT problem in 1950–51, 321, 353, 355, 361, 366; Intelligence Service in Switzerland during the war, 133; and introduction of Italian law in Zone A and Yugoslav protests to, 208 n.15; and Italian rearmament, 353, 355; and landing in Istria, 132; last U.S. troops leave Trieste, 466, 468; life of U.S. troops in Zone A, 372–73; and London talks, 450, 451–52, 453–55; military and civilian personnel of Zone A and visits to Zone B, July 1951, 377; and 1952 London Agreement, 387–92; and Nov. 1953 riots, 447; and Oct. 8, 1953, announcement, 427–28, 432–33, 433–34; official statement by, on 1954 London Agreement, 460; and peace conference, 1919, 28–31; and peace negotiations, 1945–47, 240–52; policy toward Julian Region during war, 1941–45, 123, 129, 131, 132, 168, 194–96, 198 n.101; presidential elections and peace treaty with Italy, 1920, 31; relations with Yugoslavia after Cominform Resolution, 315 n.14, 353; and Tripartite Proposal announcement, 281; and Yugoslav claims, 1941–45, 130–31; Zone A, FTT, and foreign relief program of, 284
United States Eighty-eighth Division, 168
University of Maryland, 372
UNRRA (United Nations Relief and Rehabilitation Administration), 219
Uomo Qualunque, Il (The Common Man), 309
Uradni list, Bollettino ufficiale, Službeni list (official gazette), 322
Uršič, Rudi (alias Karl or Carlo), 141, 172, 177
Uršič, Slavko, 266
Ustashi, 66, 88, 153, 183

Valenčič, Alojz, 38 n.33
Vaške straže. *See* Village Guards
Vedetta d'Italia, La, 344
Velebit, Vladimir, 450–51, 451–52, 457
Venetian Slovenia, 62, 109, 176; claimed by Slovenes, 1941–45, 60, 100, 103, 105, 120, 155; and Council of Foreign Ministers decision, 246; and Duino agreements, 201; land and people of, 4, 11 n.12, 15 n.17; and report of commission of experts, 1946, 244; and Yugoslav claims, 1919, 29;

523

INDEX

and Yugoslav reduced demands, 1946, 247
Venezia Giulia. *See* Julian Region
Venice, 3, 12, 14 n.16, 16, 191, 341-42
Vesel, Dr. Franc, 266
Vesnić (Vesnitch), Milenko R., 32 n.23
Vesnitch. *See* Vesnić
Vetrinje (Viktring), 155
Victor Emmanuel III, 95-96, 97
Vidali, Vittorio, 299, 300. *See also* CPFTT (Vidali)
Vienna, 113, 131; meeting, Apr. 20-22, 1941, 46, 50-51
Vietinghoff, General Heinrich von, 133
Viktring (Vetrinje), 155
Vilfan, Dr. Jože, 107, 177
Villach, 196
Village Guards, 85: beginning and organization of, 54-56; and Chetnik movement, 57; and Major Novak, 79; and Slovenian Catholic party, 78; and Slovenian National Army, 80; and Turjak defeat, 81-83
Villaggio del Fanciullo, 408
Villa Opicina, 408, 468
Villanti, Colonel, 439
Villi, Claudio, 191
Vipacco. *See* Vipava valley
Vipava valley, 61, 243
Vis, 92, 123
Visconti Venosta, Marchese, 131
Vital Statistics Office, 294-96, 302
Vitelli, Gian A., 396
Vivante, Angelo, 15 n.18
Vladimir Gortan brigade, 67, 111
Voce di Fiume, 344
Voce Giuliana, La, 190
Vodopivec, Colonel Vlado, 162 n.2
Vojaška uprava jugoslovanske armade (Military Administration of the Yugoslav Army). *See* FTT, Zone B; Julian Region, Zone B
Vran, 114
Vratuša, Dr. Anton, 114
Vyshinsky, Andrei, 317, 449, 460-61

Waldock, C. H., 242 n.6
Wallner, Woodruff, 430
Washington, D.C., 127, 361, 414, 415
Western Allies (Great Britain, U.S., France), 69, 105, 156; CLN from Trieste handed memorandum to embassies of, 191; and Cominform Resolution, 301; compromise proposals by, Apr. 1919-Jan. 1920, 30-31; and FTT, Mar. 1952-June 1953, 383-84; and liberation of Trieste, 157; and Pella, Aug. 1953, 421; policy of, toward Julian Region during World War II, 125, 129-32; policy of, toward Yugoslavia after Cominform Resolution, 315-16, 334, 431; position of, toward Trieste, by Sept. 1951, 361-62; and rearmament of Italy, 359; seek compromise, Oct.-Dec. 1953, 434-35, 448, 449; and Soviet Russia, 277-78, 353, 354; statement by, on 1954 London Agreement, 460; support Italian claims, 1945-47, 242; sympathetic to CLN activities in Trieste and Gorizia, May 1945, 192; and Yugoslav claims during World War II, 130-31. *See also* United States; Great Britain
Western powers. *See* Western Allies
White Guard. *See* Village Guards
Williams, Major (British), 441
Wilson, General Henry M., 99, 122, 124
Wilson, Woodrow, 28-31
Wilson line, 30-31, 241, 244, 245
Winterton, General: and AMG reorganization, 1952, 390, 396, 398; announces London Agreement, Oct. 5, 1954, 464; appointed commander of Zone A, FTT, Mar. 14, 1951, 357; blamed for 1953 riots in Trieste, 444; and flying of Italian flag, Nov. 1953, 439; and Irredentists, 380, 384, 386; and new AMG policy, 363; proclamations by, ending AMG, Oct. 26, 1954, 466-67; and prohibition of all public meetings, Oct. 13, 1953, 438; and protest from Count Carrobio on Mar. 1952 riots, 386;

INDEX

rumors of plot to kill, 467; and Slovenian geographical names in Zone A, 405 and n.39; special message by, Oct. 8, 1953, 435–36; special message by, Nov. 6, 1953, 442; and tense situation on borders, Nov. 1953, 447
Wolff, General Karl, 133, 134 n.4
Wolfrom, Jean, 242 n.6
Wolsegger, Dr., 72 and n.4
Workers' Unity, 65, 110, 146, 147–48, 149
World War I, 23–27, 119
World War II: and Adriatic Littoral, 1943–45, 71–88, 100–119; and end of Mussolini and Hitler, 133–34; and fall of Fascism, 70; and German evacuation of Greece, 1944, 91–92; and German surrender in Italy, 133–34; Great Powers' policy toward Julian Region during, 129–32; and independent Croat state, 50; and Italian armistice, 70 and n.1; Italy, Allied, and German occupation during, 1943–45, 95–100; and Julian Region, 1941–43, 57–69; and liberation of Trieste, 135–60; and Ljubljana Province under Italian occupation, 51–57; and rise of Tito, 89–95; Rumania and Bulgaria surrender to Russia during, 94; Slovenia occupied and divided during, 49–51; and Stalin-Tito agreement, Sept. 1944, 94; and Vienna meeting, Apr. 1941, 46–47; and Yugoslav armistice signed, 47; and Yugoslav government-in-exile, Athens declaration, Apr. 19, 1941, 47; Yugoslavia attacked and dismembered during, 46–49

Yalta conference, and Italian government, 123, 127, 132
Yugo-lira, 237, 327–28
Yugopress release, 420
Yugoslav Committee, 25–27, 25 n.9
Yugoslav Communist party, 48; claims Julian Region, 102–5, 233; and CLN in Trieste, 117–18; and Cominform Resolution, 299–301, 314; and Comintern letters on Istria, 67; and communication link between Massola and Comintern, 59; Oct. 1944 agreement, 104. *See also* Croat Communist party; Slovenian Communist party
Yugoslav Fourth Army. *See* Fourth Army
Yugoslav government-in-exile: and anti-Communists, 77–78; Athens declaration by, Apr. 1941, 47; and claims to Julian Region, 120–21, 120 n.1; toward coalition government with Tito, 92–94, 132; recognized by Slovenian and Croat democrats, 56, 65, 69; Teheran conference and, 89–90
Yugoslav London government. *See* Yugoslav government-in-exile
Yugoslav National Liberation Committee, 49
Yugoslav National party in Slovenia. *See* Slovenian Liberal party
Yugoslav Partisans. *See* Partisans
Yugoslav royal government. *See* Yugoslav government-in-exile
Yugoslav secret police (OZNA), 175
Yugoslav Socialist party in Slovenia, 49
Yugoslavia, Yugoslavian, Yugoslav: administration of Julian Region (*see* Julian Region; Trieste [Trst]); administration of Trieste (*see* Trieste [Trst], to June 1945); administration of Zone B, 322–32, 373–80, 401–4; anti-Communist forces, Apr. 1945, 153–56; attacked and divided, 1941, 46–47, 49–51; bank, in Trieste, and Banco di Roma, 290; and Belgrade negotiations and agreement, June 9, 1945, 196–200; city command in Trieste, 170; civil administration, recognized by AMG in Zone A, Julian Region, 199–200, 201, 221; claims, 1919, 28–29; claims, 1941–47, 120–25, 130–31, 132, 184, 241, 242; and a Communist victory, 1945–46, 168–70, 182–83, 235; and consequences of Cominform Resolution, 299, 314–19, 353–54; consulate general

525

INDEX

in Trieste, 459; and Eden proposal, 414–15; establishes diplomatic relations with Soviet Union, May 1940, 52; executive committee (*see* AVNOJ); favors partition of FTT, after 1949, 316–19; and implementation of 1954 London Agreement, 466; international position of, 1953, 381, 418–19; interpretation of Nov. 1953 Trieste riots by, 445; and Italian armistice, 89; and Italo-Yugoslav nonaggression pact, 1937, 44; and London talks, 450, 451–52, 454–55; and making of Italian peace treaty, 1945–47, 240–52; minority in Italy, according to Rapallo treaty, 32; nationalism (*see* Nationalism, Croat; Nationalism, Slovenian); and 1949 election in Zone A, 302, 304, 317; 1954 census, 7–12; 1954 London Agreement ratified by, 464; opposes revision of Italian peace treaty, 1951, 354–55; and peace negotiations, 1919–20, 29–32; proposal to Italy, May 1953, 417; protests increase of Italian influence in Zone A, FTT, 277, 286–87, 289–90, 297; protests introduction of Italian law in Zone A, 208 n.15; protests 1952 London talks and Agreement, 388–89, 391–92; reaction to 1954 London Agreement 461–62; reaction to Oct. 8, 1953, announcement, 430–33; reaction to Pella's military pressure, 421–23; refuses Italian proposals for plebiscite, 363, 388, 426–27; reject two compromise proposals, Dec. 1953, 449; remove troops from Italian border, Dec. 1953, 448; and Teheran conference, 89–90; and Tito and Soviet Union 1944–45, 94, 132; and Tito-Churchill meeting, 93–94; and Tito-Šubašić agreement, 92–93, 94–95; and Treaty of Rome, 1924, 34; and the Tripartite Proposal, 282–83; U.S. airplane incidents with, Aug. 1946, 256–57; Yugo-lira of, 237, 327–28. *See also* Yugoslav—

Zadar (Zara), 3, 32, 121; claims, 1945–46, 242, 244, 245, 246, 267
Zagreb, 156, 176
Zanella, Riccardo, 34
Zapotok, 82
Zara. *See* Zadar
Zaule (Žavlje), 451
Žavlje. *See* Zaule
ZAVNOH (Zemaljsko antifašističko vijeće narodnog oslobodjenja Hrvatske) (the Provincial Anti-Fascist Council of National Liberation of Croatia), 48, 66, 101
Zgonik. *See* Sgonico
Zone A, FTT. *See* FFT, Zone A
Zone A, Julian Region. *See* Julian Region, Zone A
Zone B, FTT. *See* FTT, Zone B
Zone B, Julian Region. *See* Julian Region, Zone B
Zone commissioner, 291
Zone president, 292 and n.40
Zoppi, Vittorio, 421, 455
Zoratti, Umberto, 171, 173, 191
Zrenjanin, 391